JOHN A.
WIDTSOE

JOHN A. WIDTSOE

A BIOGRAPHY

ALAN K. PARRISH

DESERET BOOK
SALT LAKE CITY, UTAH

© 2003 Alan K. Parrish

Visit us at deseretbook.com

Library of Congress Cataloging-in-Publication Data

Parrish, Alan K.
    John A. Widtsoe : a biography / Alan K. Parrish.
        p.   cm.
    Includes bibliographical references and index.
    ISBN 1-57008-770-9 (alk. paper)
    1. Widtsoe, John Andreas, 1872–1952.   2. Mormons—Biography.
3. Scientists—United States—Biography.   I. Title.
BX8695.W542 P37 2003
289.3'092—dc21   2002153649

Printed in the United States of America   72076-6914
Publishers Printing, Salt Lake City, UT

10   9   8   7   6   5   4   3   2   1

CONTENTS

FOREWORD

———————————————

I WAS baptized a member of The Church of Jesus Christ of Latter-day Saints in the baptismal font of the Salt Lake Tabernacle on 28 October 1952. It was the last public appearance of my grandfather—John A. Widtsoe. Afterward we stopped briefly at Deseret Book, where he purchased a teacher's edition of the Holy Bible for me—a possession I cherish to this day.

He passed away 29 November 1952. I remember his funeral a few days later. It was my first personal experience with death. But what I would like to review is the music selected for that solemn occasion.

My mother has told me that Elder Widtsoe did not consider himself to have a good singing voice, and yet he loved the hymns of Zion and other great music.

The prelude—played by Alexander Schreiner—was the B. Cecil Gates setting of "I Know That My Redeemer Lives." Brother Gates was Sister Widtsoe's brother. As we gathered to our places at the front of the Tabernacle, the music brought familiar comfort of the reality of our belief in the resurrection. I have thought since how appropriate that the services for one of the special witnesses of the name of Jesus Christ should reference and reverence the reality of the resurrection.

The opening hymn was the Gates setting of "The Lord's Prayer"—sung by the Tabernacle Choir, for whom it had been composed. Grandfather Widtsoe often testified of the power of prayer. His childhood story of finding the lost gold piece after petitioning an all-knowing Heavenly Father has been a favorite that many of his descendants have retold in talks in Primary, family home evenings, and elsewhere.

Following the tender remarks of Elder Richard L. Evans, the Tabernacle Choir sang the musical setting of Tennyson's "Crossing the Bar." Grandfather loved inspiring literature. We were often reminded that as a college student, young John Widtsoe would often read Tennyson just prior to a scientific or other exam to refresh his mind and spirit before entering the examination room. As I dealt with my own eight-year-old sorrow at that occasion, I have pondered the comfort conveyed in the poetic phrase "and may there be no moaning of the bar / When I put out to sea."

At the end of the service, the choir sang "Praise to the Man Who Communed with Jehovah." It was the familiar Welsh melody and brought to mind the more than six years of the Widtsoe service in Great Britain and Europe presiding over the European Mission. It was in Kensington in 1933 that my young missionary father first became acquainted with this remarkable family and was introduced to their youngest daughter—my mother—Eudora. Grandfather Widtsoe had a lifelong devotion to Joseph Smith and his role in restoring the gospel of Jesus Christ to the earth. It is clear that aside from the Savior, no one person so influenced John A. Widtsoe throughout his life as the Prophet Joseph. I have been told this was his favorite hymn.

As we left the Tabernacle for the Salt Lake City cemetery, we emerged into an early December blizzard. Alexander Schreiner played the Norwegian composer Edvard Grieg's "Morning" as the postlude. The morning of John Andreas Widtsoe's life had been in the midst of the Norwegian winter of 1872. Now, in spite of the storm that raged about us, we could contemplate the morning of the first resurrection and consider Elder Richard L. Evans's words: "We know not how much we shall miss him. But the years go quickly, and John A. Widtsoe is still himself, and should we ever come within reach of so high a place as where he is, we should like to take his outstretched hand and resume our talk where last we left it."

The family of John A. Widtsoe is very grateful for the many years of research but more especially for the obvious affection that Alan Parrish has for Brother Widtsoe. On many occasions as he would meet with us, he would say his greatest hope was that "the family would be pleased." We are, and we thank Alan Parrish for bringing the remarkable story of our ancestor once again to our attention and the attention of others.

George H. Durham II

PREFACE

In my early days in Church education, as director of the LDS Institute of Religion at UCLA, I had the privilege of moving the institute into its current home. Most difficult was lugging the large library, box by box, up three long flights of concrete stairs. Soon everything was properly shelved except for a large barrel of loose fragments. When spare hours arose, I shuffled through them, organizing, filing, or discarding as appropriate. Near the bottom of the barrel was a bundle of yellowed, onionskin pages. As I looked, I sensed that an important story lay behind them. They were an impressive typescript copy of lecture notes Elder John A. Widtsoe had prepared for religion classes at USC many years earlier.

A few years later, amid my doctoral studies in American Higher Education at USC, I thought of those pages again. That led to reading some articles about Brother Widtsoe in some old Church magazines. From them I gained the impression that he was Mormonism's model of the great champions of higher education I was studying. My attachment to him began to grow.

Then I was transferred to Cambridge, Massachusetts, as director of the Cambridge Institute of Religion, located near Harvard. In the early months there I acquired a copy of Brother Widtsoe's autobiography, *In a Sunlit Land.* I was gladdened to learn of the book and to read the terrific stories of his life, especially those at Harvard. It was so descriptive of trials my own students were facing that I gave each of them a copy of three of its chapters, discussed them in our first class meeting, and recommended that they make him their patron saint.

As my impressions grew I began to gather materials about John, chiefly about his connections with Harvard. I especially enjoyed the biographies he wrote for seven "facebooks"—class reports that accompanied each class reunion. In them I first read his explanations of the love he had for Utah's people and her institutions of higher learning. I also felt his personal testimony as he described to revered Harvard classmates his reasons for leaving the presidency of a prestigious American university to accept a full-time position with a church that, to them, had little station.

I carried my meager collection of Widtsoe materials with me to BYU and my new position on the faculty of Religious Education. In discussions with deans Robert J. Matthews and Robert L. Millet, and with other valued colleagues, ideas of preparing a biography first came to mind. As my interest grew, doubts and fear lurked in the shadows. I was not a scholar. My successes in college were chiefly athletic and little resembled Dr. Widtsoe's prominence in laboratories and classrooms. I also lacked his gift for the pen. My qualification—the driving force— was the deep admiration that had grown and a strong conviction that his story needed to be told. Perhaps it was more than coincidence that to each place I went in my teaching career, he had already been, and in a very impressive fashion, had opened the way. It was also significant that he was a Cache Valley boy and an Aggie, and that his professional life coincided well with my doctoral studies and my love for the campuses of higher learning. Important also is our shared notion that nothing mixes quite so nicely as the restored gospel and the college campus.

Why does John's story need to be told? The heights a man attains are probably the best measure of the importance of his story. Another measure is the way he got there and the potential his life has for helping others reach higher in their life's pursuits. Overcoming major obstacles, rising to greatness out of obscurity, and leaving a life-trail of unusual accomplishments add to the need to tell that story. Those are the things that forge the outline of John's life. He was a European lad raised in a single-parent family by a fishermaiden. The gospel found the widow, Anna Widtsoe, in her most difficult years, and it soon swept her and her two boys into its net and off to Utah. John knew privation and persecution. Yet, guided by the devoted fishermaiden, and clinging tightly to a hope-thread left by his deceased father, John found unusual greatness. Because John's life was shaped by circumstances in the Church, he was never able, nor ever sought, to live life and church separately. His attainments were an extension of what had been caught in that gospel net, part of his hallowed commission.

Seeking the life of a schoolmaster, John trod the difficult path to Harvard. There, it may be said, he found his element—so much so that it may further be said that he achieved the highest accomplishments, or as high as any student had achieved while at Harvard in its 365-year history. That flourishing set him on paths in Utah higher education that prompted President Heber J. Grant to label him "the greatest educator that Mormonism has ever produced." Prior to that bold claim, John had achieved academic greatness and international acclaim. He had also been president of the Agricultural College and of the University of Utah in some of their most pivotal periods. John's work in higher education alone merits a significant biography. To college students, John's life offers much inspiration. To those whose lives have been interlaced with Utah's colleges and universities, John's life is a landmark of accomplishment. To those who follow significant professional accomplishment and economic development in Utah's history, John's story is invaluable. To students of world agriculture, his life is a Mt. Everest.

At each stage of John's growth, his attachment to The Church of Jesus Christ of Latter-day Saints grew through trial and searching. Trusting in his mother's faith was not enough in his earliest years, and at her urging he deferred his baptism until testimony was born in his own heart. His biggest "religious battles" came in college, at Harvard, where, immersed in the trials of science, a real search for truth brought him "certain knowledge that the restored gospel is true and that Joseph

Smith was indeed a Prophet." Thereafter, the teachings of the Prophet Joseph always remained close to John's pen, and the *Doctrine and Covenants* became his favorite book of scripture.

Church trials continued through his appointments in the Agricultural College and the University of Utah. His church devotion was always the major banner raised against him by opponents. Those rebuffs were painful to John, because he had pursued his academic preparations in the hope that he could add his contribution to the work of others who had unselfishly advanced the Church and her people in Utah. His professional hope was to help bring fulfillment to prophecies of the flowering of the American west. His first audience in every pursuit was his brothers and sisters in the Church, yet he was equally serviceable to people of any faith. Indicative of that is the extreme favor he gained in the Middle East among Muslims and Jews, and through the rest of the world's people on arid and semi-arid lands.

As an apostle, John put his skills to work in Church assignments. They were especially useful in resolving complicated problems of genealogy and family history. He became the most devout Church authority in gathering the worldwide histories and genealogies that generated the vast collections of the Family History Library. As Church commissioner of education in two separate terms, he brought vast experience to critical developments in Church schools, academies, junior colleges, religious education classes, and seminary and institute programs. In special governmental callings, he added to the stature of the Church internationally.

The death of a fifth Widtsoe child led, in part, to the Widtsoes' six-year assignment to preside over the Church's missions in Europe. Improving the media image of the Church, bringing to European Church members all the blessings of membership, helping them gain that devotion enjoyed by the best of the members in Zion, making much-needed improvements in their health through teaching the Word of Wisdom, preparing them for the great war that seemed imminent, and guiding young missionaries to success in their missions and in their lives—all were epoch-making achievements in Europe.

Other assignments included long stints with Church Education; the

Church Radio, Publicity, and Mission Literature Committee; the Church Security (Welfare) Committee; and the *Improvement Era,* which, under John's editorship, became the "Voice of the Church." Devotion to those assignments, and continuing service as a director of the Utah Genealogical and Historical Society, the Church Board of Education, and the Melchizedek Priesthood Committee, along with the constant demands of quarterly stake conferences, brought him partial blindness and a relatively early decline in health. In November 1952 he died at age eighty. Left behind was a tremendous legacy of world, national, state, and Church citizenship that few others have achieved.

John felt that the best chapter in his autobiography is "The Love Story." Beyond his devotion to God, his life with Leah Dunford was the greatest of all his achievements. Theirs was a love story few have achieved. Theirs was a companionship of equals. Whether on their knees in prayer; at work in the classroom, laboratory, or lecture hall; or even at their writing desks, they created a life of uncommon togetherness, a model love story.

My study of John's life has been a very rewarding journey. It has taken me through many adventures of life in Utah from more than a century ago, to the highest levels of educational experience at Harvard and Göttingen, through many inner-workings of Utah's universities, and into the life and work of revered Church leaders. It has taken me through many thousands of files in nearly 500 crowded archival boxes of John's papers at Utah State University, the University of Utah, Brigham Young University, the Utah State Historical Society, and the Historical Division of The Church of Jesus Christ of Latter-day Saints. At each of these I have been generously assisted by excellent and willing staff members too numerous to name. I sincerely appreciate each one.

In gathering and reporting these many pieces of Elder Widtsoe's life, I have been assisted by many student assistants and secretaries—too many to name, but to each, my sincere thanks! I am especially indebted to Dale J. Pratt and Kerry M. Muhlestein, my chief research assistants in the beginning, middle, and ending stages of the research. Alison Coutts rendered valuable assistance in cutting the original manuscript to a manageable size. Cory Maxwell has been a friend and a rock of unflinching encouragement. Jack Lyon edited the book and saw it through production. Kent Minson and Shauna Gibby have added the sparkle in the typesetting and design of the volume. To each, special thanks. I should note here that quotations have been edited as needed to improve clarity and to modernize spelling, punctuation, and capitalization.

In writing this book, I have learned much of greatness. I have been deeply touched and much inspired by a life so devoted to God, to truth, and to his people, whether of a shared faith, a shared institution, or shared challenges in arid soils. My hope for the book is that it will find its way into the hands of many who will be lifted by this life sketch of a European convert to Mormonism, a college man, a schoolmaster, a leader of young men, a scientist, a theologian, a family man, an apostle of the Lord.

PART I

YOUTH AND EDUCATION

1

"MY VIKING ANCESTORS"

JOHN Andreas Widtsoe was the son of a "fishermaiden" and a man who had been a teenage runaway, born with his wrist attached to his head (requiring the desperate last rites from a priest) on an almost unknown island in far-off Norway. From that beginning John A. Widtsoe became Harvard's prize student—the outstanding student of his decade, the world's foremost authority on irrigation and raising crops in arid conditions, the president of two universities, an apostle in The Church of Jesus Christ of Latter-day Saints, and arguably the Church's most prolific author on doctrine and history. How was this possible? The simplest and most complete answer is the direction and example of his mother, Anna Karine Gaarden.

The life of John A. Widtsoe is such a success story that it is difficult to remember he sometimes had to consciously reach into a reservoir of inner strength. Of those moments he typically said, "I summoned the courage of my Viking ancestors." Even when he did not refer to this heritage, the fortitude, strength of character, and venturing inclination that brought him so much success had their roots in the soul-sculpting soil of the rugged, treeless, windswept fishing village Titran, on Norway's outermost island.

Titran was the ancestral home of John's mother, Anna, whose guiding hand directed him through so many triumphant accomplishments. Beyond her parental hand was an intrepid nature inherited from generations of hardy, venturing Vikings. A written portrait of the life of John A. Widtsoe must begin with this proud maternal heritage. John's father died while John was young. The trials Anna endured and the difficult life in which she raised her son required the fortitude gained during her upbringing. John recognized her direction and was intensely grateful for her training. In gratitude, he wrote a book about his mother; it was so well received that it was often used to teach the women's auxiliaries of the Church.[1]

The story of John A. Widtsoe's life has vast significance to audiences both in and out of the church on which he centered so many of his achievements. From his remote beginnings, John became one of the most outstanding citizens of Utah, Mormonism, America, and the world.

From John's Viking roots he summoned the courage to succeed. The Vikings came from all over Scandinavia, but their name is considered to have originated in Vik, a harbor village on the southern coastline of Norway not far from Anna's village. Rapid population growth in Scandinavia reduced the amount of available farmland, put a strain on available employment, and forced many people to leave home in search of new work and other places to settle. This was called "Vik-ing" and was originally undertaken with peaceful intent; only later was it associated with hostile, warlike activities. Although the majority of Scandinavians were fishermen or farmers, many found the Viking life irresistible as they developed new technology that enabled ships to travel farther than ever before. Thus the Viking Age was named.[2] Whatever else may be said of the Vikings of old, no one would argue against the hardiness of their character or their venturing spirit, both so apparent in John's life.

The island of Froya (then Froyen) on the southwest coast of Norway was for many generations the home of Anna's ancestors. Her father, Peder Olsen Gaarden, was the "King's Pilot," as were his father and grandfather before him. And because Anna (born in 1849) was the oldest child, with no brothers, her firstborn son (John) would be Peder's apprentice—the next king's pilot. The ferocious North Atlantic, concealing treacherous reefs, made access to the rich fishing harbors extremely perilous. When the king of Norway sailed in their area, the experienced Gaarden seamen took the helm of his vessel to guide it safely through the narrow channels, twists, and turns of the dangerous island coastline. As the king's pilot, Peder's experience and training set him apart from other local seamen, and his piloting skills were always in demand. Heavy traffic around the outermost island often kept him away from home. But his position brought him a good income, and contact with seamen from many cultures gave him a more cosmopolitan outlook than his fellow islanders, a substantial benefit to him and his family.

Where the original inhabitants of these islands came from is not known, though some suspect they were part of the northward-moving tribes of Jacob (Israel). Scientific data describe them as one continuing race back to the Stone Age. People had lived on the island of Froya at least a thousand years before the birth of Christ, and churches dating to 1000 A.D. still stand. In Anna's day, life on the tiny island centered around fishing, Norway's major industry. Little coastal fishing villages dotted the island. Anna's home, Titran (then Titteren), was on the tip of the southwest corner of Froya, where the land juts into the ocean.

Titran is an expanse of grey-white domes of granite spattered with pockets of green. There are no trees, and the shrubs reach barely three feet in height. In the shortened spring and summer seasons, the island is carpeted with multicolored wildflowers, whose changing variety remains resplendent until the harshness of fall and winter sweep the island bare again. Winter brings storms and a relentless barrage of high waves. The few bleak hours of daylight keep people housebound. The occasional daring fisherman ventures out to sea, but most stay at home with their families. Since Froya is treeless, fuel comes from the peat bogs. When the milder months return, much anticipated after a cheerless winter, the island is again an ever-changing patchwork of picturesque beauty. The storms subside, the days lengthen, and the sea is calm. The festive landscape of spring and summer is enhanced by a vast variety of birds and the ripening of blueberries, tytteberries, and multeberries.

In Anna's day, the villages buzzed with life as families absorbed the summer warmth and cheery countryside while working and playing together. The fishermen prepared their boats, readied their nets, and spread out across the water. Some went out many miles, courageously searching for a bigger catch. The generous streams that wash the coastline of Norway were its most valuable resource. In 1881, two years before Anna left Norway, the fisheries employed about 120,000 men with average profits of about $1,700,000. Only 41,500 were employed in manufacturing, and the mines raised only an estimated $322,000.[3]

The population of Norway on 31 December 1882, when John was ten years old, was 1,913,000. Of those, 1,509,000 lived in the country districts, while only 404,000 were in cities or towns. Norway was the most sparsely populated country in all of Europe, having an average of 18 people per square mile. *Bloodletting,* the term used to describe the emigration from Scandinavian countries to America and Australia, had taken a great toll. But in spite of it, the population of Norway more than doubled between 1800 and 1880.[4]

Political life in Norway was tied to Sweden and Denmark. For many centuries they shared monarchs. There were many disputes, but the federation survived. The king had executive powers, but legislation and taxation were the responsibility of the elected Parliament (Storthing), which met each year at the beginning of February. In John's day the Storthing consisted of 114 representatives, 38 from the towns and 76 from the country.[5]

Education in Norway was among the best in Europe. In the country districts 208,000 students were instructed in 6,400 schools, while 41,000 children filled 144 schools in town districts. Seventeen thousand students were enrolled in 150 middle schools and high schools. The Christiania University in Oslo had 1,000 students and 50 professors.[6]

Communities that based much of their economy on the fishing industry faced their own hazards. Each year these communities began the fishing season with a special religious service and a blessing pronounced on the fleet by their leading ecclesiastical authority. In Titran, fishing casualties were heaviest in the fall, during the time of the herring run. Fishing vessels dotted the coasts, and the fishermen, concentrating on the abundant catch, sometimes lost sight of the darkening skies and gathering winds. When they awoke to the danger, they cut their nets, lowered the masts, and readied boat and crew in every possible way to fight their way to safety. Everyone knew that at such times friends would inevitably perish. Every fishing family had suffered an untimely death. But fishing was more than an economic need; it was also a passion. Fertile fields with the promise of a rich harvest surrounded the people, but they shunned farming; they were fishermen.

Living so close to nature, accepting its risks and its blessings, kept them close to God. They were strong in body and mind. Such people may not have made the most orthodox of congregations, but they were deeply religious, relying in threatened times upon their faith alone. Worship was as much an instinct as mending nets and seeking the right places to cast them. The Bible was as much their guide as their sea maps. They lived too close to nature to be atheists.

Anna's maternal grandfather, Jorgen Arntsen Haavig, came from the mainland. He moved to Froya and settled in the village of Hovik. There he married an island girl who came from a long-established Viking family. By his industry and acumen, he gradually acquired practical ownership of the village of perhaps a dozen families. Both sides of Anna's family attained unusual prominence on Froya, evidence of the indomitable spirit and survival instinct that Anna inherited.

The Gaarden family lived in the oldest, largest, and finest house in Titran. Peder made himself quite a leader among his people, and his piloting duties took him to foreign ports. From each trip came gifts for the family and stories that held the youngsters spellbound. Though the family was small, the home was usually full. It housed the hired help that looked after the family fishing business while Peder piloted. At set hours each day, whatever the weather, he climbed to his lookout point and scanned the horizon through his spyglass, looking for ships signaling for a pilot. Destitute friends were also welcomed, as were visitors from the mainland. Anna's mother, Beret Martha Haavig, worked as hard in the family business as she did at home, so she was grateful for the help of

Engeborg Mikkelson, the beloved nurse and family companion who looked after Anna and her sister Petroline until the girls left home.

Beret, Anna, Petroline, and Engeborg prepared the daily catch for merchants and cooked for visitors, who were especially numerous during the herring season in the late fall and early winter. Much was required in the preparation of cod. After the fishermen had made their catch, cleaned it, salted it, and left it to soak, Beret, Engeborg, and the children laid it out on the granite rocks and turned it twice a day to prepare it for market. Cod livers were kept in a large barrel until ready for cooking. Cod liver oil was extracted and sold for medicinal purposes.

Anna and Petroline helped prepare meals, did housework, gathered in chunks of peat for the winter, and helped supplement the family income by gathering boatloads of seaweed, which they carefully burned to form the ash from which iodine was extracted in England. They made candles from the fat and livers of small fish and the accumulated fat from household cooking. On special occasions, Engeborg helped Anna and Petroline make baby candles and Christmas candles. Leftover fat was mixed with alkali and peat ashes and made into soap for use around the house. Throughout the summer, they maintained vegetable gardens for food storage. In early fall came the berry excursions and tedious work of making preserves. In spring the sheep were sheared and the fleeces carefully stored until fall, when there was time to wash, dry, and card the wool. Then they wove it carefully to make next year's clothing.

This hard training was good preparation for the important journey that lay ahead of Anna and Petroline, as the forces of nature in which people develop shape their character. John said of his mother, "Anna Karine Gaarden was born with the gift of vision and sensitive feelings. The tremendous natural manifestations of her native island thrilled her, taught her, helped her understand God and man, and fitted her finely tempered nature for noble endeavor. As she developed, her own nature seemed to reflect the strong wild winter tempest, and the flower-bedecked, sunlit summer beauty of the island."[7] If there were disadvantages to her rough island life, they were offset by lessons learned. Each fall, when the herring swept round the island in shoals by the million, thousands of visitors crowded the island. Each visitor brought a glimpse of life in a different environment. Anna learned much from these visitors, especially when she accompanied her father as he piloted merchants from many ports. John compared his mother's cleanliness of mind to the white foam of the wind-driven waves on the ocean, her firmness for right and truth to the storm-washed granite that dominated her island home, and her desire for freedom and truth to the seabird that winged freely over surf and reef.

Home life for Anna and Petroline had a strong religious influence. The church on Titran had been destroyed; a new one was built on the neighboring island of Hitra. Though it was several miles away, once or twice a month the whole household set off by boat for Sunday morning services. When weather or other circumstances prevented their journey, Peder led family services at home. Almost daily, the family gathered around the table to sing a favorite song, read a chapter from the Bible, and share other songs, poems, or stories.

Anna was a natural leader. She regularly took baskets of food and bunches of flowers to those in difficulty. She loved reading and stayed up late during the long summer nights reading poetry and stories. She also loved to write poetry.

Just before Anna's twelfth birthday, her mother died without warning. This loss deeply affected the family. Peder's singular love for Beret kept him from marrying again. To fill some of his loneliness, Peder often took Anna with him on his business trips. She became his chief confidante and friend. Petroline was still a child, so Peder, Anna, and Engeborg shared the duties of raising her. Petroline grew up in Anna's shadow, but she loved her sister. The trials they overcame together built a friendship that increased with the years.

Anna excelled in school and enjoyed being kept busy. The year after Beret's death, a young man from the mainland came to teach school at Titran. School officials and parents all felt he was an exceptional schoolmaster. His name was John Andersen Widtsoe. He was twenty-one years old, of medium height, square-shouldered, and athletic, with dark hair and grayish-blue eyes. Because of him, Anna was even more attracted to learning, and she quickly became fond of him. Although recognizing that she was too young for a romantic attraction, the schoolmaster wrote in his diary that he intended to marry the attractive, bright Anna Gaarden. Having found her so appealing at twelve, he kept careful watch over her development into young womanhood. Anna was popular among her peers and long remembered by all:

> She was full of pranks. She must have led the village a merry chase. The wise ones said, "Peder Gaarden (Per Gaarn in the vernacular) has some job on his hands in that girl." But they loved her; she galvanized them into joy. After ninety years, she is still a bright memory there. The old survivors of that day chuckle and sometimes they weep as they tell of the mad escapades and deeds of the heart in the day when Anna Gaarden (Anna Gaarn) had the village by the ears. That father and mother had to take her severely in hand at times was only to be expected. The world is organized for the average, not for the exceptional person.[8]

Despite the unspoken attraction the schoolmaster had for her, Anna obviously enjoyed a routine development. Each step along her way was carefully coached by Engeborg and her attentive father. Family life, school life, social life, and community involvement proceeded normally.

> Anna was budding into womanhood. There was no doubt now of her beauty. Suitors came from far and near. Her fame for looks, vivacity, and understanding had spread beyond the island. Among them came the scion of an old, distinguished family, owners of stores, fishing outfits, fishing grounds, related priests and advocates. She was but a fishermaiden, but she had beauty and intelligence. Her father who dreaded the separation that her marriage would bring, nevertheless felt that the opportunity of union with this family, through the manly, competent son, could not be set aside, for it would ensure life's comforts to his beloved, elder daughter. Gently he urged Anna to accept the wooing; but she was not ready. Ever the glint of the schoolmaster's eye was in her memory.[9]

At age nineteen Anna was engaged to the schoolmaster. Some thought this an unwise decision, for she could have her pick of men, and surely prosperity was more promising in others. Yet the community who had come to love the schoolmaster saw in this union unusual happiness, and "happiness is the child of love."[10] Three years passed before they were married because the schoolmaster wanted more education. Anna saw the wisdom in this decision and realized that this was a time for him to acquire the advanced training he desired. This devotion to academic training and the sacrifices needed to obtain it became the hallmark for her sons in the years that followed. Petroline was a young woman, and having Anna near for a few more years was a blessing that deepened their lifelong bond. Petroline's suitors came and went, but she never married. Some speculated that for Petroline, no others could measure up to Anna's schoolmaster.

2

LEGACY OF THE SCHOOLMASTER

J OHN Andreas Widtsoe's father, John Andersen Widtsoe, was born 9 June 1840 in the district of Hemne (then Hevne), some forty-five miles south of Trondheim, Norway. The Widtsoes were established on an estate in the upland fertile valleys of Orkedalen and Meldalen near Trondheim. The Widtsoe men were farmers, schoolteachers, and often public office holders. Several held a position similar to that of probate judge (lenslend). They had generally prospered and had good reputations. John Andreas's paternal grandfather, Anders Johnsen Widtsoe, was an apprenticed carpenter who moved into Trondheim to further his career. There he married John's grandmother, whose family had also come from the southern valleys near Trondheim. Her family found success and happiness in politics, the priesthood, and professional and artistic fields. John Andersen had an older sister, Johanna, and a younger brother, Sivert.

On 11 November 1851, when John Andersen was only eleven years old, his mother died. The family housekeeping chores fell largely to Johanna, and all the family endured a difficult loneliness for a long time. Eventually Anders remarried, but his marriage brought conflict and contention. Anders was happy with his new wife but John Andersen could not come to terms with her. The transition was not helped by his frequent visits to members of his natural mother's family with whom, for a few weeks at a time, he found more happiness than he could in his own home. Anders was distressed over John Andersen's unhappiness, but he was caught between his love for his new wife and his love for his eldest son. He trusted that time would resolve the discord. But it did not.

The Widtsoes were Lutheran, and Anders hoped that John Andersen would be confirmed at the customary age of fourteen, but he feared their increasing estrangement would hinder it. Confirmation typically followed six months of weekly study with the priest. Since John Andersen would not talk to his father, Anders grew frustrated over his seeming indifference toward confirmation. The boy was seldom at home, but just before the planned confirmation, he admitted that he had met with the priest a few times and would be confirmed. Anders showed his approval by giving John money for a new suit of clothes.

Confirmation day arrived; Anders, sitting in the church, could not see his son and began to fear the shame his absence would bring. The boys, as customary, lined up according to their success in the class. Suddenly Anders saw his son—in first place. In his new suit and white collar Anders had not recognized him, nor did Anders expect to see him in first place. As with many things, John Andersen had kept his success from his father. Anders was overcome. He was much pleased and earnestly hoped this would bring about a reconciliation. However, John Andersen, self-reliant and self-willed, decided to leave home and shortly after boarded a ship going to Norway's outermost island, Froya.

Although young, John Andersen was able to fend for himself. However, Anders kept a subtle eye on him and arranged with the priest who had confirmed the young man to have him return to the mainland and attend the seminary near Klaebo. Through the auspices of the priest, three men in charge of Froya's schools found John Andersen and proposed to support him through his schooling in exchange for his promise to return to their island as a teacher. John Andersen accepted their terms, unwitting of his father's participation. Klaebo suited John Andersen very well, and his unhappiness was soon replaced with a challenging and rewarding life and strong friendships. All of the subjects John Andersen had to learn to become a teacher delighted him; he had found his niche in life.

Following his studies at the seminary, John Andersen fulfilled his part of the bargain and returned to Froya to begin his teaching career. He was twenty-one when he took up his assignment to the village of Titran. His skills as a teacher took hold on the community quickly. He was a refreshing addition, and his work took him beyond the school-room into the homes and hearts of many families. As there was no priest on the island, he was consulted in matters of sickness and aging, wills and letter writing, and especially in advising parents on the welfare of their children. The people of the island adored him, and he was very much at home with them. In his first class in Titran he saw the clever girl who would one day become his wife.

By 1868 John Andersen and Anna, then nineteen, were engaged to be married, so they agreed that John should return to the seminary to obtain his certification and open the way to greater opportunities. John Andersen had two more years of school to gain his full certification. Though they were two lonely years for Anna and John Andersen, they were very successful ones. Their son recorded their feelings:

> Year after year he planned to go back to school to finish his work, but the people begged him to stay a little longer; he knew enough for them; and then the fishermaiden had not yet plighted her troth to him.
>
> Eight years after his arrival, they became engaged; and began to plan for life together. She urged him, though the years would be lonely, to return to school and finish the work there.
>
> The fishermaiden was to be his! With a song on his lips and in his heart, he went away another two years. Rich years they were. He was ripened now. Powerful friendships were established. He had a definite objective: wife and home and family. His love letters to the fishermaiden, often in rhyme—for he, too, had the gift of the poet—reveal in beautiful words and rich imagery a nature of delicacy and nobility, and an aspiring soul of depth of feeling and warmth of expression. How the fishermaiden thrilled to the richness and sweetness of such a love.[1]

John Andersen graduated from the seminary with high honors and took with him close friendships with colleagues that would continue for his remaining years. He returned to Froya and built a large two-story family house in Daloe, an hour's walk across the island from Titran. The house also served as a school for the island children. It was a center that would obviate the need for a traveling schoolteacher, though for some time John Andersen continued to teach the children of Titran and Hovik. On 29 December 1870, Anna and John Andersen were married; he was thirty, she twenty-one. The marriage ceremony was performed in the Dolme church on the island of Hitra by the old pastor Brodtkorb who had baptized Anna. This was the church the Gaarden family attended. The whole wedding party had to row back and forth between the church on Hitra and the home on Titran.

John Andersen, having lived in the city, felt anxious to contribute to the social life on the island and to replace some of the traditional activities of cardplaying and drinking with better forms of leisure and intellectual attainment. A movement called the Society for the Promotion of Popular Enlightenment was spreading across Norway, and John Andersen was the representative on the islands. The society published widely, and John's library was available to all. He also made it a regular practice to read poetry to groups who gathered at his house. Not satisfied with these efforts alone, he set his sights on a large community center consisting mostly of a reading room, built on the pattern of the assembly hall at Klaebo, that would also host concerts and religious services. He raised the money, and the eight-sided hall became a local landmark. A contemporary wrote of John Andersen's work on Froya, "John A. Widtsoe created life, so to speak, on these islands, where life had almost ceased; he started a movement to lift the people, which even today shows the power that was in him and his labor. He awakened the people as from a slumber."[2]

Over the years of teaching on the island, John Andersen experienced a growing dissatisfaction with the contribution he could make on Froya. He yearned for the experiences and opportunities that teaching in a larger school could bring. But Anna and John both felt an obligation to remain on the island to be near Anna's father. In February 1871, a little more than a month after their marriage, Peder died. The way seemed open for them to move to Oslo to pursue a degree.

The arduous work of settling the affairs of Peder's estate slowed their plans. On 31 January 1872, a little more than a year after their marriage, their first child, John Andreas Widtsoe, was born. But his birth was not without challenges. He later wrote:

> I am told that upon my birth (January 31, 1872) the wrist of my right hand was attached to the right side of my head. The separation was made at once and necessarily at great risk. Since there was no doctor on the island, and the job was crudely done, the scars still remain. It was thought, of course, that the day-old infant could not survive the shock and loss of blood. So, to save his son's soul from misery in hell, my father, with courageous friends, rowed across the angry fjord in midwinter, brought back an equally courageous priest, who sprinkled water on my head. Thus I was saved from abode in hell, and became a member of the Lutheran Church at the same time. It was a narrow escape; but I survived. Such dangers are not so great in our more enlightened days, for the midwife is now authorized to baptize dying infants, and thus to cheat the devil of the joy of torturing innocent children through an eternity or two. I am still wondering how a man with a trained mind, as was my father, could believe such evil nonsense.[3]

The child brought new priorities, and raising their son became the new parents' foremost interest. Some thought this new child ought to become the next king's pilot, as his grandfathers before him had been. But John and Anna were determined to raise this son in the mold of his father. The life of a schoolmaster was a worthy one, and they resolved that he should accomplish great deeds. Childhood memories of life on the island were few for young John, but he remembered the big house in Daloe and the frequent storms when the waves beat their way over the reefs and onto the shore so fiercely as to be heard in every corner of the house. "The angry ocean has beaten upon my memory all my life,"[4] was his comment.

It took almost three years to settle their affairs in Titran, but the family finally moved to Namsos, a small town some eighty miles north of Trondheim. In Namsos, there was a much larger school where John Andersen could have daily contact with stimulating colleagues and face the challenge of greater teaching opportunities. The local newspaper in Namsos learned of John's talent for writing and employed him as a regular contributor. The priest heard his musical voice and called on him to be the congregation's song leader. Life in Namsos was rich. Anna too found her social calendar filled. There were dances, musical performances, and theatrical productions. In Namsos, Anna had ample opportunity to expand her education, and her interest in the Bible was enlivened by contact with other churches. The couple was faintly aware of Mormon missionaries, but they only felt pity that bright young men from America had traveled so far for no real purpose.

The years that followed were the happiest for the small family. Their little son, inclined to get into mischief (several times he was nearly killed), had a lively childhood. To Anna, young John was the fullness of earthly joy.[5] John Andersen loved his little son and hoped that he would follow in his footsteps and become a schoolmaster. He took great delight in trying out educational experiments on young John, who was so often at school with his father that he became well acquainted with the faculty. John later remembered:

> My first clear memory reaches back to my fifth year. It was the glorious early summer time of Norway, in the town of Namsos, whither my father had moved. I was on the edge of the forest, in the midst of waist-high flowers. Birds were chirping and flying all about. A medium-sized, square-shouldered, athletic man, with blue eyes and coal black hair, was with me. He was teaching me how to make a whistle from a piece of young willow, so full of sap that the bark could be removed easily. It was my father. I blew that whistle with full lungs. We had a great time together.[6]

On 12 December 1877, about two years after they arrived in Namsos, another son, Aasbjorn (Osborne) Johannes Peder Widtsoe, was born. A few weeks later, in February 1878, John Andersen was suddenly taken ill. He was diagnosed with a telescoped intestine. Local doctors did all that was possible in those early days of surgical science, but on 14 February 1878, at the age of thirty-seven, John Andersen Widtsoe died. Anna was ill-prepared for this death, despite being raised in the hazardous fishing community. Writing about this difficult time, her son simply said, "The story of the weeks that followed would best be left untold."[7] Petroline, faithful and steadfast sister always, rushed by first boat to be with Anna and the boys, comforting them through the darkest days.

So distressing was her husband's death that Anna seemed barely conscious of the throngs who attended the funeral at the chapel and followed the procession to the grave. It was evident that the schoolmaster was dearly loved. The words spoken of their continued union were too shallow for meaning to Anna. Her heart received no comfort. Yet she had rehearsed how she might forge a bond between her two beloved Johns, the schoolmaster father and the gifted son. Young John was barely six, but he recalled that moment:

> The chapel and the streets outside were crowded, and hundreds
> followed the procession to the grave. The baby, of course, was left at
> home in the cradle, but the fishermaiden and her oldest son stood by
> the open grave while the cold words of the church funeral service
> were spoken, "Dust thou art, to dust returnest," with no promise of
> future meeting in a happier place than man's earth. Before the first
> shovelful of earth was cast into the grave, the schoolmaster's son, his
> namesake, threw a bright crimson rose upon the casket. That was the
> child's farewell, and his promise to carry on, in every high ideal that
> the schoolmaster had left behind.[8]

The crimson rose and the pledge that accompanied it were a driving force in John's life and his brilliant career. The vision, courage, warmth, and success of his father became beacons around which he piloted his course. John remained loyal to his father's desire that he would gain a devotion to God and family, and a love of truth, of learning, and of teaching. John recalled, "Just after my sixth birthday, my father died. Though young he had served his generation well. He was gifted, capable, farseeing, and wise, and was much beloved among the people. In my childish appreciation of him, I pledged, as his grave was filled, to keep his good work going."[9]

3

A NEW FAMILY COURSE

THE promise "to carry on, in every high ideal of the schoolmaster," supported young John through many decisions. The symbolic gesture of the crimson rose did much to remind him of that promise. Anna became his chief mentor. Throughout their lives, sometimes at significant sacrifice, Anna made every effort to provide the best opportunities and to open every way for John and Osborne to train as schoolmasters, or failing that, as priests. The people of Namsos, especially John Andersen's colleagues, opened their hearts to the family. Anna was given a position in the school. But it held too many memories and was too painful.

Anna decided to leave Namsos and return to her family in Titran, expecting to find solace, but too much of that life had gone; her parents were dead and Petroline had moved to the city. After a year on Froya, Anna decided to move the family to Trondheim, where the opportunities she sought for the boys were more readily available.

With her inheritance, the proceeds she received from several book auctions dispersing the schoolmaster's enviable library, and the small pension she was awarded for his school service, Anna had sufficient means to provide for her family. They moved into a two-room apartment on Steensbakken (Steens Hill). Below them was the beautiful

panorama of old Trondheim: its thousand-year-old cathedral reaching
to the sky, the fjord, and the harbor lined with ships. Framing the city
were fir-covered hills, beautiful in all seasons. A historic old fortress
stood above them on the hill.

John was seven, and his education was of primary importance to
Anna. Her husband's former colleagues in Trondheim offered to tutor
John privately, and Anna knew that surely no finer instruction could be
acquired. Consequently, she accepted. John recorded his memory of his
early school experience and the splendid beginning it gave him:

> School attendance began when I was nine years old. School
> friends of my father took me in hand and gave me private instruction,
> which prepared me for the special, more classical schools I was to
> enter, to become either a school teacher or a priest. I think my mother
> had some misgivings about the priest idea—but then a priest was bet-
> ter paid and higher in society than a teacher! Again, as I look back, I
> had a narrow escape.
>
> My mother taught me early to read. At five years of age I read
> easily. My father had an unusually well stocked library. My parents
> held me closely to the Bible; but I spent much time browsing among
> my father's books, many, of course, far beyond my understanding.
> However, I recall that in those earliest days of reading—I must have
> been about eight years old—I waded through a wonderful book
> called The Merchant of Venice. My mother helped me along. How I
> despised Shylock! Perhaps we do not do justice to the capacity of
> children for substantial reading. It is possible to oversimplify the
> offerings to children.[1]

John began at an early age to love books. Folklore, fairy tales, and
ancient adventure sagas ignited his lively imagination. Early he saw that
those who are free work best and are happiest. He developed a deep and
lasting aversion to tyranny. Truth and freedom became basic credos; they
were the framework for his view on life. Anna wanted her boys to stay
close to her family, so each spring when school was out, John was sent to
Froya for the summer. He remembered, "Fishing, catching crabs and lob-
sters, curing fish, and making fish nets were the routine of the day. When
we were not so engaged or swimming, Bruno, the dog, and I feasted on

wild honey. The dog found the hives, and snapped at the bees, while I took out the honey combs. Then, as a fair division, I ate the honey, and Bruno disposed of the wax. Such life was good for small boys."[2]

Anna was still very young and made many friends in these difficult years. She received several proposals of marriage, but she remained committed to her husband. Petroline sacrificed her own work and many of her plans to live with Anna and help raise the boys. The sisters turned to the skills learned on Froya and ran a successful sewing and dressmaking business in Trondheim.

Anna and Petroline had a strong Lutheran background, although John remembered that Anna had some reservations about her religion: "I soon recognized that my mother had serious doubts about some of the doctrine taught by the dressed-up priests and bishops. . . . Earnestly she prayed and read and studied to understand the purposes of the Lord with mankind, especially with herself. She acquired a new nearness to God. Truth appeared holier than ever before. Her sorrow became tinged with the glory of faith. In the language of the day she became one of the 'awakened.' Yet, she did not find the solace that she had expected in the church of her girlhood."[3]

Anna probed deeply those questions about life's purpose and how best to seek happiness and fulfillment in the service of one's family and one's God. She also made the acquaintance of a ship's captain who lived in their apartment building. When Anna needed to have John's shoes repaired, the captain recommended the shoemaker, Olaus Johnsen:

Anna Widtsoe's hand was on the door latch, when the shoemaker said, somewhat hesitatingly, for the business was concluded and the lady was a stranger, "You may be surprised to hear me say that I can give you something of more value than soles for your child's shoes." She was surprised. She looked into the eyes of the man, who stood straight and courageous in his shop.

"What can you, a shoemaker, give me better than soles for my son's shoes? You speak in riddles," she answered.

The shoemaker did not hesitate. "If you will but listen, I can teach you the Lord's true plan of salvation for His children. I can teach you how to find happiness in this life, and to prepare for eternal joy in the life to come. I can tell you whence you came, why you are upon earth, and where you will go after death. I can teach you, as you have never known it before, the love of God for his children on earth."

Understanding, happiness, joy, love—the words with which she was wrestling! But, this was a shoemaker shop. This man was clearly a humble man who knew little of the wisdom of schools and churches. She felt confused. She simply asked, "Who are you?"

"I am a member of the Church of Christ—we are called Mormons. We have the truth of God."

Mormons! It was terrible. She had innocently walked into a dangerous place. Hurriedly she thanked the shoemaker, left the shop, and climbed the hill.

Yet, as she walked homeward, the words of the shoemaker rang in her ears; and she remembered a certain power in his voice and majesty in his bearing when he delivered his message and bore his testimony. He was a shoemaker, but no ordinary man. Could it really be that the Mormons had the truth of the Lord? No, it was absurd! But, it made her thoughtful and restless. When the repaired shoes were brought to the house a day or two later, by the shoemaker's young son, Arnt Johnsen, Anna Widtsoe found, carefully tucked into each toe, other Mormon tracts. The shoemaker was valiant. He missed no opportunity to fulfill the obligation of a Latter-day Saint, to bear witness modestly and properly but steadily, to all the world.

Then began two years of struggle.[4]

What could a shoemaker know that trained priests could not? What new could be offered her by a small, almost unknown sect whose only reputation was for polygamy, a social practice disapproved of by all Christian churches and repugnant to all of Western society? As a schoolmaster's wife Anna was socially in a different class from the kind of people she perceived Mormons to be. But the desire to find truth, nurtured by her schoolmaster, kept their conversation and Olaus's testimony in her mind.

Anna started to attend meetings on Sunday. The meeting room was on the second floor of the Johnsens' house and, as she had thought, the congregation was made up of people of a lower class than herself. She did find the peace she had been seeking in this new religion. But what would acceptance of this religion do to her social standing?[5] "Must I step down to that?" she asked. Determinedly, she would have to say yes, "If it is the truth I must do so."[6] Her acquaintance with the restored gospel, missionaries from the States, the Johnsens, and other Trondheim Mormons continued. Nevertheless, it was a struggle to adjust to the differences from what she had learned from her youth. She took the Bible as her authority and through her independent self-assurance finally concluded that the book was primarily on the side of the Mormons.

Anna underwent many mental and spiritual battles that kept her awake through many long nights. If she joined the Church, how would it affect her deceased husband? How would it affect her boys and the future she wanted for them? Could she stay in Norway? Would she keep her social standing and her friends? She felt terribly alone, yet she knew that her decision had to be based on feelings revealed to her heart and mind. John described her battle: "Those who have charged that men and women accept Mormonism for ulterior motives know little of the intense search for truth and exhausting conquest of self that have preceded conversion."[7] Anna cast aside her fears and thought no more of the sacrifices for the sacred truths of the gospel, only of the blessings that flowed from accepting and abiding by those truths.

On 1 April 1881, a little more than two years after Anna's first meeting with the shoemaker and the Trondheim Mormons, Elder Anthon L. Skanchy baptized Anna into The Church of Jesus Christ of Latter-day Saints. "Thin ice still lay over the edges of the fjord, which had to be broken to permit the ordinance to be performed. The water was icy cold. Yet, she declared to her dying day that never before in all her life had she felt warmer or more comfortable than when she came out of the baptismal waters of old Trondheim's fjord. The fire within was kindled, never to be extinguished. The humble people of the branch became her brethren and sisters. She loved them and rejoiced in their company."[8]

John was naturally affected by this change in Anna's life:

> I liked the spirit of these new people called "Mormons." It was good to be with them, despite their humble surroundings. They were so fervent and so certain in all their sayings and actions.

*Elder Anthon L. Skanchy.
On the back of the photo is
written "1st missionary in
Widtsoe home, baptized the
widow."*

After my mother had been baptized, she explained to me that she
desired that I postpone baptism until I understood the gospel for
myself. She was loyal to my father's memory. She must not influence
me unduly, she thought.

A change then came into our lives. Friends and relatives became
cool towards us. Gradually we were left alone. I wondered what we
had done. We were "Mormons!" Somehow there crept into my mind
at last a comprehension of intolerance, of the dark evil called bigotry.[9]

Anna lost many of her friends, especially school colleagues. The
local clergy threatened to cancel her pension unless she returned to the
state church. Her relations with her family became strained; one visit
left her "heavy-hearted, slightly embittered, but more determined than
ever to keep the commandments of the Lord, . . . Her faithful, devoted
sister Petroline was then living with her, but even she could not understand the behavior of her sister. It seemed so foolish. Truly the fishermaiden was alone in the world. But, she had found the truth; she had

entered God's earthly kingdom; she was preparing for a great eternal blessing; she trusted the Lord."[10]

New friendships with Church members became increasingly important to Anna. Her family and her home were open to all who were affiliated with the branch in Trondheim. In addition to the Johnsens and the Trondheim Mormons, Anna made treasured friendships with the missionaries. Elders Anthon L. Skanchy, Christian H. Steffensen, Niles H. Borresen, Thorvald A. Thoresen, and Hans O. Magleby were among those long remembered.

The fruits of her conversion were sweeter than she had imagined, for there was more genuine happiness in her life than since the death of her husband, and her business prospered—all despite the unfriendliness of immediate acquaintances and family members. For many years there hung in the Trondheim meetinghouse a framed verse written by Anna in these difficult days. Loosely translated, it reads:

> *Jesus, our Brother, is King,*
> *For us He the victory won;*
> *Rejoice, dear brethren and sisters,*
> *In the newfound light and life.*
> *Our Zion awaits the Savior.*
> *We hope to meet Him there;*
> *His bride He will fetch to His home,*
> *Only be humble and true.*[11]

4

GATHERING TO ZION

―――――――――――――― ▪ ――――――――――――――

CONVERSION to Mormonism in 1881 included answering the call to gather with the full body of the Saints to build up the latter-day Zion. For two years the months were filled with the new friendships Anna developed in the Trondheim Branch, but they passed slowly as she longed to gather to Zion. Familiar questions went through Anna's mind: How would the children fare? Could they accept life in a new land with a new language and culture? Would they be accepted? Could they endure the separation from family and friends? Could the boys still become schoolmasters?

God's prophets were in Salt Lake City, and they had instructed the Saints to gather to Zion. True to the faith that burned in her heart, Anna prepared to immigrate to Utah. At first the problem of raising enough money seemed insurmountable, but it became possible with the help of friends and her own industry, together with small donations from missionaries Anthon L. Skanchy and Christian H. Steffensen, and from Ole Berkhoel, a gifted violinist who had known the schoolmaster in Namsos and was a convert to the Church. Once the finances were organized, it was easy enough to get the boys ready; John was nearly twelve and Osborne was five. But the hardest part was leaving Petroline, who had not responded to the message of Mormonism and had no desire to leave Norway.

Before leaving, out of a sense of responsibility to the family, Anna took her sons to visit their relatives one last time. She earnestly desired to maintain in herself and in her boys close ties to family roots, and she consented to let John spend the summer of 1883 with Aunt Johanna. He later wrote:

> My aunt was scandalized that any member of the family had become besmirched with Mormonism. She was determined to prevent the oldest son of her beloved elder brother from going to Utah, there to live an evil life with "Danites" and "avenging angels." Therefore, she arranged that a few days before my mother's expected arrival, I was to be sent into the mountain districts, so far away that I could not be brought back in time for the sailing of the boat. And should the stubborn mother miss the boat to recover her son, no one would know where her son was. It was a perfect plan, which, of course, was unknown to me. I understood only that I was going into the mountain for an outing.
>
> The day for my departure came. My belongings were all packed. The horses were at the door. We were at breakfast. Suddenly there was the sound of the daily mail cart, which also carried passengers. It stopped in front of the house. Out stepped my mother with my brother Osborne, just one week earlier than the set date! My aunt's consternation was inexpressible. Even now I must smile at the episode. Yet, even then, my aunt wanted to take me into the mountains, "for a change." She also was of the stern kind. But my mother was unyielding. "We leave for Oslo this afternoon." Thus, I was not kidnapped, and another "best-laid plan" was foiled. Why my mother left her home a week early she could not explain. "I just had to leave then." So the Lord guides his faithful children.[1]

On 20 October 1883, Anna Widtsoe and her two sons boarded ship on the first leg of their voyage to America and Zion. Twenty Norwegian Saints made up their emigrating company. Members of the Oslo Branch of the Church lined the pier to bid them a fitting and memorable farewell. Songs of Zion rang from the pier and were answered by the hearts of the Saints on the deck. Handkerchiefs were waved briskly, signifying love and a longing to be reunited in Zion.

Two days later they arrived in Hull, England, from where they went by rail to Liverpool. There Anna first saw an apostle of the Lord, Elder John Henry Smith. She remarked that he was as kind and good a man as her heart expected of one who held that high office in the holy priesthood. While waiting to set sail from Liverpool to New York, they took in what they could of England: "There is revealed in the boyish scrawl of a beginning diary a very open-eyed boy with an ocean-hating stomach. In Liverpool he gasps, 'Spent the afternoon in a museum, in which there was more to see than I thought could be collected in one place.'"[2]

On 27 October 1883, the Widtsoe family and their Norwegian party of emigrants were joined by other Saints gathering to Zion from Denmark, Sweden, and England. Together, they embarked on the SS *Wisconsin.* The eleven-day voyage was filled with seasickness, homesickness, and a fear of the unknown, offset by the joy of being in company with others who had heeded the Spirit and joined the Church. Gospel discussions, religious services, and shared experiences met empathetic and longing ears. Lasting associations were formed on the high seas of the North Atlantic.

They arrived in New York on 7 November 1883. The next day they boarded the train for their long journey to Utah. One week later, on Saturday, 15 November 1883, Anna and her sons arrived in their Zion: Logan, Utah. The blue sky, brilliant sunlight, resplendent mountains, and wide-open valley gave them the assurance of a good and happy home.

Elder Skanchy and his family welcomed the Widtsoes under their roof for a few days, helped them secure the necessary furniture items to get their new life started, and oversaw their move into a one-room house on a large lot on the southern edge of Logan. Although this little house was a far cry from Anna's houses in Titran, Daloe, or Namsos, she looked upon it as a mansion, located as it was in Zion under the light of the restored gospel. But life in their new Zion was a stark contrast to the comfort of Norway. Froya, Namsos, and Trondheim had been settled for well over a millennium. Settlers had been in Utah only a little more

Anna with sons John and Osborne, one week after their arrival in Utah.

than a quarter of a century. Instead of being surrounded by the sea, they lived in the shadow of the Rocky Mountains. The humid sea air was replaced by a dry climate with extremes of temperatures. Fishing was replaced by farming and cooperative religious living. Unity, shared concerns, and common devotion replaced family roots.

Some things did not change. Anna was determined to have a settled household with well-organized and well-maintained flower and vegetable gardens. The children had to be clothed and fed. Their education was as essential as their study of scripture and prayer.

They divided the single room in this house into four, a living room, dining room, bedroom, and kitchen. Naturally they faced the trials that accompany settling in an unfamiliar land and learning a new language, but their faith, and the help of neighbors and friends, kept them going. About a month after their arrival in Logan, John was attacked by a mad dog that bit and tore his legs and arms so severely that he was bedridden for six weeks. This was a difficult time for mother and son since the recuperation took most of their first winter.

Anna had again set herself up as a seamstress and was soon quite busy. She sewed by hand, late into the night, because it took more than a year to acquire a hand-driven sewing machine. However, the necessity of spending that first winter looking after John meant that their small financial reserves were taxed to the limit. In addition, their late arrival in November meant that they had no food storage. Getting through that first winter was a great test of their sturdy Norse character, their humility, their faith, and their determination. Recalling these days, John wrote of blessings at the hand of the Lord:

> Actual want there was not. The organization of the Church provided against suffering, should it occur, and kindly friends and neighbors were anxious to give the newcomers a helping hand. One evening during the first, bitter cold winter in Logan, the widow put her last stick of wood into the stove. Then she called her two boys to her side. Together they knelt down and told the Lord of their condition, and asked him for fuel so that they might keep warm. Within five minutes after their prayer was over, there was a knock on the door, and Brother Larsen, living some distance up the street, and barely an acquaintance, came in with a big sack of coal upon his back, for the emigrant family. The prayer had been answered, almost before it was uttered. The luxury of that coal, the first they had in Zion, and the knowledge that the Lord was near, made the evening one of rare joy.[3]

In March, John, now recovered from his encounter with the dog, was able to work. They put him to work toting slabs at the old U.O.M.&B. Lumber Mills at Logan at twenty-five cents a day. One worker wrote, "The job was alright with the exception that the slabs came off the saw faster than they should."[4] The family was able to move into a two-room house closer to the center of town where Anna could expand her business. Her sewing business was beginning to flourish but was slow in winter. John wrote:

> Collections were slow one month; John was out of work. At last the family had only a sack of "shorts" left. [Shorts are a by-product of wheat milling that includes the germ, fine bran, and some flour.] For three weeks, they lived on "shorts" and water. Never before, in man's history, had "shorts been served in so many different forms as the

An old house in Logan. A note on the photo reads, "One of daddy's first houses in Logan."

widow's ingenuity devised." Nevertheless, the diet was frightfully monotonous. They did not know, then, the high nutritive value of "shorts." One day, after nearly three weeks of rations on "shorts" and water, the Sixth Ward had a ward reunion. A Mormon ward reunion includes a feast of nearly all the good things of earth. When the meal was ended, there was food left over, and the good-hearted Bishop Skanchy—and no man was ever kinder to the poor—filled a large basket with roast chicken and lamb, vegetables and bread, cakes and desserts, and sent them by a messenger to the widow and her sons, who now lived in the First Ward. When the "shorts"-filled boys saw the well-filled basket of goodies uncovered upon their table there was eager, anticipatory swallowing, and much inward joy; all of which was changed to darkest despair when the widow drew herself up to her full height and said, "Brother, please take the basket back to the bishop with my thanks, and say to him that Sister Widtsoe is not a beggar, yet." To the boys, the departure of that basket with its contents was the darkest moment of their first years in Zion. It seemed a foolish pride, but perhaps it was better for the family to nurse a stubborn independence.[5]

In those early years, John received a strong witness of the power of prayer:

There were not many after-school jobs in Logan when I was a

boy, but I found one that took only two or three hours a day. One day my employer told me I had done very well, and he gave me a five-dollar gold piece for my several weeks of work.

Five dollars! That was money! I was jubilant! I would give half of it to my mother, buy a new book, and save the remainder. Into the pocket of my trousers went the bright new gold piece, and off I ran to tell my mother of my good luck.

On the way home, I put my hand in the pocket to feel and caress the money. It was not there! Instead, I found a hole in the pocket through which the coin had slipped. It was terrible! I was so sorry that I sat down by the ditch bank and cried.

Then I slowly walked back the way I had come, looking every step for the gold piece. The sidewalk on Logan Main Street was made of planks. I looked in every crack for my lost fortune. Not a sign of it! Then I walked back over the same road, stopping, looking every-where. No little shiny gold coin was there to lighten my heart! Again I walked slowly back and forth over the road I had been following when the precious coin was lost. But it was not to be found! It was lost for good.

Then I remembered that the Lord knew where that gold piece was, and that if he would help me, and wanted me to find it, it could not be lost for long.

So I got down on my knees behind a big tree and told the Lord all about my trouble, and asked him, if he thought it was the best thing for me, to help me find it. When I got up I felt so much better. I felt sure the Lord had heard my prayer.

Dusk was gathering. One would not see anything on the ground very clearly, especially a small piece of gold. But I walked right on, not so slowly this time. For I knew the Lord was helping. About halfway up the second block, there in the grass lay my lost five-dollar gold piece. It gleamed in the darkness, as if to say, "Come and take me; I want to make you happy." I almost shouted with joy. I leaned up against the fence and said, "Thank you, O Lord, for finding my money for me." Since that time I have known that the Lord hears prayers. And, since that day, I have been careful to have no holes in my pockets.[6]

Anna had trouble learning English. John had learned some English in school, and Osborne was fairly new to any language, so English came easily to him. Anna mourned the loss of the expressive and beautiful language in which she had composed her poetry and read the literature that touched all the finer things of life. In later years much of her time was spent in Norwegian literary associations and among Norwegian immigrants to Utah. John noted, "A copy of *Leslie's Weekly* became the first instructor, followed by the Book of Mormon and the Bible. By the time the first year in Zion was over, the little family had pretty well battered down the language wall. The mother, however, never overcame the accent inherited from the language of her childhood. But she learned to love the English language."[7]

Logan was a Mormon pioneer town with wide streets crossing at right angles. They were either muddy or dusty according to the season. Most of the houses were small log cabins, waiting to be replaced by the family home when prosperity and time allowed. Each log cabin had a plot of ground for a kitchen garden, and in the back were farm buildings. Their culinary water came from wells, while the rivers supplied water for the gardens (as soon as they were able to get their canals and ditches in place). When the Widtsoes arrived in Logan, there were four small meetinghouses, a large modern tabernacle, and a beautiful temple nearing completion on the hill above them. Logan was a melting pot of Britons, Americans, and Scandinavians. In their homelands they had been tradesmen and craftsmen, but here survival demanded they become farmers. A return to their trades would come as the community grew and life became more settled. Meanwhile, they were a happy people. They treasured the truths they had found in Mormonism and sought to live in the harmony of the gospel. John wrote:

> The desert lay about them. Settlements such as Logan, dependent upon irrigation, were as oases in the surrounding wilderness which in the main remained unconquered. Industrial conditions and means of transportation, despite the coming of the railroad (January 31, 1873), were such as to compel each unit to be largely self-sustaining, or meet defeat. Little money was in circulation. Instead, the business houses issued, in return for work done, "store orders" of various denominations, redeemable in merchandise. These passed from hand to hand as currency does today. Every family was required to produce most of its

own foodstuffs. Therefore, every family had a garden, chickens, cows, and other livestock. My mother's little garden, cultivated by my brother and myself, contributed largely to meet our food needs. The majority of the people by force of circumstance were farmers. It was not always an easy matter for tradesmen of the older countries to make their living from the soil, but it had to be done.[8]

Anna missed Petroline very much. She had been her strength in Norway, and without her, Anna felt very much alone. So it was with great joy that in 1885, Anna learned that Petroline had received a personal witness of the truth and would rejoin her family. After her baptism and confirmation as a member of the Church, Petroline began preparing to emigrate. Anna wrote her a letter asking for the things she missed most from Norway:

> In this letter I send you five dollars, which use as you desire, but . . . if you can, buy and bring with you . . . two myrtles with strong roots, several bulbs of Mrs. Rian's white lilies, as many bulbs as you can secure of Jacob's lilies, and as many rare flowers as you can conveniently secure. Place them in a tight cigar box containing ripe good garden soil. Water them carefully on the way . . . I hope this box will not give you any more trouble than John and Osborne caused me.
>
> The Lord has blessed this desert so that the poor among His children who come here in faith, are not disappointed. . . . I desire to bear witness to you my dear sister of the covenant, that this gospel that we have accepted is of God, and I say to you and all members of the Church, be faithful in the midst of your tribulations and a glorious and beautiful day will dawn for you. . . . This work is the last call to the earth from the King of Glory.[9]

Petroline arrived in Logan on 7 July 1885.

5

A NEW LIFE

JOHN A. Widtsoe's youthful impressions of the Saints who had chosen, or had been sent, to live among their brothers and sisters in Logan indicate clearly their love for the truths of the gospel:

> I was not conscious in those days that Logan, with the life within it, was as a social-economic laboratory, yielding results of far-reaching meaning.
>
> The four or five thousand people in Logan, with a handful of exceptions, were converts to the "Mormon" faith. They were chiefly American, English, and Scandinavian. There were a few Southern Europeans and a family or two from Australia. The city was a veritable melting pot of nationalities.[1]
>
> Few among the citizens of Logan were poor, fewer were rich. . . . All in all, there was practically a financial equality among the people. All knew one another and tried to be of service in time of need. Life there, compared with the present cluttered, panting day, was idyllic.[2]

Though life in Logan approached the ideal for frontier living, there were problems the citizenry had to confront. For instance, there were three saloons, one of which had a billiard hall. There was, even in Zion, a criminal element against which the people took action. When a man raped and murdered a local girl, they hanged him as was common in less-civilized towns. It was John's impression that the hanging led to an increased respect for law and order.

Utah communities were strengthened by the common sacrifices made to follow the Mormon faith. Beyond the shared religious devotion was their uniform dedication to education as evidenced in the elementary, secondary, and college institutions established in that generation. In his youth, John saw the beginnings of the Brigham Young College and the Utah Agricultural College, both outstanding accomplishments for a community so young and small. He wrote, "The families one by one bore silent testimony to their sincerity, honesty, and devotion to what they believed to be the word of God. Their common faith was the cement that held together the human elements, widely different in origin and experience."[3]

Part of settling into their new life in Zion was exposure to all the trials the Church faced. In Norway they encountered ridicule over "strange" beliefs and practices, but in Utah they had firsthand experience with those beliefs and practices. When the Widtsoes arrived in Zion in 1883, the crackdown of federal marshals against faithful Mormons practicing polygamy was in full swing.

Prominent Church leaders in Logan and Cache Valley were a prime target. Along with stake president C. O. Card were Marriner W. Merrill, president of the Logan Temple; Samuel Roskelly, the temple recorder; and Henry Ballard, who had been bishop of the Logan Second Ward for almost four decades. Finer or more devout men could scarcely be found in any other age or community. A recent history of Cache County sheds light on this troubled time:

> In 1885 federal marshals organized a number of raids on Cache County. Roskelly became a target for prosecution because of his position as temple recorder; he also had been a bishop for two decades in Smithfield. Since, as a polygamist, he shared time among his four families, he easily developed methods to avoid capture. He often stayed inside the temple, frequently spending the night there, and only moved through the city after dark. He moved through Logan at night dressed shabbily with an unlit pipe in his mouth and an axe on his

shoulder. His sons would meet him at a prearranged place and put him in a wagon covered with hay. . . . Roskelly kept up this resistance until prosecution ceased with the Manifesto of 1890 issued by Mormon church president Wilford Woodruff.[4]

John's personal reaction is instructive:

> At the time we reached Logan the polygamy persecutions were moving towards their height. There were a number of men with plural wives in the city, though forming a very small percentage of the population. I became intimately acquainted with several plural households. They were the most peaceful, wholesome, God-fearing families in the city. They were a challenge of decency and high living to many monogamous conditions I have observed in my life. Since I did not come of polygamous stock nor have entered into polygamy, I have viewed the situation with unprejudiced eyes.
>
> When the crusade reached its height, the Logan boys took sides against the deputy marshals who sought to bring the "offenders" to trial. The boys rejoiced when the "persecutors" were foiled. They were jubilant, for example, when C. O. Card, president of the stake, escaped from his captors on a horse, bridled and saddled and placed conveniently near, under the very eyes of the marshal.[5]

John's account of a presentation on Utah that he attended while at Harvard provides an interesting contrast:

> I remember the sickening, lying Reverend Doctor George Washington Hill, who spoke on Utah in a Cambridge, Massachusetts, church in the autumn of 1891. The plural wives of Mormon polygamists lived with their children, he said, in dugouts in the foothills of Cache Valley; the man lived in a fine house. The wives and children began their work in the fields at sunrise; he rode among them a couple of hours later, and used his blacksnake whip on the backs of the women and children. To save these poor things from such terror he had come to ask for contributions. The collection plate was pyramided with offerings that night; but I have no doubt that in a higher court provision was made for the entrance of this deliberate liar into whatever place is reserved for those who, under the cloak of religion, deceive their fellows and injure the innocent.[6]

In spite of all of the obstacles of getting the family settled, Anna flourished in this desert environment. She found excitement and great joy in the activities of the Church, even in that first year. "Association with faithful Latter-day Saints and participation in the activities of the Church were really her life's vocation," John wrote.[7] Anna raised her boys in the light of the gospel and the communion of the Spirit, but they themselves made the decision to join the Church. John was baptized on 3 April 1884 in the creek that flowed behind the Brigham Young College in Logan. Osborne was baptized in the font of the Logan temple in 1886. They were both active in the Sunday School and Mutual Improvement Associations. John gives a glimpse into the life of a deacon:

> Soon after my baptism, at my own request, on April 3, 1884, I was ordained to the office of a deacon in the Aaronic Priesthood. I served as secretary of the quorum. We were trained for the work of deacons. We sawed logs and chopped firewood for the widows against winter's need. We looked after the room in the Stake Tabernacle in which the ward held its meetings; we were taught that possession of the Priesthood meant participation in the work of the Church. It was good medicine for the boys who in time would assume Church leadership.[8]

There were many sacred occasions when Anna experienced spiritual gifts. At times she received the gift of tongues and spoke in an unknown language, followed by a fluent interpretation from another faithful sister. John knew her to spend the remainder of her life "in close communion with the spiritual forces which she invited by eager, never-failing attention to her duties as she learned to understand them."[9] Anna learned much about the gospel and in time encountered the Word of Wisdom. She had drunk coffee and occasionally tea. She never bothered with alcohol, but she often sewed well beyond midnight, and her cup of coffee seemed to give her the necessary lift. John wrote, "After two months' struggle, she came home one day, having given serious consideration to the Word of Wisdom problem. Her mind was made up. She stood in the middle of the room and said aloud, 'Never again. Get behind me, Satan!' and, walking briskly to her cupboard, took out the packages of coffee and tea and threw them on the fire. From that day she never used tea or coffee."[10]

When the Widtsoes arrived, the Logan Temple was nearing completion. It was a monument to the faith of these gathering Saints, and, as it progressed, there was more and more discussion among the people about the sacred building, the sacred ordinances, and the nearness of loved ones who had passed beyond the veil. They had all given much for the restored gospel, and the temple was a sacred presence that testified of the worth of all their efforts. The great events that led to the temple's coming to Logan soon became an important part of the Widtsoes' spiritual moorings. In the years that followed, each of them made unusually important contributions to the work that was to be accomplished in the temples of the Church.

The people of Logan spoke openly of a prophecy uttered by Wilford Woodruff with President Brigham Young at his back in the old bowery that served as a meeting place before any church buildings were erected. Elder Woodruff recorded the events of 21 August 1863, when a large number of young women, dressed in white, stood on one side of the road while young men in their best attire stood on the other, awaiting the arrival of President Young and his party to Logan. In a sacred service the following morning, President Young called on President Woodruff to speak. He paid tribute to the youth for the respect they had shown for the prophet and apostles the previous evening. He admonished them to treasure the teachings and sayings of these prophets while they were yet living rather than waiting for them to pass on. He then said:

> A few days and President Young and his brethren, the prophets, apostles, Brothers Benson and Maughan will be in the spirit world. You should never forget this visitation. You are to become men and women, fathers and mothers; yea, the day will come after your fathers and the prophets and apostles are dead and passed away into the spirit world, you will have the privilege of going into the towers of a glorious temple built unto the name of the Most High (pointing in the direction of the bench) east of us upon the Logan bench. And while you stand in the towers of that temple, and your eyes survey this glorious

valley filled with cities and villages, occupied by tens of thousands of Latter-day Saints, you will then call to mind this visitation of President Young and his company.[11]

President Young then arose and said, "What Brother Woodruff has said was Revelation and will all be fulfilled."[12]

Fourteen years later, on Friday, 18 May 1877, President Young and a large company of Church leaders met to select the exact site for the temple. Joy filled the hearts of all present as they witnessed a prophet select the sacred spot: "Brigham Young put his heel down on the southeast corner, walked 171 feet west, 95 feet north, and back to the east and south corners. He asked James Anderson and William Hyde, with four other brethren, to dig holes where the present towers are, so he could see the formation of the ground. They found it was difficult digging, and when the hole was down eight to ten feet, Brigham said: 'that's far enough, brethren, it is like that clear to the bottom.'"[13] Many years later official surveys determined that the temple stood on a thousand feet of gravel.

Activities that centered around the completion and dedication of the temple kept Bishop Skanchy very busy. He was bishop of the Sixth Ward, an official in the dedicatory services, and the informal head of the Scandinavian Saints. The Norwegian converts had a special interest in the temple since a gifted Norwegian artist, Danquart Anthon Weggeland, had been commissioned to paint the beautiful murals in two of the rooms.

The excitement that preceded the dedication of the temple aroused the interest and enhanced the expectation of nearly everyone in the area. The doctrine of eternal families brought to Anna an increased nearness to her father, her mother, and her beloved husband. John wrote, "In that principle, as it was unfolded before her, she verily reveled. . . . It threw a flood of light upon the whole meaning of the gospel as well as upon the nature of God. She became a diligent searcher for her genealogy, and did much temple work for her dead. The doctrine of universal salvation was to her one of the greatest gifts of the gospel. The day on which temple work was done for her father, mother, and husband was the notable day of that year to the family."[14]

The city council and the mayor passed a resolution that all of Logan's streets were to be specially cleaned three days before the dedication ceremonies began. Excursion trains coming to Logan ran at reduced rates to accommodate all who wished to attend. Admission to the dedication ceremony was by ticket signed by President John Taylor and issued by the bishops. President Taylor announced that all who were worthy and desired it could attend the temple. Henry Ballard was the bishop of the neighboring ward. An unusual event occurred in his life in connection with the temple dedication that captured the spiritual interest of many. Sister Ballard wrote:

> My husband Henry Ballard, being Bishop of the Logan Second Ward, was busy writing out recommends to all who wished to go to the temple, when our daughter Ellen, age eight, came in with a newspaper in her hand and asked for her father. I told her that her father was busy, but to give the paper to me and I would give it to him. She said: "No, a man gave the paper to me and told me to give it to no one but father." I let the child take the paper to her father, and when he took it and looked at it he was greatly surprised, for he saw that the paper had been printed in Newbury, Berkshire, England, his birthplace, and was only three days from the press.[15]

The Ballard family had moved from Newbury, their family seat, to Logan. It had taken them thirteen weeks on the ocean and another thirteen weeks on land to get to Utah. The Newbury newspaper contained tombstone inscriptions of the pertinent data of some sixty direct ancestors of Bishop Ballard that had been copied at the cemetery. The paper so startled Bishop Ballard that he took it to the temple president, Marriner W. Merrill, who told him, "Brother Ballard, that was two of the three Nephites who brought that paper to you, for it could come in no other way in so short a time. It is meant for you to do the temple work for these people."[16] Bishop Ballard was the father of apostle Melvin J. Ballard, who was born a little more than a year after John had been born. Later, as apostles, Melvin J. Ballard and John A. Widtsoe were loyal friends, sharing many parallel experiences up to Elder Ballard's death in 1939.

The dedicatory services were held 16–18 May 1884. Anna and John had obtained tickets for 17 May. "A never-to-be-forgotten day was May 17, 1884, when the Logan Temple was dedicated. The spiritual enrichment of the day was ample reward for whatever sacrifices [Anna] had had to make for the gospel. It seemed to her as if the heavens had opened and the very voice of God had been heard by her. She had never been so near the heavenly hosts before. The same spirit was upon her when she received her own endowments on April 15, 1887."[17]

The official Logan Temple history book recorded the events of the days surrounding the dedication. Excerpts from it were published as part of the first 100 years celebration of the temple dedication by Nolan P. Olsen, secretary, recorder, and president of the temple for many years:

> Saturday, May 17, 1884: At length the auspicious day arrived, the day most memorable in the history of Logan City. It had been looked forward to with unspeakable pleasure and delight by thousands of Latter-day Saints who have contributed of their means liberally to erect the House of God, and by many hundreds of others.
>
> The day was serene and beautiful. The sun shone in glorious majesty and shed his benign influence over all the face of nature, which seemed to be in harmony and sympathy with the object and purpose of the occasion.
>
> The people of Logan and vicinity exerted themselves to their utmost to ensure the comforts of their numerous guests. It was not ascertained how many people visited Logan during the dedication days, but there was a much larger number than on any previous occasion. The number of arrivals by train varied from 100 to 320 on every train that came. Thousands of Latter-day Saints assembled in Logan from all parts of Utah, Idaho and other places.
>
> Shortly before ten o'clock in the morning the east doors of the Temple were opened and the people commenced to enter and were conducted up the spiral stairways to the assembly hall. They were seated in the body of the hall in reversible benches, facing east when the speaker was in the east stand, and west when the speaker was in the Aaronic priesthood stand.
>
> When all were seated, a holy sacred solemn stillness filled the House, and an almost unspeakable peace filled the hearts of the vast assembly. At 10:30 A.M. President Taylor arose in the stand, with the

spirit of the Living God beaming in his face, and requested the choir to sing 'Come Swell the Grandly Solemn Strain,' a hymn composed for the occasion by H. W. Naisbitt.[18]

Seated behind the Melchizedek Priesthood pulpits were the men who would significantly shape John's life. They included President John Taylor and his counselors, George Q. Cannon and Joseph F. Smith, and apostles Wilford Woodruff, Lorenzo Snow, and Heber J. Grant. The words these great brethren uttered from the pulpit, carried by the Holy Spirit in that solemn stillness and unspeakable peace, were fundamental to the spiritual foundation of John's life.

The counsel in President Taylor's dedicatory prayer seemed especially applicable, as if providing a blueprint for John's future. The prophet prayed that the temple would be a house where the people would be

> further prepared to carry out Thy will, to administer Thine ordinances, to purify and instruct Thy Church, and to build up and establish Thy Zion on the earth. . . . To become acquainted with all good books, . . . and obtain a knowledge of nations, kingdoms, governments, and laws. . . . And as all wisdom dwells with Thee, and, as all light, truth and intelligence flow from Thee, we humbly seek unto Thee for Thy blessing to rest upon this house, that it may be indeed a house of learning under Thy guidance, direction and inspiration . . . that we may be enabled to act justly, prudently, righteously and intelligently in all the various relations of life pertaining to social, religious, political and other duties devolving upon us, and that we may comprehend always fully the relationship that we sustain to this nation, to other nations, and to the world generally. . . . That Thy people may be preserved from the errors of vanity, the follies and corruptions of the world; that they may progress and excel in every principle of integrity, intelligence, virtue, until Zion shall become the praise and glory of the whole earth.[19]

Throughout John's life, temples and temple work were so important to him that his contribution to the understanding and proliferation of temple work is perhaps unparalleled (see chapter 23). In the preface of

President Olsen's history of the Logan Temple is an excerpt from John's teachings:

> Apostle John A. Widtsoe said: "Spiritual power is generated within temple walls and sent out to bless the world. Light from the House of the Lord illuminates every home within the church. The path from the temple to the home of man is divinely brilliant. Every home penetrated by the temple enlightens, cheers, and comforts every member of the household. Temples are for the benefit and enlightenment of the members of the church. In them are revealed the keys of the priesthood, and there power is given men from on high to meet the many issues of life. The ordinances and ritual of the temple, profoundly meaningful, set forth completely and comprehensively the truths of life, explain the mysteries of existence, and make the gospel more understandable."[20]

6

PROSPERING IN ZION

THE early years in Logan saw at least some prosperous times for Anna and her boys. Her success as a seamstress led to the suggestion that she open a sewing school, so Anna rented some rooms and taught many a mother and grandmother in Logan to sew. However, such was the success at the school that it began to affect their family life so, after a couple of years, she closed it and returned to her seamstress work.

John had received a splendid primary education in Norway, much of it being given by individual tutoring from his father's colleagues, some of the best teachers in Europe. "In Logan," he wrote, "the duties of life were taken up in a new environment and with a new language. Since English was strange to me, I was placed in the second grade, but advanced in one week to the seventh grade—where my previous training had led me—a record-breaking achievement, which in my youthful mind was unique in the annals of men!"[1] Because John was well ahead of his age group, the family decided that he would forgo school and seek employment to help provide for the family needs. He was employed at the sawmill, a milk house, and a flour mill. Perhaps most valuable was his work at the newspaper office. A reporter many years later wrote:

Strange that a newspaper man should forget it, but I neglected to mention that young Widtsoe had previously been through the journalistic mill at the Logan Journal, from printer's devil to "editor." One day he reported a meeting of the city council. Just as things were getting good one of the wise old birds said: "that young feller is too young to report these doings. Let's go into executive session," and they did, leaving the aspiring journalist out in the cold. He told me that his newspaper experience was invaluable to him later in life, which has been devoted to literature of all kinds and to the preparation of many valuable reports on his scientific investigations.[2]

His most productive job was at the United Order Store that had grown out of the Logan Cooperative Mercantile Institution and was eventually turned over to the ZCMI group. He was there for three years, showing great promise for a mercantile career. One of the best things John derived from that work was contact with a valued acquaintance who deepened his love for Church history and the trials earlier pioneers had faced:

It was one of my duties to take our eggs and butter accumulation, commodities of exchange in those days, to the egg and butter house of Z.C.M.I. It was a small building a little to the rear of the large Z.C.M.I. store building. The worker in charge there was a man who to my boyish eyes was old, perhaps in his sixties. His name was James Holton Haslam. He and I became good friends. Eager for knowledge I discovered that he was the courier who twice traveled the road between Salt Lake City to Parowan and back to help President Young establish friendly feelings among the emigrant company, the settlers and the Indians. The Indians were giving chief concern. He described minutely the first trip from Cedar City to Salt Lake City riding 300 miles in three days, to warn President Young that trouble for the traveling company was brewing in the South. Brigham Young was greatly troubled. Within a few hours after his arrival Brother Haslam was again in the saddle to instruct the people at Parowan and neighboring communities to do everything in their power to protect the emigrants. When he reached Parowan, the massacre had already occurred. He had come too late!

He described to me in detail his meeting with President Young.

As he remembered the events of the massacre as far as he learned them, and he had every opportunity of knowing them intimately, President Young wept. The President did everything in his power to prevent any tragedy. He knew that if he failed his people, trained to live in peace and to give love for hate, they would be charged with the commission of the crime. He had suffered persecution with his people for many years. Moreover, he understood the horror of taking life.

In righteous anger Brother Haslam defended to me as he had done in the courts and elsewhere Brigham Young against the charge of being an accessory to the criminal act of the Mountain Meadows Massacre. He was very convincing to me; and a boy's feelings are not easily fooled.[3]

This was the beginning of John's lifelong drive to use whatever skills and knowledge he could gain to further the cause of Zion.

About six years after arriving in Zion, Anna felt it was time to purchase a lot and build a house. Before long, she settled on an idea she was certain would succeed. She wanted to buy and sell enough land to produce sufficient excess money to keep a lot for herself and the boys. She selected a piece of land she planned to develop, thinking it could be particularly attractive, and went to a friend, a man of some prominence in the community, with the idea. Unfortunately, he was so persuaded of the viability of the plan that he bought the land himself. Anna was not daunted by this experience, able to divorce the ideals of the Church and Zion from the practices of men. She soon found another property that she bought and sold in parcels until she realized enough extra money to buy her own lot of land and have her home paid for.

Once again Anna attracted proposals of marriage from good men. But her devotion to the schoolmaster still held fast, and she chose to remain a widow.

John inherited a love for books from his father and, as a very young man, was a regular customer of James T. Hammond, proprietor of the only bookstore in Logan. "One day I bought a set of Chambers' Encyclopedia," he wrote. "It was a tremendous financial venture. But, who should care, when the books contained the world's knowledge for

The house Anna built in Logan.

which I was hungering."[4] "The love of reading has been with me from my boyhood. To leave the routine of the day for a visit with great minds has ever been a delight. Throughout the years the books have accumulated, and though I have given away hundreds, they yet crowd shelves, tables and room after room in home and office."[5] Hammond became one of John's better acquaintances in Logan and a lifelong friend.

John flourished in all of his jobs and was highly praised by all who were closely associated with him. His work habits and business acumen showed them that he was a youth with unusual promise. To John and Anna, these jobs were temporary necessities meant only to sustain the family. They still planned that he would be a schoolmaster. He wrote, "My daily employment made it impossible for me to obtain a formal education in schools. Therefore, I sought private instruction after working hours. W. H. Apperley, an educated English convert, who later became a professor in the Brigham Young College, started me out in English and Latin. The instructor's personality was unique, but his teaching was good; and we were friends throughout his life."[6] From similarly devoted convert teachers John studied other subjects. His private instruction and self-study continued until he was seventeen. His mother saw to cultural training by providing music and art lessons.

For John, this was a time of searching and growth, during which he received two patriarchal blessings in a six-month period. Those blessings further opened his eyes to the life ahead of him:

> I place my hands upon your head and seal upon you . . . every blessing pertaining unto your office, calling and administry upon the Earth, and dedicate and consecrate thee unto the Lord, that you may be a Laborer in his vineyard, yea even until the Lord and Master shall come, for it will be your privilege to preach the Gospel of the Son of God both Loud and Long both home and in foreign Lands, and help to gather scattered Israel from the four quarters of the Earth. . . .
>
> You shall travel in safety on Land and at sea, and be full of faith and of the testimony of Jesus, . . . and you shall stand as a Savior unto your kindred which are dead and become a Mighty Leader among the Living, gain the victory over Sin, Hell and Grave, through your faith in the Lord Jesus Christ.[7]

The second blessing commences, "I promise and seal upon thy head a patriarchal and a Father's blessing because thou has no father to bless thee." It continues:

> I bless you . . . with the Blessings of the everlasting covenant and say unto thee thou art good in the eyes of the Lord and his eye is over thee for good and thou shalt have mighty faith in Jesus and thou shall proclaim the Gospel of Salvation and assist in the gathering of the scattered Israel of God from the scattered condition and thou shall live long upon the Earth to perform a Work for thy Progenitors that have gone behind the veil in asking their redemption thou shalt be inspired by angels and the visions of heaven shall be ever before thee, thou shall have wisdom given unto thee and knowledge shall be imparted unto thee and I bless you that you will be prospered in all the temporal affairs of life.[8]

As the family became financially secure, their attention and energy was again directed toward John's education. He wrote, "At last when I was seventeen years of age, it was decided that I should break away from my employment and enter the Brigham Young College." John had completed three years of work in the United Order Store, and when he divulged his plans to leave it for college, the bishop was most opposed to the decision, for he felt that John had a particularly good career ahead of him with the store. Anna fretted over her bishop's valued counsel. "But, the Lord had given the boys to her and not to the bishop," John wrote. "They were her responsibility, not his. She had obligations to the living and the dead which he did not know about. Besides, he did not understand, as she did, that the training of the mind is as necessary as the training of the muscles."[9]

> So from my earliest youth, education became my objective. And, there was a real relish for learning in my soul. In a little red diary from January 28, 1888, to June 7, 1891, there is a constant cry and prayer for more education, high school and college. That urgent desire made educational achievement more easily possible.
>
> Success comes more certainly where it is preceded by strong desire. They who fail have a weak, wavering, feeble desire. Indeed, success may be foretold by the strength of desire. If it is as a tidal wave, backed by action, success comes begging for acceptance.[10]

Brigham Young, while visiting in Logan in 1874, announced the establishment of a free educational institution for upwards of 1,000 young people. It was to have a practical focus so that all of its graduates would have mastered a trade—each would be supplied with a "free set of tools for his particular trade, a team and wagon, farming implements made at the institution worth about $500 so he could start right out producing results."[11] The practical plan of the college seemed to be modeled after Oberlin College in Ohio. Like Oberlin, the first American college to admit women to the student body, the Logan college was to train women in spinning, weaving, sewing, dairying, poultry-raising, and gardening. The school began operation in 1878 under the name of Brigham Young College (BYC), though the word *college* was used more in the sense of a high school. In 1885 it had its own campus, and it flourished until it was closed in 1926 because of the expansion of Utah public education and duplication of mission with the land grant college created in 1888.[12]

John registered at the Brigham Young College in the fall of 1889. The curriculum consisted of theology, rhetoric, German, Latin, physics, chemistry, geology, bookkeeping, algebra, geometry, and the theory and practice of teaching, and he took them all: "As I learned easily, I had time to forge beyond the set lessons of the day. The journey led into fields formerly unknown; fields of beauty and delight. That which I learned, all of it, was as food to my soul. One thrill succeeded another as new knowledge was uncovered. I look today with half envy upon the youth to whom the doors of new knowledge are being opened. It has been a joy to me that the zest for new and more knowledge has continued with me throughout the years."[13]

John's natural propensity for knowledge and education was reinforced by outstanding teachers at BYC, all of whom he revered. They were Joseph M. Tanner, Douglas M. Todd, William H. Smart, W. H. Apperley, and F. K. Nebeker. John noted, "They were not holders of high academic degrees, but their learning was sound, and their teaching abilities surpassingly good. I have known none better. Though library and laboratory equipment was meager, it served its purpose well. The teachers simplified their subjects, and led the students onward by easy steps. There was no attempt to make a show of learning, or to confuse the student by requirements beyond their reasonable reach. It was real teaching, the good results of which I learned to appreciate in my later college and university years."[14]

Part of the training at BYC entailed regular classes in religion and theology. All of the faculty were able teachers in religion, but Joseph M. Tanner, a gifted teacher and noted orator molded under the watchful master's eye of Karl G. Maeser in Provo, was particularly well remembered. Looking back over six decades John recorded the general feeling of the student body: "Theology became our best loved subject. It formed our outlook upon life; and made us more sensitive to right and wrong. It shaped our characters and conduct in life. From my own experience and from the observation of the lives of those who have had parallel training in secular and sacred subjects, I have been throughout life an unchanging, firm believer in religious education for youth." Though aware of the legal issues, he added, "In state-supported schools, religious education should at least be on a par with secular subjects."[15] Each student had a signed "Rules and Regulations" card that stipulated faithful efforts to prepare lessons, keep clean and tidy, obey parents, and live the Golden Rule. Use of tobacco, visiting places of bad reputation, defacing college

John, standing third from left, as a student at Brigham Young College.

facilities, leaving school, and being noisy or disorderly in school were also prohibited.

Despite these restrictions, John's brilliance in chemistry did allow him to indulge in some harmless, youthful mischief. He had a teacher who moved slowly, deliberately, always with a measured tread:

> It was always a live question whether he could under any condition walk faster. Therefore, when we learned in the chemistry class to make nitrogen-iodide, which is inert when wet but explodes with terrific noise if touched when dry, it seemed only to be for the advancement of human knowledge to place a bit of the compound on each step of the stairway just before said teacher returned from his lunch! The knowledge we sought was virtually hurled at us. As the stuff exploded on the first step, the victim jumped to the second step to encounter a fiercer noise, which led to more jumps, swifter and swifter, with each successive thunderous explosion. He reached the top at a speed equaled only by the speediest airplane. There was an ominous calm in his class that afternoon, such as precedes a thunderstorm; but we cared not. We were seekers after knowledge, and we had added to our stock.[16]

John and his fellows indulged in another experiment:

One sultry June day, the business section of Logan—chiefly the
one block facing the tabernacle—lay in profound slumber. It seemed
as if the town should be awakened and brought into life. Therefore,
it became very natural to bore a hole through the wall separating
Squire's barber shop and the adjoining clothing store, managed by a
young Jew, who was our chief opponent in chess. It seemed equally
natural to insert a rubber tube through the hole and connect it with a
bottle generating hydrogen disulphide, popularly and properly called
"rotten egg gas." The workers for civic activity withdrew to the tabernacle grounds across the street where they could witness developments. And they came. First came the clothing store manager, fleeing
from his shop, holding his nose and looking wistfully at what was once
his abode. Then his chief salesman was catapulted to the sidewalk, he
also having trouble with his nose. A sedate citizen, doing the world
no harm, came along the plank sidewalk. Suddenly he stopped, took a
deep sniff, held his nose, looked at the sidewalk, back, front, and at
the side of him. Then, with a reproving look at the clothing merchant
and his clerk, he walked out into the street, to be as far as possible
from the offending clothing store, from which there issued a steady
flow of unspeakable stench. Other citizens wandered along the sidewalk, to have the same experience. At length a crowd collected on
the street, at a safe distance, and there was much talk and gesticulat-
ing. Logan was awake! When all was going well, the leading citizen
appeared, majestically moving towards the business section, intent no
doubt upon the deep problems of city building. He stopped. He blew
his nose. He blew it again. He looked lion-like at his city. He was
about to charge—but went out into the street where the timorous
populace had assembled.

That was victory. The reformers withdrew and hid. But, a poll
was taken of those who knew the commercial backyards, and also
chemistry. The guilty ones were soon found; and they apologized pro-
fusely with fingers crossed in both pockets.[17]

On one memorable day John was the victim of someone else's sad
mischief, much more damaging. Like most boys, John was deeply
endeared to his dog, Thor. Thor was John's companion, help, and friend.

On 15 March 1891, when John was nineteen, Thor was mercilessly slaughtered. He wrote:

> Thor is dead. Poor Thor! I found him lying dead on the morning of the 13th of this month. He had been poisoned. Swinyard's dog was also found dead the same morning. Poor Thor! I miss him very much. He crawled back after taking the poison to his accustomed sleeping place, and there he had laid down and died. True to the last to those he loved! Oh, that we all might be that way! Oh, the miserable wretch that killed with poison! What a low-souled person he must be! How his soul must be black as ebony ! May the cur—No, I will not curse him. It will do no good. Poor Thor! No one meets me now when I come home for dinner, and in the evening. There is no one now to accompany me on my walks. No one for whom to buy a piece of meat or a bone with a spare 5¢. No one to play with when study is over. No one to make speak for a cold potato. No one to make kiss the cat and chase her. Poor poor Thor! But we will see him in the future when this life is but a dream of the past.[18]

The BYC teacher who had the most impact on John's life was Joseph Marion Tanner. In 1877, less than a year after Karl G. Maeser arrived at the Brigham Young Academy in Provo, Tanner made application with Maeser and the board of trustees to have a night class for him and many of his companions employed at the Provo Woolen Mills. Twenty-seven enrolled, but Tanner was the only one who completed the class. By the time he reached nineteen (in 1878), he was fully engaged in the academy. His mother recorded in her diary, "Marion attends the Brigham Young Academy as normal and assists Bro. Maeser, the principal, in teaching. He is doing well but it is amusing to think of his being a school teacher when we think of his fondness for everyday life."[19] Of those night sessions that brought him and Maeser together, Tanner wrote, "Professor Maeser was fully convinced that I possessed the essential elements of a teacher, and there a close friendship sprang up which increased with time. I was a member of the first class of graduates, but continued my studies the second year, working during vacation for means which I need to continue my studies."[20] Upon his graduation in 1878, Maeser asked Tanner to accept a position on the BYA faculty.

That fall he married Jennie Harrington, who later headed the "Ladies Department" at BYA.

The Widtsoes had been in Utah only a few weeks when Tanner, at the age of twenty-three, took his second wife, Annie Clark, in December 1883. Six months later he married Josephine Snow. He and his wives had been raised in polygamist homes and knew the hardships the favored practice imposed, and they entered it in good faith. In 1884, two years after passage of the Edmunds Act, polygamy prosecutions were in full swing. Tanner escaped much of that threat by leaving for three and a half years of service in the European Mission just two weeks after his third marriage. Though he traveled through much of Europe, the greater part of his mission was spent in the Middle East—Greece, Turkey, Egypt, Palestine, and Syria. He wrote on leaving that area, "I feel like saying a lasting farewell to the land (Jaffa in Israel) still I must acknowledge that the happiest hours of my life have been spent here, for the goodness of god has been most abundantly bestowed upon me during my labors in this country."[21]

Tanner returned to Utah in 1887, just after passage of the Edmunds-Tucker Act, imposing great hardships on polygamist men and forcing polygamist families even deeper "underground." When Tanner returned in December 1887 he was made "acting president" of Brigham Young Academy because Maeser was very ill. When that school year ended, he was appointed the third principal of Brigham Young College in Logan and a member of the LDS Church Board of Examiners with Maeser and Talmage. With them, he was awarded the degree of Doctor of Didactics and Arts. Life in the underground was unpleasant for him, his wives, and his children, so in 1891, Tanner decided to move to Massachusetts and take his most outstanding students, one of them John A. Widtsoe, with him to study at Harvard. George Thomas, a member of the group who later became president of the University of Utah, wrote that Tanner "was the inspiration of the small group of young men who went east to Harvard to go to school. He secured the money in the way of a loan for several of them. It was through his influence that the money was loaned through the board of trustees of the college at Logan. Those who did not need the money at least received his instructions and inspiration to grow, . . . and that was the first group of students who went to Harvard from this state."[22]

John graduated from at BYC in 1891, planning to secure a teaching position in the territory. But his years at BYC "had created dreams of the years to come."[23] Tanner envisioned his eight students pursuing the best training in the land with the intent of returning with him to Utah to provide for better higher education in the state. John felt that "Dr. Tanner was not only a great teacher; he was also an inspirer of men. A teacher's duty is not done when he only passes on to others the facts of his special discipline. Facts are forgotten; but the memory of guidance and inspiration never dies. Inspirers of men are the world's great need."[24]

Harvard was expensive. John obtained a $1,500 loan from the bank at 12 percent interest, and Anna mortgaged her new home and then rented it for income during those Harvard years. The rest was obtained from notes signed by five teachers and friends who believed that the gamble on John was worthwhile. Anna and Osborne moved to Salt Lake City, where opportunities for employment were more plentiful. John wrote, "In June 1891, about seven and a half years after their arrival in Zion, the little family were separated, the oldest boy going to Harvard University for study. The widow knew that everything depended upon the outcome of the venture, but she had faith that all would end well. . . . Her heart was heavy as she left her little home which she had occupied less than two years. But she was realizing her ideal."[25]

The date of departure for Cambridge was 13 June 1891. John had a vivid memory of that day, the separation it required, the risk it seemed he was taking, the fears it aroused, and yet the sense that it was the correct course—the one he desired to follow and one his mother and his schoolmaster father would choose for him. "As the morning train climbed the western valley heights, I looked long at the city and the temple. Gratitude for life in the city and for its people swelled within me. I resolved with God's help to make good."[26]

7

HARVARD

JUNE 28, 1891: "The slow horsedrawn street car stopped at Harvard square. . . . In a moment I was in the College Yard. History, tradition, science, books—the dream had come true! My prayers had been heard. Who cared for the past, in full view of a glorious future!"[1] To explain John's high regard for Harvard and its academic standing in the late 1800s, it is necessary to review its development.

Harvard College was established just sixteen years after the Pilgrims arrived at Plymouth. Their primary goal was to provide an education for ministers who needed to be the best trained, the most literate, and the most moral. John Harvard, a young Puritan minister, died in the fall of 1636 and left his modest library and half of his meager estate to the college. A tablet on Harvard's Johnston Gate memorializes his thoughts: "After God had carried us safe to New England and we had built our houses, provided necessaries for our livelihood, reared convenient places for God's worship, and settled the civil government one of the next things we longed for and looked after was to advance learning and perpetuate it to posterity dreading to leave an illiterate ministry to the churches when our present ministers shall lie in the dust."[2]

Attendance at daily chapel exercises was mandatory for 250 years

(1636–1886). As the years went by, the number of students interested in training for the ministry declined in favor of students with secular interests.

> In the middle of the eighteenth century there appeared a new sort of Harvard graduate, namely, the citizen who . . . became an advocate of independence and was called a "patriot." As the years passed . . . more and more Harvard graduates appeared as leaders of the patriot party. Several of them became conspicuous in advocating resistance to the orders of the English Government. Samuel Adams, Joseph Warren, and James Otis spoke often in the old South Meetinghouse in defense of the cause of freedom and independence. And this quality in Harvard graduates is recognizable from that time on—liberal, free, independent thinking in politics, society, and religion. A Harvard tradition![3]

The founding aims of the college changed more slowly than the makeup of its student body. Orthodoxy and moral character were Harvard's core, and for two centuries its curriculum remained the classical trivium of Latin, Greek, and arithmetic. A few years before John arrived, modest increases in curriculum began to occur. Ralph Waldo Emerson's oration on "The American Scholar" called for Harvard to grow beyond its British roots. In 1847 the Lawrence Scientific School was founded for students who wanted more specialized training than the classical core. Darwinism accompanied the rise in scientific interests, and Harvard responded with Asa Gray, Jeffries Wyman, Louis Agassiz, and Josiah Parsons Cooke.[4] The "Philosophical Four," Josiah Royce, George Herbert Palmer, William James, and George Santayana brought a new intellectual dominance to Harvard's open classrooms.

The national mood for expanded elective courses had begun. In 1869, its new champion, Charles W. Eliot, was elected Harvard's president. By Eliot's careful persistence the "Elective System" was well established by the 1890s. In fact, John's arrival at the mid-point of Eliot's brilliant career fell at the peak of "Harvard's Golden Age": "Eliot's Harvard had jelled by about 1890 and with one arguable exception he did not conspicuously undertake to alter its fundamental character in the twenty remaining years of his tenure. Eliot's principal blind spot was his incapacity or unwillingness to recognize that continually increasing numbers might affect the *quality* of life at Harvard, and not necessarily for the better."[5] Eliot is still universally regarded as this country's foremost educator. John said of him, "Such men as he have the power to shape the world, and always for good."[6]

Eliot's belief that men of eighteen could best choose their own courses soon became broadly attractive. One Harvard historian wrote, "Groups are like ready-made clothing, cut in regular sizes; they never fit any concrete individual."[7] Other Harvard experts noted that many people who lived through Eliot's later years felt that "the difference between having 150 classmates and having 580 was the difference between living in a humanely apprehensible situation that everybody could share, and alternatively, huddling together for warmth in mutually exclusive miniature Harvards that had less and less in common."[8]

If Harvard had lost dominance with the growth of other colonial colleges and new liberal arts colleges spreading across the land, it was quickly made up by Eliot's "New Education." "One after the other, the greater universities of the country followed the reforms that Harvard had adopted; it was clear by the middle nineties that the Harvard of Eliot, instead of striking off on an individual line toward Germany, had set new standards for higher education in America."[9]

THE GREENEST OF HARVARD FRESHMEN

It was a giant leap from a "Mormon village" to one of America's most metropolitan cities, Cambridge, Massachusetts. John wrote, "All around were the old buildings and the new ones that the University catalogue enumerated and named. Just beyond to the left, over the low two-planked fence, was the Washington elm, under which the Father of His Country took command of the Continental forces in the War of the Revolution. To the right, over the tree tops, beyond the Yard, loomed the tower of Memorial Hall, built in honor of the Harvard men who laid down their lives in the war of the rebellion. Behind me was Boylston Hall where chemistry was taught and where I was to spend much time."[10]

Dr. Tanner had rented a house at 421 Cambridge Street for his little

John at Harvard, 16 July 1892.

flock from Logan. (They later moved to 46 Russell Street.) This kept expenses down and provided a spiritual home. John quickly set about conquering his most immediate fear, the entrance examinations. In the language requirement alone the catalog called for specified minimums in several subjects listed and "a definite maximum attainment in any two."[11] Similar requirements existed for each area of Harvard's curriculum. Families and students so feared the examinations that grammar "prep" schools on the English model grew up all over New England, their primary purpose being admission to Harvard. A commentary on Harvard stipulated, "You really should have gone to a private school . . . and you probably did—at any rate, 80 percent of your classmates did. The best thing is to enter from Groton or St. Paul's, although Andover or Exeter will do."[12]

John did what he could to prepare: "I took a summer school course in German, and also taught myself trigonometry and analytic geometry (conic sections). My self-study, resulting successfully at the fall examinations, taught me the possibility of education without a teacher, if one has some degree of preparation, and power of application. . . . I found also, that first summer in Cambridge, as later, that if a person learns to concentrate upon the subject in hand, progress becomes rapid and safe. My life-long power to forget all else than the job before me has been a chief factor in whatever little success I have attained."[13]

The eight students from Logan passed the entrance examinations, and John did so well that one subject was applied toward his requirements for graduation. Years later he replied to a harsh newspaper report of the inadequacies of Utah high schools, "More than thirty years ago I presented myself at the doors of Harvard university and asked for admission. All of my high school work I had won in Utah. I passed my entrance examinations and even had some advanced credit when the fray was over. Consequently it is fair to assume that thirty years ago Utah high schools had standards that enabled Utah high school students to enter Harvard! Perhaps, however, in that day Harvard was wickedly careless of her standards! If so, think of the mire of Harvard inadequacy that Theodore Roosevelt must have waded in ten years or more before my day."[14]

John's second academic hurdle was the selection of a major:

> During the summer, and after much prayerful meditation, I had decided to follow the prescribed course in chemistry. Mathematics and English battled for recognition but my Scandinavian common sense determined my decision. I had the responsibility for the future of my mother, aunt and brother; I could teach chemistry, or practice it in mining or manufacturing. There were several strings to the chemical bow. Moreover, I was interested in the subject. It was an eye-opener, for there was a chemical aspect to everything on earth and in the heavens. Besides, there was about it an air of mystery, which intrigued my information-seeking mind. Thus I became a chemist. While the decision smacked of cool consideration, I learned to love chemistry and do so to this day.[15]

In later years John gave some insight into a more private motive. To President Heber J. Grant he wrote that behind his study of chemistry was a desire to enable himself to better understand and defend the Word of Wisdom.[16]

With the entrance examinations out of his way and the choice of a major made, John was ready to settle into Harvard life, but this was not without its problems:

> Classwork had scarcely begun when I was stricken by a terrific attack of homesickness—my first and last attack. The sun was wiped out of the heavens; blackness filled my heart; pain raged through my mind and body. The only apparent remedy was to return home, to live the quiet life with mother and family. It required two months to effect a cure, due no doubt to a growing and enthusiastic interest in the work at hand. But ever since I have had an understanding sympathy for student or missionary suffering from this real malady. I suspect that the cause of this attack was a hidden fear of my ability to hold my own in this great institution and in competition with students prepared in the famous schools of the land. Such fear, if it existed, vanished after the first examinations. I travelled usually far ahead of most of my classmates in scholastic grades. As the days went on, the doors of knowledge swung open, more and more. Vast vistas of truth appeared. A desire to pursue every known subject possessed me.[17]

John's distinguished scientific career best illustrates his remarkable attainments at Harvard. Most of his time was spent in the prescribed courses that brought mastery of chemistry and related biological and earth sciences. "Half of my time was devoted to chemistry," he wrote. "Its facts and theories, history and philosophy, fascinated me; and I found real enjoyment in the laboratory work. As I advanced, research in the subject became my dominant desire."[18] John's professors left a remarkable imprint on his life:

> Four men of unusual caliber constituted the professional group in the department of chemistry. Theodore W. Richards, the youngest, was only beginning his work, but in every class he showed the power which later made him a Nobel prize winner. The next two, Henry B. Hill and Charles L. Jackson, had already attained high distinction. They were essentially research men, but also excellent teachers, a rare combination. These three men were not only chemists, but trainers of men. The head of the department, Josiah Parsons Cooke, was often spoken of as the foremost man in his field in America. Wealth had

enabled him to travel widely. His tastes led him into science. He was a notable investigator and theorist. He conceived the famous periodic law before Mendelieff put it into writing. Cooke was also a writer of books, among the first dealing with modern chemistry in our land. He had taught and trained President Eliot, who was a chemist before being overtaken by administrative duties. These teachers became my friends, and my friendship with them continued as long as they lived.[19]

John left a similar imprint on them. Professor Jackson recorded his impressions: "I knew him during his period of study at the Lawrence Scientific School, of Harvard University, and have since then kept track of him by correspondence, so I am well qualified to speak about him. He is one of the most able men who has come under my instruction, and you should remember that my advanced students are picked men from all parts of the country. He showed remarkable power in his work. . . . This letter sounds exaggerated, but it is not, as he is a very rare sort of man."[20] Professor Richards added, "While he was here he distinguished himself both in English and in Chemistry, having been among our best students. Besides intellectual power he possessed rare patience, as well as energy. His bearing and demeanor gave an impression of dignity and reserve power."[21]

The greatest imprint on John came from Josiah Parsons Cooke. John described him in this way: "Dr. Cooke was a religious man. He had thought upon the meaning of life. To him there was no conflict between science and religion. All of nature was but God's speech. He was a popular speaker on such themes. He also wrote books in this field. One, *The Credentials of Science, the Warrant of Faith,* is as good today as yesterday."[22] This great man dignified matters of faith in the rational world of science and helped John find unity in the search for truth. "Dr. Cooke influenced my life greatly. He took a special interest in me. In his great library he would talk at his ease about the philosophy and the mystery of life and the best manner of picking one's way among contending doctrines."[23]

John was by no means a laboratory recluse. He wrote of "other sweets" in the college and often thought English was his favorite subject:

Learning was easy for me. Therefore, though I carried a full load of classes, as many as were permitted, I was a listener in one or two courses each year. Three of these stand out. One year with the famous and loveable William James convinced me, since the professor had a stomach ulcer that year, that he lived in a dark and uninviting universe. A course with the great Josiah Royce failed to convince me that all things had existence only in the human mind. The gentle Dean L. B. R. Briggs twisted his legs about the legs of the lecture table, and proceeded to open the mind and the very heart of Shakespeare. It was good to sit under such masters. And there were others: Dean and geologist N. S. Shaler, whose personality filled the room; E. L. Mark, the zoologist and materialist; E. H. Hall, the physicist and optimist; and the others who helped open the doors of the world for me.[24]

Occasionally John found surprises in this academic world:

One day, walking down Cambridge Street, a dwarfish figure wearing a battered straw hat passed me. What could a figure like that do near the University campus? I thought. So, having passed the somewhat ungainly dwarf I turned to get a better look at him. To my surprise he had also turned and stared at me. He probably thought he saw the greenest of Harvard freshmen.

When the Autumn term opened I selected among my listening courses the first course in philosophy given by the famous professor Josiah Royce.

At the appointed hour I was in the classroom, crowded with students eager to see and hear the great man. At last the door opened and in stepped the lecturer. I could not believe my eyes—it was the "dwarf" I had met on Cambridge Street![25]

John contributed to the student newspaper, the *Harvard Crimson*, and the university magazine the *Harvard Advocate*. On graduation day, 27 June 1894, a special afternoon issue of the *Boston Herald* featured one of John's stories. So good was his writing that upon graduation he was offered employment on the editorial staff of the *Youth's Companion*, which many at that time considered the foremost magazine for youth in America.

Prominent in the academic environment in John's day was the battle being waged between evolution and religion. Around John were many of

the world's strongest voices both advocating and opposing scientific discoveries that seemed to threaten religion. Blind faith did not satisfy
John's highly charged mind, and he had to learn to maintain a balanced
search of truth:

> At that time I was having my religious battles. Was Mormonism
> what it pretended to be? Did Joseph Smith tell the truth? I read, lis-
> tened, compared, thought, prayed. It was a real search for truth. Out
> of it in time came the certain knowledge that the restored gospel is
> true and that Joseph Smith was indeed a Prophet, and restorer of the
> simple true gospel of Jesus Christ. There has never been any doubt
> about it since that time of deep study and prayer. I must confess that
> in finding my way to spiritual truth, Dr. Cooke's steady certainty of
> the pre-eminence of religion was a great help. Remember, in that day
> materialism was the order of the day, and permeated every classroom.
> I owe much to Josiah Parsons Cooke.[26]

Within a short time, John had a burning testimony of the gospel.
He wrote:

> Why do I not take for my example that noble Child whose life
> was so true that could I live purely enough to see but a tenth of its
> beauty, it would bring me eternal life? I dare not lift my eyes to follow
> the Master's steps but I hear His voice which reaches all—even my
> sinful ear. O! hear it now. My blood surges within my veins—my heart
> will burst with the presence of such infinite love, "Father, forgive
> them, for they know not what they do." What burning coals upon my
> head—forgiveness for me who have crucified Him so often in my evil
> thoughts and actions!—on the story below me lies a young girl—
> dead. Just two days dead. I shudder. Is death so near us then! But
> receive death's lesson—Be prepared. Follow in the footsteps of Him
> Who taught us to say, "Father, Thy will be done, not mine," and who
> further promised that, "to those who knock it shall be opened." Let
> Christmas bring with its festivities—earnestness.[27]

A BATTLE OF LOVES

The boys from Logan formed a close brotherhood that fortified their
faith and courage. John kept track of each of these men throughout

The "little flock." A note on the back reads "Students from Utah and Idaho in Boston and Cambridge Fall of 1893." Back row, left to right, George Thomas, Arthur Snow, Lewis T. Cannon, George W. Thatcher Jr., Caleb Tanner, Arthur F. S. Thomas. Middle row, left to right, H. A. Anderson, Clarence Snow, Moses C. Davis, J. M. Tanner, Jean C. Thatcher, John A. Widtsoe, Joseph Jenson, R. A. Shipp. Front row, George L. Swendsen, Arthur Shepherd.

their lives, and in his autobiography he recorded their many accomplishments. Their mentor, Dr. Tanner, and his wives (often two of them concurrently) provided the family atmosphere. Tanner's second wife, Annie Clark Tanner, who lived at 222 Prospect Street, where some of the boys stayed, recorded, "Each Sunday we all assembled in the home at East Cambridge and held a Church service. For a good many years there were no Mormon missionaries in New England."[28] There were regular discussions and a much-needed camaraderie that Annie enjoyed as much as anyone. She wrote, "With regret I left my Cambridge home where the culture and refinement there suited our condition. We were free from the interfering curiosity which characterized the West and which was so prevalent during the persecution."[29] Visitors were welcomed. John recorded:

> The little Mormon colony in Cambridge and Boston was of interest to many at home. Prominent people traveling in the East stopped to visit us. Acquaintanceships so made often lasted through life and

Leah's picture Susa sent to John. On the back is written: "To John A. Widtsoe from Leah and her mother. Leah age 18. Cambridge, Mass, Aug. 15, 1892."

grew into friendships. George Q. Cannon, of the Presidency of the Church, and Moses Thatcher, of the Council of the Twelve, each of whom had a son in the group, came to visit us.

In the summer of 1892 Mrs. Susa Young Gates, Editor of the *Young Women's Journal,* and later of the *Relief Society Magazine,* came to Cambridge to study English in the summer school, which was open to women. She was a woman of superb intelligence and magnificent power—a worthy child of her great father Brigham Young. We became good friends and spent much time together.[30]

After Susa returned to Salt Lake City, she and John maintained a regular correspondence. Susa had told John many good things about her daughter, Leah, and she often wrote to him about her. Soon after reaching home she sent him Leah's photograph. But before long John was afraid that thoughts of Leah might distract him too much. His duty was to complete his schooling, pay off family debts, and provide for Anna and Osborne. Out of youth and inexperience, he attempted to terminate the friendship with Susa. Susa was surprised and told him that though she did not understand, she did not want to stand in the way of duty. Somewhat wounded, she asked that John return her letters and photographs. "May God bless you in all your walks and works, and raise up friends to you who will be deserving of your confidence and esteem."[31] But such a friendship was not to be deterred so easily, and soon the letters resumed.

In her visit to Harvard, Susa developed a great friendship with Maud May Babcock, a member of the Harvard summer school faculty. Before the summer was over, Susa persuaded her to apply for a position at the University of Utah. Miss Babcock duly moved to the University of Utah, from where she later retired having organized both the departments of physical education and speech. In her first year in Salt Lake City she was baptized into the Church. Thereafter her influence through her speech students did much to enhance drama and the spoken word throughout the Church. In the following year, the summer of 1893, she returned to Cambridge to conduct a summer-school physical education class at Harvard, accompanied by four attractive young ladies from Salt Lake City, Mae Taylor, Belle Salmon, Kate Thomas, and Leah Eudora Dunford. Leah Dunford was Susa's daughter from her first marriage.

A few minutes after 10:00 on a Saturday evening in June 1893, Sister Babcock arrived at 46 Russell Street with her four young women. Although Maud had written to Dr. Tanner about their arrival, he had not received the letter, so the ladies were a complete surprise. A fifth girl, a friend of Sister Babcock from New York, joined the company. John admitted to quietly inspecting their new guests: "Women had had little place in my thinking. There were big things ahead of me. I must not be troubled with sweetheart or wife—for many years. So I thought. The year before, Mrs. Gates had told me of her daughter Leah and had taken my photograph to her. But, the year had passed, and we had both forgotten the remote acquaintance. I resented a little the prospective loss of time in showing these girls around interesting New England, and resolved to be too busy to notice them. I was attending the summer session also and was busy."[32]

The Harvard girls in the summer of 1893. On the back of the photo is written:
> "First comes one of talents rare,
> Who chaperoned the whole affair.
> Number two is fair and tall,
> In many ways the best of all.
> Quite a belle is number three,
> Full of fun and jollity.
> Number four is trim and neat,
> Just the sweetest of the sweet.
> Number five you know full well—
> No one ought of her to tell.
> Number six [Leah] is like her verse—
> Couldn't possibly be worse."

At times like these even the most resolute of men may have been powerless to control their own destiny. John later wrote, "I was not aware of Fate holding Miss Dunford by the arm and looking straight at me; but the rascal was there. The girls were a jolly lot, to warm the hearts of college grinds, in a college that opens its doors to women, and that with a shrug, only at the summer session. We had the day and dinner together before we sent them to 18 Sumner Street (Charles Sumner's house), where they had secured living quarters. We had, as per our custom, a brief religious meeting that Sunday morning and then dinner with much talk and laughing. It was June and youth together."[33]

Within a week John described Leah to a friend: "Miss Dunford has the happy faculty of keeping the whole household in good humor for an indefinite period; she also has a very vigorous constitution which will prevent my ever trying the infallibility of her good humor."[34]

Despite John's avowed intent to keep away, he did accompany them on visits to the famous sites around Boston, Lexington's Battle Green, Concord's Old North Bridge, Bunker Hill monument, Mount Auburn cemetery, Plymouth, and Nantasket Beach. Through the summer the two groups of five managed to do many things together. "By the steady interference of Fate! Leah and I were nearly always together. My diary says, 'Went to Concord yesterday, Saturday, with the girls. Had a very pleasant time.' . . . As for me—I had Leah and—well, again I was satisfied, and more, I was pleased."[35]

More than seventy years later, when Leah was ninety-one years old, she recalled their meeting:

> The year after Mother went to Harvard, Miss Babcock came out here that winter you see, and the next [summer] Miss Babcock went back as a teacher and she took five of her promising students with her, and I was one of them. [M]y mother had been there the year before. She'd told me of all the Utah boys that were there, the most interesting was this little Norwegian lad, John Widtsoe was his name, and she said he's really a very fine man and I've told him he can have you, Leah, and she says send me your photograph. I wrote back and said, "Mother forget it. For goodness sake, if you like him, I know I wouldn't, so forget it." I knew he was there, and I wondered what he looked like. Finally when I saw him sitting over there, I went up and introduced myself to him. I said, "I guess you're Brother Widtsoe, aren't you? I heard my mother talk about you." Ha, I looked at him. I weighed a hundred and fifty pounds and he weighed a hundred and thirty-five. . . .
>
> I had pictured him as . . . great big tall. . . . And here I was robust and vigorous and I said that I wouldn't marry a light-complexioned fellow. And I thought what on earth did Mother see in him. I couldn't imagine. And it was Sunday, as I said, and all the other girls went out to—we were to have dinner there—to have a walk. He wanted me to go and I said, "No, I think this girl needs help; she's getting dinner for

The Harvard girls with their class. Leah, right of middle, second row from the top, marked with an x in her hair.

us." So I stayed and helped the girl. I noticed that when it was ready for the meat to be carved she called Brother Widtsoe. I thought, well at least he's useful. Then we knelt down and had prayer and she called on him to pray, and that prayer went straight to my heart. I said, there's the man. That was the beginning.[36]

Though both of them put up a fight against the development of anything serious, human nature again had its way. Both of them needed company, both sought a good summer's fun, and both enjoyed taking in the historical, cultural, and entertainment events. John was enthusiastic: "Things went on from good to better. There were long walks and longer talks together by us two. There was a discussion of world problems, after a storm, on the Mount Auburn Cemetery tower. She and I elucidated the moot questions of life and living, in Longfellow Park under a full moon in a clear sky. On Nantasket Beach we decided on travel over land and sea, and laid out the routes that we should take— and it really came to pass! Soon we met between classes, and ate lunch together in the famous Foxcroft Club. We learned as youth will to understand each other."[37]

John's diary expands on his feelings:

> Last Thursday, July 27th, I took Miss Leah out to the band con-
> cert, but as there was none, we went to Longfellow Park. The moon
> had just risen and it was full. The Charles glittered a short distance
> below the park, and in the far distance among the trees came the
> lights of Brookline, throwing themselves into the river, breaking them-
> selves on the faint billows of the water, like brilliants set in pearl. The
> effect was soft, soothing. The mellowness of the night would soften
> any temper, and mould it to the occasion. In the background was
> Longfellow's house with a light faintly visible through the shutters of
> his study. On the right and left was a dense mass of trees with an occa-
> sional chimney top showing between the branches. All the surround-
> ings, all nature, tended to the peaceful quiet which gives a fulness of
> heart. And there, sitting on the stone bench facing the river and
> moon we talked long together. I talked to myself and to Leah of the
> beauty of the evening, of all the beauty in the world, of the moon, of
> the stars, the worlds beyond, the stars of space, illimitable, beyond our
> comprehension, of heaven and of God. Then coming back to earth,
> we spoke of the light trembling on the waves, the messages of life and
> death passing over the telegraph wire clearly outlined against the blue,
> cloudless sky.[38]

John described Leah in detail, the excellence of her complexion, her
fair skin, her golden hair, something of her build, her good intelligence
and cultivated mind, noting even her beautiful voice and the skill with
which she played instruments and the piano. He noted her comfort in
conversations, her acute intellect, and her native intelligence. Finally,
John admitted, "I begin to like, not love, Leah."[39] A few days later, following an outing to beautiful Plymouth, reveling with Leah in the historic influence it had upon the founding of our country, he wrote, "I
think I enjoyed myself more today than I ever have before, since leaving
home."[40] A few more days passed with similar splendor before John
began an inner battle between love and duty: "Have I done anything
wrong in taking so much interest in her? It will take 2 or 3 years to pay
my school debt; then 4 more years of schooling; and 4 years to pay my
second debt; then 3 years to save enough for beginning housekeeping—

Picture John sent to Leah. Written on the back is "Cambridge Ma., March 1894. In memory of many pleasures I am with great respect the original. 1894 Harvard College, to Leah."

14 years which will make me 36 years old. No, John, do not lead any-one to think of things that never can be. I cannot have a sweet heart, if I wanted one. . . . John, be careful. There is a future ahead of you probably, if you only take care not to ruin it. . . . I was thoroughly in love, but did not dare to mention it. It was a wonderful summer. In it we began our love story."[41]

On 1 August 1893, Leah went home, but the friendship deepened through correspondence. "Letters with discussions, arguments, and explanations, moved back between us."[42] On Christmas Day John wrote, "Dear Miss Leah, Do I write you too often? . . . The church bells are chiming; the morning sunshine falls through my window upon my table; there is a delicious stillness in the air which gives happiness. Can I do better than to write to my friends when everything tends so much to put me in a pleasant mood?"[43] Careful not to intimate more than a close friendship, he added, "I can see you among your friends and rela-tives, chatting, laughing, feasting and dancing—making Christmas tide a time of joy. Dance it out. Let the old year go and the new come, both attended with song and happiness. I wish I could see you, and other friends, enjoy yourselves—but stop—can I not think, and is not the day pleasant?"[44]

At times misunderstandings arose. Once John compared Leah's hair color to that of his window casing. After being taken to task for such a comparison, he wrote, "I beg your pardon for ever suggesting any affinity between your hair and my window casing. It was a most unpoetical comparison, but a true one as to color. I have just discovered that a ribbon book-mark I have is just the same color. I shall make comparisons with it."[45] They engaged in friendly competition as to who wrote the longest letters. They inquired and learned of each other's friends and activities, exchanged ideas about poetry, and went through all that seems common in courtship. John inherited his mother's aptitude for poetry and wrote this of Leah:

A Fragment

Late the night. I wait in silence
For her gentle step upon the mat—
Lightly will she clasp her hands about me,
Saying, What is this that you are at?
Don't you know 'tis time for rest?
I will kiss her, then, and promise
All the while she is on my bosom pressed,
Promise that my life is hers forever,
Promise her that day is night without her,
Promise all that I may hold her longer.
Gently will she chide me then and withdrawing
Tell me that indeed I wrong her.
Do I think she trusts me not unbound
By oaths and such, that are but words at best?
And she will smile a sweet goodnight
And leave me happier for her tender love.
Leave me dreaming in a golden fairy land
Where all is love, the season summer
Rich and full with cloudless sky above

Where death can never enter, while life
Is breath forever, floating down the stream
Of eternity—in love, in love, in love.
And she is there: her eyes long beam
Their tender light of everlasting love
Upon me—Thus I fall asleep.[46]

A REMARKABLE GRADUATION

John's fears about distraction were unfounded; his academic achievements continued to mount. And he enjoyed the pace.

> In my junior year, I was given the task of determining from its chemical composition whether a piece of ancient pottery was of Greek or Egyptian origin. The problem was solved, and the results published. During my senior year I was given a year-long research in a complex corner of organic chemistry, which thrilled me through and through as new compounds, never before known, came out of my work. In my senior year, I was elected president of the Boylston Chemical Club, the one chemical organization of the university in that day. Finally, just before graduation, I walked bravely into the honors examinations in chemistry, and walked out happily with highest honors. Chemistry and research became my college passions.
>
> I must have paid for whatever I won, for under date of June 12, 1894, I wrote concerning the honor examination; "Awoke at 5 o'clock A.M. very restless, and could not go to sleep again. Finally got up at 6:30. A pinched feeling about my stomach, and a clamminess of my hands made me very uncomfortable. Shaved, and went to breakfast; then reviewed the whole of Chemistry 1. At 10:37 left my room feeling a sickness pervading my whole body. Met the boys who were to take the Honor examination in the Yard talking over matters. All together went to the library and finally landed in the Chem. 5 lecture room. I gave first an account of my research work; then a blackboard demonstration of it; then told how $H_2S_2O_7$ was made, and finally discussed sugar analysis. Went to lunch. No one said anything about our success or failure. Now, as I am eating I feel a terrible pain in the small of my back—terrible in the extreme. What can be the cause of it?[47]

What John had won for his academic work was remarkable, a Harvard hallmark. "So, the last examinations came; then graduation day, June 27, 1894, with its cap and gown parade, its lunches and dinners, its talks and orations, its lightheartedness, and at last the gathering in Sanders Theatre, where President Eliot conferred degrees upon us all."[48] As the crowd gathered to witness the celebration, all across Boston people read one of John's essays that had been published in the *Boston Herald* afternoon edition as the best representation of the literary abilities of the graduating class. After finding his diploma amid the scramble, he read with surprise the inscription imprinted thereon. His reaction: "It was difficult to believe, but it was printed in clear type in the program, that I was one of the small handful who had graduated *summa cum laude*, that is, with highest honors. . . . As I read my name and the honor, something akin to awe overtook me."[49]

John's writings are silent on other honors bestowed that day, but those close to him described his achievements. Susa Young Gates had this to say: "The standard of his scholarship was higher than that attained by any student of the institution ten years previous to his graduation."[50] On his plaque hanging in the Beehive Hall of Fame is this inscription: "He graduated from Harvard in only three years with the highest honors, including two awards which had never before been presented to the same man: one for demonstrating the greatest breadth of knowledge, and the other for demonstrating the greatest depth of knowledge in his field."[51] Numerous tributes by his son-in-law, G. Homer Durham, and by his closest friends, Franklin S. Harris and Richard L. Evans, confirm these achievements.

John wrote affectionately of his educational experiences in Cambridge: "The years sped on too rapidly, but I felt growth within me. I was developing. Since that time I have seen thousands of young people undergo the transformation. The training that we call education has great virtue. It gives added stature to the mind and spirit of man. I have always, therefore, been an advocate of education, but by teachers who have the correct view of life. Harvard was good to me. It was literally my alma mater. I have tried in my life to be worthy of that which I received from this great university."[52]

John, right, in graduation
gown on commencement day,
June 17, 1894.

John kept in touch with many classmates, but, for the most part, his isolation in the West deprived him of more constant association. There were periodic class reunions and with each a published class report. In the *Class Report*, on the 15th anniversary of their graduation, John summarized his feelings for Harvard. After describing his attachment to chemistry and his fondness for the elective system, he wrote, "The time spent in Harvard I found so profitable that I made no attempt to work my way through, but, rather, borrowed money with which to meet my expenses, so that I might get full benefit of the years spent at Cambridge. For two years I held a University scholarship. As far as I know, the distinction won during my undergraduate career has had little effect upon my subsequent career; but the Harvard training and ideal helped me every day."[53]

In 1944, John was honored by his classmates in being asked to speak at their 50th anniversary. In the printed *Class Report*, they wrote, "Pioneer scientific investigator of the arts of dry-farming and irrigation; eminent professor of chemistry and agriculture and college president; a

Mormon Apostle . . . and missionary for his faith; sympathetic with the daily round and the souls of common men." John himself wrote in that report that while he had found so much of good at Harvard, the eternal questions Whence? Why? Where? gave him a battle, but, he wrote, "when the battle was over, I had found the best answers, most complete life philosophy, in the teachings of the so-called Mormon Church."[54] In his memoirs he noted, "I attended the class reunion. I was on the program as one of the speakers. It was delightful to meet some of the old friends—nearly one half of the class had survived. Many had risen to real distinction. But, when I saw the manner of their lives, the manner of the world, I was happy that the gospel had found me."[55]

For the Harvard years, John's mother, Anna, rented her Logan house and moved with Osborne to Salt Lake. Life there was wonderful; Petroline filled much of the hole John had left, and many of their countrymen were nearby. Anna attended the Tabernacle with its constant flow of Church leaders. The Salt Lake Temple was in its final building stages, and she and her boys gladly contributed their share despite their Harvard expenses. An important friendship with Leah, a significant addition to the family, had begun. Gratitude arose in the mother's heart for John's success and the fulfillment it meant in her obligation to her own dear schoolmaster.

PART II

CAREER IN HIGHER EDUCATION

8

BEGINNING A CAREER

IN the weeks before John's senior year at Harvard, Dr. James E. Talmage, president of the LDS University in Salt Lake City, visited the "little flock" in Cambridge. When he learned of John's abilities in chemistry, Talmage invited him to return to Utah as his personal assistant following graduation and pledged university assistance with John's expenses at Harvard. However, 1893 brought economic crisis.[1] In a letter to John, Talmage described it as a time of "unparalleled stringency," adding, "It seems absolutely impossible to raise money with any kind of security here, and the Church has been greatly and particularly embarrassed, so much so as to be utterly unable to pay its few salaried employees."[2] The crisis necessitated closing the LDS University, and Talmage was appointed president of the University of Utah. Despite the crisis, Talmage's interest in John continued. "Were it within my power," he wrote, "I would send you the amount you need herewith, but I have never been in such a state of helplessness as I now am; however, I regard your continuation in Harvard to the completion of your course as a most desirable thing, for your personal advantage no more than for the people's good, and I feel to assure you that the means shall be raised in some way before the time you have named."[3]

Subsequent letters from Talmage indicate that he not only arranged financial help but also did everything else he could to secure John a position at either the University of Utah or the Brigham Young Academy. President Benjamin Cluff wrote to John, "I am pleased to be able to offer you a position in the Academy, as I met with the Presidency yesterday. . . . We can start you in as Professor of Sciences at a salary of One Thousand dollars a year for the first year, about half cash and half tithing pay, which is almost equal to cash."[4]

The high respect John had earned from notable Harvard professors led to offers of a coveted assistantship in the Harvard laboratory, an affiliated position in the chemical industry, or one in the gold mines in South Africa. Joshua H. Paul, president of Logan's BYC, wrote, "Are you willing to accept a position in the Brigham Young College? You would probably be assigned chemistry and biology, or physics and chemistry, to be determined later."[5] The offer included a $1,200 salary. Two months later, Paul accepted the presidency of the Agricultural College of Utah (ACU)[6] and sent yet another proposal to John:

> I have given careful consideration to your future relations with the Brigham Young College, and have concluded that the position there would be less satisfactory than one that would give you more scope as a chemist and analyst. . . . I therefore offer you, with the advice and consent of the trustees of both colleges the position of Chemist for the Experiment Station for the ensuing year. The present incumbent was to receive $700; but you will receive $1,200,—the same that the B.Y. would have paid you the first year. If your work as Chemist shall prove satisfactory, of which I doubt nothing, you will be made a professor with increased salary. The position of Station Chemist is the most desirable of any known to me, for a person of your inclinations and training. The results of your investigations will be published. You thus have the opportunity not only for research and original work, but also to lay before the people of the Territory, the results of your work. I have been working steadily for three weeks past to bring about this result, for the good of the college and yourself.[7]

The letter arrived the day before John boarded the train for Utah. The financial crisis of 1893 had caused nationwide upheaval. *Public*

Opinion reported, "Never had the nation witnessed a spectacle of greater despair or more serious labor disturbances. The panic of 1893 paralyzed the industrial structure, demoralized wages, and reduced to idleness three million workers."[8] In his acceptance of Paul's offer, John wrote, "I was caught in the [Pullman] strike and have been on the road continually since, having just arrived in Manti, where I was compelled to go first of all to meet my employment in the summer school. The position you offer me is of course much more to my liking than the position at the BYC, more in fact than any other position in the territory, and therefore I accept it at once."[9]

John's appointment is noted in the minutes of the board of trustees, 14 September 1894: "Mr. Widtsoe, the chemist recently engaged in place of Mr. Irwin . . ."[10] John's mother had been "careful to hold before the boys the ideal of service as well as education. What was the value of learning if not used for human good?"[11] Work at the Experiment Station and the ACU provided the best opportunity for John to support the family and pay their debts. In the early 1900s more of Utah's workforce was involved in agriculture, forestry, and animal husbandry than in any other occupation. A career of service and a good income were reason enough for choosing the ACU, but more compelling was his longing to be at home. "My heart beat for the West and my people," he wrote.[12] He began as chemist of the Experiment Station in September 1894. Though founded in 1888, the ACU first opened its doors in September 1890, and its first graduates were awarded diplomas in the same month that John received his from Harvard. The people of Logan were delighted:

> Last week one of [Logan's] favored sons returned home from the greatest institution of learning on the western hemisphere, laden with honors for his scholarly attainments. And now comes John Widtsoe, the poor boy printer, clerk and general roustabout, who by hard work and indomitable perseverance and determinations, managed to scrape enough money together to take a term at the B.Y. College in this city, where he very soon graduated at the head of his class. . . . [At Harvard] he graduated at the head of a class in chemistry of 250

Picture of the ACU campus when John arrived. Front, left to right: Experiment Station director's home, college president's home, Experiment Station, Old Main building.

students, and now he comes home to take a position as Station Chemist in the Agricultural College of Utah.

By inquiry we learn that Mr. Widtsoe not only conquered the mysteries of chemical science, but that he has discovered a number of compounds before unknown in the domain of organic chemistry. In his new position at the A. C. his talents will have a rare chance and his light will not be hid under a bushel, but will enlighten the way of the students under him.[13]

Though schooled at Harvard, John still had important lessons to learn from his mother. One came from the case of Moses Thatcher, an especially prominent man in Logan who was suspended from the Quorum of the Twelve. In the midst of this controversy the ward teachers called on the Widtsoes.

Soon the visitors began to comment on the "Thatcher episode," as it was called, and explained how unjustly Brother Thatcher had been treated. The widow answered not a word, but there was a gathering storm in her stern eyes and high-held head. After some minutes of listening to the visitors find fault with the Quorum of the Apostles with respect to Brother Thatcher, she slowly rose from her chair and as slowly walked to the entrance door of the house which she threw wide open. With eyes now blazing she turned to the two brethren and said: "There is the door. I want you to leave this house instantly. I will not permit anyone in this house to revile the authorities of the Church, men laboring under divine inspiration. Nor do I wish such things spoken before my sons whom I have taught to love the leaders of the Church."[14]

John served in the Sunday School and assisted the bishop with the members of the Aaronic Priesthood. But his constant search for truth took him further:

The gospel impressed me as the foremost, all-encompassing system of truth. I liked to discuss its many implications. At length I organized a group of my truth-loving friends . . . to spend one evening a week, at my mother's home, in the study of the gospel. As our text we chose Parley P. Pratt's *Key to Theology.* All went well for a few weeks. Then one afternoon a messenger informed me that Stake President Orson Smith wanted to see me. His first remark after I was seated in his office, was something to the effect that I was a bright young man. Then he added that instead of using my education for the benefit of many, I closeted myself once a week with a group of my intimates to talk over things that might benefit many. He looked at me disparagingly. It has seemed to me that the next few minutes changed the course of my life. I could have answered that I was doing nothing wrong and had the right to meet with my friends as I desired. But the right spirit led me, and I said, "President Smith, what would you like me to do?" He smiled. I think I saw a tear gathering in his eye. "Then," he said "meet me in the First Ward meeting at 7:30 next Monday evening, and bring the members of your group with you."[15]

In the Monday meeting President Smith had John sustained as the first counselor and instructor in the elders quorum. John wrote:

We undertook to read and study the Doctrine and Covenants. However, we found it difficult to remember the places in the Book where certain thoughts were expressed. We needed to have an index to which we could refer. So I made a concordance of the ideas in the Book, which was used effectively in card index form. Some years later this concordance was presented to the Church and published. In all my priesthood work, none has been more enjoyable than in this elders quorum. The happy associations came to an end after four years, when I went abroad for more learning. But the love of the Doctrine and Covenants has been kept alive. It remains one of my favorite scriptures; and I have written and published much about it."[16]

So began John's work on a concordance of the Doctrine and Covenants. An entry in the Church's Journal History, dated 11 April 1898, reads, "Professor J. A. Widtsoe presented to the First Presidency the Mss of an elaborate concordance of the Doctrine and Covenants, which he had prepared with great labor and completeness, and offered it as a gift to the Church, hoping that it would prove acceptable and useful. The Presidency thankfully accepted the gift in behalf of the Church, and expressed the belief that it would prove very useful."[17] This concordance eventually became the source of the concordance published in the 1921 edition of the Doctrine and Covenants, which was not replaced until 1981.

A CLASH WITH INTOLERANCE

Although John's "recreation" in church interests was compelling, his main focus was on the work of the experiment station and his chemistry classes. The college, a product of federal legislation, was perceived as more specialized than the state university. Faculty members were recruited mainly from eastern universities, making them "outsiders" in the eyes of the citizens of Cache Valley. The faculty were uncomfortable in this unusual religious setting.

In January 1890, Jeremiah W. Sanborn from New Hampshire was employed as director of the Experiment Station. In May the board of trustees also made him the first president of the faculty, in which office he served until 1894.[18] He was replaced by J. H. Paul, a member of the Church who came to the presidency from his post as president of Brigham Young College. The board of trustees saw the presidency as an important political appointment. For the next hundred years, all of the presidents were members of the Church. The faculty, especially in the early years, was composed of non-LDS scientists. The issue reached its peak in John's appointment to the college:

> I became, in the summer of 1894, the first "Mormon" to enter the collegiate division of the faculty. To this I gave no thought, and the situation gave me no concern. I was ever a consistent member of the Church, but also I formed a sincere loyalty to my much older faculty colleagues. Moreover, they treated me with every courtesy. It was a shock to me, therefore, when, towards the end of my first year of service, one of the leading members of the faculty approached me to tell me that at a private meeting of the faculty, it had been decided to ask me to resign. They had nothing against me, but they did not want to have the college "Mormonized." They would try to secure the resignation of the "Mormon" president also. With both of us gone, there would be no blemish upon the institution. It was my first personal contact with intolerance in a place flying the flag of academic freedom and tolerance. My temper rose sharply and I begged my visitor to take back my answer. "I would not resign; and, moreover, I would remain with the college until everyone who sent the request had left the institution." . . . The experience left a bitter taste. Of all places, there should be no intolerance in institutions dedicated to the discovery and dissemination of truth. I am of the opinion that such persons in any institution of learning should be dismissed for the good of the cause. One does not need to be intolerant to cling firmly to his beliefs.[19]

This division did not come to the people's attention, and newspapers made little mention of it. Overall, although those "outsiders" who came to help establish the college may have had some reservations about the religious makeup of the community and student body, their correspondence shows an appreciation of the intellectual abilities, educational desires, and inbred work ethic of the students at the college. John noted that "the beginning students were more mature (well over twenty years). . . . Yet, these very students, despite their greater age and imperfect preparation, learned quickly and well. It soon dawned upon me that maturity counted much in acquiring knowledge. It was a lesson confirmed by later experience."[20]

LAND-GRANT COLLEGE WORK

At the college, "the key appointment was perceived as the Director of the Agricultural Experiment Station."[21] An early report stated, "The agricultural experiment station is a department of the college the main purpose of which is the determination of the scientific laws that may be applied in the art of agriculture. The station consists of the departments of agronomy, animal husbandry, horticulture, chemistry, irrigation, poultry and entomology. Each department makes special investigations, while a number of the departments do co-operative work covering a broader field."[22] This was starkly different from Harvard's emphasis on America's privileged citizens being prepared as gentlemen for the elite professions of national society. Students in land-grant colleges came from farming communities. Their object was to prepare themselves for more success in agricultural production. John described his developing appreciation for this new kind of institution:

> The four years following graduation from college (1894–1898) were a period of continued education. During this period I added knowledge and experience to my store by study and experimentation.
>
> I had been an eager, ardent, ceaseless seeker for knowledge. The joy for seeking truth was mine. I had also come to understand that culture and personal development follow orderly, well guided study and exploration of man's truth possessions.
>
> Now I was led, by my employment at the Utah State Agricultural College, to ponder upon the place and use of knowledge in the every day occupations of man—of all men. It was in these years that I formulated the philosophy of education which was to guide me through life.
>
> The Utah State Agricultural College . . . was one of the sisterhood of land grant colleges. These institutions were authorized by a Federal Statute of July 2, 1862, signed by Abraham Lincoln. They were to provide farmers, housewives, tradesmen, and mechanics with the opportunity of a higher education, to which such people had had scant access in the past. They were further to teach the possible application of existing knowledge to the respective pursuits of the common man. So that the toil to make a living, whatever the work, might be raised to professional dignity, and at the same time be made more

profitable. In short, they were dedicated to practical education—to the vision of a nation, each member of which had been educated in the knowledge of the day as well as trained for his post.

The learning-loving Lincoln, with his feeling for human brotherhood, must have thought of his own rail-splitting youth, and his education by the flickering fire of the hearth, as he signed his epoch-making bill.

My sturdy belief, from earliest boyhood, in the rights of the common people, and my equally strong dislike of kings and dictators, and also of position and wealth by birth instead of one's effort, as well as all that savored of domination of man over man resounded quickly and happily to the doctrine implied in the land grant college and experiment station acts of 1862 and 1888. They seemed to foreshadow a greater equality of man. Educationally they were but as an extension of President Eliot's elective system, which was free education from the academic shackles of placing one discipline above another in mental training and of programming required subjects and sequences. I rose like a fish to the fly to this new conception of education. In the years that followed I clung to this ideal.[23]

Though federal land-grant legislation led the way, a bill in the Utah territorial legislature, sponsored by Representative Anthon H. Lund, created the ACU. Paradoxically, John, the Harvard graduate with credentials in chemistry, gained his reputation in agriculture without a background of farm life. Before John's ACU appointment, the experiment station had operated with only an assistant chemist.[24] John observed, "No independent investigation was undertaken by the Chemical Division in 1894." That would change drastically. John added, "The Chemists of the Station propose, for the coming year, to study as fully as their time and the means at their disposal permit—first, the air and the waters of the territory; second, the soils of the Territory, and, third, cattle feeding and the feeding values of fodders and combinations of fodders."[25] He also wrote:

It was the experimental work that fascinated me. As chemist to the experiment station, a good part of my time was devoted to investigation. Some odds and ends left by my predecessor were soon out of the way. Meanwhile there were days of thinking. Agriculture begins

with the soil. What is the nature of Utah soils? It had been held that
all experimentation should be confined to the College farm. With the
consent of President J. H. Paul, who was sympathetic with my ideas, I
broke that precedent and traveled over the State, made observations
and took soil samples in many parts of the state. Some of the results,
many of them unique in that day, were published in bulletin form or in
chemical journals. The great variety of the soils of the State, and the
astonishing fertility of some of them, led to the formulation of suitable
cropping systems.[26]

Statewide exposure to the soils, the workers, and the essential crops
was critical to John's future work. He developed a strong determination
to help the common man in his chosen pursuit. He wrote to George H.
Brimhall, "The toilers of the world are making the world, but they need
assistance. Under present social conditions they can do little else than
toil; for that reason I feel a genuine happiness in applying, to the best of
my ability, the results of modern science to the betterment of the lowly
pursuits of life."[27] He made many visits to these people. "A longer trip
was undertaken by myself and Joseph Jenson, professor of Engineering at
the College. We traveled by team, with a driver and a companion, my
brother, from Provo to Price, through Emery County, Last Chance
Canyon, to the settlements on the Fremont River, then up to Loa, over
to Circle Valley, down to Kanab, then to the St. George Country, northward through Cedar City, Beaver, Fillmore, Nephi, back to Provo.
Meetings were held with the farmers in nearly all the settlements on the
way."[28] A love for the people was increased by a love for the land: "This
first long trip was the beginning of my lifelong love of the desert. I have
driven, ridden, and walked over it, and heard the music of it by night
and have enjoyed its heat by day. The earth appeals to me most in the
contradictory phases of ocean and desert. The first years after graduation taught me much beyond the walls of science."[29]

Despite John's best efforts, not all of the farmers accepted his innovations: "During these early years the first problem was to overcome the
natural conservatism of the farmers—less in Utah than elsewhere if I
have read other state reports aright."[30] There was a natural suspicion of
new methods. "Among some there was polite opposition to 'book

farming.' In one city some of the venerable leaders of the community, seated on the stand, expressed their desire to end the meeting by continually opening and closing their hunting case watches—the regular clicks upsetting the speaker. On the whole, however, we were kindly and gratefully received, and our message given serious thought."[31] John did not let this opposition deter him, and soon the farmers looked forward to learning from the experiment station.

With a detailed awareness of the air, water, and soils of Utah, the young professor moved his investigations to crop research that would be most useful to his farm constituents. Lucern, or alfalfa, was, according to the *Utah Church and Farm,* "one of our principal crops."[32] John wrote:

> It was often said, facetiously, that Brigham and alfalfa had made the state of Utah and that neither one could have done it alone! Yet very little was known concerning the composition and growth habits of the crop. The resulting studies, which I undertook, covering 3 years, opened doors to much new knowledge. The rate of growth at each stage, the composition at various periods of growth and the digestibility fed to farm animals, with the determination of the effect of a crop upon the growth and well-being of livestock, were given careful attention.[33]

John's monumental findings on alfalfa were published in two experiment station bulletins titled "The Chemical Life History of Lucern."[34] Among farmers there had been considerable disagreement about when to cut hay for the greatest yield, when it contained its highest feed value, and which summer crops had the greatest value. John found that "to obtain a large yield of dry matter and the largest quantity of albuminoids, lucern should be cut, not earlier than early bloom, and not much later than the first week of early flower." He also found that "period for period and pound for pound, the three [Lucern] crops seem to have just about the same food value. Of the three the second crop has the least value." He further found that leaves have less fiber, but more albuminoids than the stalks.[35]

Dr. E. W. Allen, the federal government's assistant director of experiment stations, praised John's work to the board of trustees: "The bulletins of this Station on the subject of Alfalfa comprised a large part

of the Government knowledge on Alfalfa, . . . this bulletin being the
best ever issued on that subject."[36] Franklin S. Harris, an agricultural
scholar and subsequent president of BYU and the ACU, wrote of
Widtsoe, "His studies of the chemical life history of lucern gave a
scientific basis for handling that crop that has resulted in saving great
sums of money not only to the farmers of Utah but also to those of the
other parts of the world where lucern is raised."[37]

Sugar beets were another important crop of rapidly increasing significance to Utah's developing economy, and John tackled that problem, writing, "The battle for a beet sugar industry was on. There was
some doubt as to whether sugar beets could be grown generally throughout the State. Two years' test . . . found that sugar beets could be grown
successfully everywhere in the State."[38] One history of Utah's sugar
industry reported the problem of convincing farmers of the gain they
could realize by growing beets.[39] The sugar factories constantly pled for
local farmers to plant more beets.

Before 1891 Utahns had to import sugar from the East. By 1902,
with new factories in Lehi, Ogden, Logan, and Garland, half of Utah's
production was available for shipment to other markets. In 1906, consumption was about 20 million pounds while production reached 88
million. One government report stated that it was "not probable that
any standard crop would . . . yield better net returns . . . than beets."[40]
The economic boost sugar gave to the Utah economy is a good measure
of John's work.

Many other research projects were undertaken during John's years
as chemist. In a single year there were numerous lucern studies, 57 soil
studies, 90 sugar beet studies, 75 studies of animal feed and digestion,
70 samples of milk, and 400 determinations of soil moisture in connection with tillage of corn. In all, they completed 3,000 single determinations.[41] Attributing increased farm activity to the college and its
experiment station, one historian noted, "A major revolution took
place in agriculture in Utah after 1890. Between 1890 and 1900 the
number of farms and the total number of acres of improved farm land
doubled."[42] In the Widtsoe years, the station became highly regarded
in and out of Utah.

In 1895, John helped inaugurate farmers' institutes. The station's seventh annual report noted, "By an act of the State Legislature, the trustees of the Agricultural College, with the aid of the faculty, are authorized and required to hold at least one farmers' institute annually in each county of the state. For the instruction of its citizens in the various branches of agriculture and for presentation of the results of the most recent investigations of the Experiment station."[43] Prominent members of the faculty energetically trained local farmers to take advantage of the increases gained through research.

Two years after John arrived at the ACU, his friend and mentor, Dr. Joseph Tanner, was elected its third president. Tanner had a fervor for learning and an ability to skillfully combine secular and religious dimensions of honest and searching inquiry. Following John's lead, Tanner worked hard to make the farmer's institutes successful. John wrote:

> It [1896] was the first attempt by the state to place the application of modern science to the art of agriculture and then to the tillers of the soil. The following year, the summer of 1897 . . . farmers' institutes were held in practically every town south of Provo. These initial trips were the beginnings of the agricultural extension work which has grown to vast proportions, and gave me an understanding of the possibilities of education outside the classroom. This method of carrying knowledge to the farmer and his wife and to others, has always appealed to me as a sane method of education and has always had my full support. There are many paths to the educational paradise.
>
> The trip taken in 1897 was the greatest value to me. In the kind of work the college has to do an intimate knowledge of the state is necessary. We traveled with team and wagon. We could not go very rapidly. There was need of time for observation. The endless sage covered deserts lay before. Sage, greasewood, rabbit brush and other native plants we learned were safe indicators of varying soil quality. I was fired with a desire to help cover these millions of acres with crops valuable to man; the dream that such a conquest is possible remains with me.[44]

Besides his Station work, John now had classes to teach and students to guide. He wrote, "I had had little experience in teaching—

Sunday School, a class in algebra at the B.Y. College, and tutoring at Harvard summer school in mathematics—but I soon discovered that teaching was much to my liking. Chemistry and physics were my assign-ment, but occasionally, as need arose, I had classes in applied mechan-ics, geology, and mineralogy. I made some mistakes in those early days, but fortunately they spurred me on to greater efforts to become a really good teacher."[45]

9

AN HELP MEET FOR HIM

IN their Cambridge summer's courtship of 1893 John had found true love. At their separation his diary recorded his despair and his hope: "August 1st, 1893. The curtain fell at 3 o'clock this afternoon. Miss Taylor, Mr. Croxall, and Leah left for Chicago—and Utah. A cold, distant farewell as behooves friends—but a kiss blown through the window, for whom?—by Leah. Thanks. Thanks. The curtain is not quite down yet—wait. I await the new and next act."[1] These were new and strange feelings to John, and his pen recorded their depth as he confessed being "Lunatics about Leah."[2] Some stanzas of a poem from his compilation of nearly a dozen indicate his state of mind following her departure from Cambridge. The little compilation echoing the fantasy and fact of his youthful yearnings is the poetic foundation of their love story.

A HEAVY MOMENT*

> The sky is gray and dreary
> It holds an untold gloom.
> My soul is oh so weary
> Bereft of its finest bloom.

The heavy clouds did gather.
They hid my rising sun.
And life was only sadder
For beauty that was gone.

The wind moaned soft and sadly
A dark and doleful dirge;
And heaven, feeling madly
Her tears with mine did merge.

My sun is lost forever
Behind the darkling cloud.
'Twill shine no more—no never;
From out its steel cold shroud.

No light! Then darkness ever.
A life of long despair—
From earth will nothing sever
My soul? Forbear, Forbear!

The sky is gray and dreary.
It is one endless void.
My soul is, oh, so weary,
From every hope devoid.

The sky is gray and dreary,
It chills my wounded breast.
My soul is deathly weary
Oh, could I hope for rest!

*As far as can be learned This very
Touching piece was written on the
Occasion of the departure of a woman
Who was known as Leah Dunford
from the City of Cambridge.

Though John was ever the gifted student, things of the heart were completely normal with him. He was thoroughly smitten by Leah. She had what he felt then and ever after was the perfect blend of social, mental, spiritual, and physical charm that would bring the fullest marital companionship.

LEAH'S YOUTH, A DIFFICULT STORY

How Leah acquired the depth of all of her qualities speaks more of her heritage than of her training. Her childhood and youth do not make for a good story in her eyes or in the eyes of either of her parents. Though her mother, Susa Young Gates, became one of Mormondom's greatest women, the story of her first marriage is a chapter of her life she would like to have mostly erased. In a letter to John after he and Leah were married, Susa wrote of it: "Of course, you know the one thing I disliked was the use of Leah's maiden name, especially since I was mentioned as her mother. This sets people guessing and asking questions at once, which is not very agreeable to me. However, I suppose I must pay my own price always for my past mistakes, and it wasn't a mistake when it brought Leah to my arms and heart."[3] Leah and her brother Bailey seem to be the only happy memories of Susa's youthful marriage.

Susa was probably the brightest, most devout, and most accomplished of Brigham Young's fifty-six children. Born in 1856, she was the first child of Lucy Bigelow Young, who married Brigham in 1846 at age sixteen. Lucy worked to make her celebrated marriage a happy one, and she was a devoted wife for the thirty years that remained in her husband's lifetime. Susa, Brigham's first child born in the Lion House, enjoyed a close friendship with her father that enabled her to write a personal biography of him.[4] Her youthful marriage ended in 1877, the year Brigham died.

Like many young women of her time, Susa married at an early age. Leah stated, "I was born when mother was 16. When mother was 17 I was two months old, so as I grew we became more like sisters rather than mother and daughter."[5] The natural drives that lifted Susa to the great heights she attained took her out of that early marriage, away from her two children, and into the Brigham Young Academy, both as a student and a teacher. Those same drives took Susa to Harvard, where she visited John in Cambridge in 1892, whence came the association, romance, and love, of John and Leah. The friendship Susa won with John that summer grew into a remarkable relationship marked by unusual mutual respect for more than forty years. Because she remained so close in those years, frequent mention of her follows in many chapters of this volume. So great were her many accomplishments and so full and faithful her life that she deserves her own biography.

Leah was born to Susa Amelia Young and Alma Bailey Dunford on 24 February 1874 in a home on the site where now stands the Joseph Smith Memorial Building in Salt Lake City, Utah. When Leah was three, her parents were divorced. In 1878, on the advice of Elder Erastus Snow, Susa departed for the Brigham Young Academy in Provo. Soon after that, on the advice of Joseph F. Smith, she went to the Sandwich Islands (Hawaii), where she renewed an acquaintance with Jacob F. Gates. They were married in January 1880 in the St. George Temple. Leah, living with her father and his new family, was then six years old. Between 1880 and 1896, Leah's youth and adolescence, Susa had eleven more children. With them and all of her other duties, there was little time for Leah, a fact that burdened both of them to the grave.

In an impassioned letter from Leah to Susa in later years, Leah undraped her feelings of those difficult years of separation from her mother, whom she so resembled. Addressing the letter as always to "Mother Darling," Leah wrote:

> I remember your telling me that when you came to see me in St. Charles Idaho—had me sent for & brot to you—which is also my first memory of you—that you asked me what I had been doing. (You told me after I became well acquainted with you of this event, or I should not remember it so clearly.) I quickly responded that I'd had a patriarchal blessing. "Oh what did the Patriarch tell you?" "He said I should be a mother in Israel!" I couldn't remember anything else; that was all that had registered. It's the only thing that's ever registered in my life.
>
> When I think of my long and lonely childhood—a loneliness that *ached* & suffered filled it, in spite of an indulgent father. I never knew you, Mother, till I was fifteen years old (& at that time I was a mature (almost) woman)—except as a Beautiful Lady who sent me occasional

shell trimmed cards . . . with sweet verses & a few lovely, dear, letters. I had only a memory of seeing you but a few times Mother dear, till my 15th birthday. In my childhood home I was worse than alone—for with no one could I unbosom my childish desires—except my family of dolls. I feared & dreaded my Step-mother. She did not love me, I sensed it & for her I always did the wrong thing: if I was reading it was wrong I should be doing the sweeping; if I was sweeping it was wrong I should have been doing the dishes. And I was always alone—never "one to wash & one to wipe"—& never anyone to blame things on to, & I guess that was harder to face all my misdeeds *alone.*

But I never could approach my Stepmother—I was just a dis-agreeable child to her—& I must have been a great cross to her—who lived a hard life. But by ginger she often made it harder than need be. Thank Goodness, that with the years has come understanding, for-giveness, & friendship. But it all came too late to affect the life of this lonely child.

My father I knew loved me—most of the sunshine of my child life came thru him. But he didn't dare show it—I was conscious of that too. So I early learned to keep myself to myself.

Then the sun of life came up to me: you came home from the Islands and settled in Provo—& I could visit you occasionally. From you Mother dear has come the greatest joy of my life. How richly you have made up to me for the loneliness of my childhood. Never if I filled pages could I tell how grateful I feel to you. . . . You have been such a wonderful Mother to all your children that it hurts me doubly that I could or have not measured up to your expectation of me.

During my lonely childhood I promised myself that if the Lord would ever grant me my great desire & let me be a Mother in the flesh to some of his spirits that I would give my *all* to make for them a happy home where they should be loved &—*understood* which at times is better than love.[6]

One author who looked closely at Leah's childhood saw that through it came the drive that took her to so many successes in the years that followed: "Leah's less-than-ideal childhood germinated the desire to be a crusader for proper home upbringing for the future generation. She wanted to spare other children the kind of childhood she had without a trained mother's influence."[7]

LEAH'S LIFE AND EDUCATION

The thing Leah most credited Susa with was her introduction to the young Norwegian, John A. Widtsoe. She often acknowledged that but for Susa, their meeting would probably never have happened. Following their introduction in Cambridge in 1892, Susa arranged a teaching position for Maud May Babcock at the University of Utah beginning in the fall of 1892. Leah fell under Miss Babcock's influence that winter. The following spring, in 1893, Miss Babcock gathered to Harvard, where she again taught in the Summer School a group of young women from Salt Lake City who seemed most interested in her work. Leah was in that group, and in following Miss Babcock's course to Cambridge she met John. When the course was ended, and the summer romance with John, Leah noted her feelings and those she perceived in John: "We were both gone, oh so far. I had been corresponding, writing a letter every day to a tall, brown-eyed fellow here in Utah. I never wrote any more letters to him."[8]

When Fall came Leah was back in school. "I continued my course of study at the U. of U. and assisted Miss Babcock in my spare time," she wrote. "However, the more I worked in these courses of Physical Education the less they appealed to me as a major for my educational study. I obtained my diploma from the University of Utah in the spring of 1896. Then came the question whether I would go on to college and finish the type of work I was doing with Miss Babcock or go into some other field."[9] Leah's desire for college was inherited from both her father and her mother. Susa fanned it frequently, and it was deepened by Leah's work in the Twelfth Ward School. At the university she took many difficult courses in many of the sciences, among them, physics, chemistry, biology, geology, and bacteriology. There were also difficult courses in history, English, and German. In them she did so well that she was chosen to represent her graduating classmates as valedictorian.[10]

Leah liked the work she had been trained in, but she wrote, "It didn't satisfy my inner longing for something higher and better with which to devote my time and any advance training I may pursue."[11] Nursing occupied her interests for a time. It was a noble profession, but after a while, the notion of being around sickness all the time dissuaded her from pursuing it further. She wrote, "Sickness did not appeal to me then or ever. Why should people be sick anyway? Why can't they learn to take care of their bodies and be well? The Lord intended it to be so, and gave us the inspired Word of Wisdom only three years after the restoration of the Gospel in our day."[12] These sentiments grew in her, and she equated them with the growing national interest in Domestic Science: "To these subjects my thoughts and desires gravitated. The more I thought about them the more they appealed to me and I felt that they had much greater implication than either Physical Culture, so-called, or Nursing or even teaching the usual subjects in grade or high schools. There could be nothing finer for young women to do than to learn how to become efficient, trained, dedicated home-makers and mothers."[13]

Then followed many conversations with Susa and numerous inquiries to her friends, including Susan B. Anthony, who was a leading light on women's educational opportunities, and Maria Parloa and Fannie Meritt Farmer of prestigious cooking schools in Boston and Philadelphia. Through their search they became acquainted with the Pratt Institute in Brooklyn, New York, which was devoted to training people in the "necessary pursuits of life," including a great variety of courses under the heading of Domestic Science and Domestic Arts. It appeared to have the best of all they had reviewed. "So we decided that I should go to Pratt Institute to study for my chosen field of making better homes for more intelligent and educated home-makers," Leah wrote.[14] Donetta Smith, daughter of Joseph F. Smith, was attracted to Pratt's kindergarten program, so with her Leah went to the Pratt Institute for the school year of 1896–97. "The training I received at Pratt Institute was inspirational," she wrote. "The teachers were full of their subjects and eager to pass it on. I had a little introduction to the subject by studying in the University a course which was given by Dr. James E. Talmage. In this subject we used as a text a book written by Dr. Talmage called *Domestic Science*.[15] In part, because of the work she had done at the U of U, Leah was able to finish the course at Pratt in one year.

The flame of domestic science had also been ignited in Susa. Leah

Leah in a chemistry laboratory at the Pratt Institute. Leah is standing second from the left facing the camera. Florence Willard is fourth from the left in the far corner facing the wall (both are marked with an x).

noted, "My mother being eager to help out and very near to the president of the institution (BYA) Dr. Benjamin Cluff, got his permission to use a room in the basement of the Education Building on the lower campus, in which she outfitted a primitive laboratory for the study of these subjects."[16] Susa had opened the door of the BYA, and they were ready for Leah and her new program to be launched. Leah was the first westerner to graduate from Pratt and hence the best trained in the vicinity.[17] She was also anxious to put her training into the foundation of the work that followed at BYA. She noted, "Fortunately, the fine teachers at Pratt Institute had instilled into us that the teaching of any subject depends not so much on the equipment of the room as upon the spirit and preparation of the teacher. . . . So with the vigor of youth and eagerness of a crusader for a righteous cause the Home Economics Department of the Brigham Young University was founded."[18] The catalog shows twelve courses in the department for 1897–98, and "Miss Dunford" is listed as the teacher of all twelve. They include "Cookery," "Invalid Cookery," "Advanced Cookery," "Fancy Cookery," "Emergencies," "Home Nursing," "Household Economics," "Marketing," "Household Art," "Laundry," "Waitress Course," and "Diatetics."[19] As Leah looked back on them in later years, she noted, "How eager is youth and how undaunted against any difficulty."[20]

In Leah, John found the ideal life's companion, an help meet for him. *Meet,* whether used for Eve or for Leah, speaks of a wife who is equal, suitable, proper, ideal, or the perfect complement in marriage. So it seemed to be in extraordinary ways, including her personal and professional interests. John wrote of her training and work in the years of their courting, "Her training in Home Economics made her very sympathetic with nutritional problems. She was a pioneer instructor in Home Economics and the education of women for women's work. When the newer knowledge of nutrition came like a deluge upon the world, it explained the causes of many physical ills. This strengthened her interest in the subject. She felt that all should be informed, for their advantage."[21]

Numerous accounts on Home Economics education at BYU indicate that Leah's work was monumental in setting the foundation on which the program has flourished in the years that have passed since she launched it in 1897.[22] Of her leaving school she wrote, "Fortunately for me, but unfortunately for the work which I wished to do for the school, a very handsome young man persuaded me in the beginning of the year 1898, that I should leave professional teaching in a regular University and establish a private institution of my own under his guidance. Being very much in love I yielded to his reasoning and my career as an active teacher at the Brigham Young Academy, as it was then called came to a close."[23]

10

BECOMING DR. WIDTSOE

———————————————■———————————————

JOHN'S continuing success at the Experiment Station increased the
esteem shared between him and the ACU's president, Dr. Joseph
Tanner, who had this to say about John in a report to the board of
trustees in April 1898:

> The prospects of the beet-sugar industry in our state, and the
> demands for scientific information at our hands, induce me to con-
> sider the propriety of encouraging our Chemist to spend at least a year
> in Germany. As this policy has been and is being adopted by neigh-
> boring states engaged in the development of this industry, I consider it
> equally important to Utah. Prof. Widtsoe would go to one of the lead-
> ing university and agricultural stations of Germany, where he could
> pursue his investigations along a line of work affording at the present
> time great interest to the citizens of our state, and I recommend to
> the Board that he be released for that purpose on a furlough for one
> year. . . . It is always advantageous to an institution, when its leading
> men adopt a progressive spirit, and the habit of allowing them a vaca-
> tion periodically, in which to work up the most recent investigations
> in their profession, is highly commended in all the educational insti-
> tutions of our country.[1]

Between 1894 and 1898 John had been initiated into the life of

practical academia in American higher education. Classroom instruction, laboratory research, and farmers' institutes had been the focus of
his professional pursuits at the ACU. He described his work to his
Harvard classmates as "unexpected" and "almost accidental" but added,
"I became enamored of the problems of the land-grant colleges, which
deal with the education of the common man and the development of
natural resources for human good. In helping to solve these problems I
have found much joy."[2] In his autobiography he recalled these years with
fondness:

> During these four years I also pursued industriously my work in
> agricultural chemistry. More and more chemistry of life fascinated me.
> There were processes within living plants, animals and humans which
> must be determined. It seemed a field to which I could give my life.
> So the decision was soon made to go forth again in search of knowl-
> edge—of discovered truth and methods of investigation—this time in
> Europe, for the foremost workers in what was known then as physio-
> logical chemistry (now bio-chemistry) were in European universities
> and laboratories. Harvard generously appointed me to one of its
> Parker traveling fellowships, with a substantial stipend. I borrowed
> more and was ready for a new adventure.[3]

The board of trustees approved President Tanner's recommendation for John's European studies to begin 1 September 1898. In a separate request for preparation time, his furlough was moved up to 1 July.
Foremost among those preparations was marriage to Leah. Through
very busy lives their love had remained strong since their magical time
in Cambridge five years earlier. Little is said in his memoirs about the
long waiting time, but he did admit, "Letters with discussions, arguments, and explanations, moved back and forth between us. Then after
graduation, came four long years of waiting. I was doing foundation
work for my future. She graduated from the University of Utah in 1896;
then studied in the famous Pratt Institute for a year, and then took her
bachelor's degree from the Brigham Young University. . . . In 1897–98
she taught Home Economics at B.Y.U."[4] While Leah completed her
studies in Salt Lake City, Brooklyn, and Provo, John lived in Logan but
traveled much across the state. The trip from Logan to Salt Lake or

Provo took much of a day. Distance slowed the courtship down, but despite the obstacles they knew where they were going.

> One evening in the fall of 1897, on Provo Bench we decided that the time had come for us to marry. She set the date June 1, 1898, her maternal grandfather Brigham Young's birthday, when also her contract with the [BYA] would expire. It was a winter of long waiting, but at last spring came, and on a beautiful sunlit day, in the Salt Lake Temple, President Joseph F. Smith performed the ceremony that made us one, for time and for all eternity. A meal in Salt Lake City, at the home of Leah's father Dr. A. B. Dunford, followed. Then we took the train to Provo where a reception, followed by a dance, was held for us in College Hall, under the auspices of her mother, Mrs. Susa Y. Gates.[5]

Seventy years later Leah described the excitement surrounding their marriage, most particularly the efforts of her famous mother:

> Well, Mother was a very prominent member of the Brigham Young family, and when we were married she asked the . . . girls [in my home economics class] how they'd like to cook my wedding dinner. They said they'd be glad to, so mother decided that I was to be married.
>
> The plans had been set; I was to be married at 10:00 in the morning, by President Joseph F. Smith, and then we were to have breakfast with my father, Alma Dunford, who lived on 17th South then in a large mansion he built. . . . And I had breakfast then with my father and my Salt Lake family, and then in the afternoon we went down on the train to Provo, and Mother had invited all of her friends, or all of our intimate friends. Of course, a good many; it was a large group, Mother had many friends. And her wedding invitations were out of the ordinary. Mother never did anything like everybody else did. They read something like this: "Will you dance at Leah's wedding on June 1st at room D of the new Academy Building, at such and such a time." [It read "Will you and your dear wife come down to Provo on the evening of June 1st and dance at Leah's wedding. She is to be married to Brother John A. Widtsoe in the Salt Lake Temple, on that date. Our modest supper will be prepared by members of Leah's Domestic Science class. There will be music, recitations, toasts, and old-fashioned dancing. No style, no presents. Entertainment for the

night will be arranged. Carriages will meet the train. Reduced rates on the DRGW Railway can be obtained of Brother William Spence. Your friend and sister, Susa Gates, Provo. May 14, 1898. Please reply."] And it was a dance!

We danced at the wedding, all kinds of new dances. Unfortunately I married a man who never danced, and I would rather dance than eat! To this day, if I could have a good dance with a good dancer, I'd rather have it than a good meal. I love to dance. And to think I'd marry a man like that! I told him once that was the only fault I found in him. He was Norwegian, and I couldn't understand why he didn't know how to dance. But his father died when he was six years old, and he was the man of the family, and his mother made him feel that way. And he said he never had time to dance. He never learned. Oh, he'd try once in a while, and hop around with his daughters, but it was a sorry dance. He never made a success of it, never enjoyed it. . . . Anyway, they danced at the wedding. Mother had an orchestra there. And I guess there would be over 150 people went down.[6]

Because of Susa's position as editor of the *Young Woman's Journal*, her family connections as a daughter of Brigham Young, and her personal friendship with almost all Church leaders, the wedding had many prominent attendees. John's later memory of Leah forms a vivid portrait:

Leah was then 24 years of age, in the full bloom of her young womanhood. She was 5'6" tall, straight and lithe. She had a mass of golden hair. Her skin was white with cheeks so pink she was often accused of using rouge, which was very uncommon in those days. She made a striking figure where ever she went. A description of her fell from the lips of a German child "Sie sieht wie eine Gräfin aus." "She looks like a countess." There was something regal about her, no matter what she was doing.

She had a splendid intelligence, which was continuously developed as the years went on, by reading, wide travel, and association with thoughtful, informed people. Her native wit often led her brilliance in talk and action. She met the enemy head on, rather than by the devious ways of diplomacy. Shyness was not in her nature. She was not forward, but neither afraid of people. Public questions intrigued her. She fought if necessary for her views.

She was of a social disposition. She danced, played, and sang well. She liked people and they liked her. Where ever she was, social events were soon in evidence. This made her unusually successful as the wife of a college and university president.[7]

Susa made a strategic announcement to the audience of the *Young Woman's Journal.*

> The Journal regards this marriage as an event worthy of self-congratulation. The lofty ideals of "The Home" and the advanced theories "Foods" are combined to establish a Bureau of Science wherein ideals and theories will be reduced to practice. From this new domestic experimental station will be issued monthly bulletins, the primary object of which will be the encouragement of matrimonial ventures.[8]

John married well, for Leah had a spiritual and emotional grounding that would match the bounteous opportunities that lay ahead of them. Leah's reputation in the field of home economics made her a popular public speaker. She stayed on the cutting edge of nutrition and taught that diet and health were the foundation of good living. John proclaimed her the soundest missionary for maintaining human health. Their first difficult decision concerned Leah's employment at the BYA. She was at the end of her contract, which added to her sense that the time for marriage was right. Just before their marriage, she approached John with a practical notion: "Why don't you leave here and let me go on teaching because I know they would be glad to retain me for one or as many years as I want to stay and we'll save a little money and we'll have that much toward our home." John's answer was decisive: "Pack your things and get ready for Europe; you're going with me. We're marrying for time and eternity and this is time, and you're going with me and we're going to have the same experiences in our lives."[9]

So the "golden-haired, pink-cheeked, blue-eyed young lady who had bewitched [him] in Cambridge, five years before," was to accompany him to Europe so that, as John wrote, "we might have common memories of the new lands and ways."[10] Separation was not, in his opinion, an option

John and Leah around the time of their marriage and departure to Göttingen in Europe.

in marriage.[11] With confidence they started a new adventure. Leah's charm, wit, and spirit were the perfect complement to John's studious, practical nature.

Traveling to Europe seemed a perfect way to celebrate their marriage and a rich beginning for their life together. In a similar way, it was the celebration of a fulfilling career John had courted for four years and the beginning of a higher professional goal he wished to achieve. Fulfillment came in his distinction as a scholar, teacher, and scientist, and in the unusual service he could render his Church and the farmers of the West. There were mountains to climb in attaining his professional ambitions, and obstacles to overcome in being a husband and father, but the time was right for combining those concerns. Thus their double honeymoon brought them the greatest joys of family life and the world's best scholarship. Leaving sometime after their wedding, Leah explained, "We didn't go off for a honeymoon. Our honeymoon came later, it was a honey two years."[12]

During their "honey two years," Emma Lucy Gates, Leah's sister, was a traveling companion and housemate. Lucy, who became a singer of significant repute in the years that followed, went to study music under the European masters. She became the wife of Elder Albert E. Bowen, a fellow son of Cache Valley, an associate of the BYC, and John's companion in the Council of the Twelve for many years.

Just before their departure, John was called to be a missionary and was ordained a seventy by Elder Brigham Young Jr. The threesome departed from Salt Lake City on 6 August 1898 and reached Göttingen on 5 September, well in time for the new semester. They sailed from Philadelphia to Liverpool aboard the *Waesland*. In Britain they visited relatives in Leicester and stayed at the home of H. B. Bruce, a wealthy manufacturer, where they took time to recover from a strenuous ocean voyage. There were daily carriage rides through Bruce's estate and nearby parks, and many strolls through the beautiful countryside. The newlyweds were especially charmed by their surroundings.

From England they sailed to Holland and then made their way by train. John saw to comfortable seating for Leah and Lucy and then checked on their luggage. Lucy's trunk was missing. John spotted it on a flatboat about to set sail. He quickly retrieved it and had it loaded onto the train, but before he was aboard the train left. He later recalled:

> That was not the worst. Foreseeing the possible dangers of travel, I carried the railroad tickets, and my young wife our money—under the assumption that a woman was more immune than a man from robbery. The station agent, hearing of our state of affairs, telegraphed the train conductor to put off the train, anywhere along the line, two American women with plenty of money but no tickets. Humbly I boarded in the middle of the forenoon, a slow, local train, a "Bummelzug." The conductor called Rotterdam, Amsterdam, and many other "dams." Towards the late afternoon, near the German boundary, on the station platform, sat two most disconsolate women. Never before or since had I or have I been so popular. But from that time on, in our travels, I have carried both tickets and extra money.[13]

THE INFLUENCE OF GERMAN UNIVERSITIES

Early in the nineteenth century, German universities, beginning with Halle and Göttingen, shifted their emphasis from teaching to research. "The essence of the German university system, which gave it intellectual leadership in the nineteenth century, was the concept that an institution of true higher learning should be, above all, 'the workshop of free scientific research.'"[14] From Germany there flowed an unparalleled devotion to the "disinterested pursuit of truth," the freedom to follow the path that truth uncovered and to teach accordingly. *Lernfreiheit* (freedom of learning) and *Lehrfreiheit* (freedom of teaching) characterized those universities. "German universities became world famous for their success in joining teaching and research and for their ambitious goal of producing, not just the practitioner, but the creative scholar and original investigator in every field of professional endeavor."[15]

As word of the universities spread, a great migration of American scholars began. Before the outbreak of the First World War, ten thousand American students enrolled in German universities. "Returning to their native heath, they were anxious to revolutionize the whole system of American higher education by introducing higher standards."[16] John's training at Göttingen became a blessing to American institutions. "In the transplanting of these considerably modified forms of the German university to American soil . . . the decisive role was played by a highly influential group of persons destined to become presidents of the most important universities in the United States."[17]

Göttingen adjoins several scenic travel routes, the "German Holiday Road," "Harz-Heath Road," and the "German Fairy-Tale Road." It was a seat of learning from 1311, but in 1734, Georg Augustus, a local ruler of nearby Hanover, founded the university. "The international reputation of the university was founded by many eminent professors who are commemorated by statues and memorial plaques. 42 Nobel Prize-winners have studied or taught in Göttingen and many students attained a place in history."[18] Nestled in the beautiful Harz mountains near the ruins of two castles, "it was a pleasant place of quiet, a good place in which to study," John wrote.[19] John was there to focus on particular parts of the chemical makeup of foods: carbohydrates, sugar, starches, and protein. He wrote:

> The most famous worker in the carbohydrate field was Bernhard Tollens, author of the one great work on the subject, and Director of the Agricultural-Chemical Laboratory. . . .
>
> This great university, the second oldest in the German empire, was famous. Illustrious men, makers of our modern day, had taught or studied there. It was a gathering place for students of many countries. In the advanced laboratory in which I worked, the ten students represented eight different nationalities. Americans had sought out the institution of learning for more than a hundred years. Marble plaques on the houses gave the names of men who had become famous, who had lived there. Bancroft and Longfellow were among the Americans so honored.
>
> Herr Geheimrath Doctor Professor Tollens, for whose wisdom I had crossed continents and an ocean, was a short, full bearded, pleasant faced man, who was equally at ease in German, French, or English. He moved quickly from place to place, usually muttering words of help in the native language of the student. His favorite pose was to hold a test tube against the light, looking intently at the contents, meanwhile shaking his head vigorously, whether in praise or condemnation no one knew, until the oracle spoke. But he knew his subject, and was an exquisite experimenter. The laboratory was filled with the spirit of discovery. Men grew under its influence. Soon all of us learned to love the kindly, helpful, "Herr Geheimrath," (Privy Councillor) a title which the government bestowed upon him soon after our arrival in Göttingen.[20]

Tollens had brought about new advances in food research. John's dissertation was about an ancient product used widely in medicine and industry known as gum tragacanth. Its constitution had long evaded researchers, and for a while it appeared that it would also elude John, but finally it yielded to him:

> It was found unexpectedly to be a rare five-carbon atom sugar with a group of one carbon and three hydrogen atoms (methyl group) attached. It was known as the fucose. The gum was a methyl pentosan. This was unexpected. A different carbohydrate was supposed

to be in such gums. The next step was then to devise a test by which such substances might be recognized. This was done by the aid of a spectroscope. Armed with the new method of detection, I found the methyl pentosans to be of general occurrence in the plant kingdom. Nothing more in the field of research was needed for the thesis which I wrote and which was promptly accepted.[21]

John's enthusiasm for the German universities was evident: "If . . . you want to get the true spirit of research there is not a place like Germany or the German schools. . . . I can say that I got out of German universities, not so much information, as a tremendous enthusiasm for the work in hand."[22] John attended extra lectures and courses and visited museums, libraries, galleries, and related institutions, often with Leah. With other American students they formed an enthusiastic group to take advantage of local events.

In April 1899 came the most exciting event of their stay in Göttingen as related to Lucy Bigelow Young, Leah's grandmother and wife of Brigham Young:

> Dear Grandmother Young: Yesterday morning at 8 minutes after 12—Sunday April 2nd—Leah gave you another great grandchild. It is a girl, and she has but one great grandmother and so sends her best regards to you.
>
> She weighs seven pounds; has a large complete nose; large ears; dark blue eyes; a German mouth, and long black hair. She sleeps during the day, and cries during the night; she has not yet learned the best way to suck its mother's breast.
>
> Leah is very well, and we know that she will pass through this time without any serious complications.
>
> Saturday morning Leah and I took a long walk. In the afternoon she served, and took her sitz bath about 6 o'clock; then went to bed to rest. About 8 o'clock she felt uneasy, but we thought nothing of it at first. As the indisposition did not pass off, I went for the midwife, who came about 9:30. From 10 to 12 Leah suffered much, but to-day she is strong and laughs and eats heartily.
>
> She has a midwife waiting on her and a trained nurse, and a physician looks after her every morning. With love to you all—John.[23]

John and Leah with baby Anna, summer 1900, Göttingen, Germany.

John and Leah decided to name their newborn after her Grand-mother Widtsoe. John wrote, "April 2nd, 1899, Anna's birthday, was Easter Sunday, and her first day on earth, in the quaint, little town of Göttingen, was marked by the ringing of many bells, and more celebra-tion of divers kinds, by the citizens of the town."[24] Great-grandmother Young responded to the birth announcement and soon joined the little family and Lucy in Göttingen. She was deserving of a special family memory, as John wrote, "[Our daughter's] great grandmother Lucy B. Young, lived next door. Her great grandmother took care of her often, while her parents were out, and from her she received many choice blessings."[25]

Seven months later, just fourteen months after their arrival in Göttingen, preparations for John's Ph.D. were complete:

> On November 20, 1899, having come down from Berlin, where I was then studying, and having made the usual calls on my profes-sors, in full evening dress attire (including the tall "stove pipe" hat), I took my doctor's examination in the "Aula" of the University. Sixteen or eighteen professors sat around the long table and asked questions, some of them inopportune, for two or three hours. After waiting half an hour in the adjoining waiting room, I was called back, and

The family in Göttingen. Left to right: Leah, John, Anna on Great-Grandmother Lucy Bigelow Young's lap, Emma Lucy Gates. Lucy Bigelow Young was the wife of Brigham Young.

informed that I had passed the examination "magna cum laude" (with high honors). And that the University was pleased to bestow upon me the degrees of master of arts and doctor of philosophy. A special certificate was also awarded me to use should I decide to teach or enter the chemical industry of Germany. I thanked the professors, notably Geheimrath Tollens, telegraphed my wife the good news, slept soundly that night and lunched with friends at our old "pension," owned by the sisters von Keudell, arranged for the publication of my thesis, and hurried back to Berlin, glad that this milestone had been passed. I recognized that my four years of diligent work at the U.S.A.C., with the several research publications of that time, had served me well in securing the coveted degree. And I never forgot God's help for I had always placed my needs before Him.[26]

OTHER DELIGHTS IN EUROPE

Their Mormon way set the little family apart and offered frequent opportunities to present the Church to the world's elite, though not always without some embarrassment and humor. Professors at Göttingen often gave parties for their students. Once, Professor Tollens, having been made a privy councilor (Geheimrath), gave an elaborate ball, a formal dress affair to which the Widtsoes were invited. John wrote, "Since my wife was unable to go because of her near birth of our first-born, Lucy came along, and in due time on the arm of a full-blown Prussian officer was escorted to the dinner table. When she refused wine, beer, and coffee, her companion in desperation, asked 'What do you drink?' and nearly collapsed when she quietly replied, 'Water.' 'Wasser!' said he. 'Mein gott, Wasser ist nicht zum trinken, es ist zum waschen,' (Water! Why, water is not for drinking, but for washing!)"[27]

There were occasions when missionaries passing through Göttingen stopped to visit. Arnold Schulthess, president of the German Mission, made a special trip for a personal visit. Louis T. Cannon, a friend of many years stopped for a visit on the return from his mission. "Such contacts were like a summer breeze from our canyons," John wrote.[28] Berlin, Zurich, and London had well-established branches of the Church, but in Göttingen, the Widtsoes were the only members. John recalled:

> Every Sunday the three of us, Lucy, my wife, and I, took an hour and a half for worship. We sang, prayed, partook of the sacrament, and studied the gospel. The minutes of these meetings, kept by Lucy, show that we were regular and diligent in our worship. This practice kept us spiritually fed, and made the week's work easier to do. Students away from home often drift away from the best in life because they do not observe Sunday worship. No one is too busy, if he really desires happiness in life, to give a few hours a week to the Lord. I know that our Sunday meetings did much for us, though alone in our faith in the city.[29]

In Germany and Switzerland, surveillance of Americans was high. Even their move between apartments in the same building required registration with the police. In Zurich, proving their marriage was a problem. John noted, "When I answered that they were my wife and baby, I was asked to produce documents of proof. Our marriage certificate had been left at home, so we were obliged to enter into a Swiss civil marriage. Thus I was married twice to the same woman, with no divorce between."[30] The military presence was troublesome, and they learned to give a member of the military a wide berth on the sidewalk. Even ordinary citizens seemed hostile. "It was a surprise to find that America and Americans were unpopular in every European country that we visited. We arrived near the end of the Spanish-American War. Over and over we were taunted with the remark that our upstart nation had no right to do injury to a European kingdom like Spain, with a government dating back many centuries. It will have to be admitted that Europe was not all together a pleasant place for liberty-loving Americans."[31]

At Göttingen John minored in physics and mineralogy. He also undertook some innovative research into the measurements and optical properties of crystals. In Berlin he studied under Emil Fischer, an authority on the chemical composition of sugars. At the Polytechnicum, now the University of Zurich, John spent the winter of 1899 studying in the laboratory of Dr. E. Schulze, an expert on protein, and with Dr. Winterstein, a master of toxicology. His lab mate, Dr. J. Posternak, was a kind, gentle Russian nihilist who had escaped from Siberia. He taught John much about the evils of Russian politics. Spring and summer were spent in London, which John considered the most interesting city in the world. Most memorable was his time at the Rothampsted Experiment Station, the world's oldest agricultural experiment station. Lengthy discussions with Dr. J. H. Gilbert, its longtime chemist, reviewed about fifty years of their discoveries and showed him the results they were currently exploring.

Like John's professors in Göttingen, these men represented the world's best work in chemical studies of nutrition. "During this sojourn in Europe," John wrote, "I gathered technical experience everywhere. I met many persons of note, learned many of their views. One of the products of my labors was a world view of scientific endeavor. Such knowledge gave courage to undertake the probing nature of her mysteries."[32]

It was John's lasting impression that Joseph F. Merrill and he were the first of a large group of "Mormon Boys" to earn the Ph.D. degree in residence. Merrill finished in the spring of 1899 and John in the fall. Of its importance John wrote, "The real meaning of the Doctor's degree is that the institution that confers the degree, thereby certifies that in its opinion, the recipient is now able to advance his special subject unaided by teachers."[33]

In the summer of 1899, John was finally able to return to his beloved Norway. He visited the villages of his infancy, their home in Namsos, and the familiar sights of Trondheim. He enjoyed lengthy visits and renewed acquaintances with extended family members. He was given to much introspection about the path the gospel had set him on. Though it had taken him away from this land of rugged beauty and from precious associations with family, it had enlightened his mind and enlarged his soul. Following its trail had exposed him to opportunities none of his kinfolk could rival and, doubtless, far in excess of what he could have obtained if they had not gathered to Zion. His family ties were still strong. He noted:

> Trondhjem (now Trondheim), the home of my father and grandfather, brought back memories of my childhood. Out on the outermost island I relived the summer vacations of my boyhood. I saw Norway for the first time with mature eyes, and was proud of my origin. There was a pathos in my leaving. I had to go by row boat for some miles to the nearest steamer port. We were six young men, all cousins. Four were at the oars, one at the rudder, and I was the honor guest. Each was a descendent from one of the five sons and the one married daughter of my maternal grandfather. That day the water was smooth; the sky only lightly overcast; every splash of the oars was carried over the water; the eider-duck floated lazily on the ripples; we all thought long thoughts. Human hearts are much the same, in every land, under every condition.[34]

ON THOUGHTS OF HOME

John missed the daily association with the young minds that filed into his classes in Logan, and he wanted to share with them the insights he was gathering. The *Improvement Era,* the Church magazine for young men, was in its first year, and John wished to contribute to its success. From Göttingen he submitted many articles on science and religion to the *Improvement Era.* They were especially appreciated by Church president Joseph F. Smith (see chapter 16).

While the Widtsoes were in Europe, Elder B. H. Roberts was elected to the U.S. House of Representatives. However, the House voted to exclude him because he was involved with polygamy. This led to an investigation of polygamists employed by the ACU, a federal land-grant college. In February 1900 the House amended the agricultural bill to withhold appropriations for the ACU unless all known polygamists left; John's guide and friend, President J. M. Tanner, was a casualty. John wrote, "A month or so before our return to the United States I learned that Dr. J. M. Tanner was to leave the presidency of the Utah State Agricultural College. He asked me to make application for the presidency. Despite my own feelings, but trusting in my old instructor and friend, I sent on a half-hearted letter of application to the Board."[35] Seven other men submitted applications. In a meeting of the board of trustees of the ACU on 11 June 1900, a new president was elected. Only William Jasper Kerr and John A. Widtsoe were nominated by members of the board. "On the first ballot William J. Kerr received four votes and John A. Widtsoe received three votes. William J. Kerr was declared elected President of the Agricultural College of Utah." One trustee protested against the appointment because Kerr was a polygamist and his appointment would also endanger their appropriation. The board then took up the election of a director of the Experiment Station. Several applications were on file but only two were placed in nomination. On the first ballot, "John A. Widtsoe was declared elected Director of the Experiment Station."[36]

A few weeks before they left Europe, John received a cable from the president of the board of Brigham Young College stating that he had been elected president of the college. Another cable came from a close friend asking him to refuse the offer. Then came word that Kerr had been elected president and that John was elected the station's director. "Apparently there had been a battle. The old disgusting Mormon and anti-Mormon fight had been revived. President Kerr even though he had been a polygamist apparently was satisfactory to the anti-Mormon contingent, and my name had been bandied about as the Church candidate. That was 'all right' with me. Besides, the station position suited me perfectly. I had learned to love the type of experimentation for which the station stood, and was ready to dedicate my life to it."[37]

When John returned to the college he was particularly pleased to read the letters of praise Dr. Tanner had solicited from seven of his former mentors at Harvard and Göttingen, including Charles W. Eliot and Bernhard Tollens.

11

DIRECTOR OF THE UTAH EXPERIMENT STATION

O N 16 August 1900, the *Logan Journal* reported the return of the Widtsoe family. Two weeks later, on 1 September, John began his term as director of the Utah Agricultural Experiment Station. There is not the slightest evidence that John was disappointed at not having been elected president of the college. Rather, he had an evident desire to create something to rival the Rothampsted Experiment Station in Britain. John approached the work of the station with enthusiasm, eager to apply the new learning gained in Europe to the special problems found in Utah. In a letter to the Church's presiding bishop he explained, "Among our people [LDS] I think I am the only person who has so fitted himself for the kind of work required of the Director of the Agricultural Experiment Station that no serious criticism could be offered against him."[1] As director he was given the use of a charming campus house and a team and buggy.

The achievements of the Utah Experiment Station at the ACU during the years John was its director were landmark feats that established the station, the college, and the state as dominant forces in international agricultural studies. The ACU belonged to a land-grant college sisterhood that grew out of the Morrill Act signed by Abraham Lincoln. In

Home of the Experiment Station director, UAC campus, Widtsoe family residence from 1900 to 1905.

1888, Congress supplemented that bill by allowing an additional $15,000 for experiment stations. Utah took advantage of these measures by creating the ACU with the Utah Experiment Station. John, as its new director, was determined to achieve the goals of land-grant college architects and help the common man succeed. He saw the experiment station as the best means of facilitating this ambition.

Considering John's educational attainments, it might be thought that his work would have been directed toward states and institutions of greater significance, but John's main desire was to serve his state. This was not just driven by feelings for his family, Leah's family, and the memories of his youth. John's firm belief in the Church and its struggles to settle Zion were also paramount. Preparing the Utah soil and helping her people farm it in accordance with the vision he described in his early *Improvement Era* articles (see chapter 16) was the core of his motivation.

The Utah Agricultural Experiment Station on the UAC Campus.

As director and chemist, John charted the course of both the Chemical Division and the Experiment Station. He noted, "The years that I served as director of the station was a period of almost complete absorption in service to the farmers of the State."[2] Since his predecessor had concluded all previous research, John was free to explore. "The Station, if it serves its purpose well, must discover something new that meets a distinct want in the State, and which can be applied by the farmers, so as to be of economic or other value."[3] Following this course he decided to "choose problems for investigation of first importance in Utah."[4] He had successfully addressed some of those special needs earlier as station chemist. As director he felt the need to develop a much larger research plan.

John didn't rely on his training alone to determine the station's research agenda. He wrote, "We must lay aside our preconceived notions, our prejudices and even our views of what may be the nature of the truth to be discovered in order that we may gather from nature all that she has in her keeping for us."[5] Accordingly, he again sought insight on Utah's needs by boarding a buggy and visiting settlements from Logan to Kanab, over to St. George, and back to Logan. Not a single night was spent in a hotel, nor a single meal taken in a restaurant. He lived right with the farmers and learned from them about their problems. It took nearly four months, but he declared, "When I got back I knew what our experiment station should be working on."[6] The work of the station could never be stronger than the union it had with the men and women on the farms of the state.

A circular entitled "A Day at the Utah Agricultural Experiment Station" gave a helpful outlook of the station's mission: "The aim has been to discover the unknown facts of nature's laws that would promote the agricultural prosperity of Utah and to make these facts known to the people of the state in order to enhance their happiness and material welfare. To meet the demands of the present and to prepare for the needs of the future, the energies of the Station Staff are being vigorously directed."[7]

John had been trained for the academic life, so his success as a leader in agriculture was an anomaly. He was concerned that he might be labeled a "book farmer." In some of his remarks, humor veiled the tension he felt:

> Frankly, it must be said that much prejudice had to be overcome. Farmers are "set" people. In those days especially, they were doubtful about "book farmers." Up in Heber, the leading citizen, examining my hands, looked heavenward and remarked, "Oh Lord, that the time should come that a man with such hands should teach us how to farm." Down in Richfield one of the farmers arose in the institute meeting to remark that he had helped build the bridges and kill the snakes in Sevier County, and that he knew more about farming in the county than I would ever know. He concluded his oration by inviting me to return to my hotel and take the first train out of Richfield and never to return. Five years later he was one of our most enthusiastic supporters. Dr. E. D. Ball and I held the well advertised first farmers' institute in Springville. Only two men came out. Nevertheless we practiced on them. After the meeting we discovered that one of the two was stone-deaf, who passed time by attending meetings, and the other was the janitor who had to be present. Eight years later when

John, second row left, as a young chemistry professor. On the back of the photo is written "Class in chemistry, Utah Agricultural College, taken in March 1901."

our agricultural train reached Springville, we were met by the mayor, city council with a brass band, and the meeting hall was crowded to capacity. It did not take long to convert the people of Utah. They needed only to be convinced that we came as bearers of truth and that "book-farmers" so-called had much to teach the pioneer who had to learn only through hard experience. Then, the old prejudices vanished.[8]

In time John's teachings were closely followed by most of the farmers in the state. His teachings regularly appeared in the columns of the *Deseret Farmer*, a weekly newspaper he helped establish. In an article appearing in the 30 November 1905 issue, he wrote:

Don't laugh at the man with a book, for you will live to regret it. The man with the book has made the world what it is. Who transformed the small beet with 5 per cent of sugar, of 150 years ago, into the modern sugar beet, containing 15 to 17 per cent of sugar? The book farmer. Who has produced the valuable varieties of fruit? Who has bred and selected the varieties of wheat and other grains that are used on our farms? Both were done by the book farmer. Who has taught us the nature of plant diseases, and the right way to combat them? The book farmer. Who chased the apple worm out of his hole,

Portrait of John. Written on the back in Leah's hand is "Taken April 1902, age 30 years." In John's hand: "That's a mistake, isn't it? Wasn't this taken about the time I was courting Leah in earnest, about 1897? or 1898?" In Leah's hand: "No, that is not a mistake. This is your 30 yr of age picture."

and told us how to get rid of him? The same old book farmer. In short, all the advancement modern agriculture has made, is due to the efforts of the book farmer. . . .

The farmer who works with head and hand is the one who is going to succeed.[9]

This article, titled "A Word to our Boys about 'Farming,'" was directed to the next generation of farmers as encouragement to seek an agricultural education:

The farmer of the future is a man who combines theory and practice. With a trained mind and skilled hands, he subjects nature and makes her obey him. His intellect controls his work, and makes it high and dignified. He holds his work divine and reaps all the joy that belongs to the artist.

What he learns from books and from experience he executes with his hands. He works fewer hours, because of his intelligence he can accomplish more in less time. His home is comfortable; his surroundings beautiful and sanitary; he has books and magazines, pictures and music, because his intelligent mind, producing greater wealth, can

In Logan, young Anna Widtsoe is being held by her grandmother, Anna Widtsoe, John's mother. Photo taken in 1901.

procure these desirable things. He deals with God and nature in his work; and because of his freedom from other servitude, is a king among his fellows. He believes in work and play, fatigue and rest, judiciously combined.[10]

IRRIGATION AND ARID FARMING

John drew the conclusion that "the future development of Utah will necessarily depend on the extension of the old irrigation systems and the creation of new ones."[11] The irrigation work of the station brought the highest commendations from government officials and irrigation experts. Cooperative efforts and substantial research contracts with the United States Department of Agriculture followed. Utah's work in irrigation became so well known that in 1903, the conference of the National Irrigation Congress was held in Ogden. A Logan newspaper reported:

> The Agricultural Department at Washington is convinced that
> the methods adopted by Professor Widtsoe in this department are the

best in the world, and were therefore willing to co-operate on the basis above mentioned. Too much praise cannot be given Professor Widtsoe and his aides who have brought this system of irrigation to such a state of perfection as to induce the officials of the Government to form a co-operation with our institution. This means a great deal when the number of experiment stations in the country are considered. The amount thus invested is aside from the general appropriation from the government.[12]

In 1903 only 1.15% (983 acres) of Utah's land area was under irrigation, yet the land was among the most fertile in the world, and the conditions of sunshine and temperature were nearly ideal. Land rich in plant foods but without water was worth from $1.50 to $2.50 per acre, while land with ample water commanded between $100 and $300 per acre. For John the conclusion was evident: "The value of a farm in Utah does not reside largely in the land, but rather in the quantity of water under the control of the owner. The smaller the possible returns of the farm without irrigation, the greater the value of a water right for it."[13] As a result, John initiated a series of elaborate irrigation experiments. Some of the most notable ran over a ten-year period (1902–1911) and involved fourteen crops. From these he learned that the law of diminishing returns applied to the increase in yield gained from an increase in water. "At this break in the curve," the amount of water used was called the *consumptive use*.[14]

Because of the abundance of fertile land beyond the reach of irrigation, the station conducted numerous studies on the feasibility of raising crops without irrigation. In them John pioneered the concept of "dry farming" as a distinct branch of agriculture for the purpose of reclaiming desert or semi-desert lands. He wrote:

> The fundamental problems of dry-farming are, then, the storage in the soil of a small annual rainfall; the retention in the soil of the moisture until it is needed by plants; the prevention of the direct evaporation of soil-moisture during the growing season; the regulation of the amount of water drawn from the soil by plants; the choice of crops suitable for growth under arid conditions; the application of suitable crop treatments, and the disposal of dry-farm products, based

upon the superior composition of plants grown with small amounts of water.[15]

The goal of the station was to conquer the desert by scientific study. In John's copy of an 1895 station bulletin he wrote, "Calculate: the amount of materials (inorganic) furnished by the water and retained by the soil; then the amount of material removed from the soil by the crops. This, to learn the rate of exhaustion—if any exist."[16] Systematic studies of the amount of water needed for specific crops were made and the findings published in station bulletins and in newspapers across the state.[17] A key finding was, "It has been calculated that to produce twenty bushels of wheat to the acre would require an annual rainfall of 11.4 inches. In the northern section of Utah, that is all that portion north of Provo there is an annual rainfall, including snow, of about 13.47 inches. This shows that the northern section receives an annual rainfall which if properly conserved in the soil, should be sufficient to produce twenty bushels of wheat to the acre, without the artificial application of water."[18]

Station Bulletin No. 75, the first published treatise on dry farming, described important techniques, such as when to plow, when to let lands lie fallow, when to plant seed, and what kind and how much seed to use. It noted that vast areas of Utah never brought under irrigation "in most cases would make splendid dry or arid farms."[19] Where water could be taken to arid lands, even at great expense, it was considered wise to convert dry farms into irrigated land. "Good land with water can be depended upon to produce a crop each year, and forty acres of it is worth more than one hundred and sixty acres of dry farm with no certainty of a crop year after year."[20] As a reward for its work, the station received an appropriation from the state legislature to establish six farms across the state to study dry farming. John described one of them:

> I met with the Juab County commissioners to secure county co-operation, which was readily given, though with some misgivings as to the outcome. The chairman of the commission advised me to place the farm on the southern slope of the hill, since on the northern side we could only expect failure. So challenged, of course, we located the farm on the northern slope. We ourselves could only guess at the

results. Early the next spring, when only a few blades of wheat were showing, we were frankly more hopeful than certain. But in early July the farm was covered with bountiful yields of several dozen varieties of useful crops. The farm looked like an oasis in the stretch of sage brush covering hill and valley. At our invitation the people joined an excursion to the farm. They were interested and at the end of the day convinced and jubilant. They gave three cheers there for the College. As I was leaving, there stood at the farm gate a depressed looking man. I volunteered help if needed. "No," he answered, "I am just trying to figure out how those d—— fellows at the College could pick out the only forty acres on this hill where crops could be grown without irrigation." He also became a convert and the prosperous owner of a dry-farm on Levan hill.[21]

Experimental farms were established in Iron, Juab, San Juan, Sevier, Tooele, and Washington Counties. On these farms people could see demonstrations of growing crops without irrigation. The demonstrations enabled them to acquire a firsthand understanding of how the work was done and what results were obtained. Scientific farming yielded splendid stands of rye, wheat, barley, and oats on land that was commonly supposed to be valueless.

Utah was the oldest of the dry-farming states, and national articles about dry farming saluted Cache Valley residents as its pioneers.[22] Dry farming had one more test to pass—surviving a year of drought. Lewis A. Merrill answered by analyzing the harvest of 1910, a heavy drought year. Returns from all sections of Utah and surrounding states confirmed the teachings promulgated by the experiment station. Tests proved that it was possible to store two years' precipitation in the soil. Merrill noted that farmers who followed those practices "have this year reaped an ample harvest."[23]

Visitors came from other states and countries to see firsthand the station's success. L. H. Bailey, the prestigious dean of Cornell's College of Agriculture, asked John, then a member of the Irrigation Congress and president of the Dry-Farm Congress, to write textbooks on irrigation and dry farming.[24] These texts were used in France, Palestine, Africa, Spain, Hungary, Australia, and all of North and South

America.[25] For his role in pioneering irrigation and dry farming, John A. Widtsoe was dubbed "the father of the system of Dry Farming in the West."[26] During the 1890s the amount of land farmed in Utah increased fourfold, and in the early 1900s it extended further into the Uinta Basin, the west deserts, and San Juan County.[27] Dry farming alone increased Utah's crop land by one-fourth.[28] As late as 1967, 37 percent of Utah's crop lands were without irrigation.[29]

The ACU and the station sent several exhibits to the St. Louis World's Fair in 1904. Competing with 64 agricultural colleges and 60 experiment stations, the Utah station's irrigation model won a silver medal.[30] The accolade prompted this remark: "It is again a pleasure to mention the harmonious manner in which three departments, involving the labors of nearly twelve men, have worked together to carry out successfully the plans of the irrigation experiments. It is believed that this series of experiments stands alone in the history of irrigation, when its comprehensive, thorough and strictly scientific treatment is considered."[31]

Irrigation and dry farming were the principal focus of the station, but scientists also continued work on soil surveys and reclaiming alkaline lands. They experimented on the feed value of Utah crops, analyzed sugar beets and sugar-beet pulp, and considered the development of new crops suited to arid farming. During his time as director, John oversaw the publication of an average of five scientific bulletins yearly on an impressive variety of subjects.

Research and publication were not enough for John. He wrote, "Carrying the principles of modern agriculture to the farmers always seemed important to me. Unused truth has little value."[32] He felt that not one farmer in ten realized what was available to him. He urged farmers to "at once put themselves in touch with information freely imparted through the bulletins of the A.C. of U."[33] Experimental farms were effective learning centers. The state also set aside money for the teachers of the ACU to travel the state and hold institutes for farmers.[34] John recalled, "As time permitted, with specialists from the Station staff, I travelled over the State discussing with groups of farmers their problems. While we taught them something, they in turn set our faces towards

Plowing college hill.

problems to be solved."[35] Despite an occasional lapse, institute work became very successful, farmer turnout was impressive, and enthusiasm echoed in the press. As the Logan newspaper proudly proclaimed, instruction at the institutes was "disseminated in the delightful manner that comes natural to the average professor at the big school on the hill."[36]

A successful farm operation required teamwork. The farmer's wife—a homemaker, housekeeper, cook, and merchant—was a vital part of the concern, as John recognized: "Since the farmer's wife must also work intelligently if the household is to be happy, from the beginning of this period women's institutes were held with great success. My wife, well trained, and enthusiastically in support of the work of the college and station, conducted most of the early meetings throughout the State in which the problems of the home and household were discussed."[37]

With Lewis A. Merrill and J. Edward Taylor, John founded a successful newspaper called the *Deseret Farmer* and served as the general manager. The *Deseret Farmer* published articles about irrigation, dry farming, livestock, horticulture, fruit-growing, and all else having to do with farming in Utah. John wrote articles encouraging farmers to take advantage of the opportunities modern science was yielding.[38] The paper announced the farmer's institutes and reported their proceedings. John

The ACU Campus. In the front, from left to right, are the President's Home, the Experiment Station, and the Old Main building.

felt it had "done much to help the tiller of the soil and the husbandman in the arid region."[39]

All of these efforts to reach farmers were very successful. The consensus, more than eighty years later, was that "in no feature were good times more marked than in the application of science to agricultural practices and farm life. Irrigation passed from rule of thumb to technology. . . . Dry farming became first a field of research then a way of life."[40]

Any assessment of the Utah Experiment Station must consider the economic impact it had on those it was designed to serve. The Logan newspaper believed it was impossible to estimate the financial value of the work of the station, but some computations indicated that "were the directions given in the station bulletins generally followed, there would be an annual gain to the state of hundreds of thousands of dollars."[41] One significant statistic is the increase in the average value of a farm, which grew from $2,619 in 1900 to $9,499 in 1920.[42]

In 1905, just before completing his service as station director, John wrote an article estimating the economic impact of several research activities of the station. He showed that the varieties of wheat used by farmers in the state, as a result of the station's research, resulted in a total increase of at least 189,235 bushels or $113,541. Station research on feeding horses netted a statewide savings of 20,000 tons of lucern with a cash value of $80,000. Studies on the optimum time for cutting lucern showed that the value could be increased by at least one tenth, or 58,132 tons with a cash value of $275,000. By following station guidelines on when and in what quantities to irrigate wheat, statewide yield was increased by 378,470 bushels or $257,082. The increase in sugar-beet yields resulting from station research represented a statewide gain of between $150,000 and $600,000. John's analysis continued:

> Of still higher importance have been the results which indicate that by the more economical use of water the irrigation area may be increased at least one-fourth without the building of any new canals. There are now 620,120 acres of irrigated land in the State. To increase that area one-fourth would mean an increase of 157,280 acres, each of which would certainly yield $10, which would result in adding to the annual wealth of the State $1,572,800. The value of such results is a fact beyond estimations.
>
> Our work in showing the possibilities of arid lands will certainly result in adding materially to the wealth of the State. There are at present 51,972,480 acres of land in the State which are not irrigated. If only one percent of this land can be made to yield fifteen bushels per acre without irrigation, and it does not seem at all impossible, the State would gain annually 7,795,860 bushels of wheat, with a value of at least 50 cents per bushel, or $3,897,930. If only one acre in a thousand can thus be reclaimed, the annual value to the State would be nearly $400,000.
>
> Calculations similar to these may be multiplied and the numerous experiments of the station can be connected with their financial value in such a way as to show that the Utah agricultural experiment station has done work which may make or is making for the State millions of dollars. As a money-making institution for the state the agricultural experiment station takes second rank to none, save it be to the public school system, which gives to men and women powers to use the results obtained by modern science.[43]

The Utah canning industry started in 1888. In 1914, 32 canning factories produced 1,338,497 cases of fruits and vegetables. These "factories employed 1,500 workers who received one-third of a million dollars in wages. By 1914 Utah ranked fifth in the canning industry among the United States."[44]

Though irrigation had been practiced for several millennia, its refinement into a science and the peak of productivity is attributed to the Mormon settlement of the Great Basin. Many whose lives were tied to irrigation saw it as the divine miracle that fulfilled the biblical prophecy that the desert would blossom as a rose. As the science of irrigation unfolded, some proclaimed it a continuous miracle. Not willing to be so presumptuous, John wrote, "Today with our greater understanding, irrigation is less of a miracle; it is more of an intelligent conquest—a continuous conquest of the untoward forces of the desert."[45]

These were happy years for the Widtsoe family. Looking back John wrote, "I do not know of any half decade in my life which I have enjoyed more thoroughly than my directorship of the Utah State Agricultural Experiment Station."[46] But his time at the Experiment Station was to come to an abrupt and ugly end. Many citizens felt that Utah was too small to support both a university and an agricultural college. A move was afoot in the governor's office and in the legislature to consolidate the two institutions by making the ACU a college in the University of Utah. The controversy became particularly nasty at the ACU. The statewide impact of the experiment station, and John's devotion to agricultural education, led William Jasper Kerr, president of the ACU, to label Dr. Widtsoe disloyal.[47] As a result, he was dismissed from the station and the college in 1905. The dismissal came as a severe shock to him and was without doubt the low point of his professional life.

John expressed some personal feelings about the controversy:

> The dismissal shocked me. It was not so much because of losing a job; I felt I could get another. But it was unfair, the kind of thing big men don't allow. I was subjected to much unfavorable newspaper notoriety inspired by the President or his friends as means of self-defense. Most of all, I wanted to bring toward conclusion the experimental work initiated by me. I had so completely identified myself with the work of the Station that I felt as if I were leaving a child. It was some comfort to know that the Station and its work had been

brought to national recognition and that I was leaving behind a group
of men trained in the progressive policy of the Station.[48]

While the legislature resolved the consolidation controversy, John
went to BYU and founded its School of Agriculture. His two years at
BYU were triumphant and highly acclaimed. They were also his last
opportunity for significant research. In 1907 the consolidation controversy was resolved by the state legislature and Kerr's policies so condemned that he resigned his presidency. The board of trustees then
elected John as his successor. Administrative duties thereafter precluded
significant experimental research.

John's 1905 dismissal, in light of his accomplishments, was a far
more outrageous violation of the sacred shield of his academic freedom
than the 1895 petition of his faculty colleagues that he resign over the
fear of his "Mormonizing" the college. It was the lowest point of his professional life. From it he became an ardent believer that politics should
never ensnare educational accomplishments.[49]

12

BYU'S FIRST STEPS TOWARD UNIVERSITY STATURE

ON 28 August 1989, Rex E. Lee, newly appointed president of BYU, spoke of "Circles, Bells, and the College That We Love" in his inaugural address to the faculty. He noted that in the school's earliest years, its focus was on preparing teachers to guide the young minds of the state. The academy matured, and by 1903 it was poised for the step up to university life. No one else was as able to perform that task as John A. Widtsoe. Lee noted, "Our first academic endeavor that attracted any attention beyond Utah County was in agriculture, under the leadership of John A. Widtsoe."[1] The official university history records that "John A. Widtsoe's agricultural program was serious university work and could have established BYU as an agricultural school if Widtsoe had remained at the University."[2]

Harvard's president, Derek Bok, wrote, "From Germany came the idea of a university dedicated to research conducted by the specialized professor with the help of student apprentices. From England came a strong emphasis on the teaching of undergraduates and a broad conception of education that embraced the moral and emotional as well as the intellectual development of the student."[3] This was the foundation of the American universities of the twentieth century. But another dimension made it stronger. "Americans tended to look on higher education as a means for providing the knowledge and the trained manpower that a rapidly developing society required."[4] John was a decorated product of Harvard, the American Cambridge, and Göttingen, the preeminent German model. He had also become a decided advocate of land-grant colleges and thereby embodied the broadest ideals of the American university.

In 1894, Brigham Young Academy president Benjamin Cluff worked to secure John's appointment to the faculty. James E. Talmage pressed for that appointment when one closer to him could not be opened. Incoming president George H. Brimhall continued Cluff's desire: "Many times have I said to myself and others, 'How I wish Brother Widtsoe could be in the Brigham Young Academy.'"[5] Brimhall even pursued John's employment with Church leaders who knew of his prowess and the advantage he could give the academy. Finally he had to concede, "Upon consulting with my brethren, I have found a strong sentiment in favor of your being 'let alone,' and so, as in all other things, I try to make their will mine."[6] Brimhall wanted Widtsoe because of his academic record and his example as a devoted Church member, a budding theologian, and a brilliant chemist. His reputation in soil chemistry, dry farming, and irrigation had already made an impact in agricultural colleges across the world.

John also had a real determination to make learning useful in improving the lives of the working class. He replied to Brimhall:

> The toilers of the world are making the world, but they need assistance. Under the present social conditions they can do little else than toil; for that reason I feel a genuine happiness in applying, to the best of my ability, the results of modern science to the betterment of the lowly pursuits of life. For that reason, also, I try to make myself contented to remain in my present work, though my heart goes out— as you know—to the special interests of the great latter-day cause. Should I follow my own inclinations alone, I would not hesitate, but should choose work similar to that which are you doing, by the Church, for the Church and under the Church.[7]

Before a year had passed, the inclination became a reality. The

fierce political crisis that threatened to consolidate the ACU into the
U of U was raging, and John had been caught in the crossfire. On 15
July 1905, he was elected director of agriculture at BYU,[8] becoming
BYU's first faculty member with a doctoral degree.[9] BYU officials held
high expectations for John, and farmers throughout Utah heralded his
appointment. In little more than a year he launched a whirlwind program that "brought agricultural work at BYU to the fore."[10] Agriculture
had been a part of BYU's School of Arts and Industries. It was headed
by Edwin S. Hinckley, who had little time to devote to it since he was
also second counselor (vice president) to President Brimhall.[11] Through
John's personal touch and that of those he gathered around him, the
number of courses more than doubled, and they became as specialized
as similar courses in the best institutions.[12] Utah's chief farm newspaper
reported:

> Agriculture is to be made a prominent feature in the courses of
> instruction at Brigham Young University at Provo. Dr. John A.
> Widtsoe, who has gained a reputation in the west second only to that
> of Dr. Hilgard of California, as a scientific agriculturist, is to be Dean
> of the Agricultural School. It is expected that this school will draw
> hundreds of young men from all over the arid west to that popular
> institution and the results will soon become apparent on the farms
> and in the orchards of the tillers of the soil from Canada to Mexico.
> Experts along the various lines of agriculture are to be engaged and
> farmers who desire their sons to become acquainted with the scien-
> tific facts and truths of their profession will have no hesitancy in
> entrusting them to Dr. Widtsoe.[13]

Brimhall had procured the man President Heber J. Grant labeled
"the greatest educator that Mormonism has ever produced."[14] John's
vision was ambitious: "B.Y.U. had and now has no other reason for existence than to make well-educated Latter-day Saints."[15] It "must offer
complete education conforming to the doctrine and practice of the true
Church of Jesus Christ."[16] Franklin S. Harris, who became BYU's longest
serving president, looked back on his experience as one of John's BYU
students:

> His splendid personality has always attracted students to him and

John A. Widtsoe, Ph.D., director of the BYU School of Agriculture from 1905 to 1907.

his vigorous intellect has been so thoroughly stimulating to them that many of the leading scholars of the West trace their incentive to advanced study directly to his influence.

Some teachers have a way of impressing their own importance on the pupils, particularly on the young ones. They convey the idea that all knowledge centers in themselves and that the chief function of the pupil is to sit in awe at the unattainable heights reached by the teacher. This is just opposite to the attitude assumed by Dr. Widtsoe before the class. With the modesty that characterizes everything he does, he puts himself in the background and impresses on the student the sublimity of the great universe of truth and fills him with a desire, which reaches almost a passion, to seek relentlessly for truth wherever it may be found.[17]

In November 1906, Brimhall reported, "We have an Agricultural School here now larger, perhaps, than any other aggregation of its kind in the State, having an exceptionally strong faculty in that line."[18] Congratulations came from Harvard: "Read, with satisfaction, of the good work you are doing for agriculture in Utah."[19] In 1907 the

Southwestern State Normal (School) of Oklahoma felt a report about American Agricultural Education would be incomplete without including BYU.[20] John's longtime mentor, J. M. Tanner, had become the general superintendent of the Church School System with responsibility for BYU. When a significant government post was opened for John, Brimhall, fearful that he could not turn it down, appealed to Tanner:

> It would be simply calamitous to the Brigham Young University to have him leave within the next few years. We would be worse off than if we had never had him. His withdrawal would foster the sentiment that the Church School service can not hold high grade men, and that the money pull of the outside is stronger than the interest pull for the welfare of Zion's youth. His remaining will increase the feeling that the educational interests of Zion, and those having in charge its affair, hold to the policy that nothing within reach is too good for the young people of Zion. . . .
>
> We recognize in Brother Widtsoe superior talent, and the highest kind of preparation, but we do not recognize in him anything that is too good for the Brigham Young University.
>
> At an early date, we shall lay the matter before the Presidency of the Church, and fortify ourselves in every way possible against . . . cutting off of one of our educational heads.[21]

Tanner's response conveyed his continuing esteem for John and his firm knowledge of the trust John put in the Brethren: "I heartily coincide with all you say about the desirability of having Brother Widtsoe remain with you. You will, of course, lay the matter before President Smith and the brethren of the First Presidency and represent as strongly as you can our interests. Brother Widtsoe will not take any action without first conferring with President Smith."[22] John remained at BYU the two years until the consolidation issue was resolved by the state legislature and President Smith gave him instructions to accept the appointment to return to the Agricultural College as its president.

John impressed upon students the need to be well grounded, and he imbued in them the urgency of using their knowledge for the practical benefit of mankind. Harris wrote, "In those days at Brigham Young University scores of capable young men clustered about him and were

fired with the ambition that drove them to get the training necessary
for leadership. Best of all, he implanted in them a philosophy and an
attitude toward religion that has kept them in balance during the vicis-
situdes of a turbulent world."[23]

In John's view, too many universities followed the "vicious practice"
of assuming all students were candidates for advanced degrees.
Beginning courses were so choked with remote difficulty that freshmen
lost interest. He wrote, "Were the fascinating descriptive parts of the
science taught first, with laboratory work, a successful return to the laws
now heavily stressed might be made. If students are thought fit to enter
a class, it should be so taught as to be within the easy understanding
of the students and taught in such a manner that the student will
thoroughly enjoy learning the new facts presented. Learning new truths
is an exhilarating experience and a good teacher awakens that joy."[24]

Clifton Kerr labeled Professor Widtsoe his "most influential
teacher" because of his well-honed knack for impressing on students the
need of knowing how and where to find truth. He demonstrated the
preeminence of inspiration over rote facts.[25] A quarter of a century after
John left BYU, his influence was still felt. Franklin S. Harris wrote to
him, "You may be interested in knowing that a group of students of agricultural tendencies recently organized a social unit and call themselves
the Widtsonians. You see, you are still held in fond remembrance in the
Institution."[26]

John loved teaching and research and felt sorrow for anyone not
similarly absorbed. "I have seen so many who have forgotten their work
for self-interest," he wrote. "They have added little to the welfare of
their generation, and less to their own happiness."[27] An examination of
John's pocket diary at BYU shows relentless devotion. While helping
conduct an extra "Farmer's Course," he wrote, "Am lecturing about
6 hours these days."[28] Following several days of illness, he taught until a
terrible cough forced him to stop.[29]

Because of excessive demands President Brimhall petitioned the
Brethren for two assistants for John.[30] William H. Homer Jr. was secured
by a special appropriation of $1,400.[31] Homer specialized in horticulture,
entomology, and botany at Cornell.[32] Another assistant was funded by

the farmers' courses and institutes. Widtsoe convinced his former ACU colleague, L. A. Merrill, an animal industry expert, to accept the position.[33] Widtsoe, Merrill, and Homer formed an exceptionally qualified agriculture faculty. Brimhall was pleased.[34]

John lured many agricultural experts to Provo to teach the latest developments in their specialty. The school of agriculture also began to acquire land and equipment. John selected sites for orchards and kept farms running in Beaver, Dog Valley, Nephi, and Utah Valley. He had the support of the First Presidency and met with them to discuss the agricultural needs of the school.[35] First-class equipment was furnished for soil physics, horticultural, bacteriological, and veterinary laboratories. He assembled a significant agricultural library by acquiring the best periodicals and books available.[36] When he left BYU he donated many of the materials he had written and much of his personal library:

> Upon my leaving the University towards the end of last June, I left in the agricultural laboratory between seven and eight thousand pamphlets of an agricultural nature. These pamphlets represent the collection of my life since I entered active agricultural investigation. If the agricultural work is to be continued at the B. Y. University, they will be of considerable value to students and teachers. Many of the pamphlets belong to the first period of agricultural investigation in this country, and can be obtained only with the greatest difficulty. If your Institution should care to accept these pamphlets, I desire to leave them permanently with the Brigham Young University; the ownership to remain wholly in the University.[37]

John, wholly devoted to experimental work, began a vigorous program at BYU. He took his classes on excursions to orchards, the Lehi Sugar Factory, and the Utah Central Experiment Station. He started a program to examine the typical soils in all LDS wards by requiring students to conduct experiments in the neighborhood from which they came.[38] He circulated word that "small experimental farms will be established in cooperation with up-to-date farmers in the various wards. Any farmer who would like to have an experiment conducted on his farm, under expert advice, or to have certain soils examined, should write to the University at once."[39] His aggressive experimental program enhanced the stature of BYU across the state. The Agricultural Society and Farmer's Organization strengthened the program through informative activities and guest lecturers.[40]

John's class rolls verify his unusual appeal. Besides many traditional students, several established faculty members attended his classes, including E. S. Hinckley, who headed the program before John's arrival, and Chester Van Buren, a biologist known for his participation in the Cluff Expedition. Several students who later achieved academic distinction began their careers in John's classroom, including R. J. Evans, Harvey Fletcher, Ernest Carroll, George R. Hill, and Franklin S. Harris. Harris is a prime example of John's influence on students. He studied agriculture under Dr. Widtsoe at BYU and followed him to the ACU. He then obtained his doctorate at Cornell and joined the faculty of the ACU. He became BYU's president in 1921 when John was unable to fill the slot. Harris stayed for twenty-four years, from 1921 to 1944, when he too left to preside over the ACU. Harris oversaw BYU's conversion from a small college to a nationally respected university.

At BYU and the ACU, George R. Hill obtained B.S. degrees in agriculture in 1907 and 1908. He also pursued doctoral studies at Cornell and then joined the faculty at the ACU, where for ten years he was director of the school of agriculture.[41] Thomas Martin came to BYU a year after John left. He studied under William H. Homer Jr., who maintained the program Widtsoe had established. Homer was replaced as principal of the school of agriculture by Amos N. Merrill, who, like Homer, was brought to BYU by Widtsoe.[42] Martin finished his undergraduate work under Merrill and obtained his Ph.D. at Cornell. He was a candidate for a staff position at Cornell but was passed over, he felt, because of his Church connection. He filled a distinguished career at BYU instead.[43] After his retirement he was recognized by the American Society of Agronomy for "having inspired more men to go on for a Ph.D. in soils than any other teacher in the nation."[44] He trained R. B. Farnsworth, who carried the work of agriculture on after him.[45] From mentor to mentor, the agriculture program at BYU can be traced back to its founder. BYU president Ernest L. Wilkinson wrote, "Serving as head of our Department of Agriculture from 1905 to 1907, from which he was called to be President of the Utah State Agricultural College, he gave an impetus to that work which has culminated in 124 of our graduates in Agriculture now being on the faculties of 28 Agricultural Colleges, and Universities, and Extension Divisions throughout the country, and one of our Agricultural graduates, his brother in the Quorum of the Twelve, has now been honored with appointment as Secretary of Agriculture to our beloved country."[46]

An especially valuable asset John took with him to BYU was his wife, Leah, who founded the school's domestic science program before their marriage. From 1906 to 1907 she served as the dean of women (matron). Wherever they went, John and Leah Widtsoe were champions of the importance of educating women. At BYU they created the first agricultural class for women in the West.[47] In a *BYU Quarterly* Leah wrote, "In the Domestic Science department, girls study those things that they must daily apply in the home: House-hold sanitation . . . house-hold art . . . home-nursing . . . methods and principles of cookery, with attention to the chemical and physical principles underlying each practice. . . . In the department of Domestic Art, the girls learn how to do all kinds of plain sewing first; then dress-making and all its branches; also all kinds of fancy work. . . . She learns how to draft, cut, and fit the clothing she makes."[48]

John and his faculty traveled around the state conducting weekend farmer's institutes. Brimhall and John C. Swensen often went along to promote other programs of the university.[49] John conducted institutes at Provo, Springville, Spanish Fork, Lehi, American Fork, Pleasant Grove, Nephi, Tooele, Manti, Mt. Pleasant, Moroni, Wales, Hinckley, Abraham, and Castle Dale. They were well attended: "Institute at 10 A.M. About 100 men and 75 women present. Inst. again at 2 P.M. 100 men and over 100 women present. I spoke." And for the next day: "110 men—100 women at 10 A.M. Abt. 400 men and women at 3 P.M. One of the very successful institutes of my career."[50]

An added dimension at BYU was an intensive winter course for farmers. The first of these, in 1906, lasted four weeks. "This Winter Course is especially adapted to those who can not leave the farm at the regular opening of school, and who must leave for the spring work. The classes close on March 30."[51] Fifty-five farmers attended a series of one hundred lectures: twenty on theology, twenty on economics, thirty on general agriculture, and thirty on animal husbandry.[52] Prior to the second year's course, President Brimhall reported "the hearty approval of the president of our board, Joseph F. Smith, and other leading brethren of the Church." He also described specific endorsements from class participants: "A number of the members of our last year's class have sent in to us most flattering results of their labors as being beneficial to themselves, and to the community from which they came. One young man went out on the dry land of Kane County and following out the instructions received in the class he produced a crop that awakened a great interest in arid farming in that locality."[53]

The winter farmer's course was the featured topic in the next *BYU Quarterly*: "The University offers this course because it is needed by the farmers of Utah. Modern investigation has developed a science of agriculture concerning which the farmers of Utah ought to know something."[54] The next farmer's course included twenty lectures on theology, with some given by B. H. Roberts. John delivered twenty lectures on soils, waters, and plants; Merrill gave twenty lectures on animal husbandry; and Homer delivered twenty lectures on horticulture. There were also twenty lectures on the economics of successful farming and a series of guest lecturers. In 1907 the course was expanded to include a curriculum for the women of agriculture.[55] John wrote, "Last day of farmers class. At 3 P.M. students met with farmers. All kinds of nice things were said about me and a handsome easy chair was presented me. Thank God for appreciation."[56]

To promote further growth, John wrote an article entitled "A Talk With Young Men About Agriculture."[57] He described its desirable lifestyle, its profitability, and the advantage of its study in college. The article was published in the *BYU Quarterly* and the *Deseret Farmer*.[58] In October 1905, John reported, "The enrollment in the Department up to this time has been phenomenal."[59] By 1 February 1906, 135 students had registered in Agriculture, and by the 22nd there were 205 students. BYU grew to double the number of agricultural students at the ACU.[60] The *Deseret Farmer* commented, "The class has the distinction of being the largest ever organized in Agriculture during the first year of its introduction into the curriculum."[61] Brimhall reported that in October of 1906, BYU was 35 percent larger than the year before.[62] He further commented, "Aside from the course in Theology nothing is more popular in our school today than the work given in our Agricultural School."[63] At his termination John reported, "All together, not counting those attending the Institutes or the girls' class, systematic instruction in agriculture was given during the two school years, 1905–07, to approximately 450 individuals."[64]

The enrollment increases kept pace with advances John sought: "I had become convinced that people must live together in communities drawing their sustenance from nearby lands, if a state acceptable to civilized man is to be built and maintained. My own observations led me to believe that such a commonwealth can not rest upon mining or manufacturing alone. These activities prosper best in the wake of agriculture, which is the beginning of economic, social, and political wisdom. In the words of Daniel Webster, 'When tillage begins, other arts follow.'"[65]

Brimhall was overwhelmed with requests for Dr. Widtsoe to address groups ranging from stake conferences to teachers associations.[66] John represented BYU at an exhibit in Boise and at the Dry Farm Congress in Denver, where he delivered a lengthy lecture on arid farming.[67] He also wrote several articles and started his own agricultural textbook.[68]

While John felt strongly about practical education, he held to the English ideal that a university must do more: "Education should not only enable us to earn a livelihood; it should also help us to earn our bread and butter in the midst of intelligent joy. Not only should it give us greater mastery over our profession by explaining the laws involved; it should also teach the relation of the man and his work to the world about him, and the liveliness of the things to which our spiritual sense responds. Above all, it must teach the holiness of all truth. Culture, as well as vocation, should be the aim of education."[69]

John was also an instructor in theology at BYU, sometimes spending four hours a day consulting with students.[70] Brimhall labeled him a "mighty man in theology."[71] John thoroughly fulfilled Brimhall's wishes to have "science based on revelation."[72] It was later said of John, "A scientific thirst for new information, blended with a staunch faith in the eternal verities, equipped him to bless mankind as few men ever have."[73] While at BYU John wrote *Joseph Smith as Scientist* and several manuals for Church auxiliaries. He also published his concordance for the Doctrine and Covenants.[74]

When William Jasper Kerr resigned as president of the ACU, John, who had been considered for the position twice before, sensed that he might be asked to go back to Logan. The diary records, "Long talk with B.Y.U. Presidency abt. A. C. matters."[75] Three days later he was elected president of the ACU. He wrote to Brimhall, "I am fully satisfied that I ought to go to the A. C. this coming year. I have sought every help known to me, with the same result. I think you know my feelings. I want to go where I *should* do my work."[76] Keeping John at BYU had been Brimhall's constant battle.[77] On this occasion Brimhall sought First Presidency aid in getting him to stay.[78] "Pres. Brimhall spoke of my leaving. Said 'Brethren must be obeyed.'"[79] John recorded, "Talk w. Brimhall. He does not feel right."[80] John did not accept his new position without serious reflection.[81] Finally he sought guidance from the First Presidency: "Visit w. First Presidency. I want to do what is right and for the best."[82] "Called at office of First Presidency. Was set apart for the A. C. work by Pres'ts. Smith, Winder and Lund and Apostle Smoot. Prest. Joseph F. Smith was mouth. He blessed me abundantly and promised me much and told me to go ahead. Thank God for His kindness."[83] The day after this blessing, John left for Logan.

The contributions John A. Widtsoe made during this period were not without parallel personal trials. During his two years at BYU, family members were beset with illness, miscarriage, and death. The hardest trial was the death of their son, Mark Adriel. On the day of his death, John wrote, "My poor Markie is dead! The last week I spent in his presence was marked by the fact that he smiled at me and knew me. Thank God for that. Why was he given us?"[84] The next day he wrote, "Markie lies with a peaceful smile on his features. He looks better in death than he ever looked in life. God! Why should I lose him! He has wound himself about my heart."[85] After describing the funeral he simply wrote, "My

Leah with Mark Adriel, born to the Widtsoes while they were at BYU.

heart aches!"[86] With the anguish still fresh, two months after Markie's death, John wrote, "Marsel down w. intestinal fever again. Our last boy! We must raise him!"[87] Eight months later John spent a day pondering his ACU decision at Markie's graveside.[88]

John felt that agriculture at BYU would continue to grow.[89] Part of his heart was at BYU, and he continued to help the school. He wrote Brimhall, "I am still very much interested in the work of the B.Y.U., and especially in the agricultural work going on there. I shall be glad at any time to assist in planning for the future success of the department."[90] Brimhall accepted: "It really seems as though you were one of our faculty still."[91] He later asked, "Have you any recommendations to make for our needs next year?"[92] Another time, "Brother Widtsoe, you know just about what our needs are, and are in a position to help us in making selections."[93] John made many suggestions for teachers at BYU, in agriculture and other programs. Upon hearing of Homer's departure, he recommended Amos N. Merrill as his replacement.[94] Merrill wrote,

"From what I can learn from Dr. Widtsoe, the conditions surrounding your [Brimhall's] institution permit of the building up of a department which would conform more nearly to the ideal which both you and I have in mind."[95]

Brimhall's desire to have John at BYU never diminished. At Brimhall's retirement in 1921, fourteen years after their separation, his foremost desire was that Dr. Widtsoe would be appointed as his replacement. He was working to that end when his plans were superseded by John's call to the Quorum of the Twelve Apostles.[96] He wrote, "Your selection as an apostle was a disappointment to me because my desires have been so intense and my hopes so high in the direction of your standing at the head of a great Church University growing out of the B.Y.U. that my expectations never ran in any other direction." As John was leaving BYU he told Brimhall, "The work of the last two years has been a constant pleasure, and I expect never again in my life, wherever my lot may be cast, to live happier years or find more appreciation of my efforts than the two years spent in your employ. For this I am grateful."[97] In his diary he added, "God be thanked for the happy years spent in Provo. It is a beautiful city. May the future be happy."[98]

13

CRISIS IN UTAH HIGHER EDUCATION

WHILE John was at BYU, a battle was waged over the maintenance of Utah's institutions of higher learning. At the center of this controversy was the question of whether to consolidate the ACU with the University of Utah (U of U). In addition to fomenting serious divisions among Utah's principal educators, the issue divided both houses of the state legislature and was the governor's chief political agenda item. The outcome shaped Utah's higher education profile for decades. The most immediate impact was on the lives of three of Utah's most distinguished educational leaders, John A. Widtsoe, William Jasper Kerr, and William S. McCornick.

Kerr was born and raised in Richmond, Utah. He attended the University of Deseret and Cornell. He was a faculty member at the U of U, president of Brigham Young College, president of ACU, president of Oregon State Agricultural College (Oregon State University), and commissioner of higher education for Oregon.

McCornick was the first president of the Salt Lake Chamber of Commerce, twice a member of the Salt Lake City Council, first president of the Alta Club, and president, vice-president, and director of several banks, mining companies, railroads, and land and cattle companies. He was treasurer of Rocky Mountain Bell Telephone Company and an original member and president of the board of trustees of ACU, serving from 1890 to 1907.[1] McCornick's influence is of particular note because he was not a member of the LDS Church.

Within a two-year period all three men left the ACU. At the regular meeting of the board of trustees of the ACU on 8 July 1905, John was dismissed. On 21 March 1907, McCornick resigned as president of the board of trustees. One week later, on 28 March 1907, Kerr resigned after serving seven years as ACU president. The consolidation controversy brought these giants to the lowest ebbs of their professional lives.

The Land Grant Act of 1862 (Morrill Act) granted each state 30,000 acres of federal land per number of senators and representatives. Proceeds from the sale of such lands were to be used to establish and fund college programs for the industrial classes of the nation. Their emphasis was on agriculture and mechanic arts. The Hatch Act of 1887 made an additional $15,000 available for experiment stations associated with the land-grant colleges. With these acts in mind, Anthon H. Lund presented a bill in the House of Representatives on 28 February 1888 that created the ACU. It passed unanimously in both houses and was signed into law by territorial governor Caleb W. West on 8 March 1888. The Lund Act also provided $25,000 from state funds to purchase lands and erect buildings. Logan was chosen as the site for the college. The cornerstone of the main building was laid on 27 July 1889, and its doors were officially opened in September 1890.

As the college progressed, some lawmakers worried that courses at the ACU duplicated those at the U of U, creating a substantial waste of money. Although the land-grant ACU was a product of federal legislation, the legislature could decide whether to use the funds for the existing university or for a separate institution. This question was carefully considered by the legislature in 1894 and resolved at the constitutional convention in 1895 when the delegates affirmed the existence of the two separate schools.[2]

Nationally, nineteen states and one territory chose consolidation to achieve land-grant legislation at existing institutions, while seventeen states and two territories established separate institutions. In the fall of

1906, the stage was set for the debate over whether to consolidate the ACU and the U of U. The issue became a major political controversy in the state elections and in the sessions of the state legislature. Across the state public education was still undeveloped, and secondary education was not available in many places. Many felt that funding high schools was a higher priority than maintaining two institutions of higher education. Most citizens thought the small number of students attending the two colleges did not justify the operating costs. The strongest advocate of consolidation was Governor John C. Cutler,[3] who, on 2 February 1905, appealed to the Senate and House to appoint a joint committee to study the situation and "formulate recommendations as to legislation."[4]

The ten-member committee presented two reports to the legislature. Five members favored an amendment to the state constitution, arguing that "the State cannot possibly maintain two separate institutions aspiring to become universities, and make each one an institution creditable to the State of Utah."[5] They recommended that the ACU be made a department of the U of U permanently located in Salt Lake City. Their proposed constitutional amendment required a two-thirds majority vote of the Senate. Only ten of the twelve needed votes were obtained, and the bill failed. The other five committee members felt that "the duplication of courses at the institutions mentioned is a matter of serious and mature thought."[6] Their view, Senate Bill #150, passed by a unanimous vote.[7] It recommended formation of a special college commission to find a way to control the two schools and to avoid the "duplication of studies consistent with the finances and the educational advantages of the State."[8]

On 30 June 1906, the College Commission submitted three reports. The majority report filed by five members found expensive duplication in the two institutions and recommended a constitutional amendment to combine the two schools "on one site."[9] The report bore the signatures of two members from Salt Lake County and members from three counties south of Salt Lake County. The first minority report, signed by two members from Cache County, where the ACU is located, argued that the constitutional provision for the maintenance of both the U of U and ACU had passed by an overwhelming vote of 98 to 3. An extreme emergency did not exist and, therefore, a constitutional amendment was not needed. They recommended continuation of both institutions, with each school limiting its work to specific departments to minimize duplication. The second minority report, signed by the member from Weber County, which lies between Cache County and Salt Lake County, recommended that the two institutions be united under one president and one board to eliminate their "unseemly rivalry."

Governor Cutler, who had been an ex officio member of the commission, offered his suggestions to a joint session of the legislature on 15 January 1907. The budget requests of the two institutions concerned him greatly: "They are now asking for over $579,000, or over one-third of the expected revenue for the next two years." To satisfy "even a reasonable part of these demands," he asserted, would "deprive the primary and secondary schools of the State and other institutions and departments of funds absolutely necessary for their support." The governor believed the legislature should at least place the ACU and the U of U "under one board, with the proviso that one sum be asked for both schools." He decried the intense rivalry for state funds that had developed between the schools and the persistent lobbying by school officials who "should work together for the educational betterment of the youth."[10]

At the ACU the consolidation controversy ran deep. The composition of the college seemed to justify opposing views. President Kerr oversaw the faculty, academic programs, welfare of students, and fiscal maintenance of the college. Dr. Widtsoe supervised research, the operation of laboratories and experimental farms, and the dissemination of information through published bulletins, a farm newspaper, and farmers' institutes. President Kerr held the traditional view that college work should extend to all areas of learning. He endeavored to build a faculty and student body that would advance classical academic subjects. Dr. Widtsoe had produced rich benefits to the agricultural industry of the state. His statewide "student body" followed the plow, planting and reaping efficiently as a result of their learning on the college's experimental farms and in its laboratories. Although John did not oppose academic learning, Kerr's broad educational agenda threatened the program of agricultural education.

Guided by his broad curriculum philosophy, the seven years of the Kerr administration represent a period of remarkable expansion: "The whole Institution started moving and spreading, especially in the Engineering department."[11] Faculty rank advancement policies adopted the criteria embraced at traditional colleges, and college governance and the rights of the student body evolved similarly. In 1901, the semester system replaced the quarter system. In Kerr's first biennial report, he noted that the college had expanded into six schools with each school growing to meet the needs of the expanding curriculum. The school of general science expanded into mathematics, language, history, and literature.[12] In 1902 the board of trustees added courses in mining and electrical engineering. In 1903 a school of music was established, and summer school was added to the college calendar. Kerr sought to establish "a real college expanding into the various fields of knowledge."[13]

Kerr was the principal proponent of expansion at the ACU and thus the principal rival of consolidation. Ironically, the debate that ensued in the Senate, the House, and the press often focused on Kerr's earlier views as a delegate to the 1895 Constitutional Convention, where he had been the most ardent supporter of consolidation, stating that "under no circumstances" would he favor separate institutions. His lengthy testimony, published in the proceedings of that convention, became convenient fodder for opponents who favored consolidation ten years later.

John reported that he lay low in this controversy, limiting his opinions to official faculty meetings. That was an understatement. Available materials do not reveal his personal assessment of the matter until much later. Three years after the controversy was resolved, John responded in a lengthy letter to an official in Alberta, Canada, where a proposed agricultural college was the subject of debate. The official wanted to know if John thought agricultural colleges were "most successful when combined with a university or when each is conducted separately."[14] He answered that duplication was an unnecessary concern if attendance at one institution required additional staff. Another argument for consolidation was more compelling. When agriculture is taught as part of many other professional subjects, he said, "the prospective farmer has a chance to measure himself with men in other pursuits and in that way acquires a certain dignity and faith in himself that only comes by such contact."[15] He emphasized the need to have at the head of the college someone devoted to its agricultural mission. He concluded, "There is a very much larger number of separate institutions that stand high among the schools of the country. It would generally be found that the attendance of agricultural students is, in proportion to the population, very much greater in a separate agricultural college than in one combined with a university. All in all, while the question is difficult of full solution, it seems clear that the agricultural college of the future which is to serve the people in the best way will be a separately maintained institution."[16]

To approximate John's views during the crisis, it is useful to look at those expressed by his assistant, Dr. L. A. Merrill.[17] In the *Deseret Farmer*, Merrill charged that the expansion of the ACU under the Kerr administration was detrimental to the school's programs of agriculture. This overarching concern clouded the consolidation issue. Had agriculture been given the money and attention intended by the legislature, any views Merrill or Widtsoe expressed on consolidation would have been significantly different.

Changes in the ACU Board of Trustees aggravated the tensions. Governor Cutler, who opposed Kerr's policies, attacked them through the appointments Cutler made to the board, replacing three of seven members with his loyal supporters—Thomas Smart, Lorenzo Stohl, and Susa Young Gates—early in 1905.

The scrutiny of Governor Cutler, the examination of the Joint Committee and College Commission, the composition of the board of trustees, and the growing sentiment for consolidation in the legislature brought burdensome pressures to Kerr and the ACU Board. During the summer of 1905, board president William S. McCornick was traveling abroad. Reports of a board meeting scheduled for 12 May indicate that the three new appointees opposed continuance of the meeting and forced an adjournment against the opposition of the three members of the old board. News coverage reported that action as the first shot in an armed conflict. The primary purpose of the meeting was to confirm appointments for the next year and take action against those the president opposed. The *Logan Journal* reported, "President Kerr has discovered that two of the professors on his staff are not in harmony with him, if they are not altogether disloyal."[18]

On 2 June 1905, pursuant to the appointment of the new trustees, a meeting of the board was held. Motions for the election of college officials in a bloc vote failed in a standoff between old and new board members. Trustee Smart had moved that Kerr "be elected President of the College Faculty for the ensuing year" and that Widtsoe remain as director of the experiment station and professor of chemistry, with Merrill as station agronomist and professor of agronomy.[19] It was evident from the vote that either Widtsoe or Merrill or both would not be rehired. With the growing tension, both Widtsoe and Merrill considered leaving the ACU.[20] On Saturday, 3 June 1905, the *Deseret Evening News, Salt Lake Tribune,* and *Provo Daily Enquirer* reported that the two men had submitted their resignations from the ACU following the 2 June meeting. The *Tribune* got to the crux of the matter:

> Of course the refusal of the old members of the board to support the motion simply means that they do not intend to consider the two professors at all, and that they will make no concessions whatever. It was so taken by the two men in question, who, upon hearing of the action of the old members, immediately resigned and accepted other positions.
>
> When seen by the Tribune last night, Dr. Widtsoe said: "This is all I have to say—I have resigned because of the conditions which exist at the Agricultural college at the present time, and because of unjust and false rumors circulated upon the streets of Logan and throughout the State, which the directors of the institution have not seen fit to correct, though they knew these rumors were false."
>
> Professor Merrill was equally brief and to the point—"I must frankly state that I am not in harmony with President Kerr's policy in administration of the Agricultural college. It is not favorable to

agricultural work. He is attempting to make a university out of it instead of an agricultural college.[21]

On 5 June when the board of trustees met in regular session, no allusion was made to the reported resignations. Kerr read his report with recommendations in faculty changes for the ensuing year.[22] Adopting Kerr's report would amount to the dismissal of both Widtsoe and Merrill. In the afternoon session a motion to sustain Kerr, Widtsoe, and Merrill by a bloc vote was made repeatedly by Trustee Stohl, a new appointee. Each time, it failed or was ruled out of order. The minutes of the next board meeting, 8 July, reveal that Kerr intended to stick by his report.[23] By then, McCornick had returned from his travels and stood solidly behind the embattled president. Kerr's report lists the names and salaries of the college faculty for the following year; Widtsoe and Merrill are conspicuously missing. According to the minutes, Kerr's opinion was that:

> These Professors had given ample evidence that they were not in harmony with the faculty or in sympathy with the policy of the Board of Trustees or the President. One of the fundamental requisites to success in all educational institutions is that there shall be harmony among its employees and unquestioned loyalty to the institution and its authorities. He further stated that he was prepared to prefer specific charges against each of these professors, and to call witnesses before the Board and submit other evidence in proof of the charges. He would be pleased to go into the whole matter in as great detail and to as great extent as might be desired by the Board.[24]

Kerr's report carried, with McCornick and the three members of the old board prevailing against Cutler's three appointees. As a last-ditch measure, an amendment to a motion to reelect Kerr as president of the ACU was advanced; it called for election of Dr. Widtsoe as president of the college instead of Kerr.[25] The amendment failed by the same 4-to-3 margin. The board's action dismissed Widtsoe and Merrill from the ACU. John's disagreement with the expansionist ideas of Kerr hardly justified the severe action taken against him. The specific charges against him were not read into the minutes, and the files containing other information pertinent to the meeting have been lost.

The offices of the *Deseret Farmer* were moved from Logan to Salt Lake City following the dismissals. Several letters to the editor suggested that the agriculture programs would be improved if consolidation occurred. Others focused on the balance in the overall educational interests of the state and asked for a better distribution of educational monies, "pleading for consolidation on the grounds of the greatest good to the greatest number, and for an extension of the privilege of acquiring at least a high school education by the young men and women of this State."[26]

Another view alleged that Kerr had used money appropriated for agriculture for other desires of the college, including tile floors in the president's residence and oak tables in the library. "Let the dean of the Agricultural College be responsible for the expenditures and leave the amount to be appropriated with the Legislature as is now done with the Mining School and Utah will have the greatest Agricultural College in the West in a very short time."[27]

Joseph F. Merrill, director of the School of Mines at the U of U, wrote a letter favoring consolidation. He pointed out, "We already have two state schools existing as departments of the University—the School of Mines and the Normal School—and so satisfactory is the union that no officer of either school would consent to its separation from the University."[28] Both of these schools had achieved distinction quickly on small appropriations as compared with independent operations. Merrill asserted that the ACU would enjoy the same benefits through consolidation. Each school controlled the curriculum, faculty selection, course development, and admission and graduation requirements, and each enjoyed all the freedoms of a separate college. Rather than absorbing and destroying the ACU, consolidation would liberate and strengthen it, he claimed.

The consolidation controversy continued to polarize those who believed they had a major stake in the outcome. L. A. Merrill's editorial response in the *Deseret Farmer* to a letter printed in the *Logan Journal* illustrates this. The writer had charged that "every great and good cause has its traitor. The Agricultural College cause has its L. A. Merrill."[29] Merrill's editorial argued for loyalty to the institution's best good:

> It is a little strange that every one who does not support the President of the Agricultural College is classed as traitor to the College. There is a difference between loyalty to the institution and loyalty to the man who for the time being stands at the head of that institution.
>
> As a matter of fact, we do not consider Mr. Kerr disloyal to the State University because he is now against consolidation, though he is a graduate from a two years course of the University. Neither is any alumnus of the Agricultural College a traitor to that institution if he happens to favor consolidation. He may honestly believe that a greater and better Agricultural College may result from such union,— and such being his views, he is certainly justified in working towards his ideals.[30]

The controversy spread. Local citizens and businessmen joined in the struggle through the Logan Chamber of Commerce. Cache County organizations and related groups from surrounding counties (Weber, Rich, and Box Elder) also joined forces.

On 4 March 1907, a bill proposing consolidation of the ACU with the U of U was advanced in the Senate.[31] It passed on 7 March by a margin of 12 ayes, 6 nays, and 0 absent and not voting—the necessary two-thirds majority for a constitutional amendment. When the bill reached the House of Representatives, however, members opposed to consolidation accomplished a political near-miracle. Although defeated in the Senate vote, Senator Herschel Bullen of Logan continued to lead the legislative fight against consolidation. When the vote was taken at 11:00 P.M. on the 57th day of the session, the bill failed to receive the necessary two-thirds majority on a roll-call vote: 24 ayes, 20 nays, and 0 absent and not voting.[32] Bullen added, "If ever a group of men entered into a compact, dedicating every ounce of energy and every spark of ability they possessed, it was this loyal group of defenders."[33] The fight against consolidation had been won.

In 1905 the legislature and Governor Cutler had thwarted Kerr's expansionist policies by limiting the courses that could be taught at the ACU and refocusing the school's efforts on agriculture and industry. Those legislative sanctions against Kerr's policies marked the defeat of the Kerr/McCornick regime. The *Logan Journal* reported, "After mature reflection and careful investigation, President W. S. McCornick of the board of trustees of the Agricultural College, reached the conclusion that the seeming intention of John C. Cutler and the party behind him, to destroy the Agricultural College, was real, and declining to be a party to such an outrage upon the people of the state, he has tendered his resignation."[34]

One week later Kerr submitted his resignation to the board of trustees. He pledged to finish the year's work, prepare the annual report for the board, and cooperate in any desired way. After the board accepted Kerr's resignation, "on motion of Trustee Smart, Dr. John A. Widtsoe, head of the School of Agriculture of the B. Y. University at Provo, was elected President of the College . . . to begin at the pleasure of the Board, and end June 30, '08."[35] The motion passed, and a new chapter in the history of the ACU began.

14

FIFTH PRESIDENT
OF THE ACU

JOHN A. Widtsoe became ACU president on 28 March 1907 and inherited the difficult task of overcoming the animosity of Kerr's departure and lingering questions of his own loyalty. Grasping for the courage of his Viking ancestors, John pressed forward. He wrote, "I felt as if I was to wash dirty State linen."[1]

Logan had to be won over. After all, Logan was the home of the College. If it remained unfriendly, we could scarcely expect the State to be otherwise. The *Logan Journal* was distinctly unfriendly. It missed no opportunity to send out a barbed sentence about the new order at the College. It was politically a Democratic organ. The outgoing president was a faithful Democrat. A Republican state administration had caused the changes at the U. S. A. C. It was too much for a party organ! The businessmen had been fed on the dream of a great college development, surpassing the State university, with state moneys in abundance flowing into Logan. The grandiose plans for U. S. A. C. expansion . . . had actually been believed. Businessmen in a college town usually value the institution because of the money it brings to the town. Only occasionally does the shopkeeper raise his eyes to the true meaning of education. Seldom does he realize that by that somewhat intangible thing called education, prosperity is produced and made secure. Admittedly, it was not pleasant to feel that the college had a half-hearted support from the town. Of course, I had the friendship of the majority of the plain but non-vocal people.[2]

Educators hailed John as the most qualified man to take the college in the strict land-grant direction mandated. Their sentiment was confirmed several years later in the *Deseret Evening News,* which noted the international acclaim given his publications on irrigation and dry farming, "which rank among the best work ever done in America and undoubtedly surpass anything yet done in the educational institutions of the west. This work established him as one of America's foremost scientists and placed the Utah Experiment station among the first few in the world. This work was empire building; it was monumental. All the world has read of it and it has and is playing a great part in the conquering of the world's deserts and in carrying forward man's great conquest of drought."[3] The official college history also applauded John's appointment:

> President Widtsoe was eminently prepared to direct the activities of the College. Scholarly, idealistic, peace loving, conciliatory, impulsive, generous, ambitious, and prodigiously industrious Dr. Widtsoe possessed the ability and determination to guide the institution from the troublesome waters of his predecessor into a quieter haven. In appealing to the people to support the College, he pointed out that the courses of the School had been especially planned with the needs of their sons and daughters in mind. Fortunately President Widtsoe's own struggle for education made him sympathetic with the intellectual yearning of the young people to whom he appealed and his educational philosophy found ready and enthusiastic response throughout the State.[4]

Influential people wrote: "He is a prophetic educator, a man who feels and sees, long before he knows, the great factors that are weaving themselves in the structure of the future."[5] "Mr. Widtsoe . . . is recognized throughout the nation as of eminent ability in that line, and he enjoys the very highest credit with the agricultural department at Washington."[6]

Besides disgruntled townspeople and their angry newspaper, many in the faculty and student body perceived John as an enemy. Winning the

The President's Home on the campus of the Utah Agricultural College.

goodwill of the campus and the town was necessarily, and by choice, John's highest priority. If they could see that he intended to make the college their institution, serving their interests, they could not long harbor ill feelings toward him, or, more importantly, toward the college.

To curtail duplication in the ACU and the U of U, the legislature issued legally binding manifestos restricting academic offerings at both institutions. In addressing the board of trustees on 23 April 1907, John referred to those manifestos as passed on 20 March 1905:

> From the action of the last two legislatures, there can be little doubt as to what the state of Utah expects of its Agricultural College and its University. It has definitely and specifically forbidden duplication and declared that the course of instruction in the Agricultural College, until the law shall provide otherwise, shall include Agriculture: Horticulture, Forestry, Animal Husbandry, Veterinary Science, Domestic Science and Arts, elementary commerce, elementary surveying, instructions in irrigation as applied to the measurement, distribution and application of water for agricultural purposes, military science and tactics, History, Language, and the various branches of Mathematics, Physical and Natural Science, and Mechanic Arts with special reference to the Liberal and Practical education of the industrial classes.[7]

With that sharpened focus, John felt that to gain the appropriate vision he again needed to visit with farmers on their turf. Ideas gained from an earlier tour as director of the Experiment Station had borne much beneficial fruit. An associate reported, "Again he stayed with people and asked them what were the kinds of things they thought the university should be doing to serve them in their rural communities, on their farms, in their families and everywhere else. He told me again that 'When I got back I knew what the job of the university was.' This put him in a position to tell some of the teachers what they ought to be doing, and he told some of them if they really wanted to find out anything, they should go out and live with the people and learn their problems."[8] His personal visits allowed the people to experience his interest as president. His affable manner won friends, and people became convinced of the sincerity of his desires to help. To the board of trustees he reported, "The Agricultural College is essentially an institution of service to the State of Utah, and our duty has been conceived to be to serve as widely and as well as State law permits."[9]

Acclaim for John's contributions to industrial education spread across the country and into Europe.[10] Several of his addresses were compiled into a book titled *Education for Necessary Pursuits.* John never departed from his desire to improve the life of the common man through education.

> To educate all; to make common pursuits intellectually desirable; to make the scheme of education respond to the country's needs; to make the school a servant and not a master; to "ring out the old and ring in the new," and to give to every man an intense joy in his work; these are the hopes of the new education, whether men call it industrial or vocational.[11]

> The blacksmith, who has been trained to understand the chemical and physical processes occurring in the welding and shaping of iron, and who does his work thus intelligently, leads as high a life, intellectually, as the lawyer or doctor.[12]

> Life is more than vocation and vocation is more than drudgery. Education should enhance all that one's vocation can be and contribute to the cultural joy life holds.

Education should not only enable us to earn a livelihood; it should also help us to earn our bread and butter in the midst of intelligent joy. Not only should it give us greater mastery over our profession by explaining the laws involved; it should also teach the relation of the man and his work to the world about him, and the liveliness of the things to which our spiritual sense responds. Above all, it must teach the holiness of all truth. Culture, as well as vocation, should be the aim of education.[13]

In the past we have planned an education for the few—the conditions compelled it; today we must plan for the many. The one of the hundred who has been touched with the fire of genius transcends schools. He will work his will in spite of men. It is for us to plan for the ninety and nine.[14]

As John's views spread, people in Logan, Cache Valley, and Utah felt increasingly drawn to what the college was trying to do. To further align people with its success, John tried to make the college more available. Establishing night classes for easy access by local adults was one solution. He reported to the board of trustees, "In line with our determination to make the people acquainted with the College, the faculty thought it well to institute night schools. . . . Our teachers by some extra effort, can do this work. It will tend to build us up greatly in Logan, our hometown. . . . The night school students are among the representative citizens of Logan and without doubt this work will redound to the credit of the school."[15]

In his memoirs he wrote, "It worked. The rooms were crowded with men and women, anxious to learn. Even *Logan Journal* employees and their families could not resist the temptation. These 'students' for the first time really learned to know the institution, its equipment, and faculty. It was a venture that implanted confidence in the new administration."[16] During his second year he wrote, "We have this year a splendid school. The conditions and the spirit generally are better than they were last year, which of course was a year of transition."[17]

A TREATY WITH THE UNIVERSITY OF UTAH

John believed that a healthy relationship with the University of Utah was essential to establish the college on a solid footing. "The decade of

The Widtsoe family in the president's residence: John, Anna Gaarden (born 2 April 1899), Leah, and Karl Marsel (born 27 November 1902).

consolidation talk and the consequent friction had really engendered bad blood between the State University and the State Agricultural College. That must not continue. Therefore, I presented myself at the university to talk things over. I found the president, Dr. Joseph T. Kingsbury, as courteous and generous as could be. Getting together performs wonders. Strangers are always likely to misunderstand each other's motives."[18]

Widtsoe and Kingsbury set the tone for cooperation and united effort. Kingsbury had been a leader in the drive for consolidation. A year afterward, he requested consultation with John prior to presenting university matters before the governor.[19] There were frequent meetings, and the two presidents went so far as to write up a formal treaty agreement between the schools.[20] The university sponsored a newsletter, the *Educational Review,* which served educators across the state. The editor often sought John's contributions. John assigned professor C. W. Porter to write a weekly newspaper column about the ACU.

In spite of the restrictions the legislature imposed on both institutions, there were projects they cooperated on that improved the work of both.

The Widtsoe family after the birth of their last child, Leah Eudora, born 4 July 1912. Marsel, Leah, John, and Anna surround Eudora.

Scientific irrigation principles required engineering expertise, but, by law, the ACU could not teach engineering. The two schools combined efforts in the development of irrigation engineering. A similar venture was undertaken with the University's Normal School. The Normal School focused on training teachers. As the demand for high-school agriculture teachers arose, a dilemma developed. The ACU wasn't allowed to train teachers, but the university wasn't allowed to teach agriculture. A cooperative arrangement was established, and their relationship was enhanced. Exchanging professors between institutions led to the finest training teachers could wish for. Exchanges took place in the programs of the college's summer school.[21] These cooperative efforts brought about the harmony the legislature sought in the state's institutions of higher learning.

PLANNING FOR GROWTH

John next needed to set a pattern of growth. In some ways, the legislative manifestos restricted growth. In other ways, they set the appropriate foundation on which proper growth should occur. "In my opinion progress comes more naturally and effectively by growth than by revolution," he wrote. "When each man has his duties clearly defined, is respected in his work, and leaves other men to their work, there is abundance of available energy with which to search out new truths and to teach the young and old all discovered truth."[22]

John started a vigorous advertising campaign to let the people of Utah know that a desirable and useful education was available at its agricultural college. "The summer months, from July 1st until the opening of school on September 17th, were devoted almost entirely to advertising the school, having necessary repairs made, and making preparations for the opening of the school year."[23] During that time the ACU sent out 20,000 circulars, 3,000 catalogs, and had the *Deseret Farmer* distribute 15,000 copies of a special edition about the college.[24] John and fifteen of his most experienced teachers traveled across the state to promote the work of the college.[25] "His friendliness and sympathetic understanding and impressive speeches attracted people to him. As he previously had been an outstanding teacher in the classroom, he was now a teacher to the people of Utah wherever he found them."[26] Newspapers throughout the state carried large advertisements. Favorable articles covering the college and its work were also featured.[27] John wrote, "While the money actually expended for advertising purposes . . . is somewhat less than that expended last year, yet I am under the impression that the College has never before received so systematic a canvass in its behalf. A conservative estimate would place the number of persons reached by the summer's advertising at not less than 150,000."[28] John had catalogs sent to the bishops of the LDS Church.[29] He originated a program for recruiting in Utah high schools. E. G. Peterson was appointed to oversee publicity for the college.

The success of the campaign brought additional classes to accommodate an increasing student body. John expanded the departments that were within the domain of the ACU. "What I am anxious about now," he wrote, "is that the Institution formulate a series of college courses in agriculture which will be strictly up to date and, as far as possible, anticipate the coming years."[30] The effects of the emphasis on the agricultural program can be seen in this excerpt from a later report on the School of Agriculture:

> From 1894 to 1907 inclusive, only twelve students graduated in
> Agriculture. Five of these classes contained no agricultural students

at all, and at no time was there more than two. During this period one hundred and thirteen persons were graduated, of whom approximately ten per cent graduated in the agricultural course.

[Upon Widtsoe's efforts to upgrade the program] there was an immediate and definite response in the increase in number of college students in Agriculture. In 1907 the agricultural faculty was materially strengthened, the standard of the courses raised, and the institution became an agricultural college in fact as well as in name.

Even more remarkable gains in the number of graduates in Agriculture have been made in the past eight years. Four hundred and twenty-five degrees have been granted, of which two hundred have been in Agriculture, or approximately fifty per cent.

Expressed in percentage of the population this means that the Utah Agricultural College has averaged in the last five years almost one student in Agriculture for every thousand inhabitants of the state, and one graduate for every 10,000. This record is much higher than can be shown by any other state in the union.[31]

The 1912 biennial report highlights the advances in agriculture and domestic science. "During the last five years the number of students registering with agriculture as their major subject has increased from 126 to 659 or more than five-fold. . . . During the same period the students of home economics have increased from 87 to 201."[32]

In 1911, John lobbied successfully for courses in agricultural engineering. In 1912, "several new departments were organized. Notable additions and reorganizations occurred in the departments of bacteriology, botany, agronomy and animal husbandry; but, in fact, every department has of necessity been extended materially, both in floor space and equipment in order to meet the needs of the larger Student Body."[33]

John felt that many people in the state would like some schooling but had neither the time nor money to enroll full time. So, he established what he called "practical courses" to be made available to anyone desiring to take them.[34]

By 1913 John started an elective system.[35] "The course of study has been changed, in conformity with the ruling of the State Board of Education and with the best recent thought, so that only English is a required subject; all others may be chosen, under Faculty guidance, to conform with the special needs or gifts of the student."[36]

Another expansion of classes came through the ACU summer school aimed primarily at training teachers. During John's first summer, "a vigorous campaign was instituted which brought many teachers from the various parts of this and surrounding states."[37] In 1909, "the summer school closed in glory. I think nearly all the students were more than satisfied with their work here. The teachers also seemed satisfied with the students and all in all I believe the session was a great success. I had lunch on the last day with the domestic science girls and they were all in a very happy frame of mind."[38] During John's first five years as president, the attendance of the summer school increased from 56 to 224.[39] In 1910 he appointed a permanent faculty for the summer school, which grew steadily through the rest of his tenure.

Since its inception, the ACU was attended by many high school students, and part of its work was teaching high school classes. As the schooling system of the state developed, John phased out the high school work at the college. In 1913 the ACU dropped its first year of high school work. In the next two years, the second and third years were dropped. John wrote:

> To place the institution in harmony with the increasing high school movement and with the best academic practice, it seemed wise to increase the entrance requirements in accordance with the standard practice to four years. This met stubborn resistance on the part of many faculty members, who could not visualize the future, and were content with the beaten way. There was great fear that this would reduce student attendance, which it did momentarily in the college division. Nevertheless, it was accomplished. In 1911 the catalogue stated an entrance requirement of three years, and in 1914, of four years. I breathed more freely that year. With the raising of faculty scholarship and entrance requirements, the College could claim standard recognition among the sisterhood of institutions of higher learning.[40]

15

INITIATIVES TOWARD STUDENTS, FACULTY, WOMEN, AND COMMUNITY

AT the beginning of John's tenure, the students were loyal to President Kerr, whose actions had portrayed John as a villain. But John's gregarious, genuine nature soon won them over. He was devoted to them, and they knew it. John said, "The loyalty and good will of the Student Body . . . are the enduring characteristics of the students of the Agricultural College."[1] In his memoirs he wrote:

> One of the great satisfactions of this strenuous period was the constant association with the students of the College. . . . The student body was small enough to permit individual acquaintanceship with most of them. Some came of well-to-do families; others from poorer people; and some fought a heroic fight to remain in school. Many a man now prominent in public or private service arrived at the College with the announcement that he had no money. But they had ambition and courage. Some way was found to help them along by work or loans. No investment pays larger dividends than the help given aspiring youth.
>
> An equally great satisfaction came from contacts with the fathers and mothers who at any sacrifice would give their children the best possible opportunities for successful lives. There were countless long

discussions of family problems in which the loving hearts of father and mother were revealed. As I recall them, my heart grows warm.[2]

PRESIDENT TO THE STUDENTS

The students' support became a strength John relied on and invested in. As one example, John wrote, "One of the teachers [John T. Caine Jr.] has been released from nearly all of his teaching, and his main work will be in supervising the home lives and moral attitude of our students. I feel as I always have felt that since the Agricultural College is located in a state, the people of which are distinctly Christians, that the school should be conducted according to the teachings of Christ. This we shall do to the best of our ability without making of the Institution a long faced or sanctimonious place."[3]

John felt that the students could be responsible for their own discipline: "It seems to me that . . . our student body consists chiefly of more mature men and women, that it might be an interesting experiment, resulting in much good, to turn over to the student body the disciplinarian responsibility, which in most schools is rather too jealously guarded by the faculty. Our organization is nothing more than a small republic governed by its members and self-perpetuating only as the student body feels disposed."[4]

The Widtsoe correspondence at Utah State University (USU) contains several hundred letters from students asking about schooling. Each one received a personal response and appropriate materials to assist. A newspaper reported, "Dr. Widtsoe, however great his intellectual and scientific achievements, is most richly endowed in temper and spirit. . . . His friends marvel at his indomitable faith and his all-inclusive charity. Young men by the thousands remember his stirring words when the future to them was not promising."[5] Ernest L. Wilkinson, as president of Brigham Young University, later lauded this virtue: "One of the great contributions which Dr. John A. Widtsoe made during his lifetime was that of encouraging young people to go on with their education. There are literally scores of individuals throughout the Church who have made notable successes and who were inspired to go on by Dr. Widtsoe."[6] Some examples:

I am anxious to see all of the young people of the State who have been blessed with a good intelligence obtain a good education. It is the person whose mind is well trained who will in the end have the greatest happiness in life and do the greatest amount of good for his fellow man.[7]

You will find that no acquirement of man gives so great a joy in life as that of an education. It may not always lead to the greatest wealth, but it does lead to a kind of happiness which can not be secured by the use of money.[8]

Remember that during the years of early manhood we have the opportunity of laying the foundation for our later life. The man who builds right, between fifteen and twenty-five, usually is successful at forty or fifty. In fact, it may be written down as a law that the successful man of middle life did some mighty serious preparatory work at twenty.[9]

Most students had to earn their way through college, and John helped them. He noted, "I am making it a practice to give liberal assistance to all the students I can who are going through college and need assistance to finish their course of study."[10] He often offered them employment in his own house, as shown in this typical comment: "I have talked the matter over with Mrs. Widtsoe and she is willing to have you join her household during this first year until you become better acquainted in Logan."[11] He worked closely with John T. Caine in finding many more jobs around Logan. He once wrote to a parent, "An education is worth a great deal and don't let your son hesitate because he can not see his way throughout the whole year just now. Let him start in and something may turn up that will enable him to finish the year. You can give your son nothing better than an education. It will remain with him throughout life."[12] John's own past made him sympathetic. In other encouraging letters, he wrote:

There is only one thing for you to do and that is to get your education in spite of the difficulties that appear to loom up before you. You can not afford to let the debt of $100.00 or $1000.00 stand between you and the completion of your school work. If you work as hard as you can and worry as little as you can, things will come out alright.[13]

I should not feel very sorry for you either if at the end of your college course you should be in debt a few dollars. A debt is always a disagreeable thing to have hanging over you, but when it is contracted in the attempt to secure an education it is justifiable. Don't let the temptation of earning a few dollars a month take you away from your educational ideals. Seventy-five or a hundred dollars a month look tremendously big right now, but they will seem very small in late life if you have paid for your present earning with the loss of an education.[14]

The rugged lifestyle of early Utah robbed many a family of a parent. John's own trials had prepared him well for assistance with such crises: "I think I realize the difficulties that a widow has in educating a large family, and it shall be a real pleasure to me to aid you in your struggle."[15] Other examples:

I know what it is to grow up to childhood and youth without a Father and I imagine it would be just a little harder to be without a Mother. Such things, however, come in some form or other in every life and the only thing to do is to meet them manfully and without question. From what I can read between the lines of your letter, I believe your Mother, were she living, would urge you to complete your education and I certainly hope that you will let the memory of your Mother spur you on to secure an education in the near future.[16]

I was told a few hours ago that a message had reached Logan to the effect that your father had just died. Permit me in behalf of myself, students and Faculty to express my sympathy to you at this time of your great loss. While you will never find another man who will be to you what your father has been, yet you will find with increasing years that a greater power watches over you and is able to guide you and does guide you in all the affairs of life.[17]

PRESIDENT OF THE FACULTY

John maintained that "a main duty of an academic administration is to encourage students and faculty to seek the best training for their life's work. Usually men are not self-starters, though they desire the best. A little help yields large results. The scholarship progress of the faculty is a result of successful administration."[18] John identified two major problems in building a strong faculty: high turnover and low salaries. He reported to the board of trustees:

> There has been a complete renewal of the Faculty about every three and a half years since the opening of the College. . . . Naturally the former scarcity of well-trained Western men was chiefly responsible for this condition. The experience of the College shows clearly that a Western educational institution which of necessity cannot offer the inducement held out by the larger colleges, must depend for permanency in its faculty upon men and women whose interests are in the West. However, a number of properly qualified Western men have left the service of the College to accept better positions elsewhere. Many of those who have come from the East would have remained, had the opportunities here been sufficient. . . . In fact, the second chief cause of lack of Faculty permanency can be ascribed safely to the low salaries paid at the Agricultural College.[19]

John tried to attract good local students to the college and excite in them a love of agriculture. He encouraged the most able to pursue higher degrees at the best institutions. He maintained an active connection with Cornell, the prime source of agricultural education in the United States. He corresponded with his students there, encouraged their pursuits, and nourished their interest in the ACU. He also worked to open faculty slots for them. He also gave faculty members liberal opportunities to enhance their expertise, encouraging younger instructors to take leaves of absence and go to graduate universities to gain greater knowledge. He encouraged a group of young men who followed him from Brigham Young University to the College to go East after graduation to study for advanced degrees, offering them positions in the school when vacancies occurred. This group included Dr. Franklin S. Harris, Dr. George R. Hill, Dr. Reuben L. Hill, Dr. Robert J. Evans, Professor Byron Alder, Dr. Earnest Carroll, and Dr. C. N. Jensen, who came from the University of Utah. All of them eventually returned to teach in the college.[20]

The proposition of a permanent faculty from the West was compelling. "In fact," John wrote, "I feel so strongly that the department needs permanency that I am very much disinclined to take a chance on any person who is likely to be a temporary addition to the Faculty. If our feeling in this respect is not changed it may be necessary for us to sacrifice technical ability to an assurance of permanency."[21] To students he sent to graduate schools he wrote, "You are needed in Utah and the field is large enough if a man gets into it properly."[22] His personal touch often induced them to return. One student wrote, "This work I like so well, that I am intending to continue along this line next year. Before doing so however, I would like to get your advice upon the subject, as you know better than I the conditions out in Utah, and also the openings along this line of work."[23] From another came this testimonial: "I sometimes feel that the thing that holds me most strongly to Logan is my love for you and my wish to help you in any way I can to make the work you have undertaken meet its fullest measure of success."[24]

John directed prospective teachers to the most beneficial path. "My idea," he wrote, "is to encourage men of the Faculty to take up as rapidly as may be possible some certain line of investigation peculiar to the West in which he will make himself eminent and authoritative."[25] "Above all things, try to get the spirit of the researchman. We are sadly deficient in our State in men who are possessed with a love of discovering truth for truth's own sake, or even for the sake of applying it to the needs of mankind. . . . We must all be willing to give a fair share of our lives and training for the upbuilding of the State and people that we love."[26]

> Young men of the West, usually graduates of the School, who showed marked ability in any one department of human knowledge were encouraged to go away for further study and qualify themselves for positions on the College faculty. In no case was a definite promise given to these young men, but the condition was explained to them. After they had done the necessary work, if a position existed here, they were offered the position, though in no instance was any person relieved of duty in order to make a place for one of these young men. Gradually, by this method, during the last seven years, we have been building up at the Utah Agricultural College a faculty which is undoubtedly the strongest in any agricultural college of its size in the whole United States. The only fault with our faculty at the present

time is it is not as old in years as it will be in a few years. However, we will probably outgrow that difficulty altogether too soon.[27]

John's carefully selected contingent led the ACU for many years. Franklin S. Harris was one of the first to leave for training and return for service, both at John's urging. E. G. Peterson was another whom John urged to attend Cornell and come back to Utah. Both served as presidents of the ACU. George R. Hill, another of John's protégées, served as director of the School of Agriculture at the ACU. In 1912 John reported, "The scholarship of the Faculty has been greatly advanced during the last two years, in fact the present Faculty of the Utah Agricultural College measures up with the best agricultural college faculties in any part of the United States. More than forty of the world's leading colleges and universities are represented on the Faculty."[28]

By 1914 he was able to comment, "By training and temperament the Faculty compares favorably with the best and is well fitted to conduct investigations and to give instruction in the subjects assigned by law to the College. Moreover the longer tenure of office, resulting in closer associations of the professors with each other and with the work of the College, has led to a more perfect unity of understanding and purpose."[29]

High scholarship was not John's only faculty priority: "It is really more important for a school to secure a man who understands the method of teaching the subject than to have a teacher who is only a good mechanic."[30] He added, "There are great scholars who are infidels. They have the right so to believe. But out of their classes have not come the power that shapes life for happiness. Teaching facts is not the chief purpose of an educational institution. The building of character, and the fitting of youth for the best manner of living are most important."[31]

In John's eye a teacher held a sacred trust and a high responsibility:

> There has been a tendency to over-value high learning as a means of good teaching. Out of profound scholarship comes the material used in teaching. It does not follow, however, that the man who discovers truth is a good teacher. Frequently a man of lesser learning, if what he knows is sound, is better able to teach discovered truth

than the discoverer himself. A university must possess the research spirit and teach man's knowledge effectively, else it fails in its purposes. It is one of the most difficult problems for university administration to find men who combine good research and teaching ability. Many a young college life has been marred by the vain efforts of a learned man to impart his knowledge to others. Learning new truths is an exhilarating experience and a good teacher awakens that joy.[32]

John was clear in his aim: "The Institution has only one request to make of its employees, namely, that they give the very best in them to the Institution. In return the College is duty bound to do the best it can for its employees."[33] He also offered financial incentives: "If the man who is appointed makes good and shows himself able to build up a history department in this Institution his salary will be increased from year to year as the finances of the Institution will allow."[34] John undertook significant improvements in faculty salaries and sabbatical leave. "Faculty salaries were extremely low. It took some years to secure approval of a fixed schedule for various ranks, nearly 20 percent above that which had prevailed. Yet that was too low. The board also agreed to a sabbatical leave program for the teaching body. Whether from the point of view of scholarship or fretted nerves, the teacher needs occasional freedom from the routine of the class room."[35]

INITIATIVES IN THE EDUCATION OF WOMEN

John's views on education for everyone embraced a special emphasis on women because they had not been widely welcomed in higher education. Leah's views reinforced his own. He wrote, "It is often thought that girls do not need as much educational training as do the boys. I doubt the truth of this statement, since every man or woman is entitled to a complete preparation for life. Woman's work is very important and there is no reason whatever why she should not be fully prepared by careful training for her life's work, whatever it may be."[36]

In an address to the International Congress of Farm Women, John said, "Women's work has lagged behind. We must now dignify the work of women, as we have made that of the man. . . . You women represent one-half of the people of the earth. You have rights."[37] John felt that the

duties society demanded of women could be met with greater success
and a higher reward if women were better trained:

> Society now knows that the mission of women must be dignified
> by intelligence and made equal to that of man, else the foundations
> of society will crumble. . . . Women are now coming quickly to under-
> stand the value of such special education and the great power of their
> position as the mothers and makers of the race. When every mother
> knows the laws of health, more children will be strong. When every
> mother is broadly and sympathetically trained in the application of
> science and in the arts, more children will be intelligent. The church
> and the school are great factors in the training of the coming men and
> women, but compared with the home they sink into insignificance. If
> the formative years of a child's life are spent in a home of health and
> intelligence, a man is produced. If the reverse occurs, crime, disease,
> filth, the reform school, the police court, and the house of prostitu-
> tion, are the result. The picture is unpleasant, but it is common. Upon
> the proper education of the women will depend almost wholly the
> future of the race.[38]

> The experience of the last quarter of a century has shown con-
> clusively that the new agriculture succeeds only as the farm family life
> is improved. . . . For that reason agricultural education gives practi-
> cally as much attention to home economics—the modern name for
> home-making and house-keeping—as it does to agriculture proper.[39]

Immediately after his election as president, John expressed to the
board of trustees his determination to extend educational opportunities
for women and to build up the program of domestic science: "The state
demands a first-class school of Domestic Science and Arts. The School
of Domestic Science and Arts should be thoroughly remodeled, in harmony with the best knowledge at the present time. Instead of offering
only one course for women, dealing exclusively with Domestic Science
and Arts, another course could probably be added covering . . . such
branches of Agriculture as can be followed by women as a means of
livelihood. . . . The time has come when many women must depend
upon themselves for support."[40] Some positive steps were under way
when he wrote, "I am especially anxious that we shall succeed in

The Women's Building, home of the School of Domestic Science and Arts.

building up a strong department of domestic science. . . . We have [plans] proposed to the State Legislature for building up a college course in domestic science second to none in the West."[41]

One of his first problems was a shortage of classrooms. Building funds were unavailable, but he succeeded in coaxing the legislature to appropriate enough money to convert a dilapidated old dormitory into a first-rate domestic science building in 1909. To ensure that it was equal to any in the nation, he asked Susa Young Gates and Zina Card, both members of the board of trustees, to travel the country examining the facilities and programs of other successful colleges. They investigated twelve key schools, returning with first-class ideas on how to design and furnish the building.

As a result, John wrote, "the State Legislature . . . authorized the establishment of the most complete and best equipped college in the West for the teaching of homemaking. A building of five floors is devoted entirely to this work. It is equipped in a modern way for all . . . subjects that belong to a woman's course of education for home-making. It is a thing to be proud of, that Utah among these Western states is leading out in this direction. However, it is only in harmony with the spirit of the founders of the State."[42]

John organized two departments in the college of Domestic Science and included programs for women in the Farmers' Institutes and in the programs of the extension division. John noted:

> In the beginning scarcely a handful of women attended the lectures. Then an awakening came, until the domestic science lectures and schools are now usually crowded to overflowing. Over twelve thousand women gathered to take part in these discussions last year. This year two-thirds of this number passed through the special institute [railroad] car carrying exhibits of woman's work, as it passed through the settlements of the State. Women are beginning to understand that housework has received the caress of science and has been made beautiful. It is no more simple drudgery, but a glorious conquest for the welfare of new generations; and in truth it contains no more drudgery than other professions. The pioneer women who have made this State are frequent visitors to these gatherings throughout the State and, while homework to them had been labor, most exacting and often bitter, they have rejoiced to see it exalted to a new and great dignity. . . . Blessed be the eager minded, ever hoping women of our State who have looked for and accepted every new and good thing for the uplifting of their kind.[43]

John also succeeded in getting an auxiliary for women added to the International Dry Farm Congress. An associate wrote, "It is a fundamental policy in the Extension Division, emphasized at least ten years ago by President Widtsoe, that farm and home training must go hand in hand. It is thought that extensive development cannot take place in agricultural science until comparable development has taken place in the home. For that reason we aim to have at every farmers' institute a women's institute, and at every farmers' 'Round-Up' a housekeepers' conference."[44]

In his memoirs he added:

> In the midst of this work for farmers we observed that all experimental provisions by Congress for the Land Grant Colleges were chiefly for the farms and farm animals. Their wives whose work is as intricate as that of the husband and more far-reaching for human welfare were ignored.
>
> It seemed to my wife and myself that something similar should be

A view of the college on the hill, looking up 5th North from downtown Logan.

done for the promotion of women's work experimentally, through the Agricultural Experiment Stations.

It was evident that new knowledge was needed in many womanly activities, from the food to serve a family, to the rearing of children. Stations and funds for agricultural experimentation had been authorized for every state; why not similar experiment stations for the fields of home improvement? A bill was drafted with the approval of the College Home Economics Department and the help of my wife, who was always a champion of woman's work. Through letters and personal discussions she converted Reed Smoot, a dear family friend, to the need of home and family improvements as well as farm welfare.

Senator Smoot introduced the bill in the U. S. Senate and fought for its passage. It was first introduced April 7, 1913, as Senate Bill 250, but was not passed for several years. The measure finally emerged as the Purnell Act—to furnish funds for the home as well as farm improvement.[45]

Two especially valuable programs grew out of the college of domestic science. First was the training of home economics teachers for Utah high schools. Second was the preparation of home demonstration agents for every county of the state. Both programs made invaluable contributions to the state and opened more college doors to women.

PRESIDENT OF A STATEWIDE STUDENT BODY

As Utah was largely rural, the ACU was a great boon to the majority of the population. Even many who were unable to attend benefitted from the information it disseminated. "An educational institution that confines its work to the college campus fails in our day to render full service to its constituents," he wrote. "The progress and practical applications of knowledge should be made available to those beyond ordinary school age. Therefore, in 1907, the old faculty committee on farmers' institutes was replaced by an authorized extension division. Professor L. A. Merrill . . . was made director with headquarters in Salt Lake City."[46]

Widtsoe and Merrill felt that many farm people were so occupied with building canals and clearing sagebrush that they were not aware of the benefits of the college. Merrill wrote, "For this reason the Extension Department has been organized and the responsibility of carrying the glad tidings of the new Gospel of Agriculture and Domestic Science, placed upon it."[47]

Everywhere Utah farmers looked forward to the Farmers' Institutes. Important problems filled their agendas, but there was always ample time given to open discussion. Women's Institutes were integrated, and evening sessions were held conjointly. A friendly press was always a helpful ally, as this news report shows: "The greatest friends of Utah farmers, Dr. John A. Widtsoe President of the Agricultural College, and six of his expert professors will deliver all the gilt edge information that we can hear in the space of four meetings as stated above. Spread the word to your neighbors. Raise the cry everywhere and let the Big Chiefs of Utah see such a multitude of farmers as will give them an unforgettable picture of this vast empire. They will give us pointers worth gold."[48]

Utah farmers became some of the most knowledgeable in the West. Merrill wrote, "There is a genuine respect and mutual confidence between the farmers and the professors from the College. Recently an able scientist from the U. S. Department of Agriculture, in traveling through this State, remarked to the Director of the Experiment Station that he had never been in any place where the farmers had so much confidence in the Station workers and where the Station workers were so completely in harmony with the farmers."[49]

When John was at BYU, President Brimhall shared an idea that John implemented at the ACU.[50] In cooperation with railroad companies, traveling classrooms were set up in railroad cars. Some were equipped with exhibits, and others were used as lecture halls. As the train traveled through the state, it stopped for an hour or two in small towns and for a day or two in larger ones.

> The farmers' institute train has been traveling from Salt Lake to Milford and return, meeting the farmers of this State at the average rate of something over one thousand a day. This evening the train returns to Salt Lake and a great gathering will be held in the Assembly Hall, under the presidency of Governor Spry, in which agriculture, domestic science and the Agricultural College will be boosted. Next Thursday the train starts out again, this time over the D. and R. G., to visit Sanpete and Sevier counties and then to go eastward toward the Colorado line. We are keeping a lot of things going, but I believe that most of them are being done well and systematically and that the State is being benefitted largely by the work we are doing in behalf of the common people.[51]

In 1916 a newspaper reported: "The train of this year consisted of thirteen cars and made the trip through most of the towns of Utah and as far west in Nevada as Panaca. Next year it is aimed to enlarge the train to twenty cars."[52]

In his memoirs John described another successful outreach program:

> Next was the attempt to bring the farmers and housewives of the State to the College. On the College campus were the teachers and equipment needed, such as livestock, for example, more than could be carried on a train. There would be available also comfortable classrooms and regular periods for the consideration of special topics.

Besides, it would be a change and an outing for the farmers and their
wives. As a result of such a venture, the cause of the College would
be furthered.

In accordance with these plans, the U. S. A. C. Farmers' Round
Up was created. A two weeks' program was formulated. The time was
set in January, after the Christmas celebrations, and in the farmers'
slack season. Unexpected success followed this offering. Farmers with
their wives came from all parts of the State.[53]

The round-ups were a huge success. John and his faculty taught the
latest developments in agriculture. The program quickly expanded into
divisions for farmers, county agents, and housekeepers. In 1916 it was
estimated that about 1,650 people participated in those meetings.[54]

One more innovation was necessary: "As the work progressed, it
seemed clear to us that all farmers would be benefitted if a trained man
could be placed in the various localities of the State, ready to answer
the questions of the farmers, and to show them what should be done. It
seemed a proper use of the moneys appropriated for extension service.
The first man so appointed as County Agricultural Agent was Luther
M. Winsor, who in 1911 was sent into the Uintah Basin, then in special
need of help. This was probably the first "county agent" in the United
States. . . . Utah was a pioneer in the county agent movement."[55]

John maintained close contact with Winsor, and the venture was a
great success. By 1914, eight counties had agricultural agents, and R. J.
Evans was appointed to coordinate their work. One historian wrote,
"The impact of county agents was immediate and substantial."[56] In addition to battling many agricultural problems, they helped sponsor youth
farming groups, threshing groups, dairy-cow testing associations, and
poultry and egg marketing cooperatives.

E. G. Peterson was appointed Merrill's successor in 1912. Peterson
wrote, "The farmers' institute has been to some extent responsible for
the wide spread awakening in agriculture."[57] Farmers' Institutes became
more like farmers' schools and housekeepers' schools. Peterson informed
Widtsoe, "It is planned during the coming year to conduct twenty-four
of these, of five day's duration each, in many of the principal districts of

the State."[58] Round-ups were soon held in Logan, Cedar City, and Richfield.

John pressed for agriculture in elementary and secondary education. "Teach agriculture properly in the public schools," he wrote, "and in one generation every acre will be made to produce three fold its present crop value. We have the raw materials here if only human intelligence can be made to play upon them. The school master, however small his salary may be, or however much he is despised as impractical, is the power in every land that shapes the destiny of the nation. Teach the children and the result is inevitable."[59]

High schools welcomed John's ideas and often requested guest speakers from the college. He helped outline high school agriculture courses, and by 1912 it was reported that "the majority of the high schools are now giving elementary instruction in agriculture, home economics, commerce, and mechanic arts."[60]

John continued to use the *Deseret Farmer*, designed to put the results of careful research within the ready use of the common farmer: "The writings, taken in connection with the vast fund of information printed in the columns of the Deseret Farmer in answer to inquiries, make the publication of everyday, practical value to the farmer, and it is the only farm journal that can perform the service for its readers, because of the fact that its staff is right on the field."[61] Important information given at the institutes and round-ups was published for all who were unable to attend or who needed follow-up information to help implement new discoveries.

John loved his statewide student body, noting, "I have found much joy in my life as a result of my work in connection with the educational up building of the State and my only regret has been, which every honest man I believe feels, that incompetency to do all that might be done."[62]

By 1915 the average yield per acre in Utah had doubled over that in the latter part of the 1800s.[63] One historian wrote, "In no feature were good times more marked than in the application of science to agricultural practices and farm life. Irrigation passed from rule of thumb to technology. . . . Dry farming became first a field of research then a way of life."[64] Another measure of the prosperity of Utah agriculture was the increased value of farms. "From 1900 to 1920 the comparative value of farms in Utah increased from $2,619 per farm to $9,499."[65]

COLLEGE GROWTH: BLESSINGS AND CHALLENGES

Despite the academic pruning that accompanied John's appointment, the college experienced increased attendance in 1907.[66] John wrote, "Last year's attendance was the largest in the history of the Institution. The spirit of the Student Body was excellent and we had an increase of over 50% of students of college grade."[67] In his second year he wrote, "Since the opening of the College, in 1890, 15 students have been graduated in agriculture. This year, however, ten students have been accepted as candidates for graduation in agriculture."[68] In 1912 total enrollment was 1,366, a record-breaking year.[69] John noted that the number of college students, graduates of high schools, "must be five times as great as at . . . any other year in the history of the School."[70]

He also wrote, "During the last five years, the Agricultural College has grown so rapidly that the strength of every employee has been over taxed to meet the new demands. . . . Total attendance has increased from 717 to 1380 students and the present school year (1912–13) shows . . . the largest attendance in the history of the Institution."[71] By the end of John's term in 1916, the college had 97 faculty members and 1,453 students. The number of graduates with degrees increased from 3 in 1907 to 110 in 1916.[72] During John's nine years, enrollment of college-grade students increased nearly eight times. Eighty percent of all ACU graduates graduated under his administration.[73]

An important measure of a college's success is its ability to place its graduates in good positions. The files bulge with evidence that John went overboard to assist, including countless letters of recommendation. He often wrote to students of openings at the ACU and elsewhere. There are circulars to the schools informing them of graduates who would be available.[74]

Placing ACU graduates well also enhanced the reputation of the college. John recalled, "The college graduated more men trained in

The hillside of the campus toward the end of John's years as president. The letters UAC are embedded into the lawn in front of the Experiment Station.

agricultural science than the neighboring states. We succeeded in placing many of these men in important state positions in the West. Others
found positions with the federal government. The demand for trained
workers was such that for several years few graduates found their way
to farms of their own. The South American countries became so interested that we placed in 1912 one graduate in Uruguay and in 1913 five
in Argentina. . . . It was a fascinating challenge."[75] To memorialize their
success, the ACU published a book titled *The Graduate* that tracked the
progress of each graduate.

Qualitative growth was equally important to John, who wrote, "We
are looking now very definitely towards the making of a great agricultural and industrial college. It must be a school not inferior in any
respect to any other schools of collegiate rank."[76]

From the college's opening, funding from the legislature fluctuated
dramatically each session. The ACU and the U of U campaigned as
rivals for state dollars. In 1911 presidents Widtsoe and Kingsbury
pressed a mill tax through the legislature that provided a steady income
to each. John wrote, "For the first time we can look into the future and
plan with some certainty concerning our work."[77]

The winner of the master plan contest of 1912.

Expansion required new buildings. The Domestic Science Building had become a feather in John's cap. A gymnasium and student activities center became another: "The College is now able to . . . foster desirable athletic activities. The Thomas Smart Gymnasium has already become the center of the social functions of the College. This enables the Institution to exercise a close and helpful supervision over the social affairs of the Student Body, which is always desirable in the training of young people."[78]

The chemistry department was housed in various rooms in the school's main building, but the labs were grossly inadequate for many demands and not properly built for others. John worked hard to obtain funds for a new chemistry building, including a lab for his own research. In honor of his many accomplishments in chemistry and his contributions to the ACU, the building was named after him.

The progress of the school was so promising that a contest for a long-term master plan was held. The plan became the campus over

The "Quad" in the 1920s as developed according to the 1912 master plan. The tent village in the background housed farmers and homemakers on campus for summer programs.

many years that followed. A newspaper recapped the building program. President Widtsoe "secured several new buildings, such as the Gymnasium, the Woman's Building, Stock Judging Pavilion, Chemistry Building and Heating Plant; remodeled the Mechanic Arts Building, and built up new laboratories in practically every science taught in the college; . . . [and] renovated nearly all the old buildings."[79] The college also built an electric power plant that served the ACU, the Deaf and Blind School in Ogden, and the State Hospital in Provo.

CONTINUING PROFESSIONAL WORK

John's contributions to irrigation were milestones, but his work in dry farming was unique, almost revolutionary. One farmer referred to him as "the father of the system of Dry Farming in the West, and the foremost . . . in the whole country."[80] John looked for alternative methods of farming in arid Utah because of the practical limits of irrigation. Were there enough nutrients in the soil and enough natural precipitation to produce needed crops? John wrote:

The . . . original problem of dry-farming is the extension of the area now occupied by man, by devising methods whereby lands that receive little rainfall, lands that may be said to be in a state of permanent drouth, may be made to produce profitable crops also. These so-called deserts cover more than one-half, nearly six-tenths, of the entire land surface of the earth, and offer an opportunity of conquest unequaled in any other domain.

. . . It must reclaim by correct methods of soil tillage and every other means, the largest possible part of the unirrigated half of the earth which is under a low rainfall. This is a vast program of ambitious purpose which of necessity must be carried out by dry-farming, as that branch of agriculture which concerns itself directly with the utilization for the production of crops of the water that falls from the heavens.[81]

As its feasibility became more apparent, so did the need to get the information into the hands of farmers across the state. John set the ACU to the task of compiling that information, noting, "A certain portion of my time goes every day to the study of dry-farming and keeping up with the literature of the world."[82] He published widely and helped organize the Dry-Farm Congress. As word spread, attention from arid regions across the world focused on the ACU. Inquiries and visitors from many nations poured into Logan. Franklin S. Harris wrote, "In recognition of his authority in the subject of dry-farming he was made president of the International Dry-Farming Congress and it was during his presidency that this organization reached its highest point of usefulness."[83] Everywhere dry farming went, knowledge spread about its founder and the college.

Dr. L. H. Bailey, renowned dean of Cornell's College of Agriculture, the definitive source of agricultural education in the nation, produced an international series of books on successful agriculture. He wrote to John, "I have no mind to look any further for a person to write the book on 'Dry farming.' I should like to have you prepare it yourself. . . . What we need now is a thoroughly sound and conservative book on the whole subject, such as I know you can write."[84] John noted, "I am anxious to do the work only for the sake of the cause involved."[85] He spent a year researching and writing the book *Dry Farming: A System of Agriculture for Countries Under a Low Rainfall.*[86] In the introduction he explained the importance of the subject:

> Nearly six tenths of the earth's land surface receive an annual rainfall of less than twenty inches, and can be reclaimed for agricultural purposes only by irrigation and dry-farming. A perfected world-system of irrigation will convert about one tenth of this vast area into an incomparably fruitful garden, leaving about one half of the earth's land surface to be reclaimed, if at all, by the methods of dry-farming. The noble system of modern agriculture has been constructed almost wholly in countries of abundant rainfall, and its applications are those demanded for agricultural development of humid regions. Until recently, irrigation was given scant attention, and dry-farming, with its world problem of conquering one half of the earth, was not considered. These facts furnish the apology for the writing of this book.[87]

Dr. Eugene W. Hilgard, the foremost agriculture scholar in the Western United States, wrote, "In this treatise on Dry-Farming, Doctor Widtsoe has produced a most timely and useful book in which both the intending and the actual farmer may find both the principles and the practice of farming in regions of deficient rainfall, discussed in a simple and practical form. Doctor Widtsoe's book, carries with it the convincing quality of a wide personal experience in the matter treated. It should be in the hands of every farmer from the Plains country to the Pacific Coast."[88]

John Burns, secretary of the Dry-Farming Congress, wrote to an investigator in Hungary, "You will find this book of immense value to all of your people who are interested in dry-farming information. This is, by far, the best thing yet issued."[89] Burns also wrote Dr. Widtsoe, "I wish that the Dry-Farming Congress could afford to place the book in the hands of every farmer in the United States. It would be worth millions of dollars to every state in the Union within the first year."[90]

The text quickly became an international bestseller, with translations in French, Spanish, Italian, and Hungarian. When John was inducted into Utah's Beehive Hall of Fame in 1986, the plaque detailing his accomplishments noted, "His book, *Dry Farming, a System of*

Agriculture for Countries Under a Low Rainfall, which was published in 1911, remains the definitive work on the subject and is still in use throughout the world." It was further reported that "he spent considerable time in the Middle East instructing farmers in his methods of dry farming and his book was eventually translated into the languages of the Middle East to better communicate its principles."[91] John modestly said, "My book became almost a best seller, for books of its class."[92]

Because irrigation progressed so much under John's tutelage, he was regarded as the dean of irrigation also. While president of the ACU, John served on the Advisory Board of the National Irrigation Congress. In an address to the congress, he summarized many of his findings on irrigation.[93] He wrote to Utah's Governor Spry, "Irrigation and dry-farming, hand in hand, will reclaim the desert portion of the earth—neither can do its work effectively alone."[94]

> The experiments in dry-farming and irrigation, undertaken under my directorship of the station, had been continued during my interlude at B. Y. U. But the results since I left had not been published. So I set myself the task, in the midst of crowding duties, to assemble and prepare for publication the mass of available data. Several bulletins, chiefly on the relationships among water, soils, and plants, resulted from the toil. The outstanding finding was that after a certain quantity of water is applied to a crop, further additions do not increase the yield or increase it very lightly; also that the composition of crops can be controlled measurably by the quantity, time, and method of irrigation. These were major and new findings, with many others of derivative value.[95]

Following the success of the dry-farming book, Dean Bailey asked John for an equally good international textbook on irrigation. John wrote to Bailey, "I am still engaged in the work of tabulating, digesting and publishing the immense amount of data that we have here. It will take some six or eight months to get the experimental work published and until that is done I would not be able to begin on any general treatise of the subject."[96] Bailey consented, and in 1914 John published *The Principles of Irrigation Practice.*[97] One scholar wrote, "In this work you have presented matter that practically all Western people have long desired to have thus easily available. . . . The fact that we are already using this book as a text in our classes in the University of Utah tells in the strongest way how much we like it."[98]

As John Widtsoe's books spread across the world, his reputation and that of the ACU reached heights seldom attained in agricultural science. Forty years later, Franklin S. Harris said, "I have witnessed the fruits of his scientific work in many lands, from the tiaga of Siberia, the highlands of Iran, the hills of Palestine, the farms of Canada, to the arid lands of Latin America."[99]

FAME AND FAMILY

As John's reputation spread, he was asked to serve on many committees and commissions at national and international levels. Representatives of many of the best institutions and experiment stations across the world maintained contact. Officials at the United States Department of Agriculture and the Office of Experiment Stations called on him regularly.[100] One notable experience gives an indication of the respect John commanded. Susa Young Gates (his mother-in-law) and an associate traveled the nation to examine domestic science departments. Of their visit to the Pratt Institute, she wrote, "When we arrived, I just mentioned that we were visitors from the West, and we were coolly told by the Secretary to walk about and look for ourselves. I then hauled out my introduction [one written by President Widtsoe] and presto! She got up and went with us herself."[101]

John was especially gratified by the international attention afforded the college. He was pleased to contribute to an improved world view of the LDS people and their accomplishments in Utah. He wrote to President Joseph F. Smith, "A remarkable interest seems to have been developed recently in the work done by the Latter-Day Saints in the reclamation of regions formerly thought valueless. During the last few weeks we have had official representatives in Logan from half a dozen of the great nations of the world for the special purpose of getting first-hand information concerning the methods employed by the people of Utah."[102]

High government officials from many nations, most notably Asian nations, maintained contact with President Widtsoe through written correspondence. A large number of them also traveled to Logan to learn from John the secrets of dry farming firsthand. These international friends always left Utah with a positive impression. Representative of them is a letter from a member of the Imperial German Consul: "While travelling towards the North East, my thoughts are still in Utah, where I spent such an interesting time. Especially the two days at Logan I will always recall for the many delightful impressions I had there. Allow me, dear Mr. Widtsoe, to express to you once more my heartiest thanks for the many courtesies shown to me and for your kind advice you gave me with regard to the problem of dry farming. On a most pleasant trip through the dry farm district I saw with my own eyes what wonderful results can be obtained by the right way."[103]

Acclaim for Dr. Widtsoe's uncommon industry spread. Many attributed his successes to that industry. It is difficult to determine which was his greatest asset, his industry, his brilliance, or his devotion to his people. In the face of all those successes, John confided to a friend that he found it trying to give public addresses, and that he always suffered from stage fright.[104] Despite this personal hardship, he spoke frequently on behalf of the college. "Permit me to assure you that in all my work I have thought only of the welfare of the Institution, standing as it does as one of the greatest servants of the State of Utah."[105] Although he didn't expect praise, he was grateful when his efforts were noticed and appreciated. After receiving a salary increase, he wrote to the board of trustees, "In my work for the Agricultural College, since my early manhood, I have never taken time to think of salary, and I cannot now work any harder or more conscientiously than I have done in the past—but, the unspoken appreciation of my work that was carried with your action, I value with my most treasured possessions, and it will lighten greatly every burden of the day."[106]

Much of John's fame was linked to his pen. His professional and his religious writing usually came at the requests of professional and ecclesiastical colleagues who thought he was uniquely qualified for each offering. While at the ACU he wrote, "As usual, my pen was restless. I wrote many articles for periodicals. Often I had to defend our college work in the daily press. . . . I wrote also rather steadily for the Church publications. Many study courses for the Mutual Improvement Associations and other organizations took much time. I probably wrote too much. When I look at the volumes of the bound writings, I wonder that I found time for them all. Also, I wrote numerous addresses which have not been published, chiefly for other people who were frightened by pen and ink."[107]

A vibrant faith had brought the Widtsoes to Utah, and it never dimmed with time and experience. John continued to exercise his faith and his religion:

> In the midst of the heavy duties of the U.S.A.C. Presidency, my Church work was not forgotten. To pay tithing was a privilege. To keep the Word of Wisdom brought daily physical as well as spiritual benefits. Our daily family prayers brought a spirit of peace and joy into our life. In the Logan Fifth Ward, to which our family belonged, I taught the advanced theology class in Sunday School, which had been organized during the days of my station directorship for the benefit of students away from home who needed steadying help as the new world of knowledge opened to them. From these studies and at the request of President David O. McKay [then Church Superintendent of Sunday Schools] I wrote a priesthood course of study, *A Rational Theology*. This has gone through several editions. I was also a faithful attendant at my priesthood quorum meetings. In the 64th Quorum of Seventy I was a member of the council and also the class leader. Later, when the 178th Quorum of Seventy was organized, I became the senior president, and also the class leader. In these Church teaching positions I had capable assistants, such as Professor William Peterson and Dr. F. S. Harris. As best I could, I also attended to my work as a member of the Young Men's Mutual Improvement Association General Board, to which I had been called in 1905.[108]

The family was of supreme importance to John and Leah Widtsoe. John noted, "During these U.S.A.C. years we lived a very happy family life."[109] The Widtsoes had three children born to them while John was the president of the ACU. Helen was born in 1907, Mary in 1909, and Leah Eudora in 1912. Helen lived only one day, and Mary lasted only a few hours. The Widtsoes had previously lost two children, Markie almost exactly a year before Helen. While sorrow tugged at their heart-strings and lingered with them throughout life, John carried on, undaunted. His faith in God did not waver, and his work for the college did not suffer.

Leah was an equal partner in all matters. John praised her contributions, which he felt enabled his successes. He wrote, "She left me free to do my special work; and I could not have accomplished my life's assignments without such a division of labor."[110] In his memoirs he added, "My wife, capable in any position assigned to her, assumed the duties of a college president's wife with grace and success. Innumerable dinners and receptions were carried out with dignity and precision. Numerous people of national and international distinction were our guests. But she served also in Church positions, ward MIA president, Stake counselor in the stake MIA and long time temple worker."[111]

Franklin S. Harris, a close family friend and frequent house visitor, wrote, "We have never ceased to marvel at the resourcefulness of Aunt Leah, as we affectionately call her, and we soon became aware of one of the chief sources of the strength of this great man. She supported him without reserve, and he constantly relied on her judgment, particularly in the work for women and in the extension activities which he initiated in all three of Utah's institutions of higher learning."[112]

THE DECISION TO LEAVE

John enjoyed his success at the college. He was happy and intended to remain there many years. Nonetheless, his reputation, his skills, and lofty public regard made him an attractive candidate for higher stations. At that time, significant institutional problems invaded the University of Utah. Changes were necessary, and John was considered the primary catalyst in resolving the problems of the state university:

> Inscrutable fate again took a hand in my affairs. In the forenoon of January 14, 1916, General Richard W. Young called by telephone to ask if I would do him a personal favor and meet him in Salt Lake City that evening. He took me to meet the executive committee of the Board of Regents of the University of Utah. Without much ado,

they told me that President Kingsbury, of the University, was to be retired, and then offered me the presidency.

I promised to think it over, with the mental reservation that I would have none of it. I would have to leave work which I had learned to love. The salary was $2,000 less than I was drawing. My expenses in Salt Lake City would be higher. Some of my hopes for later life would have to be laid aside. Worst of all, the University was in bad repute among the institutions of the land, as well as the State, and the faculty was in a state of commotion. It was a bad muddle. I valued the confidence thus placed in me, and I had no fears about the future of the school; but why should I have to carry the burden of straightening things out? I had already had a good deal of that to do for the State of Utah. Washing dirty linen for a state is always an unpleasant task.

Before deciding I sought out the friends whom I could trust in such matters. Everyone, my wife and all the others, said, "Take it; you are needed there. Someone must do the work. You are none too good."

On January 20, 1916, I was formally elected president of the University of Utah, the term of office to begin July 1, 1916. I was in the southern part of the State helping in one of our round-ups the day after the public announcement of the selection was made. I returned to Logan somewhat heavy-hearted.[113]

John was to leave his boyhood home, the college he had served more than twenty years, and the vital work that had endeared him to the people. Beyond that, he wrote, he was leaving "a body of colleagues and associates who include my dearest and most intimate friends; a loyal, industrious, wholesome, devoted and outward looking student body, which is nowhere surpassed; and a governing board of trustees, who as kind and gentle friends, rather than as superior officers, have given me unanimous support in my every endeavor to promote the interests of the college. Only the deep conviction that, just now, my best efforts belong elsewhere, could compel me to take this step."[114]

The board of trustees was saddened with John's decision, as they prized his leadership. In their view, "a new man, with abilities equal to those of Dr. Widtsoe, [would] require several years time to become as thoroughly acquainted with local conditions as was Dr. Widtsoe."[115] In a special meeting urging him to stay, they offered a thousand-dollar increase in salary. John, however, had determined that he had chosen the correct course, so the board expressed their sincere gratitude for his contributions: "While naturally, we regret to lose the man who has done so much to place the Agricultural College of Utah in the front ranks of such institutions in the United States, and who has raised the standards of the school in such a gratifying manner, Dr. Widtsoe, feeling as he does, that he is simply answering a call that comes from the citizens of the state to do service in another branch of work, leaves with the heartiest good will and support of the members of the board, and the assurance that in his new work he has our very best wishes."[116]

Public expressions of appreciation were forthcoming from many with whom he had close association. The faculty resolution was typical of many expressions, public and private:

> The institution is losing an educator whose scholarly achievements have brought him local, national, and international renown; and
>
> Whereas, he has been untiring and effective in his efforts to dignify the common pursuits of life; and
>
> Whereas through his keen, broad conception of education for service he has met, during his incumbency, not only the immediate needs of Utah but has also outlined her future agricultural and industrial possibilities, and had advanced the college to the first rank among Agricultural colleges of the world; and
>
> Whereas, we have the utmost confidence in his continued success as President of the University of Utah, be it therefore,
>
> Resolved, that we now, in token of our friendship and esteem, pay this tribute to him upon his entrance into his new field, expressing at the same time our deep personal and institutional loss.[117]

It is difficult to catalog the impact John A. Widtsoe had on the college he loved and the state he served. During his service and for years thereafter, agriculture was Utah's leading industry and the backbone of her economy. A Utah historian noted, "The quarter century from 1890 to 1915 has often been referred to as a golden era for agriculture. . . .

This was especially true in Utah."[118] Rather than evaluating his accomplishments from the viewpoint of a modern society in which agriculture occupies less prominence, it is best to heed his contemporaries:

> Probably more of Dr. Widtsoe's manhood energies have been devoted to problems of administration than to any other single field. In this work he has been eminently successful. The openness of his method of dealing with people, his obvious honesty of purpose, his desire to give all a fair hearing, his sagacity in understanding the real problem before him, and most of all his unfailing ability to estimate men have given him the respect of those over whom he has presided. . . . Dr. Widtsoe has had a number of very difficult administrative situations to meet, but his diplomacy and tact have enabled him to overcome the difficulties and in a large measure to bring harmony out of chaos.[119]

The *Journal of Education* announced his appointment as president of the University of Utah:

> President Widtsoe has made a college of National reputation at Logan. As an author, as a scholar, as a specialist, as one skillful in handling problems of human nature . . . he is one of the distinguished administrators and leaders of the country. . . .
>
> In Dr. Widtsoe the state of Utah has one of the most active educators in the United States. He is level-headed, conservative, energetic . . . a scholar whose ability will be felt for progress in the reconstruction, development and advancement of our beloved University of Utah. Give him half a chance, and he will place that institution upon a basis of national recognition, side by side with the greatest institutions of learning in our country.[120]

16

THE YOUNG MEN'S MUTUAL IMPROVEMENT ASSOCIATION

———————————◼———————————

IN June 1875, President Brigham Young called Junius F. Wells to organize the young men of the Church. Wells reported, "The spirit of the work fell upon me from the moment I was chosen to undertake it. I seemed at once to know what I should do."[1] Wells summarized his instructions from Brigham Young: "We want to have our young men enrolled and organized . . . so that we can put our hands upon them at any time for any service that may be required. We want them to hold meetings where they will stand up and speak—get into the habit of speaking—and of bearing testimony. These meetings are . . . to be composed of young men for their improvement—for their mutual improvement—a society of young men for mutual improvement."[2] Wells implemented the inspired counsel, which included these words:

> At your meeting you should begin at the top of the roll and call upon as many members as there is time for to bear their testimonies and at the next meeting begin where you left off and call upon others, so that all shall take part and get into the practice of standing up and saying something. Many may think they haven't any testimony to bear, but get them to stand up and they will find the Lord will give them utterance to many truths they had not thought of before. More people

have obtained a testimony while standing up trying to bear it than down on their knees praying for it.

Your society is not for debates—debating on foolish and absurd questions, which prove nothing, is a bad practice and leads to infidelity. You must not permit it, but avoid contention of every kind in your meetings.[3]

John was a member of the first YMMIA organized in the Logan First Ward in January of 1886. Its mission well suited John, whose mother encouraged his active participation. Harvard interrupted his formal YMMIA training, but its influence continued with his fellow LDS students. When John returned to Logan, his quest for learning, teaching, and testifying of gospel truths was evidenced in the study group he formed and his subsequent call to elders quorum leadership.

After returning from Europe, John and Leah served as presidents of the YMMIA and the YWMIA in the Logan Fifth Ward. From there John was called to be a member of the general board of the YMMIA. John valued his service on the General Board and direct contact with many Church leaders, especially President Joseph F. Smith.[4] During that time he published his extensive concordance of the Doctrine and Covenants, which led to several requests for instruction manuals by various Church auxiliaries. From 1902 to 1904 John wrote a series of twenty-eight lessons for the Young Ladies' Mutual Improvement Association under the title *The Book of Doctrine and Covenants.* In 1903 he wrote another series of lessons for the fourth-year theological department of the Deseret Sunday School, *An Outline for the Study of the Book of Doctrine and Covenants.* In 1904 he authored another series, *The Study of the Book of Doctrine and Covenants.* In 1906 he prepared *The History and Message of the Doctrine and Covenants* for the YMMIA.

Throughout his terms as president of the Agricultural College and the University of Utah, he continued his affiliation with the General Board, noting, "My duties on the General Y.M.M.I.A. Board were performed fairly regularly and with much pleasure. I served as chairman of the M.I.A. committee appointed to work out plans for M.I.A. care of young men of high school and college age. Out of the investigations and considerations came the M Men movement of the Y.M.M.I.A., which, in association with the Gleaner Girls of the YWMIA, has been a powerful factor in steadying the religious pulse of youth."[5] The reputation of these organizations was widespread. "They won the patent of true nobility. Truth was their motto and coat of arms. The badge that a mortal ruler might confer, is, by comparison, dross and worthless."[6] The success of the program of M-Men and Gleaner Girls was a tribute to the noblest pioneer accomplishments. John added, "They have shown themselves worthy of their noble ancestry. Satan is making his last stand, and a determined one. It should be your concern to battle against every corrupting practice. Tell the tempter, whoever he may be, 'Get thou behind me!' You are a flying wedge of men and women who can cure the world of its moral sickness. In the work of upholding the traditions of your people it will give you courage to remember—'*Noblesse oblige.*'"[7]

FRIENDSHIP WITH JOSEPH F. SMITH

John had rich spiritual memories of the "kingly figure" of President John Taylor at the Logan Temple dedication and YMMIA conferences, and he revered presidents Wilford Woodruff and Lorenzo Snow. But, over nearly a quarter of a century, he treasured an intimate association with President Joseph F. Smith. Their friendship began when President Smith performed John and Leah's marriage in 1898. John had studied under many of the world's greatest teachers at Harvard and Göttingen, but the records show that Joseph F. Smith was the teacher he held in highest regard. That is most evident in his desire to compile Joseph F. Smith's teachings in the book *Gospel Doctrine: Sermons and Writings of Joseph F. Smith*, which was "a matter of love for the work at hand." In tribute he gave this praise: "President Smith's sermons and writings breathe the true spirit of the Gospel, are sound as gold in tenet and precept, and express the will of the Master in every word."[8]

In his last twenty years President Smith oversaw more than fifty of John's carefully written articles to the young men of the Church. Over those years John's esteem for President Smith knew no bounds. John's closest mentor, Joseph Marion Tanner, wrote to BYU president George H. Brimhall in 1907 that John, in a darkened hour of his life, would do nothing without conferring with President Smith. A few months later, at age thirty-seven, John was asked to consult with the prophet as he sought divine direction in proclaiming doctrine on the origin of man. John's journal for 27 September 1909 reads, "Met w. First Presidency and Apostles to hear paper by O. F. Whitney on Origin of man."[9] Two or three drafts of that proclamation passed between 47 East South Temple Street and John's office on Logan's College Hill.

In 1914 John was busy writing an unusual Melchizedek Priesthood manual that David O. McKay had requested. John described it as "almost breaking into a new field as far as Mormon literature is concerned."[10] Answering a telegram from Elder McKay, he wrote, "How would 'Rational Theology' suit you? If that has a foreign sound I think any number of names can be suggested. A name after all has the least meaning." John was also a busy college president, yet in 1914 he published, at Cornell's request, the definitive international irrigation textbook, *Principles of Irrigation Practice*. He was the father of a young family and still supported his mother. John also translated and published seven articles from their missionary's autobiography in 1914. Besides doing all this, John wanted to mark President Smith's seventy-sixth birthday. His thoughts filled eight printed pages. He showed them to Edward H. Anderson, President Smith's assistant editor, and wanted to share them with the whole Church. Self-conscious of the personal nature of his tribute, he asked that it be printed anonymously. An interesting exchange followed over the impossibility and the seeming impropriety of keeping secrets from the president of the Church, who was also the *Improvement Era*'s editor. John wrote:

> The leaders of the people are subjected to searching consideration by the people, and the confidence given them is in proportion to their deserts. It is therefore, a noble tribute to the worthiness of the man, Joseph F. Smith, that he is the synonym for all that the people respect and hold dear.[11]

> A fighting apostle, he has always been fighting for the cause of truth. Yet, Joseph F. Smith is temperamentally a man of peace. Gentle and kind are his ways. A gentleman, is the instinctive appellation bestowed upon him by all who meet him. In character, voice and

manner he is the dignified peacemaker. Nevertheless, his loyalty is such, and his convictions are so firmly established, that evil may not be spoken about truth, without arousing the lion within him. To measure the ground; to give the foe full place and warning, to try strength according to the laws of decency, but never to give quarter to evil or untruth or injustice, that is the method of Joseph F. Smith.[12]

President Smith knew of John's high regard for him, and surely such eloquence bears its own signature. The anonymity John sought was from some who might have found grounds for criticism that would obscure the purity of his true appreciation. Brother Anderson wrote John:

> I will let your article go in under the initials J.A.G. I told President Smith about it, and he read the proofs and at the bottom of one of them which he sent over afterwards, he wrote the following:
>
> "Oh! What a glorious standard my friend has set up for me! I would that I could fill every measure of it. And I feel that he would have me do so if I could. I thank him for his friendship, and his good intent; and while the noble standard he has raised to my life and works seems far above my reach, I recognize it as worthy of the best and truest efforts of all the powers of mind and soul, with the help of God, to rise as near to it as possible. God bless the bright mind and noble soul who would voluntarily do so much to encourage his brother to such worthy deeds! It makes me feel mighty humble, to say the least. [signed] With very best wishes I remain sincerely your friend and brother."[13]

Three years later, John found another way to express appreciation: "One day, hearing President Joseph F. Smith say that he would be forgotten because he had no written work to leave behind, as had B. H. Roberts and other writers, I conceived the idea of collecting the essence of President Smith's sermons and editorials into a book." That was the background to producing *Gospel Doctrine*. President Smith's time was ending, so John gathered a small circle of friends to expedite production of one of the most widely used doctrinal texts in the Church.

At that time John presided over the University of Utah, which became an army encampment because the United States had entered World War I. More serious was the worldwide epidemic of Spanish

Influenza, which took the lives of many students and forced the closure of the university.

On 1 November 1918, four nicely bound typewritten copies of *Gospel Doctrine: Sermons and Writings of Joseph F. Smith* were ready. The committee presented the first of them to President Smith just seventeen days before his death. Franklin S. Harris wrote of that occasion, "In company with J. A. Widtsoe, [Osborne] J. P. Widtsoe, L. N. Stohl, A. E. Bowen, and Joseph Quinney, Jr., presented to President Joseph F. Smith a volume we had compiled from his writings and sermons. He gave a strong testimony of his help from God."[14] As full as John A. Widtsoe's life had been and would yet be, at its spiritual foundation was the influence of Joseph F. Smith, whom John saw as a man near to perfection. He wrote:

> It is common knowledge that when the children were young, his rest was not easy if he had not seen the little ones properly tucked away for the night. The same father-heart beats for the people whose accepted leader he is. The hearts of the people ache over the long hours he spends in the office working out the affairs of the Church. . . . But, he is not to be dissuaded. He must see his people tucked away for the night, before his heart will be at peace. So works love! And who shall say him nay, whose care from boyhood has been the welfare of his people.[15]

THE IMPROVEMENT ERA

Joseph F. Smith was second counselor to presidents Wilford Woodruff and Lorenzo Snow through the difficult 1890s. One-eighth of America's families controlled seven-eighths of her wealth, and much of the rest of the nation wallowed in poverty. Few appropriations were given to Church education, twenty schools were closed, and preparations for opening the new Church university were abandoned. The First Presidency wrote, "Every day urgent demands for cash are made of us, which we cannot meet for the simple reason that we have no money. . . . We never saw such a time of financial stringency as there is now."[16] The severity of those trials were memorialized by the revelation on tithing to President Lorenzo Snow in St. George on 17 May 1899.

That depression spurred a general move for auxiliary reform and "re-baptism of Mutual Improvement."[17] The *Contributor,* the magazine to the YMMIA for seventeen years, failed for lack of money. Heber J. Grant, deeply troubled over that failure, feared for the young men of the Church. He wrote, "I prayed to the Lord that I might be chosen as one of the general superintendency."[18] The following day while he and other brethren were assembled in President Woodruff's office, President Smith said, "I suggest that Brother Grant here and Brother B. H. Roberts be counselors as well as myself."[19] Grant wrote, "Brother Woodruff turned to me and asked me if I would be willing to serve. I told him that I would be delighted to do anything he wanted me to do."[20]

During their first meeting, a new magazine was discussed. Years later, as president of the Church, Heber J. Grant recalled, "I felt from the start that it would receive great support because of the wonderful ability of Brother Roberts as a writer, my willingness to work as the manager, and the prestige that would come to it through having one of the Presidency as the Editor-in-Chief."[21] Success was sure: "Our capital was the interest of the young men of the Church of Jesus Christ of Latter-day Saints in the Mutual cause; and that had only to be appealed to and drawn upon in order to be sufficient and permanent in the maintenance of the Young Men's organ."[22] In 1897 the *Improvement Era* began its mission to bolster the well-being of the young men of the Church.

The progress of the *Era* and Dr. Widtsoe (who was associated with it from 1898) were parallel in their development. The *Era* sought to enrich the lives of young men through teachings on the written page. John sought to enrich them in the classroom, the laboratory, and the crop field. As the *Era* became the voice of other Church auxiliaries, John became director of the Experiment Station and president of the Agricultural College and the University of Utah.

President Smith maintained a firm hand as editor-in-chief, noting, "It is better for us to save our own boys who are being misled at home, than it is for us to go out into the world."[23] He reemphasized that theme by drawing on Brigham Young's teachings: "The field to be occupied is religious, social and educational. The religious work is not to be formally theological in its nature, but rather to be confined to the limits outlined by President Brigham Young, when the organizations were first established: 'Let the keynote of your work be the establishment in the youth of an individual testimony of the truth and magnitude of the great Latter-day work; and the development of the gifts within them.'"[24]

By example and precept John Widtsoe was a perfect complement for the YMMIA. Surprisingly, the first volume of the *Era* did not include a contribution from him. He had already published more than a dozen articles in professional works, and a series entitled "Foods from the Point of View of Nutrition" was already in print in the *Young Woman's Journal*. A closer look reveals the demands of his research projects that hatched eight scientific articles that year, while preparations for marriage and his doctoral program consumed his excess capacity.

JOHN'S EARLIEST ARTICLES

Once John and Leah had set up house in Europe, John began an article for the *Era.* His experiences at Harvard and Göttingen put him in a position to soften the trials of faith that would come in the emerging scientific age. His article addressed the dilemmas he had seen in the confluence of science and religion. A letter he sent with the article explained the problems so well that it was printed as a preface to his article. He wrote:

> I have been a careful reader of *The Improvement Era.* . . . Its evident enthusiastic spirit of helping the young men of Zion in every possible way has encouraged me to send the enclosed article. . . .
>
> To the thinking boy, brought up in the fear of the Lord, comes a stage when there is a desperate effort to reconcile science and religion; but the task is made difficult for want of deep scientific knowledge and a mind trained in discrimination; and often the faith of the boy is weakened for a season. Of course, there is no real conflict between science and religion; and no reconciliation is needed except by the drifting mind. Yet as long as science is what it is today, and the teachers of science half-taught, this condition will exist in our schools. I have myself gone through the critical period when science and religion seemed to rise up against one another; and can sympathize keenly with every young person who is in the same condition.[25]

John described the conflicts as being largely due to "insufficient knowledge" and the failings of science—"Science is imperfect; the gospel, as far as we know it, is perfect."[26] But his love for both science and the gospel helped him relieve doubt for many who might have shunned one in favor of the other. "Such are the thoughts that prompted me to select a humble subject in science, and to arrange it in a way to indicate how it may be a strengthener of faith. It is one out of a thousand."[27] The article, "A Voice from the Soil," showed that a small range of science may communicate large lessons in science and religion. The article was exactly what President Smith had in mind. It was "educational," "not formally theological," and it built "individual testimony of the truth and magnitude of the great Latter-day work."

John wrote, "Were our knowledge perfect enough, every phenomenon in nature would be a testimony to the truth of the gospel."[28] The phenomenon he examined in "A Voice from the Soil" was how Utah and the Rocky Mountains compared with the great capitals of sacred societies in ancient times. The semi-arid lands of Mesopotamia, Palestine, Egypt, Peru, and Mexico became barren because of neglect. The success of those was largely due to the fertile soil. Precious soil nutrients are easily washed away in more humid climates. "If, on the other hand, only a small quantity of rain falls upon the soil—an amount sufficient to soak the soil without draining through—the water will gradually be evaporated back into the air, and there will be no loss of plant food. In such a district, the soils, if they are treated right, become richer year by year, even though subjected to tillage."[29]

Joseph Smith's prophecy that the Saints would become a mighty people in the midst of the Rocky Mountains would come true, in part, because of the soil of that semi-arid region. Bringing the Saints to Utah was strong evidence of the guiding hand of God. "A Voice from the Soil" launched John's writing career with the *Era,* and this career continued aggressively through fifty-four years and more than 730 entries.

John's second article, "We Walk by Faith," demonstrated how science and religion operate on the same principle of faith—the substance of things hoped for and the evidence of things not seen. It, too, was "educational," "not formally theological," and built "individual testimony of the truth and magnitude of the great Latter-day work." In typical simplicity John addressed a question scientists had long sought to answer: "Is it possible to keep on dividing a dust particle of sugar (or any other substance) forever; or is there a particle of sugar so small that it can not be divided again?"[30] He then described what scientists consider that final state to be. To describe that in his day required one to believe in things no man had seen.

> This smallest piece of sugar, is called a *molecule* of sugar. The mortal eye, though aided by the most powerful microscopes of modern days, could not distinguish a sugar molecule, or even a pile of thousands of them; placed on the tongue, there would be no sensation of sweetness, for the sense of taste is far too gross to recognize one molecule; though it were hurled against our body with the velocity of lightening, we should not feel the impact. To all our senses, the molecule is wholly unknown; and, no doubt, shall remain so while the earth is as it is. Yet the existence of such a particle is as certain as is the existence of the sun in the high heavens.[31]

> If the faith of science is compared with that of theology in the greatest detail, the superiority of the science of God may be shown in many ways, especially in the fact that God has been seen and heard by mortals, while no man has claimed to have seen the atoms believed in by the chemists. That is, after all, the final difference between god-science and man-science; the ultimate idea of the former, may be seen and heard and felt; while the ultimate ideas of the latter, must remain abstraction to the human mind forever.[32]

Following these were fourteen other articles dealing with science. Utah was still agrarian, and most of her citizens were required to work with soil, water, air, sunshine, manure, and tillage. Similarly persuasive and compelling analyses examined a wide range of topics from their lives.

Edward H. Anderson was co-editor of the *Era* and the liaison for President Smith. In the midst of this science series, John expressed some fears that his subject matter was not sufficiently interesting to young men. Anderson replied, "You need not have any fear that your articles

. . . will not be suitable for our magazine. I am constantly in receipt of compliments upon your writings. . . . Rest assured that they are appreciated in this office, and by the brethren connected therewith."[33] He often expressed his appreciation and that of President Smith: "We thank you for the interest you have taken in *The Improvement Era,* for the assistance you have rendered the editors, and for the good you have accomplished among the people, by contributing your writings for its pages. It is appreciated by us, and has added much to the value of the magazine."[34] Many of Anderson's letters were petitions for more articles, and he annually sought permission to use John's name and photograph in the prospectus of the coming volume.

JOSEPH SMITH AS SCIENTIST

In September 1903 President Smith wrote, "I have your note of Sept. 11th, in which you refer to a series of articles you have just finished and mailed to the *Improvement Era* on the subject, 'Joseph Smith as Scientist.' Please accept my thanks for the same, and believe me your efforts are highly appreciated, especially as we are not prepared at the present time to pay you for the labor which you have done." He added that John's only pay was "the knowledge that you have done good work for the benefit of the boys and girls of Zion."[35] The articles in this series became the lead article appearing on the *Era's* front page almost every month between November 1903 and October 1904. "The purpose of these articles," John wrote, "is to show that even though the mission of Joseph was chiefly of a spiritual nature, yet he recognized definitely the fundamental laws and many of the facts of science; and that, in many cases he stated natural laws which later have been discovered and accepted by men of science. Such a demonstration will not of itself be sufficient to establish a testimony of the truth of Joseph Smith's mission: but it may remove an obstacle from the way of those who are seeking for truth."[36]

That Joseph Smith did not use the language of science was further proof of his divine inspiration: "In the following papers it will be shown, by a series of comparisons, that, in 1833, the teachings of Joseph Smith, the Mormon Prophet, were in full harmony with the most advanced scientific thought of today, and that he anticipated the world of science in the statement of fundamental facts and theories in physics, chemistry, astronomy and biology."[37]

In the December 1903 issue John wrote about "the persistence of matter and force." He reviewed the history of alchemy and the cult sciences that grew from the belief that men could, through mystical powers of supernatural order, annihilate matter or create matter from nothing. In Joseph's day chemistry was newly discovered, and scientists began to gather data that exposed fallacies in cultist teachings. One discovery found that when coal was burned, the matter did not cease to exist; rather, the weight of the gas collected as it issued from the chimney was the same as the coal from which it came. Another found that rain came from invisible particles present in the air. In time, with many similar findings, scientists concluded that matter is eternal and that the quantity of matter making up the universe can neither be increased nor diminished. "This great generalization, known as the law of the Persistence of Matter or Mass, is the foundation stone of modern science," John wrote.[38] Again he turned his pen to showing that Joseph Smith taught those things substantially before their popular acceptance in science:

> No doctrine taught by Joseph Smith is better understood by his followers than that matter in its elementary condition is eternal, and that it can neither be increased nor diminished. As early as May, 1833, the Prophet declared that "the elements are eternal," and in a sermon delivered in April, 1844, he said "Element had an existence from the time God had. The pure principles of element are principles which can never be destroyed; they may be organized and reorganized, but not destroyed. They had no beginning, and can have no end."
>
> It is thus evident that from the beginning of his work, Joseph Smith was in perfect harmony with the fundamental doctrine of science; and far in advance of the religious sects of the world, which are even at this time, slowly accepting the doctrine of the persistence of matter in a spiritual as well as in a material sense.[39]

In article after article, John showed the parallels of the truths of science and the revelations of God to Joseph Smith.

Joseph Smith as Scientist was republished in book and manual form many times for nearly a century.[40] In 1908 and 1920 the YMMIA used it as their lesson manual. In those early years, John completed the first concordance of the Doctrine and Covenants, a ten-year project that was published in 1906 as a volume of 205 pages under the copyright of Joseph F. Smith, trustee-in-trust for the Church.[41] On 31 December 1906, John recorded in his journal, "Finished lessons for Y.L.M.I.A. Walked down town w. Leah. Went to bed early. Thank God for this year. In spite of Markie's death it has been a very happy one. Things accomplished: MSS for J.S. as Scientist finished. Y.W.M.I.A. manual written. D&C. Concordance printed. Agrl Dept. at B.Y.U. placed on firm basis. Articles galore. Phosphate deposits sold. Arid Farm placed on safe basis."

KELVIN AND THE ORIGIN OF MAN

A few months after John became president of the ACU in the fall of 1907, he wrote a tribute entitled "Lord Kelvin, the God-Fearing." It was well received across the Church and seemed to trigger deeper trust from President Smith. Lord Kelvin was ranked with the world's greatest men of science, certainly "the greatest of all living students of nature."[42] John felt that Kelvin's death was an opportunity to recognize his closeness to Latter-day Saint teachings, particularly on the origin of life. Kelvin wrote: (1) "Careful enough scrutiny has, in every case up to the present day, discovered life as antecedent to life. Dead matter cannot become living without coming under the influence of matter previously alive." (2) "I confess to being deeply impressed by the evidence put before us . . . that life proceeds from life, and from nothing but life." (3) "How then did life originate on the earth? Tracing the physical history of the earth backwards, on strict dynamical principles, we are brought to the red-hot melted globe on which no life could exist. Hence, when the earth was first fit for life, there was no living thing on it."[43] After a review of Kelvin's ideas, John added:

Not only did Lord Kelvin believe that God lives and rules, but he had no sympathy with the idle notion of the day that life began upon this earth and will disappear with death. He believed in the eternity of life, and that life had come to this earth from other heavenly bodies. True, he did not understand the full philosophy of life's beginnings on this earth, but certainly with all the power at his command as the great scientist of his day, he refuted many of the modern theories which teach the origin of life on this earth without the intervention of an overruling Providence.

. . . Lord Kelvin did not believe in the origin of life without the assistance of God, yet he makes himself a great deal clearer in the somewhat long extract which follows. Carefully read, this paragraph will be found to teach that life is eternal; that life on this earth came from other spheres; that the law of natural selection is imperfect, and does not account for the variety of living things; that the law of evolution is true only as it conforms to the law of progression; that the whole of nature teaches the existence of a great designer or great governing power; and that finally, the power of free agency encircles our lives.[44]

This tribute appeared in the April 1908 *Improvement Era.* In November 1909 the official statement of the First Presidency entitled "The Origin of Man" was published. Many years later, in compiling the *Messages of the First Presidency,* James R. Clark found an association between the two articles. He noted that the First Presidency's official statement "opens with the sentence: 'Inquiries arise from time to time respecting the attitude of the Church of Jesus Christ of Latter-day Saints upon questions which, though not vital from a doctrinal standpoint, are closely connected with the fundamental principles of salvation.' This sentence seems to indicate that (1) the statement was being made to answer repeated inquiry on the subject the statement treats and (2) that the subject of the inquiries may be closely connected to vital doctrines of the Church."

Clark concluded that since the *Improvement Era* was an official organ of the Church and so widely read, some of the statements in the Widtsoe article were responsible for many of the "inquiries . . . respecting the attitude of the Church" on the subject. John's final paragraph read, "Does 'Mormonism' agree with the sane talks of Lord Kelvin? All who understand it will say, yes. The science of the world is, and can be no more than one phase of the everlasting gospel of Jesus Christ which embraces all truth."[45]

As John's career advanced, his contributions to science became more renowned worldwide. Through those years his contributions to the *Era* increased, covering the topics of science, Church doctrine, and Church history. There were articles on the authenticity of the restoration scriptures, the importance of the gospel and education, the need and development of teachers of spiritual inspiration, the causes of war, and the effects of the gospel on human lives. He published sixty-four articles in the *Improvement Era* prior to his call to the apostleship in 1921. In those busy early years, his pen pressed onward with inspired intensity, driven as much in the domain of his religious beliefs as in the domain of his scientific beliefs. The search for truth and the articulation of its principles, whether in fields of science or religion, was to him one passion and one duty.

17

PRESIDENT OF THE UNIVERSITY OF UTAH

———————————◼———————————

I N the early 1900s, the University of Utah found itself fettered by growing tensions between the faculty, the president, and the board of regents. Many critical decisions were made by the president and the board without due consultation with the faculty. At the center of the controversy were decisions involving faculty retention, advancement and promotion, and academic freedom. The consequences of the decisions made were less serious than the blatant disregard of the faculty. In the spring of 1915 the aggravation peaked with the resignation of seventeen professors and eventually that of President Joseph T. Kingsbury. The "unholy row" in Utah's capital city drew the attention of the entire nation.

Two and a half years after their arrival in the Salt Lake Valley, the first Mormon settlers created the University of Utah (then Deseret). Their efforts in the face of privation and struggle made an important statement about the values of Utah's people. For many years the university's main function was to oversee the educational system of Utah Territory. Hence, one of the main focuses of the university was training teachers. Dr. John R. Park was elected president in 1869. Under his administration the school became a university in fact as well as in name.

Aerial view of the new campus (post-1894), taken in the 1920s. This photo shows how the campus looked while John A. Widtsoe was president.

He was succeeded in 1894 by Dr. James E. Talmage, who served as president until 1897, when Dr. Joseph T. Kingsbury was elected. The university increased rapidly in enrollment and scholastic achievement. On the surface, things appeared to be moving splendidly under Kingsbury's administration.

Dirty Linen and the "Unholy Row"

Kingsbury was described as "cautious and conservative. He was especially sensitive to off-campus criticism and quick to seek appeasement."[1] "The faculty . . . had no regular means of contact or communication with the Board excepting through the President, who in practice came to conduct himself as a representative of the Board rather than as a spokesman for the faculty. Thus he sowed seeds of discontent."[2]

Because of this mistrust of Kingsbury, the faculty felt compelled to seek a clear definition of their rights and powers. In 1906 a code committee was chosen to clarify faculty rules, bylaws, and regulations that

The Central Building or Administration Building in 1914, the year it was finished. It was renamed the John R. Park Building in 1919 in honor of Dr. Park, who was U of U president from 1869 to 1894. It is the building in which the central administration of the university is housed.

had been adopted over time. Although some problems were resolved, tensions increased.

On 13 September 1913, the faculty presented a petition signed by Dr. Joseph F. Merrill, director of the school of mines, and forty-six other faculty members. It wasn't until December that the board even considered the petition and then only long enough to table it indefinitely. In the petition the faculty expressed their concern that the board was limiting the "proper freedom of the individual instructors" enough to make them question their "security of tenure of office."[3] They expressed further outrage that there had been a "lack of mutual understanding"[4] between the two parties, so they asked for occasional meetings with the board to consider questions that addressed their concerns. Though the petition was signed by most of the university faculty, it had little impact on the board. The discontent grew, and public awareness spread. When the matter was addressed by a student speaker in the June 1914 Commencement, an angered governor wrote to the board of regents expressing his fear of taxpayers' reactions.

Early in 1915, discord in the whole campus community erupted. On 26 February, Kingsbury informed two professors and two instructors that they would not be reappointed. On 2 March, a mass meeting of the student body was held. A petition was signed by more than half the student body to "strongly disapprove of the President's action and petition the board of regents to investigate the reasons and motives for the removal of these men and make public the results of the investigation."[5] The situation intensified with the announcement that George M. Marshall would be demoted and replaced by Osborne J. P. Widtsoe, principal and teacher of English in the Latter-Day Saints' High School. Because Osborne was a prominent member of the LDS Church, and the dismissed faculty members were neither LDS nor from Utah, many people felt there was interference from the Church. That fear was long regarded the "lingering ghost" that always arose when problems plagued the university.

On 5 March 1915 the Alumni Association and the Senate passed resolutions to form committees to call on the board for a formal investigation. Kingsbury eventually explained that the actions were taken against the professors because they had worked against the university administration. The board justified its actions, claiming that the breach between the faculty members and the president was such that "one or the other must go."[6]

On 17 March 1915, Kingsbury's proposal was passed and the four men were dismissed. Because of this decision, fourteen members of the faculty submitted their resignations immediately and others followed in succeeding days.

The resignations brought repercussions throughout the community, but the board created its own faculty relations committee to demonstrate their desire to bring fairness to the controversies. A "peace meeting" between the citizens' committee and the faculty relations committee was held on 14 April, but the board refused to reconsider its actions, and the reconciliation was stalled.

In April the matter was investigated privately by the American Association of University Professors (AAUP). Several notables from Johns Hopkins, Columbia, the University of Pennsylvania, and Princeton formed the investigating committee. They found that of the four charges the president had leveled against the dismissed faculty members, one was entirely without basis, and the other three had "no . . . grounds for such action."[7] They further found that the president and the board had demonstrated that an unfavorable opinion shared in private conversation had become grounds for dismissals. As to the allegations of outside influence by the LDS Church, they stated:

> This charge does not, as a rule appear among the reasons originally given by the resigning professors for their action. But it is clear from subsequent statements that in the case of several of these teachers one of the principal motives for resignation was that the President had of late been subject to increasing pressure to fill important positions in the Faculty with men selected, not primarily on grounds of scholarship and teaching ability but because of their connection with the religious denomination to which the majority of the people of the State, and a majority of the Board of Regents, adhere. . . . It was further believed by some of the resigning professors that the President had more than once yielded to this pressure.[8]

On 27 March 1915 the board decided that a faculty committee should be formed to facilitate harmony between faculty and administration. That committee recommended creating an administrative council composed of the president and deans (as ex-officio members) and faculty members numbering two more than the ex-officio members.[9] This administrative council, subject to the approval of the board, was to determine all matters of educational policy and administration, including requests for appropriations, the use of funds, and the appointment, promotion, demotion, or removal of faculty members.

President Kingsbury and Dean James L. Gibson toured several of the eastern universities and readily replaced the faculty members who had resigned. The reconstituted faculty expressed willingness to work with the administrative council and Kingsbury. But when the widespread conviction that Kingsbury would be a continuing source of ill will and prejudice was conveyed to him by members of the board, he submitted a letter of resignation in the board meeting of 20 January 1916:

> I believe that a condition, if possible, should be brought about by which all the people of Utah could unite in building up a strong University commensurate at least with the wealth and dignity of the state.
>
> To be sure that I shall not stand in the way in effecting this

desirable end, I have decided not to be a candidate for reappointment as President. . . .

I trust that I shall always lend my influence for the advancement of the University in the future as I have done thru the many years of the past.[10]

The board accepted his resignation and voted to designate him president emeritus and professor of chemistry for the 1916–17 school year.[11] Moments later, Regent Van Cott, with Mattson's second, moved that John A. Widtsoe be employed as president of the University of Utah during the year 1916–17.[12]

BOARD CONSIDERATION

John A. Widtsoe, a veteran of Utah crisis resolution and educational leadership, was only a few valleys away, at the ACU in Logan. He had already successfully quelled the discontent arising from the consolidation controversy. The ACU had become a model of cooperation and accomplishment, and many saw President Widtsoe as the "man who practically made the Agricultural College."[13] The university's board of regents recognized that his administrative skills, his scholarly pursuits and attainments, and his educational experience would enable him to bring peace to their university and raise its scholastic status.

After nine years under Widtsoe's presidency, things were going well at the ACU. The scholarship of the faculty rivaled that of any similar institution; the college, world renowned, had obtained the best available equipment. Debts were paid, and the ACU was financially stable. John was just forty-four years old, and a smooth and successful life of discovery with a reputation among the most notable scientists in the world lay ahead of him in his beloved Logan. Another call to manage dirty state laundry was not what he had anticipated.

While the majority of the board of regents strongly favored his appointment, there was stubborn opposition. Some concerned his qualifications, but most of it was a reaction to the activities of the majority of the regents in the selection and notification process:

We are opposed to and protest against the election of Dr. Widtsoe to the Presidency of the University of Utah:

First: Because we are not advised nor have we had the opportunity of advising ourselves as to his ability to fill this position.

Second: Because no opportunity has been given to consider other available men. This matter has not been taken up with an open mind, nor has due and proper deliberation been given to it. As far as we are informed no one other than Dr. Widtsoe has been given any consideration.

Third: Assuming the ability of Dr. Widtsoe, we believe his election is ill-advised and not for the best interests of the University. We believe that a man can be found who is as well or better fitted than Dr. Widtsoe, of greater experience and against whom the objections that will no doubt be raised with respect to Dr. Widtsoe, would not exist.

We are opposed to and object to the manner of Dr. Widtsoe's election. Not only was the decision to ask for the resignation of Dr. Kingsbury coupled with the election of Dr. Widtsoe as his successor, but Dr. Widtsoe was decided upon, the matter settled, the position offered to him and accepted by him without any consultation with us. . . . We believe that the action of the majority offering it to him without discussion by the whole Board and without investigation as to other available men, and without the knowledge of a number of the members of the Board is not only in poor taste and with scant courtesy, but in direct violation of the spirit of the law creating the University of Utah and providing for its government by a Board of Regents each with equal authority.[14]

The covert activities of members of the board of regents became fodder for reporters of the campus newspaper, the *Utah Chronicle*. In criticizing the activities of the board, the paper reported, "For three years the regents have been discussing the selection of a new president and . . . among those whom they have been considering was Dr. Widtsoe."[15] At such times public speculation usually outstretches the consideration of those who carefully study the matter. Chamberlain's history of the University of Utah addresses the concealed activities of board members on the matter. "It was obvious and admitted that the majority members of the Board had previously caucused and that Dr. Widtsoe knew well in advance that he was to be nominated."[16]

Of the regents, Porter felt that the board had acted too hastily and that a more thorough search should have been made; Gemmell said that "if President Kingsbury was not to be reappointed, the Board should seek a President outside the State"[17]; Van Cott had also considered that but had concluded that "Dr. Widtsoe, through his wide knowledge of the state, was best fitted for the position."[18] Justifying the majority's actions, Major Young said, "We felt that it was of the first importance to the growth and development of the school that its president should be a man thoroughly and intimately acquainted with the people of the state, and should have their confidence and support; that he should be well informed as to our resources, our commercial, agricultural and mining problems, and deeply versed, without prejudices, in the sociological differences that, to a certain extent, unhappily, have marked our history."[19]

Some felt that John was chosen because of his LDS affiliation. Anthon H. Lund, a member of the Church's First Presidency, denied any Church influence. "It had been asserted in some quarters that the Church had been using its influence to secure their appointments. This, Mr. Lund said, he wanted to emphatically deny. Nothing of the kind had occurred, he said. The matter of the appointment of both men, in fact, had originated from outside the church."[20] There is no indication of Church contact in John's journal. Despite opposition, the proposal carried with the majority of two votes.[21]

A DIFFICULT DECISION

Once again a heavy cloud of controversy hung over John's head. Again it was his Church affiliation, not his academic qualifications, that created tensions over his suitability for the position. Having set the ACU on a steady course, was it now time to move to a larger battlefield? He wrote, "It seemed that perhaps I could go on for some years without the strenuous labors that had taxed my powers to the utmost. I was about to relax a little."[22]

Before responding to the board's invitation, John mulled over the positive and negative factors to be considered. His salary was to be $2,000 less, and his expenses were to be considerably higher. Many of his interests for later life that were tied to the agricultural work of the college seemed at peril. More serious was the disrepute of the university and the commotion in the board and the faculty. He appreciated the confidence of most of the board of regents, but he hesitated at taking the reigns in rescuing the university so mired in controversy and conflict. Acting on the advice of his closest friends and that of Leah, and out of his sense of duty to his state, John accepted the offer.

The ACU board of trustees was understandably chagrined. They valued John highly. "A new man, with abilities equal to those of Dr. Widtsoe, . . . would require several years time to become as thoroughly acquainted with local conditions as was Dr. Widtsoe."[23] In a special meeting they raised his salary another thousand dollars to entice him to stay in Logan. On 7 February 1916, after much deliberation, John resigned the presidency of the ACU.

> I will not deny that my heart is heavy as I write, for I am leaving much. . . . Only the deep conviction that, just now, my best efforts belong elsewhere could compel me to take this step. I believe that by entering the new field that lies before me I can, at this particular time, be of greater service to our beloved state than by remaining in my present happy and congenial surroundings.[24]

> I can not really tell you how I feel unless I let my feelings overcome me. This is not the time or place for that. I love this institution. I believe I know it better than any man, even the superintendent of buildings; I have seen these buildings go up brick by brick. I climbed to the second story of the first building, the present south wing of this structure, when it was being constructed and scratched my initials in the sandstone. My best and dearest friends are on this faculty. I am proud and happy in my associations with this student body and the ones that have been here before you. It is a sad wrench to leave all this, but I am going into the new place to do my level best there and hope to find much joy in the work.[25]

In a letter to F. J. Alway of the University of Minnesota, John gave further insight: "You must know what a wrench it is for me to sever my connections with the Utah Agricultural College, but I hope it will turn out for the best. I shall not cease my agricultural investigations, but shall continue them as far as my time will permit and I hope also in my new work I may find some place for the ideals that govern the agricultural colleges."[26]

On 7 February 1916, John accepted the presidency of the University of Utah.[27] Some voiced opposition but many more heralded his selection. A Salt Lake City newspaper lauded his scientific reputation: "All the world has read of it and it has and is playing a great part in the conquering of the world's deserts and in carrying forward man's great conquest of drought."[28] Ralph V. Chamberlain, a member of the faculty and historian of the University of Utah, noted:

> I am writing to express my pleasure and satisfaction on hearing of the election of Dr. Widtsoe as president of the University of Utah. Many alumni besides myself would have felt serious disappointment had a man been brought from outside when within the state there is such splendid material. Dr. Widtsoe is by instincts and training a scholar of the first rank as well as a proved executive leader who has the advantage of "knowing his parish" thoroughly. He knows well the modern university, its purposes and tendencies; and I feel every confidence that under his guidance a distinct period of solid development along lines of the highest ideals of scholarship and education will ensue. I much doubt whether another man could be secured anywhere who could win any longer and maintain a more united and sustained support.[29]

Letters of congratulation poured in. True to their friendship over many years, Kingsbury was first to write. "You were elected to the Presidency of the University of Utah last night. Permit me to congratulate you and wish you success in your new position."[30] John replied, "Upon my return from Monroe I found your letter of January the twenty-first. Let me express my deep appreciation of the fact that you were the first to write me after the Regents had decided on their course of action. I shall not attempt to write you at this time and tell you of the admiration in which I hold you and the understanding I have of the splendid work you have done for the State of Utah during your long life of service."[31]

In response to a letter from D. R. Allen, secretary of the board of regents, John wrote, "Accept my sincere thanks. . . . In the new work that lies before me I shall desire only to be of service to our State and shall ask all the lovers of the State to give me all the assistance that they can for only by united action can we achieve great work. . . . Like you, I am sad to think that Dr. Kingsbury could not have been continued in the office. I have a deep and affectionate respect for Dr. Kingsbury."[32]

It was to be expected that L. H. Bailey, famed dean of agriculture at Cornell and firm advocate of John's agricultural genius, would comment: "Let me congratulate you on your appointment to the Presidency of the University of Utah. I hope that this will be all to your liking. I cannot quite reconcile myself with the idea of your going out of the agricultural college field but I shall hope that it is all for the best."[33] John's response to Bailey perhaps best explains his reasoning:

> I am not a deserter nor am I tired of the splendid work in which I have been engaged all the days of my life since I came out of college, however much it must seem so to many of my friends who have heard of my transfer.
>
> A very peculiar and urgent educational situation has arisen in this State and I have decided that it is practically my duty as a good citizen of the State to lay aside my personal feelings and to serve our State University for a few years. I want to assure you, of all men, that in making this change I am not actuated by selfish motives. I may be making a huge mistake, but if I am it is because I cannot see things clearly. I believe it will be for the best good of the educational institutions of the state and ultimately for my own good to make the proposed change. I can say to you that when the change was first proposed I simply laughed at it. Only after some time did I come to the conclusion that I must try the new work.
>
> I hope that I shall be able to continue my agricultural work. Whether it is possible for me to do so without being connected with the Agricultural College remains, of course, to be seen. I have many plans. I should like to realize some of them. I am too old and moreover have not the slightest desire to work up another field to which I could devote my energies during the remainder of my life. I am going

to [stick] to the old specialty, though I suspect that I shall have to find new ways of working at it.[34]

Responding to a letter from W. M. Jardine, director of the Kansas Experiment Station, John described more deep feelings for the ACU:

> After much debating I have decided to accept the University Presidency. The educational issues in our State are such that I believe it is my duty even at a personal sacrifice just now to accept the position and do what I can in behalf of the University. It is a wrench such as I have never experienced before in my life. I love the work I am in, I belong in it and had no greater ambition than to continue in it until it should be placed on younger shoulders. In any event, I want to say to you that in my spare time, and I hope I may have some, I will be able to devote part of it to my favorite agricultural studies; and if I do anything at all for the University it will be to make it acquainted with the fundamental, important, educational spirit which is the dominating one of the agricultural colleges.[35]

Offsetting discouragement from friend or foe were the opinions of noteworthy observers. The *Journal of Education*, a national publication, wrote, "President Widtsoe has made a college of National reputation at Logan. As an author, as a scholar, as a specialist, as one skillful in handling problems . . . he is one of the distinguished administrators and leaders of the country. He will come to the state university with the prestige of ripe scholarship from Harvard and of uninterrupted success in educational affairs. Whoever thinks in large units in Utah, or in the rest of America, will welcome him to the larger field."[36]

A local journalist wrote, "A more capable, scholarly, and able man for the position than Dr. Widtsoe could not be found in the United States. The state and the University are to be heartily congratulated on securing him."[37]

Because of his lifelong devotion to Church leaders, a letter from President Heber J. Grant was much appreciated, especially for the message it bore:

> Permit me to tender to you my sincere and heartfelt congratulations that you have been chosen as the president of the chief educa-

tional institution of our state. I consider the honor one that you have justly earned, and I am pleased that you saw fit to accept this position. I believe, as you have stated in your letter that was given to the press, that it opens to you a wider field for usefulness. Knowing your great ability and capacity as an executive and instructor, I rejoice in having an enlarged field of labor given to you. I know of nothing that has been more pleasing to me than to have so many of our Utah boys "make good," who have gone East and prepared themselves for usefulness.[38]

John's devotion to the Church was known, and while he did not desire to parade it before the public, he never felt it necessary or desirable to make his allegiance a secret. To him there was no church/state conflict in the performance of his responsibilities. While he carefully honored his responsibility to the state and the federal constitution, he also carefully honored his faith in seeking divine guidance in his daily activities. It was obtaining such religious liberty that led to the very constitution some felt he could not abide by. In his desire to do well in his new appointment, he wrote, "The die having been cast, I set to work. First I asked the Presidency of the Church to bless me that I might be of service. That was not mixing Church and State, but asking through authorized channels for higher help. The administrator who does not ask for such help, loses much. There were things to be done in the University before the next year's opening, which the incoming man alone could do. The College needed the usual attention. As a result, my health taxed me. With my wife I sailed in May for Hawaii, land of beauty, to secure a three months rest."[39]

Before leaving for Hawaii, John sent a letter to the board of regents of the university asking that the salary budget be approved, that the medical school be continued, and that Kingsbury be in full authority during the months that Widtsoe would be gone concerning matters pertaining to the next school year.[40] By early August the Widtsoes had their formal move well under way. He wrote Major Young, "Hard at work getting ready for the move to Salt Lake and shall be there ready to stay not later than the last of this month."[41]

18

WORK AT THE UNIVERSITY OF UTAH

Since his years at Harvard, John had become a major proponent of "practical education." He believed that good education was basic to the survival and prosperity of the nation. He wrote, "Education is a producer of wealth, in a large sense, which leads to prosperity, which in turn leads to a high civilization."[1] He took that credo with him to the university, where he preached the importance of useful, practical, and moral education: "We recognize that the permanence and prosperity of our republic depend upon the proper education of all citizens. . . . Schools with their teacher and courses of study become therefore of paramount importance in the conduct of the affairs of our State."[2] John had a keen sense for the broad responsibilities of educators, especially those in Utah: "The longer I am in the teaching business, the more strongly I feel that the work derived from the text book and the technical lecture is only a part, though perhaps it may be a large part, of the service that we are to render the students that come to us for instruction. It is only upon a basis of moral life, a return to what men are pleased to call religion, that we shall remove from the earth the chaos which now threatens it."[3]

The importance of fundamental educational values seemed only to increase with his experience. In 1919 John wrote, "The universities are facing the problem of how best to steer by instructional methods the young people of our [up] and coming generations into safe channels of life activity. I think I have never in my educational work felt the responsibility of the labor so much as I do at the present time."[4] John taught the faculty that the directing and controlling influences of the institution are the timely virtues mothers teach around the fireside: "A hearty kindliness towards all; respect for each other; the trust that each man is doing his best in his own imperfect way; the willingness to speak good rather than evil of all men; the steady hope that good is gaining daily triumph over evil; and the continuous, unchanging love of truth in all our walk and talk."[5]

John looked with confidence on the university. He told Senator Smoot, "Without question, the University of Utah is destined to become [the] great intellectual center of the Intermountain country. . . . Its attendance will increase very rapidly, and its need for ground increase correspondingly."[6] To Regent VanCott he added, "I feel so confident if we can preserve peace at the University of Utah for a few years and be successful in building, slowly, perhaps, but securely, toward increased service, we shall secure, for the State and for the West, in the University a most magnificent educational machine, the reputation of which ultimately will become equal to the great Universities of the land."[7]

In taking the reins, John was not a novice in dealing with the kind of faculty tensions that had rocked the university. He had twice been the victim of assaults on academic freedom. He was a good friend of President Kingsbury, and he abhorred the conflict that had brought his dismissal. That Osborne, his brother, was a figure in the issue added to his anguish. "Into this mess I was thrown by my acceptance of the presidency of the university," he later recalled. "It would be my job to restore order and good feeling in addition to performing the normal duties of the position. Clearly, I did not relish the task. For nearly sixteen years I had been placed in positions where human nerves were bare. I was weary of that sort of work."[8]

Before undertaking the task, John sought a blessing from the First

Presidency as he had done before his return to the problems in Logan. Those blessings fueled the energy with which John pursued his difficult tasks. When the work was especially daunting, a lift from spiritual advisors was much appreciated.

> In a late afternoon of a warm, sultry day in August or September, I sat in my office rather tired after the day's work. The University of Utah had had internal dissensions which had been fanned by enemies into a nationwide scandal. I had been called in to assist others who were trying to return the institution and its work to a normal condition. It was the third time in my life that I had been obliged to serve my state in such a capacity. I was weary. Just then there was a knock upon the door, and in walked George Albert Smith. He said, "I am on the way home after my day's work. I thought of you and the problems that you are expected to solve. I came in to comfort you and to bless you."
>
> That was the way of George Albert Smith. . . . Of course I appreciated that; I shall never forget it. We talked together for awhile; we parted, he went home. My heart was lifted. I was weary no longer.[9]

Despite the uplift from his friends, John had battles with discouragement. He wrote, "At this moment, the U.S.A.C. looked upon me somewhat as a deserter, and the U. of U. looked upon my arrival with doubtful eyes. There was only one thing to do, to go to work with a smile and trust the corrective power of time and honest effort."[10] Some of that corrective power and honest effort were reflected in a message to the campus: "A University that does not advance is useless. . . . For true progress in any institution, the regents must increase in their sympathetic understanding of the University; the faculty must increase in scholarship, teaching power and sympathy with the students; the alumni must work harder for their alma mater, and the student body must increase its confidence in the faculty and regents and become more and more efficient in its class room and outside activities."[11] He focused his efforts on four distinct groups, the board of regents, the faculty, the student body, and the alumni.

THE BOARD OF REGENTS

One of the pillars on which John's success would stand was his relationship with the board of regents. He had been successful with the board of trustees at the ACU and knew the importance of such relationships. Many of the disruptions that had taken John to the U of U could be ascribed to the confusion of the board:

> It did not take long to discover some of the causes of the late upheaval. There was a State act authorizing the establishment of the university, another dealing with the composition of the Board of Regents, and several lesser acts dealing with various university matters, such as the schools of education and mines. Then there were the biennial appropriations, with incidental requirements. These legislative acts had been observed by the university officials. But, there was no set of Board regulations, derived as by-laws from the general State laws. Nothing had been crystallized as to relationship among regents, faculty, and other employees. Almost my first task, even before entering officially upon my University duties, was to formulate a series of Board rules and regulations for the guidance of all connected with the institution. These rules were printed and have been in force ever since, with such amendments as the years have brought. The consequent certainty and order made me feel easier about my work, and, in fact, were a protection to the university family.[12]

John, blessed with a penchant for diplomacy, brought order to the university community through an understanding of defined administrative roles and adherence to specific responsibilities within those roles. He was a conciliator, yet he was driven by his convictions and usually achieved his purposes. He wrote to one of the regents, "I have tried to stand squarely to what appears to me to be for the best interests of the Institution. . . . I have learned in my administrative experience that one of the chief rewards of serving in positions where criticism and misunderstanding will always have to be met, is the enduring friendships so often established between the administrative servant of the Board and the members of the Board themselves."[13]

THE FACULTY

John immediately set out to establish goodwill with the faculty. One of his earliest acts was to spend three days at the university meeting with deans, department heads, and faculty members. He announced that there would be no personnel changes for the coming year.[14]

> Naturally, the faculty were ill at ease. The fight had unnerved them. Many of them, peaceful scholars, were shaken deeply by the events that had invaded their quiet academic domain. Then, to add to their misfortune, they were to deal with a new president, strange to them, whose ways might add to their bewilderment. At the most ordinary contact, these people quivered with anxiety. However, as they discovered that open sincerity was to guide university affairs, they settled down to their work at ease. The past was gradually for-gotten. The new events of the day entered the center of the stage.
>
> Other faculty members sought to capitalize on the situation. There were positions to be filled; promotions to be made; and increased salaries to be gained. Human nature is in full operation on college campuses as elsewhere. One professor who had been much trusted by the board during the upheaval was bitterly disappointed that he was not chosen president. He was thenceforth anything but a supporter of the new administration. Before I had actually entered upon my university duties, but was clearing the way, one of the deans who also had ambitions requested me to sign a document which gave him full control over more than one-half of the faculty. My refusal left him soured. Deans and departmental heads have their definite, impor-tant duties, but for the welfare of the institution they must not be allowed to usurp the duties of the president.[15]

John sought a collegial relationship with the faculty. In a letter to each of them he solicited suggestions. "I realize thoroughly that the wis-dom of this Institution is not centered in one man or in one office. . . . I ask you, therefore, to take a few minutes of your time to suggest to me any views that you may have concerning the greater welfare of the Institution. I am sure that every member of the Faculty can suggest something that may be considered with profit in the building of the

University of Utah."[16] The responses demonstrated fresh trust in their president.

John's administrative experience enabled him to see problems that could engender anxiety among the faculty: "There was much difference in opinion as to procedure and decisions. Former decisions had been forgotten or ignored. Nearly every question led to debate. I took the time, therefore, to prepare a code of faculty regulations. This code settled many a question in faculty meetings. . . . This code has been kept up, with necessary amendments, through the years. With these Board and faculty statutes in hand, progress became easier. Much time, temper, and energy are lost because of uncertainty."[17]

That code was a thirty-page document entitled *Regulations of the Faculty of the University of Utah.* It delineated the rights of the faculty in governing the university, including the right to regulate the requirements for admission, degrees, and certificates; the right to decide upon curricula; and almost every other aspect of successfully achieving the mission of the university. The president of the university was chairman of the faculty.[18] To implement decisions recommended by the faculty, an administrative council was created. This council comprised the president and several deans and professors.[19] They met frequently and earnestly sought to represent and implement the desires of the faculty as a whole.[20]

President Widtsoe always tried to clarify his view in affirming his earnestness toward them: "Am I right in this understanding of the situation? Is this the view that you hold of the function of the University relationship?"[21] He trusted the judgment of faculty members: "This office is looking to you for the recommendation of someone to fill the vacancy now existing in your Department."[22] He welcomed information from the faculty: "I am always glad to receive reports that will help to keep us in touch with what goes on in any or all of the departments of the Institution."[23] His genuine concern and his ability to communicate that concern facilitated success with the faculty, as can be seen from this passage in a letter to John about a personal problem: "I am particularly glad that you had a long talk with her. She has written me that the talk was extremely gratifying to her and she leaves with the best of feeling.

You are so signally successful in such conversation, that I regret that you aren't three or four people so that we might all talk to you more and longer, for those personal conferences with you are more enlightening and productive of more real understanding and cooperating than any number of committee meetings. But I know too that one lone man could scarcely have more conferences in twenty-four hours than you do as it is."[24]

John was quick to commend laudable efforts. He was especially helpful in times of personal and family crises. His natural instincts to communicate with the faculty, his desire to treat them with fairness, and his congenial nature quickly brought good faculty relations. "The great majority of the faculty," he wrote, "were excellent, high-minded men and women, sometimes caught in the net of their prejudices, but always honorable. For these my associates for five years, I have retained sincere admiration, and many are counted among my dear friends."[25]

John felt the scholarship of the faculty should rival that of any university in the nation, noting, "The University of Utah is a young, rapidly-growing institution, in a young and rapidly growing section of our country, and backed by an education loving people. If the right kind of people are gathered in this Institution, we should be able to do a great deal for ourselves and for the State. There is no reason why we should not here in this Institution gradually build a world wide reputation."[26] "Only in an atmosphere of scholarship can true education survive."[27]

The desire for a highly qualified faculty required a strategy to assure success. John wrote, "Special attention was given to the scholarship of the faculty of the institution. From early pioneer days, higher academic degrees were none too common in the institutions of America at the time I served the U. of U. Even Harvard, the mother of them all, had only a handful of men on its faculty who carried early doctorates. Therefore, I did as I had in Logan, encouraged young men to go away to study and receive their degrees and for everybody to maintain the high standard of scholarship in their teaching."[28]

John traveled throughout the nation searching for faculty and boosting the image of the university. To a colleague at Harvard he wrote, "I believe I heard you say that you have not been West. You want to take a trip out here and see the part of our great country which in time, because of its resources and climate, will probably become the most important section of our land. The N.E.A. meets in Salt Lake City next month. We shall be glad to see you here."[29]

Excellent teaching was continually emphasized. John wrote to the dean of the school of education, "It is conceded that chemistry, physics, mathematics, and even the principles of mechanics no longer make an engineer: in addition he must be taught the application of these sciences to his business. It should be even more necessary to fit the prospective teacher, who not only has to make truth applicable to life, but who has the special business of helping in the growth, ripening, and maturing of the human mind as the instrument by which our future progress is to be accomplished."[30] He felt strongly about students succeeding in all classes with ordinary diligence: "As I have previously said, in many a science, the beginning courses are so taught as if the whole class were intending to become candidates for the Ph.D. degree in the subject. Students fall out in despair. . . . He is a poor teacher who confuses his students or fails to make his subject interesting."[31]

In an address to the faculty, John spoke of his expectations: "The man who gives of himself to his class, who stimulates students into new desire to learn or to act, who awakens within students greater respect and love for truth, who becomes a worthy example that students desire to follow—such a man usually teaches well. . . . They [students] must go out from us possessed of useful facts held by disciplined minds, clean and helpful, lovers of their fellow men, tolerant of the issues. . . . When the last measure is taken . . . our success will be determined by the degree to which we have produced such a generation of manhood."[32]

In remarks delivered at the university's centennial celebration in 1950, thirty years after leaving, John again addressed the university's teaching mission: "A college degree does not make a teacher; it only helps develop the inherent teaching power of the individual. Men differ. Some are teachers; some are research men. It is an educational crime to subject students to the meanderings of a person who cannot teach or will not learn to do so. . . . Teachers in an educational institution must above all other things be lovers of men."[33]

John's efforts to increase unity, scholarship, and quality teaching in the faculty were gratifying. As his term ended he wrote, "I recognize the fidelity and fine service rendered by the Faculty of the University during this period. My personal associations with the Faculty members have been most delightful. The support of the Faculty has been the one great reward as duties have come and gone."[34]

THE ALUMNI

A critical pillar in John's plan for progress in the university was increased participation of the alumni. They were a large group, and their influence was more significant than their numbers would tell. But they too had to be won over. John recognized that his appointment strained their devotion: "For years there had been a fighting rivalry between the U. of U. and the U.S.A.C. The U. alumni had been inclined to look with contemptuous eyes upon the 'cow college' in Logan. To have the U.S.A.C. President chosen to head their school was a somewhat bitter pill to swallow. . . . Yet, I am happy to say that while I served the University, full support was given the institution by the alumni. . . . The U. alumni were a group of splendid, loyal men and women, in whose hands the destinies of the school could well have been trusted."[35]

THE STUDENTS

The student body was the final pillar in the outline Widtsoe gave to the board of regents. He felt that the students were the primary purpose for the university's existence.[36] As he began his first year, the student newspaper reported, "President John A. Widtsoe announced yesterday that he will reserve his time between 11 and 12 o'clock on every regular school day during the year for consultations with students. Anyone desiring to talk matters over with him will be welcomed at this time."[37] John's files are filled with letters to students. Every kind of hardship was addressed, but the most common contained ageless wisdom on advancing through the system. To one he wrote, "My advice to you is to decide upon your getting an education. Let nothing stand in the way of winning for yourself the trained mind and the abundant knowledge that a college education can give. As you go along in your work, you will discover the tendencies of your gifts, and gradually, before you know it, you will be in the field for which you are best fitted and which, therefore, in all likelihood will bring you ultimately the greatest return."[38] To another he said, "I am very glad to hear of your educational ambitions, and hope that they may be fully realized. Whether they are or not depends entirely upon yourself and the degree of ambition which you maintain throughout your life."[39] To a third: "I am glad that you are going to gather more knowledge and acquire more discipline of your mind, for in life's race, it will be the best equipment that you can possibly have."[40]

The president often assisted students from his own pocket, which made writing this letter painful: "It really grieves me to tell you that during this coming year I am afraid I shall not be able to lend money to any students. It grieves me doubly because I think it will be the first year in the last twenty-five years that I have not been able to use some money for such purposes. However, I have just built myself a little home under war prices, and have been under certain other very heavy expenses, which have made it necessary for me to borrow considerable sums of money, which I must repay during the year."[41] For many students he found financial help. That number grew so large that he organized a Faculty Committee on Student Employment.[42] Soon there followed a Faculty Committee on Boarding and Lodging Houses.[43]

Related to the problem of employment and upkeep while at the university was the matter of securing suitable employment after graduation. John again took personal interest in helping graduates find jobs, addressing them through the student newspaper: "I am especially anxious to give what help my office can render in placing all seniors in suitable positions. It is the intention of this office to make a business of this work and I regret that a suitable beginning has not been made this year. Some things, however, may still be done. I ask, therefore, that members of the senior class, who desire this office to assist them in securing proper employment, to file with my office a statement of their qualifications and desires."[44]

John believed in the university's social duty to students. Most student groups met off campus, so he worked to make the campus more

serviceable to them. Fraternities and sororities had garnered bad reputations, but he believed in the good in the individuals that comprised
them. Of one group he wrote, "From my personal knowledge of these
men, I can frankly say that they form a particularly strong student
organization. The men are of excellent character and reputation, coming from some of the best families of the State. I can personally vouch
for their excellent virtues."[45] To another group he wrote, "Fraternities
have within their hands the power to be of great service to the
Institution with which they may be connected, or they may also be a
detriment. I am very glad to be able to say that the disposition of the
members of the Phi Alpha Epsilon has always been to protect and help
the Institution and its administrative officers."[46]

While many complained at the pranks and mischief of fraternities
and sororities, John looked to the good and encouraged their members
by his support: "May I say to you that I am very greatly pleased with the
communication and the resolutions which you have taken. I believe
that as a result, we shall have fully as much college spirit as a result of
the Skull & Bones activities, without any after effects that will tend to
injure the Institution. . . . I want to say to you further that when initia-
tion stunts are in progress, if they do not offend the ordinary standards
of morality and good taste, I enjoy them immensely, and should be very
sorry to have the feeling back of the Skull and Bones society disappear
from the campus."[47] Widtsoe did hold the view that fraternities should
put off rushing students to their sophomore year, thereby enabling them
to first engage fully in the purpose of their schooling. He told the faculty, "Let us increase the number of social groups, with emphasis on the
class groups, and delay the time of pledging, and in a very short time,
the fraternity problem will cease to trouble us."[48]

Rules were worked out for association between fraternities and
sororities. While on the whole serious problems were infrequent, some
did arise. One foreign student, misunderstanding the intent of a student
prank, pulled a pistol on a group of his fellow students.[49] At another
time a group of sophomores had a row with a group of freshmen and
turned a fire hose on them inside a building.[50] In cases like these, John
proved to be an excellent administrator, often leaving the discipline up

to the students themselves. He wrote, "From the organization of the University there had been a tradition that there should be no smoking in the buildings or on the campus of the school. After the first World War many young men returned with the smoking habit. Frequent complaints were heard. . . . To settle the question I called for a mass meeting of all students and put the question up to them. Almost unanimously they voted to uphold the tradition against smoking and selected their own officers to find and discipline offenders."[51]

Of his personal relationship with the students, John felt that "with the students I always had cordial relations. Necessary discipline was received in the spirit in which it was given. Some remnants of uncollege practices were in operation. They were pretty much eradicated. I was a regular attendant at nearly all student affairs, athletic games, sports, dances, and other social functions. The visit might be very brief, but it had a good effect. There was no attempt to place the student body in [straitjackets]."[52]

His genuine interest in students did not go unnoticed. Upon his resignation, the students organized an assembly in his honor. Looking back he wrote, "It was great fun to labor with the student body."[53] In a related sense he wrote, "I have spent my life in endeavoring to save souls, chiefly the souls of young people. As a school teacher that has been my responsibility. My own children were nearly all taken from me, and that made it important that I devote myself to the children of other people."[54]

John's love for students was highlighted many years later by Richard L. Evans, who said, "What we haven't told is the endless hours of time he has given from his crowded days in the building of men, young and old, inspiring them to greater effort, giving them a thirst for knowledge and a high regard for truth."[55] Franklin S. Harris said, "Even though he was the highest official in the institution, he had the ability to get close to the individual student who was always inspired by his interest and his wise counsel. Today in every part of the country these former students are mourning his passing but feel gratitude in their hearts for what he has done for them."[56] David O. McKay added, "Elder Widtsoe is one of the rare men who knew how to praise. It is that

quality, I think, which has endeared him to so many tens of thousands
of young men and women. . . . It is this quality expressed, I repeat,
wherever merited, that has encouraged and stimulated many students,
who sought Brother Widtsoe's advice, and were encouraged thereby to
press on to achievement."[57]

19

WAR AND EPIDEMIC

———————————◼———————————

Though World War I broke out in 1914, the United States did not enter it until 1917, during John's first year as president of the university. He wrote, "The campus became a military camp. Male students were organized into an S.A.T.C.—Student Army Training Corps. The U. of U., just emerging from a war within itself, was now in a war of the nation. The experiences during this period were anything but happy. I have never found suitable words to express my feelings about war and its consequences. War is of the devil."[1] There was one positive impact— the war helped bring an end to the discordant elements that had divided the university.

"Pro-ally sentiment in the University of Utah, as in nearly all other universities of the country, developed more rapidly than among the general public."[2] Early in 1916 general preparedness brought some military activity on the campus, but the response was sluggish. Regent Richard W. Young, a major in the United States Army, backed a proposed system of military training at the university. In March, announcement was made of the formation of a Citizens Training Camp in Utah. University students were urged by the general committee to join the camp for the ensuing summer. Campus interests centered on preparedness, and in

The Student Army Training Corps (S.A.T.C.) in front of the Park Administration Building in October 1918. The corps is being addressed by Col. Wright. This photo portrays the military presence that dominated the campus during the war years (1916–1918).

March 1917, the students signed a petition "that a department of military science and tactics be established at the University of Utah."[3] The campus newspaper also reported great excitement among students, who felt that international relations in the United States had been weakened. The student newspaper went on to report that a previous plan for training students in military affairs was abandoned because of declining interest: "The men of that time probably thought the United States immune from attack or trouble or else they themselves were sufficiently prepared to defend their country. . . . The United States now realizes its perilous condition in world politics. The methods of warfare have changed. Men must be trained or the organization will be inefficient and likely to fall easy prey before an up-to-date fighting machine."[4]

Within a week it was reported that a student petition had been successful and that "President Widtsoe has already made application to the war department for an officer, and recruiting for actual activity will

Photo taken at the time of an S.A.T.C. retreat, October 1, 1918.

likely begin in a short time."[5] The department of military science and tactics was created just one week before the United States declared war. Despite the excitement at the university, the federal government "was not able to supply an officer to take charge of the military drilling, but soon gave the University a list of retired army officers who might be used in giving military work, the University to assume the financial responsibility involved."[6] Under these limitations the department of military science and tactics began its work. All male students attended regular military drill, and all women students reported for instruction in Red Cross or other preparedness work. University credit was given for all this training.

The faculty joined the war effort by pledging to "keep clear the light of learning before the eyes of the coming generation, so that, whether in war or peace, men and women of strong character shall be produced and the heritage of years not sink into oblivion." They continued, "To this end we do as a body and individually hereby renew and reaffirm our faith in the American institution of which we are a part."[7]

To further rally American sentiment for the war effort, the Division of Publicity in Washington, D.C., "called into service some fifty of the most distinguished writers of the country."[8] Among them was John A. Widtsoe, whom they asked to write an article on some appropriate aspect of the war. His response: "I shall be very glad indeed when the spirit moves or earlier to prepare something that may be of use in your propaganda. I am enclosing in this letter a circular just published by the University of Utah to show you that we are not hesitating at this Institution in our attempts to bring before the people the causes and meaning of the war."[9] The Treasury Department also asked him to "devote a portion of each address . . . to an appeal to the people to sub-scribe for our Country's Bonds."[10] In an address to a large audience of LDS Church youth leaders, he proclaimed his views on the cause of the war:

> We are at war; that we are in the business of winning the war; that we must remain in the war until it is ended; and that we must come out of the war victoriously, so that the world may be free. . . .
>
> I suppose every Mutual worker and all the members of the Church are familiar with the few simple facts upon which rests our attitude with respect to the war. If these facts are not understood, they should be known by every member of the Church; for there is no organization in the world that has a deeper interest in the progress and the outcome of this great world war than the organization known as the Church of Jesus Christ of Latter-day Saints. . . .
>
> I may remind you that this great war is an effect of many causes—some very evident and near, some not so evident, but remote. This war did not come out of a clear sky. It did not simply happen, but came as a result of things that have occurred through generations of time. When the war broke out in 1914 . . . we desired no quarrel with the world. We attempted to keep out of all kinds of disputes with our neighbors. . . . We were going about in our own way to develop our natural resources, and contending simply for the right to work out on this land, in this hemisphere, our form of government—a government by the people, so that the people may be free—a government which does not depend upon a king or upon a military class, but which does depend, for its power and influence, upon the will of the people gov-erned. That was all we asked of the world; and we were determined, as we are determined today, that no power on earth shall come in and destroy our experiment in free government. On that point we are all united. We propose to stand together to the last in behalf of this great

experiment in free government which we believe, and which all sane thinkers of the world today believe is a solution of the social difficulties that vex the world today.

During all these years, in order to maintain our right to work out our experiment in free government, we had asked the world to recognize three things, three main principles. If the American people will keep them in mind, it will be easier to understand the causes back of this war:

First: We insisted upon the recognition of the Monroe doctrine, which simply meant that we would not permit any European or foreign power to come to these shores, or to this hemisphere and become a power here, so that our work for the freedom of the world might be endangered. At the same time we agreed that we would keep out of Europe; we would not attempt to interfere with European politics. We wanted to be left free to work out our big experiment for the good of mankind.

Second: We insisted that the world recognize the freedom of the seas, so that we might carry on commerce with the world. In spite of the fact that we were located thousands of miles away from the older and more thickly settled domain of the world, we might still, by the use of the seas, have free communication with our neighbors in every part of the world.

Third: We insisted that all our disputes with other nations should be settled by the method of arbitration. . . .

Let me now call your attention to the fact that the German government, which stupefied this country when it began the war in Europe, has been unwilling to recognize any of these fundamental principles upon which we rest our claims with respect to the world. . . .

Almost at the beginning of the war an anti-United States propaganda was started by the German government at home and abroad, based largely upon the claim that we were furnishing munitions to other countries; and we were asked to stop our trade with other nations. We were requested to remain here, as if we were on an island of the sea, quiet and subservient, taking orders from a power which was showing itself unfit for leadership among the nations of the world.

We soon learned that spies, sent out by the German government, were honeycombing our country and other countries. They were down in Mexico, over in Japan, in the Latin republics of America.

They had one message to deliver: "Let us all get together and destroy the United States of America." The Monroe Doctrine was being ignored absolutely by the German government in its propaganda. . . .

Soon after the war broke out, sea troubles also began. . . . After some time this submarine warfare became ruthless, until there was nothing left but to believe, at least as far as our government was concerned, that the freedom of the seas was no longer a principle held in respect by the German government. . . .

Long before the war broke out, in spite of our repeated requests, the German government, almost alone in its views among the great powers of the world, had said to us defiantly: "We will not submit any of our difficulties to a treaty of arbitration; we will not have such a treaty."

In other words, all the things for which we have stood, sacred rights to us because upon them depends the future of popular government, were all dishonored by the German government. There was nothing else for us to do than to declare war on such a government, that we, ourselves, and the great cause of our land, might live and be protected. . . .

Finally, we may as well remember that the great, big overwhelming cause of the war, the reason why we are in the war and wish to remain in it to the end, is that one great system of government is opposed to another system of government. The one system says that a man, ordinarily in power because he is born of a certain father, shall stand at a head of a nation, and through a controlling, self-protective military machine, shall speak to the people and compel their obedience. The people under this system shall have little or no voice in the management of their own affairs. The other system declares that within the majority of the people lies the power of government, and that they may select men to govern them for one, or twenty, or a hundred, or more years, but that the power remains with the people. This latter system says that there is no place in this world for war; that this is a world in which justice and peace must reign; and that our government must be so established that cannons and rifles and poisonous gases will be removed from the possibility of destroying human life; that there is nothing more precious upon the face of the earth than human lives, and that these lives must be guarded and guided and allowed to develop to serve the God they worship, and to develop the earth which has been given them. Shall autocracy rule, or shall democracy prevail? That is the question.

We are fighting today, in a small way, the fight that was waged in the heavens, according to our own doctrine, long before we came to the earth. We were assembled in a great gathering, to discuss the journey to the earth and the life we were to lead here. The Father of the race laid before us his plan. "I will send you down there. I am the Master of men, because I am the possessor of the largest knowledge; and we shall so arrange things that you, my children, may know the law; and as you succeed in obeying and living the law, so shall your greatness before me be." It was not wholly an inviting program, because men are likely to fall, always, when they have the freedom of choice, but it was God's plan, a pure and perfect plan. Then Lucifer arose and said: "I have a better plan. I will take these people with me. I shall be the master. I shall see that every one of them shall live in joy and happiness. They shall have all they want to eat and fine houses to live in, and I shall see to it that the life journey is a beautiful, happy one, and I shall save every one of them without any effort on their own part." By God's plan every soul would be obliged to earn its own salvation; by Lucifer's plan, salvation will be forced upon every one, irrespective of deserts. God's plan is natural and wholesome— Lucifer's plan was unnatural and forbidding. One was good; the other was evil.

Today the world is fighting out the age-old issue. Shall man govern himself, though he makes mistakes at times,—or shall government be imposed upon him, even though the government be of perfect precision? We of this land and this Church have long since answered the question. Government by the people is a right; government imposed upon the people is wrong. We shall remain with the right. Though our lifeblood be shed, we mean to fight for the right to be free against any evil power, like that of Lucifer's, that would impose its sugar-coated bitterness, its "kultur" upon us.[11]

With America's entry in the war, food conservation took on

heightened importance, and the need for more farm workers became urgent.[12] The university changed its academic calendar because fall semester began before the harvest and winter semester encumbered planting: "The four-quarter plan possesses the flexibility needed at this time, because it provides the beginning of classes in the fall, early winter, and early spring, which may be completed with the securing of proper credit after approximately twelve weeks of study. . . . Nearly two hundred universities and colleges in convention assembled last May advocated the adoption of the quarter plan, at least during the time of the war."[13] The Federal Food Administration ascertained what each state institution was doing to contribute to the food conservation movement.[14] President Widtsoe reported that university officials gave a series of lectures in conjunction with the office of the United States Food Administrator to all female students except those already at work with the Red Cross. General lectures to the entire student body persisted through the crisis. "I am quite sure the University is doing everything in its power to help in the matter of food conservation," John wrote.[15] In a separate letter, he further described the university's war effort:

> During the school year 1917–18, all the male students of the University of Utah, physically fit, were required to take military drill three hours a week. Those who were not able to take this drill were required to take the lectures on Food Conservation, or to devote their time to some form of war work. . . . The latest information we have is to the effect that 773 of our Utah boys were in the service . . .
>
> All the girls of the Institution were required to join a knitting section or a surgical dressing section, or take the Food Conservation courses. . . . The number of surgical dressings made by the girls of the Institution reached the tens of thousands, and a very large number of sweaters, helmets, socks, etc. were made by the knitting section.
>
> In June of this year the Institution entered into a contract with the Government to give intensive courses in auto mechanics, gas engine work, radio telegraphy, electrical construction, carpentry, blacksmithing and concrete work. The contract specified that the University of Utah should house, feed and instruct approximately 440 men for two months, the Government to supply the necessary officers

Women from the U of U Red Cross units knitting clothes for soldiers during the war years.

to give the boys military drill and to see that military discipline was enforced during the time the men were here. . . .

The United States government also made a temporary contract with the University to house, feed and instruct in collegiate subjects, approximately 900 men who could enter the University of Utah as fully matriculated freshmen, or who had presented at least 13 units of approved high school work. . . . As soon as inducted, these men became privates in the United States Army, but they were allowed to select subjects in the different fields specified by the War Department. . . . The subjects required by the Government in these sections practically required us to discard the old college curriculum, and to substitute a new one.[16]

As the draft came into effect, males from eighteen to forty-five were nominees for military service. The army did not have facilities to house the numbers who came into service. To help absorb and train these men, colleges and universities across the nation were converted into military camps. The result was the Student Army Training Corps (SATC). John wrote:

As you know, Salt Lake City is the center of the intermountain

Women of the U of U Red Cross units training in the library.

country and has excellent railroad connections. If the War Department should designate Fort Douglas as an educational training post, the men could be transported easily, and undoubtedly could be trained at this Institution at less expense than at almost any other University in the country. . . .

If the government would ask us to train a certain number of men in specified lines of work, we undoubtedly could make the necessary shifts and form the necessary cooperative agreements with concerns interested in such work, so that we could meet the Government's demands—all of which can not clearly be shown on a questionnaire. . . .

It has occurred to us that the proximity of the reservation to our campus, the Government could well afford to designate Fort Douglas as one of the educational training posts of this inter-mountain country. . . .

May I close by saying once more that the University of Utah is extremely anxious to serve our Government, and that we ask only that the Government specify definitely just what we are to do.[17]

The proximity of Fort Douglas made the University of Utah an advantageous choice for the federal government. It was suggested that

Fort Douglas be made into a reconstruction hospital for rehabilitating soldiers. John wrote, "The University of Utah a modern, up-to-date state university will count it a pleasant duty to assist in carrying onward this undertaking to a successful issue; and especially will the Institution be happy to help use the fortunate placing of two great institutions to accomplish work of a high order."[18]

The university was not given adequate time to prepare for the traffic that followed. "The SATC plan for the training of officers was ill-conceived and greatly belated. It allowed the administrations of the various universities and colleges less than a month to make the transformation of their campuses into military camps."[19] At the height of the confusion came an epidemic of Spanish influenza, which was especially dangerous in close quarters. "The University . . . declared a vacation pending the clearing up of the epidemic and sent home all students, including the draftees. The Army, however, quickly ordered the latter group back to their quarters on the campus, with the result that the Fort Douglas hospital was soon taxed to its capacity."[20] Widtsoe felt that "it was unwise for the military authorities to call back the boys at a time when it was very certain that the influenza would break out." He tried to circumvent it: "Every method was used, honest and dishonest, to create a sentiment that would release the boys and allow them to go back home to their anxious parents."[21]

The SATC caused the university further grief. Governor Bamberger received complaints that the SATC was not warmly quartered and that their food was both bad and meager. He wrote to John, "The student army is cared for by the University under contract and any irregularities in that respect can not be charged to the military authorities."[22] Widtsoe countered, "The barracks occupied by the S.A.T.C. unit have been selected by the military authorities. . . . I believe that they have been made comfortable and warm. . . . In fact, we were directed by the Commanding Officer to return the blankets loaned by the citizens of Salt Lake City as there was an ample number of army blankets on hand. . . . I have no greater desire . . . than to provide abundantly under the law for the comfort, physical and otherwise, of the young people entrusted wholly or in part to the University."[23]

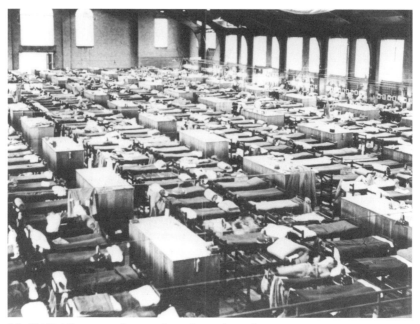

U of U Fieldhouse, used as a military barracks in the war years.

With demobilization, some of the men left the campus without completing their courses. Others, who never would have entered the university except for the SATC, continued their studies and pursued successful careers. However, because of the excitement of victory at war, attendance suffered, and "in the end it was decided to omit all final examinations that year. On the whole, however, disorganization on the University campus due to the war was considered less severe than at most universities."[24]

World War I prompted the War Department to urge expansion of the ROTC. Widtsoe encouraged its adoption at the university. He urged Senator King to exert "influence in securing the establishment of such a corps at this institution."[25] The board of regents passed a resolution stating that the government agreed to furnish up to $300,000 in equipment and five commissioned officers to operate the program, while the University agreed to erect necessary buildings for seventy-five men to care for horses and equipment furnished by the government. The seventy-five men could be recruited from the students, but they would "have to enlist in the U.S. Army for one year and would be the same as regular soldiers but would have some time to pursue college work. Stables for 100 horses would have to be erected and sheds to protect the guns, equipment and the men to look after the work."[26]

The war effort and the expansion of the ROTC brought new buildings. The SATC buildings were made permanent. The war ended earlier than expected, and the government grant left them with a deficit of $100,000. The ROTC used another $30,000 building for horses and equipment. "These two debts . . . form the only deficit of the University of Utah," John wrote.[27] The new buildings led to increased efficiency of several departments in the university. Within a short time, they were filled to overflowing with students.

In a documentary entitled "Influenza 1918," the Public Broadcasting System reported that "Influenza 1918" was the worst epidemic the United States has ever known. Before it was over, the flu would kill more than 600,000 Americans—more than all the combat deaths of that century combined. "For the survivors we spoke to," said producer Robert Kenner, "the memory is one of horror and fear—which may explain why many Americans were willing to let those few terrible months fade into obscurity. Schoolchildren know more about the Black Plague from centuries ago than they do about this episode in our recent history."[28]

Within a week of the opening of the 1918 fall quarter, the university was hit so hard that it was put in quarantine. Along with the university, all public institutions, even churches, were closed in order to control the spread of the disease. To assist, faculty members "proposed a statistical study of the influenza situation in Utah . . . to try to deduce from the data obtained some of the conditions surrounding the development and control of the disease."[29] Keen disappointment followed the government's refusal to endorse the study.

By mid-December churches were allowed to hold worship services, but the university remained under quarantine because of projections that the flu would continue through the winter. At the height of the epidemic, John and Leah's only living son, Marsel, became seriously ill, adding severely to the stress of their situation. Happily, Marsel recovered. The press of the war led to the recall of the students to their campus quarters. As a result of these hasty orders, "twenty-eight of the boys made the supreme sacrifice. In addition, fifteen of the regular University students fell victims of the epidemic."[30] John mourned those deaths to the end of his life. "Before the evil was over, someone in Washington ordered the boys back. I protested that it was still unsafe, but in vain. Newly commissioned lieutenants and captains stuck to orders. Washington was too busy to consider health matters. Hence, the boys had to return; but gathered from all parts of the State and living under unnatural conditions, it proved death for about 18 of them. The local military officers, our own citizens in uniform, might have avoided the catastrophe. Give a man a little authority, and he loves to show it off. The war period was a sad one."[31]

Despite the severity of the situation in the university, the PBS documentary indicates that Utah was hit minimally by the epidemic, October being the worst month with about 195,000 deaths nationally attributed to the disease. On 6 January 1919, the university was permitted to reopen its doors after missing an entire quarter. John faced the difficult dilemma of helping students whose graduation plans had been interrupted by the quarantine. "In order not to work an injustice against our students," he wrote, "we are allowing them to register for 20 hours of school work a term instead of 15 which was the normal, with a maximum of 23 hours. . . . By allowing students to carry 20 hours a term, they will be able to complete almost a full year's work."[32]

When several students contracted flu the following year, John canceled all social activities and issued a caution to all students that if they felt even slightly indisposed, they should stay home.[33] Dire as it was, the influenza epidemic was just one of the extra burdens that fell upon Widtsoe's shoulders during the first World War.

20

UNIVERSITY DEVELOPMENT

AFTER the war, John concentrated on helping the university become what he had envisioned. In his opening faculty address in the autumn of 1919, he said, "The great state universities must be research as well as teaching institutions. Unless truth be discovered, continually, the process of teaching becomes stale, civilization falls to a stationary level, and life becomes tasteless."[1] He taught that "research is fostered at the University of Utah under the belief that great teaching can be done only in an atmosphere which is favorable for the discovery of truth."[2] He encouraged the faculty, "Keep the research flame alive! There is none better for those who are to devote their lives to academic work."[3] "Every member of the faculty should, if possible, become actively interested in some sort of research; if not of the survey kind indicated, in some other form that will result in contributions of value, more or less directly, to mankind."[4]

Although John missed conducting his own research, he took pleasure in his work. "Personally," he wrote, "I have never enjoyed any work so much as that which I did when I was wholly in research work, but I have found a daily joy also in the duties that have come to me the last 15 or 20 years as administrator of the affairs of public institutions."[5] In

the summer of 1919, however, he was able to combine both. Notable
research activity in this period came from mining, chemistry, engineering, public health, and sanitation. To foster more research, John sought
membership for the university in a national institution: "I would suggest
. . . that the Sigma Xi Society send someone at our expense to investigate conditions here. . . . The institution has a faculty of excellently
trained men, drawn from the leading institutions of the world. It gives
fully as much time and money to research as any other State university
of its size and with its income. We want to develop more and more the
spirit or the feeling for the discovery of truth."[6]

Research at the university necessitated improved reporting. John
noted, "I have always felt, as a research worker, that my work[s] were
only partially done until the results of my investigations were published.
In fact, I have long preached to investigators the doctrine that there are
three parts to every investigation, each one of equal value, first the planning of the work, second the execution of the plans, and third the
preparation of the results for publication and the publishing of them. I
hope we may with vigor see that all the original work done in the
Bureau of Mines be published."[7] To Dr. Joseph F. Merrill he added,
"Personally I am of the opinion that researches that are carried on and
not published might almost as well be left undone. They may benefit a
very small number, but the truth discovered is not given to the world at
large—which is the solemn duty enjoined, I believe, upon all seekers
after truth who have the good fortune to discover new truth."[8]

Similarly, he encouraged the publication of master's theses. It just
wasn't right, he felt, to let good information lie buried on the library's
shelves.[9] "I am hoping with all my might that we shall be able to place
the University of Utah with its face squarely toward the research idea,
and that we shall be able to render large service in advancing knowledge as the years go by."[10] He summarized his strong conviction at the
end of his term:

> I am very conscious of the need at the University of Utah of a
> larger research spirit in the School of Education, . . . and I am con-
> vinced that by no manner can we build a true University, whatever its
> size may be, without the spirit of research and the employment of that

spirit in advancing the boundaries of human knowledge. Investigation and teaching must go together on the same campus if great educational conquests are to be made. I do not mean by this that every man shall be a research man, because there are many cases of excellent teachers who lack the feeling and equipment for research work. But there must be a large proportion of the Faculty to do research work and to leaven by their spirit of research the whole teaching lump of the Institution.[11]

REACHING THE PEOPLE

From his youth, John was a strong advocate of making education accessible: "What was the value of learning if not used for human good?"[12] As president of the ACU he developed extension work in the experiment station to bring to Utah one of the best programs in the nation. Before taking up the presidency of the university, he announced that "one of the chief aims of the institution will be to make it as nearly as possible approach the needs of the state, and to become daily more potent in directing the life of the state."[13] He continued to preach the university's responsibility to the community in commencement exercises in 1919: "With equal earnestness must the University contribute to the intellectual and spiritual well being of the people of Utah, to their character development. The desert is not fully conquered if the conquerors are not wide-visioned and honest, clean, gentle, tolerant, and believers in the mighty forces which control human destinies. . . . Out of the halls of this Institution must issue a full respect for the intangible things of life; the imponderables; the quiet influences which in their effect on humanity are greater than the artillery of steelbound cannon. The University must teach the way of moral conquest."[14]

John felt the university's first duty was to seek solutions to the problems of the day and to find ways to reach those who would not attend the university: "We must touch with a more intelligent vision those who, this very day, must decide upon the fate of their country. The campus of a state university is the whole state, and its students all of the citizens of the state. Workers, whether with head or hands, should be served by us. . . . It is a primary duty of each state supported institution to seek out service especially needed in the district from which it derives support."[15]

In his memoirs John recalled that the university was a Salt Lake City institution with little concern for the whole state. "This was not fair to the people," he wrote. "In our day a State university must devise means and methods for helping all who are suitably prepared, and who desire academic advancement, wherever they may be. In the first year of my administration, therefore, I recommended to the Board the creation of an Extension Division to serve the people of the State beyond the university campus. Correspondence work, classes conducted by faculty members in any part of the State, and many other kinds of help, were received with enthusiasm by the citizens of the State."[16]

Development of extension work had to be delayed while the nation was at war. But as soon as the war ended, John sent a message asking that each department develop at least one course to be offered through the extension service. "The motive which impels men and women to seek education is partly the wish for fuller personal development," he noted. "It arises from the desire for knowledge, for self expression, for the satisfaction of intellectual, aesthetic and spiritual needs, and for a fuller life. It is based upon a claim for the recognition of human person-ality."[17]

Pamphlets were circulated throughout the state announcing new adult education programs.[18] There were classes in advertising, selling, teaching, business, mining, and auto mechanics, as well as general collegiate courses.[19] Attendance was often so great that additional teachers were needed.[20] John wrote, "For the good of the Institution and for the good of the Faculty . . . all members of the University staff could well be required to give at least the equivalent of two weeks of exten-sion service during the school year—providing, of course, that no one call would be of longer duration than one week. . . . I really believe the great majority of the Faculty members, once they were brought into the Extension service, would enjoy the work, and would understand its full benefits to themselves as well as to the Institution."[21]

By February 1920 the extension division reported increased success in reaching over the state.[22] John pushed for a larger extension staff and a larger extension curriculum. "Since we had the first two years of the full medical course," he wrote, "we felt justified in offering extension work in health matters, notably in child health and welfare. This was well received by the mothers of the State."[23] A great amount of time was put into researching and teaching on infant health.[24]

Other popular courses in the extension division were educational administration and general education,[25] health education, petroleum geology, analytical chemistry, metallurgy, bacteriology, and advanced stenography. There were also informative lectures on such topics as social democracy, the ethics of citizenship, the making of modern nations, our daily lives as citizens, and social aspects of the contemporary drama.[26] An intensive two-week course was introduced in teacher training for executives and technicians from sugar plants in the state. Classes in dressmaking and millinery were provided free of charge in civic centers. The division sought to establish good relations with the high schools by sending musicians to perform at school assemblies.[27] They also held a large powwow for the Boy Scouts in Utah. As a result, "the number of regularly registered extension students . . . increased . . . nearly fourfold that is, from about 650 to nearly 2500."[28]

As the university reached out to more of the state, John expanded his vision. "Utah is yet practically undiscovered," he wrote. "It is a fundamental duty of the educational institutions, especially those of higher learning, to discover Utah's resources and the eternal relations of forces that will enable man to win the wealth upon which civilization rests. Research must be fostered."[29] As to their priority, he added, "I believe that we can do few things of greater interest to the people of the State, or of greater value to the State itself, than to deal in any proper manner with the natural resources of our commonwealth."[30] For Utah to become attractive to live in, resources had to be developed: "It no doubt would be somewhat of a sacrifice at the present time, after the sacrifices of the war, to make many of these improvements, but we are facing a condition of a practical nature, and I believe we should proceed to the utmost of our ability to meet it and to establish conditions that will relieve us of the possible difficulties that might arise should our returning soldiers fail to find sufficient and enjoyable employment."[31]

John believed that the university had to assume the burden of discovering and teaching the means of conquest over natural resources.[32] For that purpose, he created a Bureau of Economic and Sociological Research that would also conduct biological surveys.[33] He also promoted geological and research surveys[34] and instituted a "Know Utah" campaign, "by which it is planned to extend information about Utah throughout Utah, this by means of lectures, illustrated in the main, dealing with specific subjects on Utah's resources, achievements, attractions, and life."[35]

John wrote five articles about Utah's resources for the *Salt Lake Tribune* under the heading "Map of Utah's Future" that were printed over the span of a month. Entitled "Utah, an Empire of Undeveloped Resources," "Crops That May Be Manufactured," "A Foundation of Iron, Coal, and Related Resources," "Establishing Our Chemical Industries," and "Utah As a Playground," the articles focused on Utah's natural beauties and wonders.[36] The last article prompted a letter to Senator Smoot: "It has been called to my attention that the Water Power Act, in its present form, may jeopardize the attractiveness of our National Parks and Monuments. I have a great love for the National Parks with which I am acquainted, and it does seem to me that the few wonderlands that have been set apart from the thousands of other watered lands should be preserved in their natural beauty, if possible."[37]

To increase tourism, John invited national organizations to hold conventions at the University of Utah. The National Federation of Women's Clubs, the American Association for the Advancement of Science, and the American Nurses Association were a few that accepted the invitation.[38]

HELPING THE HIGH SCHOOLS

Viewing the entire system of formal education as one integrated whole was fundamental to John's educational vision. He later wrote, "The relationship of collegiate institutions to high and elementary schools had always interested me. High schools are feeders of the colleges, and the elementary schools are feeders of the high schools. They merge into one another. The educational system is one. The demarcation between college and high school, between high school and elementary school should be slight. Failure to observe this has often worked injury."[39]

He instructed his department heads that "the future growth of the University will depend in large part upon the cordial relations that may be established between the University and the group of high schools in our State."[40] He felt that personal contact went far in creating good relationships. To this end, he held banquets designed to allow the leaders of the school system to get to know each other. The principal of Park City High School was duly appreciative:

> I want to congratulate you upon the remarkable success that is attending your get-acquainted and get-together banquets at the University. I have attended both, and consider the move not only a great advertising scheme for the University, but the best individual thing done of late to get the whole of the school system of our great State pulling together, and getting to the place where they can understand each others' problems. It looked for a while as though this last one was going to lead to unhappy complications (a reflection being cast that the U. of U. is getting far too much of the State's money). But there again, your good judgement and diplomacy came to the rescue; in that closing speech of yours, I consider, you cleared the whole stage of complications, and did it in a dignified and liberal-minded manner.[41]

John simply wanted to make the resources of the university more widely available. "The Extension Division wishes to be of as much assistance to the teachers in the schools of the state as it possibly can," he wrote. "To this end it has organized the work in health education into a special correspondence course and has completed arrangements by which persons taking the course are exempt from the examinations required by the State Board in this subject." "Besides the health course the Extension Division offers a great many courses by correspondence, many of them in subjects relating to teaching. . . . We think we know the needs of teachers and are willing to try to select the right courses for applicants if they will tell us just what their problem is."[42]

The *Utah High School Journal* was a part of this effort. In the first issue John wrote, "We hope, by this publication, to establish a close relationship between the high schools and the colleges and universities of our State."[43] An annual High School Day was established on which the university hosted visiting seniors and their teachers from high schools around the state.[44] The university invited the participation of the high schools whenever "an unusual investigation intended to ascertain and classify by years and seasons the most necessary and desirable content of reading courses for high school pupils."[45] Beyond these supplementary training and public relations programs was the formal training to prepare teachers for the public schools. John strongly opposed a negative attitude toward professionally trained teachers: "I believe that there is only one way to combat the condition, and that is to make it impossible for those who have not been trained properly in our day to enter the profession of teaching. I voiced that at the last meeting of the State Board of Education. I believe in it still. You had better reduce the number of our teachers, let our children go to school a half or a third of a day, rather than to allow the feeling to continue that anybody can teach school."[46]

In 1919 the William M. Stewart Hall, a teacher-training laboratory, was completed. As president of the State Board of Education, John encouraged cooperative efforts of the school system to train teachers. A typical note read, "I have suggested to Dean Bennion that he and I, with members of your Department, if you feel so inclined, make a trip over the State after this campaign is over, to encourage high school seniors to enter the State School of Education next year."[47] In one meeting they addressed the efforts the board was making to meet the "emergency" of a shortage of teachers: "Upon motion of President J. A. Widtsoe, Dean Milton Bennion of the University of Utah, with two other persons to be named by the Board, were appointed a committee to inaugurate and conduct a campaign among high school seniors and others for the purpose of inducing more young people to enter normal schools in preparation for teaching."[48] The university offered a number of scholarships to attend their normal school, the school designed to train teachers. As a result, a great number of teachers embarked on their careers in the Utah school system.

SUMMER SCHOOL

The University of Utah had held a summer school to train teachers throughout the state. As with other programs of the university, John worked to upgrade it. In his usual manner, he sought the advice of all parties involved. Several graduate students asked for more graduate classes to be taught. In 1919 a letter was sent to all Utah school superintendents asking their advice for the summer school.[49]

John pursued the idea of summer programs beyond the boundaries of the campus. He wrote, "If it would be for the health advantage of 50 to 100 Utah School teachers to spend from 4 to 5 weeks in Brighton or some other similar place, carrying on part of their summer school studies, we should take steps to supply the need. Our canyons, with their cool and beautiful retreats, should be made available for our profession."[50] John held high hopes for the potential of a Brighton summer school: "We might be able to start something that would be very attractive, not only to our own teachers, but to those from other states. We of the state have made entirely too little use of the great, scenic, and health pursuits offered especially in the summer time by our splendid mountains and canyons."[51] Along with the traditional courses in teacher training, classes in English, history, and other subjects that didn't require laboratory facilities were offered. On 4 March it was determined that if one hundred applications were received for the Brighton Summer School by 1 April, it could be held in the canyon. In July John reported that more than 700 students attended the school.[52] The astonishing success of the school brought expanded plans for the following year. To the Brighton Summer School was added a school in art held near the lakes on Mt. Timpanogos.[53]

SAVING THE MEDICAL SCHOOL

Another university program that needed bolstering was the medical school, which had so deteriorated that it was no longer accredited. In March of 1916 John wrote to the chairman of the Council of Medical Education, saying, "I am writing to ask you what must be done to have the University of Utah Medical School again enter Class A."[54] The war slowed his efforts, but after the war he undertook to establish the medical school on respectable ground. He wrote to the Medical Council and other universities asking why they wouldn't accept the university's credit. "The two year medical school was young. The American Medical Association was not certain that the Utah school could retain an A rating. Consequently, I made several trips to the Chicago headquarters of the association. The rating was maintained."[55] Soon credit was given to the school even by Harvard. Improvements were made. A course in pharmacy was offered; a building was dedicated wholly to the work in medicine; a medical fraternity was created. The medical school flourished from that time forward, receiving recognition from institutions throughout the country.

REVAMPING FINANCES

John also had to deal with the problems of limited funding, noting, "We are running at the present time upon the smallest per capita cost of any State University."[56] Although running an institution on a small budget was not new to John, he felt that it was harder to raise money for the University of Utah than it had been for the Agricultural College.[57] There were further complications: "This year's attendance is approximately 20% higher than the attendance of last year. This is making the financial problem more difficult than ever."[58] "The salary pressure upon the Institution is crowding everything else out of the way until it seems that everything beyond salaries and the bare maintenance of the Institution must be practically forgotten for some time. The departmental budget, considering equipment and supplies, is smaller than it was last year, and will not suffice, even as it stands, to meet the actual needs of the departments. I am hoping against hope that something may 'turn up' to provide us with relief."[59]

Dr. Widtsoe tried draconian measures. In April of 1920 he said, "Since just before Christmas until within the last two or three weeks, I have spent practically all my spare time in overhauling the financial situation of the University."[60] Besides the logistical headaches, he also had to worry about whom he would upset, noting, "I tried to get some results without awakening the usual row, and up to date have succeeded fairly well."[61] As with other things, John sought the input of all involved.[62] He received both aid and pressure from the board of regents, who wanted him to determine what departments were expendable.[63] It was decided that the minimum enrollment for junior college classes would be twenty, and for senior college classes, ten. Classes not meeting those requirements would be canceled.[64] This was done to "serve the largest possible number of students at the least possible expense."[65]

After rearranging the finances, John determined that to build, or even to maintain, the kind of institution that the university should be, more money was needed. He told a group of men at a Kiwanis Club meeting, "Our great need now is to obtain a small additional appropriation to place our present activities on a safe basis, so that we may avoid the necessity of reorganizing our work with a view to eliminating some of our work and excluding students. That which has been built should be maintained."[66] He viewed private donations, with which he had become familiar during his Harvard days, as only a partial salvation. He felt that a concerted effort had to be made by the entire university family to obtain the needed funds: "To win large financial support for the University of Utah is not the work of one man or of a small group of men. All must help. Efficient work in the classroom and loyalty outside will help establish a safe reputation for our Institution; but in addition we must individually seize every opportunity to speak the word or to do the thing that will in time bring increased revenues from State or from private sources."[67]

The president also felt he needed more support from the state: "We need more money; we need an adjustment of existing laws; and we need to have a better State appreciation through the legislature of the intangible work of the Institution."[68] John's efforts paid off, and before he left the university he wrote, "I am spending most of my time at present in the lobbies of the State legislature, asking and answering questions concerning education in the State of Utah. . . . The Governor in his budget, however, has made an allowance, which if approved by the legislature will give us a fairly easy year next year."[69] This budget was passed, and Widtsoe's successor reaped the benefits.

21

PROGRESS OF
THE UNIVERSITY

———————■———————

Insufficient financing hampered the advancements Widtsoe sought, but the university made impressive and steady growth. To a colleague he explained, "We shall probably have to effect the changes and additions of which you speak little by little as money becomes available."[1] By 1920 he was able to report, "We are fast becoming a university. University spirit is developing within the Institution, and both students and faculty are reacting to the new conditions."[2]

Substantial growth in attendance had a broad impact on the university. In 1919 the freshman class was so large that courses had to be rearranged to accommodate the students.[3] The increase was unexpected because Utah already had the largest per capita state university attendance in the United States.[4] John recalled, "During my five years of service to the University, the college enrollment increased over two and one half times; and in total enrollment the increase was threefold."[5] Physical facilities expanded to keep up.

By 1920 there were six schools at the University: Arts and Sciences, Education, Mines and Engineering, Medicine, Law, and Commerce and Finance.[6] New departments were added, including military science, anthropology, sociology, business practice, and economics.

The graduate school had languished for several years, but under John's direction it made significant progress.[7] One of the more remarkable changes during the Widtsoe years was the adoption of the Harvard elective system. This put the academic practices at the University of Utah on a par with the great universities of the land.

A SHADOW OF TROUBLE

One of the controversies that led to Kingsbury's resignation and Widtsoe's appointment persisted, however: the influence of the LDS Church on the university. "A cloud of irreligion was cast over the institution," John later wrote. "This was objectionable to the people who paid taxes for the support of the school, and whose forebears had fought and conquered the desert in the spirit of religion. Also, men employed from other states, looking with unfriendly eyes upon the Mormon faith, undertook to say and do things in the classroom derogatory to the traditions of the State."[8]

John believed that teaching morals was as essential as instruction in any other subject. Governor Cummings felt the university became "a safer place to send our young folks, and this is as it should be."[9] Though a mutual respect grew slowly, the perception of Church influence spread. The great majority of the community saw the university as one of the many inspired endeavors of the Mormon settlement of the Great Basin; others desired a complete severance between the university and the interests of the Church. John was straightforward from the beginning: "When the executive committee of the regents tendered me the position, my first answer was that they unknowingly had made a mistake and really did not want me. When asked to explain, I assured them that wherever I went I intended to perform the duties of my religion, to attend my priesthood and other meetings, and to be active in the Church, though I should keep my views on religion to myself. I suggested that they would prefer another type of man, perhaps a so-called 'jack-Mormon,' one a Mormon in name but not in practice. This frank statement saved me much later trouble."[10]

I was warned soon after entering upon the U. of U. presidency, by a member of the faculty, a Mormon, that it was not the thing to mention on the campus anything concerning the founding of the university by the Mormon pioneers. Everything concerning them should be soft-pedaled, to "let sleeping dogs lie." That was a challenge. A week later I gave my first address to the faculty and students, and took as my theme the debt of the University of Utah to the pioneers of the State. That served warning, on the faculty especially, and also to all who were interested, of my position. During my entire administration the old shameful attacks upon the Church, if entertained at all, were kept under cover.[11]

Though some felt the Church influenced policy and hiring decisions, Dr. Widtsoe was adamant: "During my administration the religious adherence of persons nominated for various positions was never discussed in Board meetings, nor anywhere else, with me."[12] He further explained, "During my state service of over a quarter of a century, no official of the Mormon Church, of which I was known to be a faithful adherent, attempted by word or intimation to influence my official acts. I had personal acquaintance with the leaders of the Church, and met them frequently, yet never a word was spoken to secure for someone a position, or even to suggest policies of action."[13]

OTHER SERVICE OPPORTUNITIES

John A. Widtsoe's prominence generated many opportunities to serve in capacities outside his presidency. The list of boards and committees he served on is long. He was on the State Text Book Commission, helped direct the Utah Academy of Science, was elected a fellow of the American Association for the Advancement of Science, was on the American Scandinavian Foundation, served as a member of the National Economic League, and was elected president of the State Historical Society. "In 1918," he wrote, "I was elected president of the Utah Education Association. I had always avoided the honor, since I felt I had honor enough. Because of war conditions I had the unprecedented privilege of serving two terms. During these two years the House of Delegates over which I presided, of the association came into action."[14] He was the secretary to the State Board of Education, and the senior member of that board the entire time he was president. He was also elected a vice president of the National Education Association.

John was a scientist through and through but had to subdue that facet of his life. He wrote, "My time is taken up with my various duties, and I have very little time left to do any great amount of outside reading."[15] "The U. of U. days were filled excessively with labors. As the diaries are scanned, only scanned, I grow restless. Nature intended some leisure for the human body and mind. There was not only work at home, but travels east and west, to attend meetings in connection with university problems. I maintained my irrigation and dry farming associations, but could give very little time to them. There was also a heavy drain from local demands, to speak, visit, advise, and so on. My days were too full of work but they were happy days of worth-while accomplishment."[16] He spoke of times when "the old dry-farming fever" came upon him.[17] He followed quite closely the agricultural news and attended the International Dry Farm Congress.

John's university experience was detrimental financially because of a lower salary and the need to provide his own accommodation suitable for hosting:

> I was obliged to draw upon our meager savings. I have never recovered from this financial setback. Fortunately, I have never been a lover of money. If the needs of the day were met, I was inclined to be content. However, in Logan I was well on the way to independent, financial comfort. Going to the U. of U. destroyed that future. The demands made upon me were such that no time or strength was left for the care of personal affairs. The university had needs. The situation was critical. The man at the head could not think of himself. Always the institution came first.[18]

> One thing was made clear to us. A dinner to be socially perfect cannot be given successfully in a public place, not even in a room in a university building. The home atmosphere is wanting. University presidents can hardly be expected to own homes suitable for such occasions. Every State educational institution should have a president's residence, furnished and equipped for these worthwhile requirements. That was not possible at the University though it has long been

The Widtsoe family home at 1425 Sigsbee Avenue, at Salt Lake City.

practiced at the U.S.A.C and most other State universities. The cost
would soon be repaid by the good will gained. Having lived in the
president's residence at the U.S.A.C., we know the difference in
advantage to the school. After three years of renting we built a home
near the University, and it helped us much. But, it was not a proper
burden to place upon an underpaid university president, for location
and architecture were controlled by university needs.[19]

During this busy time, John revised an edition of *Joseph Smith as
Scientist*, wrote articles for the *Improvement Era*, and was a frequent
Church speaker. Leah, as always, was an especially stalwart support to
John. Franklin S. Harris, president of BYU and the ACU wrote of Leah
that no woman could have contributed more to a man's success, noting, "Her temperament and training are such that they have fitted
exactly into the work required of her and her husband. They were both
born to leadership, and circumstances have given them constant opportunity to exercise this quality."[20] John agreed: "There were numerous
social engagements. Many of them were, of course, given in our own
home—dinner after dinner and luncheon after luncheon! In this
responsible part of the work, my wife as usual led out with consummate
skill. She was the perfect hostess. In addition, she entered into the public life of the city, and made hosts of friends for us and the university.
For two terms she served as president of the Salt Lake City Federation of
Women's Clubs, later the Salt Lake City Council of Women. While she

The Widtsoe family, at home, in the U of U days. Left to right: Anna (John's mother), Anna, Eudora, Leah, Marsel, John.

gave first allegiance to her home and to religious duties, she did not hesitate to undertake worthy civic responsibilities."[21]

Unfortunately, the years the Widtsoes spent at the University of Utah were filled with personal trials. The first of these was John's mother's death. On 11 July 1919, she passed away after suffering through a lingering illness. John had always been close to his mother, and her death was a great loss. On the day of her funeral he wrote, "She was a most devoted mother, loyal to the last degree. Her devotion to the cause of truth was almost sublime. She was self-sacrificing beyond expression in behalf of her own and those who needed help. Her mind was transparently clear. The great issues of her life always swept before her. To her I owe my inspiration. Thanks! Many thanks! dear Mother. Goodbye, until [we] meet again on the last stretch of the endless journey."[22] He wrote to a friend, "The year had been heavy, and especially hard during the last two or three months, so, as I had a good opportunity, I ran away and took a three weeks trip in to Alaska, spending eighteen days or more on board ship."[23] The trip provided him much-needed rest:

I am, myself, very fond of the Coast country, and go there every once in a while to get a taste again of the places where the land and the ocean meet. You know I was born, and my earliest years spent in such a country, and my education, nearly all of it above the high school grade, was gained near the sea-coast; so many pleasant memories cluster about the coast countries of the world. It was partly the boyish longing for the old scenery that drove me into Alaska this summer, where we sailed for two or three weeks along the quiet waterways and among the wooded hills that are so characteristic of the shore line both of Alaska and of Europe.[24]

The following year John's brother, Osborne, passed away, the victim of a sudden cerebral hemorrhage. A day after his funeral, Aunt Petroline and Mother Gates were in an automobile accident for which John held himself responsible—since he was the driver.

Osborne's death was, of course, a terrific blow, the effects of which I will feel for some time. I try to keep the event out of my mind, and refuse to talk about it to any extent with anybody, but nevertheless it follows me by day and by night. Then too the care that the other family will need in one way and another takes a bit of time and thought and adds its mite of burden. Just why I should have the only automobile accident of my career the day after my brother's funeral must be answered by someone wiser than I am. The injuries done to the two women I loved best on earth save my own wife was, of course, a shock that I have not yet quite overcome. Mrs. Gates, however, is now able to walk about a little with a cane. Yesterday we walked a few rods outside of the house. My aunt is still in the hospital and likely to have to remain there for some weeks to come. Both of her hip bones were fractured, and being an elderly lady, the healing process is slow. Neither one of them can yet turn on her side.[25]

John still pressed forward: "In spite of all these troubles, life and its chance to serve the world looks good, and I do not need to allow myself to be depressed, but intend to go right on doing a day's work each day, and getting such joy out of the days as best I can."[26] There were many sympathetic letters from friends. After Osborne's death and the automobile accident, John wrote to A. C. Carrington, "During the summer especially it may be necessary for me to clear out of the office for some time. I have felt the strain of the year much more than I expected, and somehow I must get myself in shape for the coming year."[27] He took the time to gather himself together and maintain the drive and optimism needed to direct the affairs of the university.

ADMINISTRATIVE ABILITIES

John's administrative skills were manifest in his unusual success at the college and university. In recognition, he was asked by the Church to speak on the topic of "The Executive and His Control of Men."[28] In welcoming David O. McKay as a new member of the board of regents, Widtsoe revealed his feelings: "It is a high and dignified office, which, while fraught with much responsibility, also carries with it the satisfaction of being able to render much good to the thousands of young people who, at the University of Utah, are preparing for leadership in our State."[29]

Though occasionally frustrated by those who could not adapt to needed change, he was patient with them. He encouraged one dean, "I am exceedingly anxious, as I have said to you frequently, that we be courageous enough to do what the successful schools of the country are doing everywhere, to lay aside the old established academic harness, and proceed to serve our constituencies according to their special needs."[30] In later years he added, "College faculties make rules, usually very good. But, having once made them, they fear to revise them with the changing day. There is not a larger proportion of men with independent initiative among college professors than among other men. It often became necessary, therefore, to remind ourselves that our regulations are man-made, not God-made. That often gave courage to battle against an outworn tradition which threatened to stifle progress."[31]

John worked hard to deal squarely with what appeared to be in the best interest of the university regardless of the consequences that fell to him. Upon his resignation it was reported:

> Probably more of Dr. Widtsoe's manhood energies have been devoted to problems of administration than to any other single field. In this work he has been eminently successful. The openness of his

method of dealing with people, his obvious honesty of purpose, his desire to give all a fair hearing, his sagacity in understanding the real problem before him, and most of all his unfailing ability to estimate men have given him the respect of those over whom he has presided. To say that he has never had opposition would be far from the truth. All men of action find difficulties to remove. Whenever a stand is taken for the right, the opposite forces are naturally antagonized. Dr. Widtsoe has had a number of very difficult administrative situations to meet, but his diplomacy and tact have enabled him to overcome the difficulties and in a large measure to bring harmony out of chaos.[32]

MOVING ON

John accepted the presidency of the university out of a sense of duty to the state he loved. He planned to stay in that service as long as he felt he could contribute, or until a higher calling came.

On March 17th, 1921, as I was nearing the end of my fifth year with the university, my future was changed. That sunshiny morning, I had gone directly from my home, with the superintendent of buildings and grounds, to plan for a recreation area for the children of the training school of the School of Education. My office did not know of my whereabouts. When I returned about noon, I was told that Dr. Richard R. Lyman had telephoned for me repeatedly. When I called, he asked me to come to his office without delay. He took me directly to the temple into the room of the Presidency, in which, with the Twelve, they were holding their regular Thursday meeting. Even then, I did not guess the purpose of the visit. After some business items had been transacted President Grant turned to me, and told me that I had been called to fill the vacancy of the Council of the Twelve, occasioned by the death of President Anthon H. Lund. Was I willing to accept the call? There flashed before my mind the probable result: The laying aside of many a cherished desire; the constant service to the end of life; the complete change in life from that for which I had been trained. But, the biggest thing in my life was the restored gospel of Jesus Christ. It had full claim upon me. Was I worthy of the office? Could I perform its duties properly? I have always been conscious of my limitations. Question after question rushed through my mind. For a moment all time and space were mine. Then, without hesitation I answered, yes. I had never refused a call by the priesthood. It was too late to begin now. The vote of the Council was taken. Under the hands of all present, President Grant ordained me at once an apostle and set me apart a member of the Council of Twelve. His accompanying blessing has always been a comfort to me. The prayer circle that followed cleared my mind. As I left the temple that day, I knew the time had come to turn my back on the projects of the past. On Sunday, the following April 3, 1921, at the General Conference of the Church, the action taken by the Presidency and Twelve was confirmed by the people, and I was sustained as a member of the Council of the Twelve.[33]

After John received the new calling, a newspaper reported that he "said yesterday that he was not sure as to whether he would be allowed to hold an apostleship in the Mormon church and at the same time act as head of the state university, which is a non-secular institution. Dr. Widtsoe said that he presumed he would be obliged to fulfill his contract with the state which would expire July 1, 1921, and that he did not think he would be asked to serve in the two offices at the same time."[34] The article continued by saying that "President Charles W. Penrose, first counselor to President Heber J. Grant, expressed the opinion that it would be perfectly proper and right for Dr. Widtsoe to hold the two positions at the same time, citing as an example Senator Reed Smoot, whom he said was an apostle in the church and also served his state as senator."[35]

However, John did resign, noting, "The Church to which I belong has called me into its service. My convictions make it both a duty and a privilege to accept the call. Therefore, I tender you my resignation from the Presidency of the University of Utah."[36] He further wrote, "I thank you for the courtesies that you have shown me; the support that you have given me, and the personal friendships I have enjoyed with you. Whether officially connected with the University or not, I stand ready to assist the Institution in every manner within my power. I shall lay down the burdens of my post with deep emotion, for I leave my life-long profession, a daily association with clean, eager and hopeful youth, and

The John A. Widtsoe Building on the University of Utah campus. In the past it was the Physical Science Building, the Chemistry Building, and the Mathematics Building. In 1976 it was renamed in honor of President Widtsoe.

the opportunity to serve an institution which, properly guided, will rise to mighty power and influence in our land."[37]

John also bade farewell to the student body: "It has been a delight during the latter part of this generation to meet with you and your predecessors and to see your splendid development."[38] He sent a memo to the employees of the university: "Much of the heavy detail work has fallen upon this body of University servants. I know how well it has been done. I congratulate you upon the fidelity and the earnestness that you have manifested in your work. I thank you also for the courtesies you have shown me personally and in that way helped to make it a joy to serve at this Institution." To the faculty he wrote, "My personal associations with the Faculty members have been most delightful. The support of the Faculty has been the one great reward as duties have come and gone. As I leave the office, I am sending out this last President's Office Bulletin, to thank the members of the Faculty for their courtesies to me, for the friendship they have given me, and for the loyal and diligent efforts that have made possible a successful period in the history of the University of Utah."[39]

The university expressed its appreciation for their departing president by conferring on him an honorary doctorate of literature. In doing so the chairman of the board of regents said:

> This diploma evidences that the board of regents of the University of Utah regard you as worthy to receive the highest honor in their power to bestow, and in their behalf I can say that their act in voting you this honor was not done in a mere routine and perfunctory manner, but through a sincere desire to show you the high esteem in which they hold you; and I believe the citizens of this state also hold you in like esteem. We think your life and labors so far are and will remain an inspiration to every young man whose ideals are that he may lead a life of honor and usefulness to his fellow citizens.
>
> When we consider that you were not reared in the arms of luxury and ease, but rather your early life was one of privation and struggle and that you have come to this honor through untiring and persistent work, it has more than an ordinary value and meaning, and now, dear Doctor, let me assure you of our desire that your future may be as successful as your past and that you may continue to enjoy the high esteem in which your fellow citizens now hold you and that you may continue to render to your state the same quality of valuable services that you have done in the past. To this end the members of the board of regents again express their esteem by presenting you this token of it.[40]

His work at the University of Utah was the last professional position Widtsoe would hold. It was the second time he had rescued one of Utah's institutions of higher learning from troubled waters. His service had a remarkable influence on higher education in Utah. Even today we can learn much from John Widtsoe about educational leadership and the educational foundations on which Utah's institutions of higher learning securely rest.

PART III

WORK IN THE APOSTLESHIP

22

THE NEW APOSTLE

I<small>N</small> The Church of Jesus Christ of Latter-day Saints no higher recognition or public honor can be bestowed than the call to be a member of the Quorum of the Twelve Apostles. The First Presidency has a higher profile in leadership than the Council of the Twelve, but members of the First Presidency are almost always selected from the Twelve. The call to the Twelve is the determining call to the leadership of the Church.

> They are the Twelve Apostles, who are called to the office of the Traveling High Council, who are to preside over the churches of the Saints, among the Gentiles, where there is no presidency established; and they are to travel and preach among the Gentiles, until the Lord shall command them to go to the Jews. They are to hold the keys of this ministry, to unlock the door of the Kingdom of heaven unto all nations, and to preach the Gospel to every creature. This is the power, authority, and virtue of their apostleship.[1]

John felt he was adequately qualified if not the most qualified candidate for the presidency of the Utah Agricultural College and the University of Utah, but he had not sought, anticipated, or aspired to the sacred calling of apostle. As the weight of the new responsibility settled upon him, he pondered deeply. "Faith was mine," he wrote. "A reasonably correct life was mine. Could I serve the cause acceptably? That was my urgent question. I knew that hundreds, perhaps thousands of men could fill the position to full satisfaction. But the call had come to me. . . . At the best, my own powers would be inadequate."[2]

In the call to the Twelve, his faith stood preeminent over acclaim and professional achievement: "It is not given to us to aspire for Church positions and as one who had his time and energies fully occupied with very congenial work, I had never thought seriously about being called into any Church position that would take me away from the profession of teaching."[3]

Of John's many associates in Utah higher education, no one knew him better than Franklin S. Harris, his student, colleague, neighbor, and traveling companion. From so many perspectives he knew John well:

> John A. Widtsoe the man is even more outstanding than John A. Widtsoe the scholar. . . . It is those who know Dr. Widtsoe under these acid-test conditions that love him best. . . . There are . . . few men who spend all their lives in vigorous building. Wherever they go or whatever they do they attract attention. They are always veritable centers of activity. Where they are something is going on. Everything they touch is made better by the work of their hands. Every day they live they add a brick to the structure of human welfare.[4]

From Church members came warm congratulations and good wishes, although George H. Brimhall, president of Brigham Young Academy, expressed some disfavor: "Your selection as an apostle was a disappointment to me because my desires have been so intense and my hopes so high in the direction of your standing at the head of a great Church University growing out of the B.Y.U. that my expectations never ran in any other direction."[5]

From other colleagues came more guarded responses requiring more difficult explanations. John later recalled, "Those not of my faith sent doubtful good wishes. Several of my professional colleagues in other states wanted to know what kind of madness had overtaken me, to resign a most honorable post for one that had no standing and little meaning in the world."[6] One of his most intriguing explanations was made to cherished friends and fellow students in the Harvard class of

1894. Class reports were published in conjunction with each of several regular class reunions over the years. In each one John had published impressive accounts of his accomplishments. As one of the reunion speakers, he weighed carefully how to adequately explain his sudden departure from one of the most distinguished career records in the class. He desired to keep his classmates' respect, maintain their friendship, and yet be faithful to the convictions of his heart and his high calling. He explained:

> I felt early that life would be short of the best unless reasonable answers could be found to the eternal questions, Whence? Why? Where? My search was not helped by College. James and Royce confused me. The faculties of the sciences were remote from such questions. Most help was given by Josiah Parsons Cooke, instructor of Eliot, illustrious scientist, sound philosopher, believer in God, and great human being. When the battle was over, I had found the best answers, and most complete life philosophy, in the teachings of the so-called Mormon Church. Thenceforth I lived my religion faithfully, and have found much joy in so doing.
>
> Therefore it was easy for me to accept the call of the Church, which separated me in middle life from my beloved educational and research activities. I should then be better able to pass on to others that which I had found to be good. It was possible for me to do the required work, since the Church does not maintain a trained or paid ministry, but expects every member to be able to explain and defend its doctrines.[7]

David O. McKay conveyed the regard of his fellow apostles: "I rejoice[d] when you were chosen a member of the Council of Twelve, for I realize[d], then, that our friendship, which hereto had been warmed only by occasional association, would now be cemented by the glow of brotherly affection. . . . I esteem you as my friend, and love you as my brother!"[8]

Fellow Scandinavian Saints added to the many voices that acclaimed John's call. They were especially pleased that he filled the vacancy created at the death of Anthon H. Lund, a fellow Scandinavian: "A heavy gloom fell upon the hearts of the Scandinavian Saints at the announcement of the death of our Beloved Brother, Anthon H. Lund, but which has now been removed by your being called to the same position."[9]

Public acclaim was echoed in press coverage that enumerated John's well-rounded qualifications: "Elder John A. Widtsoe, who has been chosen by his brethren and ordained by President Grant to step into the vacant place in the quorum, is excellently qualified for the mighty responsibilities connected with the calling. His fine mental attainments are supported by and indeed based upon an unswerving faith in the revealed truth which the Gospel implies. He is sound in doctrine, convincing in speech, and abounding in energy."[10]

Despite the extreme change in focus, John maintained a dogged determination to keep one foot in his scientific studies. He wrote, "My time, while fully occupied, will not be so crowded with Church duties that I shall be wholly removed from the scientific studies which have occupied a good part of my time all my life."[11] He therefore sought membership in the National Association of State Universities.[12]

Franklin S. Harris briefly described John's remarkable record of Church activity and publication:

> While his new labor as an apostle will call for a more complete attention to spiritual matters than he has previously given, he is by no means unfamiliar with Church work. As a young man he made a concordance to the Doctrine and Covenants, and since that time his pen has been constantly busy in defense of faith and saints. He has written numerous articles for the various Church periodicals and has outlined many of the lessons studied by different organizations. His little book "Rational Theology" is one of the clearest expositions of the essentials of "Mormonism" that is extant. He has always been a diligent worker in the Priesthood, particularly as a Seventy in which calling he labored for many years as class leader and president. His membership on the General Board of the Young Men's Mutual Improvement Association has kept him constantly in touch with that organization, and he was for several years the teacher of what was said by some to have been the best Sunday School class in the Church.[13]

The transition from the office of president of the University of Utah to the office of an apostle so crowded John's time that he was unable to fulfill even demands that he especially liked: "You know Logan is always home to me, and it is the one place that I like to serve without question and with all my vigor, but the transition which I am about to make from one kind of work to another, together with certain appointments which I have already accepted, make it practically impossible for me to accept your invitation with any certainty that I shall be able to keep it."[14]

FAMILY LIFE ADJUSTMENTS

Recognizing the lifestyle change that would come with this new position, John and Leah determined to make it as successful as their other appointments. "This will bring about a great change in our lives," John wrote, "but both Mrs. Widtsoe and I are going into it with good courage and in the hope that we may be of even greater service to our fellow men than we have been in the past."[15] But adjustments were necessary:

> I had earned well for many years, and, until the university appointment, with the help of a wise wife, had been moving towards financial independence. Now, the Church allowance, supposed to be sufficient for a modest support, was about a third of what my annual earnings had been, going on to two decades. . . . We had just built a home near the university. . . . Not much of the savings of earlier years was left. The two older children were ready for missions. There was only one thing to do: to rearrange the family mode of living to come within the reduced income. So, the automobile was sold, and the hired help was dismissed. The family did not complain. My wife, true to her pioneer ancestry and her faith in the gospel, went on under the changed conditions cheerily and with a smile.[16]

Their silver wedding anniversary was just one example of their frugality:

> There was no money for silver, and going into debt was foreign to our code of living. Automobile there was none. So I put the whole matter up to the lady involved; and she reached a quick and possible solution. She asked that for an anniversary gift I stay with her three whole days. That was an unusual request in a household where the

husband spent much time in travel and the other time in office and public service. But, in consultation with President Rudger Clawson of the Council of Twelve, that was arranged. Then on the anniversary I asked her what we should do. She suggested that since we had no automobile we take a street-car ride. We boarded the Fort Douglas street car, and traveled to the end of the line. We had never seen the whole car line before. It was a real adventure on that glorious spring day (June 1, 1923). Other inexpensive events followed. If one so desires, great satisfaction may be found in simple pleasures. That is a lesson well to learn.[17]

The life of an apostle demands much travel. During the early years John and Leah spent nearly half of their days apart. But they were determined "to be together as much as possible, for thereby love is nurtured. Long separations are never good in married life."[18] On long assignments arrangements were often made for Leah to go with John. On an assignment to attend the Alberta Temple dedication, he wrote, "It was a splendid outing, a spiritual feast, and an unusual opportunity for both husband and wife to share in the things that feed the spirit. Since coming into my present service I have often felt that benefit would come from a closer association of the wife with the spiritual matters that engage the attention of the husband so constantly."[19]

Since Osborne had not long died, John kept in contact with his widow, Rose. He wrote to her, "You have had to pass through a severe trial, severer than any of us who have not tried it can possibly understand. Take comfort in the fact that so many people are sending you quietly messages of sympathy, goodwill, and new cheer. The Lord is with you, He will bless you, and I am sure that great happiness will yet come into your life. You have the most splendid memory to carry with you all your life. That in itself is a gift given to few people."[20]

John's first six years as an apostle were eventful. Soon after his call, his daughter Anna and son Marsel were of age and ready for missionary service. Anna served in the Southern States. Elder Charles A. Callis, a fellow apostle, was her mission president. "Anna has a fine personality," Elder Callis wrote to her father. "She is well liked by her missionary associates, members and investigators. She has for a companion now a sister who has just arrived from the West. This indicates the satisfactory progress your daughter has made."[21]

Sister Callis took a special interest in the new missionary: "We enjoy having Anna come to our home. She is always welcome. Our daughters love her and she fits in as one of the family and brings sunshine into our home. Aside from her being a missionary, I have a love for Anna personally. . . . There is one quality in her that especially excites admiration and that is her intense love for her parents and her great desire to be a credit to them. I think Anna has done wonderfully well. . . . The glimpse which Anna has given me of your home life has increased my esteem and admiration for you and your wife."[22]

After her mission, in 1926, Anna announced her intention to marry Lewis J. Wallace, an attorney from Washington, D.C., with just two days' notice. To a friend John confided, "Leah is still in a state of mourning. She has not quite gotten over the shock. Meanwhile, we are happy for Anna's sake."[23] A year later, Anna returned home to have her first child and the Widtsoe's first grandchild. "The baby seems to be in tip-top condition," John recorded. "He is one of the finest looking babies for his age that I have seen, and I venture to express this opinion after having consulted with unprejudiced people not members of the family."[24]

K. Marsel Widtsoe was the only Widtsoe son to survive to adulthood. Marsel wrote to his mother, "I could not ask for a better mother than you. You have given us a good start in life and I hope that now we, your children, might do those things to make your life enjoyable and happy."[25] He served a mission in England under the presidency of David O. McKay. It pleased John very much that Marsel could experience the spirituality of President McKay, who reported that Marsel was making good in every respect and was successful.[26] At the mission's end, John was pleased to report to President Grant that Marsel was "able to do his work well and to be worthy of an honorable release."[27]

ASSIGNMENTS AND RESPONSIBILITIES

As one of the Twelve, John was given numerous responsibilities. Most prominent were his calls to be a director of the Genealogical Society, the Church Commissioner of Education, and a guiding member of the general board of the Young Men's Mutual Improvement Association (YMMIA). In addition, there were regular and frequent (almost weekly) assignments to preside at stake conferences across the Church. There were also regular assignments to tour Church missions and to prepare lesson manuals for the Melchizedek Priesthood quorums, the Genealogical Society, and the YMMIA. The lesson manuals, the spoken addresses, and numerous articles and papers led to a steady stream of questions and requests for more information on many difficult topics. John spent many hours almost every week drafting careful answers. Because of his analytical skill, his insight on the teachings of the Church, and his gracious and gentle writing style, he became one of the most sought-after authorities on questions of Church doctrine.

In addition to a heavy ecclesiastical load, John was under strenuous demands in matters unique to his professional expertise. Issues centering on the Agricultural College and the University of Utah continued to demand his time and attention. Individual requests for counsel on matters of career and education poured in from all corners of the Church and the state. John sought conscientiously to answer each one. Particularly demanding were national and international requests for his participation in developing large-scale resolutions to irrigation and land-reclamation problems. All of these matters were a pleasure to him, but altogether the demands would have far more than overwhelmed an ordinary man. His very success in managing and contributing to all the endeavors that demanded his attention is in a great way the measure of his genius.

John's travel to stake conferences in all parts of the Church put him closer to the people of Utah than his college and university travels had. Questions about career and college were especially frequent, and scores of letters passed between him and the young men or women, or their interested parents. Often there were letters of recommendation. Franklin Harris summarized this aspect of John's life: "During the 17 or 18 years I have known you, you have been a constant stimulation to me, as you have been to thousands of students who have come under your influence, and I am glad to see that so many of them still go back to you for counsel."[28] Some examples of more general concerns provide a view of this time-consuming role. He advised a young man that by all means he should attend college after his mission: "The time will soon speed away, and before you know it the work will be behind you, and then you will be happy and your life long because of the effort you made."[29] John also had advice for those looking to leave Utah: "I hesitate always to advise any of our brilliant Utah boys to leave the State [for] we have need of the best that we produce."[30]

His students were grateful for the example and friendship they found in him. As one student wrote, "The interest that you have shown in me and my affairs is truly an inspiration that will help me succeed and strengthen my feeling of brotherhood for my fellow man. . . . I am sure that I have found in you, Dr. Widtsoe, a friend whose interest extends far beyond the superficial kind. I take great pleasure in congratulating you upon the occasion of your having been elevated to such an important and worthy office and desire to assure you that, after having lived among your people for five years, I feel closer to them and to your Church, and, as God is my judge, I shall always consider the wronging of my fellow man a betrayal of the confidence of you, my dearest friend."[31]

People wanted John's viewpoint on all subjects, and he responded. For example, to one correspondent he wrote, "If our children were encouraged to enjoy the common pleasures of childhood more, we would have less trouble with them as they grow into maturity."[32]

> I am very grateful that early in life I decided to avoid alcoholic drinks and every other substance that tends to dull the senses to sleep; to avoid every and all entanglement with women that might lead to a weakening of my moral nature; and to keep out of debt. These three maxims have helped me a great deal from my boyhood up. . . . To do a full day's work every day when one is at work; to play every once in a while so that life will not be too monotonous; to see the good in the people with whom you associate and forget, if you can, any of the human weaknesses that you may observe; to love God and to serve Him and to give to His cause a full tenth of your time: these have been the qualities that, as I have observed men, have always led to happiness and to success.
>
> In my observations with young people, it has never yet failed that

if a person would do every task as request[ed] and at the proper time, he has never failed to achieve the good will of his fellow workers and a reasonable degree of distinction in his field of endeavor.[33]

Widtsoe remained fond of J. M. Tanner, under whom he had served at the ACU and the BYC. Tanner's death came at a critical time in John's life. He wrote to the family, "I am . . . taking this opportunity of telling you of my love for Dr. Tanner, and my deep and thorough appreciation of his goodness to me from boyhood to the day of his death. . . . I have not, at any time, worked with a man who is more congenial to myself, or who had a bigger or broader vision of the possibilities of institutions of learning. . . . He is gone, and not only have you lost a husband and a father, and I a friend, but thousands have lost an inspirer and safe counselor. He was a remarkable man in his gifts and graces, and I have met few like him in my career."[34]

THE DISCOURSES OF BRIGHAM YOUNG

It is difficult to establish a chronology of John Widtsoe's first six years as an apostle. He was deeply involved in several concurrent activities, including many writing projects. His most constant roles were serving as commissioner of education and working with the YMMIA Board. His work on the Colorado River Commission, the Fact Finders Commission, and the Board of Survey and Adjustment, though recommended by President Grant, were voluntary commitments to the United States Interior Department and the Bureau of Reclamation. Even in the six months he resided in Washington, D.C., as a special advisor on reclamation, it is difficult to tell from his journal that he had broken his normal ecclesiastical stride. Most noticeably absent during those months was the regular, at least weekly, entry, "Temple Meeting" with the Twelve and the First Presidency.

During that period, John's fascination with the life of Brigham Young became a writing project that would become a classic of LDS literature. This fascination began as early as 1892 at Harvard when Susa Young Gates, Brigham Young's daughter, first began to share with John the research she was doing on the Young family in New England. As the years passed, John reaffirmed his admiration for Brigham by giving him credit for innovations in irrigation.

On John's fiftieth birthday, 31 January 1922, Susa wrote him a commemorative letter on formal letterhead, "The Relief Society Magazine, . . . Editor, Susa Young Gates":

> My dear son John,
>
> Today you are fifty years old. I am writing this with my beloved father's pen, which I shall this day entrust to your keeping—as the representative of father's family, in the leading Quorum of the Church.
>
> It is a disappointment to me that none of our sons seem disposed to represent their noble grandfathers before the Lord. But I am so grateful that you are that "man to stand before the Lord" for Brigham Young. If one of our sons, or grandsons, even so stand, in your day, pass on to them this most precious relic. For the inspiration of the Lord will flow from this pen, if the worthy one holds it![35]

While this compliment must have touched John deeply, there is no mention of it in his journal. An entry does say that the Widtsoes had dinner with the Gates family and then went home to Sigsbee Avenue, where a large party was a complete surprise to John. Later there are many entries of his working on Brigham Young's sermons and discourses, but the first and most complete reference that has surfaced is in a letter written almost a year earlier:

> It may interest you to know that I am wading through Brigham Young's sermons, and have behind me four-fifths of them. I think the study has given me a most excellent insight into Brigham Young's character. There is a clear thread running through the discourses that ties together states of mind and feeling and connects up with the events of the day. I did not expect to find the work as illuminating as it has been. To what extent do you think a man preaching from the pulpit, as Brigham Young did, succeeds in covering himself and his real self from the people?
>
> I have been interested to find in the sermons frequent references to the Missouri persecutions, which confirm measurably. . . . Brigham Young's practical common sense made him often see the end from the

beginning, and thereby gave him a power which seemed almost prophetic to many of his colleagues.

Perhaps the most remarkable thing about the evidence of the sermons is the development of the man as he grew in years. Whatever personal traits may have developed in him during his long life, the sermons are splendid evidence of a rather fine growth of quality and sympathy as the years moved on.

This is no time or place to write you any of my impressions. I hope to have the work completed in a short time, and then, if the typewriters can be secured and paid, I hope to whip the thing into readable shape, ready for use by myself or others.[36]

In the immediate months following his fiftieth birthday, John's duties seem to have taken precedence over the sermons. The journal references center on his supervisory duties with the *Deseret News,* the YMMIA, the Temple Committee, religion classes, seminaries, six junior colleges, BYU, the Colorado River Commission—including a ten-day float trip—and many conferences and meetings, manuals for the Young Men and the Quorums of the Seventy, Anna's and Marsel's mission calls, and preparations for beginning biographies on presidents Young and Grant. On New Year's Eve, 1922, he was most grateful for a happy year, for the maturity and goodness of the three children, and for the happiness he and Leah shared.

A day in bed with pharyngitis gave John some unexpected time. "No visitors," he recorded. "Read Journal of discourses, Brigham Young sermons." Some notable references appear after his 1923 mission with Senator Smoot, amid his reclamation meetings and report preparations, and while he was preparing a manual on prophecies of the Doctrine and Covenants: "Nov. 20, Routine on Reclamation work all day. Made some calls. Work on Brigham Young sermons in evening." "Nov. 22, B. Y. sermons in evening. Work of classification begun." "Nov 29, Thanksgiving dinner in Café Louise—tough turkey. Home. Read. Worked on B. Young, etc., until bedtime."

Irregular spurts of activity characterize the next two years, but the work picked up when John was released as commissioner of education in April 1925: "April 12, Worked on sermons of Brigham Young for 4–1/2 hours." Through April and May, he conducted the surveys of the northern reclamation projects, but often every other day he found several hours for the sermons. "June 22, Getting things in shape for B. Young's sermons." "July 3, End of Irrigation Economics course (USAC Summer School). Routine. 19 chapters of B.Y.'s sermons done." "July 11, Completed sorting of B. Young's sermons. 40 chapters. Much work yet." "July 27, B.Y.'s sermons until head ached." "August 3, All day on B. Young's sermons. From 12:30–5 P.M. in Historian's Office working over sermons in Deseret News." "August 10, B.Y. sermons revision."

He worked on the manuscript through August: "August 28, Routine w. Brigham Young all day. Finished work except for odds & ends!! Had binder bind MSS. for easy handling of brethren. Drive. Thank God! I hope Pres. Young is satisfied." On 9 October he sent half of the manuscript to the printer, and during October he made this entry: "In evening had surviving sons & daughters of B. Young & partners. Read extracts from discourses of B. Young. Very pleasant evening." On 20 October he reported on the book to the First Presidency and the next day went to Washington, D.C., where he worked on the index. Thereafter there is no mention of the book's completion or publication in the journal.

While working on the discourses, John spoke at a three-day celebration of Brigham Young's birth, noting, "The acid test of greatness comes after a man is dead, when his life may be viewed through the perspective of many years. Brigham Young has been dead fifty years and his fame is increasing. Brigham Young found his God early in life and . . . he never forgot Him or failed to give Him honor. In the sense that he was loyal to God, he was loyal to his church and his people."[37]

He described some of the things he had discovered about Brigham Young to a psychologist in Los Angeles just a few weeks before the book was published: "I am just coming out of a study of the discourses of Brigham Young . . . and I am convinced that the greatness of Brigham Young rested not nearly so much in his dominant personality as in the fact that he used consistently the full gospel of Jesus Christ in bringing material and spiritual happiness into the lives of his followers."[38]

On his travels in the Eastern states he found public libraries to be deficient in LDS works, so he suggested to the First Presidency, "In view of the well-known name of Brigham Young, it might be quite worth while to place some copies of the Discourses on the shelves of at least the more prominent libraries."

The Discourses of Brigham Young was used as the study guide for the priesthood quorums of the Church in 1926. In commending its use, John remarked, "President Young studied under the teachings of the Prophet Joseph Smith and he names no higher privilege than to teach the people that which the Prophet had taught him. I doubt whether any of our leaders has been more correct in his doctrine than has President Young."[39]

MISCELLANEOUS PROJECTS

In 1927, because of his many projects, John asked the First Presidency for permission to have a typist or stenographer: "I have numerous requests for articles, manuals and other writings to carry our work forward; and besides I have in my heart the desire to do certain other literary work that may be of value in behalf of the great Cause to which my life is committed."[40] He hoped someday to write the story of Joseph Smith from his view.[41] He also received many requests to translate his books for the Norwegians and Danes both at home and in America.[42]

John used his Washington, D.C., trips to further missionary work and made a recommendation to the First Presidency: "I became greatly impressed with the need of recognizing the importance of Washington, where the legislative leaders of the country assemble, as a place where much work may be done in behalf of our cause. . . . It seemed to me as I observed conditions there that a good publicity man, a member of the Church, instructed to keep our people in Washington before the public, could be of great service in many ways."[43] He felt that the world was full of people, who, if the gospel was preached to them, would accept it.[44] "Those who are clean, virtuous and honest and seekers after truth are the people who we seek and who, if they are preached to properly, are impressed with the great latter-day message. The world is in confusion. The simple truths of the gospel have vanished very largely from the people."[45]

Missionary work in Scandinavia was of special importance to John: "The field in Scandinavia remains ready for harvest. With more laborers the harvest would be much greater."[46] He did much to maintain relationships among Scandinavians in the Church. He wrote to Oluff Peterson, "I am always proud of the fact that both of us who have come out of the Scandinavian country are developing into honest, conscientious, useful and reliable citizens in this great new country which we have adopted, as well as in the Church which we so dearly love."[47] The Scandinavian Saints had an annual conference.[48] At the death of Anthon H. Lund, John assumed the responsibility for these summer conferences and organized a committee to run them.[49] When the possibility of disposing of foreign newspapers was raised, John reacted strongly:

> The first result of the closing of a Church foreign paper would probably be the establishment of corresponding private papers, over which the Church would have little or no control. Moreover, it is unquestionably true that there are still a number of people in the Church who do not read English fluently, or who, even if they have learned to speak or read English fairly well, still look back in great fondness upon the language which they learned in their youth. To these people the paper published in their native tongue is of considerable comfort.
>
> There is a great sacrifice in many cases, back of the decision of any person to leave his native country to find a foothold in a new land where a new language is spoken. For that reason I would suggest that the matter of foreign papers be gone in to carefully, and with a feeling for those who are not so familiar with the English language, before definite action is taken.[50]

Though the call to Church service removed John from professional duties in the colleges and universities of Utah, he noted in an address given to the Liberty Stake:

> The educational system of the State of Utah is one of the very best in all the world. We have here a great university, the state university, founded in 1850, the oldest state university west of the Missouri river. By a very interesting coincidence, that university occupies today the

site selected for it by Brigham Young about 1850. We have the distinction of having more students in that university considering our own
population than any other state university in our country, and its
scholastic standards have long been among the best in the land. As
soon as the bill was passed by Congress providing for agricultural
experiment stations, President Anthon H. Lund, who was then in the
territorial legislature, introduced a bill providing for the establishment
of an experiment station and an agricultural college. That college has
also become famous in the educational circles in America, and as far
as I know, it is the largest per capita agricultural college in the United
States. All this indicates an unusual love of education among the
people of the State.[51]

In John's mind, the finest result of higher education was "a more
intimate acquaintanceship with nature and with Nature's God."[52] He
also felt a strong responsibility to encourage young people to get as
much education as their gifts and resources would allow, realizing that
the safety of the republic depended on educated citizens.[53]

23

CONTRIBUTIONS TO
MODERN TEMPLE WORK

───────────◼───────────

Since the Quorum of the Twelve Apostles was restored in 1835, nearly one hundred exemplary men have been called to the office of apostle. From that noble group, John A. Widtsoe and Joseph Fielding Smith have been the most deeply involved in the developments of genealogy, family history, and modern temple work. Their contributions are well documented in the many lessons, addresses, books, and articles that detail the developments of that branch of the Church's mission. They also dominate the recent centennial history of the Genealogical Society of the Church.[1] John Widtsoe's attachment to modern temple work steadily deepened throughout his life. That temple work rose to such prominence amid the strains of his demanding schedule is compelling evidence of his conversion to it.

In an address to the Genealogical Society, John told of an acquaintance that kindled his initial interest. He was a student at Harvard in 1892 when Susa Young Gates visited Boston on a genealogical research trip. Her remarks, public and private, gave an emphasis to temple work that profoundly shaped his life:

> I first met Sister Gates in 1893 [1892], in Boston, Massachusetts. She was there then to gather genealogy for the Young family, and she

discovered a number of things with respect to that genealogy which has made the extension of that family record possible. Ten years or more after that time, illness overtook Sister Gates. She was ready to die, or at least we thought so. A servant of the Lord, later the President of the Council of the Twelve, declared that her time to go had come, and then, under the power of inspiration, he said in substance, "No, the edict of death has been revoked, on the condition that you dedicate the remainder of your life to the cause of salvation for the dead." She accepted life and the challenge, and as far as I know . . . she never faltered in helping to establish this work. She was the one who turned my interest in the direction of genealogy. Her fiery faith lighted my faith and gave me courage to undertake the work.[2]

John developed strong feelings that the most vital element in modern temple work was expressed in the words of Moroni and Malachi when they spoke of turning the hearts of children and fathers to each other. Mutual concern for the ultimate happiness of each family member was the divine intent behind gathering family data and performing sacred temple ordinances. It was so in John's own family, and in his early years he had a rich conversion experience to temple work. His mother, Anna, and his Aunt Petroline spent almost a year in Norway collecting their family genealogy. After finishing the essential temple ordinances for almost one hundred ancestors with whom they had established a direct link, discouragement set in and interest waned because they were unable to establish adequate relationships. That disappointment, however, was soon overcome by a remarkable spiritual experience John remembered to the end of his life. He wrote, "One Sunday morning when I awoke I had a distinct impulse to examine the book the sisters had brought with them, containing the list of blood relatives that they had collected. Obedient as I have always been to spiritual messages, I sought out the book, and studied it for five hours. I found that morning the key which has enabled me to secure thousands of desired names."[3]

John became an ardent believer in divine assistance that comes to diligent temple workers: "I feel so strongly that the work of the dead must be done in the very best manner possible, but I have no fear about

The determination in John's eyes reflects his commitment to temple work.

ultimately finding means of any nature whatsoever with which to accomplish the work."[4] Despite the work he had done for his family, John shared with a fellow officer in the Genealogical Society his fear of inadequacy: "The limitations in my life [were] such as to make it difficult for me to do the amount of temple work that my long list of dead requires of me."[5] Because he was not able to do all the work for his deceased ancestors, he enlisted the service of others to help him. To one of them, he wrote, "I have been so caught by circumstance[s] the last few years as to make it very difficult to do the temple work that is really required of me, and this generous action of yours has done much to make amends for that which I myself have failed to do."[6]

A shared love between ancestors and descendants is the key to bringing the entire human family to eternal life in the kingdom of the Father. To obtain this goal will take more time than this life for most.

Agency and opposition, the elements that guide human progression, require time to master and perfect, and the opportunity of perfection extends beyond mortality. So, to John, the doctrine of universal salvation became the foundation of modern temple work.

The Doctrine of Universal Salvation

It was John's testimony that temple work is at the center of the plan God devised for the happiness and progression of his children. Although the plan has many intricacies, underlying everything is the doctrine of universal salvation. This doctrine extends the blessings of eternal life to all people if they choose to accept it, but that choice remains with the individual. This doctrine was the root from which the work of ancient and modern temples grew and the effectual core of the restoration of gospel doctrines through the Prophet Joseph Smith. John relied on the assurances of Joseph Smith that without turning our hearts to our dead kinsmen, we cannot be made perfect (see D&C 128:18). The Prophet further said, "The greatest responsibility in this world that God has laid upon us is to seek after our dead."[7] He also warned, "Those Saints who neglect it in behalf of their deceased relatives, do it at the peril of their own salvation."[8]

> The basic reason for the importance of the work for the dead, is that the Lord would save all his children. The plan of salvation is absolutely universal. The work of the Lord will not be completed until all who come on earth have had a full and fair chance to accept or reject the gospel. The power to do so remains with the dead in the spirit world, where the gospel will be preached to them.
>
> However, the possible blessings of salvation are conditioned upon obedience to the principles and ordinances of the plan. The dead as well as the living must comply with the requirements for salvation. These requirements are of a two-fold nature: Those that can be met in the life after this, in heaven, and those that must be performed on earth. Faith and repentance may be developed in the spirit world. Baptism with water (strictly an element of earth), a necessary ordinance of the gospel, can be performed only on earth.
>
> This makes the dead dependent on us, the living, for help. Since the dead cannot themselves submit to ordinances, which are specifi-

cally of the earth, yet by divine edict are requisite for entrance into the kingdom of heaven.[9]

The scriptural passage "this is my work and my glory—to bring to pass the immortality and eternal life of man" (Moses 1:39) echoes through all of John's teachings on temple work. Because that work extends through eternity, temples are universally the shrines of God's plan for the eternal life of man and the workstations for bringing about his work and glory. John taught that salvation for the dead is the great keystone in the gospel arch that holds all other parts of the gospel together: "We shall not progress very far here or hereafter, until we are tied to our fathers back through our natural family lines to Father Adam. We cannot move on to our full exaltation until this is done. Let everyone help in this work."[10] He further spoke about the worth of redeeming the souls of the dead in furthering our own eternal development and advancement. A seldom-considered yet impassioned viewpoint concerning their worth was revealed when he wrote:

> The foundation of this work is love, born and nurtured and developed in sacrifice. The worth of a soul now becomes great to me. I go into the temple, and give a half day to opening the doors of salvation for a dead person; or I spend many precious hours searching for, planning, gathering genealogy in order that he and his brothers— my brothers—may have those saving ordinances done for them by my fellow-workers who have access to the Temples of the Lord. I only know him by name, and never shall know him nearer on this earth; but out of my own understanding love of the cause, no matter how humble it may be, and out of my willingness to sacrifice to prove that love, I take a step toward the likeness of my Father in heaven. It is a tremendous thing—this soul for whom I labour. Without that soul I might not find the same opportunity of approaching the likeness of my Father. That soul is of immense worth to me. . . .
>
> . . . A soul becomes of indescribable value, since it offers a means of service by which we ourselves may rise to the position and power of godhood. . . .
>
> The worth of a soul can best be measured in its effect upon man's realization of his highest ideal. Without my brother I cannot attain my highest. Without loving him I cannot look forward to the highest

place. Without sacrificing for him I cannot hope to win the fullest recognition. Without him I cannot achieve my likeness to the Lord. We are bound together, one great human family, moving on to a glorious destiny.[11]

The divine desire of a loving Heavenly Father for the eternal life of every child is unquestioned. That very desire underscores the divine worth of every soul born into mortality, for each is bound up in the love of an infinite Redeemer who fulfilled the sacred atonement. Further, when men and women accepted the great plan of God in the Grand Council in the premortal world, they became parties to the salvation of every person under that plan. Thus the immortality and eternal life of every man and woman became the work and glory of each mortal brother and sister.

Through temple work, the great mysteries of eternity are laid open to the minds of men and women who prepare themselves for the revelations of God given there. Anyone who has the opportunity to participate in the divine work performed in modern temples and refrains from doing so deprives him or herself of some of God's greatest blessings. John wrote:

> The instructions and all other parts of the endowment ceremonies are of such a nature as to exalt the spirit of man. The sealing powers of the priesthood, exercised in the temples, uniting parents and children, and husband to wife, for time and eternity, give indescribable satisfaction to the soul. The vast meaning of the temple ordinances opens the human understanding to the mysteries of eternity. . . .
>
> Those who fail to receive their endowments and sealings, who enter into marriage outside of the temple, are losers beyond expression. Those who have had their endowments but who do not work for the dead fail to receive the refreshing of their souls that comes by repeated communion with the Spirit of God so abundantly manifested in the temple.[12]

In a 1921 address in the Assembly Hall on Temple Square, while serving as president of the University of Utah, John described man's voluntary choice to place himself under the plan, to fulfill part of the plan by performing temple work, and to participate in the progression encompassing the universal salvation of mankind. He taught that through modern temple work both our premortal and mortal existence are connected to our potential for exaltation:

> The human race were "in the beginning with God," and were created spiritual beings in a day before the[ir] arrival upon this earth. Mankind is here because of its acceptance of the Plan of Salvation, and satisfactory pre-existent lives. We have won the right to be here; we have not been forced to come here; we have won our place upon the earth. We shall pass into another sphere of existence, and shall continue upward and onward forever and forever, if we obey the high laws of eternal existence.[13]

Behind the various beliefs surrounding eternal life and universal salvation of mankind lay some of the greatest religious battles. Such beliefs were at the heart of the religious excitement that Joseph Smith encountered around Palmyra, New York, the very spark that led him into the Sacred Grove.

> The vicious doctrine had been preached for generations that only a few men and women were destined to be saved in the presence of God. In that battle, questions were asked. Is there power of repentance beyond the grave? At death does nothing remain of the old life? Is memory blotted out? Is the power of free will then a thing of the past? Around such questions, asked by intelligent men, a great battle was waged. That was after the Lord had turned the key, through the Prophet Joseph Smith, and laid bare the doctrine of universal salvation, which declares that all who repent, either here or in the hereafter, may achieve salvation in one or the other of the great glories that the Lord has prepared for His children.[14]

John also taught, "The fact that such corruptions of ordinances and ceremonies have always existed is a strong evidence of the continuity of temple worship, under the Priesthood, from the days of Adam."[16] The mysteries that lie behind the means of attaining eternal life make up the mystique of the world's temples, a fascination that has intrigued mankind for centuries.

Let me suggest that the reason why temple building and temple worship have been found in every age, on every hand, and among every people, is because the Gospel in its fullness was revealed to Adam, and that all religions and religious practices are therefore derived from the remnants of the truth given to Adam and transmitted by him to the patriarchs. The ordinances of the temple in so far as then necessary, were given, no doubt, in those early days, and very naturally corruptions of them have been handed down [through] the ages. Those who understand the eternal nature of the gospel— planned before the foundations of the earth—understand clearly why all history seems to revolve about the building and use of temples.[16]

Temple work centers around the duties of men and women in this world and the influence of their work on the degrees of glory to be attained by others in the worlds beyond. Thus temples are the undisputed intersection between the mortal world and the worlds of glory that extend even to God's own habitation. The varied views of man's immortal salvation are evident in the work of the world's temples. Such temples, from whatever century or sect of religious thought, were raised in acknowledgment of God and his plan for the eternal life of mankind. The great shrines built by people throughout the ages connect ancient and modern temple work and provide evidence that obtaining eternal life is the shared duty of mortal kinsmen. Over the ages, men have tried to maintain the correct form and meaning of revealed temple ordinances, even at times when God has withdrawn the necessary power and guidance for correct performance. These attempts in all ages gave rise to the corruption of temple ordinances. Awareness of this corruption sheds important light on the history of revealed temple work and is essential to any consideration of modern temple work.

HISTORICAL DEVELOPMENTS

The seeds Susa Young Gates planted in John developed early roots. Throughout his busy academic career, many years before his apostolic appointment, he maintained a constant vigilance in matters of temple work. The Utah Genealogical Society was organized a few months after his graduation from Harvard in 1894. He followed the society closely for many years and was an active participant by 1910, when their publication, the *Utah Genealogical and Historical Magazine,* began. At that time he was on the Committee on Preparation of Genealogical and Historical Papers, Lectures, etc., chaired by his brother, Osborne.[17] On 6 October 1910, Osborne read a paper written by John for the quarterly meeting of the society. John was in Washington, D.C., on business for the Agricultural College. In the address, John described some key theological elements embodied in the work of the society that culminated in vicarious temple ordinances. One of them was the restoration of priesthood keys that ushered in the sacred temple ordinances to be administered before the sons of Levi could make their offering as prophesied by John the Baptist (see D&C 13:1). That offering was based on the restoration of temple work:

> The life of man began with loving sacrifice, and received its crowning mission in the work of redemption for his dead kindred. The mystic allusion in the Doctrine and Covenants which refers to the time when the sons of Levi will offer an offering in righteousness would be clear and beautiful in the light of the principle of vicarious salvation; for the sons of Levi would offer upon the altar, which the Prophet Joseph Smith declared was the acceptable offering in righteousness—the books containing the records of their dead, who had received vicarious salvation at their hands. Man's endeavor throughout the history of the world has been a constant search for joy. Whatever his work, however diligently he pursues one line of endeavor or another, the purpose is always the same—the circular line of upward progress leading him ever back to the quest for joy. As all other activities in the great and grand plan of the world work by upward evolution, so the course of God is an eternal round of love.[18]

In a lesson on temple work, John wrote of temple ordinances and symbols performed on earth in tandem with ordinances and realities accomplished in heaven: "The earthly ordinances of the Gospel are themselves only reflections of heavenly ordinances. For instance, baptism, the gift of the Holy Ghost and temple work are merely earthly symbols of realities that prevail throughout the universe; but, they are symbols of truths that must be recognized if the Great Plan is to be fulfilled. The acceptance of these earthly symbols is part and parcel of correct earth life, but being earthly symbols they are distinctly of the earth, and cannot be accepted elsewhere than on earth."[19]

In several addresses John discussed the instrumental role of the Prophet Joseph Smith in restoring modern temple work and the importance he attached to it. Almost the first and last duties in the administrative ministry of the Prophet dealt with building temples. From the dedication of the temple site in Independence shortly after the Church was organized to the preparations for the temple in Nauvoo just before his death, Joseph held a constant vision of the importance of building temples and getting temple work under way. Joseph's attention to the dedication of temple sites and his many revelations about temples all point to his deep understanding of the necessity of temple work and the redemption of the dead.[20] John noted, "The main concern of the Prophet in the restoration of the Gospel in these latter days was the founding, building, and completion of temples in which the ordinances 'hid from before the foundation of the world' might be given. In fact, the Lord declared repeatedly to the Prophet that unless temples were built and used, the plan of salvation could neither be in full operation nor fully accomplished."[21]

John studied the inspired teachings of Joseph Smith throughout his lifetime and became the Church's leading scholar on the revelations of the Prophet as recorded in the Doctrine and Covenants. In addition to the first extensive concordance on the Doctrine and Covenants, he wrote two books and many articles about the Joseph Smith. Through it all he shared the Prophet's enthusiasm for the fundamental role of temple work. In an address to the Genealogical Society nearly a year before his call to the Twelve, he declared, "I doubt whether association with any other organization would give me greater joy than this one, because it seems to me that the work in charge of the Genealogical Society is the very keystone of the Gospel arch. If the work entrusted to us in this organization is well done, the Lord's work is safe, and will go onward, according to the will of the Lord; but if it be poorly done or slighted, the work of the Lord to that degree will be hindered."[22]

John also had a strong testimony of personal revelations received in the temple. One particularly valuable experience illustrates the kind of revelation available: "For several years, under a Federal grant with my staff of workers we had gathered thousands of data in the field of soil moisture; but I could not extract any general law running through them. I gave up at last. My wife and I went to the temple that day to forget the failure. In the third endowment room, out of the unseen, came the solution, which has long since gone into print."[23] Such revelations are answers to the greatest problems that vex the lives of righteous men and women.

Those who enter the temple to perform service for the dead may be the recipients of blessings and revelations as a consequence of that service: "That is the gift that comes to those who enter the temple properly, because it is a place where revelations may be expected. I bear you my personal testimony that this is so."[24] To emphaze this gift and privilege, he added, "Does it mean that once in a while God may come into the temples, and that once in a while the pure in heart may see God there; or does it mean the larger thing, that the pure in heart who go into the temples, may, there, by the Spirit of God, always have a wonderfully rich communion with God? I think that is what it means to me and to you and to most of us."[25]

Soon after John's call to the Twelve, he was made a director of the Genealogical Society. Though he had been a stalwart contributor to the society for many years, he was able to devote more time and attention to it as part of his apostolic appointment. Bearing that mantle, his spiritual convictions grew deeper. He also carried greater influence on the policies and directions the society would follow. After a few months as one of the Twelve, John provided a glimpse of the significance he attached to the restoration of temple work: "I haven't the slightest doubt that unseen forces all about us are guiding us into the proper performance of the important work for the dead. In fact, the longer I study the Gospel of Jesus Christ the more convinced I am that salvation for the dead is the cementing principal which hold[s] together all the other doctrinal divisions of the Church. . . . It seems to me that [the] spirit of temple work is growing by leaps and bounds among the people."[26]

In 1995, in commemoration of the one-hundred-year anniversary of the Utah Genealogical Society, a detailed history was published by three reputable historians. Of Widtsoe's appointment, they noted, "A respected scholar and academician, Widtsoe brought broad perspective and foresight into guiding the direction of the society for the thirty years he served on the board."[27]

THE TEMPLE INDEX BUREAU

In 1921 a substantial and divisive problem arose because of duplication in research efforts and ordinance work. Harry H. Russell, an energetic worker in the library of the Genealogical Society, became the leading voice in the urgency of the duplication problem. An incident from his own temple activity illustrates the magnitude of the problem. Russell was progressing well with work on one of his family lines. After spending 360 days in performing the proxy ordinances for those ancestors, he discovered that other members of his family were doing work on that same family line in St. George. Elated by the discovery of further family involvement, he quickly arranged a trip to St. George to celebrate and compare notes: "To his dismay, he discovered that they had the same book and had been doing work for the same names he had done in the Salt Lake Temple. His training as an accountant and businessman led him to quickly calculate the hours lost if such duplications were taking place in all the Church's temples."[28] Though Russell was one of the Church's most conscientious genealogists, he refused, at least for a significant time, to perform further endowments for his own ancestors, though he continued his work as a temple officiator.

Elder Widtsoe reported similar aggravations among other diligent Church members:

> I heard of a sister recently who said she had quit doing Temple work because she had just expended $500 in Temple work only to find afterward that someone had preceded her in doing it. She became discouraged. Another sister expressed herself along the same lines for the same reasons. This should not be, but we should strive to overcome such possibilities. . . . I may say also in this connection that a plan is being devised, in connection with the Genealogical Society, to reduce

the possibility of duplication by a card index system containing the names of those whose work has been done, and which will be valuable, and available to everyone who is interested.[29]

Attempts to resolve this problem began in the 1890s, but it wasn't until John chaired the society's Activities and Programs Committee that the problem was finally solved.[30] In 1921 he and his committee set their sights on finding a solution. Russell devised a plan for an index bureau to act as a clearinghouse to approve all names before essential temple ordinances could be performed.[31] John initially approved Russell's plan and brought it to the attention of Anthon H. Lund, president of the Genealogical Society, and Joseph Fielding Smith, then Church historian and recorder.[32] The idea was endorsed, and John was left to work out the details with elders Joseph Fielding Smith and Joseph Christenson. A meeting with temple presidents and recorders was held during the October 1921 general conference to refine the plan. On 3 November 1921, Elder Widtsoe explained the system and outlined the steps to the board of directors of the Utah Genealogical Society who, after some discussion, instructed him and his committee to finish their plans and bring their final recommendations with an estimate of the costs of operation before members of the board and the First Presidency. Later in November Elder Widtsoe outlined the proposal in a letter to President Heber J. Grant. His eloquent justification gives a clearer view of the problem and why they diligently sought to resolve it:

> The work in our temples has now grown to such proportions that a knowledge of the work done in the temples is called for by very many people to avoid duplication, and to guide in the preparation of family records. The financial loss due to duplication is large; the discouragement that follows duplication is larger, but the fewer spirits provided with the blessings of the endowment when duplication occurs is the most serious consequence. To make the records furnish this protection, an index is necessary. . . . The Directors of the Society; the presidents and recorders of the temples, and the committee on classwork and activities, are unanimous in the opinion that the time has come when the index should be made.[33]

Elder Widtsoe stressed the urgency of forming the index and

recommended that young people familiar with the typewriter be called on short-time missions to get the project in place. The cost of the cards—which he estimated at $1,500–2,000—was about all that was required. Two months later he wrote to the First Presidency, suggesting that stakes in temple districts call qualified women to serve six-month missions to complete the cards and establish a central filing office where work could be checked to avoid duplication. He also recommended that Harry H. Russell be called to supervise and oversee the work.[34] The recommendations were approved, and Russell was made director of the Temple Index Bureau.

FUNDAMENTAL PRINCIPLES

In major addresses to the Genealogical Society, Elder Widtsoe frequently spoke of fundamental principles of Mormon doctrine that are firmly established by temple and genealogical work. The following excerpts briefly capture his view of some of the most important principles of church doctrine.

On the eternal existence of man:

> Every person who goes into the temple tacitly admits his belief in the principle of the eternal existence of man. This is the first thought that must possess any intelligent worker in the temple, otherwise why spend time on the work.

On the eternal life of man:

> Man is not only indestructible, but is subject to growth. . . . Every time we go into the temple we accept the doctrine that not only shall man live forever, but he shall either grow or retrograde.

On the agency of man:

> The eternal spirit of man is characterized by its free agency. . . . Certainly we could not conceive of the true meaning of temple work, unless we accept the eternal principle of man's free agency; and that the dead as well as the living may receive or reject the opportunities of the Gospel.

On the judgment of man according to works:

The spirits sent to this earth will be judged by their works. . . . Moreover our punishment stands, at least measurably, throughout the endless ages, because, as we go onward, those above us go onward also, and the relative positions remain the same. . . . Temple work . . . assumes this principle of eternal justice.

On the love of God for humanity:

My spirit and yours, and the spirit of every man or woman are guided and will be guided by a loving Father. . . . In the presence of His love we grew and developed in our spiritual existence, as today we live out our physical existence, and as in the hereafter we shall continue our eternal life. Temple work best represents the quality of the infinite love of God for his children. . . . Unless we know the eternal love of our Father for His children we gather only a partial meaning of temple work. God's plan is to save His children.

On the authority of God and the great plan:

Then, also, to perform these ordinances of the earth officially, and to make them valid, God has delegated authority to His servants on earth, whereby the work of the Great Plan, as pertaining to the earth, can be consummated. . . . Hence, living men and women may act for and in behalf of the dead under the direction of the Priesthood. Those who die in unbelief, but who later obtain belief, must have the chance to go on, otherwise justice is not satisfied.[35]

Guided by these fundamental principles, Elder Widtsoe often spoke of the accountability all people share for their dead. In general conference, on 3 April 1927, he taught, "We have been told by the Prophet Joseph Smith that without our dead we cannot be saved; or, as he stated it, 'Their salvation is necessary and essential to our salvation.'"[36] In remarks to a family organization, he stressed that family members currently on the earth cannot progress to eternal life until their family lines are tied back to Adam. Guided by this conviction, Elder Widtsoe wrote, "I believe the Lord requires of us that we all set our houses in order in this respect, that each man and woman, every family, set about to secure just as completely as may be possible a record of their dead, so that thereby the genealogies of the human family may be gathered and increased in number, and we may have ample material with which to labor in the Temples of the Lord."[37]

POPULARIZING TEMPLE WORK

To help place all organizations in close touch with the Genealogical Society and to educate members about genealogy and modern temple work, Widtsoe headed a committee that included representatives from the Sunday School, the Young Men's and Young Women's Mutual Improvement Associations, the Primary, Church Education, and Brigham Young University.[38] He wrote to Adam S. Bennion, superintendent of Brigham Young University, to inquire about having instruction in genealogy and temple work added to some of the curriculum.[39] In a letter to the general Primary president, he wrote, "I feel that you are sowing seed on very fertile soil. If our children can be taught some of the elements of Temple work, however small, it will mean much to the Temple workers of a generation hence when these little boys and girls shall be grown men and women."[40]

The *Utah Genealogical and Historical Magazine* had carried some brief outlines for lessons on genealogy. Topics centered on record keeping, the Genealogical Society, the doctrine behind genealogy, and the history of genealogy. His background as an educator gave Elder Widtsoe a constant place on the committees assigned to formulate genealogical lessons. In February 1923 he shared a personal wish about the lessons: "Some day I hope that the central office will have complete study courses for the genealogical societies of the Church."[41] Some lessons on genealogy were being taught in the Church at the time, but no universal system was followed. His wish for a study course from the central office was fulfilled in 1925 when a three-year course on genealogy and temple work was begun. The lessons, published in the *Utah Genealogical and Historical Magazine*, were designed for weekly study classes. The foreword explained the intent behind the lessons:

> The lesson work presented herewith is the beginning of a three years' course in genealogical and temple work, based upon the new genealogical handbook, published by the Genealogical Society of Utah.

> Each lesson is grouped into four parts, designed for weekly class study for genealogical workers, and others interested in the work of redemption of the dead.
>
> The outlines and lesson-statements have been purposely left brief to enable the class to work out its own details and otherwise delve into the work in a manner best suited to the conditions at hand. With the handbook of easy access and an abundance of material in the Scriptures to supplement its teachings, there is now at the disposal of all Latter-day Saints sufficient material to give them a working knowledge of genealogical procedure, if they will but devote the necessary time to master the intricacies of this wonderful art. Even those who do not desire to become practical genealogists will find much satisfaction in a careful study of the doctrine presented.[42]

The signature beneath the foreword reads, "Genealogical Society of Utah, Lesson Committee, Dr. John A. Widtsoe, Chairman. Salt Lake City, Utah. Dec. 1, 1924."[43] These lessons focused on fundamental doctrine. They included frequent examples from scripture and an emphasis on world history and world society. A notable difference between these lesson outlines and previous ones was that about every third lesson was devoted to genealogical procedures. This allowed every student to gain an understanding of the skills needed to do his or her own genealogy. Students also learned how to use various sources of genealogical information and how the Genealogical Society functioned. Elder Widtsoe was determined to teach every Church member about the importance of temple work and how to proceed with that work for his or her own family.

BUILDING A CENTRAL LIBRARY

While traveling through Europe with Senator Reed Smoot in 1923, John assessed the work required by each country to maintain accurate genealogical records and surveyed their sources and repositories. As he visited Great Britain, Denmark, Sweden, Norway, Germany, France, Belgium, and Holland, he found out how to obtain genealogical information from them. He carefully observed what procedures they followed and tried to secure as much information as he could for the Utah

Genealogical Society's library.[44] At the conclusion of his trip, he sub-mitted his observations and recommendations:

> It is very clear that in all the countries visited there has been for
> some time an active interest in genealogical research. Our mission-
> aries, following the suggestion of Brother Morton, could help greatly
> in locating such collections. Selections of books and other materials
> should be made, however, only by some one who is experienced with
> books and who has a deep interest in genealogy. My Frankfurt
> [Germany] experience was confirmation of this view.
>
> Clearly also there is quite as much genealogical material in
> Scandinavia as in any other country, if it only may be made available.
> The Society should proceed vigorously to supply its library with all
> valuable printed material on genealogy. The collections made on this
> trip will make a good foundation. Such library facilities will do much
> for the cause here at home, and will furnish leads for more detailed
> work abroad.
>
> Our genealogical work abroad is done in a very haphazard man-
> ner. I fear that some of it is inaccurate. It seems to me that steps must
> be taken to organize for this work. Competent men should be placed
> in Scandinavia for genealogical purposes. There is work enough to
> support them. It may be the wisest plan to form some organization at
> home, a genealogical bureau, which will undertake to act as a medium
> between the person seeking the names of his dead and the expert
> worker who will collect the names. The system as now practiced is not
> commensurate with the cause, or with the provision made for temple
> work.[45]

Whenever Elder Widtsoe was on assignment in Europe, he consci-entiously sought to purchase worthy genealogical books and already published family histories. In the 1931 Genealogical Convention, Elder Joseph Fielding Smith announced that the purchases made by Elder Widtsoe had kept the society nearly broke. President Widtsoe responded, "I regret that, of course, but I am not very sorry. Nearly every book will be of value to us in the course of time."[46] In many of his endeavors to obtain important books, he had felt the direction of the Holy Spirit. He shared one of his most memorable experiences:

I know of no work that I have done in the Church which has been so filled with testimonies of the divinity of this work as the little I have done in behalf of the salvation of our dead. I could tell you a number of experiences, but the one that impressed me most happened a few years ago when I accompanied Brother Reed Smoot to Europe. We came to Stockholm; he had his work to do; I decided to see what I could do in the way of finding books on Swedish genealogy. I knew the names of the two big bookstores in Stockholm. I went to the one, made my selections, and then started across the city to the other bookstore in the hope that I might find some more suitable books. As I hurried along the street filled with people, I was stopped suddenly by some voice which said to me: "Go across the street and down that narrow side street." I looked across the street and saw a little narrow street. I had not been in Stockholm before. I thought: This is all non-sense, . . . I have to do my work, and I walked on. Almost at once the voice came again, as distinctly as any voice I have ever heard. Then I asked myself: What is your business in this city? Are you not on the Lord's errand? And I crossed over; went down the little narrow street, and there, half-way down, found a little bookstore that I had known nothing about. When I asked for books on genealogy the lady said: "No, we do not carry books on genealogy. When we get such books we send them to the bookstore"—naming the store for which I was headed. Then, just as I was leaving in disappointment, she said: "Stop a minute. A leading book collector, a genealogist, died about a month ago, and we bought his library. Many of his genealogical books are in the back room ready to be sent to the bookstore, but if you want to buy them you may have them." Thus we secured the foundation of Swedish genealogy in our library.[47]

From these inspired beginnings, the Church's genealogical library has become the largest and most useful repository of genealogical information in the world.

A PROGRAM FOR GENEALOGICAL EXCHANGE

The European trip with Senator Smoot deepened Elder Widtsoe's conviction of the need for Church members and interested genealogists to coordinate and share their research. Travel to distant lands to

research ancestral lines was too costly for most to consider, but in almost
all of those distant lands were fellow Church members or interested professionals who could exchange research information for work on their
lines in yet another part of the world.

The emphasis given temple work from the beginning of the restoration of the gospel to the Prophet Joseph Smith underscores the importance of making genealogical information and temple ordinances available to everyone as expeditiously as possible.[48] This was the underlying
message of an address on the beginnings of modern temple work by Elder
Widtsoe.[49] In 1928 he published the names of key workers and the
addresses of the significant archives and libraries of genealogical information in the Scandinavian countries. From each library or archive he
requested information on local researchers who could be employed on an
individual basis to do research for Church members who wished to obtain
their information but could not travel to these countries. The information was most helpful in furthering the work.[50] Yet this was not enough;
the need for greater success drove him to find more successful methods.

From 1928 to 1934 Elder Widtsoe was the president of the
European Mission, which consisted of eleven missions across the various capitals of Europe. He became starkly aware of the feelings of dep-
rivation among European Church members, who were without a temple
where they could receive their own endowments and sealings or do the
work for their dead ancestors. Under the leadership of President
Widtsoe, the mission presidents in Europe established a program for
genealogical research and exchange. Each branch organized a genealogical class in which members studied the best-known manuals on genealogy in the Church. A mission genealogical agent was called to coordinate the classes and the research results. Within each country, Church
members could aid each other. For example, a member in Liverpool,
England, could do research for someone in Glasgow, Scotland, and
thereby eliminate travel and lodging costs for the Saint from Scotland.
In exchange, someone from Glasgow could do local research for the
Liverpool member or someone else from the branch with family roots in
Glasgow. Global exchanges were even more intriguing. Without a
temple, the only work European Saints could do was gather genealogical

data. On the other hand, they had an advantage that those in Utah did not have—they were in the very lands from which the Utah members or their ancestors had come and could readily research the family records. The following excerpt is from a reprint of one of Elder Widtsoe's *Millennial Star* editorials:

> It is further proposed that Latter-day Saints of European descent, living in temple districts, may be willing to do work in the temples for the dead of those who live in Europe, in exchange for genealogical help. Such valuable mutual assistance could be arranged . . . through the mission genealogical agent. A definite basis for exchange will probably be suggested, as, for example, three new names in a given family line or four hours of actual research work done by someone in Europe would pay for the endowment of one person in one of the temples[51]

This editorial includes an excerpt from a letter President Widtsoe wrote to the Genealogical Society to report the success of the exchange program in missions that had undertaken it. This same editorial, later reprinted in the *Utah Genealogical and Historical Magazine,* instructed Saints in the United States to send their research requests to President Widtsoe's office. The mission genealogical agent would then process the requests and forward them to someone who could assist the American Saints. John's mailing address in Liverpool was included as well as a description of the information needed from all who wished to obtain research help in Europe. To assure fairness in the program, the editorial included a standard basis on which the users could plan: "Members living in Temple Districts will do ordinance work for names of those living in Missions at the standard rate of 50¢ for a female and 75¢ for a male. Members living in Missions will copy information from parish or probate registers at the rate of 25¢ per hour. Thus two hours research will pay for the endowment of one woman and three for that of a man [whose work includes additional time for priesthood ordination]."[52]

In April 1931 Elder Widtsoe, though still living in Europe, spent time in Salt Lake City to attend general conference. His attendance was requested by the First Presidency because he had not attended for three years while residing in Europe. Held in connection with the conference was a convention of the Genealogical Society. Responding to their request, he gave a moving report of genealogical interest among the Saints in the missions of Europe. He reported that it was a matter of great sorrow to many Saints in Europe, especially those of second- or third-generation Church membership, that they must live their lives without the blessings of temple ordinances. Moreover, the members lamented that they didn't have the privilege of enjoying the blessings of regular temple attendance. He spoke of their concern about the thousands of Saints who had faithfully lived the principles set forth in the Restoration and who had gone on to a splendid reward beyond the grave but who most often were required to wait substantial periods for their temple work to be done. They waited in the spirit world with those who had rejected the gospel or never had it. The living descendants of these faithful Saints were, of course, anxious that temple ordinance work become more efficient, with unnecessary delays eliminated. Elder Widtsoe requested that the society take up this matter and, through the Index Bureau, get the temple work of deceased members efficiently accomplished. He reported disappointment that the work of the Exchange Bureau had developed so slowly, yet he spoke with confidence and urged patience and greater effort to make it successful. As a result of this interest and at his recommendation, the Research Bureau of the Genealogical Society was established. Despite his sincerity and the intrinsic merit of the idea, it did not flourish. "The Society did not adopt the worldwide supervisory program Elder Widtsoe had in mind, but it did establish the Research Bureau, which supervised all research done at the library, hired researchers, made contacts with foreign researchers, transferred money to foreign countries when needed, conducted classes in genealogical research, assisted in obtaining information not available in the library, and acted as a general clearinghouse in coordinating research activities."[53]

TEMPLE WORK TO THE END

In 1923 Elder Widtsoe was asked to attend the dedication services of the Alberta Temple. The experience seemed to invigorate him further and intensify his advocacy of temple work. He was particularly

The inscription reads "President Heber J. Grant and Apostles G. A. Smith, Jas. E.
Talmage, and John [A.] Widtsoe and others of the Original Student body of B. Y.
University, Provo, Utah, U.S.A. Taken on Alberta Temple Grounds, Aug. 30, 1923."

moved by the spiritual impact temple work had on the rest of the gospel
work in the latter days: "The Alberta Temple . . . is an architectural
gem, beautiful inside and out," he said. "The architects have produced
an exquisite harmony such as I think I have never known before in any
structure whether in the new or old world. The dedicatory exercises
were very impressive. There were eleven sessions and the spirit which
actuates the great latter-day work known as 'Mormonism' was present
abundantly so that every person present was touched by it."[54]

Elder Widtsoe continually strove to deepen the appreciation and
understanding of Church members regarding temple work. He was convinced of the "need to lay out with great care a general plan for the
future development of this work, having in mind the tremendous importance of it according to our faith."[55] Additional concern arose over those
in the mission field who did not have the knowledge to do their own
genealogical work: "I do think that the Saints residing in the mission
field would be greatly benefitted if some definite help could be tendered

them. They need to know something about the sources of genealogical information, often lying near at hand, and the methods of building their genealogy for Temple work."[56]

Through the remainder of his life, Elder Widtsoe participated in the decision making that guided the society and the Church in matters of temple and genealogical work and salvation of the dead. In 1935 he taught that of all the gospel principles, probably none contributed more toward developing one's spiritual power and strength than work associated with salvation of the dead. From his own experience and the experiences of his friends, he assured Church members that "those who give themselves in wisdom and with propriety to this work will round out their spiritual experiences, enrich their lives, and find a new and abiding joy in all duties pertaining to life under the Gospel of Jesus Christ."[57] During Leadership Week at BYU in 1935, he spoke of the doctrine of universal salvation again: "If the Gospel is not for all men—if God has a few chosen spirits whom He loves and who, irrespective of their labors in the past, in mortality, and in the hereafter, shall be brought into His presence—then the whole latter day work falls to the ground as a set of separate and distinct unorganized principles."[58]

In 1937 he described the urgency with which the Church must proceed: "The dead are so many that we cannot hope, unless we use the utmost expedition, to keep pace with the gathering of the names made available in our genealogical research."[59] In 1939 and 1940 he prepared outlines for lessons that were carried in the society's magazine. From 1940, when the Church ceased publication of the *Utah Genealogical and Historical Magazine*, through 1954, a genealogical section was included in the *Improvement Era*.[60] Elder Widtsoe was editor of the *Improvement Era*. A 1943 editorial carried his ideas further:

> To give glory to the Lord, members of the Church must seek the blessings offered by the temples. To build with a flaming faith, and then, when the building is completed, to fail to use it, is folly and unacceptable to the Lord. The flame of faith must not burn low. Every member of the Church should so conduct himself as to be worthy of receiving the ordinances offered within temple walls. Further, he should seek opportunities to labor there for the dead, so that they, if

the work is accepted by them, may also win membership in the kingdom of God. Then we do honor to the Lord, and win blessings for ourselves and our ancestry.[61]

In moving remarks growing out of the worldwide horrors of World War II, especially its devastation among his beloved European countries, he gave a sobering challenge to Church members. His address was given in recognition of the fiftieth anniversary of the dedication of the Salt Lake Temple:

> These are trying days, in which Satan rages, at home and abroad, hard days, evil and ugly days. We stand helpless as it seems before them. We need help. We need strength. We need guidance. Perhaps if we would do our work in behalf of those of the unseen world who hunger and pray for the work we can do for them, the unseen world would in return give us help in the day of our urgent need. There are more in that other world than there are here. There is more power and strength there than we have here upon this earth. We have but a trifle, and that trifle is taken from the immeasurable power of God. We shall make no mistake in becoming collaborators in the Lord's mighty work for human redemption.[62]

The great emphasis Elder Widtsoe and other society officials put on gathering family names and performing temple work in time created a serious dilemma. Inflexible policies of proving familial relationships in the clearance process for names submitted to the temple, combined with increases in temple attendance, led to a shortage of names for temple work. Elders Joseph Fielding Smith and John A. Widtsoe were the main advocates for processing names regardless of family connections to members of the Church. Their views gave rise to the current name extraction program. Historians have noted:

> In September 1943, Elder Widtsoe anticipated the policy that eventually developed when he declared that the Society ought to obtain all published manuscript and microfilm records as fast as possible and use the names for temple work. "Why don't we use the names for temple work which cannot be tied to any Church families? . . . The Lord has provided these names by inspiring genealogists to compile and publish them. In an extremity like the present, why not

use the names from such records? . . . For what purpose have these books been compiled, if not to make the names available for temple work?"[63]

The urgency Elder Widtsoe had always expressed for this sacred work did not diminish as he neared the end of his life. Addressing the general conference in April 1950, he urged once again that the Saints turn their hearts steadily and forcefully toward the duty of laboring for the dead. He said, "We cannot be saved without doing so. The earth cannot continue to its destined end unless we so do."[64] As always, he pointed to the outstanding spiritual benefit that flows to all who actively participate in the work: "Let us do our duty for ourselves and for the future of this earth upon which we live and which we hold so dear. And let us remember always that the spiritual forces centering in our temples are more powerful than atom rays or any earthly force discovered by man."[65]

In the last year of his life, he summarized his lifelong view: "Temple work is the cement that holds together all gospel principles. Genealogy is the first step in universal salvation, as far as we on earth can contribute to this great human destiny."[66] The *Improvement Era* published excerpts from an article on the temples he was working on at the time of his death. Illustrating his article are color photographs of the interior and exterior of the St. George Temple. These final comments returned to the essence of modern temple work—the work and glory of God. Lifelong devotion to the salvation of the dead draws Church members closer to those so served and to God, whose work it is. Reminding readers that we are not expected to comprehend the details of the temple in a single visit, Elder Widtsoe declared:

> Therefore, the Lord has provided means of repetition. Temple work must be done first by each person for himself or herself; then it may be done for one's dead ancestors or friends as frequently as circumstances will allow. This service will open the doors of salvation for the dead and will also help fix upon the mind of the living the nature, meaning, and obligations of the endowment. By keeping the endowment fresh in mind, we shall be better able to perform our duties in life under the influence of eternal blessings.[67]

Wherever one turns in the revealed gospel of the Lord Jesus Christ, and particularly in the temple, the conviction grows that the work of God is re-established for his specific purposes in the latter days. Temple service is to aid and to help us in qualifying for this mighty work: " . . . to bring to pass the immortality and eternal life of man." (Moses 1:39)[68]

A strong testimony of an intimate connection between the powers of heaven and modern temple work illuminated the life and teachings of John A. Widtsoe. It began to burn its way into his heart while he was a young student at Harvard. Those feelings grew ever stronger until the day he himself passed through death's portal. His study of scripture and the revealed teachings of latter-day prophets brought conversion to the doctrine behind temple work, while personal experiences in gathering genealogical data and participating in vicarious temple ordinances brought conversion to the divinity of the work. John's testimony deepened through his life as he became one of the foremost spokesmen for modern temple work.

24

A MISSION WITH
SENATOR SMOOT

A subordinate clerk with a hollow, but broad Swedish accent, waved me to a chair before I could open my mouth, after entering the door. I sat down. He proceeded solemnly to sign visas for passports for people who were going to Sweden, others came in; they were waved to the seats. The silence was oppressive. No one dared to speak. Was not this the office of the Royal Swedish Consul General for the United States! I got nervous; I rose from my chair; paced the floor; summoned the courage of my Viking ancestors, and approached the clerk, who by the way was a very good-looking young fellow of about 25 years. He frowned and waved me back, "Please take a seat." I answered weak but courageous that I did not think he could do anything for me, but that the Consul General could be of assistance to me. Well, what did I want to see the Consul about, well, that I preferred to tell the Consul myself. And then, I sprang on him one of my professional cards. He read a title, the card looked good; he softened in manner, disappeared in the distance, and in a few minutes I was sitting in the presence of the Vice Consul as the Consul was off on his vacation. Thus the cost of the professional cards has already been justified. The Vice Consul and I had a long and serious talk. He is in the Swedish diplomatic service, and has been stationed in London-Oldenburg. It gradually became clear to me that they would rather not know when Mormon missionaries go to Sweden; but that the New York office has discretionary powers.[1]

This excerpt from a letter John wrote to Leah from New York City, 2 July 1923, captures the anxiety, the power politic, and the nature of the mission he and Elder Reed Smoot undertook to the capitals of Europe. Though war hostilities had ended in 1918, religious persecution had kept the Church's missionaries out of almost all European countries for several more years. Years later, in compiling *The Messages of the First Presidency*, James R. Clark explained, "A number of letters in the Smoot file in the early 1920's show evidence of considerable difficulty on the part of the L.D.S. Church in maintaining adequate missionary forces in a number of foreign countries, both in the Pacific and in Europe, due to governmental regulations denying missionaries passports or entry visas. Senator-Apostle Smoot was influential in smoothing out many of these problems."[2]

Before addressing the question of returning missionaries to Europe, the First Presidency turned its attention to the temporal needs of her war victims. In the January 1921 issue of the *Improvement Era,* a "Special Fast Meeting" was called for January 23 to "provide food for three and a half million hungry children in mid-Europe. . . . those who are confronted by long months of semi-starvation. . . . As followers of the Master who drew the little children to him and blessed them, our immediate duty is to see that no hungry child cries in vain for bread."[3]

In March 1921, President Grant asked Reed Smoot, a prominent member of the United States Senate, to arrange for significant amounts of excess food and supplies to be sold to the Church for distribution to the Saints in Germany. Then, a few weeks later, President Grant wrote to Smoot, urging him to find a solution to the prominent practice across Europe, especially in Scandinavia, of prohibiting the missionaries from entering their countries.[4] "It seems incredible to me that our missionaries are to be excluded from [Norway and Sweden]," he wrote, "and I believe that the Lord will open a way for them to remain there. There are too many good honest hearted souls in Norway and Sweden for the doors of the Gospel to be closed against them."[5]

Smoot replied that a personal visit would be in order, and President

Grant asked for advice on who should undertake that journey.[6] Senator Smoot's response was immediate:

> I have thought that the ideal way of securing a reversal of judg-
> ment against our Mormon Elders preaching the Gospel in the
> Scandinavian Countries would be for Apostle Widtsoe and myself, if
> possible, to visit those countries with letters of introduction to the
> governing powers of those countries from the President of the United
> States and the Secretary of State, asking that we be given a respectful
> hearing as to the object of our mission in those countries, the beliefs of
> our people, and call to their attention the injustices that are being
> meted out to an innocent people. If you think the work ought to be
> undertaken immediately, then I suggest that Apostle Widtsoe and one
> other member of the Quorum undertake the mission. It is impossible
> for me to leave Washington for months and months to come.[7]

Additionally, Smoot noted that Widtsoe's international reputation as a scientist, his prominence as a distinguished college and university president, and his Scandinavian birth and background were perfect complements to Smoot's political clout. Smoot, the leader of the Senate Finance Committee and a member of the (War) Debt Funding Commission, had a unique opportunity to open doors that were closed against the Church. He also thought that reason was on their side: "Our position is so just and the discrimination against our Elders so unjust and apparent that I cannot help but believe that if it were presented to the proper officials of those countries, a reversal of their position would result. Apostle Widtsoe could present the case and perhaps it would be just as well to send him, if early action is necessary, with another member of the Quorum, and I believe that with God's blessings success would attend their efforts."[8]

In the weeks that followed, President Grant received word from the mission president in Sweden advising a delay in Smoot's proposed mission until after the Swedish national election, as he felt the new officers would be in a better position and frame of mind to effect the desired change. Months passed before the political scene was most advantageous and suitable arrangements could be made, but Smoot maintained his desire that Widtsoe accompany him in this difficult mission.

Through the winter of 1921 to 1922, Smoot and Secretary of State Hughes held conferences with the ministers of Norway, Sweden, and Denmark in Washington. These ministers forwarded their pleas to the respective government leaders with no success. Smoot recorded, "So far our Secretaries of State have failed and the Ministers feel like it is useless for them to press it any further, in fact, the Norwegian Minister told me that the answer he got from his last letter indicated that if he pressed this question further that it would not be to his advantage politically."[9]

In April 1923, Smoot and Widtsoe were authorized to make the journey.[10] John acknowledged the inspiration and wisdom behind the decision: "Action has been delayed until this moment when Brother Smoot is in such a commanding position before the world, that it seems as if this is a psychological moment for him to attempt to throw the Gospel doors of Scandinavia wide open."[11] With Leah he shared more of his personal outlook about his companion and their mission: "As he is also an apostle, prophecy will be fulfilled. I pray that my modest contribution may be worthy. I go on this mission with no selfish motive. I rejoice that all ulterior motives have been taken out of my heart. I am on the Lord's work."[12]

From our modern viewpoint, it is difficult to imagine a ban against the Church in countries that had been allied with the United States in the great world war. John soon realized that the ban was imposed by the clergy, not the heads of state: "We have nothing to fear from the people; little from the politicians; but [from] the clergy of the established church in all the countries, we may expect stubborn resistance."[13] A conversation with the manager of the Norwegian section of the Foreign Information Service in New York sheds further light:

> I was received very kindly; I sat down at the desk, we sized each other up. I told who I was, and frankly told him that I had come to learn from him if he (Sundby-Hansen) knew what regulations existed in Norway against Mormon Missionaries. I soon discovered that Sunby-Hansen, a bluff Norwegian, had attended our meetings in Chicago, was half a Mormon; but was not courageous enough to pay the price of sacrifice required, should he join the Church. We got

along well. He told me the last Mormon law in Norway came about because young Mormon Missionaries were caught preaching in one of the mountain valleys. I admitted the danger to the Norwegian Nation; should two such men be allowed to go loose. He laughed. We got along well. Then he volunteered to do some work for me. He is a personal friend of the Norwegian Consul General, who was called on the telephone, yes no Mormon Missionaries are allowed to enter Norway. Mormons may go there as visitors, but not to propagate their Church. Is there such a law? Yes, it is in the constitution! Whew!! Are you sure of that? Yes I think I am. I said to Sundby-Hansen that the only weakness in that statement was that the Norwegian constitution was written in 1814, i.e. 16 years before the Mormon Church was founded and 38 years before Mormonism was preached in Norway. Well that showed there was work for tomorrow.[14]

The next day, 3 July 1923, John met with the Norwegian Consul, who gradually became more sympathetic. Although the Norwegian constitution prohibited Jews and Jesuits from entering Norway, he admitted that this regulation was rarely enforced. He added, "Maybe they might change about the Mormons, too. Well, little can be done on this side of the ocean."[15]

Elders Smoot and Widtsoe arrived in London on 11 July and were scheduled to return to the U.S. on 7 August. Widtsoe urged the senator to extend the mission to 28 August but had little hope of persuading him: "This hurry is wearing me out, and it is hard on him. However, I am here on a mission and under orders. I am obeying."[16]

Everywhere Smoot went he was the center of attention. He spoke at the launching ceremony of *Leviathan,* on which he sailed to Europe. He was treated as a dignitary on the voyage and took many opportunities to speak of the Church. He spoke at the "Pilgrims Dinner" a few hours after their arrival in London. "This was Utah's night," Smoot recorded. "The speeches of [Justice] Sutherland and myself brought forth great cheers. I was very happy in my remarks and received many congratulations at the close of the dinner."[17] The London *Daily Express,* which had regularly printed "very nasty articles" about the Church, was unusually favorable. On Monday, 16 July, Elder Smoot was invited to

John visiting the British Mission with Senator Reed Smoot in 1923. John is seventh from the right on the second row. Senator Smoot is on his right side, and David O. McKay (the British Mission president) is on the right hand of Senator Smoot.

the homes of two of London's most wealthy and influential elite—Lord Beaverbrook, the owner of the *Daily Express,* and Sir Edward Houlton, owner of several other London newspapers. He wrote, "In my conversation with Lord Beaverbrook the question of the *Express* publishing bitter attacks on the Mormon church came up and he told me he had become convinced that the attacks were unjust and upon my assuring him they were he told me they would not occur again."[18]

The senator had arranged for John to handle the finances on the trip. This caused problems when entering Denmark: "Dr. Widtsoe got into trouble as they claimed he had too much money and were going to take it away from him. When he stated he was with me the officers changed their minds and let him go."[19] There were only eight missionaries in Denmark, and the Church was in very poor condition. John noted, "The senator did some splendid work of which I must not write; but I can say that he had a two column interview in *Politikaher,* the first time that our people have had such recognition, and he got to the bottom of the quiet antagonism to our people."[20] Both brethren felt the article would do the Church a great deal of good in Denmark. They met with Count Reventlow, the acting minister of foreign affairs, and had a refreshing exchange. Elder Smoot wrote, "We talked over American politics, conditions in the Ruhr and World affairs and finally reached the troubles we were having in getting our Missionaries into Denmark and I told the Count I had come all the way to have conditions changed. We talked over the present attitude of the Church as to polygamy and I gave him a history of Polygamy in the Church and conditions today and actions taken by the church and why regarding polygamy. He saw no reason why we should not be treated as all other church organizations and would do what he could to help to that end."[21]

Most of the problems were misunderstandings that were resolved simply by face-to-face meetings. John wrote, "Such trips should be taken often. To stay too closely to one part of the work is to serve the cause less valiantly."[22] In Stockholm they met with the prime minister of Sweden. Elder Smoot recorded:

> Greetings were cordial. The Prime Minister had heard of me. We first discussed conditions in Sweden and at home. I then for 1/2 hour presented to him the present position of the Mormon Church, the difficulty we were having with the entering into Sweden of our Missionaries and that those in Sweden were here in some cases beyond the time allowed in their Visaed passports. I explained the attitude of the Church on polygamy. My opinion of the Scandinavian people and their conditions in Utah. If ever I was blessed with a power of presentation of a case it was on this occasion. I wound up with the following statement. For the love I have of my Scandinavian mother, and upon my honor as a United States Senator I tell you the statements I have made regarding the Mormon people and Church are true. The Prime Minister answered immediately and said he believed what I had so well stated. . . . The interview was a success. Our Minister complimented me on presentation of case. I know I was blessed in so doing.[23]

The two apostles also met with reporters from five major Swedish newspapers, Archbishop Nathan Soderblom, and several of the high-ranking authorities of the national church. At each meeting Smoot responded to questions on plural marriage; polygamy was the chief issue straining Sweden's relationship with the Church.

From Stockholm they went to Christiana (Oslo), where they met a Mr. Swenson, the American minister. Swenson was most helpful in arranging meetings with the king of Norway, the secretary of state, and the secretary of education and religion. Elder Smoot wrote, "I presented to them both the treatment our missionaries were receiving by Norwegian Consuls refusing to Visa their passports. I explained to them the church's attitude on Polygamy since the manifesto and assured them the church sanctioned no more polygamist marriages. . . . We will send a copy of the proceedings of the conference in 1907 approving of the discontinuance of polygamist marriages to our Minister and he will follow the question up with the hope of final success."[24] The minister of foreign affairs asked what specific allowances the Church wished to be made. The senator asked for two- to four-year visas for missionaries and the same for two married couples as presiding officials in the mission.

Leaving Norway they visited Munich and Paris. Similar efforts were made to meet with state officials and lift the bans against the missionaries. In Switzerland they received word that President Warren G. Harding had died in San Francisco. Senator Smoot wrote, "A great, wise and good man called home. One of my dearest friends."[25] On 7 August 1923, they left France for America aboard the *Leviathan.*

On 3 November 1923, Senator Smoot telegraphed some good news to President Grant: "Just received word that on October eight the Norwegian Minister of Foreign Affairs received word that the Department of Justice and police had decided that hereafter an American citizen intending to proceed to Norway should not be refused a visa on the ground that he is a member of the Mormon Church or travels as a missionary of such Church. I feel better towards my mother's country."[26]

Two days later Smoot sent copies of a letter of acknowledgment to Minister Swenson of Norway. He also sent copies of his letters to John Dyneley Prince, American minister in Denmark, and Robert Woods Bliss, American minister in Sweden. He noted, "I feel if the question is followed up in Sweden and Denmark as it was in Norway by our American Minister there, the results will be the same."[27]

Widtsoe's visit to London included a special bonus: "When we

The family during Marsel's mission and John's early years as an apostle. Left to right: Anna, Leah, Eudora, John.

pulled into London . . . the crowd surged around the Leviathan train. With my satchel in hand I marched down the platform, for a moment forgetting that I had a son in London, when I suddenly heard a familiar voice cry out 'Here he is!' And then a pair of young arms tried to squeeze the breath out of me. It was the boy."[28] John reported to Leah, "This morning Marsel came to the hotel about 10:00 A.M. I drove out with the Senator to the Embassy, the Consulate and Commercial Attaché, while Marsel remained in our suite of rooms playing his new banjo/uke, eating."[29] That afternoon he took Marsel with him to interview genealogists. "We were kindly received. I wanted Marsel to be present and hear the proceedings. We spent two hours there. It was a revelation to me. I feel that we have just been scratching the surface in our methods of research."[30] The following morning they met with officials at the headquarters for Religious Education and had an enriching session. John noted, "I am certainly getting first hand information about the things with which I am working at home. Surely, the Lord has helped me these two days."[31] Father and son spent many good hours together: "Yesterday afternoon Marsel and I went to the British Museum, and had a good time for about two hours. Then Brother Smoot, McKay and I with Marsel as our guest had dinner at the Royal Palace Hotel. Marsel has eaten dinner with us at the Hotel each evening since we arrived."[32] At the conclusion of his visit, John told Leah, "In your son Marsel you have a clear, clear headed, thinking, sweet spirited boy, of whom any parent may be proud. By the way, his success in preaching is largely the result of your efforts. Your weekly motors have become texts."[33]

As it was Sunday, they attended services in North London. John recorded, "At the close of my remarks in the afternoon two little girls came to the stand, each with a bouquet of flowers, one for Bro. Smoot and one for me.—The gift of the North London Branch. I met many of the saints. My heart is tender over them. I also sought out the three men who are doing genealogical work."[34]

Widtsoe had an opportunity to talk to David O. McKay, Marsel's mission president, and reported to Leah: "The boy so far has conducted himself most satisfactorily. I was pleased last Monday night to hear him say that he would not go out with certain groups of missionaries because they were not above taking a drink while out for trips! He also said 'what is the good of doing anything that you will regret? Why not do the right thing, then you will have nothing to regret?'"[35]

Marsel turned twenty-one in England. Elder Widtsoe wrote, "My dear son Marsel—I send you my heartiest congratulations upon the attainment of your full citizenship in your country."[36] He wrote of the privilege of voting and appealed for the right to tag along on his first visit to the polls, "to swell up with pride because I have such a son." He wished him a long and useful life filled with activity. "May you find the life work you most love, and which you can most successfully do. . . . I am very proud of you, for I believe that you are true in character, and love the best things of life. I am proud of you because you have kept yourself free from the lower faults, and have sincerely tried to reach higher levels as new light has come to you. I am very grateful for your faithful service in the mission field, and for the great awakening which has come to you there."[37] The letter is filled with John's fatherly advice:

Don't be satisfied until you know some one thing as well as it may
be known. Then the world will seek you. It does not matter much
what it is, so that you are a master of it. . . . Be patient. To him who
labors faithfully all good things will come. But, curiously enough, it
seldom comes at the time or in the manner desired by the person himself. To rise high, one must go down into the depths. Yet who cares for
trials, delays and misunderstandings, when one knows his high ultimate destiny on earth and in heaven! I have tried it. For example, it
was mighty hard for me to go down in disgrace so to speak from the
U. A. C.; to come back somewhat unwelcome—yet the ultimate success was such as to make the trials dim memories of the past.[38]

John reported to President Grant that the journey was more successful than they had expected: "I went on this trip with some mis-
givings, as you know. Things went pretty much as I expected. I did my
best to support Brother Smoot, and to make things easy for him, but of
course his influence was the real vital factor in the work in hand."[39] He
was dissatisfied as to his own contributions. Given the time restraints,
he knew things would be rushed and many of the good things would be
left undone. He added, "As a trip it was unsatisfactory. I had no time to
call on my colleagues in the scientific, professional world where I
thought some good for the Church might have been done."[40]

Their trip took them to London, Scandinavia, Germany,
Switzerland, and France. John noted that opposition to the Church
originated with the priests of other churches. His report to the First
Presidency concluded:

The fact that it is generally understood that the Mormon Church
urges its proselytes to go to Utah has a bearing on the case. There is a
quiet, determined opposition, in Scandinavian governmental circles,
to American emigration. Even Denmark, with its relatively crowded
acres, wants her people to remain at home and help make a greater
country. Sweden and Norway, which have vast undeveloped
resources, dream of the day when they may be mightier nations; and
are urging their people to remain at home. Both Sweden and Norway
have organizations dedicated wholly to checking American emigration from the Scandinavian countries.

Moreover, and curiously enough, men and women in high position really believe that polygamy is still a practice of the Church and that immoral conditions prevail among the people. A campaign of education should be provided for among the leaders of the Scandinavian peoples.

There is also some resentment against the use of the term missionary. To those not of our Church, especially in Europe, a missionary goes out to convert the black or yellow heathen. The unfortunate connotation of the word in Scandinavia awakens hostility.

Finally it must be said that the anti-Mormon feeling among governmental officials in Scandinavia is due in part to our own failure to use the existing American governmental machinery as represented by the American ministers and consuls. It would seem that our mission presidents have not felt free to ask for such help as of right they could demand. [41]

25

SPECIAL ADVISOR
ON RECLAMATION

FOR much of his first six years as an apostle, John A. Widtsoe, with the consent and recommendation of President Heber J. Grant, worked on the enormous problem of making the great stretches of barren lands fertile. While politicians had important visions of vast settlements in the arid Western states, their success required scientific knowledge. The population surge westward depended most of all on correct management of vital water resources. Agriculture had to pave the way, since the food supply needed to keep pace with growth.

The great rivers of the West, properly managed, could be spread onto millions of acres of barren lands. But those waterways had to be harnessed and brought under the control of farmers for the millions of acres to be reclaimed for crops.

Reclamation became the lifeline to settling at least seventeen of the Western states. Though individual irrigation programs had been put into operation by many families, it was increasingly evident that to attain real success, the federal government needed to help the farmers and undertake the massive projects reclamation required. Mounting pressures from the increasing population brought national attention to the problem, and despite Eastern and Midwestern opposition, the federal government began to invest in large irrigation projects in the West.

Congress passed the Reclamation Act in 1902, creating the U.S. Reclamation Service within the U.S. Geological Survey. This act compelled Congress to finance the construction of large dams and their many attendant canals, roads, drainage systems, and settlements. It compelled the consumers, whose livelihood depended on these projects, to repay the construction and operation costs. By 1907 about thirty projects were under way, and despite many efforts to eliminate every obstacle, because this was new territory for Washington bureaucrats, problems increased. Some of the lands were not as suitable for irrigation, settlement patterns did not follow as anticipated, land speculation drove up prices, inexperience with irrigation led to unanticipated problems of water-logging and drainage, and there were construction cost overruns of enormous proportions.

The problems of the Reclamation Service reached a critical apex in the early years of John's apostleship. His involvement was inevitable, given his reputation as the reigning dean of dry farming and of Western American irrigation. In 1921 Governor Mabey put John on the Utah State Water Storage Board. In 1925 Governor Dern appointed him to the Utah Water Storage Commission. In his later years he was a member of the Utah Water and Power Board. In the fourth annual meetings of the Utah Irrigation and Drainage Congress, he presented a paper entitled "The Duty of Water," a phrase used to describe the quantity of water needed to grow successful crops. In August 1921 at the fifteenth annual convention of the Western Canadian Irrigation Association, John gave two addresses that stirred wide interest. His water doctrine echoed the predominant feelings of water consumers.[1] He made a similar appeal on water usage in October in the closing address of the Irrigation Institute in Yakima, Washington. The *Yakima Morning Herald* reported, "Being a man of vision he spoke of the future and the task confronting the leaders in irrigation development. Temperamentally a preacher with almost religious zeal for constructive agricultural methods, Dr. Widtsoe made a strong appeal."[2]

The Colorado River Commission

Herbert Hoover was secretary of commerce in December 1921, when President Warren G. Harding appointed him to be his representative in establishing a compact among the several states through which the Colorado River flows, all of which felt they had a claim to its valuable water supply. Hoover was regarded nationwide as the key man in negotiating American domestic policy. His appointment marked the beginning of the Colorado River Commission, which led to the Colorado River Compact, signed by the commissioners of the respective states in November of 1922. The law under which the commission was begun stated that they were to "negotiate and enter into a compact or agreement providing for an equitable division and apportionment among said states of the water supply of the Colorado river and the streams tributary thereto."[3] The great dams and other reclamation projects on the Colorado are the children of that compact.

Between January and November of 1922, the commission met twenty-seven times to hammer out the details of the economic and legal issues. There were also numerous public hearings in each of the affected states, including meetings in Phoenix, Los Angeles, Salt Lake City, Grand Junction, Denver, Santa Fe, and Cheyenne.[4] In several of these John was the chief voice on using the water for reclamation. Other voices were raised over the need for flood control, drinking water, and electric power. R. E. Caldwell was the Utah State engineer and the commissioner for Utah in the commission's investigations. John was asked to be Caldwell's advisor. Thus he became a key voice in the decisions that led to the Hoover Dam, the Glen Canyon Dam, and other reclamation projects along the Colorado. John was tagged "Advisor for Utah."[5]

The hearings in Salt Lake City were held on 27–28 March 1922. John spoke in behalf of Utah and strongly urged that the whole Colorado River Basin be developed independent of state lines. His proposals set forth an orderly priority that embraced all the interests represented in the development of the river and provided a plan for reassessing matters following a suitable trial period: "Since the foundation of any commonwealth is agriculture, it follows that in arid and semiarid countries irrigation is the first compelling practice, which, once properly established, will lead to the development of all other resources. Brigham Young understood this clearly for he advised his people, and the advice was almost a prohibition, to do no mining until after the land had been won from the desert, homes had been built and cities founded."[6] The proposal was carried in article IV of the compact.

John insisted that the question of power development on the river be secondary, since the matter of irrigation was by far the most important factor in the development of the river, and that whatever power might be developed must always be subservient to that of irrigation. Based on investigations of the Reclamation Service, there was water enough for all in the Colorado River if it was properly cared for by storage.[7]

In September 1922 John was part of a ten-day Colorado River expedition designed to give commissioners and advisors direct observation of the river's potential and some of the Reclamation Service's proposed dam sites. Following the expedition John reported, "The Colorado River is one of the remaining undeveloped resources of the United States. Among the possibilities are great power dams and irrigation schemes allowing possibilities of 6,000,000 horsepower. Flood control there is indispensable to the Imperial Valley for which one or more dams is essential. Our party investigated a number of dam sites and undoubtedly as a result of our trip a more exhaustive investigation of the water power of the river will be made."[8]

The final meeting of the Commission convened for ten days in Santa Fe, New Mexico. On 24 November 1922, the Compact was made. John reported that all of Utah's interests were upheld and that the proposed Glen Canyon Dam would be built, yielding inestimable value to the state.[9] An account in the *New Mexican*, by a "Mysterious Observer," makes light of many of the dignitaries involved with the meetings, but when it turned to the Utah delegation it was notably complimentary. The technical expertise of Elder Widtsoe and his membership in the Quorum of the Twelve was noted. Then the writer described him as "one of the gentlest and rarest souls of the land."[10] It is fair to say that Dr. Widtsoe was the primary scientific advisor on the commission.

The final paragraph in the compact as agreed and signed by the seven commissioners states, "The major purposes of this compact are to provide for . . . the equitable division and apportionment . . . ; the relative importance of the several beneficial uses of the water; to promote interstate comity; to remove causes of present and future controversies; and to secure the expeditious agricultural and industrial development of the Colorado River Basin."[11] The provision John was so instrumental in obtaining, the value of which is immeasurable though not so apparent, states, "Subject to the provisions of this compact, water of the Colorado River System may be impounded and used for the generation of electrical power, but such impounding and use shall be subservient to the use and consumption of such water for agricultural and domestic purposes and shall not interfere with or prevent use for such dominant purposes."[12]

The Fact-Finding Commission

Following the Santa Fe meetings, Hubert Work, secretary of the interior for President Calvin Coolidge, invited Widtsoe to be one of seven special advisors on reclamation to sit on a "fact-finding committee" to carefully examine all of the projects of the Reclamation Service. Hundreds of millions of dollars and many thousands of farm families were at stake. Secretary Work, on 8 September 1923, sent a letter to each special advisor describing the magnitude of the problem and his views of the needs that the committee should address:

> It is generally reported that relatively few of the original settlers on projects now remain on them as water users. One hundred thirty-four millions of government money have been expended. Fourteen millions have been returned and six millions are due and unpaid as of December 31, 1922, to which must very soon, be added computations for the present calendar year. Time extensions for payment of both construction and maintenance charges have been asked which, if granted, would multiply deferred annual payments, it is feared, beyond

the ultimate ability of the settler to pay, entailing probable loss of his home and to the Government the loss of the investment.

The purpose of this inquiry, in which I very much hope you may participate is to have the processes of administration of this trust reviewed by men of affairs applying their best thought to this important governmental agency. Reclamation has done much toward the development of the West but it now clearly requires to be adapted to existing conditions, so that its future success may be achieved and the possibility of home ownership be assured to settlers.[13]

President Heber J. Grant thought it an important service and urged John to accept the appointment. John's best description of the work is contained in a letter to Marsel, still a missionary in England:

I did expect to spend the fall and winter at home, to catch up with delayed duties and tasks, but this call from Washington upset things. Twenty-one years ago Congress enacted the Reclamation Law, by which the moneys received from the Public Lands were to be used for the building of irrigation reservoirs and canals. More than $145,000,000 have been spent under the act; about 2,000,000 acres of land reclaimed and tens of thousands of families settled under the projects. Nevertheless, the government reclamation has not been wholly satisfactory, and attempts are being made to undo it. For that reason a commission has been appointed to look into the whole matter and work out the future of government reclamation attempts. It is a great responsibility, but I am glad to give the service to the government and to my beloved West, where irrigation is practiced. It seems only proper also that a representative of the people which founded irrigation should be on the commission. As for the honor—well you know I have had all the honor I care for.[14]

At the opening meeting of the committee, 15 October 1923, Secretary Work further described the problems that had developed around the massive governmental projects of reclamation. Repayment from the farmers, without putting them out of business or under such duress as to cause them to flee to other opportunities, was his focus. Reclamation was still a new course in the country, and there were many new projects under study and many more to follow as the West

"Fact Finding Commission," January 19, 1924. Left to right: James R. Garfield, former U.S. secretary of the interior; Thomas. E. Campbell, former governor of Arizona (chairman); Dr. Elwood Mead, world-renowned authority on reclamation; Dr. John A. Widtsoe, vice chairman and secretary; A. C. Cooky, member of the bureau plant industry representing the Deptartment of Agriculture; T. E. Brown, corresponding secretary of the commission.

expanded. He concluded, "Your committee is requested to survey the whole subject in its entirety, give to the bureau your opinions concerning our operating methods that we may avoid errors, and finally your recommendations which Congress may study and which should ultimately preserve the sanctity of contract, secure to farmers safety for their investments already made, and insure a return of invested funds."[15]

This group of special advisors on reclamation, labeled the "Fact Finders Committee," included Thomas E. Campbell, the former governor of Arizona; David W. Davis, the newly appointed commissioner of reclamation; Oscar E. Bradfute, president of the American Farm Bureau Federation; James R. Garfield, Theodore Roosevelt's secretary of the interior; Clyde C. Dawson, representing Julius H. Barnes, the president of the United States Chamber of Commerce; and Elwood Mead, a professor of agriculture at U. C. Berkeley. Of the seven, it was reported that "none is better qualified than Dr. John A. Widtsoe, whose life-long study of irrigation has brought him an international reputation as an authority on this subject. His vision of the possibilities of reclamation and his knowledge of irrigation practice will . . . strengthen their findings. In the appointment of Dr. Widtsoe to this commission, Utah not only takes pride; she feels confident that he will help to accomplish for reclamation the greatest possible good."[16]

The committee reported that 13.8 percent of the farmers were "prospering." Contrasted with that figure, 21.6 percent were "very poor," another 34.4 percent had "not broke even," while the remaining 31.2 percent merely "broke even."[17] These figures demonstrate the two opposing crises. Either the Reclamation Service faced failure through non-collection of revenues from farmers, or thousands of farmers faced failure and withdrawal from their lands. The fact finders, though mobilized by the Reclamation Service, worked for the success of farmers. John expressed that view in an impassioned exchange over a "very hopeless" description given by a delegate from the Uncompahgre project. Most of those farmers had been unable to pay any of the government charges, even though they were spread over a long time at low interest. Widtsoe asked, "The farmers, of course, are our main concern. Do you think that the project is incapable of producing from the soil under, say, ordinary farm management, to make it a successful project?"[18]

The daily record of the activities of the special advisors shows that their meetings began on 15 October 1923 and ended on 10 April 1924, when their final report was submitted to Hubert Work, secretary of the interior. In the 15 October meeting they elected former governor Campbell as chairman of the committee and John A. Widtsoe as vice chairman and secretary. Many entries show sporadic attendance by all except Campbell and Widtsoe. The entry on the last day states, "Dr. Widtsoe left the office this evening, with the understanding that this would be his last day of service, but that he would drop in every day until he left the city, and it was his intention to stay on for a week or ten days longer."[19]

In an early meeting it was decided "that Dr. Widtsoe continue his work on the outlining of a plan of procedure for a study of the general question."[20] His detailed "Plan of Inquiry" was presented to the committee on 29 October and guided their investigations to completion. The old label of "book farmer" aptly fits John's activities on the Fact

Finders Committee. On page after page of their minutes, John is the central figure, and he often acted alone. In the first three months, more than 130 witnesses paraded before the committee. Most of them were experts on the government side of the problem. They included congressmen and senators from the states involved in the Reclamation Service.

Having been immersed in the government issues, the Fact Finders turned to the issues farmers faced at each Reclamation project. Campbell and Widtsoe were appointed as a subcommittee to assemble the data requested and to have it ready for the whole committee's review as they were able. On 8 December they discussed the organization of their final report and decided that John's Plan of Inquiry would be followed. For each project, Campbell was to look into the engineering questions, Garfield was to look at matters dealing with the organization of the Bureau of Reclamation, and Widtsoe was to "undertake the other sections as indicated in the 'Plan' for which data have accumulated."[21]

On 5 January 1924, because of Congress's urgent need to act on legislation that depended on their report, the Fact Finders resolved not to visit each of the twenty-eight projects but to call "a general meeting of all organizations and individuals representing water users on the U. S. Reclamation Projects, to convene at the Hotel Utah, at Salt Lake City. . . . At this conference the problems confronting the irrigation projects will be discussed freely and in such a manner as to assist the committee."[22] In opening the conference, Chairman Campbell said, "This is a fact-finding commission. We want facts and not fancies, regarding the condition of the farmer upon these projects, to the end that we ascertain in this manner the true existing conditions."[23]

The Salt Lake City Conference was held 17–27 January. The committee conferred publicly with more than 120 witnesses from all of the projects. They were asked to prepare their report in advance and were given an outline to follow. Those written reports supplemented the 1,764 page transcription.

It is apparent from the transcription that John listened carefully and entered the exchange only when critical points needed to be made for the benefit of the committee's report to the president and the Congress.

The central issue was the matter of repayment of obligations due the federal government. No one seemed interested in having their debt canceled, only in fairer treatment by their government in light of increased understanding of their problems.

Two exchanges in the projects conference illustrate the feelings that moved the committee to their recommendations. From the Yuma, Arizona, project a farmer pled, "When the war over in Europe broke out, you remember how gladly our boys volunteered, how they went to the service of the flag, how they went across the pond without any forcing at all, were more than glad to go. I fought and fought with my son to keep him from being a volunteer." The man told his boy that getting their wheat to the battlefield was service enough, yet when the government called, off he went. The fathers picked up the extra burden their sons left to them, but because of bad economic times, they couldn't pay their water bills. The government reacted by increasing their obligation 1 percent more per month, and some received notice that their water would be shut off. The same government officials chose to forgive or reduce interest assessed in the English debt, and the debts of France, Belgium, Italy, Russia, and Germany, yet they assessed further penalties on the families who shouldered the burdens their sons had left behind.[24]

Helping the farmers produce better crops in greater quantity was a remedy to the problems they all shared. This important point was made in John's exchange with a man from the Minidoka project in Idaho. Widtsoe said, "You say it is not fair to judge these projects by the poor farmer but we do have a great many poor farmers, and when we undertake to change agriculture or to produce new crops, very many of us are poor farmers. . . . Can you make a better farmer out of the farmer if you were to give him some sort of direct supervision, do you know any other method by which it may be accomplished?" The man replied, "I attribute a large share of our success directly to that class of work, we found it was cheaper to get a good agricultural expert like we have to go out and help a man on to his feet than it was to hire a lawyer to throw him out, costs us less money to make a good Indian out of him than to make a bad one. We have increased our production very largely through this very helpful work."[25] Always the teacher, John pursued this point of training with many of the delegates at the conference. It crystallized in him the idea that a better basis for repayment from the farmers, and increased productivity through training farmers on each project, was the road to resolution of the reclamation crises.

The committee resumed work in Washington, D.C., on 2 February 1924 by carefully classifying the information in the transcript of the conference. On 7 February the committee approved six chapters for the report. Over the next few weeks, committee members reviewed parts of the report almost daily as urgency over its completion mounted in Congress. Through most of March only Campbell and Widtsoe consulted over the report and the many resolutions that needed to be included. On 31 March they discussed reorganization of the Bureau of Reclamation. On 3 April Dr. Elwood Mead was sworn in as the commissioner of reclamation. He would oversee passage of the provisions in the report and implementation on all of the reclamation projects.

The special advisors introduced their report in a letter of transmittal dated 10 April 1924. The letter summarized the problems the fact finders identified and the solutions they recommended. They wrote, "The situation that has developed on the Federal reclamation projects is serious. Three projects have been abandoned, and unless remedial measures, of a permanent character are applied, several more of the projects will fail; and the Federal reclamation experiment conceived in a spirit of wise and lofty statesmanship, will become discredited."[26] Their desire was to correct conditions at each project to turn impending disasters into imminent and lasting successes.

The report was submitted to Interior Secretary Work, who presented it to President Calvin Coolidge. Coolidge attached his personal message and presented it to Congress for passage and enactment. The report was entitled "Federal Reclamation by Irrigation, a Report by the Committee of Special Advisors on Reclamation, April 21, 1924." Excerpts from President Coolidge's message summarized the problems identified, the remedies considered, and the recommendations of the fact finders:

> Many occupants of our reclamation projects in the West are in
> financial distress. They are unable to pay the charges assessed against

them. The heretofore adopted repayment plan is erroneous in principle and in many cases impossible of accomplishment. It fixes an annual arbitrary amount that the farmers must pay on the construction costs of projects regardless of their production. In its place should be substituted a new policy providing that payments shall be assessed by the Government in accordance with the crop-producing quality of the soil.

The facts . . . show that of the Government's total investment, $18,861,146 will never be recovered. There will be a probable loss of an additional $8,830,000. These sums represent expenditures in the construction of reservoirs, canals and other works for the irrigation of lands that have proven unproductive. I recommend that Congress authorize the charging off of such sums shown to be impossible of collection.

The probable loss and the temporary difficulties of some of the settlers on projects does not mean that reclamation is a failure. The sum total of beneficial results has been large in building up of towns and agricultural communities and in adding tremendously to the agricultural production and wealth of the country. Whatever legislation is necessary to the advancement of reclamation should be enacted without delay.[27]

Assessments to farmers based on construction costs were grossly inequitable. It was obvious yet bold to recommend that the farmers be relieved of the federal assessments. John wrote:

Reclamation by irrigation is the result of the joint efforts of the engineer and the farmer. The engineer builds the irrigation works; the farmer must pay for the works and make a living from the reclaimed lands. There can be no irrigated farm without the competent engineer; but there will be no payment for the works nor community development under them without the successful farmer. A fundamental error was made in believing that the construction of irrigation works would of itself create irrigated agriculture. The reclamation act was based on that assumption. It has been demonstrated that the Government can build irrigation structures of the highest quality; but how farmers on the Federal irrigation projects can repay the cost of these structures within reasonable time limits is yet to be demonstrated.[28]

The committee recognized that training, though difficult to achieve, was necessary for farmers to master reclamation. The deeper they looked into cost issues, the clearer it became that repayment had to be tied to soil productivity: "The expense of changing rough, desert land into irrigated fields, and of adding the new implements and improvements needed, involves a large outlay of money which must be won from the products of the farm. It will be necessary to put into effect a new plan of repayment . . . in our opinion one based upon the inherent power of the soil, under intelligent cultivation, to produce crops."[29]

On 5 December 1924, early in the next congressional session, "the Fact Finders' Act with sixteen specific provisions was passed into law. Major provisions required the Secretary of the Interior to approve all new projects after due scrutiny, that applicants under each project be carefully screened, that irrigable lands under each project be classified by the Secretary according to their power to support a family, that all construction charges shall be based on the productive power of the land, that when feasible the operation of the project be given to the water users, and that the results of each survey with the Secretary's recommendations be reported to the Congress."[30]

Historians praise the work of the fact finders, emphasizing that they demonstrated a thorough understanding of the status, the possibilities, and the weaknesses of reclamation. Their work constituted the major turning point and the most critical modification in reclamation policy, revamping the Bureau of Reclamation and becoming the basis of Dr. Mead's policies as commissioner of reclamation during the Coolidge, Hoover, and Roosevelt administrations.[31]

THE BOARD OF SURVEY AND ADJUSTMENTS FOR RECLAMATION

With Senate assurance that the Fact Finders' Act would pass into law in December, Secretary Work and Commissioner Mead made plans for quick action. Subsection K authorized the secretary to conduct surveys on each reclamation project to see if the farmers' inability to pay

Caption on photo reads "Delegates to the Reclamation Conference Denver Colo. Jan 6 1925."

was attributable to mistakes made relative to the project, lack of fertility, inadequate water supply, or other site-related physical problems. For those problems the secretary was to recommend adjustments in relief of farmers. On 15 September 1924, Mead asked Widtsoe to chair a committee to survey the Northern projects—all those in Colorado, Utah, Nevada, Oregon, Washington, Idaho, Montana, Wyoming, and Nebraska. A representative of the Interior Service and a trained economist would join him, and in each state a local expert would be added. Mead concluded, "I have come to realize more fully, from our recent contact, what a delightful friend and splendid citizen you are."[32] Governor Campbell chaired a similar committee to survey the Southern projects.

Wanting badly to see the resolutions of the fact finders bring needed relief to farmers and lasting security to the reclamation projects, John praised the plan: "Much of my regular work had to go untouched last winter while I was in Washington. However, having set my hands to the plow, if you think it desirable in order to complete the foundation upon which you and others will have to build the future of reclamation by irrigation in the United States, I shall be glad to try to secure a proper leave of absence to undertake the work you may desire to assign me."[33] Work began with a conference in Denver for delegates from the reclamation projects to consider implementation of the surveys. Mead then called Widtsoe and Campbell to Washington for final preparations. He concluded, "It is a great relief that we are to be associated together again and that the Government is to have your valuable assistance in these studies."[34]

From the Washington meetings came their official title, the Board of Survey and Adjustments for Reclamation. A plan for conducting the surveys was devised and letters were sent to officials at each project outlining the information they were to provide to expedite efficiency in the committee's visit. Formal authority and direction is in a 30 January 1925 letter from Secretary Work. He directed that the surveys be made with "painstaking care" and the "greatest expedition" to see that every factor was fully considered, that the benefits "may be realized by the settlers on the reclamation projects at the earliest possible date."[35]

The work of the Board of Survey and Adjustments proceeded rapidly between January and July. In a short time John reported to Secretary Work a more uncertain state of mind in the farmers than had been anticipated, and he urged that a definite announcement soon be given of the three-year moratorium they were recommending.[36] A similar letter went to Commissioner Mead: "It is important for the successful outcome of the work that the water users be told early what the action of the officials at Washington will be."[37]

From his reports three things stand out in the project surveys. First, "that an immediate moratorium be put in place allowing sufficient time for thorough survey and adjustment programs to be put in place." He noted, "The Board is convinced . . . that final arrangements must now be made."[38] Second, that "all recommended adjustments be made to give relief to farmers for ills of soil infertility, water shortages, or other physical limitations, for which the farmer is not liable. Third, that the management of each project be put in the hands of the water users as organized water districts as early as possible. . . . To accomplish this, speedily, will do much to bring about project success."[39] As the surveys proceeded, it became more evident that classification of lands and a repayment plan tied to the per acre productivity of each farmer was the fairest method.

In this survey work John felt that the entire system of irrigation was on trial and that the success of reclaiming land through irrigation revolved around two basic considerations: There must be a national need for the goods produced and due reward to those who made it succeed. He noted, "Only those who are content with the normal rewards of rural life will succeed and be happy on the farm. The activities necessary for development of the vast resources of the west will cluster about and depend upon the irrigated centers. Our venture in irrigation will not be wholly satisfactory until the irrigated area has been extended to the full utilization of the water resources of the west."[40]

He outlined five suggestions for reclamation:

> Faith in western irrigation must grow from an awareness that it is a national need.
>
> A comprehensive study of the projects should show the productive value of the West.
>
> The treasures of irrigation knowledge need to be utilized by all who live by the irrigation ditch.
>
> Reclamation by irrigation must be viewed through an increased appreciation of the economic and social principles it provides.
>
> Training must be provided to irrigation leaders by schools that have the expertise.[41]

A Montana newspaper heralded John's viewpoint as the best that had been offered on reclamation:

> His committee was in Great Falls. . . . To our mind, his presentation of the whole reclamation question, as it pertains to the western country, was the most sensible and unprejudiced of any we have heard at any time or in any place. He has a vision of the great good that will be worked out for the whole nation, as well as an understanding of the difficulties that confront the reclamation service at this time. His conclusions are wholesome and his opinions are eminently fair. We do not think the president of the United States could do better than to

follow the irrigation doctrine as preached by Dr. Widtsoe in this year, 1925.[42]

By August 1925, the surveys were complete. The water users were convinced that John and his board were in their corner. Goodwill was being established because fairness dominated the study. John wrote, "After six months' intensive work on this subject, I am more hopeful than ever about the ultimate favorable solution of federal reclamation problems, but if the possible success is to be won more attention than ever must be given to the human problem as it is found on the projects." He emphasized that tact and diplomacy needed to dominate the transition period to overcome the hostile sentiment of past years: "Just now I would fear the use of a whip in winning project success. The soft answer and friendly hand will accomplish more."[43]

With the survey work done, the reports designed and compiled, and adjustment recommendations submitted, John wrote to Mead, "The labor of the last few months in behalf of the Bureau has been a very pleasant experience. I thank you for the opportunity. I hope that some good may come out of the efforts that I have put forth with the other members of the Board. As I have written you repeatedly, the work . . . has strengthened my faith in irrigation."[44] Later he concluded, "To work out with the people the findings of the committee, the next summer and fall two committees visited all the projects. I was the chairman of one of these. In accordance with our final report, Congress charged off nearly $28,000,000, due to mistakes on the part of engineers and farmers. But, the experience gained by the Bureau was well worth the money, for the development of the West is far from being completed."[45]

In these years of government service, John presented his ideas in a series of lectures in the summer school of the Utah State Agricultural College. His work with the fact finders and the Board of Survey and Adjustments, refined by his classroom presentation, were published: "After nearly two years' work with the Reclamation Service, I prepared my conclusions in a book entitled *Success on Irrigation Projects*."[46] He wished to furnish, in nontechnical writing, "the main principles, by the use of which the irrigated and irrigable area may be made to serve more completely the needs of modern, civilized man."[47] A few months later he presented his "rules of reclamation" to the student body at BYU and indicated that the work of reclamation, of taming the desert, was a part of his own religious interpretation and zeal.[48] "The destiny of man is to possess the whole earth; and the destiny of the earth is to be subject to man. There can be no full conquest of the earth, and no real satisfaction to humanity, if large portions of the earth remain beyond his highest control. Only as all parts of the earth are developed according to the best existing knowledge, and brought under human control, can man be said to possess the earth."[49]

While it is too much to assert that John's committees set right all the ills of reclamation, it is nevertheless generally accepted that their work set it back on course. On a visit to Utah, Secretary Work stated, "When the history of reclamation is written Dr. Widtsoe and Dr. Mead will be regarded as 'the fathers of modernized reclamation.'"[50] Work was also gracious to President Grant: "Please allow me to express my thanks to you for making it possible for the Government to have the services of Doctor Widtsoe in reorganizing the Reclamation Service in this Department. No one within my knowledge could have brought to this tremendous task the knowledge and industry, with the unusual ability to express their results, that he did. With his associates, I believe he has accomplished a piece of constructive work that will save Federal reclamation."[51]

The *Great Falls Daily Tribune* lauded Widtsoe's work and all but called for his appointment as secretary of the interior: "We haven't the slightest information as to what his political affiliations may be. But we would like to see a fellow just like him made secretary of the interior at Washington for one administration."[52] The editorial went on to describe the public reaction to his addresses: "We have taken occasion to say in these columns on several occasions that his talks in this part of the country during the last year or so, while he has been engaged upon this fact finding work, have been the most sensible of any of the presentations that have come this way. They have been fair and truthful. They have criticized where such comment was needful. There has been no political banter. There has never been a word of lacking faith in the final outcome."[53]

His books and his work on commissions and committees in Washington brought foreign dignitaries seeking assistance with their agricultural needs. The Canadian government continually sought his assistance through the remainder of his life. Indication of some of the influence he had was given in an announcement in the *Lethbridge Herald* on 30 January 1926:

> In order to put the District in a way to meet its assessments, the province enacted the Colonization Act which, in effect, permits bona fide farmers to meet their assessments in easy installments over fifty years. This legislation was framed on the recommendation of Dr. John A. Widtsoe, Utah, an eminent authority on irrigation and land settlement, who made an examination of the situation for the government.[54]

In the midst of his activities with reclamation projects, authorities in Russia were making plans to publish Widtsoe's textbook though two decades old. The *Deseret News* wrote, "While in Salt Lake, he [Shumakov from Russia] conferred with Dr. John A. Widtsoe, whose book, *Principles of Irrigation Practice,* is being translated into Russian for use there, and according to the professor, is considered in Russia to be an invaluable contribution to agriculture."[55]

Official duties as an apostle in the Church curtailed his active participation in the problems of reclamation and irrigation for the following six years. On 7 October 1927, he submitted his resignation from the Utah Water Storage Commission to Governor George H. Dern, noting, "I have been appointed to take charge of some of the work of the Church in Europe."[56] He continued, "I have enjoyed the work of the Commission very much. Properly conducted, there is probably no activity in the state which has greater or more far reaching consequences for the future development of the State of Utah."[57] Weeks later John, Leah, and Eudora sailed for Europe to fill a six-year assignment as president of the European Mission.

26

COMMISSIONER OF CHURCH EDUCATION

———————■———————

K<small>ARL</small> G. Maeser was the first president of Brigham Young Academy and the first superintendent of the LDS Church School System. He was followed by Joseph M. Tanner, Horace H. Cummings, and Adam S. Bennion. While Bennion was superintendent, David O. McKay was appointed the first commissioner of education. In 1922 Dr. Widtsoe took over for McKay.[1] While John was commissioner, Bennion pursued his doctor's degree. When it was completed, Bennion returned. John's journal reads, "April 1, 1925, on recommendation of Comm. Of Educ. I and colleagues were released; Comm. Disbanded. Supt. made executive officer. It has been a very pleasant experience. Informative. I am grateful for the experience."[2] Bennion was followed by Joseph F. Merrill. In 1933 Merrill and Widtsoe exchanged roles; Merrill became president of the European Mission, and John was again appointed commissioner of education.

Of his first appointment, the *Improvement Era* announced, "Dr. John A. Widtsoe was appointed commissioner of education of the Church, on motion of Elder David O. McKay, Jan. 26, 1922. Elder McKay resigned that position owing to a desire to devote more time to foreign missions."[3] Stephen L Richards and Richard R. Lyman were the

assistant commissioners, and Adam S. Bennion continued as the superintendent. Orson F. Whitney recorded the view of many: "I know of no
one better fitted for the place, and I am sure your appointment will
redound to the great advantage of the cause."[4]

. To John, BYU was "the academic head of the Church Schools
System."[5] Its entrance and graduation requirements were to compete
with universities of high quality across the land. But he stressed that the
university should also emphasize "training for the activities in which the
Church is most deeply concerned. All students are given instruction in
theology; and are expected to participate in the religious activities of
the institution. All the activities radiate from the central idea of the
institution that it is a place in which to train forceful and devoted
Latter-day Saints."[6] He was determined that BYU would be recognized
as "a first class college worthy to be placed by the side of many other
similar private institutions in the country."[7] He gave numerous talks on
BYU's campus and kept a close association with President Harris, which
he found "a most attractive prospect."[8]

Beginning in 1890, religion classes in the public elementary schools
in Utah were conducted on the model of religious training common in
other churches. As John wrote, "The classes are held usually once a
week after school hours and not in the school building. We have not yet
secured the opportunity of having the children give one hour of the
school day to religious instruction outside the school room, of course.
We hope that this may be possible in the near future."[9] Almost 60,000
children were enrolled. John held frequent meetings with those who
oversaw the program and prepared its materials.

John detailed the role of seminary, to "supply religious instruction
to young people during this period and help make of these young people
faithful members of the Church."[10] He added, "Young people are asked
to leave the high school during one of their study periods each day and
join the classes in the so called seminaries . . . built very near the high
schools."[11] Seminary teachers were to be college-trained, with an appealing nature and considerable Church experience.

Many families could neither spare their children at home nor afford
to support them at college in Salt Lake or Logan. Accordingly, Church

leaders instituted junior colleges. John felt that the junior colleges offered "more persons the opportunity of some college training . . . , more individual attention to students; it enables parents to guard better their children during the critical first years of college life; it makes it possible to give religious teaching and direction during the years when coming leaders are most frequently crystallizing their convictions regarding the fundamental issues of life."[12]

When John was made commissioner, six junior colleges had been established: Gila College in Thatcher, Arizona; Ricks College in Rexburg, Idaho; and in Utah, Dixie College in St. George; Snow College in Ephraim; Weber College in Ogden; and Brigham Young College in Logan. Similar work was provided at the LDS University in Salt Lake City. Along with the standard college fare, courses in theology were offered by faculty of the highest quality.

The Church School System was governed by the General Board of Education, presided over by the president of the Church. The Commission of Education consisted of a commissioner, two assistant commissioners, and the superintendent. Each junior college had a board of trustees composed of presidents of the Church stakes that fed the college. Each stake had a board of education responsible for religion classes, teacher training, and seminary. The commissioner's office provided specialized training in educational sessions that ran concurrent with general and stake conferences.

Utah education and the commission had some notable triumphs. In 1923 John wrote, "We have in the Church 8.6 young people attending college out of every thousand members . . . whereas, in the whole United States there are only 4.9 per thousand of population attending college. There are 60.6 individuals per thousand attending high school in this Church; whereas, in the United States as a whole, there are only 20.8. That is, nearly three times as many."[13]

A 1942–44 study showed that Utah was still maintaining that impressive record in Utah [74 percent LDS]; 24 percent of young people between fifteen and seventeen years of age attended high school, compared with a nationwide figure of 19 percent. In the United States 3.3 percent of the school population had graduated from high school, while in Utah 4.5 percent had graduated. During the same time period, more students graduated from college in Utah than in any other state.[14] Men of Utah had a median attainment of two years of high school, one year above the national average.

In 1946 a book entitled *Education—America's Magic* attempted to assess the educational success of each state. Noting that Utah ranked first in several measures of the study, it concluded:

> Utah has first place among the states by a wide margin. While ranking thirty-second in ability to support education with an income of only $1,680 per child, and fourth in effort, it still ranks first in educational accomplishment, in the degree in which accomplishment is commensurate with ability, in efficiency, and in the level of adult education. Indeed, this combination of great effort and high efficiency in the utilization of school funds seems to have operated in a remarkable manner to overcome the handicap of relatively low ability. Utah easily outclasses all other states in over-all performance in education.[15]

A Carnegie Foundation study searched for men of outstanding accomplishments. It drew names from three classic works, *Who's Who in America, Leaders in Education,* and *American Men of Science.* Utah led the list by about 30 percent.[16]

Just before his call as commissioner of education, John wrote, "Mormonism [is] a system of truth which includes all truth, which accepts all truth. . . . . A system which leads its followers into a life-long pursuit of truth."[17] In 1952 he reflected, "The two major activities of my life were the gospel, and education."[18] His devotion to professional education was an extension to his discipleship in the Church: "I have only joy in the knowledge that I received the training which the Church Schools gave in my day. I should not have joined in taking any step which would not increase the efficiency of this system as I knew it first as a student and later as a teacher."[19]

THE UNIQUE COMPONENT IN UTAH EDUCATION

When John became commissioner of education, more than thirty years had passed since he entered Harvard and began his illustrious career in education. As a student, John knew what affected him most and what was lacking in American education. As a professor, he became even more aware of its strengths and weaknesses. As a college or university president, his awareness of those educational weaknesses and the issues that surrounded them deepened. Through all of those years, he was devoutly religious and especially aware of education's shortcomings with respect to religious training. John was a uniquely qualified expert on education and religion.

John favored education that included "general religious principles upon which all citizens can or should agree."[20] On the relationship of education and citizenship he wrote, "We are spiritual, as well as mental and physical; and our education, to be complete, and fully satisfactory, must take into account the demands of the spiritual nature of man, and provide for religious instruction. The man whose mind and body alone are trained is not necessarily a safe citizen. . . . Spiritual education is the best known means of causing men to use their powers for human good."[21] In an October 1922 general conference address he said, "The man whose mind only has been trained may be likened to the ship with great engines and a huge propeller ready to drive the ship forward, but without rudder, chart, compass, or definite destination. When we add to the man, so trained, spiritual training, then it is as if we add to the ship, with its wonderful machinery, a compass, a chart, a rudder, and a dependable intelligence which controls the whole machinery, above and below deck, so that the vessel may reach a safe haven, according to a definite purpose."[22]

In an extensive review of the history and design of the Church School System, John noted that the very spirit of the gospel awakens the desire for ever-increasing knowledge in all fields of interest. Moreover, the sacred revelations that guide the Church instruct its members to "seek all truth; and 'truth is knowledge of things as they are, and as they were, and as they are to come.' Knowledge of itself possesses no saving grace; but with greater knowledge, larger service may be rendered."[23] He further noted that the Church had fostered educational institutions from its beginning. In Utah it founded almost all of the early elementary, secondary, and post-secondary institutions.[24]

John sustained forging a line between secular and religious training, and he turned to revelation for support: "We do not believe it just to mingle religious influence with civil government, whereby one religious society is fostered and another proscribed in its spiritual privileges" (D&C 134:9). Addressing the graduates of the Agricultural College, John described the highest good in education: "The love of truth must be fostered if men are to travel the road to happy useful life. Unless you have learned to love truth your college course has been in vain. Almost the prime purpose of college training is to enable men to distinguish between that which the powers of men have found to be true, and the inferences . . . that are drawn from such facts of observation. . . . Men must cling to truth at whatever cost. That must be the constant, most important teaching of the schools."[25]

The Church has been unwilling to trust the spiritual training of Zion's youth to public education. John wrote, "Spiritual perfection, under the true laws of God, should be the aim of all men; the trained mind and the vigorous body may be used in winning such perfection. The will for righteousness transcends in importance, any intellectual accomplishments. It is for the development of the greater power that the Church Schools have been established."[26]

> As a nation we believe in God. The religious society over which I have the honor to preside teaches that those who laid the constitutional foundations of the United States were divinely inspired and led in their work. Faith in God is built into the very structure of the nation. If we lose this faith, we shall lose our strength. Likewise, many of the principles of truth woven into the governmental fabric of the United States have been derived from the Holy Bible. The spirit and purposes of the republic would be greatly promoted if a few moments each day could be devoted in our public schools to readings from the Bible. An acquaintance with the Bible remains a foremost help toward the living in this incredibly changing day.[27]

In marking the centennial of the pioneers' arrival in Utah, John emphasized that the second act of those pioneers provided for the establishment of the University of Deseret, now the University of Utah.[28] The education conceived in the eyes of those pioneers "included the training of all the powers of man."[29] Mechanism and practical education were advocated vigorously by Brigham Young. "Above all, however, they believed that schools should provide spiritual education. They were much afraid of the results in character building if the spiritual natures of people were not developed and fed during the formative years of school life."[30] John told President Grant, "As you have said so often, it is the making of Latter-day Saints which alone justifies the existence of the Church School System. While the present members of the Commission remain at this work, the effort will be made to develop throughout the System those spiritual ideals and activities which have always been contemplated by those who have founded the Church School System."[31]

As the twentieth century began, Utah public high schools were becoming established. As public high schools became the champion of home and American values, the Church sold its academies to the public schools at a small fraction of their cost. The cost of operating the Church schools represented a large proportion of the revenues of the Church. John proposed, "In justice to the many needs of the Church, the present cost of Church School education should be reduced. The duplicating of the state school system, even were it desirable, is impossible for financial reasons."[32]

As the Commissioner of Education, Widtsoe was the first LDS Church representative at the Religious Education Association's annual conventions. Members of the association harbored resentment toward the Church and its religion classes. John stood his ground: "America cannot go on in advancement as she has in the past unless our educational systems are supplemented by religious training. . . . What is rapidly becoming the most important phase of American education [is] namely the unifying and vitalizing of all of our educational activities in the public schools by giving them a religious purpose and motive."[33]

Upgrading the junior colleges was another of John's priorities. The *Deseret News* reported, "The junior colleges of the Church will be placed on a strictly collegiate basis announced Dr. John A. Widtsoe. . . . The Church board of education intends to introduce two-year standard college courses, in all junior colleges under its jurisdiction. . . ."[34]

Dropping high school classes made room for students who were ready for more advanced study.

The Church maintained some high schools where people were not able to support their own schools with public funds. Otherwise, the funds formerly spent on high schools were used to strengthen its junior colleges. John wrote, "The Church now plans to strengthen its . . . junior colleges and to make them first rank in their field. I need not go into the argument in favor of this change, but you know that there a[re] a great number of reasons why young people should be kept near home in the junior colleges during the rather tender age represented by the high school graduates."[35]

As his term as commissioner ended, John gave this summary:

> The day of the Church high schools was ending; the seminary, giving religious education to students in near-by state high schools, was in the ascendancy. Many parents could not accommodate themselves to the change. They wanted their children to have the privileges of Church high school training. The growth of the Church, with the many demands made upon its funds, clearly made inadvisable a system of Church high schools paralleling and duplicating the state high schools for the support of which the saints paid twice in taxes as well as tithing. The seminary system, already tried out in several places, seemed the nearest and best substitute. Soon, nearly every Latter-day Saint locality made application for a seminary near its high school building. It is hoped this may be possible wherever our people are located. Then all the children of all our people may have a chance to gain some special religious training instead of the few who happen to live near the special Church institutions. The success of the seminary venture has attracted the attention of educational leaders everywhere.[36]

Aspen Grove Summer School, 1927

John often taught faculty groups in their summer schools in Aspen Grove. One of the most acclaimed series of lectures was given to seminary teachers and the BYU faculty in 1927. A short time thereafter, BYU president Franklin S. Harris recommended their publication, and the YMMIA Board requested permission to use them as a lesson manual for their Senior Department.

The Aspen Grove lectures (titled *In Search of Truth*) are the most formal presentation of John's views of science and religion. They were a classic in his day, and they are still a valuable analysis of the subject. What follows is a brief summary of some of his lectures, showing his insight into the tension between science and religion. It is a well piloted path. The lectures addressed two questions: "What is science?" and "How does the Church view science?"

LECTURE 1: NEW LAMPS FOR OLD

In this lecture Widtsoe referred to Aladdin of *Arabian Nights* fame, whose wife traded his seemingly shabby old lamp for a bright new one. The old lamp had hidden powers by which Aladdin had acquired his palace, his wealth, and his station. Similarly, in human exchanges involving fundamental beliefs, Widtsoe maintained there is the greatest need to ascertain the truth in the new offering before jettisoning one's security and faith. Yet, to resist change when new thoughts and opinions are an improvement would jeopardize advancement: "A new definition of God, a new theory of man's relationship to God, or a new interpretation of the purpose of life, are matters which must be subjected to the severest tests of truth. One who loves truth cannot follow the multitude with respect to such matters. He must know for himself. "Since in every proffered exchange may lie hidden a thrust at fundamental truth, every offering must be examined."[37]

The scientific age demands that men and women understand the processes and limitations of science and be able to test the doctrines drawn from scientific advancements. As modern advances are products of the scientific activity, "the new offerings are in the main children of the scientific laboratory."[38] All proper human activity anchors itself to truth, and the honest mind loves truth above all else. In the proffered exchanges of new things for old, religion and science have often appeared to conflict. Because truth is the aim of both science and religion, those conflicts have been more apparent than real:

The Gospel accepts and embraces all truth; science is slowly expanding her arms, and reaching into the invisible domain, in search of truth. The two are meeting daily; science as the child; religion as the mother. Earnest attempts at reconciliation are rewarded with full success. Occasional failures are usually due to the mistake of alone trying religion, the more comprehensive and better established, by the newer and less dependable standards of science. Religion has an equal right to try science. Either method, properly applied, leads to the same result: truth is truth, whether labeled science or religion.[39]

LECTURE 2: THE FACTS OF SCIENCE

In 1927 the scientific age was well under way with electricity, steam locomotion, air flight, and radio. John noted, "Science is knowledge, all knowledge of mankind, systematically classified and arranged. The sum of human experience is the sum of scientific knowledge. To possess all truth is its hope; without increasing truth it perishes. It is never complete; it is ever increasing; 'it knows in part and it prophesies in part.'"[40] Widtsoe maintained there was no limit to the domain of science: "Only one condition is imposed upon knowledge by those who build science: it must be arranged systematically for the easier comprehension of man. The facts of nature organized about human life, that is science."[41] The fourfold objectives of science and its disciples are: "to gather existing knowledge; to discover new knowledge; to give man an increasing control over natural forces; and to make love of truth the greatest human passion."[42]

Man's ability to observe natural phenomena is the fundamental limitation set on science: "However weak or strong a man may be, the facts of science come by observation; he has no other means of obtaining them."[43] Scientific instruments are aids to man's senses. The progress of every avenue of science is closely tied to perfecting those aids: "In truth, there was no real scientific progress until instruments of precision and magnification were devised, and whenever a new instrument has been constructed, a new science or a new branch of a science has come into being."[44] These instruments have determined the progress of science.

Widtsoe was insistent about the basis of science being facts grounded in "verifiable and verified observations. . . . They are the building blocks of science, and there are no other. Failure to recognize facts as the only foundation of science is the cause of most controversies within science, or between science and religion.

"To walk safely with science and religion, facts must be of first consideration. Every inference, every hypothesis or theory, is based upon and drawn from facts. The faith of science is in facts, not in conjectures, however valuable the latter may be as guides to new discovery. There would be no science without facts."[45] Science uses any and all hypotheses that assist in correlating facts, but science can never commit itself to any of them on the basis of faith. To do so would take it out of the realm of science.

In the gospel of Jesus Christ there is no limit placed upon truth. In fact, the gospel itself declares that truth will make man free. The domains of science were expanding by 1927 to include the behavior of the human mind, the basis of human conduct, causes of social and economic phenomena, religion and the spiritual life of man, and life after death. Religious convictions were less subject to scorn. Religion was gaining in respect with each new discovery of nature.

LECTURE 3: THE INFERENCES OF SCIENCE

The inferences of science depend on the facts of science: "By inference is meant the formation of judgments, (beliefs and opinions) on the strength of, or as a consequence of other judgments already formed, it may be, on the ground of observation, or only entertained provisionally either for further consideration, or for the sake of argument."[46] The mind of man has always inclined him to further researches and new discoveries: "Without mind, there is no science, no progress, only extinction."[47] The mind is a powerful instrument that depends on speculation to help understand the facts it uncovers: "If guided and controlled [speculation] may be of much human service, but . . . untrammelled and wilful may lead mankind into deep distress."[48] The first question regarding any new law of nature is "Why?": "By pursuing the cause or causes to the last degree, we come to a land where human understanding cannot enter. The wise thinker knows and respects the limits of human thought. It is profitless to enter where there is no light. When light is obtained, that is when new facts are obtained."[49]

In the pursuit of truth there are several stages: "Laws, hypotheses and theories are used indiscriminately in common speech, and often they do overlap, but there is a clear distinction among them. A law is a description of the observed regularity of a group of facts. An hypothesis is the explanation of this law. A theory is the explanation of the hypotheses, an inference is yet further removed from the facts upon which our thinking rests. Often the hypotheses and theories are the same."[50]

Often the real mischief of a new discovery has come when the discoverer sets himself up as a good interpreter: "A man with a stern desire for truth, who has the gift of philosophic insight, is the best type for the development of scientific hypotheses."[51] "The Church has no quarrel with hypotheses or theories. It merely insists that they be known for what they are—inferences from facts, and subject to change as new facts accumulate. It further suggests, respectfully, that until the facts give final certainty to the theory, the scientific philosopher refrain from presenting theory as fact to people untrained in science."[52]

LECTURE 4: THE TRUTHFULNESS OF SCIENCE

Widtsoe felt that since the facts of science are won by observation, the human senses become a limiting variable of science. There are waves too long or too short to excite the human sense of vision and sounds too low or too shrill to affect the human eardrum. Man lives in a vast universe, only a fraction of which he understands with his unaided senses. Therefore, when many people observe the same results under set conditions, scientific facts become established. The advance of science has coincided with the development of instruments to aid human senses: "The invention of a new instrument has nearly always meant the birth of a new branch of science. The history of instruments to aid the senses would be a good history of modern thought."[53] Imperfections in the instruments developed must give rise to some suspicion in final conclusions: "While the possession of instruments enables us to penetrate more completely the region of the unknown, it does not relieve us from the necessity of carefully estimating the truth of our observations, and presenting them humbly for admission to the kingdom of fact."[54] The better trained, the more the scientist understands the limitations placed on discoveries: "In the end, the aim of science is to secure a knowledge of that part of the universe not directly sensed."[55]

The chief result of modern science is a knowledge of the unseen world: "It is noteworthy that the existence of the unseen world into which science is rapidly entering has been declared these many centuries by religion. When we go beyond that which may be directly sensed by man, we are in a field declared by religion to be subject to man's knowledge."[56]

Multiple inferences and the degrees of probabilities that go along with scientific advances must remind us that science in the end is limited by our power to observe correctly. "In fact, the whole structure of science rests upon assumptions which if false make necessary a full reconstruction of our modern thought."[57] Modern science developed with the doctrine of cause and effect. Those who advance knowledge uniformly believe that under like conditions, the same cause will always produce the same effect. This assumption, so commonly observed, has the force of final truth. This orderliness in nature allows scientific assumptions to produce facts: "We live in a reign of law. Orderliness is characteristic of law. This, also, is an assumption, but one of such high probability of truth that it approaches the dignity of a fact. Many thinkers hold that the reign of law that prevails in the universe is sufficient proof that intelligence is the controlling power of nature."[58]

Controversies centering around scientific knowledge are almost always about inferences; seldom are facts embroiled in controversy: "Scientists on both sides, warm with enthusiasm for their inferences, defend their respective views with all their might. Stories of such disputes among men of science litter the pages of scientific journals—and that is the place for them. When such controversies are carried into the field of popular interest, the very spirit of science should forbid men of science from stating claims in such a manner as to mislead a public untrained in scientific logic. The recent controversies between science

and religion have been most unscientific—and the scientists have often
been quite as unscientific as the religionists. Dogmatism is unbecoming
in everyone, but especially in a scientist. It is well for him to remember
the probabilities lying at the foundation of science."[59]

LECTURE 5: EVOLUTION

Widtsoe introduced the delicate subject of evolution with a historical overview of the idea and an explanation of what is shown in the fossil record: "This regularity of progression in the universe from the simple
to the complex, is the inference known as the law of evolution. It has
been observed or felt from the earliest day. Before the Greeks, and
throughout the history of thought, it appears and reappears. Modern
science did not originate it, but emphasized it by the discovery of new
facts. The law of evolution, thus stated, does not require that all things,
all life, shall have a common origin. It merely declares that everything in
the universe is moving onward."[60] "The history of life upon the earth as
revealed by the fossil record shows that as time went on, the existing life
forms became more and more complex. In the earliest rocks only elementary forms of life have left their fossil records; in the rocks laid down
later, the fossil records show more advanced forms of life up to the most
recent geological formations."[61]

Man and the vertebrates have many similarities: the skeletal structure, muscular construction and placement, nervous organization, blood
resemblances, and embryonic life. It is possible, if existing creation is
properly classified, to proceed from man as the highest form of life,
descending through small changes, to the lowest form of life. "The one
great difference, in such a classification, not yet bridged, is that of intellectual power."[62] Biologists have affected many surprising changes in life
forms. "No one, least of all the Church, objects to these facts if properly
verified. They are all accepted, acceptable, and welcome. The work of
gathering more knowledge in the field of biology is favored by the
Church."[63]

In space there seems to be steady movement from unorganized matter to more and more complex organized forms. On earth the geologic
record indicates a constant advancement among life forms. Simply

stated, all creation has been and is advancing, becoming more complex, evolving, or progressing. Exceptions to this rule are in such a minority that they rather emphasize the usual order.

The doctrine of universal advancement of God's creation is well established: "In no particular is the work of the prophet, Joseph Smith, more in harmony with modern thought. Throughout all time man shall increase, progress to a godlike destiny."[64] That the ancestor of all life began as a faint spark through the accidental combination of moisture, temperature, and materials in the primordial lifeless slime, as advanced by advocates of the ultra-evolutionary hypothesis, is a flawed theory, Widtsoe asserted. First, it is in violation of all observed facts that only life begets life. "If one such life germ could be formed, any number may have been so formed, for we have no right to say that only in one spot, among one group of molecules were the necessary conditions favorable."[65] Moreover, many leading scientists of the day held that there was life on other bodies in space and that germs of life carried through space gave birth to life on earth. If this could be true for one form of life, it could be true for many forms.

The view that man descends from lower animals is based on structural similarities with lower animals, the gradually ascending nature of life forms in the fossil record with man as the latest figure, and the discovery of man-like beings in glacial formations of early times. Conclusions based on these criteria are at best inferential and are far from being final. The facts are too far apart and the foundation too insecure. The story of life in the fossil record has too many gaps, and the skeletal remains of great antiquity are too incomplete.

"The doctrine of the origin of man as held by the Church has not suffered from the advancement of modern biology, anthropology and archaeology."[66]

In summary Widtsoe argued, "In the case of present-day views of the origin of man, the old is better than the new, no matter how bright and burnished the modern offering appears to be."[67]

> The Church by its own methods of winning truth, real and true to hosts of men and women who have used them, declares that man is an eternal being. That which he is, is everlasting. It had no beginning;

it can not end. Man is not inferior in eternal quality to the elements of which he is built. As an eternal being he lived before he came upon earth. He was begotten in that pre-existent state by God, whom we worship as the creator of the earth, and the Father of our spirits. From the beginning, man has been man. How the eternal spirit of man became associated, first, with the mortal body is not known; nor is the whole career of mankind on the earth known. But man was always man; else he is not eternal; nor a very child of God. True, upon the earth, as in the time before this, he is subject to the unending law of progress, and throughout the endless ages he has developed and progressed, but his relationship as a child of God has always existed.[68]

President Harris requested these lectures because he knew that Elder Widtsoe would be living in Europe for several years and that his influence would be sorely missed in the growing fuss over science and religion. The series was intended to address two central questions: "What is science?" and "How does the Church view science?"[69] Widtsoe's vigilant training at Harvard and Göttingen and his years of private study, combined with his carefully won faith and his call as an apostle, made him uniquely qualified to address those two questions. The lectures were a landmark in Church literature and a treasured publication to thousands who lived close to the fires of science, especially young students who were beginning their journey therein. President Heber J. Grant liked them so much that he gave five hundred copies as Christmas gifts in 1931.[70]

Elder Widtsoe always saw science and religion as confederates. As both earnestly sought truth, ultimate truth, they were precious to him as a devout disciple of truth. Both were sacred, and the abuse of either was an annoyance. These lectures, meant to be simple expositions, were easily understood by scientists or laymen who valued the gospel and science.

Academically and religiously, John A. Widtsoe was a disciple of truth. Whether from the test tube or the Holy Spirit, truth was something sacred—something to be revered. The fuss that arose between science and religion involved misunderstandings or misapplications of the principles of truth. John desired to eliminate the fuss through proper understanding.

COMMISSIONER OF EDUCATION

In November 1933, John was again asked to serve as commissioner of education. He said, "The Commissionership and all that pertains to it were rather dumped on me in the spring," and in the midst of this busy time for Church education, he had to immediately take action on several matters.[71] Most pressing was the seminary program: "I sat as a member of the State Board of Education and a messenger brought us the question as to what we would do as a State Board if the Church should undertake to give religious education to students of the high schools outside of the high schools. It is one of the great satisfying memories of my life that I had the honor of making the motion that we give credit for the work done in such seminaries, yet unborn, just in the minds of men; and that motion prevailed and is still on the records of the Utah State Board of Education, and I hope it will never be wiped off of those records."[72]

From that time on, John was involved in the seminary program, as a member of the YMMIA Board, as commissioner of education, and at the Seminary summer schools. It was 1934, he was again at the helm, and two crucial questions were put before him: What should be the curriculum of the seminaries? Should there be a junior seminary for ninth-graders? John felt that those who had been teaching would have the most intimate knowledge of both questions. Accordingly, as had been his practice in his ACU days, he sent out a survey: "A number of our seminary workers have suggested that the present practice of teaching the same subject in all the seminary classes in any one year, the so called rotation system, is not wholly satisfactory. Requests have been made by a number of seminaries that they be allowed to return to the old method of teaching the Old Testament, the New Testament, and Church History and Doctrine concurrently."[73]

Twenty responses favored the rotation plan and seventy-five were opposed. John wrote, "This shows that a very large majority of you are in favor of returning to the old system of doing three seminary subjects in each year. In accordance with your vote and our own good judgment in this office, the recommendation was made to the Church Board of Education at its last meeting that the rotation system be abandoned and the old system be readopted. This was approved. With the beginning of the school year 1934–35, therefore, the three seminary subjects should be given in each fully organized seminary."[74]

The second question involved junior seminaries and the place of the ninth grade in the seminary system. Junior seminaries corresponded to junior high schools. Sentiment flowed in the direction of eliminating the junior seminaries, at least in the seventh and eighth grades. Complicating this matter was the fluctuating placement of the ninth grade. Some areas included it in junior high school; others did not. Regardless of the public school system in each area, the ninth-graders had been kept with the junior seminary program. Many doubted the wisdom of this, especially with the possibility of abolishing the junior seminary program altogether.

Again John desired to know what those closest to the students felt, so he wrote for their views: "Conditions have arisen which make it necessary to evaluate anew the place of the Junior Seminary in the Church educational system. We need the benefit of your experience. . . . Will you, therefore, answer. . . ."[75] Seventy-eight favored moving the ninth-grade into the senior seminary program; eleven opposed. They also suggested phasing the junior seminary program out of operation.

RELIGION SUMMER SCHOOL, 1934

For four summers in a row, the Church's Department of Education had arranged for the seminary teachers of the Church to study the Old Testament, the New Testament, and the history of the early Christian Church under non-LDS scholars from Eastern universities at a summer school. Originally the plan had been that after four years of summer school, the teachers would be given a summer without a class. Although John was in favor of this (he had always guarded against teachers getting burned out from lack of a break), he felt that it was extremely important to help the teachers take all they had learned and put it in a Gospel perspective. Furthermore, he felt that a course that helped the teachers view their students' place in the gospel would give crucial direction to their teaching. Accordingly, Widtsoe, on short notice, organized another summer school. He gave the teachers this explanation and assurance:

> I want to half apologize for calling this convention this summer. I understand that most of you have been in summer school the past four years consecutively, and were it not for the special message we want to put over this summer, in accordance with the wishes of the Department of Education and the General Authorities of the Church, we should not have called this meeting. But let me hold out this indefinite promise. You will discover after we have been together for a while that my office does not make many promises, but I will make one half-promise, that if I am able to arrange it there shall be no summer school one year from now. You will have at least one summer of freedom in which you may visit or make money or do anything else becoming a seminary teacher. I do feel we have work to do this summer that should be done and must be done. . . .
>
> The purpose of this summer school is a definite one. Most of you have been studying the Old Testament, the New Testament, and the history of the Christian Church. You have had a wealth of information given you. You have had all the quibbles over Isaiah and all the quibbles over Matthew, Mark, Luke, and John. I hope you have made up your minds as to which quibble is the best. But during that time you have had very little direct consideration of the Gospel, and the purpose of this convention or summer school is to discuss Gospel problems, and in doing so to bring to our aid any of the information that you have gained in the courses formerly taken or otherwise obtained. In other words, we want to apply the Gospel to academic learning. This time we will reverse the process.[76]

This was no small undertaking. In the midst of his other duties, John was about to become almost the sole teacher of an intensive five-week course. "I am occupied in teaching the seminary teachers of the Church," he wrote. "It is taking all of my working time, and I am obliged to let all other matters go."[77]

The school met from 12 June through 13 July, sometimes at BYU and sometimes at the Church Administration Building. Joseph Fielding

Smith often assisted, sitting in on many classes and offering his great wisdom and experience. Over thirty-six teachers attended. They were also taught by many General Authorities, including President Heber J. Grant, President Anthony W. Ivins, Elder Richard R. Lyman, Elder Charles A. Callis, and President Antoine R. Ivins. Four courses were taught by Widtsoe: "Man and the Gospel," "The Truth of Mormonism," "Seminary Problems," and "Questions and Answers." Additionally, the group attended several temple sessions usually accompanied by a lesson on the temple. At least six times they held lengthy sessions in the upper rooms of the Salt Lake Temple, where the endowment and other matters were discussed. There were outings to parks and canyons, presentations by university presidents and teachers, and a variety of other activities.

John warned the teachers, "We have quite a bit of work to do. I do not know whether we will finish it all in the time that we have at our disposal."[78] At the same time he worked to meet the needs of the teachers and involved them in this process, telling them, "We have laid out a program, as indicated in the circular sent out, but if we should decide ourselves to change that program we have the right to do so. We are not going to be bound by any office made schedule, and when we see how things develop (and you will all help out, no doubt, in that development) we will finally settle down to the regular order of business that will suit us best."[79] Graduate credit was offered for two of the classes, pending class participation and the completion of two papers for each course.[80]

John spoke of changes they were experiencing and the future he saw: "We are in a day of change. Something is being born. We have pains accompanying birth. We are going to help bring this child into life, and then when it is born we are going to help the child become a mighty citizen in his own day. . . . I might go on to tell you my vision of this great work, which is the vision of every man who has thought about it."[81]

In "Man and the Gospel" John asked his students, "Don't you think that if God, whom we have accepted, and Christ, whom we have accepted, and the unseen world, which we have accepted here, if all these forces combined to prepare a plan by which man is to achieve what we call salvation, then the main item of concern in the whole Gospel is the individual, the man, for whom the Gospel was made?"[82] He then added, "Do you keep that in mind in your seminary teaching? Do you have your students leave the schoolroom at the end of the year with an understanding of the value of a man in God's eyes, and therefore in our eyes? . . . If I were you I would look on each seminary student, each girl, each boy, with appreciation of his importance before ever beginning the day's work or the work of the class. You will find it will help you tremendously. It is a law of all good teaching, the law of looking outside oneself for the needs of our fellow men."[83]

With the foundational understanding of the gospel's purpose, John helped the teachers come to a working definition of salvation: the removal of every hindrance toward joy and eternal progression, or Godhood.[84] As the class progressed, they came to see that a desire to bring about God's plan for all people leads to a need to understand how God would have us advance his plan. This meant having contact beyond the veil, or with "the unseen world." John taught that obedience to the plan brought joy, but also that "a man who lives the commandments, who prays, who reaches out for the truth and does it persistently, who learns the Gospel and who lives the Gospel, following the formula, ultimately becomes an instrument himself by which he may penetrate the unseen world and live in close touch with the realities of what we call 'the other side,' which is not so far away from us—perhaps is nearer than we think."[85]

Widtsoe succinctly summarized the temple endowment, explaining that it fell into five distinct parts: (1) The story of our eternal journey. (2) The conditions upon which progress in this journey depend, including warnings against digressing from its course. (3) Covenants, which he believed were the agreements that bind us to follow the path of eternal progression and give life to the exchange. (4) Tests of knowledge, something John felt would be understood by every teacher. Of this he said, "We are dealing with great eternal realities, with God who directs and overshadows all of our labors, all of our lives, and we must be able to give an account [of our lives] to Him. We must have tests. So some of the things that trouble many of the people who go through the temple are as logical as they can be." (5) The endowment bridged time and eternity, making that which had been and would take place throughout eternity fit into our time, and making that which was taking place in our time efficacious in eternity.[86]

John also taught the teachers about the teaching of the temple: "Like everything else that man obtains, temple information is given through a set of symbols. It is symbolic teaching. Some of the things that to some people seem least congruous mean the most when they are looked upon as symbols. If a man goes through a school with closed eyes he sees nothing; with a closed mind he sees still less; but with an open mind and open eyes you will find every word, every step, everything done in the temple has a symbolic meaning which fits into the great cause of the Gospel in earth and the working of the Gospel in eternity."[87]

He concluded, "I can bear testimony to you, that if one goes into the temple in the right spirit there is no question about the fact that revelation comes through him."[88]

John expressed to the summer school his gratitude for the extremely valuable contribution made by Joseph Fielding Smith:

> I cannot say how deeply appreciative I am personally and you are individually of the assistance of Brother Joseph Fielding Smith. He has spent about a third of the meetings with us, besides actually taking a part in the work. We do appreciate it, Brother Smith, and that you were able to come to this closing meeting. The Lord bless you.
>
> Brother Smith and I discuss frequently matters of interest to you teachers. We do not always see eye to eye on certain things, but on the fundamentals we see exactly alike, and I have found him to be one of the most willing, most open-minded men. He holds to his own opinions—he is a Smith. He is also himself. But he is not stubborn. What a difference that makes in a man! We love you, Brother Smith. I know I speak for all of you when I say we would like to honor those who are faithful members of the family chosen by the Lord as the instrument through which this great work was established in these latter days. . . . We honor him for his labors. We love him also because he stands for the family chosen by the Lord to usher in this work, and for many other personal qualities.[89]

The teachers were grateful. On the last day of class, while presenting John with a gold watch, G. Byron Done said:

> Dr. Widtsoe, it has been the practice of this group the past four summers to give to their teacher some token of appreciation. I think that on some of those occasions the gift was given as a matter of custom by some of the men in this group. When the idea was suggested several days ago to this group to present you with this token the response was immediate and universal. We appreciated our wise teachers who were brought to us from the East. They fed our minds. They gave us a background of the things we wanted to know about the Bible. But I speak the mind and heart of this body of men and women when I say that as a teacher you have not only fed our minds, you have inspired us, and that the spirit which you carry with you has warmed our hearts. I am sure this body of men and women will go back to their work with a greater love for it, with greater determination, with renewed faith, for you have won our hearts and our love as a great teacher.[90]

John's work as Commissioner of Education, especially the summer school, completely consumed his time from April through September of 1934. In less than a year he would be released, ironically so that he could participate further in education in Southern California. There he would have a lasting impact on the institute program.

27

MISSION CALL AND
FAMILY ADJUSTMENTS

J OHN A. Widtsoe's commitment to Harvard and to those who had lent
him the money to secure his education had precluded his earlier acceptance of a mission call. In 1896 John was twenty-four years old, his debts
were contained, and his career already showed remarkable potential. It
was time to decide among a mission, marriage, or his career in agriculture. He and his family carefully weighed the decision and decided that
John should volunteer for a mission and that Osborne (graduated from
the BYC) should teach school to support the family while John was
away. When John returned, he would then take over the support of the
family while Osborne served a mission. "The plan was well laid, but like
many man-made plans did not work out. John was told [by his priesthood leaders] that it was desired that before he take a mission, he first
'lay the foundation for a family.'"[1] The family reorganized their plans.
John looked toward carrying out his instructions, and Osborne planned
to go to Harvard. John turned his attention to the romance that had
begun at Harvard in the summer of 1892. In 1898, six years later, John
and Leah were finally married. It wasn't until the fall of 1927, on the
heels of a family crisis, that John was finally able to embark on a full-
time mission. He wrote:

We both desired a large family. This was not granted us. Seven children were born to us. Two died soon after birth, from causes that modern knowledge could have rectified easily. One, subject to the same untoward condition lived about two years, then passed away. John A., Jr., when one year old, was caught by an infectious disease from a neighbor, and died after much suffering. Three grew to maturity, Anna Gaarden, the eldest, born April 2, 1899, Karl Marsel, born Nov. 27, 1902, and Leah Eudora, born July 4, 1912.[2]

Marsel, their only son to live to adulthood, filled an honorable mission to Great Britain, attended college, and began teaching seminary in Preston, Idaho. From 13–15 May 1927, John was assigned to preside over a stake conference that coincided with seminary graduation in Preston. His journal tells the story:

> May 15: 8 A.M. meeting w. Stake Presidency about special assignment. 10 A.M., grad. Exercises of Franklin Co. Seminary. Marsel presided at morning meeting. He did very well. He has done a splendid year's work. Thank God.
>
> May 23: Tel. At 6 A.M. Marsel down w. pneumonia. Came down Saturday night after wet all day at trackmeet at Logan. Temp. Sunday 105 degrees; Monday morning 104 degrees; Monday night, 105.8. Leah left on 7 A.M. train for Preston. We are all worried.
>
> May 24: Marsel better. Temp. 102 degrees. Leah with him in Preston. Work on manual. Word from Leah in evening Marsel somewhat better. Temp. 102.
>
> May 25: Report from Preston that Marsel is no better.
>
> May 26: Left for Preston on 7 A.M. train. Arrived noon. Found Marsel very sick, but right lung free from involvement. Spent afternoon w. him. In evening Dr. C. Snow drove up to pass on Marsel's case. I am praying the Lord to spare his life.
>
> May 27: Marsel very sick. Snow & sleet. J. E. Fisher has sat up w. Marsel every night since Sunday. My heart is heavy. Leah collapsed for a while this morning.
>
> May 28: Marsel had his best night. Temp. 100 degrees in morning. Lung is clearing. Marion came in. Abt. Noon pains set in. Morphine. At 3 P.M. alarmed. Oedema had occurred. From 4–7:45 we watched his heavy breathing. At 7:45 P.M. my beloved son, my

*Photo of Karl Marselius
(Marsel) Widtsoe,
1902–1927.*

only living son, Karl Marselius Widtsoe, died. Leah, I & Marion present. Oh, the agony! Made arrangements. Drove home w. Quinneys.
Reached home abt 2:30 A.M. I am so alone. I needed Marsel. He
promised so much. I loved him so. God help me! & help Leah!

May 29: Reached home abt. 2:30 A.M. Found family up. Present
A.E. & Lou; Dr. & Mrs. Clarence Snow; Rose & Karine. Spent day
at home & undertakers. My lovely son; none better ever lived!

May 30: Home all day except to select casket. Marsel's cards most
splendid. He may well be a model for youth. How I shall miss him!
The house is crumbling before my eyes. My God, I thank thee for
Marsel—but why was it necessary for him to go?

May 31: People have come & gone the last 3 days. Marsel at
home in his casket. A beautiful man! A beautiful life! Funeral services at 2 P.M. See stenographic report. Fine music. Excellent addresses

by D. O. McKay, Hyrum D. Jensen & Pres. H. J. Grant. At cemetery until 5:30. Wallaces here. Oh, My God! My God!

June 7: Marsel graduated from the U. of U. today! It is awful! God help me forget![3]

When Marsel died he was only one month away from temple marriage and his turn at Harvard.

The answer to John's plea "God help me forget!" came on 29 September 1927: "Temple meeting. About 12:45 P.M. President Grant announced that Dr. J. E. Talmage would be released as President of the European mission and that I was to succeed him. It was a complete surprise. I thank God & pray him to help me prove worthy of the trust. I am dazed."[4] Years later, John recalled, "It was some two or three months after the death of our son Marsel. Undoubtedly that had much to do with the call. It was felt no doubt that absence from old scenes would ease the grief."[5]

In the weeks following Marsel's death, John wrote many sympathy letters to others who had lost loved ones. They illuminate his views of death and measure the healing process he underwent in this crisis: "I need not explain to you how we have felt throughout the summer, and how we still feel. It was very difficult for me to leave my home and do the work assigned me, but we have been getting along by the help of the Lord and we are grateful to Him for all his blessing[s], even though at times they seem to be in the nature of serious loss."[6] To a widow, he wrote, "I have always felt that those who passed before us into the spirit world are not wholly without power to assist us who remain. I am sure that the influence of your husband will still be with you, and will help you in the days that are before you. Faith transforms all of life, turns grief into gladness, and deep sorrow into joy."[7]

In his letters he seemed to find great comfort. To a friend who had lost his wife, he wrote, "I want you to know that I sympathize with you deeply, and wish that you may receive in great abundance the only comfort that helps on occasions like this—the assurance of the eternal duration of life, and the possibility of a reunion under more permanent conditions that characterizes the life hereafter."[8]

Making arrangements for their move to Europe helped take the grieving parents' minds off Marsel's death. Leah described her feelings to the First Presidency:

> The mission came to us at such a crucial time, when we both needed it so greatly—I especially, for I was in danger of becoming narrow through brooding and inactivity. I can see that now. All my life, since my earliest childhood memory I have cherished but one consuming ambition: to be the mother of a large family of children. . . . John felt as I did regarding children and they came to us as Nature sent them, seven of them, and every one received in joy and welcome. Naturally, we desired our children, our sons especially (we were blessed with three), to help us make the name of Widtsoe honorable in the Church and to found a large and useful family. Why we were not permitted to raise them all to useful maturity on this earth will remain a mystery— our trial.[9]

Because the call to serve in Europe usually followed seniority in the Council of the Twelve, John had not anticipated it so soon, if at all, because he had already had the opportunity of spending time in Europe. He was nonetheless eager to serve to the best of his ability and to learn from President Talmage, to whom he wrote, "Were it not for the faith that we all have that we are on the Lord's errand and that He gives strength according to the needs of the day and the desire to serve, it would be quite out of the question to enter with any degree of confidence upon the most important work of the world—the establishing of the Kingdom of God in these latter days. . . . We are happy in the privilege of serving in the great latter-day cause. There is no joy equal to that which comes from giving some little aid in the accomplishment of the Lord's purposes."[10]

ANNOUNCEMENT, ACCEPTANCE, AND PREPARATION

At the 1927 semiannual general conference of the Church, President Heber J. Grant announced that James E. Talmage and his wife had been honorably released from presiding over the European mission and that John A. Widtsoe and his wife would succeed them in presiding over the mission and the Relief Society.[11] John then delivered his formal acceptance and gave a stirring address on the hand of God ruling over all things in the advancing world: "I feel humble and incapable, of my own strength, to accomplish the work that lies before me; but I have faith, I may say absolute faith. . . . With that faith I go forth gladly at the request and call. . . . As my memory goes back to my mother country, and later to the days I spent in the European countries in my early manhood, as a student, I feel that there are in those countries a very great number . . . we may reach. . . . I am always thankful that missionaries were sent into my native land."[12]

The call received considerable attention in the press. John's international reputation made him a perfect ambassador for the Church. Moreover, his expertise in dealing with college-aged men set him apart as a good leader for the corps of missionaries in Europe. The *Deseret News* reported, "Dr. Widtsoe is a man of scholarly attainments and a profound student of Gospel principles. He has had wide experience as an educator and for years has been in close contact with young men such as those with whom he will be associated in the mission field. He knows their problems and will no doubt give them sympathetic and considerate attention."[13]

Other reactions to his new assignment were predictably mixed. The American Scandinavian Association gave him a heroic farewell, celebrating that one of their own would be presiding over advancements in their native lands. Franklin S. Harris, president of BYU, expressed the ambivalence shared by many: "In the first part of my letter I want to congratulate you on your appointment as President of the European Missions. I know of nothing that could have been done that would have been so important for the welfare of the missions. . . . There is almost a lament among our faculty members at the thought of your being so far away. You have gradually won the hearts of our faculty, and the climax was reached at the Alpine Summer School, so that now there are some of them a little upset at your going away."[14]

The Saints in Europe were happy to welcome the Widtsoes. The official journal of the European Mission, the *Latter-day Saints' Millennial Star,* reported their arrival and gave an overview of the missions under John's care:

Photo of Leah, John, and Eudora about the time they embarked on their mission to Europe.

The "European Mission" comprises ten main units, each designated a Mission and in charge of a Mission President; these are the British, French, Netherlands, Swiss-German, German-Austrian, Norwegian, Swedish, Danish, Armenian, and South African Missions. The President of the European Mission has general and visitatorial jurisdiction over the units named, and therefore occupies the position of a President-General; moreover, he holds concurrently the office of President of the British Mission.

The mission is to be congratulated on the appointment of a man of Elder Widtsoe's capability, capacity, experience, and powers of mind and spirit, to be its chief executive. None can doubt that the selection was made under the influence of divine inspiration through the First Presidency and the Council of the Twelve, by whom action was taken on September 29th, of which action immediate publicity was given through the home journals.[15]

GETTING STARTED

John A. Widtsoe was set apart for his mission on 21 November 1927. En route to Europe, he, Leah, and Eudora spent a few days with friends and associates in Washington, D.C. They sailed from New York

City on 15 December on the SS *President Roosevelt,* arriving in Plymouth, England, on the 23rd. The British official who checked their passports refused them entry, saying, "We do not want your kind of people in our country. We may tolerate the young elders, but not you who are leaders."[16] A considerable conversation followed before he asked what they intended to teach if permitted to enter. John answered, "We intend to teach the British people so far as we are able how to win happiness while they live on earth, and how to find happiness in the life to come. We intend to teach them the meaning of life, where they came from, why they are here, and where they are going." Almost in a breath this official stamped the passports and said, "Now we are done with that. Let's talk about Mormonism. I belong to a church but I am dissatisfied with it. It does not answer the problems of my life. It does not answer the questions that lie within my soul. I want to hear your teachings. Can you really tell me whence I came? Can you tell me why I am here? Can you tell me where I am going, for I know that life upon earth will end?" John later noted, "He became a fast friend—a type of millions of people in the world today who walk in darkness, feeling the need of light. Our obligation is to these people the world over."[17]

The Widtsoes arrived at the mission headquarters in Liverpool just in time to celebrate Christmas with the Talmages and the missionaries assigned to the mission home. Naturally, it took some time to become acquainted with the workings of the mission and the central office, but, though the work was demanding, it was not complicated. In a letter to President Grant, John described his plans in the immediate months ahead: "I am planning to give my first, and pretty much undivided, attention for the next few months to the British Mission. It is in need of it. Fifteen Districts, and between 60 and 80 branches, with the missionary body need careful attention for the best results. I have called a conference of the District Presidents for next Monday, January 16th. As soon as that is over I expect to go into the field to effect the pending reorganization of about one-half of the districts before the spring Conferences begin."[18]

When John had traveled through Europe with Senator Smoot in

1923, David O. McKay, president of the European missions, had discussed with them the problems the Church faced in Europe. Now, John sought Elder McKay's advice: "I trust you will be willing, whenever it occurs to you, to send me a note of suggestion. You know the situation here and your heart is with the missionary work."[19] In a letter to the First Presidency, John described the plan of action he formulated after several weeks in the European Mission:

> It is evident that our membership needs first attention. We are not holding our members well; they are inactive; or if active, too many are contentious and fault finding. We have some wonderfully fine members, but the notable exceptions only emphasize the general condition. Probably fewer than one-fourth of our membership takes part in our Church activities. There are 840 mature men holding the Priesthood, and many not ordained; yet only enough trustworthy men are available to officer a few of our branches. The time of our missionaries is largely consumed with branch supervision; and our propaganda work is suffering. . . .
>
> Our success will be measured by our power to hold our converts. . . . Whole branches are suffering from spiritual dry rot because of monotony and inactivity.
>
> The way out would seem to be, first, to use more of the Saints in official positions, and, second, to employ more vigorously the effective means offered by our auxiliaries. Brother and Sister Talmage sensed the situation keenly. They brought many Saints into more active service, and put the MIA on a new footing of missionary value. But they had barely enough time to begin the work.[20]

In the early days of the mission, the Widtsoes were greatly concerned about their daughter Anna, who was going through a divorce. She had two toddlers and was pregnant. When the third arrived, complications forced her to bed. It was an especially great comfort to have Grandma Gates at home looking after the family. Susa reported, "Anna never grunts nor grizzles. She takes it all in good part and is a very cheerful, delightful companion and associate. We all love her better every day. I too feel things will come out all right."[21] John replied to Brother and Sister Gates:

I want you to know again and again how truly I appreciate all that you are doing for me and mine, at this time in my life. Your watchful care over Anna has made me feel easy while she has gone through her recent confinement, as well as in her meeting of her present difficulties. I am sure that I could not have been any kinder to her, or more helpful than has "Grandpa," as she lovingly speaks of you . . . She has made many small mistakes, no big ones; she [has] an unusual nature full of moods, up and down, but withal as clean and wholesome and capable a girl as I have known. I shall do all I can to help her until the children are old enough and she is able to shift for herself. As to her marital future: I am closing my eyes to it, since I feel that we are all practically helpless when it comes to deciding anything in that matter. I can pray and that is about all. She cannot live on $50.00 a month, with the two children, I am quite sure of that; therefore I have written A. E. [Bowen] to let Anna have such help as he thinks proper from time to time out of my account, and of course, your judgment, particularly Father's, who has long financial experience, will be just as mine would be.[22]

The first year was particularly difficult. John confided to Elder Talmage that he felt he had let some important duties slide. "The work required of the European Mission President, if it is to be done well, is too much for my strength or for the strength of any ordinary man. . . . Since I have never been classed among the lazy ones, I take a little comfort in the thought that the work is bigger than it is ordinarily assumed to be, but I do dislike to be so crowded as not to do my work thoroughly."[23]

At the end of their first year, Widtsoe wrote a summary of the work for the *Millennial Star.* He reported that Church population in Europe was nearly thirty thousand in 1928. That year the six hundred fifty-two missionaries "distributed over five million tracts, pamphlets and books, held sixty-five thousand meetings, sold or loaned seven thousand nine hundred copies of the Book of Mormon, baptized one thousand five hundred thirty-five persons, and gave close attention to the hundreds of branches throughout the missions."[24]

The year had been exhausting but productive, and the Widtsoes took heart at their successes and at being in countries they loved. Christmas marked the first anniversary of their arrival, and as they

On back of photo is written "Elders of Liverpool District Sunday January 22, 1928."

reflected on the recent loss of Marsel and on Anna's difficulties, they were grateful to have Eudora with them. But another crisis was coming. John later described it to Elder J. Reuben Clark, Jr: "As you may have heard, on so-called Boxing Day here—the day after Christmas—Eudora came down with an acute attack of appendicitis and was operated upon that night—a broken [ruptured] appendix was found. It was a dangerous case, but the Lord blessed her and us abundantly. After about nineteen days in the hospital she was removed to our home where she is now convalescing and it seems that she is on the high road to recovery, and we hope to increased health and strength. Meanwhile, the anxiety and duties attending her illness took most of our time during the better part of three weeks."[25]

John had made two strong recommendations to the First Presidency. The first was that a separate mission president be assigned to the British Mission so that John could devote himself to the great needs of all the European missions:

> Our elders are younger than ever before and require, therefore, more personal contact with the mission president. Under existing immigration laws our members are more stationary and need new, more constant and special attention. The European Missions (excluding the Armenian and South African) now number eight, or twice as

many as a generation ago, with problems of coordination correspondingly increase[d]. Further, in this day of new thinking, new methods
must be devised to present the gospel effectively to the missions of
God-fearing people who live here. All these changed conditions
demand increased labor.

To accomplish well the work entrusted to us, I feel strongly that
the first need is the appointment of a president of the British Mission
who can devote his whole time to the British Mission—missionaries,
members, and propaganda—leaving the president of the European
Mission larger opportunity to supervise the remaining work, which
now is poorly done if the British work is well done. There is ample
work to keep two men very busy.[26]

John's second request was that the European Mission Headquarters
be moved to London, which he regarded as not only the center of Great
Britain but perhaps of the whole world. He felt that the increased efficiency would warrant the costs of both recommendations and bring
an increase in tithes and offerings. As a result of these requests, Elder
A. William Lund, assistant Church historian, was appointed president
of the British Mission beginning 1 January 1929, in the midst of
Eudora's illness.

A great burden was lifted—the guilt of having seriously neglected
nine missions in trying to meet the more immediate demands of one.
John wrote, "Brother Lund is here and took charge of the British
Mission on January 1st of this year, but it will take several weeks to
finally separate the interwoven affairs of the British and the European
Mission. Meanwhile, as soon as that has been accomplished it would
give Mrs. Widtsoe and myself, a much better opportunity to do the work
required of us on the Continent."[27]

Separating the operations of the missions, so long merged in their
work, was more difficult than John had planned. It was particularly difficult to separate financial responsibilities. Operation of the *Millennial
Star* and a bookstore also added to the complexity. The split wasn't final-
ized for a year.[28] But John felt that the process took the entire first three
months of 1929. Then he wrote, "Mingled feelings naturally accompany
this announcement: Rejoicing that the latter-day work is moving

forward, and regret that the close association that Sister Widtsoe and I have had with the Saints and Elders of the British Mission will of necessity be somewhat curtailed. It has been a delight to become acquainted with the faithful, devoted members of the Church in this land, and to observe their intelligent integrity. Upon the foundations laid in Great Britain, a mighty structure is being reared."[29]

John found that new freedom gave him greater opportunity to do good. More than a year after the separation, he wrote, "The second year was devoted to the organization problems awakened by the separation of the two missions, and to visiting the continental missions which had received scant attention the first year. At the same time, the firmer definition of the European mission as a central helping agency, instead of a part of the British Mission . . . brought much new work to the office."[30] For the final nine months of 1929 John concentrated on the problems of continental Europe, beginning on 21 March in the French Mission. This was the largest European mission, having three different governments and languages. The elders had to supervise the wards and branches particularly closely in the center of France, where members were few and unfamiliar with Church practices. Conferences filled quickly with members and elders eager to hear from Elder and Sister Widtsoe. "The visits stimulated investigators, comforted the Saints and gave new heart to the Elders," John noted, "and the instructions, I hope, to the Elders in particular, will help to unify the methods of teaching them practices of the European Missions—perhaps the outstanding need of the missions today."[31]

More than a month of touring passed before John returned to Liverpool. During his tour, he received word of the passing of his dear Aunt Petroline. John dealt with this death with his customary nobility:

> I had hoped steadily that she might live until my return—I wanted to see her again. But, I had not prayed that she might be allowed to live, for I did not want to intrude my will into the purposes of the Almighty. I shall now keep her in memory as I knew her in life, and it is somewhat curious, but since the news of her death reached me, I have remembered her more and more as the young good looking woman she was and less as the aged woman that she became. . . . She

was not unwilling to live, but I think she rather hoped that she might pass on. Those who were the nearest to her during her long life had gone on. . . . When you speak of blameless lives, hers must be included. Her testimony . . . was magnificent in its certainty.[32]

The demanding pace of the mission sometimes strained family life. Soon after Eudora's bout with appendicitis, she expressed to Grandma Gates her feelings of being lost and out of place in Europe. Again Susa came to their aid. She wrote to Eudora words of comfort and advice. She especially urged her to find an interest that would help her through hard, lonely times: "Your life, my dear, I feel will be a very long, useful, and most noble one. But with that feeling comes a hope that you will understand me when I suggest to you that you begin now from this very hour to engage in some soul-saving labor. You are there where you can realize how important it is to bring the Gospel before the inhabitants of the earth, but I want you to remember the thousands who have passed away without any chance of hearing the Gospel. Will you also recall that Marsel and your Uncle Osborne are exceedingly busy in Temple work on the other side."[33] Susa suggested that Eudora go on a campaign to get the Saints in Europe interested in temple and genealogical work. Eudora took up this proposal with enthusiasm.

Susa continued to look after Anna and the grandchildren. Anna, now divorced, began to entertain the idea of remarrying her former husband, much to the chagrin of the family. Susa reported, "She is really once more desperately in love with her husband. I have said everything I could to her, have discouraged it and disheartened her until I give it up."[34] John, who relied heavily on Susa, wrote, "I cannot begin to tell you how very grateful we all are for your help to Anna. I realize how much you have done for her."[35]

28

IN THE EYE OF THE
EUROPEAN PUBLIC

J OHN had learned the advantage of positive press coverage while working at the ACU, the University of Utah, and the Bureau of Reclamation.
In the goodwill mission he filled with Senator Reed Smoot in 1923, he
saw firsthand the power of the press in shaping the public perception of
"Mormons." As European mission president, he was eager to excite that
power again and to maintain good relations with the press. He often
invited members of the press to attend mission presidents' conferences,
where he included the importance of improving the Church's public
image in his instructions. His comments about the Paris mission presidents' conference and his tour of the Scandinavian missions are salient:
"As times change, proselytizing methods must be changed. . . . The
radio, the phonograph, the motion picture have come to benefit
humanity. The tracting age is approaching its end in missionary work.
. . . The old cheaply printed tract is left untouched; the present world
wants its reading matter in brief, concise sentences, artistically printed.
. . . We need more and more to use all of these devices, as they come
along."[1]

John was intrigued by the possibilities of using technological
advances and effective media devices to improve the presentation of the

message. He felt that many of those innovations were divinely inspired and that God would hold the Church accountable for not making full use of them in furthering the work: "The world is not Godless. It is our problem to place before them the truth as we understand it in a convincing way so that they may find the joy and happiness and the conquest of self and the forces about them which come from a fuller and truer conception and of the eternal realities about them."[2] While only a sketch of his efforts can be given here, the correspondence files, official reports, and scrapbooks give witness of the high priority he assigned to generating a favorable public image for the Church.

John wrote to Lucy and Albert E. Bowen about addressing problems with the Church's public image:

> Missionary work is progressing in these European countries. The religious unrest is increasing. The prejudice against us is vanishing in the face of increasing religious tolerance and in a wider knowledge of conditions throughout the world. It is pretty difficult now to make the people believe that Mormons have horns or build walls around their cities or that they maintain dungeons in which they keep English girls. There are yet a few ministers who dish up some such things to their congregations, but they are not taken very seriously. There is a big harvest ahead of us if we can only capitalize conditions as they are, but someone must have the time and the leisure to prepare ammunition for our army of Elders. . . . I would like nothing better than to have a year or two free from other duties, to devote to the preparation of material, both new and the reorganization of old, to put into the hands of our Elders. We have a big opportunity for publicity in Europe at the present time, and I am hoping now that the British Mission has been established I may find time to make use of some of these opportunities. During the last year we have met scores of newspapermen and without exception they have been friendly, or at least willing to listen respectfully to our message. Newspaper accounts of our meetings and interviews have been all that we could possibly desire. We have not been in a position, however, to make full use of this tolerant feeling which is developing concerning us—that will be one of the big steps forward in the near future, whether I am here or someone else comes to replace me. The entrance of our cause into

newspaper fields, into radio activities, into the usual advertising methods, is right ahead of us and must be brought into use if we are to make use of the means that the Lord has given us, for the promulgation of His cause in these days.[3]

John's desire to take advantage of the press in accelerating missionary efforts was frequently evident in his reports to the First Presidency. Getting newspaper coverage of mission conferences and regular Church meetings was among his most successful accomplishments:

> We were literally invaded by the Press of Great Britain. We had to "shoo" them off, to get our work done. . . . On several occasions the reporters sat through our meetings. It seemed wise to permit them to do this, since so much mysticism has been made to surround Mormonism. The result was a mass of publicity throughout Great Britain, and I suppose, on the continent. And, it was all fair and friendly. The reporters told the truth. . . . We shunted several reporters into the Relief Society's section of the conference, and the sisters received some very favorable publicity. Reading the reports, it must have seemed that the Mormons after all are people, not polliwogs.[4]

Missionaries who served at John's side in these efforts left impressive descriptions of their president's vision and boldness. He tried to instill a feeling for publicity in all who served. Elder Arnold D. White, mission secretary, recalled that the president "was very alert to what was going on civically. . . . He envisioned such things as exhibits and open forums. . . . He looked forward and ahead to the time when more effective missionary work could be done through that type of thing."[5] John did not miss many opportunities to change the public view: "I think Brother Widtsoe had some influence with the local press that mellowed their response to our activities. He was aware of what they were doing. Of course the mission accumulated all the clippings affecting the Church and its program pro or con. And I think he had some influence that way in tempering the feeling of the press toward our program. I think maybe his achievements as an individual . . . because of who he was, not necessarily because he was an apostle but his achievements otherwise, might have had some impact on that."[6]

John was direct with the press. He let them know when he felt they had been unfair and often responded to negative releases. The most sensitive issues seemed the more urgent press topics to him: problems surrounding the work of missionaries, work performed in temples, and questions about the practice and discontinuance of polygamy. Never had any articulate Church spokesman been so aggressive in telling its story to the public.

When a blatant denunciation of the Church appeared in an article on "Mormon secrets" by an excommunicated member, John wrote a strong response. The editors of the paper were sufficiently impressed with its articulate content that they published it:

> Dr. John A. Widtsoe, Mission President, writes to the Sunday Mercury: Sir,—Upon my return from a trip into Durham I was astonished to learn from your issue of 29 January, 1928, that you have been victimized by William E. Bowns. In the interest of British fair play and clean journalism may I make the following statement and protest?
>
> There are two main counts against the article that you published. First, it uses without permission an illustration from the interior of the Salt Lake Temple, which is protected by international copyright. Second, the article is wholly untrue. The briefest examination of the extensive and easily accessible literature concerning "Mormonism" [will show] that Bowns is selling crude fiction instead of facts.
>
> The Bowns to whom the published baptismal certificate was issued is not a member of the Church for he has been excommunicated for dishonesty; he has not held the priesthood as he has admitted to us before witnesses; he has not been near or inside a "Mormon" Temple; he was not called to be a missionary; he is a deserter from the United States Army; he took with him, when he deserted, an automobile and a camera not belonging to him.
>
> Photographs of the interiors of the "Mormon" Temples and descriptions of temple purposes and ceremonies have been long published by the Church under the title "The House of the Lord." The illustrations that you used in your article were taken from this book. Bowns' references to "Mormon" missionary work in Great Britain are untrue, malicious, and liable. The "Mormon" bogey is dead.
>
> I request respectfully that the libel against a clean and wholesome people contained in the Bowns article be corrected. We shall be happy

to furnish the facts. Shall we write you an article on "Mormon" Temples?

In view of the advertisement of this article oh would it not have been well to have required Bowns to make his affidavit instead of only promising to do so?[7]

John gave similarly straightforward defenses in many parts of the country. Some responses came in press conferences like one on the semiannual conference in the Sheffield District in April 1928. The paper commented on interesting aspects of the meetings, especially the practice of calling on any member to speak. In the press conference, John made remarks about how much the sentiment toward Latter-day Saints had changed over the previous thirty years: "That the old Mormon bogey has been replaced in England by a spirit of tolerance and generosity is the opinion of Doctor John A. Widtsoe. . . . Now there was a new feeling towards Mormons. There was a spirit of better understanding and a spirit of tolerance and generosity, which was much appreciated."[8]

For a century, the British press had enjoyed a heyday of mocking Mormon polygamy. John used this as another opportunity to publicize the Church. He went to great lengths to explain polygamy, using Sister Widtsoe's relationship to Brigham Young to tantalize and to deepen the discussion:

> Doctor John A Widtsoe, a former Principal of the University of Utah, U.S.A. . . . , was present with his wife, "Sister" Widtsoe, who is proud of the fact that she is a granddaughter of Brigham Young, the pioneer Mormon who led his little band from the persecution of the Eastern States. . . . Brigham Young had nineteen wives and fifty-six children, of whom Mrs. Widtsoe's mother was the nineteenth.
>
> "Have you told him who I am?" asked Mrs. Widtsoe with a smile when her husband introduced the "Free Press" reporter to her.
>
> "I have," replied Doctor Widtsoe, "and he never flinched!"[9]

In 1928 John learned that W. J. McKay was touring the country delivering anti-Mormon lectures for hire. His presentation included a movie and a script. John obtained all the information he could about the man's presentation and an effective way to derail it. He even turned to Senator Smoot for help, hoping diplomatic pressure could be put on Britain to stop the lectures.[10] The lectures were soon curtailed.

In 1929 Maud May Babcock went on a tour of Europe and visited the Widtsoes. She was an accomplished and impressive woman with a reputation for dramatic reading. The Widtsoes were in France when she arrived in England, but they had arranged for the British mission president to take advantage of her abilities by scheduling programs with interested civic groups and inviting the press. But when Sister Babcock joined the Widtsoes in France, they learned that her talents had not been used as planned. John wrote to his London friend William Goodair, a well-known and well-educated man, asking him to make arrangements for Miss Babcock to return to England and perform. John reported to the First Presidency:

> I think he did not wait half a day before he wired me an answer. He had already secured an engagement for Miss Babcock before a fashionable group in behalf of an organization that is providing homes for the totally disabled soldiers of the late Great War. . . . Then a fount of social events followed. She met Lords and Ladies—our Elders were drawn into the same groups, and finally arrangement was made by which the famous drawing room of Lady Beecham was placed at the disposal of the Lady McEnteyre, who was the chairman of arrangements. . . . Lords, Ladies, Ambassador, Ministers, some two or three hundred were present—mingling freely with the Mormon Elders and listening to Professor Maud May Babcock of Utah—known also as a Mormon. I am told that Miss Babcock held her audience wonderfully well during her reading, and received applause, flowers and even a poem was addressed to her and of course many invitations followed as a result. . . .
>
> I am thoroughly convinced that to win the respect and understanding of such groups of people means that much of the prejudice that has existed will be allayed. Such people are the molders and makers of public opinion and what they say is carried far and wide. I doubt if we have done enough of such things in the past, to smooth the way before our Elders.[11]

Arnold White, who worked closely with John as his secretary, described an important facet of the president's publicity vision: "I think he began pointing toward the higher echelon and began raising the sights a little. . . . I think he sensed that if we could bring the more influential people to it that they in turn would bring others. . . . I mean 'influence'—more influential people, more educated people, more financially capable people."[12] John wanted the public to see that the message of the Church is one of happiness and truth, that the missionaries were men of faith and love for the Lord who sacrificed greatly because they knew that the truths they taught would increase happiness and goodness in the lives of anyone who would heed them.

One article reported a visit with President Widtsoe in which he explained fundamental practices of the Church. The article described abstinence from tobacco and alcohol and eating only a little meat but many seasonal fruits and vegetables. John told the reporters about the Word of Wisdom exhibit being held in Dresden, Germany. He again assured them that polygamy was now forbidden and that those who attempted to practice it would face serious consequences. One reporter noted the following exchange:

> "Any dancing allowed?" I asked.
>
> "Dancing? We revel in dancing. And what is more if you become a Mormon, you will live five or six years longer than you would as a member of any other faith. . . ."
>
> "We intend to proselytize," Dr. Widtsoe continued with enthusiasm. "We have a marvelous message. If you are poor we can teach you how to overcome your poverty. Seventy percent of our members own their own houses. If you are ill we can show you how to be well."
>
> "But don't you find the name of Mormon as somewhat against you when you try to make converts?"
>
> "Sometimes," the doctor said guardedly, "people who come to a meeting of the Latter-day Saints are surprised to find they are Mormons. But we don't disguise the fact. We have no wish to deceive anyone."[13]

John found that prejudice was diminishing through their successes with the press, and he seemed pleased to report to the Church that a new day of understanding and acceptance had arrived. Newspapers that once ridiculed the missionaries now printed interviews with them. John noted, "Missionaries in the past spent more time in prison than proselytizing."[14]

John monitored media progress very closely. In November 1929 he was pleased to report the arrival of a new day:

> Can this be Europe? How it has changed from the Europe of my childhood or of my student days, thirty-one years ago! Of course, the narrow, cobblestone streets, the crowded, queer houses, the cramped mode of living, the grimy poverty, the social strata, and the weight of castled and cathedraled centuries—the face of Europe—are still here, much as in the past. The difference is one of outlook and attitude, of hope and fear, of the spirit, but as real as wood or stone. The change is remarkable. . . . There are those who would gladly flay or burn a "Mormon," but their voice is thin, and they are of the class who indiscriminately would like to flay or burn somebody.[15]

Endeavoring to change the religious beliefs of proud Europeans was a bold enough undertaking, especially so because it required them to accept that their churches grew out of the great apostasy. Bolder in the view of the British was the fact that the gospel was brought to them from America by Americans. John shared his view of the obstacle this perception became:

> Americans are not as popular in Great Britain as they might be. In fact, one of the real handicaps in our work in Great Britain today is that most of it is done by American men. Joseph Smith and Brigham Young in the minds of some people are not so obnoxious as a religion manufactured in America. The trade competition between the United States and Great Britain is increasing so rapidly that even an American-made religion seems unwelcome simply because it is made in America. Of course, we have preached far and wide the universality of the Gospel of Jesus Christ, that the place of origin is incidental and that the principles are our only concern, but there are some so prejudiced that they will not listen to anything American—for is not America compelling Great Britain to repay her war debt, and thereby compelling millions of Britishers to live in poverty and is not America entering the world's market and taking the harangue not

only on the street corner, but among many of the upper classes. Wherever one goes in Great Britain at the present time discussions may be heard as to a probable war between Great Britain and the United States. It seems to be taken for granted that it is bound to come. . . . Over on the continent a similar unrest exists—America is more popular there—in fact, is very popular there—but they have quarrels among themselves. Unless the common sense of humanity prevails, Europe is headed for another shake up and this time a more terrible one than the last.[16]

This assessment of the international anxiety overshadowing the mission work concerned John more than personal matters. In the same letter is an example of how his quest for media attention was affecting his daughter, Eudora: "In the beginning when she discovered how thoroughly unpopular we are in certain circles, she hardly knew what to make of it. Now she is coming back strong—she knows something about what we have to offer and has been able to compare it as others have and she is ready to stand up in defense of the cause."[17] At Queen Mary High School, Eudora took the requisite hour of religion, which occasioned almost daily family talks on correct interpretation. "It did not take her long to discover for herself the shallowness of the teachings that were handed out to her."[18]

Earlier in 1929, a world hygiene fair was held in Dresden, Germany. John saw it as a great opportunity to espouse one of the virtuous teachings of the Church and to enlighten the public on the Church's views on health and the impact of modern revelation. The opportunity for this exhibit stemmed from the German-Austrian Relief Society's efforts to find more lesson material. Sister H. W. Valentine, the mission president's wife, met the director of Dresden's Museum of Hygiene. He was so impressed by her explanation of the Word of Wisdom and her written account of it that he published it in the museum bulletin. Later, when asked if the Church could build an exhibit, the director gave enthusiastic approval. A collaboration of President and Sister Valentine; their successors, President and Sister Edward P. Kimball; President and Sister Widtsoe; and elders from several missions gave flesh to the idea. John wrote tracts in English and German. Thousands of people flocked to the exhibit, received a pamphlet, and met with the missionaries. John wrote:

> The Word of Wisdom—its principles and results—forms one of the most popular exhibits in the International Hygiene Exhibition at Dresden, Germany. . . . This may be both startling and pleasant news to the Latter-day Saints, who have so long found it difficult to present to the world the precious truths that they possess. The exposition itself is unique. It is dedicated to one thing: The preservation and improvement of human health. It is built around the monumental Museum of Hygiene, the finest in the world, in a vast park of shady trees, green lawns and colorful flower beds. In aim as in beauty it is unsurpassed by any of the several expositions held this year in Europe. The exhibitors from all countries have conformed in spirit to the ideals of the exposition. No European spectacle is more worth seeing. . . .
>
> The exhibit is effectively located at the front entrance of the League of Nations' building. . . . Through the open door the illuminated main wall is observed. The lighted sun—the Word of Wisdom—is rising from the sea of ignorance, and radiating from it are the rewards of the Word of Wisdom—health, long life, wisdom, etc. The rays are lighted alternately, with fine effect. In the middle of the floor stands a large globe, slowly rotating, and showing in brilliantly lighted spots the points on earth where the Church is teaching the Word of Wisdom. On the left side wall is a moving, endless lighted ribbon which tells the story of the Word of Wisdom; and on the opposite wall is a large comparative statement of the physical, educational and moral conditions among the Latter-day Saints, showing the results of the Word of Wisdom. Photographs, charts and several posters, drawn by Elder J. Blaine Freestone of the British Mission, cover the open spaces on the walls. . . .
>
> As far as possible the visitors are taken through the exhibit in groups and addressed by the attendants. Great interest is manifested in the exhibit by all. Prominent professional people from all parts of the earth have made favorable comments upon this method of preserving human health. Invitations have been received to give Word of Wisdom information in other lands. As high as 30,000 have passed

through the exhibit in one day; the average is near 5,000; about 120,000 tracts were distributed the first two months.[19]

The exhibit was so successful that the following year, when a fair was held in Manchester, England, approval was obtained to exhibit there, and the Widtsoes oversaw the creation of another high-quality display on the Word of Wisdom. Leah was put in charge, and John sent most of the office staff and the mission-home cook to assist. The exhibit met with similar success.[20]

In March 1929, John reported to President Grant the success across the European missions and a steady change of feelings toward the Church in the British Mission, noting, "We need now to provide more modern and effective means for the use of our army of young men. . . . The pressure of work has been such that neither Leah nor I have been able to enter the publicity field as we should have done and as we must do in the near future. The ground must be prepared for our elders, and we must supply them with the proper ammunition, if I may so word it, for the battle."[21]

As time passed, John felt that prejudice against the Church throughout Europe was diminishing significantly. He had found almost all press representatives receptive to the right kind of prompting, and they had taught him that cooperation and opportunity were possible if carefully nurtured. While much work remained to be done, he could see that favorable reporting and image-building would soon overtake the wildly distorted public image of the Church.

Of particular pleasure and surprise was the greater tolerance in his homeland. John wrote, "Up in Norway, which, because of the stranglehold that the priests have upon the country, the anti-Mormon feeling has always been great, there was a complete change of sentiment upon the occasion of our last visit."[22] John was excited about the crowds in all the meetings during his visit and the rising number of baptisms. He wrote, "I feel that we are reaping a harvest. . . . Moreover, the Norwegians are a truth-loving, independent-thinking people and it is inevitable that in the end they will recognize the truth contained in the message of the Lord Jesus Christ as restored by the Prophet Joseph Smith. . . . I feel that the work will go forward rapidly in Norway and that all . . . laboring as missionaries and the members of the Church will be blessed . . . as you give your strength to the teaching of the Gospel to the people of that country."[23]

Even with this remarkable progress, John was disappointed with the time it was taking. In his last year in Europe he wrote, "Work of course moves very slowly. The prejudice here is deep and more or less unyielding. One has to use a [pick]axe and dynamite at times to break the crust of opposition that has formed; but as I say, the work is going forward, and we are very grateful for it."[24]

After the 1933 elections and the repeal of prohibition, John wrote of the damaging reaction he expected in Europe: "It was bad enough to have Utah to go wet but to have the fates conspire so as to give Utah the fame of being the thirty-sixth State, the one state needed for repeal, was really terrible from our missionary point of view. I have not seen the London papers but can well believe that they headlined the fact. It will be thrown up at us a good many times and in many places. I believe that our only answer would be to point out the complete freedom under which Latter-day Saints live. Their free agency is never interfered with and they, like other people, are subject to making mistakes."[25]

Some of John's success in public relations came because of who he was. Attention came to him in Scandinavian countries because he was a Norwegian who had developed an international reputation in science and had presided over two American universities. He was entered in a new Scandinavian "Who's Who" as the first Norwegian-born man to become president of an American state agricultural college, the second to become president of an American state university, the first to be director of a state agricultural experiment station, and the first to be principal of a school of agriculture. He was the only man listed with three "firsts."[26] His work in agriculture was known worldwide and often opened doors and hearts for him.

Because of his own experience, John encouraged the missionaries to broaden the scope of people to whom they directed their message and to avoid limiting their efforts to the poor. His secretary, Arnold D. White, wrote, "I think he and Sister Widtsoe both knew some very prominent people in high echelons of government and civic life in

London that got us some favorable publicity and had some influence on the general feeling." White further described Widtsoe's ability to speak to people from all walks of life: "He could stand up at the pulpit in Liverpool, Durham House, and talk to those humble Saints gathered there in a very simple language that they understood. And yet he could meet with a group of intellectuals and speak their language. He wasn't inclined, in my judgment, to show off his learning. He was very humble over his achievement."[27]

John had a personal touch with people and experience with the press. He could inspire in them a sense of fair play, honesty, and responsibility. He was acutely aware that false ideas about the Church hindered its progress, and that changing those ideas could greatly improve the missionaries' success in talking with people about the message of the Restoration. He felt that a better public image was key to success.

29

A BOOK ABOUT
BRIGHAM YOUNG

———————— ▣ ————————

Wʜᴇɴ the Widtsoe family left for Europe, Susa and Leah had nearly finished the manuscript of *The Life Story of Brigham Young,* a biography of the world's most prominent Latter-day Saint. John, the compiler of *The Discourses of Brigham Young* and a stalwart disciple with a penchant for publicity, immediately saw that *The Life Story of Brigham Young* provided the first real opportunity for the Church to tell its own story. There was lively intrigue about Brigham Young, polygamy, and the Mormons, especially in Europe. Properly handled, this book could garner much favorable public opinion and put to rest the lurid images of the past. After two months in Europe John wrote to Susa, "I feel easy about the 'History of Brigham Young.' Out of all the difficulties that have attended its begetting, will be born a worthy and valuable child. Things are happening over here that make me feel that right now we have need of just the kind of material that you have been assembling in your book."[1]

Susa entrusted its publication to John after President Grant had given his approval. She wrote, "As I have thought this matter over, about father's history, I feel that the Lord has certainly inspired the Pres. to leave the whole thing in your hands. He was kind and gracious about it, too, as he could be. I fancy the two [Heber J. Grant and Anthony W. Ivins, his counselor] could not agree on any one but you as the final judge."[2]

John handled the negotiations for publication through Harold J. Shepstone of London, an editor and agent. Many letters passed between them, and soon Shepstone felt the best marketing course was to have the book published in serial form in prominent newspapers. John wrote to Susa:

> Mr. Shepstone has been working quite industriously on the Brigham Young chapters. They are now practically finished but not quite. Leah and I are a little behind in the reading of them. The editor of the London Daily Mail is waiting for an appointment with us concerning the matter, but I hesitate to take any of the chapters there until all are in shape so that he can get the continuity of the story. Mr. Shepstone is doing a very good job, and if nothing comes of it, he will be out a good deal of time . . . and money. On the other hand, it is beyond question that something will come of it. We shall be able to dispose of it without much difficulty. I have had two letters from the Macmillan people asking about the manuscript. I cannot undertake negotiations with them until the work now being done by Mr. Shepstone is well under way. The condensation intended for magazine articles need not in any way interfere with the publication of the book in book form, but I assure you that such work requires a great deal of time. I am putting in spare hours on the work and we will get it done.[3]

Susa, six thousand miles away, was restless over the release of the materials she had written about her father. But she was well aware of the work required of a high-quality publication. She replied, "If it shall do good there I will be more grateful than I can express. Neither Leah nor I expect to make any money out of it, but if it does the good you seem to think it will, I shall be very grateful. . . . It must be done right . . . and I do know what months of time are consumed."[4]

John had to balance his involvement in the book with his busy travel schedule among ten missions. Letters were intermittent, but finally he was able to report, "Last week, in London, Leah and I spent an afternoon with Shepstone. . . . It is now nearing completion in form for magazine publication. Unless some anti-Mormon pressure is brought to bear, there will be little doubt about its publication in the near future. . . . Shepstone has done a really big job in making out a series of articles on the subject of Brigham Young's life. They are very readable. . . . It will undoubtedly be one of the most powerful means of propaganda in behalf of our cause."[5]

By February 1929 Shepstone sent the final seventeen chapters to John for proofreading. "Now I should like to have these seventeen chapters as early as possible so that I can get along typing them out. I wish to hand one copy to a newspaper here and to send another to Berlin, Paris, New York, and to three or four of the agents here representing the Colonial newspapers."[6]

John and Leah proofread each article and returned them with some family photographs that Shepstone had asked for. "My wife and I agree . . . that you have done an exceedingly fine piece of work. Necessarily, much interesting material had to be left out; but the chapters as you have put them together are very readable and carry the story forward without strain. . . . We are also sending you a collection of photographs. Many of them are rare, and the only copies available."[7]

John and Shepstone were careful about impressions given by the text and photographs and worried over possible ridicule by newspaper editors. They were sensitive to the abuse the Church had been dealt over polygamy and how, handled wrongly, these materials could promote further attacks. The photographs included Brigham Young and his family and many views of Salt Lake City. One photograph, a picture of Brigham Young and his wives, caused a disagreement. Shepstone felt it would capture interest and contribute much to the success of the series, but John and Leah felt it would probably do more injury than good. Shepstone argued, "There are two points here that one has to remember. In the first place one is dealing with historical facts and, of course, there is the record of his wives, while the other point is that there is the risk of newspaper editors obtaining such pictures on their own and using them without saying anything about them. For these very reasons I am inclined to think that it would be just as well to give out the picture which Mrs. Gates has prepared showing Brigham Young with portraits of his wives."[8] Shepstone also worried that editors might jump to careless conclusions and put out feelers for more striking photographs. He just couldn't see the photograph doing any harm.

John's reaction to Shepstone's urging was simple: "Lets 'lay low' on the wife business that's been harped on so much that it ought to be threadbare. We're to stress the epoch-making contribution of the man to the conquest of the West. Give the other a rest."[9]

During the summer, Shepstone made final preparations while the Widtsoes were immersed in mission conferences. In August Widtsoe wrote to Shepstone, "This morning a copy of the Newcastle *Sunday Sun* reached the office with the first installment of the story. That looked as if you had been successful in placing the series. Is the story appearing elsewhere also? We shall be interested in getting some news about your experiences, with the MSS., which no doubt have been many."[10] Shepstone responded immediately with disappointing news. The articles Shepstone had compiled laid out the facts in the life of Mormonism's great leader. They were truthful, factual, and ennobling, not the image the British press wanted to perpetuate of a life they had maligned for decades. Shepstone wrote:

> To be quite frank I have been a little disappointed in placing the serial. The "Sunday Express" turned it down with the remark that they would prefer not to touch the subject. I then tried the "News of the World" "Sunday Dispatch," and "The People," and quickly discovered that the story was not sensational enough. What the journals wanted was a great deal more about the question of polygamy which you know was purposely cut down, wherein I think you were wise. I offered it to the weekly papers in Dundee, but they both refused it. I then approached the "Newscastle Chronicle" people as they are in keen competition with one of the Harmsworth papers, but the fee they are paying is very small, namely (five pounds, five shillings) per article, as you will see in the letters enclosed, which please return to me. My friend in New York writes me that he likes the story and sees no reason why he should not be able to place it in some American newspaper, and I am hoping to hear that he has been successful by every post. Then I have given a copy of the MS. to a Canadian

journalist in Paris, who has promised to deal with it in the French press and probably also in the Canadian papers. Then an agent has a copy in Berlin and so far has written quite encouragingly about it, but has not yet found a paper to accept it. I have been unable to interest the representatives of the Australian and South African papers in the Ms. but am still trying to do so.[11]

Shepstone wanted to publish the book. It was evident that the newspapers would not publish the serial in a form that he, the Widtsoes, and Susa could approve of. While this was disappointing to Shepstone emotionally and monetarily, a successful book-launch would resolve his disappointment. Rejection of Shepstone's articles was a harsh reminder that persecution's heavy shadow still lurked and that the press was not ready to treat fairly the Church or its epic accomplishments in settling the American West. John must have been severely disappointed, but there is little evidence of it. Rather, he remained optimistic and felt the series was still a victory. He wrote Susa:

> The Sunday Sun published five of the Brigham Young articles; then stopped. The ministerial pressure became rather intense. But the series has been a great victory for us. For the first time has even a part of our story been told in the right spirit in the press of England. We shall have new opportunities soon. I assure you it is entirely a matter of giving one's time and strength to the question of publicity. I feel sometimes that I am guilty for not taking my time for that sort of thing, but the regular duties must have the right-a-way and the days are only so long. The articles, so far published, have done splendid missionary work, and, of course, publication may be resumed later and, as I have indicated, other opportunities are presenting themselves. If nothing else comes of your efforts with regard to the life of Brigham Young, this publication seems to me to justify your efforts. Of course, the book will be published.[12]

The letter ended on the optimistic note: "It looks now that we shall be able to publish the Brigham Young articles in Czecho-Slovakia."[13] He also wrote favorably of the progress Shepstone was making with the book and only a month later received a letter from Shepstone:

As you see by enclosed letter Jarrolds, the publishers, are willing
to publish Mrs. Gates' work on the Life of Her Father. . . .

I sent them this MS. some five weeks ago and for the last fort-
night they have been phoning me and asking me to call about it. . . .
They insist, however, on the American rights, and the usual course
here is to go 50/50. I think on the whole this is a very fair proposition
and meanwhile I have told them that I felt sure you would be
agreeable.

What Jarrolds have is the 22 chapters which I sent you, which is
roughly about 90,000 words in length. They assured me that this is
quite long enough and that it would be only tiring to the ordinary
reader to publish such a lengthy MS. as Mrs. Gates has written. . . .
In this contention I fancy they are right.[14]

Two weeks later more good news arrived from New York. Shepstone
had arranged to send the manuscript to Macmillan. Their response was
much better:

You will be interested to learn that my journalistic friend in New
York has placed the manuscript with MacMillans. . . . I had a cable
from him last Friday, which reads: "Have placed book rights with
MacMillan. Royalties ten percent first five thousand, twelve and a half
next five, and fifteen thereafter. Advance of five hundred dollars. Can
you send duplicate of script and photographs. Jones . . ."

The moment I received the cable from New York I at once
'phoned to Jarrold's and I must say they were quite nice about it and
were quite willing in the circumstances to be content with the British
rights. As you know, it is best for a book to be published separately in
each country if it can be managed.[15]

John cabled the news to Susa. The news precipitated a discourag-
ing but not unexpected setback around the question of Church endorsement of the book. Susa reported that the First Presidency "were all
unwilling to give their approval to a manuscript which they had not
read, but Uncle Heber said he did not want to interfere with my publishing a history of my father when I had it all ready, but he was
reminded by Uncle Tone [Anthony W. Ivins], that it would be looked
upon as authoritative because it would be church history as well as

having a good deal of doctrine in it."[16] In their conversation mention was made of things printed in London by Orson and Parley P. Pratt that had to be withdrawn.

Again the question of using the photograph of Brigham Young and his wives arose. Shepstone felt it was vitally important, but John and Leah were even more determined that it was unwise:

> We object absolutely to the use of the picture of Brigham Young and his wives, for the following reasons: Many sensitive readers, who are willing to read the story of Brigham Young's marital relations, will look upon this picture as an unnecessary affront; it may lead many persons, reviewers and others, to make unfavorable comment upon the whole book; it brings into undue prominence one of the phases of Brigham Young's life; and, it will tend to turn the "Mormon" people against the book. The Latter-day Saints in Europe will probably make large purchases of this book, far larger than the publishers suspect, if the book pleases them, and the inclusion of this picture would be taken as an unnecessary flaunting of the practice which has been the center of attack these many years. The text deals with the subject fully enough; the picture would be demanded only by the morbid; it will diminish, not increase the sales of the book—and we mean to do all we can to give the book a good circulation.[17]

Because the Church was more accepted in America, Macmillan was willing to publish a larger version of the biography. John responded, "We suggest that the following chapters be added; Irrigation, Music and Drama, Literature and Education, and perhaps one on Women's activity. . . . We urge that at least one chapter on cultural arts and education be added to the British edition, and better still, two. They need not be long; but they will complete more fairly the story of the man."[18]

The difficulty of weaving work on the book into his mission routine is seen in a brief report of his activities to Susa while the book was in publication: "Brigham Young's book is now in type and will be published in the course of a month. We have space in the International Hygiene Exposition for a Word of Wisdom exhibit, incredible as it seems. Radio and newspaper opportunities are multiplying. We are short of mature people to do the work required here. . . . The future is full of promise on this side of the Atlantic."[19] At the bottom of the letter Leah inscribed a note: "I worked all day on B.Y. Proof, Eudora reading to me. This I hope will be the final. I've read & studied & arranged & rearranged so much that I practically know the mss by heart—word for word. It has taken much time but if only you and the brethren especially our dearest friends (the Presidency) feel satisfied we shall feel more than repaid."[20]

John expressed his feelings about the shortened version Jarrolds was willing to publish:

> A telegram came from Shepstone advising us that . . . Jarrolds . . . was willing to print his newspaper articles in book form at their own expense. We had to decide quickly, and after weighing the matter pro and con, concluded that the Cause that we represent would be served by having such a book on the market. It would be a distinct advantage to us to have a book written by ourselves, printed by a leading British publishing firm. I therefore wired Shepstone approval at once. True, this was done somewhat regretfully, for I had looked forward to the time when a first class popular life of Brigham Young might be worked over from your larger work, but I felt that if the popular Life were published first [it] might delay indefinitely the publication of the larger work. However, we followed the promptings of the Spirit and I have no regrets. I trust that you approve also in your heart.[21]

A month later John's news for Susa was more cheerful: "You will have considerable income from the book for it is bound to sell well. . . . The reviewers almost without exception declare the book to be one of the best ever written by a near relative of the person 'biographed;' and generally the book is praised. When we get home a set of criticisms will be sent you and you will be greatly pleased."[22] Susa replied, "I just have a letter from Shepstone, and I am sending for six more books, as the publication here in America will be delayed until September or later, and I want my children to have a book."[23] In October John wrote, "The British edition, while not selling very fast as yet, is doing a very great amount of good and sales will come. . . . We have fifty reviews or more of the Brigham Young book to send you and the First Presidency."[24] In a detailed accounting of the book, Leah was upset about its lukewarm reception. "Mr. Shepstone . . . feels that Jarrolds have not quite done the fair thing by the book. John is convinced and I agree with him that some of these high church people here in England have sent out a whisper to Jarrolds that they had 'better play low on the Brigham Young book.'"[25] Leah was surprised at the prices charged in both countries, especially in the years of the depression. Of Macmillan she wrote, "I was so disappointed when I heard of the high price. . . . It looks to me that they are just trying to 'quash' the sale of the book from that end, as well as from this end. Am I mistaken?"[26]

Twenty years later John recalled, "This was probably the first book, frankly pro-Mormon, to be published in England by others than the Church. . . . The book received a deluge of newspaper and magazine comment—almost invariably favorable. It was the best kind of propaganda."[27] He also related an unusual story of the book's effect on one interested reader:

> My wife, who had read that Bernard Shaw while delivering a talk in the United States had spoken most kindly of her grandfather, Brigham Young, informed me she was going to write him a letter telling him that her mother had written a book about her father which had been printed in England, and if he would accept the book she would be glad to give him one. I assured her that her letter would be ignored and she had better forget it. Nevertheless, one day she wrote the letter telling Mr. Shaw of the book and that she was glad there was one man in England big enough to recognize another great man. Most people in England thought Brigham Young was a scalawag.

The letter went to George Bernard Shaw. John recorded the result:

> One afternoon about a week later one of the office missionaries brought a card to my wife in the Relief Society office saying that a man named Shaw wanted to see her.
>
> For two hours they talked, mostly of the gospel and our reasons for being in England. He assured her that he was certainly interested and had come to claim the book. Finally my wife told him that her husband was on the continent but invited him and Mrs. Shaw to have dinner with us on my return. He replied, "Yes, we'll be glad to do so, unless you come and have dinner with us. That will be more fun for

you, won't it?" Naturally, she accepted, thinking he was just being polite. But the invitation came for a certain day.

It was astonishing to see on his large and well-filled book shelves in a most conspicuous place a copy of the Book of Mormon. He spoke with real zest about the accomplishments of Joseph Smith and Brigham Young. I remember he asked one pertinent question when we told him how many thousands of members we had in England. He said, "I am not interested in that. What I want to know is how many of your converts do you keep." He brought home one of the important things that Latter-day Saints must keep in mind.[28]

The Widtsoes highly valued the friendship with George Bernard Shaw. In her thank-you letter, Leah invited the Shaws to allow the Widtsoes to return the hospitality in Salt Lake City sometime later: "I do hope . . . that you will give us the great pleasure of showing you some of the beauty spots near our homeland."[29] She sent some picture books showing the picturesque scenery and beautiful colors of Utah, a copy of one of John's books answering questions about the Church, and a post-card showing Temple Square, to which she added a brief explanation of each of the buildings.

The hectic schedule took its toll. By October the Widtsoes were slowed by exhaustion and illness. John wrote President Grant, "I did not attempt to make work, but only to do that which would seem to be necessary, yet only a fraction of it could be reached. I spent more than one half of my time in travel, and attended an average of about a meeting and a half a day throughout the year, in addition to the necessary office routine which is considerable."[30] Having regular communication with John and Leah, Susa knew of their wearisome pace and wrote a concerned warning:

> You are so modest and so unwilling to let people know what you are doing that I think that few on earth will ever realize the mighty work that will be organized and re-organized under your hands. No one, since my Father's day, I feel in my spirit, has ever had the inspiration, the training, the desire and the gifts to organize and put in shape the Mission field of Europe except you and Leah. God be with you in your strenuous endeavors. But please don't wear yourselves out

as Orson F. Whitney, Brother McMurrin and Jas. E. Talmage did. Remember what Mrs. Gillman said to me: "The Lord Himself will not justify you in committing suicide even to assist in righteous work." Eight hours sleep, eight hours recreation, and eight hours work. That was Brigham Young's rule. I heard him say so, all his life. Stick to it, establish that as a precedent and you will do as much good in that Mission as any other phase of the work you are doing.[31]

John needed to heed this warning, for he still had many years ahead of him in Europe.

30

THE WORD OF WISDOM: THE FIRST CRUSADE

D URING the last two decades of John and Leah's life together, their strict adherence to and frequent publication on the Word of Wisdom gave rise to the common catchphrase "The Word of Widtsoe" across the Church. Both of the Widtsoes had made professional careers out of studying the chemical and nutritional value of foods. The first time they applied their learning to an ecclesiastical purpose was during their mission in Europe. John wrote:

> A great variety of duties were constantly before us. Not only spiritual but temporal problems had to be solved. For example, the saints of the British Mission were not as a group in the best of health. In common with the mass of British people, they lost their teeth easily and early in life. They were suffering from various maladies. At conferences much time was taken in blessing the sick. Much of this condition came from incorrect diet. My wife, with my encouragement, began a campaign for better health, largely through nutrition. A series of lessons on the positive aspect of the Word of Wisdom were prepared which were used in all the missions. Too many of our members feel that if they refrain from taking liquor, tobacco, tea and coffee, they are keeping the Word of Wisdom. They are doing so only in part. If the law be understood and lived, people would not be ill and the

blessings promised may be fulfilled. Only so may they "run and not be weary, walk and not faint." The lessons were in harmony with the newer knowledge of nutrition then coming to light and were an added testimony to the divine inspiration of the Prophet who gave us this wise law of health. The lessons became very popular. Scores testified to the benefits received. Letters came in telling about relief from pain and suffering, and actual cure of diseases suffered for years. The Church of Christ must ever try to care for the whole man.[1]

The contrast between the standard of health in the Western United States and that in Britain was disturbing. John noted, "The British government itself was aware of the situation and had organized a national health society, with the King as chairman, to examine and reform the living habits of the people."[2] Teaching the Word of Wisdom was the beginning of the Widtsoes' work with the European Saints. Leah's Relief Society lessons, published in the *Millennial Star,* were a complement to the national movement. Too much sickness in all ten missions of Europe led to the use of the lessons there. The Word of Wisdom revelation also opened the door to teaching God's interest in man's mortal tabernacle, and the prophetic role and divine call of Joseph Smith. A further indication of the immediacy of the need the Widtsoes saw in the Word of Wisdom is John's earliest series of lessons as mission president: *"The Gospel and Health: A Study Course for the Mutual Improvement Associations in the British Mission of the Church of Jesus Christ of Latter-day Saints."*[3] John emphasized that the manual "should be kept within easy reach for reference, and could well be read and re-read. It [set] forth the broad conceptions of the Word of Wisdom, given by the Lord in this dispensation."[4] In the preface he wrote, "The Gospel of Jesus Christ is designed to give man health and happiness. Health is concerned with the spirit and mind as well as with the body of man. The Gospel is mistakenly supposed to concern only man's spiritual health. Mental and physical health forms the only assurance of spiritual progress. A man who is physically or mentally ill is not truly happy, though he may approach spiritual peace. The three parts of man's nature are interrelated and depend upon one another's welfare."[5]

In eighteen lessons the manual taught the value of good health using a variety of intriguing topics, including the blessing of work; the place of exercise, play, and recreation; sleep; cleanliness, bathing, and elimination; food composition; clothing; the use of meat; water and air; coffee, tea, chocolate, sweets, tobacco, and alcohol; excesses and the dissipation of strength; and the law of chastity. John tenaciously taught that the physical body is sacred and needs to be carefully maintained in achieving both physical and spiritual well-being: "Man is made in the image of God, and possesses the possibility of becoming a fully developed, happy, healthy, joyous traveler on the road of eternal progress. But, to realize the possibility, he must obey the laws of the journey. He must never lose sight of the fact that his body is the tabernacle of the spirit, which is the offspring of his Maker and as such deserves the greatest intelligent care."[6]

Almost 20 percent of 350 articles and editorials John wrote for the *Millennial Star* dealt with one or more aspects of the Word of Wisdom. Most of those articles and editorials were either doctrinal or societal commentary. In an editorial titled "Schnaps," John wrote of how drunkenness leads to poverty and destroys families while enriching those who sell alcohol. "Would the nations take a first long step toward material prosperity," he concluded, "then let them end the liquor traffic. Within a twelve-month, men would again face the light; women would smile, and children cease to fear their world."[7] In "The Word of Wisdom in the Market Place," he described how men masked the ill effects of invasive products by claiming safety in decaffeinated coffee and in cigarettes from which the nicotine had supposedly been removed. Such reliance only demonstrated that the world was beginning to understand the real danger of these substances.[8]

John gave an analogy to demonstrate his point. A young woman had been smoking, and a young man said to her, "Your body is given to you to be a home for your immortal spirit. Through your body your spirit speaks. As you care for the body, respect it and keep it clean, your spirit gains power to express itself. The body must be looked upon as a holy tabernacle. The Lord expects you to keep it clean, pure and strong. Remember, this body is to rise with you in the resurrection."[9] In an editorial encouraging support for the Relief Society lessons, John wrote,

"The specifically prepared lessons on this subject will appear throughout the year in the Auxiliary Guide numbers of the *Star*. It is recommended that these lessons be read by all who have access to the *Star*."[10]

In 1929, the Widtsoe's second year in Europe, the Relief Society's Word of Wisdom lessons were published monthly in the *Millennial Star*. Leah wrote an introduction: "The Relief Society Program for 1929 in all the European Missions was considered at the Conference of Mission Presidents held in Paris last August. Without exception the heads of all the Relief Societies in the various missions agreed on the following outline of courses. First lesson: Theology and Testimony. Second lesson: Work and Business. Third lesson: Word of Wisdom lessons. Fourth lesson: Literary."[11] Where the Relief Society met only twice each month, the theology and Word of Wisdom lessons were to be taught. Leah commented:

> Word of Wisdom Lessons are most timely and will prove interesting and helpful to the mothers or future mothers of the Mission. They will deal with the care of the physical body as set forth in the marvelous Guide given to Modern Israel. This is most fitting too: Through the mother comes the child's physical body; she usually prepares its food from infancy to maturity. It is proper that she should herself understand and teach her dear ones how and why they should care for the most valuable instrument on earth—the human body.
>
> An attempt will be made to make the lessons very simple, yet show how the teachings of this inspired document are in strict accord with the very latest findings of science.[12]

To complement the lessons and to show great variety, Leah promised to serve some "Word of Wisdom foods" and to furnish some "health recipes" for distribution in special leaflets. "Our aim," she wrote, "should be to make all our foods and refreshments simple, but good; inexpensive, yet wholesome for body building."[13]

The opening lesson, January, 1929, "God's Laws of Physical Health," promoted the doctrinal notion that health is a human birthright and that teaching children about it exceeds the importance of teaching them reading, writing, or arithmetic. "One of the many evidences of the care our Heavenly Father has for His earthly children is the fact that whenever the Gospel has been upon the earth, He has given laws and commandments concerning physical as well as spiritual well-being."[14]

February's lesson, "Temporal Salvation," was about God's laws extending man's temporal life. Leah emphasized, "There are those who quibble even today as to whether or not the Word of Wisdom was ever intended as a commandment. To those who accept divine guidance any word 'given by revelation, showing forth the order and will of God in the temporal salvation of all saints,' would be accepted as a command."[15] To support her view she quoted from the *Doctrine and Covenants Commentary*, which explained that the Word of Wisdom (D&C 89) is the most commonly taught and the most scientifically confirmed of the revelations in the Doctrine and Covenants. "It is a Revelation that deals mainly with proper mode of living, and the rules given, far in advance of anything suggested by scientists, have been amply sanctioned by undisputed authority on hygienic laws, as soon as these have become known through research."[16]

In March Leah identified "The Five Factors of Physical Fitness": "A person in health must have fresh air, clean water for drinking and bathing, exercise, sufficient play, sleep, and good food."[17] The proper amount and quality of each was discussed, with the exception of "sufficient play." In April's lesson, "The Earth Our Home," Leah explained that mortal bodies are composed of the dust of the earth, which chemists had divided into fifteen elements that could be found only in the Lord's foods, the plants and fruits of the ground. Children should be fed with at least as much thought as farmers put into feeding their prizewinning livestock. May's lesson, "Eating for Health," centered on one chief factor, that a person's health is largely a function of the food consumed. Leah drew attention to the recent advent of the science of nutrition and some research that had recently been published in Britain: "The broad conclusion for the citizens and statesmen of this country to draw is that the quality of the food eaten by growing children determines their physical welfare. Nutrition is the foundation of the public health."[18]

In June Leah advanced her discussion of foods, "The Plant Kingdom—The Fruits of the Earth." The body, like an engine or a furnace, gets its energy from the fuel it is given. Variety is necessary for the many functions the body performs and is provided by seasons of nature. Man should partake of all the edible fruits and vegetables grown "in the season thereof." "For that reason it is a great mistake for anyone to say: 'I don't like this vegetable or that,' and refuse to eat it. Children should be taught from the weaning period to eat and enjoy all the different kinds of vegetables (prepared in milk soups at first), that their bodies may grow in bone strength and nerve tone as well as in size."[19]

In July, "Meat 'Sparingly:' The Animal Foods," divided all foods into building and fuel categories. A major part of the lesson addressed the harmful effects of meats, which are justified as a source of protein. Leah reported several studies that concluded that only one sixth of man's food should be protein, and that only one third of that one sixth should be animal protein. Moreover, she described how meats overtax the liver and kidneys and increase uric acid, gout, and rheumatism. She emphasized the cautions about meat in the revelation. "The 'Protective' Foods," a discussion of new information about the importance of food substances recently labeled vitamins, was August's lesson. It taught that bodily derangement comes from the absence of the basic vitamins. "One of the most important facts about vitamins is that they cannot be made in the human body and must therefore be supplied in the food. They are produced in plants, and vitamins found in animals have come from plant food."[20]

In September she urged a conscientiously chosen mixed diet to fill the Lord's admonition to eat "all wholesome foods" and sounded a warning about enriched foods: "In many families bread is, as it has been called, the 'staff of life.' But when all the precious germ, shorts and bran have been removed, the life has been taken out of it—and it is a 'broken staff' indeed!"[21] In October she warned about "Foods That Deceive." To illustrate, she quoted Dr. R. H. A. Plimmer, author of *Food, Health, Vitamins,* concerning the use of sugar: "The figures of the Board of Trade show that the imports of sugar have increased enormously per head of the population, thirty times as much sugar is used per head now as compared with a hundred years ago. Sugar, in its concentrated form, is not a natural food. At one time honey in very limited quantities was the only sweetening agent available. Sugar forms no part of the diet of the Indian hill tribe of the state of Hunza, whom Colonel McCarrison describes as living on natural foods and having the perfection of health and physique."[22]

November's lesson, "Foods That Tear Down the Body," arose from her adage, "If we wish health of body and mind we must obey Nature's laws; if we desire God's blessings, we must obey His laws."[23] In it she identified tea, coffee, chocolate, cocoa, cola, tobacco, and alcoholic beverages as "Anti-foods" because of the actual poisons that have been unmasked in countless laboratory experiments. After a discussion of their poisons she concluded, "Can any intelligent person in the understanding of these facts fail to heed the Prophet's warning? Are the mothers of Israel and the daughters of Zion fit to claim the title when they willfully allow their bodies to be poisoned and their minds darkened by the use of any of these deadly drugs, even though they be disguised in the tempting drinks of daily life?"[24]

December's lesson, "A Merry Christmas," concentrated on the trend to turn Christmas into a pagan holiday through eating excesses: "Where plenty abounds, it is a continuous orgy of feasting and stuffing, munching and chewing sweets and pastries, with all sorts of harmful drinks, until the body sickens because of its abuse."[25] To those who celebrate as true believers, "Christmas should be a sacrament and should be celebrated as such. . . . Not a time of gloom, nor of disgusting bodily indulgence, but a season of joy and gladness, of gratitude for life and a determination to share the best one has with those who may be most in need."[26]

In his stewardship report for 1929, John wrote to the First Presidency. "My wife has done a most notable piece of work, in addition to her many duties, in teaching the people the Word of Wisdom, both positively and negatively. The changes, physical and economic, that have come over many of our people as a result is nothing short of marvelous."[27]

In 1930 the Relief Society lessons were compiled into a manual and no longer published in the *Millennial Star*. Because the manual was not available until March, the women were asked to review the Word of

Wisdom lessons of 1929 in January and February. Leah continued her lessons on the Word of Wisdom into their third year under the heading "Home and Health."[28] "Lessons on human nutrition are to be given, paying more attention to the practical application of the truths learned in the Word of Wisdom lessons studied last year. Menus and recipes and suggestions for daily use will be given; other subjects dealing with home problems will also be made a part of this series."[29]

Leah found troubling the British custom of drinking tea and the problems it posed to the advancement of the Church. She reported a study showing that in 1926 over 395 million pounds of tea were consumed in Great Britain. As an "anti-food," she added that one pound of tea has enough caffeine in it to kill seven to twelve people if consumed all at once.[30] To help counter the British tradition in the eyes of the Saints, and as an example of nutritional science supporting the Word of Wisdom, she put an excerpt from a newspaper article in one of her Relief Society lessons:

> By reason of the emphasis recently put upon the importance of vitamins in our food, a great many purveyors of this or that article of diet have been tempted to make claims that cannot be substantiated by laboratory tests. It is now found that this was the case with green tea; in spite of what its friends were accepting as its apparent reasonableness, there is nothing to it. The Bureau of Home Economics of the United States Agricultural Department has recently conducted a three months feeding experiment with guinea pigs, using green tea as a side line, with decidedly negative results. The tea imbibing creatures did not do at all well. The presence of the highly-prized vitamin C in sufficient quantity to make tea useful in the human food scheme was thoroughly disproved.[31]

John shared some related statistics about other "anti-foods" in Great Britain. In 1928 the alcohol consumption bill was £288,000,000 whereas the public education bill was £94,800,00 and the poor relief bill £54,264,000. "Comment . . . is unnecessary. The drink bill represents the gratification of an unnatural appetite."[32] It was of further interest to John that the inception of a national movement against excessive alcohol consumption coincided with the beginning of the Church in

England. In a *Millennial Star* article, he explained how the perception of
alcohol had evolved since Joseph Smith received the Word of Wisdom
revelation:

> Teetotalism, the abstinence from all alcoholic drinks, was born in
> the town of Preston, England, on September 1, 1832. The pledge,
> there and then signed by seven men, was the beginning of public,
> organized opposition to the rule of king Alcohol. The success that has
> attended the now hundred years' old movement has been celebrated
> far and wide. While the fight against alcohol has met severe, stubborn
> opposition, the gains far exceed the losses. The world is better and
> sweeter for the battles waged against drunkenness as also against
> moderate drinking.
>
> It is interesting to note that the movement was born in the old
> "cockpit" of Preston, in which five years later the first meetings in
> Europe were held under the auspices of Latter-day Saints. It is even
> more interesting to recall that the organized temperance movement
> was born just six months before Joseph Smith, the Prophet, received
> the divine revelation known as the Word of Wisdom.[33]

A WORD OF WISDOM EXHIBITION

In 1929, when all of the European missions were promoting the
Relief Society Word of Wisdom lessons, President and Sister H. W.
Valentine presided over the German-Austrian Mission and Relief
Society. Sister Valentine, who shared Leah's enthusiasm for proper diet
and the Word of Wisdom, became interested in related work being done
by Dr. M. Vogel and the Dresden Hygienic Museum. One of their missionaries, prior to his call to open the Czechoslovakian mission, worked
with the Valentines. He wrote, "Our Mission Mother thought we ought
to make his [Dr. Vogel's] acquaintance. I accompanied her on her first
visit. We had a long and interesting talk with the doctor and received
an invitation to write up the Word of Wisdom for his magazine. We
worked together and two months later had the joy of seeing the article
in print and receiving a check for our work. Our Mission Mother kept
up her contact, with the result that in 1930 and 1931, the Church

placed a Word of Wisdom Exhibit in the great Health Exposition 'Der Mensch' put on by the Dresdner Hygienic Museum."[34]

The seed had been planted, but before it took root the Valentines were replaced by President and Sister Edward P. Kimball. In November 1929, presidents Widtsoe and Kimball met with A. T. Haeberle, U.S. consul at Dresden, a meeting that led to an official invitation for the Church to participate in the exposition. As European mission president, John was made an honorary member of the exposition committee.[35] The exhibition was open from 30 May through 12 October 1930.

Several experienced Church members participated in the planning and construction phase, and John prepared the desired tracts. John noted, "Great interest is manifested in the exhibit by all. Prominent professional people from all parts of the earth have made favorable comments upon this method of preserving human health. Invitations have been received to give Word of Wisdom information in other lands."[36] Arrangements were made for the exhibit to be located at the front entrance of the League of Nations building, which John believed was most effective and helpful in attracting guests.[37] Tracts were published in both English and German.

Commenting on the impact of the Word of Wisdom a hundred years after the revelation was given, John acknowledged the significant shortfall in the degree of compliance the commandment deserves. "But multitudes of us have laid alcohol to one side, forgotten tobacco, do not drink tea or coffee, and consequently, in a hundred years some astonishing results have been attained, such as no other group of like numbers and place in civilization can show."[38] The results of Church attempts to follow the teachings in the Word of Wisdom were published in the pamphlets given at the Dresden Exhibition. Samples of the statistics published included the LDS birth rate average of 30 per thousand of population compared with 22 per thousand of twenty-five nations. The death rates of 7.5 per thousand compared to 24 per thousand implied an increasing length of life among Latter-day Saints. Other health differences showed that deaths per 100,000, comparing averages of LDS people with those of six large western nations, from tuberculosis were 120 for the six nations compared to 9 for LDS people, and from cancer the difference was 119 compared to 47. Maternity deaths per 1,000 births were 45 compared to 10.

When the exhibition closed in October, it had been seen by 2,166,500 people. John reported in an editorial for the *Millennial Star* that 212,000 tracts were distributed, and 4,521 people left their names, requesting further information. From this experience, John concluded, "People generally desire truth, and usually recognize it if proper presentation can be made. . . . Mankind needs the regenerating influence of the Word of Wisdom."[39]

The endeavor was most successful, and soon preparations began for a similar event to be held in Manchester, England, in January, 1931. Leah took charge of the exhibit. John reported:

> The house and all the elders have gone to Manchester where, under the leadership of my wife and the chief cook in the house, a word of wisdom demonstration is being conducted, the first of its kind, I believe, in the history of the Church. We are beginning to change our methods of proselyting a great deal. Demonstrations and Exhibits are coming into greater importance than they had a few years back. The people over here are in sad need of Word of Wisdom information. They need to be taught not merely abstinence from substances that injure them, but they need also to be taught what food they should eat for their physical benefit.[40]

31

TO THE SLAVIC NATIONS

Dᴜʀɪɴɢ his first extensive European Mission tour, John received a letter from the First Presidency dated 13 March 1929 instructing him to begin preparing for proselytizing work in the Czechoslovakian Republic. He began immediately, and plans flowed easily. John planned to take several elders who were proficient in German because they would be best able to get along in the republic while mastering the language. He also planned to make the proper overtures to Czechoslovakian governmental officials and chose the first week of July as an ideal starting date in order to have things well under way before winter. To assist those elders pulled from the German-Austrian and Swiss-German missions, John requested that ten or twelve new elders be called from Church headquarters and trained in the language and culture, and that four or more be sent each month until winter had set in. He emphasized to those elders and their families that Czechoslovakia—at that time little more than a part of the former Austrian Empire—was as accessible as Berlin or Vienna, where missionaries had long labored. He reported to the First Presidency:

> I have already taken steps to secure the translation of two or
> three tracts into the Czech language, by Sister Jane Brodil—a young

woman who appears to be competent, educationally for the task and of course before publication we will make sure that the language is correct. . . . If it is possible for you to comply with this request for a small group of missionaries for the new field, I'm sure it would bring about success that may await us in this field. I am approaching this matter with much deliberation; with a prayerful heart, and with a desire that only the work of the Lord may be spread more widely over the earth and reach more of the honest hearted. I cannot help but feel that the Lord is quite willing that we should undertake this work now, since it has been brought to your attention and approved by you and that thereby the Gospel door will be opened to the great Czecho-slovakian nations. If we find those people impenetrable to Gospel truths we shall nevertheless have done our duty. I shall keep you informed of the steps taken from time to time.

I find myself exceedingly busy. Most of the continental missions have not had a visit for the better part of two years. A few have had the detailed visits that they require for a number of years.[1]

With this response John set out to finish his tour of each of the ten European missions. He developed a plan to assess their strengths and isolate their problems. The opportunity in Czechoslovakia was true pioneer missionary work and a significant step forward in the work of the restoration. John wrote:

That country had become democratized, and much liberty of thought and speech prevailed there. Under the leadership of Thomas Masaryk full individual freedom prevailed, and many enlightened enterprises for the public good had been undertaken. Moreover, if the gospel could be brought to the Czechs, a Slavic people, it seemed as if it might be a door to the mighty Slavic nations. Russia, with its great population, must some day hear the gospel. After much preliminary scouting, Elder Arthur Gaeth, who had already served a very successful mission in Germany, and was soon to be released, was called to preside over the new mission, assisted by a half dozen picked missionaries from among the American elders serving in Germany.[2]

On Saturday, 18 May 1929, the first day of the Church's centennial celebrations in the German-Austrian Mission, more than 1,800 people attended a dance and social. Sixteen hundred visitors attended the morning meetings, and there were 1,500 in the afternoon and 1,850 at night. They heard the message of the restoration of the priesthood, one hundred years earlier. The presentations included a pageant, lectures, songs, and testimony from Apostle John A. Widtsoe. Hundreds of German Saints felt blessed to be able to shake his hand and hear his voice.

In the midst of these celebrations, John told Elder Gaeth he wanted to meet with him. At that moment Gaeth had a strange feeling "that all the dreams which I had for the future would not be fulfilled, that I was not going home, but that I would be called to another work in Czechoslovakia. No one had spoken a word to me about it, for other than President Widtsoe, no one in the German Austrian Mission knew about it until his arrival in the Mission."[3]

In their meeting John explained that plans were being made to open a mission in Czechoslovakia, and he asked Gaeth to consider extending his mission another six months to go there and assess the feasibility of the mission. All that Arthur heard was familiar from the impression he had received, and he was ready to accept immediately, but John asked him to think about it overnight. Gaeth wrote:

> I knew what mother would say, for it had been her prayer from my childhood when I had become ill with pneumonia, that if the Lord spared my life, she would do all in her power to have me devote my life to His service. I knew father would not object. And there was my sister who had borne the brunt of the expense of my mission. She as well as "Dad" and mother, would say: "Go where you are called."
>
> But my training in the Church from childhood and my testimony that God is directing the destinies of His Church won out and I was prepared to accept the call with the feeling that "not my will, but thine be done, oh Lord." As I look back now, it seems that I could have given no other answer. When I was 14 years old and mother, sister and I went to the patriarch for a blessing, he had promised mother that one of her posterity would return to her native country to preach the Gospel to her countrymen. Mother was born in Undangs, in Czechoslovakia, then Austria Hungary. I, her only son, was going to Czechoslovakia to preach the Gospel.[4]

Gaeth had done unusually well in the routine duties of a missionary: tracting, holding street meetings, fulfilling branch ecclesiastical assignments, and building good relations with media and political representatives. He had served as the director of auxiliary organizations and had edited their quarterly publication, the *Wegweiser*. He was a traveling propagandist, serving at the right hand of the mission president and living in the mission home at the center of mission management. He was a creative and successful teacher, and in one thirty-day period he delivered a series of illustrated lectures on the Book of Mormon to 6,455 interested participants as the central program of the mission's centennial celebration. His assessment was published in the *Deseret News*: "Only recently have I realized how . . . each specific task, each bit of knowledge contributes to the sum total of a person's education, somehow works and makes its impression in the journey of a life-time. Each bit of knowledge, each new acquaintance, each happy hour, each period of anxiety and experience of sorrow and pain plays its part in the making of the man."[5]

Elder Gaeth filled many diverse assignments with distinction and became adroit in handling the press. Throughout Germany and Austria he had worked with more than a hundred reporters as he gave lectures on Utah and the Latter-day Saints. From one article published in an Austrian newspaper came a lengthy correspondence that led to the conversion of a prominent woman who joined the Church and translated the Book of Mormon into Hungarian. Gaeth wrote, "Who knows where a seed dropped today will sprout, what fruit it will bring forth, or how far it will be carried by the wind, before it finds fertile ground! The ways of the Lord are marvelous, His workings often mysterious."[6] Together with Sister Valentine, his mission mother, Gaeth had published the article on the Word of Wisdom that led to the Church's opportunity to place a "Word of Wisdom exhibition in the great Health Exposition 'Der Mensch!' put on by the Dresdner Hygienic Museum."[7]

THE WORK IN CZECHOSLOVAKIA

In 1913, in Vienna, Austria, Czechoslovakian Frantiska Brodil had met missionaries from the Church. She was courteous but not interested.

However, the elders left a standard tract, which she read, and she wanted to hear more. She could not persuade her husband, a minor Austrian government official, to develop any interest in the missionaries or their message. Frantiska accepted the gospel, taught her two daughters, and attended church and Sunday School with them. They were stalwarts in their Vienna Branch and helped maintain the organization when all the men went to war. As part of the war settlement, the Brodil family moved back to Czechoslovakia in exchange for a family of Austrians living in Czechoslovakia. In Czechoslovakia their circumstances were considerably worse, and Mr. Brodil soon became ill and died. The family struggled for many years, but with some aid from the new social welfare programs and from a brother in South America, they hung on, and the girls advanced in school, eventually attending business college to train for office work. One of the early missionaries to serve in the mission wrote, "Sister Francis Brodil . . . has become known and shall always remain known as the great pioneer who literally prayed a mission into existence."[8]

In fulfillment of John Widtsoe's call and the spiritual witness Gaeth had received of his work in Czechoslovakia, Gaeth sought out the Brodil family in Prague on his first day in the country. They longed for contact with the Church. "Once a year the Mission President visited them. On one such occasion the two daughters, Francis and Jane, were baptized in the Votava (Moldau) River, the first baptism to be held in the new Czechoslovakia. . . . True, they lived for such visits, but they only strengthened in them the desire to have missionaries laboring in their midst."[9] They spoke about it to each mission president and wrote several letters to the First Presidency, who then instructed John to make the appropriate preparations. Naturally Gaeth received a royal welcome from the Brodil family, who saw in him the beginning of the answer to their prayers. A year earlier Elder Thomas Biesinger, an eighty-four-year-old man who had served part of his mission in Prague in 1886, had visited them. As a missionary he was arrested and after several weeks in jail was banished from the province. Another elder named Kaiser had received similar treatment in Ceska Lipa in 1904. Now Gaeth was sent to this land previously deaf to the gospel message:

The situation was new and strange to me. The instructions I had received were to find the Brodil family in Prague and with their help, to investigate conditions to see if missionary work could be introduced. That implied, getting government permission for missionaries to enter the country so that they could work there. It implied becoming acquainted with the country, feeling out the nature of the people to see if there was any likelihood that any considerable number would take kindly to the Gospel message. It implied an investigation of the language, of living conditions to see if missionaries could live and make themselves understood there. In spite of the fact that I had been sent to investigate conditions, President Widtsoe must have felt rather forcibly that the Gospel could be preached to the Czechs, for he instructed me, if I found no serious restrictions, to seek out a place where the new mission might be dedicated. He would come to Czechoslovakia early in July.[10]

Gaeth reported that conditions were favorable, and the necessary preparations for opening the new mission were made. John contacted appropriate government leaders and press representatives to win friends for the Church. Those contacts proved most helpful when persecution from other churches arose. Gaeth continued good relations with government officials and soon counted among his better friends three of President Masaryk's four secretaries, with whom he occasionally exchanged dinner invitations. "When the Catholic Church took out after us and one of the Catholic priests tried to defame us and blast us because of the polygamy doctrine, the fellows in Masaryk's office suggested I sue for libel, and I did. I got a retraction from the priest as a result of it. It had to be published in the newspaper."[11] This happened both in Prague and Mlada Boleslav.

Official announcements and the history of the Czechoslovakian mission indicate that the dedication services for the Czechoslovakian Mission took place on 24 July 1929. John's journal indicates that the dedication meetings continued through 22–24 July. The only mention of a dedicatory prayer is on 22 July:

July 22: Elders' meeting all forenoon. Wrote report to First Presidency, also editorial on John Husback of Karlstein castle. The

On the photo is inscribed "Photo studio Prague, vaclavske num 15." These are probably the first missionaries in the Czechoslovakia Mission.

storm was over and the sun out. A glorious day for the most important event in history of the Czecho-Slovak. Republic. An hour later came Bro. Gaeth & Dresden party. (Bro. & Sister Valentine, daughter Basil, Elders Simons, Noble & Richards [visitor from Cornell] & the Brodil family: mother & daughters, Fanny and Jane.) At 11:15 services commenced, continued until about 2 P.M. All bore testimony. Singing. I spoke last & then offered prayer of dedication of the land and of our efforts. It was a very spiritual and refreshing meeting. Then we had lunch, then rest; then visit to Karlstein castle, then home by train. An historic and beautiful day.

July 23 Meeting with Elders all forenoon. Photograph of group at 9 A.M. In city all afternoon. Writing in eve.

July 24 Up at 4 A.M. Violent thunderstorm. Left w. five elders on 6:52 train for Karlstein. Walked 45 minutes through village and up the road to top of mountain.[12]

The dedicatory services all took place in Karlstein, a village southwest of Prague, where John and others had previously selected a shady spot atop a mountain. It overlooked a beautiful valley and was "just

below the walls, ramparts and battlements and towers of the old
Karlstein Castle, the most famous in Central Europe."[13] By 6:30 A.M.,
when their visitors from the German-Austrian Mission arrived, the sun
was beginning to emerge from the heavy clouds that had echoed with
thunder. Gaeth wrote:

> At 8 A.M. when we arrived at the little knoll behind the famous
> Karlstein castle, a beautiful summer day was upon us. Sixteen souls
> gathered that day, under the direction of Elder John A. Widtsoe, of
> the Council of the Twelve Apostles, president of the European mis-
> sions, to dedicate the land of the Czechs and the Slovaks to the
> preaching of the Gospel. All of the 16 bore testimony to the good-
> ness of the Lord and expressed the desire that this be one of a num-
> ber of missions soon to be opened so that all the Slavic nations
> might be given an opportunity to hear the Gospel. . . . President
> Widtsoe pointed out the importance of the situation, the unique
> combination which had been selected to make the introduction—
> Elder Carlson with Scandinavian blood flowing in his veins, Brother
> Toronto with Latin and Scotch, Brother Hart with English, Brother
> Josie with Ungarian and Mongolian, Brother Hayward with Jewish
> and American, and Brother Gaeth with Germanic and probably
> Slavic—all nationalities combined in the opening of this new
> venture.[14]

John remarked:

> There we spent the day in bearing testimony, singing the songs of
> Zion and finally at the close of the meeting, dedicated the land and
> our efforts to the cause of the Lord. . . . Now we are under way, and
> have our organization perfected. All that is left to do is the work. This
> day is not merely the opening of the door to the Czechish people, but
> to the Slovak races as a whole, which represents millions of people. I
> hope that this is just the beginning of the work. From here we expect
> to reach out to Poland, Hungaria, and other nations. The responsibil-
> ity of the missionaries is that they conduct themselves in such a way
> that the Lord may be able to use them. Look after your own fitness. If
> you will do that, I will make you the promise that the work will be
> crowned with success; not only here, but among the other people of
> this type. I feel that we are not alone. It is a glorious privilege to be in

this life. Had it not been for the hero of this land, Huss, the world would not have been ready for Luther, and what was to follow. This land fostered freedom and religious liberty, while our own land lay in darkness and was subject to it. The Huss Spirit has long prevailed and, we have no apologies to make for sending missionaries here. It is an honor to be a servant of the people. I wonder if the Huss episode has not been in preparation for this day. Did not the Father vision it in his Plan of Salvation. I have wondered if the Martyr himself, has not been here today, and added his blessings to the occasion. . . . It [the Truth] is for the good of man, and so the man touched by Truth receives the desire to give it to someone else. Our commandment is, "go ye into all the world, and preach the Gospel unto every living creature." The time will come when we will all be engaged in missionary work, either directly or indirectly.[15]

John observed the effect of the day on Gaeth: "He prayed for the blessings of the Lord upon the work, looked into the future and saw bright prospects, bore testimony to the divinity of the mission of Jesus Christ, explaining how his mother had been led to accept the Gospel in her native land in spite of all hardships."[16] The Brodils, the happiest souls among them, oversaw the preparations for a special lunch. When evening came the party was still on the hill, basking in the inspiration and joy of the Spirit. "It was a day which will long remain in the memories of those who participated," Gaeth wrote, "a day which the growing Czechoslovak Mission had tried to celebrate each year."[17] He continued, "Next day, President Widtsoe, who had been with us for almost three weeks, departed from our midst. I had been in daily contact with him, had done some of his secretarial work, had had many intimate talks with him. I began to appreciate why everyone loves, honors and respects him, why he is held an ideal by so many young people, why so many seek his advice. From him emanates the spirit of love and understanding, the true spirit of the Gospel. He is truly one of Christ's disciples of love upon the earth. He is at home in the humblest of circumstances, but can associate with the most intellectual and the mighty."[18]

To inform the Church of the momentous event in Czechoslovakia, John wrote an article for the *Improvement Era* entitled "Opening the

Gospel Doors to the Slavs."[19] In it he outlined the history of Czecho-slovakia and the hopes and experience of the Church there. He also reported the dedication of the land and the opening of the work:

> The Czecho-Slovak Mission of the Church of Jesus Christ of Latter-day Saints was formally opened on July 24, 1929. The meeting of testimony, song and dedication, hours of glorious spiritual feasting, was held in a place of unusual beauty, on a shady hilltop overlooking the famous Karlstein Castle and the picturesque valley of the river Beroanka. The gospel door was thus opened to the Slavonic race of people.
>
> To preach the gospel to all the nations is a duty enjoined upon the Church. The opening of the Czecho-Slovak mission is in obedience to this command. May the Lord prosper the work![20]

The reaction of one of the early missionaries further expresses the significance of this beginning: "Think of it! The opening up of the gospel doors to the great Slavonic world—the Czecho-Slovaks, the Russians, the Poles, the Bulgarians, and the Yugo-Slavs (over 200,000,000 souls). Stupendous and all important is the work and blessed are those Slavs who are leading out as genuine pioneers in the redemption and salvation, not only of their living but also of their dead."[21]

John was determined that they should proceed wisely and, as preparations allowed, he kept the First Presidency informed. He had learned that laying the proper groundwork and seeking the approval of the appropriate officers of a country opened many doors. He informed the Brethren:

> The impression has been with me from the beginning that we should not go into the field with a blur of trumpets. I am always afraid of the big end of the horn when I am going inward. Yet all necessary Governmental Offices have been consulted: Those of the President, Interior Department, Exterior Department, Education Department, etc.; as also our American Representatives. Everywhere the reception has been friendly, and at times cordial. Some powerful friends have already been made, and far-reaching connections established.
>
> On August 8th and 10th, the Republic's official radio station will

broadcast two lectures on Utah and the Mormons. These were written by Elder Gaeth, revised by me and translated by an educated Czech who will deliver them into the ether. And, we are to receive pay for them! Well[?] really why not? Arrangements have been made with the clubs, schools, adult and education organizations, and other similar institutions for lectures on the Mormons and Utah with and without illustrations. These will begin as soon as the summer vacation ends. You will remember that the summer vacation is sacred rite to the European. Only quiet negotiations have been made with the newspapers, as I have felt that our men should learn a little Czech before advertising ourselves too much.[22]

Anthony Ivins, first counselor in the First Presidency, replied:

The report from Prague is very interesting and hopeful. It seems almost too good to be true. Whether these people accept the Gospel . . . at the present or not they will at some future period. For they are undoubtedly of Israelitish extraction. They are exactly in the line of march followed by the ten tribes after they left Assyria, as outlined by the Prophet Ezra. As I study the question more carefully I become convinced that these people came into the Balkan States, found their way into Southern Russia and moved over to the west to Scandinavia and the British Isles. They are now there in great numbers, and sometime, perhaps it is now, the Lord will move upon their hearts and they will come to understand the truth.[23]

Tracts were prepared by the missionaries, who gave radio addresses and public presentations. The YMCA, at first cold, soon warmed to them and gave them the run of their facilities. In a short time the missionaries were teaching basketball and running a league for local participants. They formed a quartet to accompany illustrated lectures. In the major cities, beginning in Prague, there were English Clubs that opened their doors to them. Gaeth wrote:

In November President John A. Widtsoe of the European missions, and Mrs. Widtsoe, spent a week in the Czechoslovak mission. We had an extensive program of activity prepared for them. They spoke at our regular English meeting with more than 100 present. We allowed all present to ask questions of Mrs. Widtsoe, a grand-daughter of Brigham Young, so that they might obtain a new impression of "Mormon" women. Mrs. Widtsoe met the leaders of Women's Clubs in Czechoslovakia, the head of the Czechoslovak Red Cross, and she was taken on an inspection tour of the social welfare projects in the city, which ended with a trip to Krc, where the extensive Masaryk homes are located, one of the most unique social welfare projects in all the world. This institution was created at the expense of practically two million dollars and cares for Prague's sub-normal children and aged and destitute men and women. The socialistic parties in the government have always been strong and have secured favorable legislation for the unfortunate.

With Dr. and Mrs. Widtsoe we decided on a new and interesting venture. We invited ten of the leading newspaper men in the city to come to the Community House of the city and dine with us, to meet "Mormons" and see what they are like. As those we invited could speak English, we had no trouble, and seven of them accepted our invitation and sat down to a banquet with us. Well, we had a great time! We talked about Czechoslovakia and the Czech people as long as we could, until finally one of the editors broke the ice and asked us a question about Utah and the "Mormons." We spent three profitable hours together, made some interesting friends, and broke down more prejudice. We sent them all away with literature, "Fruits of Mormonism," "Philosophy of Mormonism," etc.[24]

One of these men, the editor of one of the largest news distributing agencies in the country, became a friend. He was responsible for many favorable articles and for advertising many Mormon conferences and lectures to the extent that other religions became jealous. The favorable publicity did much to break down some of the prejudice and inform people of the work of the Church, but it did little to bring about baptisms.

In the early 1990s, following the fall of the Berlin Wall and the decline of the Soviet Union, accounts of a prophecy President Widtsoe purportedly gave in a mission conference in July or August 1932 were circulated in the Church by some of the missionaries who had attended. Their accounts centered on comments he had made about the religious and political climate in Czechoslovakia, to the effect that communism would be allowed to succeed in Eastern Europe as a means of putting an end to the stronghold of Catholicism and Russian Orthodoxy.[25] Nothing that direct has been found in Widtsoe's writings, but some of the descriptions that Gaeth and others gave of religious oppression lends credence to their likelihood. The Czechs and the Slovaks were converted to Christianity in the ninth century by missionaries of the Byzantine Church. As the centuries passed, Catholicism became the predominant religion; by the fourteenth century it controlled a third of the land, and the people were its serfs and peasants. At the general conference in April 1931, Gaeth described the view of the people: "It was said at that time that the Archbishop of Prague controlled one-third of the province of Bohemia, and he had a large retinue of priests and followers who spent a good deal of their time in riotous living. This greatly incited the feelings of honest men and women who believed in the message of Christ."[26] The heroic reformer, John Huss, was burned at the stake for his opposition, and though his spirit lived on, the dominance of the church continued into the generation of Gaeth's missionary efforts. Gaeth continued:

> Then the World War came and that people succeeded in gaining their freedom and in establishing religious liberty. The educated people began to break away from the church. They began to go off into the paths of skepticism and agnosticism. The masses still remain in that church and are remaining so probably because they feel they must have some kind of a cloak and that the cloak they are wearing now is probably as good as any they could get. But the leaders and the educated people are opposed to organized religion. They want nothing of it, because the experiences they have had with organized religion have taught them that it has meant bondage to them.[27]

President and Sister Widtsoe spoke to a large audience in the Prague English Club, where Gaeth had a strong influence. They told the story of the pioneers who settled Utah. The audience seemed so interested that many of them stayed for several hours to become better acquainted with the Widtsoes. Two young women and a brother were the children of Vaclar Kralicek, a prominent government official who had met with John in Utah to discuss the possibility of sending students from Czechoslovakia to be trained at the Agricultural College. One of his daughters, Martha Kralickova, had been with him and had met with several Church officials who made lasting impressions on both father and daughter. Vaclar Kralicek had since passed away, but the children remained interested friends of the Church. Martha and her father co-authored the report on the Church for President Masaryk. Martha had kept the autographed books they were given while visiting in Salt Lake City. John told Gaeth, "She is interested in our teachings, is anxious to hear more about them; so keep up the contact."[28] Gaeth became acquainted with Martha, who was at the end of a sabbatical leave from teaching at a Chicago high school. He later said, "When she left to go back to teach school I was impressed that that was the woman I ought to marry."[29]

By this time Gaeth and the Widtsoes were very close. "I was at that time by far the youngest mission president," Gaeth said. "And I wasn't even married, which was another difficulty. But I got married after two years [in 1931]. I had a special dispensation from the Widtsoes to find a wife. . . . I baptized her in Chicago, and then we went to Salt Lake and we were married in the Salt Lake Temple."[30] In his journal for 23 March 1931, John wrote, "Performed ceremony uniting Arthur Gaeth & Martha K. Picha in marriage."[31] At the direction of the First Presidency, the Widtsoes had returned to Salt Lake City for the general conference in April 1931 and to spend time with their family. The Gaeths stayed in Salt Lake for three months while Martha learned about the operations of Church auxiliaries. She became very close to Leah Widtsoe and was of great service to the Church through the remaining five years of Gaeth's service as mission president. John noted, "We had friends among the official body of the State. . . . President Gaeth and his ener-getic wife, Martha K. Gaeth (herself a Czech-American with influential friends in Prague), performed valuable service for the latter-day work in this new, strategic mission of the Church."[32] When Gaeth's seven-year term as mission president ended, he recorded that since the day President Widtsoe dedicated the mission, "thirty-six missionaries have been called to that field. They have been instrumental in baptizing one hundred and five people. Branches of the Church have been established in five cities, Sunday Schools in four, Relief Societies in three, Mutual Improvement Associations in three."[33]

Wallace F. Toronto, one of Gaeth's fellow missionaries, was the next president of the Czechoslovakian Mission until the war forced the missionaries to evacuate. In the April 1940 general conference, Toronto spoke of the devotion of the Saints in that region and of the efforts of the missionaries, who had been evacuated twice yet each time returned with greater determination to succeed:

> I bring you the greetings, brethren and sisters, of a small band of people, Czecho-Slovaks, who know that the Gospel of Jesus Christ is indeed the most priceless possession which they have ever had. They are living in a war-torn country which has been ravaged, robbed and plundered. They are existing under the most adverse of conditions, but none-the-less they live the Gospel to such an extent as would put many of us to shame. Perhaps we need adversity, in order to fully appreciate the commandments and the blessings coming from the Gospel which we have. . . . Members of the Church in Central Europe have learned to know the deep meaning of the Gospel. They have learned to know that its core and essence is to be found in the admonition of Jesus: "Love thy neighbor even as thyself."
>
> A short time after almost two million German troops had marched across the borders of Czecho-Slovakia—during that time of tension and terror, which inevitably resulted—a young German officer, a fine, straight, clean-looking fellow, walked through the door of our meeting hall in Prague. We thought: Certainly, this is the end for us. The Secret Police have probably sent some one here to close the Mission. Coming up he said: "My name is Brother R. (for obvious reasons it is felt unwise to give his name). I am an officer in the German Army. As soon as I had completed my official duties here in Prague, the first thing I set out to do was to find this Branch of the Church in Czecho-Slovakia. With your permission, I would like to say just a word to this congregation." I replied: "Certainly, Brother R., we shall be happy to hear from you."
>
> He stood up, and in a language which most of the people of Czecho-Slovakia detested, German, he had this to say to the members of the Church and to the friends who were present: "Brothers

and sisters, I come here not on an appointment of my own choosing. I come here as a servant of my government. I know we have brought you considerable distress and dismay. We have caused already much suffering. Nevertheless, you and I have something in common, something which oversteps the boundaries of race, language, and color. You and I have the Gospel of Jesus Christ. Despite the fact that I speak German and you Czech, yet because of the Gospel we still speak in common terms. The time is coming when we shall know this better than ever before."

I wish I had time to tell you all he said. Tears streamed down the faces of those Czecho-Slovakian people. As he walked down the aisle they stood up and put their arms around him and wept upon his shoulder. Every available Sunday—he believed in keeping the Sabbath—he was at the Branch hall, doing his best to make the Gospel of Jesus Christ a living thing among a subjugated people. . . .

We regretted having to leave our members in Czecho-Slovakia. Had we been able to leave them in the hands of a successor, we should have felt good about coming home, but conditions would not permit that. Nevertheless it is my testimony to you that some thirty thousand members of the Church who have been left in Europe, who are now carrying on for themselves—despite the fact that they must suffer, and perhaps have want of the necessities of life—are being protected by the hand of the Lord.[34]

32

TRAINING AND LEADING MISSIONARIES

———————— ■ ————————

CULTURAL diversity across the nations of the ten missions of Europe, Armenia, and South Africa required that each mission have sufficient autonomy to accomplish its work well, yet the work was similar enough that good ideas were almost equally effective in all missions. In the fall of 1928, at the European mission presidents' conference, John presented a plan to emphasize both individuality and conformity in each mission and each missionary. "There are two things to be done in a mission," he said. "First; the mission should retain self-expression, and be at liberty to work out its own individuality, allowing the missionaries also the freedom of self-expression. And secondly, the missions should be able to express themselves under the law. The greatest responsibility resting upon the mission presidents is to co-ordinate the work, that is, to preserve their individuality and self-expression, yet at the same time keeping the spirit of co-operation and learning to work together as one great missionary unit."[1]

MISSION PRESIDENTS' CONFERENCES

John felt responsible for the work and morale of all the mission presidents and their missionaries. He decided their interests could best be served by bringing them together for extended conferences lasting about ten days. The minutes of the first conference reported, "The three principal aims of this convention as stated by President Widtsoe were first to derive inspiration from association with each other. Second, to obtain more coordination in our work. Third, to establish unity of purpose in proper forms of administering the affairs pertaining to our missions."[2]

The following summer, several of the mission presidents planned to attend a Boy Scout jamboree in England, so John arranged for a nine-day conference to follow immediately at Durham House, his headquarters in Liverpool. He reported to the First Presidency their efforts in again emphasizing individuality and conformity. The mission presidents also formulated the work and the instruction of the priesthood quorums and Church auxiliaries and began plans for a special program to celebrate the centennial of the Church's organization in the following year. The conference agenda covered eighteen topics, including tracting, study courses, coordination of the *Millennial Star*, self-government in the different parts of the mission, wider publicity, missionary preparation and concerns, and women's work.[3]

In June 1930, the mission presidents' conference was held in Basel, Switzerland. John was particularly happy to report to the First Presidency that the inspiration that had created the European Mission was everywhere evident. Though some mission presidents continued to build large office staffs for incidental, perhaps unnecessary work, the European office was gradually taking over those duties, allowing more time and manpower to focus on proselytizing and caring for members.

MINGLING WITH THE PEOPLE

John went among the people of Europe to observe life firsthand, feeling certain that he could better train missionaries if he could observe the public's attitude. The view from a railroad car or in the stations along the way was not enough:

> Therefore, I bought in Paris a Ford car, with a college education, that is, a Ford chassis with an elaborate French closed body, arranged by a wealthy American for tourist purposes. I paid $400.00 for it and sold it for $200.00—the loss together with the necessary upkeep, I

Photo taken at the Mission Presidents Conference, Prague Czechoslovakia, July 5–15, 1932.

gladly assumed as a personal private expense. The gain in European vision and perspective, as we drove through hundreds of small villages and large cities, I met many people, it was greater than I had expected and will make me more useful in the great work to which my life is dedicated.

As we traveled between conferences we met not only with many strangers, but with our saints and missionaries and saw them off dressed parade. In conversation with our saints, their needs and point of view were revealed. My little survey was made easier by my slight facility to speak with the people in several countries in their native tongue.[4]

On his trip, John observed a general lack of uniformity in mission and Church procedures. He brought attention to this problem by comparing it to the circumstances that had brought the great apostasy in earlier centuries. He next observed that Church services were being held in meetinghouses that were usually associated with public uses not in harmony with Church practices. As a consequence, people above the poverty level were unwilling to associate with the Church. His third observation was that most of the Saints were poor, and the missionaries were not targeting the middle-class. As a result, he made plans to train

President Widtsoe with missionaries of the Manchester Conference (England) during the centennial celebration in 1930.

missionaries to expand their reach to all classes of people and to go further out to smaller villages and towns. He also observed great waste in missionary efforts arising from their youth and inexperience. Finally, he noticed that the old tracts had become well-known and unproductive; new ones were needed.

A Policy from Church Headquarters

In addition to changes President Widtsoe wanted to make, the First Presidency sent word of a new policy concerning the migration of Saints to Utah. They instructed the missionaries to encourage European Saints comfortably situated in their homelands to stay and strengthen the Church in Europe. They explained that in earlier days of settlement, when all able members were encouraged to gather to Utah, there were sufficient lands and water to support the growing Church. In the 1920s conditions had changed. Unclaimed water-accessible land was becoming scarce.[5]

Throughout Europe, existing branches needed to be strengthened and aligned for permanent operation rather than being temporary holding units that cared for new members while they awaited their turn to gather to Utah. John was responsible to make the Church as effective for its European members as it was for its Utah members.

DEVELOPING EFFECTIVE MISSIONARIES

Ten mission presidents stood behind John. All of them were staunch, proven disciples. Missionaries assigned to them were like diamonds in the rough. Polishing missionaries was the most crucial element in bringing the Church to the level of success it needed. Solutions to the problems the Church faced in Europe rested in their hands. John described his challenges to the First Presidency: "The problems of effective missionary work have occupied much of our time, and will continue to do so, as a special issue for 1930. Of course, the spiritual meaning of our work has been emphasized everywhere; and my heart has been made very tender by the spiritual manifestations that I have witnessed and felt."[6] Church members in the branches and districts were much aided by the presence of missionaries, but the mission presidents agreed that the missionaries' primary work was with "strangers"—countrymen who did not belong to the Church.

John addressed the need for hard study of the gospel. He advised placing an easily distracted missionary with a studious companion so that the former might discover the pleasure of study. In the 1932 mission presidents' conference, he taught, "Experience has shown that there will be no spiritual permanency in a mission unless time is taken for daily spiritual food—the daily morning study hour—from the mission home to the last arrived missionaries, and that the daily use of an hour for joint gospel study be urged upon all missionaries."[7] His missionaries remembered his emphasis on study and the wise use of time. Clifton Kerr reported:

> First he recommended that a person always carry some reading material with him. In an average lifetime a person will spend countless hours waiting for someone or something. With something to read, these otherwise wasted hours can be converted to constructive improvements of mind and spirit. Second, President Widtsoe said that if a person will spend 10 minutes a day in thoughtful study of almost any subject, and another 10 minutes thinking about what he has read,

in a year, he can be an authority on that subject. He also suggested that to increase one's capacity for learning, a person should cultivate the ability to read thoughts rather than words. When one grasps the idea, the words have served their purpose. Some things may need to be memorized, President Widtsoe, said, but there is so much to know that it is more important to know how and where to find it than it is to spend much time memorizing. His fifth point was that reading commentaries on gospel subjects can be helpful, but there is no substitute for the special spirit that comes from reading the ancient and modern scriptures found in the Standard Works.[8]

John emphasized that time taken to learn the history and traditions of a country was time profitably spent, and that real effectiveness with the people required them to move from Utah to Europe mentally as well as bodily.[9] It was not as hard to teach a new language or the principles of the gospel to a missionary as it was to touch his heart and give him the spirit of the work. John noted, "Missionaries today are not as effective preachers as they were twenty years ago. The missionaries use outlines too much and do not speak out of their hearts. The Lord can do remarkable things with an unlearned elder if he is humble. The real problem is to train our missionaries in faith, humility, and knowledge. Do not accept challenges to debate. Hold street meetings at every opportunity."[10]

Nearly fifty years after his mission, an elder recalled some of the preaching skills he had learned: "President Widtsoe taught that what a person may teach by way of principle or doctrine is not as important as inspiring one's listeners to seek knowledge by their own initiative and effort. Until this takes place, one really hasn't acquired knowledge. . . . He urged his missionaries to strive to avoid trite expressions and lengthy and irrelevant introductions before getting to the subject."[11] Another missionary remembered President Widtsoe being so driven to find new approaches and increase efficiency that he urged all mission presidents to give missionaries assigned to administrative work defined office hours. Once those hours were finished, the missionaries were to proselytize. No missionary was exempt from this work.[12]

John saw that in addition to proselyting activities, the missionaries were responsible for the ecclesiastical leadership in most of the branches and districts of the missions. Ecclesiastical time was detrimental to proselyting time, but significant changes would be years in coming. Improving missionary efficiency in all of their work became a high priority. It became increasingly important as emigration slowed. President Widtsoe wrote to the First Presidency, "A definite attempt was made to increase the efficiency of the mission of the labors of the missionaries, which is unpardonably low. Nothing is now more needed here. As part of the movement, new tracts have been prepared and are being published, and other materials and methods for improving missionary work are under way. The improving of missionary efficiency will be a major concern of 1932."[13]

After interviewing some four hundred missionaries who had averaged nearly seventy hours a week teaching and proselytizing,[14] John was more convinced that only an increase in efficiency would yield a substantially greater harvest:

> Proselytizing success goes hand in hand with missionary efficiency. This campaign is yet in full service. Daily programs, simple guides and outlines, and new tools have been provided the missionaries. Meetings have been held with more than three fourths of the missionaries laboring in the European Missions. A series of new, supplementary tracts have been published in all of the missions. An information service has been organized in the European Mission office, for the assistance of the missionaries. These efforts are bearing rich and good fruits. The majority of our young missionaries are eagerly waiting for leadership. They want to become efficient in the work of the Lord; but need direction and supervision in their efforts.[15]

John gave an interesting profile of the typical missionary to his successor. They were usually under twenty, inexperienced and immature, from active social lives that made transition to missionary life quite unnatural. Were they to live as they had at home under the pressure of tremendous temptations, they "should have disaster overtake most of them in a very short time. Missionary regulations and restrictions must therefore be enforced." Many had a poor work ethic and were inclined to view their mission as a vacation. Some sought only to improve themselves, and many were scathing in their view of Europeans. John added:

> It usually takes three to nine months to train a young man into a reasonable missionary efficiency. It is very probable that soon we shall place the incoming elders in a "school" for a few days with the mission president as the leader. Much depends upon his first companion. In fact, the right start is half the battle. The majority of the missionaries after a while become possessed of the spirit of the work. They grow in a testimony of the truth and perform really a marvelous work considering their youth and inexperience. But they need constant supervision and direction. Failure to do this usually results disastrously.
>
> We have not been quite just to the missionaries in helping them achieve proper efficiency in their work. They come into the field knowing little or nothing about what is expected of them, and frequently the mission presidents see the elders only twice a year and then only just an hour or two. The elder, therefore, has to educate himself as best he can. Such a system would be inefficient in any business. We have also failed in supplying the elders with the necessary tools such as tracts and pamphlets fitting their needs. Until recently the tracts used by the elders were those which had been written nearly a half century before, fifty years of the most tremendous change the world has ever known in thought and conquest over nature. At present all elders . . . are required to become familiar with several pamphlets: (1) The Successful Missionary, covering a number of practical missionary problems; (2) Studies in the Priesthood to make them at least partially familiar with the facts that they should know and which are fairly familiar to the people in the branches; (3) Branch Supervision, covering the details of work in the branches; (4) Tracts and Tracting, dealing with the methods of tracting.[16]

THE SUCCESSFUL MISSIONARY

As part of their effort to increase missionary efficiency, especially among elders with infrequent access to the mission president, the presidents of the European missions urged John to prepare some guidelines. In response, he wrote *The Successful Missionary: Letters to Elders in the*

Field,[17] a compilation of sixteen letters that dealt with some of the problems that limit success. He drew much of his information from interviews with his most successful elders. The book was well received and quickly disseminated. Copies were also sent to the editor of the Church section of the *Deseret News.*[18]

In the opening letter, "Here I Am!" Widtsoe built on a missionary's own desire, the faith that led him into a mission. One undertakes missionary work first, because God has commanded it; second, because our world needs it; and third, because it is the finest preparation for success in life. Five steps are given to help the missionary get started: Get busy; stay fit physically, spiritually, and mentally; dedicate yourself to the work; keep your motives in line with the mission goals; and follow the rules. "It is the consensus of opinion of thoughtful observers that, aside from its inestimable spiritual value, missionary experience is worth more in winning success than the corresponding time spent in school."[19]

A letter about mission regulations taught that there is really only one regulation: "The missionary must always be a gentleman—that is, a true man. That covers the whole ground. A gentleman is not only outwardly attractive in manner, but inwardly sincere in his professions."[20] Much of this letter addressed the Word of Wisdom and chastity. "An ambassador of the Lord, sent out among the nations, to call them to repentance, is under greater obligations than the ordinary member of the Church. The missionary body must be kept spotlessly clean."[21]

"A safe measure of a man are the habits he maintains"[22] was the message of the third letter, "As the Twig Is Bent." It detailed attention to six areas that would guarantee successful missionary life: labor, study, social, recreational, financial, and moral, explaining that a sense of freedom and power comes to one who follows good missionary habits. The seventh letter, "Sowing," explained a missionary's threefold duty: finding, converting, and holding, and emphasizing that winning friends for the Church is an ever-present duty. "Finding Truth" emphasized that a missionary must be able to bear his own testimony boldly. Missionaries must know how to find truth for themselves to teach others. A missionary is to teach truth and nothing but the truth. "The approach to truth must be made reverently. Prayer, or its equivalent, the expression of real desire, is a necessary precedent and accompaniment of a search for truth. Study, continual and intensive, is required. The practice or use of truth, as a test of its verity, is an imperative requirement."[23]

The remaining letters cover how to handle being away from home ("Moving Away from Home"), the basic principles missionaries preach and defend ("The Sling of Faith and the Pebble of Truth"), how to gain the power to preach the gospel ("As a Flaming Fire"), being experts on the word being preached ("Knowing the Gospel"), the part of the universe that cannot be known by the ordinary physical senses ("The Unseen World"), overcoming hardship and discouragement ("White unto Harvest"), dealings with Church members ("Our Members"), training new missionaries ("The First Companion"), missionaries as a brotherhood ("Our Fraternity"), and issues to cope with on returning home ("Homeward Bound"). The young missionaries were the backbone of the operation of the Church in Europe. If they were properly trained, the entire mission would operate successfully.

LEADERSHIP AND RAPPORT

In a letter to Susa Young Gates, John's counselor, confidante, and mother-in-law, he described his challenge: "I think I am more concerned about the elders than about anything else. They are the means by which we have to work and do our work, and unless the tools are just right the workmanship is likely to be imperfect."[24] John sought to identify closely with the elders and wanted to help them find ways to be successful in their missions. While still presiding over the British Mission, he scheduled conferences in every district of the British Isles, having decided that he would postpone going to the Continent and working with the problems there until he had made significant progress in Britain.

John took advantage of the powerful effect a mission president could have through his example and personal contact. The missionaries appreciated his personal interest and extra efforts. David M. Kennedy, who was serving in the mission office as a district president when the Widtsoes arrived, recorded some of his experiences:

> I was there the day we put President Talmage on the train to go

to London to leave for home, and we accompanied him to the train. President Widtsoe was there. After President Talmage left he said, "Well now, brethren, what should we do? Should we go to a show or take the day off? The boss is gone, and I'm new here. You fellows have been here longer than I have. What should we do?" Well, we were all trained under President Talmage, so we all had to go back to work, we thought. He said, "Well, that's a good idea. Let's go back to work."

Other times he'd come in and say, "What are you doing, President Kennedy?" I'd say, "Well, I'm working on a letter or doing something here." He'd say, "How would you like to take a walk?" And I'd say, "Fine. That would be very interesting." So we'd go for a bit of a walk. We'd go down around through the park, and he'd look at the signs, and as we'd go he'd be talking about different things. . . .

Then I'd notice that the next week in his sermon President Widtsoe would use some of the things he'd observed on that walk that I hadn't even noticed. He had a mind for taking the little things that he saw and making a story or comparison out of them.[25]

John's example and support helped Kennedy in his mission and in later life. Kennedy ultimately achieved great private and public distinction. From 1930 to 1946 he worked for the Federal Reserve System; then he became chairman and chief executive officer of the Continental Illinois National Bank and Trust Company of Chicago. He served as U.S. secretary of the Treasury under President Richard Nixon and held the positions of ambassador-at-large and U.S. representative to NATO. President Spencer W. Kimball appointed him as a special representative of the First Presidency in gaining recognition in many nations still closed to the Church.

George Romney, also a district president under President Widtsoe, became one of the captains of industry, introducing compact cars as president of American Motors. From 1963 to 1969 he was the popular governor of Michigan. In 1967 he became a front-runner for the 1968 Republican presidential nomination. He was secretary of Housing and Urban Development from 1969 to 1973, also under President Nixon. When he was asked to select the most influential teacher in his life, he chose John A. Widtsoe. President Widtsoe had encouraged Romney and the other missionaries to find a better way and had counseled Romney to choose the career that led him to high positions.[26]

These are prominent but typical examples of the rapport John developed with his missionaries. He understood that many missionary problems were the result of their comparative youth and inexperience. To an impatient branch president who had spent a quarter of a century in the Church he wrote, "Mormon Elders are only human beings. They have the eternal truth to give to the world but they are probably under a greater temptation than any other man for that very reason. Besides, possessing eternal truth does not of itself put an old head on young shoulders, but you will admit after your twenty-five years experience in the Church that you have seen no other young man of the same age as competent, as capable, as attractive, as well behaved, as pure in their lives all in all, as the group of Latter-day Saint missionaries whom you have met."[27]

Not all of them were as qualified as John wished. Some lacked the character and discipline to live by the rules. Some were not as faithful to the Church or their calling as desired. Not all lived the commandments they were there to teach. After one woman made some false charges about mission assignments being a type of Church discipline, John wrote, "The servants of the Lord who are called in the mission field are called by inspiration and revelation. It is not true that sinful men are sent into the mission field that their mistakes may be forgotten at home or that men are sent into the mission field to be reformed. . . . We may justly say that there is no finer, cleaner body of young men and women in all the world."[28]

During that first year, the Widtsoes learned much about missionaries and mission work. Foremost was the rapport they established and the valuable lessons they taught. Kennedy, who would later create the agendas for general conferences, meticulously planned a time schedule: "When I presented the agenda to him [President Widtsoe], he said, 'Well, President Kennedy, that's a very, very good outline. You haven't missed anything that I can see. I wonder if you allowed any time for the Lord to give us any inspiration.' Oh, boy did he knock me, just with a little thing like that."[29]

Elder Arnold White gave a detailed account of life in the Widtsoe mission home. The house was always in good order, and every day the missionaries held a scripture study class: "So I studied with him, I ate with him, lived with him, traveled with him, preached with him, prayed with him, and labored with him generally in both family and Church affairs. I can honestly say that never during all of that intimate association did I see or experience one thing that I, as a rather critical and eager young man, would consider beneath the dignity of the office the man held."[30]

White recalled that President Widtsoe "dedicated himself to that new service. He pretty well divorced himself from personal affairs, from past private connections." John set the example and advised the missionaries, "Don't be here and your mind and spirit over there. This is where your labors are. Go to it."[31]

The missionaries responded with warmth. They also shared their feelings with parents, who occasionally wrote letters of appreciation. One father wrote, "It must be a great satisfaction to both you and Leah to be as father and mother to so many wonderful young men, and to have their unbound love, confidence and respect. From my own experience, I know that it will go with them through life."[32] Elder Talmage wrote that he had received many reports, "particularly by returning missionaries, of the masterly way in which you are conducting the affairs of the mission, and of the splendid work being done by Sister Widtsoe. We know that your success is of the kind that is called success by the Powers above."[33]

Members of a missionary class in the University Ward asked John about the value of missionary service. His response was that any young man who devotes himself to the work "will receive a most unexpected reward. He will grow in power, in spirit and in intellect. He will acquire an experience that he can use in his daily life, just as long as he lives wherever his work may be. He will be filled with memories that will comfort him throughout life. He will rejoice in the appreciative goodwill of hundreds. . . . Few things this world has to offer bring such rich a reward as missionary service."[34]

LIFELONG ASSOCIATIONS

John's interest in his missionaries went far beyond the confines of the mission field. He had a special attraction to men of high ambition who wanted to make the most of their lives and become pillars in the Church and community. When the Widtsoes arrived in Liverpool on Christmas Eve, 1927, they met Richard L. Evans, a young missionary serving as the assistant editor of the *Millennial Star*. An immediate bond developed between them. At President Widtsoe's request, Evans extended his mission time for many months. He became a secretary, companion, driver, and beloved friend. On the day he departed, Evans wrote, "This morning I parted company with the best man I have ever known. . . . Before we parted, he gave me the most wonderful blessing I have ever had. . . . We put our arms around each other and parted as father and son. . . . I hated to break the wonderful 1 1/2-year association—but it will be renewed."[35]

Evans was devoted to the Widtsoes. In a letter announcing his engagement, he wrote to Leah:

> Taking it all in all, she reminds me more of you than anyone I have ever known. I have told many people that knowing you had spoiled me for any other girl I ever knew.
>
> I love you, mother Widtsoe. I look forward to seeing you in the spring, I hope with all my heart that the associations with you and Dr. Widtsoe which I valued so very much will be renewed & perpetuated. I look forward to it much & think of you very often. I quote you both to Alice until she thinks that you're a pair of demi-gods—and I'm not so sure but that that's the case.[36]

When the Widtsoes returned to Salt Lake City, Evans became one of the family. They even gave him a key to their home since he dropped in so often. "Even after their passing he continued to carry that house key in his pocket until the day he died, as a symbol of what the Widtsoes had meant to him."[37] In a copy of *Evidences and Reconciliations* kept close at hand in Evans's office, John had inscribed, "To me this volume is another evidence of your goodness to me. No son could do more than you have done for me in our association together. This I appreciate beyond ordinary expression. I recognize your gifts, service to the world and to your people; and rejoice in the abundant share of your affections bestowed on me."

Another missionary who became very close was G. Homer Durham, a future son-in-law, university president, and member of the First Quorum of the Seventy. An interviewer asked David Kennedy, "I've heard Homer Durham say that John A. Widtsoe was a great man to encourage young men and that several people came out of that mission who were almost his protégés, such as Richard L. Evans and I guess Homer Durham himself. Did you have that feeling about him?" Kennedy related how Widtsoe would often ask the missionaries what their future plans were. In one instance, Widtsoe invited Kennedy into his quarters and talked specifically of where he would go to college and how he would support his wife. President Widtsoe offered to help set up Kennedy with a job while he was attending school. "He frequently asked about our family," Kennedy said. "He sent messages when our daughters were born. He also talked about school in Washington, how was I getting along, how did I like my studies, what was my principal interest, etc. This showed President Widtsoe's concern for people and their welfare."[38]

George Romney was considering medicine or law, but John advised him to go into business and economics, explaining that the principles in that field were less well known than in other areas. George wrote:

> I followed his advice. It has proven true. Inflation and economic problems remain unresolved because we haven't found—or haven't adopted—the needed answers.

> I continued to seek his advice after my mission, even though since then I have lived in the East. As long as he was alive, I dropped in to see him when I was in Salt Lake City. Even after he passed on, I would visit with Sister Widtsoe. She was a friendly, brilliant wonderful woman. I owe the basic direction of my life to President and Sister Widtsoe.[39]

The Widtsoes loved their missionaries as they did their own children and continued to welcome them throughout their lives.

33

TRAINING EUROPEAN MEMBERS IN CHURCH GOVERNANCE

IT had been customary for experienced American elders to operate European branches of the Church, but the branches needed to be ready to function on their own. The threat of a major war in Europe in the 1930s increased the need for ecclesiastical independence. Elder White, mission secretary for two years, recalled, "When I was with Brother Widtsoe, in his communications to the Presidency of the Church and the Twelve he would make quite frequent mention of the war clouds gathering over Europe. He was very emphatic in saying, 'It isn't a matter of *if*; it's more a matter of *when*. All of the elements are present for a conflagration.'"[1]

The supply of qualified leadership among local members was severely strained by emigration practices. John sought diligently to obey the counsel of the First Presidency by encouraging the Saints to remain in their homelands and by schooling them in Church leadership. "We are here to establish centers which will serve in the future work of the Church,"[2] he said. Missionaries filled leadership positions because most of the members were new and inexperienced in Church operations. As emigration declined, some resentment from experienced Church members arose toward temporary missionaries presiding over their branches.

John worked hard to train local members in effective branch and district operations.

To strengthen local leaders, John also sought to build up Church auxiliaries. He emphasized those auxiliaries in mission presidents' conferences, teaching that "their purpose was to meet the individual soul needs of the various members; to build up and strengthen their faith; and to give them diversion of spiritual activity; also holding youth and preparing . . . both old and young, to get the most out of this life and to prepare for a greater service, and in fact build life into eternal perfection."[3] He stressed that the gospel was not intended as book learning, rather, it was to become a part of their lives and actions, which included work and play. Proper recreation (dancing and the other needs of the youth) was part of the Church and their religious duty. During his second year in Europe, John wrote to Susa Young Gates, "So far, every mission, small and large, has been attempting to work out plans for itself . . . Now the same procedure, the same study course, the same general activities will be followed in all the missions and the whole group will attempt to follow, as near as possible, what is being done by the Church at home. I believe it is the only safe procedure, unless we want to repeat the experiences of early Christianity, and build up here a number of Churches which are departing, each one a little, from the organization and doctrine of the mother Church."[4]

A major impediment in getting the branches and districts in the European Mission in full step with the central stakes was the absence of properly prepared manuals. Because of the old practice of encouraging the Saints to gather to Zion, Salt Lake had not prepared manuals for foreign Church use. John found that each mission was going in separate directions, often in opposition to one another. Untrained leaders prepared study courses without uniform objectives.

John and Leah worked hard to provide each auxiliary with the appropriate literature in their language. Some missions produced mimeographed notes once or twice a month that included articles, sermons, brief editorials on news of the mission, and outlines for lessons. "It helps the Saints a great deal. . . . All together, it is a very satisfactory method of holding the Saints together and is somewhat cheaper for small circulations than printing would be."[5] The progress they were making in unifying the Church across Europe through the auxiliaries was encouraging. John reported to the First Presidency:

> The work for the priesthood and auxiliaries for the coming year was formulated . . . and many other important missionary problems received candid and helpful treatment. Possibilities for making our work more effective were set forth fully through the experience of those present.
>
> I begin to feel, now, that these missions, which have been separate, somewhat divergent entities, are coming together as parts of one organization. The strong will help the weak, and all will be benefitted. Careful guidance from the central office for a year or two will accomplish this. The European countries in which we are laboring are separated by artificial, political boundaries; the European point of view is about the same everywhere, and very distinct. Even the language barrier is minor in this day of the universal public press. A united front will help us internally and externally.[6]

Lengthy mission presidents' conferences had become annual events. They had previously been occasional and brief. John's view was, "It was . . . very profitable for this group of leaders and their wives to exchange views over a period of a week. It became a school for correct doctrine and practice. In the attempt to secure unity among the missions the annual mission presidents' conference became a very important factor."[7]

Leah presided over all women's auxiliaries for Europe as did each mission president's wife in her respective mission. They played an important part in strengthening and unifying the branches. In the 1928 mission presidents' conference, Leah led several sessions on the work of the Relief Society and its importance in caring for the women of the Church. She was insistent that the Relief Society sisters conduct their own meetings.[8] She instructed the leaders on the advancement of women and wrote many of the lessons and teaching materials. Elder White recalled her vigilant efforts to strengthen the women's auxiliaries: "Sister Widtsoe I think made a rather unique and great contribution to the sisters, particularly of Europe, in her Relief Society articles and communications in the matter of homemaking and diet and ways of improving their health and that type of thing. She was well trained in those matters and made her talents and understanding readily available to all the sisters of Europe through the Relief Society channels."[9]

John observed in Leah the great impact a mission president's wife could have. He reflected on her contributions and on each mission's need for more experienced and qualified women: "The need was felt for women missionaries from headquarters to lead out in Primary, Y.W.M.I.A., and Relief Society work. It is most unfair and unwise to expect the mission president's wife, in addition to running the large home establishment, to be president, two counselors, and secretary of the Relief Society, Y.W.M.I.A. and Primary of the entire mission. No woman can do it, no matter how capable she may be. And it seems unwise to expect the elders to be proficient in this essential work for the women of the missions."[10] John's requests were answered with the arrival of sisters Nettie Woodbury and Ileen Ann Waspe, whose exceptional work opened the door for more women missionaries in Europe.

As the years passed and local leadership matured, serious transition problems emerged. Disgruntled branch members who complained about the leadership of the American elders were often excommunicated or disfellowshipped. When these members appealed to President Widtsoe, he usually overruled the strict action of the young missionary leader, but the costs were great. Many missionaries ruled with an immature iron fist, convinced that the members were worldly and lacked discipline. John explained to President Grant:

> The inexperience of the missionaries leads them all to do foolish actions. . . . [The members] weary of being governed always by youths from a strange country, of frequent changes, of hearing the mother tongue murdered most awfully, of being disciplined by those who cannot catch the native point of view. . . . The branches are increasing in size, we would have it so, but that means a larger number of capable men calling for the reaction of active service. The saints are exceedingly patient, but the strain is often very hard to endure.
>
> I have labored persistently to teach these principles to the missionaries and mission presidents. Today, at least half of the branches in this group of missions are presided over by local brethren; and the

Priesthood and auxiliary activities are moving forward steadily, to help keep everybody busy in the Church. Three-fourths, or more of the branches should be governed locally, thus relieving our elders for proselytizing work and teaching members and investigators in classes or by the fireside. The missionaries are urged to act as advisors to local officers rather than to hold the offices. As representatives of the mission president, the missionaries are a part of the highest authority in the mission, and should act accordingly, without usurping the rise of Church experience normally belonging to local members.[11]

John's increasing sense of urgency regarding self-sufficiency was driven by signs of the coming war. He knew that the Church needed to be unified and established firmly in Europe.[12] He later wrote, "Some of the members were called to fill mission-wide positions and did so to the full satisfaction of all concerned. During World War II . . . one acting president, a local man, exclaimed in a letter, 'What would we have done if we had not been trained in self-government?'"[13]

John, who had authored Church manuals for more than thirty years, wrote, "For three years we labored at European headquarters to provide uniform lessons for all the missions so that they could all be 'in line.' My wife prepared the lessons for the Relief Societies and MIA and . . . wrote a European Beehive manual based on the one used at home. . . . Often it was found necessary to make adaptations to local European conditions."[14] White remembered that the European Mission office provided courses of study for the MIA, the Relief Society, and the priesthood, "all under the direction of Brother and Sister Widtsoe—I say Brother Widtsoe, with Sister Widtsoe being an able assistant."[15] John informed the First Presidency, "Equal efforts were made to utilize over here, as far as practicable, or wise, the study courses and plans used at home—that is to conform to our Church programs. In my own words, to which all agreed, 'We decided to join the Church.' . . . The people are responding well to the feeling that they are doing the work done elsewhere in the Church."[16]

As Church programs under local leadership progressed, John requested even greater organization in the auxiliaries, later noting, "Guides for general mission use were proposed and sent home. Such

help freed the missions in Europe and elsewhere from much unnecessary toil and for the work of proselytizing. It was also a great benefit to
the people generally for it made them feel that they were in reality an
integral part of the Church."[17]

By their fifth year, the Widtsoes' efforts in establishing self-
government across Europe were bearing fruit. Frequent lessons on tithing
and fast offerings as "the divinely provided means of revenue for the
Church," which depended "more upon the spiritual than upon the economic condition of the people," were of great help in a time of economic
depression. John reported to the First Presidency, "The future permanence of our work in Europe, or elsewhere, rests primarily upon the
development of the two principles of self-support and self-government. It
is a joy to report that at the beginning of 1933, three-fourths of the
branches or more were presided over successfully, by local members."[18]

Perhaps the clearest vision of John's efforts in training Church
members to be self-sufficient was given in the reports of the mission
presidents who served under him. It was a custom for returning mission
presidents to report in general conference. Each president saw Church
independence in Europe as a mark of the Widtsoes' achievements. In
April 1932, President Gideon N. Hulterstrom reported success in
Sweden: "President and Sister John A. Widtsoe . . . are doing a most
wonderful work. . . . I can state that more responsibility has been placed
upon the local brethren, and our auxiliary organizations are working;
they are active and they are doing a most splendid work."[19]

President Hyrum D. Jensen reported on Norway in October 1933,
touching on the conditions during the Depression: "While [the Depres-
sion] has deprived us of the missionaries from home, it has compelled
the Saints to be more faithful and more energetic in the work. . . . We
have all the organizations that you have here at home. While we
haven't them as perfectly organized, perhaps, as you have here, they are
working toward perfection."[20]

From the Netherlands President Frank I. Kooyman reported in
October 1934:

> The people at large there did not seem to be very much
> impressed with our teachings, not very much interested, so we started

to labor with our young people, to get them into uniform action with all the groups at home. . . . And by the way, what would our M. I. A. leaders say should they be over there and attend a meeting of our young people, an inspiring meeting, when the one in charge of the congregation might lean over and ask: "What would you suggest we sing?" They might say: "Let's sing 'Carry On.'" "Well, we haven't got it in our language." "'True to the Faith,' then." "We haven't got it." "'Put Your Shoulder to the Wheel.'" "Oh, no, we haven't got that translated yet, either." That was the condition. Then, if the Lord had blessed you, that you had, perhaps, a little ability to translate, you would try to put these songs into the other language. "Firm as the mountains around us"—what does the Hollander know about mountains? Not a thing. "And we hear the desert singing"—they have never seen a desert. So, of course, we have our difficulties, but still, with the help of the Lord, we have been able to translate these songs, and now the Saints are singing them.[21]

Holger M. Larsen reported success in Denmark in October 1934. He was impressed at the eagerness of the people to learn how to manage the small mission as the central stakes of the Church were managed. They were excited to learn how to take care of themselves, and they were one of the first missions to coordinate the auxiliaries and install local leaders.[22]

While the mission presidents hailed the work of the Widtsoes in Utah, European Saints expressed their appreciation at home. Arvilla Smith, a member of the Sheffield Branch in England, penned this poem:

Tribute to President Widtsoe

I've truly met a man of God,
Of uniform simplicity.
Whose mind, it is so versatile,
Whose soul is all humility.

Kindness reigneth o'er his heart,
Which in all truth is purity.
He finds no fault, nor judges man,
His friendship is sincerity.

He is a man, among all men,
His smiling face of kindness
Doth show his wondrous charm,
Truly a man of righteousness.

God's greatest love on him bestow,
Rich blessings on him pour.
God grant that I may ever live
To praise him ever more.

Examples of his glorious life
Are in demand for growing youth;
His greatest ideals to acquire,
To reverence and to honor truth.[23]

John reported to the First Presidency that self-governance was progressing so well that there was little danger of the Church in Europe ever slipping back into its previously fragmented state. "It gives me real joy to be able to make this report," he wrote. "It has been the desired goal for several years; and has involved me and my wife in more diplomacy and hard work than I would care to state."[24]

TRAINING THROUGH THE WRITTEN WORD

The *Millennial Star* was the official organ of the European mission and demanded much of President Widtsoe's time. It rallied considerable unity and provided much information for the Saints. John was the editor-in-chief and wrote valuable entries for nearly every issue. During his mission he published some three hundred editorials and almost sixty feature articles. In the summer of 1930 he wrote to President Grant, "The *Millennial Star*, which should, in my opinion, continue to be the voice, primarily, of the European mission office, demands some continuous attention, since the associate editors are young men drawn from the mission field."[25]

John's articles and editorials covered almost every subject related to the gospel. They were so popular that eighty of them were later published in a separate book titled after the first essay, *Man and the Dragon*, *and Other Essays by John A. Widtsoe.*²⁶ Mission statistics, notices of transfers and callings, reports of meetings, and regular articles on the history and doctrine of the Church filled the pages of the *Millennial Star.*

John constantly sought for better ways of presenting the restored gospel. Church tracts were well-known but largely ineffective. He reported to the First Presidency, "At the last conference, rather a heavy load was placed on the European office . . . the chief of which was leadership in the modification in our old tracts and the making of new ones to meet existing needs. Since the work devolves on me, the work goes on slowly."²⁷ To gather useful direction in his writing, he sent a "tract questionnaire" to all the European missionaries, nearly 800, "to discover what the field really needed or desired. The results obtained, I took three weeks off, and wrote a series of tracts, known as the Centennial Series, since they were produced in 1930, the Church centennial year."²⁸

The series consisted of twenty tracts that were sent in rough draft to four of the mission presidents with the request, "Please read them and have others read them, critically. Do not spare them. Rewrite them whenever necessary. You may wish to suggest other titles or subjects. Out of our united effort something good will come and that is what we are after. The work has been done amidst such pressure of work as I have seldom known."²⁹

The first tract, "About Myself," included a photograph of each missionary. Other tracts addressed the need of religion, church organization for the ordinary man, continuing revelation from a loving God, life's meaning and the guideposts to happiness, the first principles of salvation, the Book of Mormon, the Word of Wisdom, and women and marriage.

Responses in and out of the Church were positive. Francis W. Kirkham wrote, "I am thoroughly convinced . . . that the philosophy of life which you so marvelously set forth in these tracts is the only effective appeal that we can now make."³⁰ A *Deseret News* official favored putting the tracts in every home, for they "[have] the real, the perfect missionary spirit—the sweet spirit of giving others a taste of the joy we have."³¹

In addition to publishing the Centennial missionary tracts, the

Millennial Star, articles on the Word of Wisdom, and other manuals, John was continually writing. In his memoirs he noted:

> As conditions arose, other publications were produced to aid the elders. With the collaboration of Elder (now Dr.) F. S. Harris, Jr., a book called *Seven Claims of the Book of Mormon* was produced to help the missionaries . . . defend the Book of Mormon. Another booklet, *The Successful Missionary,* was addressed to the missionaries themselves. *Studies in Priesthood,* a tiny volume, proved very popular among the saints who had little knowledge in print of the meaning and functions of the priesthood. *What is Mormonism,* a very brief pamphlet, became very useful. "What Others Say," was a pamphlet in defense of "Mormon" living and so on.[32]

John and Leah worked on many publications together. John proofread *The Life Story of Brigham Young,* and they regularly consulted together on their Word of Wisdom lessons, though as he said in a letter to Susa, most of the credit for its accomplishment was due to Leah:

> Three years ago we published The Gospel and Health; then for two years Leah has written a magnificent series of Word of Wisdom lessons; at present we have in circulation a Word of Wisdom tract, first used at our Word of Wisdom Exhibit in the International Hygiene Exposition at Dresden, but are now being used by all the missions with very great success. It is a friend winning medium.
>
> Leah's lessons are bound together in one volume which has been sent to Sister Robison. Through her you can get access to the book. The pamphlet, The Gospel and Health, has long been out of print. We have constant demand for it from all the missions and from America. We have plenty of the Word of Wisdom tracts. I may have sent you some already, but I am sending you some by this mail.[33]

There were other requests for publications. *A Handbook for Quorums of the Melchizedek Priesthood* was under way when John left for Europe. A handwritten note accompanying his file copy explains that all but five pages were written by him. The year 1925 appears on the title page, but his note states that the book was published between 1928 and 1930. Another noteworthy book, *Success on Irrigation Projects,*[34] grew out of his summer-school lectures at the Utah Agricultural College and his work with the Fact Finders Commission and as a special advisor in reorganizing the Federal Bureau of Reclamation. Franklin S. Harris kept its publication alive, since John seemed to have set the project aside at least until after the mission. Harris wrote just after their departure, "I have been impressed with the desirability of publishing your book on irrigation. Now is the time, because it will be more in date now than after your return. Please do not let it drop, but let me help work out some method of handling it."[35] Harris arranged for its publication by prestigious firms in New York and London. After giving a complimentary copy to President Grant, John explained, "It only seemed that the experience in such matters that I have been fortunate in gathering should be placed, in part, at the disposal of the public."[36]

In February 1929 John sent a manuscript to the First Presidency with a note: "New and somewhat subtle problems of faith are arising among our people as a result of the changing educational conditions in this age of discovery and invention. The younger element need assistance in the solution of these problems. Particularly as regards the proper use of the vast accumulation of scientific facts and conjectures. That the leaders of youth, such as our seminary principals, need like direction was brought home to me some time ago when I was assigned to give a course of lectures to the seminary teachers. My correspondence is filled with requests for help in this field."[37]

This resulted in the immensely successful book *In Search of Truth*, which contains the lectures Widtsoe gave to BYU faculty and Church seminary teachers at the Aspen Grove Summer School in 1927, just before he left for Europe. A shortened version had been published in a YMMIA manual. Requests for a fuller version began coming almost as soon as the Widtsoes arrived in Europe. "Isn't it possible to get the lectures that you gave in Aspen Grove put into book form? You have no idea the interest all over the Church in regard to this matter. The brief lessons in the Senior Manual have been so popular that they are all out of print, and there is no apparent way of getting even one of these. They tell me in the Era office that they have scores of letters begging to get one of these manuals. I am going to see George A. about it,"[38] wrote Susa.

In a reply to a letter from T. Albert Hooper, manager of Deseret Book, John described the history behind its publication: "The manuscript, as you probably know, went to The First Presidency and received their approval; then went to the department of Education. . . . Since then I had heard nothing about it. You are at full liberty to publish the manuscript on such terms as you and your committee may fix. It was not written for profit. . . . I should want to turn the income over to the Genealogical Society."[39]

Reaction was immediate. One reader noted, "The Book of Mormon is the only book I have read which was more fascinating than 'In Search for [of] Truth.' The copy ordered sent to me came Monday evening and on Wednesday noon it was read. While meditating during the reading of it, I was wishing you would bring out certain facts pertaining to this Dispensation and found that my desires were realized. The chapter 'The Way to Truth' is worth memorizing. I shall reread the book within a week. Thursday after reading it I was in Logan Temple and before the services began, I was reflecting on many of the facts you set forth."[40]

It was so popular that the Brethren wanted to give it maximum exposure. T. Albert Hooper wrote to John, "I thought you would like to know that your book 'In Search of Truth' has been adopted and approved on the M.I.A. reading course for the year 1932–33 as the book for executives of Mutual's to read."[41]

President Heber J. Grant was the book's biggest fan. He wrote, "The chapter entitled 'The Theories of Men' fairly thrilled me. I could hardly leave your book alone . . . after I had started on it. I believe that it will do a world of good with young men who are inclined to accept anything and everything that men say who pass for scientific scholars."[42] President Grant wanted the book to be widely read and went to great efforts to ensure that it was: "I am pleased to tell you that I have ordered five hundred copies of Brother Widtsoe's splendid book, *In Search of Truth*, to send out during the holiday season."[43] President Grant even sent John fifty dollars as a token for the time put into the book. John felt he could not accept the money and sent it back. President Grant responded, "I didn't consider the fifty dollars I sent you really in the nature of a royalty. I just felt so grateful to you for having written a book like you did that I wanted to show my appreciation by sending a small check as a Christmas greeting. However, I will spend the money in sending copies of your book to all the seminary teachers in the Church. There are about a hundred of them, as I remember, and I will tell them that the book comes with the joint compliments of Brother Widtsoe and myself. I appreciate very much your using your talents in writing articles that are of great value to the youth of Zion."[44]

President Grant so liked the book that he read parts of it in general conference. He wrote to John, "I can assure you it was a real pleasure to me to read the selections from your book *In Search of Truth* at our General Conference, and I would be only too happy to have you send a message for the General Conference next October, in fact for every conference while you are away. It would be a pleasure to me to read anything you might send, and to have the saints have the pleasure of listening to your splendid writings."[45]

Other publications were also in demand. John's father-in-law wrote that many members were anxious to get John's lessons and pamphlets, "especially Dr. Joseph Merrill [Commissioner of Education] is very anxious to use them, so I understand, in the Church Schools. Will you send them quickly?"[46] The mission secretary recorded, "It was during the time that I was with them that the manuscript of the book *The Word of Wisdom* by the Widtsoes was prepared. So he was working in his spare time on two or three publications: *The Successful Missionary, The Word of Wisdom,* which I believe was largely Sister Widtsoe's publication, and I believe *Principles of Church Government,* which was published for the use of the priesthood of Europe. . . . I think out of that came a larger book that became generally used in all the quorums of the Church, *Priesthood and Church Government.*"[47]

John also wrote occasional articles for the *Improvement Era,* including some about the Church in Europe, the opening of the Czechoslovakia Mission, and the Word of Wisdom exhibit. He wrote two articles about the Church's genealogical work in Europe for the *Utah Genealogical and Historical Magazine.*[48] George Albert Smith asked him to rework *A Rational Theology* for use as the course of study for the MIA during 1932, the year that *In Search of Truth* was being used as the guide for leaders of that group.[49] He occasionally composed lyrics, writing to one translator, "[I] find that you have taken the trouble to translate one of my Gospel Hymns into German. Of course, I am pleased that you have taken this trouble and thank you for it."[50] The amount of writing John did while at the same time fulfilling an active and successful mission is astonishing.

34

AN INTERLUDE IN UTAH

THE traditional term of service for a European mission president was three years, and 1930 was the Widtsoe's third year. As the months passed, they began to wonder about the future. John expressed his feelings to President Grant: "It has been a joyous privilege. It has done a great deal for me and Leah, personally. I felt, at the time the call came, that life held very little more for me; new courage has come these last two years. I feel that I am coming back; and to Leah the work has been a real salvation."[1] When asked about his plans, he replied, "I have made it a rule, I hope not unwisely, not to suggest what I may do. I trust the inspiration of the brethren. . . . I have given my life for one great cause and it matters little how those that preside over me decide to have me spend the energy, power or gifts that I may possess."[2] President Grant felt strongly that the Widtsoes should remain in their assignment for another term. John's journal entry for 24 October 1930 simply reads, "Received letter advising us of extension of our mission!!"[3] He replied to the call:

> I thank you very sincerely for your good letter of October 14th. It is always an inspiration to hear from you. No bridges were left unburned when the call came to devote my whole time and strength

to the affairs of the Church. I am ready to do my best wherever I may be placed. Your wishes are law to me. Certainly my wife and I will be pleased and very happy to remain here just as long as you desire.

We were very glad to receive your letter, for, expecting that history might repeat itself, some things were held in advance, and others were being hurried along, in preparation for a possible early release. Now, we can tackle the waiting work with greater freedom. I only regret that we have accomplished so little these last few years, but every day has been crowded. I have never worked harder.[4]

Happy to be where the Brethren wanted him, John wrote to Elder Melvin J. Ballard, "Whenever the Brethren are ready I know they will release us. Meanwhile we are enjoying the work greatly. It is good to be busy here with these very important problems that present themselves daily. We are in good health, due primarily to the blessings of the Lord and our attempt to obey carefully the laws of health. I feel daily that the Lord is guiding the work. It takes much worry from my mind."[5] Though he noted that they could make a partial holiday of the extended term, he told President Grant, "The problems that lie before us and the new opportunities that are developing, are such that no honest man, believing thoroughly in the purpose of the Church, can feel at ease unless he is at the work with all his might. I confess that I have made labor for myself; but, even so, I feel that I have accomplished only a trifle of that which has been within my grasp. This is my chief regret."[6]

John and Leah worried most about Eudora's social development and education. They decided it would be best for her to return home to live under the watchful eyes of her sister Anna and Grandma Susa: "We felt that in fairness to her time of life she should mingle with her own people. Since her twelfth year she had been away from home with us, and our many peregrinations. Her schooling had suffered, and her friends were drifting to those near home, then being away from us might help develop her independence."[7] As soon as Eudora returned, Anna and Lewis decided to remarry. They moved to Ogden and left Eudora alone with her grandmother.

John wrote to U of U President George Thomas, "I am writing . . . frankly to ask you to keep a corner of your eye open for the little girl.

She is not timid, but a little modest, and I realize that she is going to have some difficulty before she is finally fully adjusted to the place and the people from which she had been absent so long."[8] Susa reported, "Eudora feels better, dear child she is lonely often times but all of us are doing what we can to make life easier for her. School starts next week and she will feel better, I am sure. These lessons are good for her as they are for me and her mother. I am happy to find many traits in her like her beautiful and noble mother. We have all fallen in love with her."[9]

Soon after they decided to extend the Widtsoes' appointment, the First Presidency invited them to return to Salt Lake City to attend April 1931 general conference, to look after personal and family matters, and to enjoy a break from their labors.[10] John wrote to Susa, "Going home means a lot of extra work and we are immersed in it. It looks now [as] if we shall reach New York about March tenth, and Salt Lake City about the seventeenth."[11] They were in Utah for about two months, during which time they strengthened family relationships, attended countless gatherings, and often gave addresses on the Church in Europe. The break provided only part of the relaxation they needed before they embarked on three more years overseas.

Because of John's prominence, he was a favorite target of anti-Mormons. On 1 April 1931, he recorded in his journal, "Called into Presidency's Office about charge in 'New Era' that I have a plural, deserted wife." Meetings and discussions about a libel suit followed, but no action was taken. President Grant made reference to the attack at conference and presented an "Official Statement" from the First Presidency repudiating the practice of plural marriage in the Church. In introducing the statement, he said of John:

> In most instances the misrepresentations and false accusations have been made by way of recital and innuendo, with an apparent effort to shield the authors and publishers from legal responsibility. In one recent instance, however, they have been bold enough to print a libelous attack on President John A. Widtsoe, supposedly because they knew of his expected presence here for conference. The circumstances recited are wholly fictitious and false, and are presented, undoubtedly, with the purpose of creating prejudice against him and

injuring his work in Europe. We think that the high esteem in which Doctor Widtsoe is held, not only in the Church but in his State and as a national figure, makes unnecessary any reply to such calumny. However, if he desires he may have the facilities we can afford to protect himself and to prosecute the defamers of his good name. [12]

After a three-year separation, the saints in Utah were anxious to hear from Elder Widtsoe. He included a special greeting from the missionaries and the Saints in Europe in his address about their work:

I rejoice this day that the spirit which I have felt in these gatherings yesterday and today is quite the same spirit as that which I have felt in the small gatherings in the various European countries. The Latter-day Saints who live the Gospel of Jesus Christ speak and hear by the same spirit. . . .

I bring you in particular greetings from the membership of the Church in the European lands, a body of faithful men and women, loving the Gospel just as we love it here. . . . They live in the outposts of Zion, but they are ready and willing to labor there, and to help maintain and retain those outposts. . . .

Opposition and oppression have very largely vanished from our work in the European lands. A new day has dawned, and it seems to us, who labor there, that if the Lord will only bless our efforts it may be possible, in the near future, to bring a convincing message of the truth of this work to the hearts of thousands in those lands who are honest in heart.

We have many difficulties; there is no question about that; there are difficulties on every hand; the greatest difficulty, perhaps, that we have to contend with is the spiritual or religious indifference of the present day. It is an indifference which seems to cover the earth everywhere. It takes the form of a resentment or revulsion against organized religion—not so much a contempt for religion itself, for the principles of it, but rather a contempt or near-contempt for the organized forms of religion, for the churches themselves. . . .

I believe that the spiritual resentment in the world today has resulted from the idolatry which still lingers upon the earth, the attempt to force men to worship a God that is man-made, an incomprehensible God, an essence, one who is so far from us in understanding that men cannot bow down before him as they should, and pray to him as a child should pray to his father. . . .

In the mission field, whether in Europe or elsewhere, it is the greatest message that the Church has to give to the world today—the true definition and the true conception of God our Father, the maker of the heavens and the earth. . . . I rejoice in the glorious first vision given to the Prophet Joseph Smith, the greatest of the visions and teachings of these latter days. . . .

We have the authority of the priesthood. We are teachers to all the world. As we magnify our commission and rise to the full possibilities of world teachers, we shall be blessed and made powerful. Joy will fill our hearts; power will come to our hands, and the things that need to be done we shall be able to do. So run my thoughts as I consider the work that has been done in European lands during the last few years.[13]

In connection with general conference, there was a convention of the Genealogical Society. John addressed them about genealogical work among the Saints in Europe. He reported that he was disappointed that research and temple work through the Exchange Bureau had developed so slowly. He urged patience and a greater effort to make it successful. Earlier John had also made a poignant appeal for a European temple: "The ordinances distinctly of earth . . . must be received by every soul desirous of eternal advancement. Those who have died without complying with the ordinances of earth must receive them through living proxies; and they become valid and operative when accepted by those in the spirit world."[14]

Without a temple, the only way European Saints could fulfill their responsibility to the dead was by gathering information for relatives living near the temples in America to do the work. On Monday, 18 May, Leah's sister, Emma Lucy Gates Bowen, gave a farewell party for the Widtsoes. The Bowens had handled their finances and overseen the care of their daughters, Petroline, and their house. The Widtsoes were very grateful to them.

The trip back to Utah had been profitable but strenuous. Just before his return to Europe, John wrote, "I think I have never known a busier time than that which has punctuated the last two months. I expected a time of rest and peace instead it has been one of strenuous endeavor."[15] He reported to the First Presidency, "During the year 1931, we lost three months of active labor on this side of the ocean, by a pleasant trip to 'Zion.' It was most enjoyable, and again we express our appreciation for the opportunity. Yet the time there was most profitably spent even from the point of view from the work here, for many things were done and finished that would have dragged along for months or years by correspondence."[16]

There was much to be done on their return: meetings to be scheduled; lessons, articles, and editorials to be written; talks to be prepared; conferences to be arranged; and final details for the Copenhagen chapel dedication to be coordinated. John wrote to Joseph Quinney, Jr.:

> After reaching England we were in the office a little less than a week when we left for Copenhagen where a fine new church was dedicated amidst much celebration. Then followed the annual meeting of the mission presidents which generally lasts about ten days, but this time nearly two weeks. After that President Larsen and I took a trip through the Danish Mission, visiting all the districts. When that was finished my wife and I went to Norway, making a round trip, again visiting the districts and branches. We came home a few days ago, and are now immersed in office work necessary for the opening of the auxiliary year.[17]

Things were not going as well in Utah. Lewis and Anna divorced again, and Eudora was unhappy without her parents. Susa worked at filling the gap but seemed relieved when Eudora decided to return to Europe. Susa wrote, "Eudora will be with you, I suppose shortly, and I am glad that you will look after her diet, for I think that is half of her trouble. Late nights, for she is popular and beautiful, and naturally loves pleasures and excitement. So, I will be glad to have you look after her yourself."[18] Eudora returned to England that autumn and enrolled at the University of Liverpool.

In Europe John felt isolated from the day-to-day business of the Church. He sent reports to the First Presidency and often corresponded with his brethren, but he hungered for their companionship. He wrote to Susa, "I am missing here, as much as anything, the opportunity of intimate contact with the movements within the Church." These feelings were echoed in a letter to James E. Talmage: "I think that I miss, perhaps more than anything else, the association of mature men, for in dealing with our young elders, splendid and wonderful as they are, it is almost entirely a process of giving and giving advice and suggestion, direction and encouragement, and of receiving no similar sustaining words in return."[19]

Isolation, not having "intimate contact with the movements within the Church," caused John much personal grief during a conflict between the two members of the Twelve with whom he was most closely associated. Because of the real affection John had for these two men, and the window it opens into the lives of general authorities, this incident is covered here in some detail. For almost thirty years John had worked closely with Joseph Fielding Smith in the Utah Genealogical Society. Leah had also shared a close friendship with Sister Ethel Smith. John wrote to Susa, "I love Joseph Fielding Smith. I think I understand his power, and I am always eager to point out his great possibilities of service. It is often difficult for one in his position to find the opportunity for proper self-expression. Sometimes it is easier for one lower down in the ranks. But the Lord is with him to magnify him in his work and his future is secure."[20]

Some of Elder Smith's regard for John is seen in a story related by Susa about a conversation she had with him about men who had been recommended for the post of assistant Church historian. Elder Smith was then the Church historian. Susa wrote, "I asked him if you [Widtsoe] had been proposed. 'My gracious, no,' he answered. 'I am expecting they will put him in my place when he gets home. They ought to; he deserves it.'"[21]

James E. Talmage was to John a model and a mentor in science, in religious discipleship, in faithful writing, and in university leadership. Their friendship had extended over almost forty years, beginning when Talmage asked John to be his personal assistant following graduation from Harvard. More recently, they had shared the love, the work, and the joy of Church developments in Europe. Letters of appreciation and friendship flowing between the Widtsoes and the Talmages appear in the Widtsoe papers in about the same frequency as do those between the Widtsoes and the Smiths.

In 1929 Elder Smith gave an address to the Genealogical Society of Utah that was published in the October issue of the *Utah Genealogical and Historical Magazine* and separately as a pamphlet. Part of the published address caused some concern, and the First Presidency thought it prudent to issue a response in April 1931:

> The statement made by Elder Smith that the existence of pre-Adamites is not a doctrine of the Church is true. It is just as true that the statement: 'There were not pre-Adamites upon the earth,' is not a doctrine of the Church. Neither side of the controversy has been accepted as a doctrine at all.
>
> Upon the fundamental doctrines of the Church we are all agreed. Our mission is to bear the message of the restored gospel to the people of the world. Leave Geology, Biology, Archaeology, and Anthropology, no one of which has to do with the salvation of the souls of mankind, to scientific research, while we magnify our callings in the realm of the Church.[22]

John was almost unaware of an earlier issue involving Elder Smith and Elder B. H. Roberts prior to his return to Utah in 1931. Mention is made of it in a 2 January 1931 letter from Susa.[23] It is clear from her comment that on the Smith/Roberts issue, the family sided with Smith. The only hints of a doctrinal controversy the Twelve were reviewing appear in two journal entries during the Widtsoes' ten weeks in Salt Lake City. 26 March 1931: "3–5 P.M. reading controversial papers abt. J. Fielding Smith's sermon."[24] 7 April 1931: "9 A.M. long meeting of General authorities: Pre-Adamites, life & death before Adam; free Masonry; direction of the Seventy; function of High Councils, etc."[25] A seven-page letter of the First Presidency, dated two days earlier, appears to have been the center of discussion.

On 9 August 1931, nearly three months after the Widtsoes returned to Europe, Elder Talmage gave an address titled "The Earth and Man" in a Sunday afternoon service conducted by President Anthony W. Ivins. Elder Joseph Fielding Smith gave the opening prayer. In it

Talmage gave his view of some of the things that had been at issue in Elder Smith's address.

Most of the information about John's involvement in the conflict is contained in letters between Susa and John. In August Susa wrote, "The trouble is still concerning the controversy of who was the first flesh on the earth, etc., etc., between Joseph [Fielding Smith] and James [E. Talmage]. James preached a very subtle sermon containing his views, two Sundays ago, and it is not certain but that it will be published or not. I wish they would let the mysteries alone. Who cares about the mysteries anyway?"[26] Unfortunately, Susa's letter arrived after John had unwittingly been pulled into the debate.

Two days before Susa wrote her letter, Talmage sent John a copy of his address and a letter of explanation. He wrote that many requests had been made for a copy of the address, including one for a thousand copies from Elder Joseph F. Merrill for the seminary teachers of the Church. Aware of the controversy caused by the publication of Smith's address, Talmage wrote, "On my own initiative I halted the printers, and awaited the return of President Grant, to whom I submitted a copy . . . with the request that the First Presidency consider it carefully before it went into print." That day, 27 August, the Presidency referred the matter to the Twelve to be resolved in their meeting on 29 September. Talmage continued, "In view of the fact that I send you the copy in accordance with the suggestion adopted by the Council, it may be well for you to address your reply to President Rudger Clawson."[27]

The letter was sent by airmail to the coast, in the hope that an immediate reply from John would arrive before the 29 September meeting. The letter had to be forwarded from Liverpool to London, where John was conducting mission business. The instructions were, "Write as soon as you can stating as to whether you approve the address, or think it should be modified in any particular, and what changes or modifications should be made, if any."[28] His response was immediate, dated only thirteen days after Elder Talmage's. Addressing President Clawson, John wrote, "I have read Brother Talmage's address twice and with care. The subjects therein treated, delicately yet forcefully, are of high importance to our youth who in the midst of modern-day knowledge are seeking to anchor their faith. . . . I am pleased indeed that the address was delivered publicly and hope that it may soon be published. . . . I am equally happy that the address calls attention to the nature of scientific inference. The confusion of facts and inferences lies at the bottom of many of the differences among mankind."[29]

That response, sent on 9 September, was well on its way to Salt Lake City before Susa's letter was received. John was not aware of the depth of the personal feelings of elders Smith and Talmage on the issue. He merely responded to the instructions sent to him. Deciding that the address did not clash with his understanding of the gospel and that the issues in it needed to be addressed, John did not disagree with or alter any of the theses.[30]

A week later, after John had had more time to contemplate the matter, he wrote to Joseph Fielding Smith, addressing him as "My dear Friend and Brother." John separated himself from the earlier controversy in recognizing that it had been settled by the action of the First Presidency. He then expressed his assurance that they both agreed that the "subjects raised in Brother Talmage's sermon . . . are of very great importance to our people living in this day." He added, "I have always admired you in your fearlessness in defending your point of view as well as for your apparent willingness to modify your views as new light comes to us." John was obviously concerned about Elder Smith's reaction to the letter John had sent to President Clawson: "I am writing this letter merely for fear of a possible misunderstanding of my attitude with respect to yourself. I am no lover of controversies. I think, usually they lead nowhere. The occasion that led to the writing of my letter was the invitation to make a statement of personal views."[31]

John's letter did not have the conciliatory effect he hoped for. It probably arrived after his endorsements had been reported to the Twelve. On 10 October Susa wrote to John, "Joseph feels humiliated because of your letter to James [to President Clawson, no intervening letters to Talmage have been found] but I tell him that you did not understand the situation at all. I am sure you are with Joseph as we are, first, last, and all the time."[32] Susa's letter also had to be forwarded to

John, who was traveling on the continent. His response makes clear that he hoped his explanation would alleviate the controversy:

> I was keenly distressed to read in your letter, that Joseph Fielding felt humiliated because of my letter to the Council of Twelve. I love him very sincerely, and trust him, and value him as a safe defender of the Gospel. He is very nearly the last man on earth whose feelings I should want to wound. I would rather be wounded myself. The service he is rendering is one now sorely needed by the Church. My only suggestions to him in person have been intended to be constructive, and to help direct his power into even greater effectiveness. My last ten days have been depressed ones, by the thought that by some mischance, he has misunderstood my motives.
>
> I was asked to express my views on Brother Talmage's sermon, not yet published, I think, and which seemed a good treatment of the subject, though very incomplete. It did not occur to me, that there was anything personal about it, or that personalities were involved in it. It may be that my own temperament resents so deeply the thought of allowing personalities to intrude themselves into a search for truth, especially in so sacred a place and among such persons. Perhaps I am too "innocent" about such matters. If so, let it be so continued. I have no inclination nor time for such personal controversies.
>
> As I read Brother Talmage's sermon, it dealt with only two themes: 1. Did the creation of the earth occupy long periods of time, running far beyond the traditional periods of 1000 years each; and, 2. Was Adam the last of the creations, as intimated in the first chapter of Genesis?
>
> Both of these questions, as I understand them, may be answered affirmatively—with the authority of ancient and modern prophets, and of every-day observation. I have been afflicted with these questions for a generation of time. It does seem high time that the Church answer them definitely or declare that it does not know; so that more important questions may engage the minds of young and old. I gave my opinion frankly, in my letter to the Twelve—as I was expected to do—and assumed, really, I was only speaking the mind of all.
>
> It did not occur to me, until after I had mailed the letter that it even remotely touched the Roberts-Smith controversy of some months ago. I suppose the spirit whispered to me, for I wrote my dear

brother and colleague a note in which I asked him not to consider my letter as bearing at all on the controversy of last spring. Even then, that seemed a useless precaution.

I am frankly at a loss to know, just how my letter humiliated my brother and friend. I did not intend to do so. Both you and he know that. So, may I be forgiven?

Please read this letter to Joseph if you desire.[33]

When Susa received the letter, she took it to everyone familiar with the issue. She wrote to John:

I wish I could tell you how deeply moved I have been in reading this letter which has just come on this morning's mail. I have taken it . . . into Joseph Fielding. While he read it, he was certainly touched with the lovely spirit of your letter. He told me many things about the whole situation. . . .

He admits that no one knows just how long the earth may have been in its creative state, nor do we know just when it began to be measured to Adam. I suggested that Adam of course was the first divine flesh on the earth, at least, as he helped create it according to the Pearl of Great Price. Then he says that death did not come into the world until after the fall, but just how long the fall was after creation and just how long Adam and Eve lived after the fall, he made no dates in our restrictions. He is certainly a wonderful scholar. He can turn to any passage and he is studying deeply and educating himself profoundly in the spiritual things of the kingdom.

You know how much he thinks of you and how anxious he is for your fellowship and support. I am glad he feels this way for it comforts me immensely. He says that he will write you at a great length just as soon as he can get a moment, as he wants you to understand his position in regard to the whole situation.[34]

It is evident from Susa's letter that Elder Smith felt certain that Elder Talmage wished to present a public rebuke of his teachings and that it had been so discussed in meetings of the Twelve. Elder Talmage admitted to John that his address was in direct contradiction to the *Genealogical Magazine* article in a letter telling him that after two days of lengthy deliberations, the First Presidency recommended that his address be published.[35] Elder Smith wrote to John, "I care little for the fact that it was delivered purposely to chastise me. I'm trying to say and do nothing which will offend, so I try to hue closely to the conventional lines where no dispute can arise. Even this I find to be rather a difficult thing to do. I wish I could sit down with you and talk some things over."[36]

It was not easy to be away from the Brethren for so many years, and John felt keenly the distance and responsibility of this isolation. As always, though, the work was his primary focus.

35

MISSION ACTIVITIES
IN A SECOND TERM

———————— ■ ————————

John and Leah Widtsoe returned to Europe in time for the dedication of a new chapel in Copenhagen, Denmark. This chapel was the finest the Church had built in Europe, and the historic celebration was held 14–16 June 1931. Latter-day Saints from neighboring countries gathered to Copenhagen for the dedication. There were three dedicatory meetings on Sunday. The *Improvement Era* reported, "Three inspiring meetings were held where all mission presidents and wives had the opportunity of expounding gospel truths. Each of the three sessions was largely attended and the outpouring of the Spirit of God was manifest. President John A. Widtsoe offered the dedicatory prayer and was the main speaker at the services. President Widtsoe spoke the Norwegian tongue with ease and power, using a forceful and convincing language."[1] A grand concert on Monday featured the largest LDS choir in Scandinavian history, and the MIA sponsored contests and competitive social activities on Tuesday.

President Widtsoe convened a two-week mission presidents' conference after the dedication with the theme of standardizing Church work and improving proselytizing activities. Following the conference, John toured the Danish mission with President Holger M. Larsen. Other

The new Copenhagen Chapel dedicated by President Widtsoe in services held June 14–16, 1931. On March 17, 1999, it was announced that this chapel would be renovated into the Copenhagen Denmark Temple. Construction began on April 24, 1999.

Scandinavian mission tours followed. One of John's goals was to bring the work of the European missions into harmony with worldwide Church programs. "It has taken some time to accomplish this," he wrote, "but I am very happy that it has been reached."[2]

In November John received word that the First Presidency had acted on his recommendation by commissioning Janne M. Sjodahl and Hugo Peterson to prepare a new Swedish translation of the Book of Mormon.[3] They also acted on another of his recommendations. Elder White recalled, "President Widtsoe sensed a need for the visit of a patriarch to Europe. The first to come that I recall was Brother James H. Wallis. He was vigorous and he and his wife came together, the parents of fifteen children.

"They had quite an impact on the Saints. I don't recall that they did as much on the Continent as they did in England. He traveled all over the British Mission giving patriarchal blessings. He gave hundreds of them upon recommend."[4]

John was delighted and thanked the First Presidency: "As a major advance, due to your action, I may mention the presence of a patriarch

European mission presidents and their wives attending the annual mission presidents conference in association with the chapel dedication at Copenhagen, Denmark, in June 1931. Leah is on the left in the back row; John is second from the left in the front row.

in Great Britain. Spiritual power has been developed among the Saints, through the gift of the patriarchal blessing. Brother Wallis has the spirit of his calling; and is an unusually capable and discrete patriarch. He will require two or more years to meet the demands upon him in the British Mission alone. The other missions need the same blessings."[5]

The individual mission tours taught John much about the problems of proselytizing and the feelings and needs of Church members. He wrote to Susa, "I am on the continent, alone, visiting the missions. We are having some most wonderful conferences. It is always a joy to meet the devoted missionaries and the faithful Saints. The members, now deprived of the old hope of emigrating to 'Zion,' need new encouragement and support. My heart goes out to them."[6] His desire was "to advance the spiritual condition of the missionaries and members; to organize more completely and in harmony with Church practice, the priesthood and auxiliary organizations; . . . to advance the practice of self-government among the saints; to teach the saints the necessity of self support; to make our missionary work more effective; to secure more publicity; etc."[7]

In January 1932 two broad objectives filled John's time. Naturally, his primary focus was proselytizing. Every attempt would continue to be made "to increase the efficiency of the mission of the labors of the missionaries." His second broad objective grew out of the need for improved missionary efficiency. Liverpool had been the headquarters of the British and European operations for almost a century, but it was not an efficient location. John wrote, "[A] major concern will be the moving to London, and completing the organization for efficient supervision of and assistance to the missions. I've seldom known anything so difficult of accomplishment as moving to London. . . . We must be in London as a matter of strategy if nothing else."[8]

In January 1932 the First Presidency called James H. Douglas to take over the leadership of the British Mission; it was thought that the arrival of the Douglases would be an auspicious time to make the move. In Liverpool the activities of the British and European missions, along with the operations of the *Millennial Star,* were closely linked. The move to London offered a chance to make strategic and monetary improvements. John later wrote, "In many of the missions, large homes, approaching small hotels, were and are maintained. This is not really fair to the missionaries who are chosen from all the group to live in comfort with the mission president's family, while other missionaries must seek often uncomfortable quarters. Nor is it fair to the mission president's wife, who often, with inefficient or no outside help, has to run a small hotel. With the scarcity of help, the missionaries are often expected to help with the cleaning and house-work of the large mansion."[9]

Missionary traffic for years used steamships from Montreal, the Canadian line, which docked in Liverpool. Hence, at the time, all missionaries bound for Europe entered Britain via Liverpool. In 1928 the Church changed to the U.S. Lines for its European missionaries. Thereafter, all missionaries docked in Southampton or Plymouth, and the Liverpool-based European mission president seldom met any of the new missionaries.

Durham House in Liverpool, Church headquarters for many years, was undoubtedly planned for a family of considerable wealth. It was commodious but generally uncomfortable. When the Church took it over, a heating system was installed and two of the rooms were converted into a meeting room for the Liverpool Branch. Each president, however, spent as little money as possible, and repair bills mounted. John commented:

> In London we secured a very comfortable home for office purposes at 5 Gordon Square, just back of the British museum. An apartment for ourselves was obtained at 23 DeVere Gardens in the delightful Kensington part of the town. That became a gathering place on Saturday evenings for all missionaries near-by or passing through London. There also people of influence, not of our faith, came for a visit or dinner. We had the opportunity especially to advise people who were writing books about us. Life in London gave many opportunities for gospel proselyting. The office staff found quarters with private families where the gospel could be taught. A short block or two away from the European office the British Mission, which had found London the natural home for the office work, had secured a suitable office space for the President and his wife who lived in a comfortable apartment.[10]

The Douglases were anxious to preside over British Mission activities, and the ordeal of moving headquarters was an aggravation. The notion of running a small hotel as their home and headquarters in Birmingham or London was less appealing to them than to the Widtsoes, as John remarked to the First Presidency:

> Brother and Sister Douglas, though ever so willing, and they are lovely people, looked with nervous distress, I was about to say terror, upon being placed in an unwholesome house, as told them by the former residents, and upon the responsibility of managing a large household. In fact, it could not have been done. Brother Douglas said that he would rather pay the difference in cost, than to have to live there; though he would comply with anything required of him. Moreover, extensive and thorough repairs and renovations were needed after three years occupancy of the old house.
>
> Quick action had to be taken. I felt that had you been on the ground you would have done as I did. If they, Douglas's had been young people, I probably should have advised delay until after an

exchange of mails with you. In consultation with Brother Douglas it
was decided to rent three small rooms for office purposes, and place
Brother and Sister Douglas in an apartment, and to move to London,
where, normally, for efficiency reasons, the office should be. The
actual selection of the rooms and living quarters were made by
Brother Douglas himself.[11]

After the move to London, Eudora enrolled in the University of
London. When the dust had settled and the reorganization of the central office and operating staff was complete, John toured some of the
missions on the continent. This tour lasted more than four months.
One of the more noteworthy visits was to the Czechoslovakian Mission.
In connection with this visit, he held a mission presidents' conference
from 5–15 July. Elder White reported:

> During the summer of 1932—as I remember, in early June—there
> had been appointed in Prague, Czechoslovakia a mission presidents'
> conference involving all the mission presidents in Europe and their
> wives. Elder Clifford L. Ashton, who was a co-laborer of mine in the
> European Mission office, left with the Widtsoe family to do some vis-
> iting in the missions en route to the conference. Then a little later I
> left to be at the conference to record the doings of the conference.
> President Arthur Gaeth, who at that time was president of the Czech
> Mission, was hosting the group. As I recall, we met for about ten days
> in one of the hotels in Prague and went over matters vital to the inter-
> est of the missions, hearing the reports of the various presidents and
> getting general instructions and solutions to problems that would
> come up in a meeting of that type from the presiding officer, Elder
> Widtsoe.
>
> While we were there we were also taken to a place outside of
> Prague. As my memory serves, it was Karlstein Castle. On a hill, not
> far from Karlstein Castle, a meeting was appointed—a rather infor-
> mal one, but it was appointed. I don't now remember whether it
> included all of the presidents and their wives that had attended the
> conference, but I do remember specifically it included the Gaeths, the
> Widtsoes, and I as their secretary. The other members present I can't
> fully say.
>
> I believe at that time I recorded in shorthand the statements

made by Brother Widtsoe at this meeting on the hillside. As my memory serves me, those notes will reveal that he indicated that there could very well be a temple erected at some time on that spot of earth. Now granted it may, at this point, be a remote thing because of circumstances putting it otherwise, but that has come into my mind on several occasions.[12]

After the conference, the Widtsoes and their traveling companions went to the German-Austrian Mission, headquartered in Berlin. Elder White continued:

> We happened to be in Berlin visiting the German-Austrian Mission, which was presided over at that time I think by Dr. Oscar Budge of Logan. We were visiting the mission home in Berlin, where I think we spent two or three weeks.
>
> It happened to be just the time that there was a political election being held. General Von Hindenberg was president of the German Republic, an aged man in his middle eighties as I recall. But Hitler at that time, during this election, became the Chancellor of the Reichstag. His "Brown Shirts" were walking down the street saying, "Heil, Hitler! Heil Hitler!" It just happened to be an unusual time to be in Berlin during the election that brought Hitler to power. Within a few months of that time, Von Hindenberg died, whether of a natural death or otherwise, and Hitler assumed the dictatorship of Germany.[13]

John purchased a car at his own expense so he could travel through the countryside and get a better feel for the conditions of the people and ideas on how the Church and the missions could best perform their responsibility to the world. He reported on his experiences in Italy:

> Traveling as we did by auto we had an unusual opportunity to witness conditions from the inside. One day we drove from Genoa to Florence, via Pisa. The road took us through perhaps forty villages. It happened to be a great Catholic holiday, God's day, whatever that may mean. In every village the priests had gathered the people into processions lasting all day, Monks, nuns, priests, intending priests, people and the canopied hosts, before which the people knelt upon the ground. When darkness fell the celebrations continued, under the light of candles over the doors and in the windows—by that time

people and priests seemed a little unsteady upon their legs, for there is alcohol in Italian wine. . . .

In South Italy in the Province of Palermo, Mr Vincenzo di Francesca, an educated, fiery character, has, as you know, been preaching from the Book of Mormon for the last two years. More than a year ago, he was excommunicated from the Methodist Church, in which he served as minister, for his Mormon teachings. He has asked repeatedly for baptism, but I have been impressed to put him off for a little longer. He has a group of people to whom he has been teaching Mormonism as he understands it. I did not have time to go into the situation thoroughly, though it should be done soon.[14]

Besides surveying Italy, John considered other countries that might be organized into missions in the next few years. He had Arthur Gaeth travel to Yugoslavia to investigate the possibilities. He sent elders Ray L. Richards and Garland F. Smith to Spain. But his conclusions were that the time was not right yet for that expansion.

The marvelous spiritual lift that came from having a patriarch assigned to the British Mission led John to request that the First Presidency assign patriarchs to each of the European missions:

In the fifteen months that [the patriarch] has met with the people he has given nearly twelve hundred blessings. His report will of course designate the actual number. The people have received their blessings joyfully. Men, women, and children, after having received their recommends, have set about to cleanse themselves and make themselves fit for the blessing; have often come fasting; and then, having received the blessing, are earnestly striving to live so as to have claim upon the blessings promised. The faith of the Saints has often brought tears to my eyes. It seems a miracle that the tithing of the British Mission increased in 1932 more than sixteen hundred dollars above that in 1931. England is the hardest hit of the European countries. I can not help but believe that the tithing increase is tied up with the awakening of faith through the receiving of patriarchal blessings. I pray that the other missions may soon have patriarchs assigned to them.[15]

In 1932 Senator Reed Smoot, John's associate in the Twelve,

companion in his European mission of 1923, and the longest-serving senator in the United States Senate, was defeated in Utah. John was annoyed by it and wrote to Albert E. and Lucy Bowen, wondering what in the world the people had done. He thought it impossible that the people of Utah, particularly Church members, could be so foolish as to defeat Smoot, "who in some respects has become the most helpful figure in all Mormondom in advancing the cause of the Church. After thirty years of struggle and labor, he has succeeded in arriving at a key position in the world's affairs, and then we threw him overboard. . . . That he is a Senator of the United States and Chairman of the Finance Committee, a member of the Church holding a high position, acted almost like magic."[16]

As was his custom, John sent the First Presidency a detailed report of the year's accomplishments and the problems that lay ahead. Most noteworthy were a Beehive handbook written by Leah and increases in missionary efficiency through daily programs and other new tools from mission presidents. A series of new supplementary tracts and an information service in the European Mission office aided in "bearing rich and good fruits." Because of the contribution to the Church's survival in the difficult years ahead, his comments about self-support and self-government follow:

> Special efforts were made throughout the year to teach the members of the Church the principle of self-support. The mission presidents were urged to teach and explain tithing and fast offering as the divinely provided means of revenue for the Church, and the necessity of extreme economy in these times of economic distress. In every mission where the mission presidents responded to this charge beneficial effects were observed, though the tithing increased above last year in only two missions. The old observation came out of the campaign, that the payment of tithes depends more upon the spiritual than upon the economic condition of the people. By letters, articles, editorial and spoken addresses, the European Mission office aided in this campaign.
>
> Almost as strenuous efforts were made to perfect the self-government of the European members of the Church and their branch, district and mission activities. . . . It is a joy to report that at

the beginning of 1933, three fourths of the branches or more were presided over successfully, by local members. The favorable response to this policy has been prompt and grateful. To meet the demands of the more complete auxiliary organizations in the missions, district supervisors for the different auxiliaries, drawn from the local membership, have been appointed in many districts. The results are very favorable. Such activity in branch, district and mission-wide affairs will of course develop and prepare the people for assuming the responsibility of conducting their own affairs instead of depending upon the missionaries for such service. The only obstacle found in carrying out this policy has been the feeling of some mission presidents and many missionaries that church official activity can not be safely entrusted to European converts.[17]

Their continuing devotion to their mission labors is shown in a letter to the family: "The pressure of work is such that we have little time to look back into the past, or to dream very much about the future, except as it pertains to the work at hand."[18]

36

THE FINAL YEAR

———————————◼———————————

Cʜʀɪsᴛᴍᴀs day 1932 was the Widtsoes' sixth Christmas in Europe and the beginning of their sixth year presiding over Church programs in Europe. The Church was advancing well, both the established organizational aspects and the special work of proselytizing. Eudora had become a young woman, Anna still struggled with the problems of a difficult marriage, and Susa maintained a close correspondence and remained the principal source of family and Church information. Otherwise, only a few items about the operations of the Church in other parts of the world crossed John's desk.

John was especially gratified to see his carefully crafted missionary tracts bear fruit. "Oh Sir—it's what I've wanted for years," was the reaction from a twenty-six-year-old woman who had begun her study of religion at age thirteen. "Since then I have studied almost every religion and many Christian creeds, and none of them have approached what I thought the true explanation—whence we come, why here, what follows death, who and what is God. In these few booklets I find something I can *believe,* I don't feel I need search further."[1]

Most of the needs the Widtsoes had seen in 1928 had been effectively addressed, and while they could productively serve much longer, their sixth year was under way, and it was again time to consider being replaced. Fresh mission tracts were in place. Church members were practicing self-government in their branches and districts and were making good progress with the principles of tithing and self-support. Public opinion in the printed media was much improved. The auxiliaries were functioning as they were designed to. The Word of Wisdom as a means of improving daily health was ingrained in the Saints. Organization, relocation, and realignment of missions was on track. Yet John recognized much was left to be done.

As 1933 got under way, John received a letter from Anthony W. Ivins of the First Presidency. At the time, President Grant was recuperating from serious health problems, and President Ivins became troubled about what was best for the Widtsoes and the work they had so remarkably set in motion. He wrote:

> I have said nothing in regard to the contents of this letter to anyone. With the coming of summer it will be a long time since you left home to take charge of the European Mission. If we follow an established custom you would be released, and another of the brethren selected to do the work that you are at present engaged in. I've recently asked myself this question; can another man take up the business of the mission where you leave it off, and carry it on to a successful termination, or would it be better to have you and Leah remain until the program that you have inaugurated has further developed.
>
> It does appear to me that the field there offers far greater promise of development than the one that you would occupy if you return at this time. Will you not be confidential with me and tell me just how you feel in regards to this matter.[2]

Through Susa's relationship with "Uncle Tone," John and Leah had developed a special closeness to him and were at ease in corresponding with him. John had mixed feelings. He explained that he and Leah had been familiar with problems in Europe prior to their call to the mission, and so had been enthusiastic about improving certain conditions. He knew there were good men in the Twelve who could carry on the work very well. He gave some frank comments about the needs that would have to be considered in a new president and the program he would inherit, things on which he felt the future of the Church in Europe depended, noting, "Though some phases, important ones such as the final office organization, and the publicity must be carried on vigorously until it becomes a fixed policy. It would retard our work in Europe if a leader should arrive, who . . . would fail to press the present organization and activity into permanency. Whenever we shall be released, we shall see ourselves, many times, back in this delightful European work."[3]

However, John's great concern was for his daughters. He wrote of Anna's unhappy marriage and his feelings that she could be helped by their presence. He also wrote of Eudora, who had grown more than she realized by her European experiences, "yet we feel that in justice to her, she should be home with her own people next school year, and with privileges of natural home life. . . . She prefers to stay with us rather than live in Utah under the restraint and the limitations of a boarder." Their willingness to continue to serve and their concern for family matters pulled them in opposite directions. "We hesitate to take the responsibility of decision. Perhaps you can counsel us. I am happy in the work here; to Leah it is life, to the children, as they have been placed, it has been a blessed sacrifice."[4]

Having given his response, John carried on. There was much ahead of them in this sixth year. Sensing the impending political struggles, John had pressed hard in preparing the European Saints for self-government and self-support. But he had not anticipated the economic hardships caused by the Great Depression in the United States. Those financial hardships left families unable to provide financial support to missionary sons. Moreover, those sons were needed at home to help provide for their families. As one historian has written, "During the 1920s eight hundred to thirteen hundred were called by the First Presidency as missionaries each year; this represented from 13 percent to 20 percent of the total young men of missionary age. In 1932, on the other hand, only 399 were able to respond, or only 5 percent of the potential."[5] That problem was intensified by the increased need for early releases caused by hardship in many families. An optimist always, John saw a benefit in that crisis. He wrote, "The interesting thing is . . . that

as a result, our local saints are rising in their own majesty to act as pros-
elytors. Whenever the mission president grasps the possibility of using
the local membership, he finds that he is making up for his missionary
losses through the assistance of local helpers."[6] New ways of getting the
work done surfaced: "Two elders who formerly reached just a few [by
using] the usual method are now able to reach hundreds and sometimes
thousands through the exhibit and lecture method. Other methods are
being experimented with. Of course, the final problem is to follow up
those whom we meet. One contact as you know is never enough."[7]
President Grant agreed that there was a hidden and important benefit
and wrote that it "has probably been a blessing in disguise because it has
forced us to make greater use of the local Saints."[8]

John expressed his feelings on the problems in the United States:
"The conditions at home must be terrible if echoes are to be relied
upon. Conditions here are bad enough. What the world is coming to we
cannot easily foresee, but, unless the proper principles are used, in guiding the nations, there will be no recovery from the depression. I am just
as certain as I can be that the eternal principles which form the structure and framework of the Gospel must be accepted before the world
can find peace and prosperity."[9]

A Mission Tour in Palestine

In their final year, the Widtsoes were to realize a dream of a lifetime—a visit to the Holy Land. The visit was so meaningful that it
occupies an entire chapter in John's autobiography. He wrote to a friend,
"The longest trip we have had to take since we came over here lies
before us next week, when we have to go to Armenia to reorganize the
Armenian Mission. We hope to touch briefly in Egypt, and spend some
time in Palestine where the headquarters of the mission are located."[10]

Their mission tour began in Egypt. "In Cairo we spent a week
[10–16 May]. Millenniums are unrolled there. The museum, the
sphinx, pyramids, other places up the Nile made the days never-
forgettable. In the great pyramid I became certain that, whatever may
have been the purpose of the builder, the attempts to give it prophetic
power are but poor guesses."[11] For most of their stay in Egypt, they were

hosted by William M. Jardine, the American Minister to Egypt and one of John's former students at the USAC. With Jardine they took a trip up and down the Nile to examine many local irrigation ventures. Some of the Egyptian officials he met had been educated in France, where they used his textbooks on irrigation and dry farming.

On the evening of 16 May, the Widtsoes boarded a train for Haifa. When they awoke next morning, they were passing through old Philistia. "Fields, rocks, cultivated, barren, in succession. The Holy Land! Intensely interesting," John recorded.[12] They marveled at being able to cross in one night the area that Moses and his people wandered through for forty years. "As we moved northward, over the Sharon plains, we recalled the history of the past that had been enacted there. And we were glad to see that modern man had planted fields and orchards over much of the land, using for irrigation, water which was obtained from deep (often 2,000 feet) wells."[13]

Midmorning they were met by a Brother and Sister Piranean and their daughter. Most of the next two days were spent on Mount Carmel, in the Jewish Colonization Information Bureau, and in reading the Turkish Mission history. John's journal for Sunday, 21 May 1933, reads, "At 11 A.M. meeting w. Piranean family. Sacrament Meeting with them—instructions, etc. Set them all apart. Testimonies. Dedicated house & rededicated mission. General meeting at 3, abt. 60 present of many nationalities. Meeting at 5:25 with candidates for baptism."[14] Years later, he wrote a fuller account: "On our first Sunday in Palestine, in Haifa, we held a meeting. About sixty attended, Jews with side locks, Muhammadans with the red fez, Armenians, and Turks. I spoke English; Sister Piranean rendered my words for her husband into German; he converted it into Armenian; a Turk then translated it into Turkish; and a friend made it into Arabic. I wondered really how much of the original meaning survived after these many translations!"[15]

Two days were devoted to training and orientation, but they had to move on, for much was ahead. Having buried three sons, John had one more important stop to make. He wrote, "Visited graves of Elders John A. Clark and Adolf Haag and placed flowers on their graves."[16]

John already had influential friends in Palestine. His work in irrigation and dry farming had brought frequent contact with people from that semi-arid land. In 1930 S.D. Yoffe, a Jewish agricultural official, asked John to persuade Macmillan to publish a Hebrew translation of Widtsoe's irrigation book.[17] He added an invitation to lecture: "Your visit in Palestine would be a great event for the farmers of this country as they are striving to learn the scientific and practical principles of irrigation, and they shall be very glad to get them from such an experienced and renowned instructor as you are."[18]

The book had already been published as a series of articles in a farm journal named *Hasedah* (the field). When planning his trip to Palestine, John wrote to the publisher of *Hasedah,* "Some time ago you wrote me about the publication of my book on Irrigation Practice in your magazine, and permission to do so was secured from the publishers. There is now the possibility of my visiting Palestine in the near future, and I should be pleased, when there, to become acquainted with agricultural conditions, and to be of such service as I can render."[19] This request was fulfilled. John wrote, "Dr. Eliezar Volcani, head of the agricultural work in Jewish Palestine, had visited me in Utah. He read of our arrival in the newspapers. That was the end of privacy. But it was also an open door to knowledge of modern Palestinian development."[20] At the girls' agricultural school he found both of his books well used and prominent on the library shelves. The Citrus Grower's Organization wanted him to do a six-week lecture tour. He received letters and visits from many people who wanted him to help their agricultural program.[21]

John used his contacts to spread the message of the Church, sending carefully selected Church books to several of his friends in Palestine.[22] But the import of the visit went far beyond agriculture. He was in the lands of the prophets and the mortal ministry of the great Messiah. These were the thoughts that brought renewed meaning to his own divine call to the apostleship. This visit was the fulfillment of many lifelong hopes. It was his spiritual homeland! The peak of the spiritual pilgrimage was bound to be Jerusalem, the Holy City.

Unfortunately, their visit was punctuated by some bad news about Susa Young Gates. A terrible illness had slowly weakened her, and she had finally been admitted to a hospital. She complained of intense pain in her joints and bones, accompanied by a high fever. After four weeks continually surrounded by at least three doctors and her husband, her fever suddenly left. She stayed a few days longer to be sure the illness was gone, then returned home.[23] But on 27 May, the First Presidency sent two telegrams. The first stated, "Sister Gates bedridden several weeks seriously if not critically ill."[24] The second read, "Sister Gates passed peacefully away this morning. Funeral: Tuesday assembly hall."[25] John sent his condolences to Susa's husband, Jacob:

> Leah and I were in Tel Aviv in pursuit of our work when the cables of the first Presidency came. Brother Piranean was not sure of our address, so we did not receive them until Tuesday, May 30th. We came to Jerusalem about 5 P.M. We feel the thrill of being in this city filled with sacred memories. Leah was in excellent spirits. Then, Brother Piranean gave me the telegrams. After the first shock, I decided to let Leah take the planned walk to the wailing wall and neighborhood, and then to bring her back to the Y.M.C.A. where we were staying before telling her. I thought the new scenes might help crowd out the thinking of her grief. It was a dreary hour for me, doubly so as I realized how Leah's cheer would be shattered in a short time. . . .
>
> I feel as if I had lost my best friend; for I could rely upon her loyalty and helpfulness—unselfishly and freely given. You all have reason to be lifted up in gratitude for having had such a mother. It is 41 years since I first met her—and ever since that day I have had wise intelligent counsel from her, and a priceless love.[26]

His brief journal account for the day contains heartfelt sentiment for Susa: "Left Tel Aviv early with Dr. Volcani. Drove to . . . Jerusalem. Fine ride. Put up at Y.M.C.A. Excellent. With guide went to Wailing wall, through bazaars & to wall to see sun set on Mt. of Olives. . . . Obtained mail from Bro. Piranean. Telegram informing us of the death of Mother Gates. The greatest woman in the Church is gone; and one of my best friends."[27]

In consequence of this difficult news, John cut short some of his plans. He wrote to Dr. Volcani, "The day that we arrived in Jerusalem we received word that my wife's mother had died three days before. This made it impossible for me to leave my wife any length of time, and it also hurried our visit since in all probability there would be a complete change of our plans in the near future, due to this event."[28] Their sorrow dampened the joy in their experiences in the Holy Land, yet in some ways it made them more valuable: "Mother's love of Jerusalem, of Bible scenes, of the temple, made us more conscious than ever of the loss. We had dreamed of the joy that she would have in firsthand reports of things and conditions here, from her point of view—and then we were suddenly told that she is gone beyond our reach!"[29]

After ten days in Jerusalem, they drove through the Judaean hills, passing by Bethel, Shiloh, Jacob's Well, and Samaria. After reliving so many sacred stories, they arrived in Haifa and stayed with the Piranean family. On 11 June, the Widtsoes and the Piraneans, with their daughter Astrich, "drove through Nazaret, Tiberias, by Sea of Galilee, fine views. . . . Entered Syria, drove through desert country. Reached Damascus abt. 1:30 P.M. Called for Bro. Moses Hindolan, Br. President. . . . Meeting at 6 P.M., abt. 40 present."[30] They were pleased that the Damascus Branch was so vigorous and noted with pleasure that pictures of Heber J. Grant and other leaders were pinned to the walls of tiny, humble homes.

From Damascus they traveled to Beirut and the ruins of the old temple of Heliopolis, where Solomon is said to have built a palace for his Egyptian queen. Two years earlier, John had described the place: "Beirut, the principal Syrian seaport, has a mixed population. Like most of the cities in Syria and Palestine, Arabs, Jews, Turks, Armenians rub shoulders. The Christian university just a few miles south of the city has done much to bring civilization to these peoples. Beirut is a good place for our proselyting."[31]

From Beirut they went through Tripoli and Antioch to Aleppo to fill their assignment to dedicate a monument at the grave of Joseph Wilford Booth, who had died while serving as mission president in 1928.[32] "At length we reached Aleppo and the group of faithful saints there. Brother Booth's monument stood prominently in the sand-surrounded cemetery some distance from the town. On Sunday, June 18, 1933, the whole group standing by, the grave was dedicated, and a spiritual meeting was held there. The heart grew warm in love."[33]

John corresponded with President Piranean through the rest of his mission. His agricultural contacts in the Holy Land continued as well. After returning home, he corresponded regularly with Chaim Weizmann, who was trying to establish an agricultural college in Palestine. John offered to help gather volumes for their library.[34] In Palestine, he had become close friends with Sheikh Ja'coub El-Bukhari, and they maintained a correspondence for many years.

During their mission tour to Palestine, President Grant requested a frank response about their desire to stay in Europe or come home to Utah.[35] Susa's death probably had an impact on John's response. Once again, his letter tells of full satisfaction with their life in Europe and their happiness in the service they were called to. As before, he expressed his concerns about Eudora and Anna. He felt Eudora needed to continue her growth and education at home but did not want her to have to board somewhere. He was so worried about his and Leah's separation from Anna that he requested she be sent to Europe if their mission was again extended. Whatever the decision, "when you are moved upon to release us, we shall go home rejoicing until then we shall go on here rejoicing."[36]

In mid-July, about three weeks after receiving his answer, the First Presidency announced that Joseph F. Merrill would replace John A. Widtsoe as president of the European Mission. The official letter of release was dated 25 August 1933: "In due time we hope to have the pleasure of welcoming you and Sister Widtsoe home, and we sincerely trust that the Lord will bless and prosper you and that you may be filled with peace on the completion of your successful mission."[37] It took more than three months for the Widtsoes to be certain everything was in order for the Merrills.

In the midst of their preparations, John wrote a message to share with the Church in the next general conference. As promised, President Grant read it to the congregation. For six years President Widtsoe had been combating blatant negative publicity and the more subtle, more dangerous attacks on the restored truth. His conference message reflected those twin enemies:

> Never was the universe of untruth more deeply stirred than when the Gospel of the Lord Jesus Christ was restored in this age—the beginning of the end of the reign of anti-Christ. . . . Truth's destiny is victory. It breaks down every barrier of error. . . . The masses of men love truth better than error, but are blinded by the clever presentations of the enemy of truth. Just so, the truth of the restored gospel is becoming understood in the world. . . . If persecution from without is diminishing, contention within is fanned into livelier flame. Of the two methods of destruction—persecution by untruth or discord among those who have accepted truth—the latter is the deadlier. . . . Persecution from without is gradually vanishing. . . . But, at the same time, the danger of jealousy, strife and evil speaking among the members of the Church increases. . . . There must be an honest endeavor to love our brethren and sisters as well as the Lord in heaven—the first law of Gospel living. Love begets love. Whenever Latter-day Saints live in love together, their armour and their shield, all their weapons are of heavenly workmanship.[38]

THE FINAL SEPARATION

Many fine feelings were expressed by President and Sister Widtsoe as their mission wound down. These reflections best express their assessment of the long mission term served in Europe. Their call had come to them when the weight of their cross was about to crush them through the death of Marsel. A ray of that memory and their healing is seen in an expression to President Ivins: "I know of nothing in my whole life which has been better for me, for Leah, and for my family than the years we have spent in Europe on this last mission. I think it has made life over for us. You know how deeply grateful we are to you for your part in the assignment and for your constant wise encouragement and support."[39] With his deep European roots fresh in the precious soils of his homeland, he wrote, "There have been many problems to solve, many changes to affect, due in large measure to the new international situation, especially that phase of it which . . . has prohibited emigration from

England to America. I am European born and partly bred here, as a considerable part of my higher education was obtained in continental and British Universities, and therefore I feel very much at home on this side of the Atlantic."[40]

In a letter to President Don MacDalton, he added, "We have had a delightful time here during the last nearly six years and leaving for home will be a good deal like leaving our heart's work. Not least of the regrets that we shall have in leaving is the constant and happy associations that we have had with the presidents of the missions."[41] The mission presidents, the many missionaries, their associates in the management of the mission and the *Millennial Star,* and countless members of the Church in Europe were saddened at their leaving. One member wrote:

> You are about to leave us, your present lengthy mission of presiding over the European Missions has come to an end. You have both discharged your duties with kindness, skill, and always shown valiant leadership, and I unhesitatingly say, your services are not only approved by the Presiding Authorities of the Church, but are also acceptable unto the Lord. . . .
>
> The missions here, which have been under your care, have greatly improved. . . . You will leave things in splendid shape for Bro. Merrill, unto whom we shall try to give the same service and support, for after all, isn't it a case of all of us being joint heirs together with our Lord in bringing his children into the fold of Salvation.[42]

A sister whom John promised a visit prior to his leaving wrote:

> I could just get right up and dance around for sheer joy for I feel so happy about it. To think that a real Apostle and his wife are to honor us with a visit and enter our very humble home. It will be the most eventful day in our lives and we cannot help but keep thanking Heavenly Father for being so good to us.
>
> You cannot realize what it means to us. We know that it will cost you a lot and use some of your very valuable time but I know that it will be worth it and I am certain that the Lord will reward you one hundred fold.
>
> It is the most important thing that has ever happened in our lives and we are looking forward to it with great anticipation. God bless you

both for your goodness to us. We feel much more honored than if a King and Queen were coming.[43]

Fortunately, the press of getting ready to go home kept the Widtsoes so busy that they had little time for nostalgia. John wrote, "I find that getting ready to leave when I have to turn over this rather large organization to Brother Merrill is time consuming and unfortunately I am compelled to make a trip to the continent before leaving, and in fact before Brother Merrill arrives. So my time is very crowded. In fact I think everybody at 5 Gordon Square is working pretty much up to the limit."[44] He assured the First Presidency that he would follow their instructions to do all he could to help President Merrill get started. He wrote, "A number of problems are standing at attention waiting for orders and I suppose it will take us a week or ten days before he says 'nuff.' Then there are a few unfinished matters which I must attend to in person requiring another few days."[45]

Leah and Eudora remained in London to finish their preparations while John looked after things on the continent. He made mission visits in Denmark and Norway. In a last visit to Trondheim, he gave several days to genealogical research, made valuable library purchases, paid a final visit to relatives, and bid a final farewell to his Church family in Trondheim. His journal reads, "Sept. 16: At 6:55 a crowd of saints gathered at station. Train late, did not leave until 8: P.M. for Oslo. Beautiful souvenir given me by branch. Happy days in Trondhjem. In my bag are over 2000 names of my ancestors & many more thousands waiting to be copied."[46]

While in Norway, John had made preliminary arrangements regarding his father's grave, but because he would be home far in advance of its accomplishment, he asked President M. H. Knudsen of the Norwegian Mission to see to the final details. Knudsen wrote of his "pleasure to assume the personal responsibility . . . of placing a head-stone over your father's grave. I will write to Mr. Lauritzan at Trondheim reminding him that the order you placed will eventually be fulfilled and in the meantime I will make sure that the right grave will obtain the right monument at Namsos."[47] En route to London, John spent a day with the presidents of the Norwegian, Danish, German-Austrian, and Swiss-German missions.

John prepared a lengthy report to familiarize President Merrill with the conditions of the mission.[48] The nine-page memo was filled with helpful insight into the problems that came with the assignment and the successes they had experienced in dealing with them:

> During the last few years certain definite administrative aims have been set up which are now in full operation, though many of them have not yet been brought to completion in some of the missions. These administrative aims may be summarized as follows: (1) To help the people secure and enjoy all the privileges and blessings of Church membership. This includes teaching them that a mission of Zion is just as much a part of Zion as is a stake of Zion and Zion will in time be spread over the earth as the pure in heart increase in numbers. (2) To establish more formally among the saints the principles of self-government and self-support under the direction of the constituted Church officers. (3) To secure uniformity among the missions in their practice and activities and conformity with General Church practices and activities. (4) To increase our proselyting efficiency. (5) To make the European Mission Office of direct help in promoting the cause of the Lord in Europe.[49]

In the report, John emphasized the genuine goodness of all the mission presidents but added that they all tended to do things in their own way unless his office required uniformity. He cautioned that where different languages were involved, the divide occurred more easily. He strongly advocated annual mission presidents' conferences to help stimulate uniformity and motivation. On the role of the mission president's wife, he counseled that she be "a consulting counselor of all women's activities. That is, she stands by the side of her husband giving him counsel with respect to the work of the women though without assuming official direction of any organization unless she is especially qualified and is definitely appointed to do so."[50]

He identified only two "Membership Problems." The first emanated from the practice of gathering to America soon after conversion to the Church: "The auxiliaries were primarily Bible classes teaching the gospel but having no direct relationship with the organization of the Church and the stakes. No attention was given to social and recreational programs. The members of the Church that failed to immigrate wearied of this monotony." For that reason, John had put much emphasis on social and recreational programs and stated that social evenings, contests involving the fields of debating, public speaking, writing poetry, and like activities had been very successful. The other membership problem centered on Church meeting facilities: "Uninviting meeting places have played a great part in hindering the progress of the work. Many of the so-called better class cannot be invited to our halls. The European sense of social stratification does not permit of it."[51] Building funds had been started in a few localities, and he encouraged more as soon as feasible.

John was also frank about the missionaries. Their youth and immaturity was a major problem, further complicated by the transition into the disciplined life required in the mission. He wrote, "They are taken from an active social life and placed under missionary discipline and restrictions. It is really an unnatural transition. If, however, they are allowed to live as they do at home, since they are away from home and under the pressure of tremendous temptations, we should have disaster overtake most of them in a very short time. . . . Meanwhile they are fine, sweet, wholesome boys who if they are put on the right path and helped to remain there, develop into splendid workers."[52] Under existing circumstances, he said, the majority became possessed with the spirit of the work and did marvelous things considering their age. He felt the need for greater missionary training and better support by way of printed materials and supplies.

In addition to the written counsel, John and Leah stayed several days to help the Merrills get started. President Merrill described the transition to the First Presidency: "Late Saturday evening, October 7, Brother Widtsoe turned over the responsibility of this office to me. . . . These fifteen conference-days were very delightful to us. Brother and Sister Widtsoe seemed not to tire of our inquisitiveness. . . . Brother and Sister Widtsoe certainly have the affairs of the mission at their fingers' ends."[53]

The final farewells were difficult, instructive, and indicative of the feelings shared by thousands. The letters fill many file folders, reflecting the high regard that flowed between the missionaries and the Widtsoes. From the British Missionaries Association:

> The past six years have been remarkable for actual work done alone. The missionary experiences of the Widtsoes are no doubt without precedent in Church History. Verily, here is faith and works, but that is not all. The mission of the Widtsoes has to be reckoned by some other medium than that of sheer deeds alone.
>
> Besides organizing mission-wide auxiliaries, besides this herculean effort to stabilize organization through local active participation, besides these and a thousand other things that no one but a Mission President can ever know about, in these six years, the Widtsoes have been busily at work manufacturing memories for all of us! Memories that make for character: products of the Mill of Truth. Memories heightened by imagination are what constitutes our very beings. Or in other words, as the Good Book says, "As a man thinketh, so is he."
>
> Because of our proximity to this cherished Mill of Memories, we of the British Mission, over which President and Sister Widtsoe have presided and made their home, feel infinitely more moved when we say our word of farewell than the ordinary phrase would indicate. But so say we, and add our heartfelt wish for a safe journey to the new "field." In days that are now, and days that are to come, our actions, thanks to understandable lessons of truth, may speak above the poverty of mere expression in showing to you our grateful appreciation for your true-blue missionary service. May the lights which you have kindled so unselfishly never grow dim, but grow brighter and brighter "until the perfect day."[54]

To this public expression both John and Leah Widtsoe attached a farewell epistle. In each was a particularly personal response to their requests for "our message." First John:

> The day of our departure from the mission field approaches. The farewell hour is almost here. Our thoughts turn backward to the happy times we have had with you; to your eager questioning, your heart felt testimonies, your ready devotion to the Lord's service. We are grateful for your many kindnesses to us. We shall never forget you; do not you forget us. May our missionary friendships be life-long.
>
> You have asked for our message. Let it be about the King's image.

A lump of silver is but a lump of silver in the marketplace, sold by weight under the changing market price. If that lump of silver be passed through the mint it becomes something more than a lump of silver. The King's Image pressed upon it makes it coin of the realm. Thenceforth with a value above its weight and market price it is in the King's service.

A human life is but a human life, lost in the multitude of indifferent lives, unless it enters the King's service, unless the King's image be impressed upon it. Then it becomes current coin of the King's realm, which may purchase joy, happiness, satisfaction, otherwise unattainable. Does a life bear the King's image? That is a vital question.

How may we so coin our lives? How secure the impress of the King's image? It is not a secret. By losing and forgetting ourselves in a great work, a mighty cause. Thus, we enter the King's service. Thus, we come to bear the King's image. Unselfishness! Selflessness! Great words; greater ideals! Keys to the solution of the world's problems! He who forgets himself in noble service will have success thrust upon him. Whoever mingles with his eating and drinking, with his daily toil and moneymaking, with his pleasure and his pain, the act of loving service of his noblest ideal, will rise to the heights, above the clouds, with the envying multitude below. He will be in the King's service. There is really no other way to true success.

You ask for the parts of the spiritual minting press? Here I sum! Faith in God; love of truth; obedience to law; courage to say no; sincerity in labor; temperance in all things; generosity, virtue, and industry. These are elements out of which unselfishness is born, and by which the King's image is impressed upon human lives.

Soon you shall also be home, released from your foreign missions; missionary farewells are for a few flying months only. Then, more seeking after truth, more sharing of it with others, until all of life becomes a mission of service in the King's Cause, until all may know that we are in royal service, in the service of the King of Kings. So is success won and joy obtained—everlastingly. May you so live that the missionary spirit may never forsake you.

It is understood that whenever or wherever you meet me, you

will announce your name and European Mission pedigree without waiting for me to speak first.[55]

Leah wrote:

> "Auf Wiedersehen"—from mission Grandmother
>
> My dear Mission Sons, it is but natural to judge a Cause by those who represent it. Most of the finest members of the Church I have met in Europe admit that their interests in restored truth was occasioned by the life and character of the young men who bear its message to the world. Unfortunately, one unworthy missionary can undo the work of ten good ones. Many an apathetic member or Branch, even, may trace its back sliding to one or a group of missionaries who willfully forsook the standards of the Truth they represent. . . . The path you have chosen as a missionary is full of joy, yet it demands from you a life very different from that which you have left at home. Only when you "shoot straight" and play the game fair, may you gain the joy and progress to which you are entitled. If I may leave one final bit of advice with you it would be this: don't ever make a promise to members or friends here unless you intend to *fulfill that promise faithfully.*[56]

HEADING HOME

During the three-week period between their official release, 7 October, and their setting sail for New York on 28 October, the Widtsoes finished some personal interests in London. Somerset House and the genealogical collection of the British Museum, royal societies, museums, and art collections and galleries attracted their attention. Especially meaningful to both of them was a visit on 14 October: "Leah & I had lunch w. Mr. & Mrs. Bernard Shaw at their home, 4 Whitehall Court, London."[57]

When finally they left for Southampton, John wrote, "Very cold day. 5 trunks & about 11 parcels!! After 6 years. Left for station abt. 8 P.M., train due to leave 9 P.M. . . . A big crowd to see us off at station. All elders from two offices & district & many saints."[58] About 10:30 P.M. they boarded the S. S. *Manhattan.* "Today closes a most interesting chapter in our lives," John wrote. "May the Lord bless the results of our labors in behalf of eternal truth. Thank God for the privilege we have had—Eudora, Leah & I."[59]

At about noon on 4 November, they boarded a train to Washington, D.C., where they met the First Presidency; elders Rudger Clawson, Stephen L Richards, and Reed Smoot; and several other prominent Church members. John's journal reads: "Nov. 5 The Washington chapel was dedicated today. Meetings at 10 A.M., 2 & 7:30 P.M. Abt 2600 in attendance. A splendid spirit. I bore my testimony in afternoon. A splendid structure. Lunch with Marriotts at Smoot's house."[60] On 12 November they were met by a large crowd at the Salt Lake train station and went directly to their home at 1425 Sigsbee Avenue.

The adjustment wasn't easy. "As you know," John wrote, "my work in Europe kept me away from Utah a little more than six years. During that time many changes occurred and upon my return I found myself practically a stranger in a strange land; but I am gradually recovering the home perspective."[61] For a while life at home was as frenetic as it had been in the mission. He shared another glimpse: "We have been home over two months and hectic months they have been—furniture scattered from the north pole to the south; the banks are unwilling to lend us sufficient money for building a new estate; boards, in your happy words, to be sat upon, and upholstered chairs, in your eloquent words, to be sat in. . . . We have tried to tell the multitudes of all that we know but they are not much wiser than they were before we returned home."[62]

In his first general conference address following the mission, John shared some of the greater joys he had felt in Europe: "I think there is no one here who is enjoying this conference more than I. Since my late boyhood I have sought to attend these conferences from year to year, and with considerable regularity I have been able to do so. Because of my absence in the mission field I have been able to attend only one of the last twelve . . . therefore I come to this conference hungry."[63] Though he had missed the great spirit of the general conferences, he assured the Saints that he had enjoyed the outpourings of the Holy Spirit and gave an appealing description of the Church in Europe: "At times it has seemed to me that the spirit that has moved upon those who have spoken and listened in the small gatherings in the mission field has been even stronger and more powerful, than we feel here at home. It often happens that, when far away from home, far from the sheltered protection of the temple, the tabernacle, and the stakes of Zion, we draw more heavily upon the spiritual forces about us."[64]

Next he spoke of the wonderful men and women with whom he had labored: "I have seen them make the greatest discovery of all time. . . . I have seen them discover God. I have seen them discover Jesus Christ. I have seen them discover the Gospel, its virtue and truth. I have seen them discover their own place in the great plan of salvation."[65]

Of the European members he gave a similar tribute: "The challenge is to be an example . . . to our brethren and sisters who labor in behalf of the Lord's great cause far beyond the organized stakes and wards of Zion. I love those people as I love you here. They are battling for the truth on the outposts of Zion; they are extending the boundaries of Zion; they are fulfilling the prophecies under which we shall go forward until we cover the earth."[66]

John stayed abreast of Church affairs in Europe. Members and leaders wrote to him regularly, informing him of events and asking for advice. The six-year mission had been a taxing but fruitful endeavor. John wrote, "We had been absent from home a full six years. It was harder to leave the work in the mission field than it was to leave home at first. The spirit of the mission was ours, and joyous it was to spend all one's time in attempting to teach the eternal truth to people ignorant of the gospel."[67]

37

THE CHURCH RADIO, PUBLICITY, AND MISSION LITERATURE COMMITTEE

T HE 1920s, John's first decade as an apostle, saw the world shrink through technological advances in communications. They much enhanced the Church's ability to take the gospel to all the world. John became accustomed to public scrutiny while at the university and became skillful in turning the press to his advantage. He had also learned to use the press to advance the message of the Church in Europe. Now he was quite ready for the challenge set by the new medium of radio. Broadcast stations began operation in almost every state of the USA in the 1920s. A popular slogan proclaimed that radio "changed the world."

With the Church's first radio broadcast in 1922 came the announcement that "a new epoch in methods of preaching the gospel was introduced on the 6th of May when the *Deseret News* Radio station was formally dedicated, with speeches and musical selections broadcasted."[1] President Heber J. Grant spoke directly into the radio transmitter at 8:00 P.M., dedicating the airwaves for the use of the Church. "This is my message to the people of the world, a quotation from the Doctrine and Covenants, known as Section 76, a revelation to Joseph Smith and Sidney Rigdon."[2]

And this is the gospel, the glad tidings, which the voice out of the heavens bore record unto us—that he came into the world, even Jesus, to be crucified for the world, and to bear the sins of the world, and to sanctify the world, and to cleanse it from all unrighteousness; that through him all might be saved whom the Father had put into his power and made by him; for we saw him, even on the right hand of God; and we heard the voice bearing record that he is the Only Begotten of the Father—that by him, and through him, and of him, the worlds are and were created, and the inhabitants thereof are begotten sons and daughters unto God. (D&C 76:40–42, 23–24.)

The broadcast of the semiannual general conference of 1924 was another landmark for the Church. President Charles W. Penrose, ill and unable to attend, listened through "a receiving instrument" placed in his home. When President Grant opened the conference, Penrose gleefully exclaimed, "It is the President's voice!"[3] When a men's chorus sang a hymn, he said, "That is wonderful." Church leaders began to contemplate the potential of radio. Although it would be years before the majority of the world had radios in their homes, they recognized that "in the privacy of their own homes [people] are often willing, if not eager, to listen to the gospel message. Many an indifferent person has openly admitted that radio has done more to convince him of the immortality of things and of the existence of Deity than any other intermediary."[4]

John was one of the first to address the need for the Church to use modern technology to present the message of the restored gospel. At general conference in October 1924, he said, "Today, man is able to do things that in days gone by were conceivably done only by God. Yet . . . an old thought came back to me, that the airship, the steamship, the telephone, the radio and all the other marvels of this age, are but as the clothing of the body, but as instruments to be used by man. By means of these great inventions and discoveries, great gifts of God to the people of these latter days, it is possible for the righteous man to accomplish righteousness more widely and more speedily."[5] In the general conference preceding his service as European mission president, John had sounded a warning that the Lord was moving rapidly in opening new avenues for spreading the gospel:

> I was impressed this morning by the remarks made by President Ivins, that throughout all the ages of history the hand of God has overruled the actions of mankind, that nothing is done except as the Lord may use it for the accomplishment of his mighty purposes. No truth has become more living in my soul throughout my life than this. The things accomplished by humanity become in the end God's accomplishments, as he makes use of them in working out his infinite purposes. I cannot help but believe that the mighty changes that have come in this latest day of civilization, the vast physical, economic and social changes, have all been brought about through the goodness of the Lord for the accomplishment of his latter-day work. The printing press came into existence and by it the Word of God has been brought to all people. Then in this day, when the Lord has restored the gifts and blessings of the gospel and the organization of the Church, have come other marvelous means by which we may speak the eternal truth in our keeping to all the world. The steamship came that we might carry the truth from continent to continent, across the great oceans; the railway that we might deliver the same everlasting truth to every part of every land; the telephone and the telegraph, and now the radio, that we might spread the truth of the gospel over all the world. In time we shall be able to utilize all these agencies to bear our witness to the peoples of the world, that we may stand free from blame before our Maker in the last great day.[6]

John wrote of proselytizing methods that needed to be updated: "Tracting has been a valuable means of spreading gospel news. . . . Now, however, other helps must come. The radio, the phonograph, the motion picture have come to benefit humanity. . . . The present world wants its reading matter in brief, concise sentences, artistically printed. As we move over the earth with our message, we need more and more to use all of these devices, as they come along."[7] John shared with Elder and Sister Albert E. Bowen his desire to have a year to prepare up-to-date publicity materials for use by missionaries. He wrote, "There is a big harvest ahead of us if we can only capitalize conditions as they are."[8]

The Church had been more reserved with modern technology, and

John found himself at the forefront of a coordinated publication entity. He noted, "We have not been [in] a position . . . to make full use of this tolerant feeling which is developing concerning us—that will be one of the big steps forward in the near future, whether I am here or someone else comes to replace me. The entrance of our cause into newspaper fields, into radio activities, into the usual advertising methods, is right ahead of us and must be brought into use if we are to make use of the means that the Lord has given us, for the promulgation of His cause in these days."[9]

John's pioneering publicity work in Europe was recognized by President Grant. After admitting his own failures at favorable newspaper publicity as the Japanese and the European mission president, Grant said, "I never succeeded in getting one single line of refutation printed in the papers of England. Some very pernicious articles were written about us, but the newspapers would not publish refutations of those articles. Today we are getting very favorable publicity. The newspapers are open to the president of the European Mission, John A. Widtsoe. We regret his absence from the meetings of this conference. We would be delighted if he were here."[10]

In the annual general conference of the Church, at the midpoint of his mission, John spoke of the impact of their publicity efforts: "I think I am safe in saying that the work of the Lord is going forward satisfactorily in the European Missions. Never before, because of the new inventions and discoveries for the dissemination of truth, has the testimony of the restoration of the Gospel of Jesus Christ been so widely scattered and made to reach so many people, as at this time."[11]

Soon after his return from Europe, John addressed the April 1934 annual general conference. He spoke of a "new feeling" for the Church in the public's eye, a wonderful change. But, he warned, "the eternal battle is still on between truth and error, between the Lord and the Evil One, the battle that will never end so long as men have their free agency, so long as error is possible, wherever there is truth. We have merely shifted our battle ground, we have merely changed our weapons. Three hundred years ago humanity fought with spears and shields. Today out of the sky poison gas and bombs are dropped on the unprotected cities below. Just so, in the mission field today, under the new conditions we must change our battle ground and the weapons that we use, but the battle goes forward."[12]

A SPECIAL COMMITTEE

With Elder Widtsoe back in Salt Lake City, the time to scout the "battleground" and use "new weapons" had come. The need for appealing, well-packaged information grew rapidly. It was especially acute in the missions but beyond the skills of young missionaries. John, however, had the necessary vision and experience. On 26 February 1934, Rudger Clawson, president of the Quorum of the Twelve, wrote to him, "Please be advised that you have been appointed to act as chairman of a committee of three to 'Organize the Available Material for Publicity Purposes Among the Missions of the Church.' The other members of the committee are Bishop David A. Smith and President Samuel O. Bennion, who have been notified of this appointment."[13]

On 4 April, as part of general conference, the Widtsoe committee met in the Salt Lake Temple with mission presidents serving in the United States. The purpose of the meeting was to exchange ideas on how the committee might best assist the mission presidents. The mission presidents were asked to communicate their ideas to Elder Widtsoe. President George S. Romney of the Northern States Mission submitted a list of helpful suggestions the day after the meeting. He outlined six specific areas of focus: newspapers, radio talks, window displays, Church-oriented dramas, big-screen advertisements for local movie theaters, and slide shows with prepared lectures: "We need instructions as to the best way to contact paper editors, and we hope to see some prepared features. . . . We have no idea how to contact stations, we need instructions and some new material. . . . I was very much interested in the suggestion of Dr. Widtsoe in regard to dramas etc. We shall welcome suggestions of this kind."[14]

On 11 April, Joseph Daynes, president of the Western States Mission, wrote, "Acting upon the suggestions given us at the time of our meeting last Wednesday, may I state that this Mission would appreciate very much indeed, if through your publicity bureau arrangements could be made to feature the following: First: dramatization of Church History. . . . Second: Publicity articles. . . . Third: Radio Talks."[15]

LeGrand Richards, then president of the Southern States Mission, shared similar feelings: "I am very happy to again express my delight with the appointment of the Publicity Committee. . . . I feel that I can appreciate . . . how much good this will do in standardizing the work throughout the Missions. . . . Your accomplishments in Great Britain in furnishing Newspaper stories impressed me very much, and I feel that something of that kind could well be undertaken here in the south with very beneficial results. At least, I would be happy to undertake to have the articles placed if your Committee could furnish me with the necessary stories and cuts."[16]

A testimonial of the advantages of media potential was written by the Northern States Mission publicity director on 14 April 1934: "I am sure this will . . . aid all of us to find the most efficient methods of preaching the Gospel. A short time ago we obtained a few Electrical Transcriptions of the Tabernacle Organ and Choir. In an attempt to put these into immediate use I've visited the larger broadcasting stations of Chicago. When I announced the records of the Organ and Choir they manifested quite a bit of interest. They seemed anxious to use such material, and on April 1st K.Y.W., a prominent station here, gave a fifteen minute program from a record we loaned to them. . . . There are several stations throughout the Mission calling for and are anxious to use these on their programs."[17]

Following these and other reports, the Widtsoe committee submitted a report to the First Presidency outlining the focus of the newly named "LDS Publicity Bureau":

> Newspapers: Prepare for syndication in the United States and abroad a "Church Magazine Section" similar to the Church Section now issued weekly in the Deseret News. But instead of its being only a "local" periodical, it could become an "international" weekly feature of from one full page to eight half pages (the present size of the News Church Section). . . .
>
> Radio: Connect station KSL with Brigham Young University, so that College programs carrying the spirit of youth and the power and

teachings of the Gospel could be broadcast from Provo. These programs could include music, drama, etc., particularly adapted to appeal to non-Church members.

Plays built around early and modern Latter-day Saint life, incorporating Gospel topics, but interesting and instructive in teaching radio fans the true meaning and interpretation of life, could be prepared for use on radio programs other than those originating at KSL. According to Richard L. Evans, production manager of KSL, there is a great need of this type of material. It could be produced in the radio class of the B. Y. U., or by staff writers of the Church publicity bureau.

Such programs could be sent to all missions and to all well known radio stations. Mission presidents could call for and have prepared by the bureau other fitting material for radio broadcasting.

These suggestions could be enlarged upon and a bureau for the handling of radio, magazine, news and motion picture publicity be formed.[18]

The committee began promoting work in some of these areas. Soon "film sermons" presented some aspects of the gospel.[19] Lectures, slide shows, and films were created about the Book of Mormon.[20] Within a year of President Joseph Quinney's request for a series of talks suitable for missionary radio work, the bureau released thirteen.[21] John felt that the Church needed to engage in a publicity campaign equal to that of any commercial entity. He announced in the October general conference of 1848, "Such a campaign would need some sacrifice of time, strength, and money. But the cause is the greatest on earth. Lesser causes are fiercely vocal. Millions of dollars are spent annually to advertise a brand of whiskey or cigarets. Why not shout the way to peace from the housetops? Publicity and repetition need not be confined to the material aspects of life. Our spiritual needs, always battling with evil, have greater rights. It could be made the greatest campaign for human happiness in the last two thousand years."[22]

John kept abreast of opportunities for publicity for the Church. He wrote to the First Presidency, informing them of an exposition to be held in Oslo in 1938. He noted, "I believe that it would be very helpful to our cause in Norway and the Scandinavian countries and in Europe generally, if we had an exhibit at this proposed fair. President Knudsen could perhaps be authorized to enquire as to possibilities and costs, if any, and report back to you, so that if you should decide to authorize our participation in the fair we could make our application for space early and thereby secure a good location. My own experiences at the European fairs have convinced me that they are excellent supplemental proselyting means."[23]

Soon the missions reported the effects of the committee's work. LeGrand Richards wrote:

> On January 13th there appeared in the "Constitution" of Atlanta, Georgia, I think the largest newspaper in the Southern States Mission, an article called, "Charm School Prepares Mormon Girl to Fascinate, Conquer World." When I read this article I felt sure it had come through your efforts. It covers three columns and at least twenty inches in length.
>
> The newspapers of the South are very friendly toward us. I have before me a letter from one of our Brethren in Mississippi. The country paper has been printing articles from him on the doctrines of our church. He prepared them himself, and while I commend him and the paper for what was accomplished I did feel that better results could be achieved were the articles prepared by one capable of doing that work.
>
> I am in receipt of a letter this morning from the President of the District in Florida advising that they have a publicity man in Jacksonville and that the papers are very friendly there and would be happy to run articles for us. If, therefore, you have any suggestions or recommendations to offer I will be very happy to receive the same.
>
> We have done practically nothing in our Mission in the way of radio work since I came here. I have been waiting with the thought that through your committee there would be some definite program recommended. If anything new along this line is developed I will be happy to have you so advise me.[24]

Soon after the creation of the publicity committee, on 29 March 1934, John was made the Church commissioner of education for a second term. It was a demanding assignment that immediately took tremendous amounts of his time and energy. Studies of the seminaries and the needs of the Church's colleges and university required considerable attention. Numerous letters show John's deep involvement in educational affairs that overwhelmed his work on the publicity committee. To President Don B. Colton of the Eastern States Mission he wrote, "Until I can get the pressing spring work connected with the Department of Education out of the way, I shall be unable to tackle seriously the publicity work. I hope I may be able to get at it, however, before May is over. I look upon the movement as one of the most important undertaken in recent years by the Church."[25]

John wrote of his involvement, "I undertook the supervision of the Church school system, and now I am teaching as the sole teacher or practically so, the whole group of seminary workers. It is consuming, it seems, more time than I have at my disposal."[26] He described the impact of the summer school: "We have just finished a five weeks' seminary teachers summer school and convention. Since I have been the only teacher, it has kept me exceedingly busy and all my correspondence is a month or more behind."[27]

Seven months after the formation of the investigating committee, on 24 September 1934, John and his colleagues submitted a report and proposal to President Clawson and the Quorum of the Twelve:

> Last February you appointed us a Committee on Mission Publicity, the chief purpose, from your letter of appointment, being the organization of available material for publicity purposes among the missions of the Church.
>
> We have given this assignment considerable attention. At the April conference we discussed with the mission presidents the problems of mission publicity and since then have been in communication with several of the mission publicity directors. We have also examined a number of manuscripts and projects intended for publicity purposes among the missions.
>
> It has become clear to us that there is at present an urgent and insistent demand for the kind of assistance intended when this committee was appointed. We are asked to make us aware of all available opportunities for presenting the gospel message to the people of the world, especially those developed in our recent scientific progress. Such publicity will be of great advantage to the Elders and sisters

serving in the mission field, and may determine the future progress of our proselyting activities.

The attempt to place upon young missionaries the burden of publicity direction, often involving the preparation of the materials themselves, without adequate supervision from the head-quarters of the Church, has seldom been successful. Some good has of course resulted, but too much cannot be expected from the young people sent into the field.

Moreover, the efforts made in this field need review and coordination. There is an unnecessary and wasteful duplication, owing to the lack of organization for mission publicity.

As we have considered the matters brought before us we have come to sense as never before not only the tremendous importance of the subject of mission publicity, but also the large extent of material that needs to be considered, organized, and presented to the missions. We have attempted in the attached sheets to point out some main proselyting avenues and some main divisions of mission publicity helps.[28]

Other duties took John away from the publicity committee. In January 1935 he was appointed to the Utah Water Storage Commission by Governor Henry H. Blood. Governor Blood also appointed him an official delegate to the Conference of the National Reclamation Association to represent Utah at their December meetings to be held in Salt Lake City. On 23 April 1935, John was appointed editor of the *Improvement Era,* and not many weeks thereafter, discussions of his going for a year to the University of Southern California were under way. Stake and mission conference visits were assigned to him almost weekly, demanding a great deal of time because of the amount of travel involved. He wrote, "The work of the Mission Publicity Committee has pretty much stood still for several months, owing to the large number of duties which have been placed upon me in connection with the Department of Education. Before the October conference, however, we hope to have some plans in readiness for you all, and among the things that we hope to be able to discuss with you is the question of radio talks."[29]

FORMATION OF THE CHURCH
RADIO, PUBLICITY, AND MISSION
LITERATURE COMMITTEE

Elder Widtsoe's committee recognized the urgent need for a general committee to oversee publicity and prepare mission publications. Their recommendations for specific action were twofold: (1) "That suitable returned missionaries, many of whom have already volunteered, be called to the aid of the Committee, on an unpaid basis, or at the most to be paid for actually accepted productions." (2) "That for general supervisory and coordinating purposes the part or full time of a paid man be placed at the disposal of the work."[30]

John wrote to David O. McKay, newly appointed second counselor in the First Presidency, "With respect to the Mission Publicity Committee, the requests . . . require occasional or regular help, for which no doubt the Church must make payment. The Committee felt that if a small sum, say not to exceed one hundred dollars a month, could be allowed by the Presidency, helps such as that offered by Brother [Gordon B.] Hinckley could be secured from time to time, to get the work under way. Really, I have a feeling that in these changing times mission publicity is one of the outstanding needs connected with our proselyting."[31]

Formal action on the committee's recommendations was slow in coming. Almost a year after the recommendations were made, John wrote to David A. Smith, fellow committee member: "Up to date, I have had no official communication to the effect that the Presidency has approved of our committee as a mission publicity committee, nor has any action been taken, as far as I know, upon the request of the Council of the Twelve that a small sum be set aside for assistance in this work. I find it physically impossible to go over all these matters single handed, but could do so easily if a little assistance were available. Inasmuch as the Presidency has informed me that these matters be directed to our committee, I wonder if you could ascertain what form of action has been taken."[32]

The First Presidency formed the Church Radio, Publicity, and Mission Literature Committee in October 1935.[33] That committee was to carefully consider the recommendations of Elder Widtsoe's committee and oversee the creation of slide shows, radio programs, missionary pamphlets, brochures, audio presentations, translation of materials for mission use, and anything else that could contribute to mission or publicity work. Elder Stephen L Richards chaired the committee. John A. Widtsoe, Melvin J. Ballard, Charles A. Callis, Alonzo A. Hinckley, and Albert E. Bowen were also appointed.[34] As recommended by the Widtsoe committee, recently returned missionary Gordon B. Hinckley was hired as their executive secretary.

Elder Widtsoe's familiarity with Hinckley's efficiency led to his recommendation. The Radio, Publicity and Mission Literature Committee's early endeavors were directed at satisfying the ever-burgeoning mission field. John often acknowledged the quality of the work young Gordon produced, and over the years there is frequent mention of his contributions, always with high praise.[35]

In 1944 John was released from the committee,[36] but he was so identified with it that continued association was unavoidable, and his conviction about its importance never dimmed. Two years after his release, he continued his appeal that the Church move more rapidly in accepting modern technological devices as gifts of Heavenly Father: "Missionary work must grow in foreign fields, as never before; missionary work at home must increase as never before. We shall employ every modern device: the telephone, telegraph, radio, printing press, the short wave systems as mentioned by President Smith, and the other devices that are coming. We shall use them all in our attempt to win men and women from wickedness to righteousness, from untruth or near truth to full and complete truth which is the gospel of the Lord Jesus Christ."[37]

WORK OF THE COMMITTEE

John felt the need to constantly update pamphlets and tracts while presiding over missionary work in Europe. With the committee, he was frequently involved in conceiving, writing, and editing new pamphlets, brochures, and tracts.[38] No one in the Church had a more active missionary pen than John. As a scientist and educator, he had produced more than four hundred publications, and a similar number appeared while he was an apostle. Within a month of the committee's creation, he was closely involved with Hinckley in the creation of a special publication, a handbook for missionaries. He also worked with Hinckley on a slide show that Hinckley had begun while on his mission,[39] and on a booklet about Latter-day Saint temples.

A good share of the work of the committee had to do with radio broadcasts. As one historian noted, "In 1924 the Church purchased a radio station whose call letters soon were changed to the familiar KSL. The Tabernacle Choir began its weekly nationwide broadcasts in 1929. At first the announcer had to climb a tall ladder to reach the only microphone available. The series was planned for only three months, but favorable response from throughout the United States and from Europe prompted the network to continue the program indefinitely."[40]

Soon all of the radio programs with which the Church was affiliated were under the jurisdiction of the Radio, Publicity, and Mission Literature Committee. The committee was responsible for organizing, writing and producing many radio programs.[41] John's contribution included writing and delivering regularly scheduled radio addresses. The Church was invited by the Columbia Broadcasting System to participate in its national "Church of the Air" broadcast, four times annually. Two of those broadcasts coincided with conference, and whoever was speaking during the featured session automatically participated in the "Church of the Air." In 1936, John delivered a conference "Church of the Air" address entitled "What is Man?" discussing man's premortal history and postmortal destiny.[42] In 1939 he spoke on "Foundations of Peace."[43] In 1946 he addressed the subject of "Faith in the Atomic World."[44] In 1948 he spoke about "Hunger in the Midst of Plenty." In it he addressed the spiritual famine in a world with gospel truths available.[45] In 1950 he spoke under the title "Be of Good Courage."[46]

John also participated in the Church's regularly scheduled Sunday Evening Broadcasts. His first series of addresses, given between 2 January and 29 May 1944, necessitated that he forgo other obligations: "I am advised that for the first few weeks of my radio work I do not accept any evening appointment. Several reasons for this have been explained to me, and I am willing to abide by them."[47]

John delivering an address at KSL radio station.

The series was titled "An Understandable Religion" and took the form of an introduction to the gospel. The first address, "Can the Unseen World Be Known?" dealt with revelation and inspiration as valid sources of knowledge.[48] Ensuing lectures covered topics like "What is God?" "What is Man?" "The Objective of Life," and "Religion and the Family"—subjects designed to express the ideas of the gospel in a plain, straightforward manner.

The addresses were well received. John replied to one of the many who wrote in appreciation, "Thank you for your kind comments on the radio work. These talks are addressed, as you of course understand, to a certain class of people, who probably do not listen in. However, if one soul here and there may be touched, it is about all we can hope for. You remember how Abraham talked the Lord Himself into reducing the number of righteous who might save Sodom and Gomorra."[49]

John was surprised at how many members liked the simple talks, but he understood the attraction that the addresses held for them: "The radio talks that I gave were not intended for people like yourself, for you are well versed in the gospel. But I suppose that it is always interesting to Latter-day Saints to listen to the old truths restated, no matter how well they know them."[50] John received many requests to publish the addresses, which culminated in a book entitled *An Understandable Religion*.[51]

Another of John's books, a history of his mother, was included in the committee's radio programs on early Church history. Gordon B. Hinckley wrote to John:

> You will recall that the Radio Committee decided that a new episode should be substituted for the one dealing with Mexican Colonies.
>
> After giving careful consideration to the matter, Brother Cannon and I concluded that perhaps nothing would be more effective than some good dramatization built around missionary work, which received such strong emphasis during the administration of President John Taylor.
>
> Further consideration led to your own lovely story of your mother. Using a portion of it, we have produced the enclosed script. I believe it is true to the history and to the spirit of your story, and I think that it will make up into an effective dramatization.
>
> Lest it create embarrassment for you, we have left out the Widtsoe name, although all those familiar with the story will immediately recognize it from the incidents. If you feel reluctant about permitting its use or if there is anything in it which you wish treated in different manner, we will be pleased to try another subject (although I know of none so effective) or make changes.[52]

John had been a seventy until his appointment to the apostleship. Much of his professional life was spent helping the public understand what he and the institutions he was affiliated with were trying to do. His experiences with the press during the university consolidation issue, the building of a new agricultural program at BYU, the revival of the Agricultural College, and the rescue of the University of Utah from its plummeting public image all provided a unique, intuitive understanding of how to work with the public media.

John's experience was often sought. Of a proposed pageant celebrating the hundredth anniversary of the coming of the gospel to Europe, he urged that it be accessible for the smaller branches. He felt that the most successful portrayal "should have been built around the voyage across the Atlantic of the first company of elders."[53] Elder Widtsoe encouraged participation in the Oregon Trail Pageant.[54] While teaching at USC, he oversaw the setting up of a display for the American Exposition held in San Diego and was the main speaker at a two-hour program there.[55] As the Radio and Publicity Committee participated in the World's Fair in San Francisco, John was a great help in putting up a highly successful exhibit.

John wanted to provide missionaries with a way to defend the Book of Mormon. To that end he, along with Franklin S. Harris, Jr., created a booklet called "Seven Claims of the Book of Mormon."[56] He and Gordon B. Hinckley created a "Missionary Guide,"[57] one of many collaborative projects: "With an ever-present gleam in his eye, Elder John A. Widtsoe frequently reminded Gordon that his door was always open. Gordon prized moments of one-on-one discussion with this man of great intellect, whom he found to be not only brilliant but also down-to-earth and personable."[58]

As early as mid-1936, John suggested motion pictures as a means of spreading the gospel.[59] He gave a series of lectures at the Lion House, "Modern Revelations and Modern Questions." He regularly proposed placing Church materials in prominent libraries, noting, "There is a superabundance of anti-Mormon literature in almost every library, but a pitiful scarcity of Mormon literature presenting our case properly. I have in mind libraries of certain universities attended largely by our people, also certain theological schools and students of which should have access to our point of view and also to city and other libraries in which we could profitably place some of our works in addition to the Book of Mormon which is now generally distributed."[60]

He further reported:

> There are perhaps one hundred extensive public libraries, in the large centers of population, which have fairly large collections of anti-Mormon books. It would be profitable in the near future to place a

small selection, perhaps four or five volumes, of pro-Mormon literature in these larger libraries which are patronized by tens of thousands
of readers.

In six or eight of the theological seminaries of the United States,
we should place a fair collection of our literature. My assignment dealt
directly with the universities attended by many L.D.S. students; as
Harvard, Columbia, George Washington, University of Chicago,
Michigan, Wisconsin, Idaho, Arizona, Nevada, California, California
at Los Angeles, and a few others. These fair sized collections of our
literature could be placed profitably.[61]

His participation in the committee gave him the chance to finally
put into action so many of the ideas he had long held about getting the
Church the kind of attention that would help bring the gospel to many
other people. As an aging apostle, he became one of the biggest propo-
nents of taking advantage of the newest and most modern means available for spreading the gospel net and expanding the harvest of the kingdom of God.

38

RELIGION CLASSES AT USC

───────────── ▪ ─────────────

T HE University of Southern California (USC) created the University Religious Conference (URC) to organize the many religious groups represented in their student body. In 1935 the members of the URC (including Carl Sumner Knopf, dean of the School of Religion, and Rufus B. von KleinSmid, USC's prestigious president) launched an experiment to allow university credit for religion classes of the members of the URC. They felt it was fundamentally wrong for a university to grant credit for almost any philosophy, ancient or modern, but, because of the separation of church and state, to deny credit for teachings that were at the very soul of the nation. In a radio address von KleinSmid expressed his view of the power of religious convictions as the best means of averting war, the world's great menace in the early decades of the century. Addressing political convictions he said, "None of these— nor all together—can ever take the place of religious convictions which insist that it is possible for peoples so thoroughly to understand each other's character, aspirations and necessities that war would seem to be as foolish as it is needless and ineffectual."[1] John A. Widtsoe participated in the USC experiment from the beginning and knew the feelings of all who promoted it. He wrote, "Sound, prominent thinkers felt that if collegiate youth, the coming national leadership, were made acquainted with living religions in a systematic, dignified manner, placed at least on an equal footing with all academic subjects, it might help advance the national welfare. Is it not true that when God is banished from daily life and students' minds and bodies are trained but not their souls and characters, that their outlook on life is bound to be warped?"[2]

Each member institution of the URC was invited to develop religion classes, select its own teacher, define its own program, and espouse its own beliefs. Preston D. Richards, legal counsel to the URC, and Eugene L. Roberts, a member of the USC faculty, were Latter-day Saints who helped secure the inclusion of LDS religion classes, held apart from Protestant classes. The general announcement released by USC under the department of "Biblical Literature" set the parameters: "The Church and Its Program. An analytical survey of the origin, development, international distribution, organization, and administration of a church program. Its tenets, forms of worship, practices, social services, and publications. Lectures, readings, and related work. Three hours of lectures and study each week. Sections will be formed for the following groups: (1) The Protestant churches; (2) The Catholic church; (3) The Episcopal church; (4) The Jewish synagogue; (5) The Mormon church."[3]

An important stipulation protected academic integrity by requiring that each teacher was to have the full professional rating required for faculty status at USC. Dr. Widtsoe was selected to be the first professor of Mormonism.

THE SELECTION OF DR. JOHN A. WIDTSOE

Preston Richards had been a member of the general board of the Young Men's Mutual Improvement Association (YMMIA). In 1935 he was an influential attorney in Los Angeles[4] and helped organized the University Religious Conferences at UCLA and USC. He also helped found the Church's Deseret Clubs, precursors to the Institutes of Religion at those and other colleges in the city. Richards was one of a few key Church leaders who eagerly sought to establish a strong Church presence in Southern California.

On 21 July 1935, Richards wrote to Widtsoe, "I am enclosing herewith an original letter from Mr. Evans, Secretary of the University Religious Conference, suggesting that we give a course in Mormonism at U.S.C. This letter was received just before we left for Hawaii. I read it to President Grant and also to President Clark, and they both suggested that I take the matter up with you."[5] John had been reappointed Church commissioner of education eighteen months earlier, following his release as president of the European Mission in the fall of 1933. On 19 August 1935, Richards requested a private meeting on the following Sunday when John was to be the visiting authority at the Los Angeles Stake conference: "It is my thought that this course, because of its extreme importance, should be given by yourself, as Commissioner of Education, if it is possible to make the arrangement. It will be the commencement of similar work in other institutions if the work is successful. . . . You would immediately step into a position of leadership among the faculty members of U.S.C. and all other educational and religious leaders in this community. It would be one of the finest pieces of missionary work ever done in the Church. I most sincerely hope that it can be worked out this way."[6]

August ended with no final decision, though there was consensus that the class was to proceed. On 12 September 1935, Richards sent an urgent telegram to Widtsoe: "President Von KleinSmid wants immediately name of instructor giving our course Name will be in schedules being printed if received by eleven thirty Pacific time Von KleinSmid and all our people here hope you are designated Wire me immediately Registration next Tuesday."[7]

John's telegraphed reply was sent at 11 A.M. Pacific time: "My appointment made this morning Have had no information from university Assuming first lecture on Tuesday September 24 Can you secure all necessary information for us Also secure someone to represent me at registration if necessary Stake Presidents must help secure class of reasonable size say thirty I need to remain here long as possible. Greetings and Thanks."[8]

Paul H. Dunn was instrumental in establishing the LDS Institute of Religion programs that grew out of this experiment and was acquainted with many URC members who launched it. He described von KleinSmid's personal satisfaction in Widtsoe's participation: "He used to come over to the Institute after we built the building, because he was proud he had had a part in bringing the program to campus. It was at his invitation that Dr. Widtsoe eventually received the assignment to come to the University."[9]

A more detailed response from John was written immediately after the telegram was sent: "The half-expected has happened. The Presidency are asking me to inaugurate the projected course in the 'Mormon' Church program at the University of Southern California."[10] He added:

> I only have two fears with respect to the experiment: First, that I personally may not give an adequate account of myself; second, that there may be a lack of interest on the part of our people in the course, so that we shall suffer thereby in comparison with the others. As my thoughts have begun to deal with the problem, I can see that I shall need all my time and strength for a matter of two months or more to outline the work, make syllabi for the students, and produce ample reading and study matter to keep the students busy and to make the course more comparable with that of other churches, with the Church literature which we possess. We shall make up a fair sized library of "Mormon" subjects, to be placed in the library of the University; otherwise, of course, we should be helpless in carrying on the directed study required.[11]

RESPONSES AND BEGINNINGS

The *Deseret News* announced the experiment: "It was said at the Church offices that the L.D.S. Church considers it a distinct compliment to be invited to join the other groups in the presentation of the course at a school of such acknowledged high rating."[12] It reported that USC was the first nondenominational university to offer university credit for religion courses taught by competent instructors from individual religious groups, noting, "It is hoped that out of the experiment, if successful, a movement may be generated for the same purpose in other collegiate institutions. It is characterized by competent observers as a worthy attempt, indeed."[13]

John recognized the advantage being offered the Church but was surprised that he was assigned to fill it because he had already spent so many of his fourteen apostolic years away from Utah. "This is a big opportunity for the Church," he wrote, "and while I did not for a moment think it would be my duty to participate in the work yet I am quite ready to accept the call, and shall do my very best in representing the Church as it should be represented."[14] In his memoirs he recalled the unique nature of the invitation: "I was appointed to inaugurate the work for the Church and my wife and I spent the school year of 1935–36 in Los Angeles. The classes were well attended and successful. As far as I know, it was the first time that any religion of the day, especially 'Mormonism,' was taught formally in a non-Mormon university, and for academic credit. It is an experiment of great worth and should be possible in all institutions of learning."[15]

To get things started, John sent an urgent letter to the stake presidents in Los Angeles. He reiterated the First Presidency's interest in the experiment and called on them to ensure its success through concerted efforts to identify prospective students and enlist their support of both day and evening classes. He conveyed his interest in the class and pressed the importance of its immediate success in achieving the potential good that could come to the Church. He was afraid there were not enough LDS students at USC and that those who were there were too widely spread among professional and general schools and scattered over much of the city as day and evening students. He wrote, "It would be very desirable to have a reasonably large class, one of thirty or forty members, from the very beginning of the course. Undoubtedly the other churches, with their large membership, will have crowded classes. . . . We must make good, not only intrinsically, but in comparison with the other churches. It will mean some weeks of right hard work for me to get the course under way, but no doubt should it succeed, some one else perhaps more competent than I can continue it and carry it on permanently."[16]

John lauded the courage of USC officials in pressing for the experiment to succeed and to extend it across all of American higher education: "The authorities of the institution appear to be very sincere in their statements that they hope to place religious education where it should be, on a par with other university subjects and with the same recognition given them."[17] He frequently reported successes of the experiment to the First Presidency, who, with him, hoped the program would spread to colleges and universities nationwide:

> The university authorities and many other thinking people are very much in earnest about the experiment of raising religious instruction to the level of history, science or other academic subjects by teaching it in college halls and giving it college credit. That such dignifying of religion is desirable is conceded, but the apparent difficulties and existing prejudices have deterred the schools from making the attempt. Should the USC experiment prove successful, it will open the door to similar instruction over the country.

> The decision to make the attempt, which as it seems was preceded by vigorous voicing of many conflicting opinions, was taken as you know only a few weeks ago. Consequently, there was no time to advertise it properly. Moreover, it was listed in the printed program as to make it appear to be a special part of the school of religion here maintained. The result is that the morning classes are small as yet, and may remain so until next semester. Meanwhile student interest and inquiries is increasing rapidly.

> The university authorities plead that we go on, despite pioneer difficulties, for they feel certain of the favorable outcome of the attempt, if good beginnings can be made.

> Every kind of attention is being shown me personally, my "Mormon" affiliation not withstanding. Undoubtedly, our participation in this venture has indirect as well as direct value, of a high order, to our great cause.

> I must say that it gave me something of a thrill last Tuesday morning to stand before a class of college students in a university hall on a university campus, of a fully accredited university, to give a course of lectures on the Gospel, for which credit towards graduation will be given. As far as I know, it was the first occasion of the kind.

Times have certainly changed; and new opportunities of teaching the eternal truth are coming within our reach.[18]

John was a popular speaker, and his presence at general conference during his long stay in Europe was sorely missed. He too had missed its spiritual renewal but, after assessing things at USC, he reluctantly requested that he again be excused from general conference during the first week of October, noting, "I can at best attend the coming conference only between trains on Sunday and at this critical beginning the time of travel is needed for organization and preparation. I shall miss greatly the spiritual nourishment of the conference; but unless you wish otherwise, I shall give my undivided attention to the assignment that you have given me here, even at the personal loss of attendance at this conference."[19] The Presidency telegraphed their consent: "Your letter September twenty-eighth read at Council Meeting today We join with you in the thrill received through teaching the gospel in a university hall Regret you will not have pleasure of being with us at conference but think it unnecessary for you to come."[20]

The experiment proceeded successfully for all five groups, but John's classes exceeded expectations, and it was especially satisfying when students of other faiths would "sit in" for two weeks and then drop other classes to stay. He attributed these decisions to the great holding power the gospel always has when attention is given to it:

> The evening class is much larger than anyone expected. This week it ran up to 75 more—nearly 60 of those being registered fully as university students. Most of those present at the evening class are, of course, members of the Church who are loyal and desire to make the experiment in religious education continue here as successfully as possible.
>
> My morning class is about the size of the morning class of the other denominations. The evening class is many times larger. If work is continued, doubtless many of the L.D.S. students attending this institution, who are not now enrolled will take the course next semester.
>
> I am attempting, as best I can with the time at my disposal, to make a text book out of the work that I am giving here for use in our

Institutes and for the students of the B.Y.U. and also for general purposes. Whether I should be able to write the book as I go along, will depend upon the time I find free from other duties.[21]

The First Presidency welcomed the opportunities being offered to spread the gospel and expand Church education: "The large attendance at the evening class indicates loyalty on the part of Church members which is most commendable, and also reflects credit upon your ability as a teacher and your authority as interpreter of the Gospel principles. We are impressed with the feeling that what you are doing is laying the foundation of something which will be a very rich benefit to the Church, and you have our confidence and blessing as you pioneer this important movement."[22]

Christmas brought the Widtsoes their first opportunity to return to Salt Lake City to share their experiences. It is evident in their reports that the big question on their minds was whether the gospel could be taught for university credit by Latter-day Saint professors in colleges and universities all across the nation. The *Deseret News* arranged an interview with John:

> Dr. Widtsoe says the president of the University, the regular faculty members, the school officials and the students are according the classes every consideration; the registration is relatively large and the interest is keen. There is a decided tendency, he says, on the part of university students to inquire into religion and its place in life. The classes, conducted as a part of the USC curriculum, but elective, are satisfying this want and the school officials have expressed themselves as believing that what was started as an experiment will become a permanent course.
>
> In his classes at the USC Dr. Widtsoe said he has students of the L.D.S. faith and a large number also who are not members of this Church. The class is actuated, he said, by a spirit of honest and frank inquiry and no semblance of prejudice or narrowness.[23]

In January 1936, John wrote an article explaining his experiences in the *Improvement Era*:

> Indeed, the developments from this experiment may in time

modify, to the advantage of the nation, the ideals and practice of education in the United States; and its effects may be felt beyond the boundaries of our own country. In short, religion, as understood by a group of believers, is placed on a level with recognized academic subjects, such as history, science, or philosophy.

The teaching of these courses is hedged about by only two, but necessary, restrictions. The work must be given in a strictly academic manner, by teachers of university training and fitness. The courses must be expositions of the faiths and not arguments for the truth. Proselyting belongs to the church and church institutions. These are desirable safeguards for the groups interested as well as for the university.

Running through the experiment are three main thoughts. First, that it is desirable and necessary that universities take part in religious and spiritual education; second, that fully acceptable courses of study, of university grade, may be built from the content of organized religion, and, third, that the objective of the experiment may be more effectively gained by allowing each religious group to present its history and doctrine. These will all be tested as the work progresses.[24]

INSTRUCTION GIVEN, LEARNING GAINED

In the fall and winter quarters, John followed the course title "The Program of the Church." His lectures gave detailed explanations of the operations and mission of the Church. He expanded his class notes into a textbook, which became part of the basic curriculum for the Institutes of Religion and for BYU religious instruction:

> The purpose of this book is to provide college classes, missionaries and the general reader with a connected survey of the faith and practice of the Church of Jesus Christ of Latter-day Saints. . . . The title of the book is borrowed from the catalogue name of the course, "Religion 60-B1," offered by the University of Southern California. The lectures given in that course in 1935–36 form the basis of this book. . . .
>
> The schools determine largely the kind and amount of information, the opinions and point of view of the American people. More than any other agency the schools are responsible for the behavior of

the citizens of our country. As the schools teach them so they are likely to become. We know of no better places outside of the home and the church in which to prepare American boys and girls, men and women, for American citizenship. . . .

It will not do to say that such training is the concern of the Church. The schools own the time of youth. Enough time must be spared by the school for religious training. Religion must be dignified in the eyes of youth, who look at the world through school windows, by giving religion a place by the side of other subjects of the curriculum, in methods and frequency of teaching and in the use of texts and other educational helps. School credit must be given for such work properly done, if respect is to be gained for it in the minds of those who attend our schools. All this may be done lawfully without infringing upon the constitutional provision for religious liberty.

The experiment is a noble one, which in behalf of national moral safety should be followed by other institutions. It is difficult to understand why an ancient philosophy should receive an honored place among the offerings of a university, while a living philosophy of life accepted by multitudes of people should be excluded from the academic realm.[25]

The purpose of the Church was the focus of John's first few lectures: "Salvation is the common term applied to the objective of life. . . . Whoever is on the way to happiness is approaching salvation. Whoever has attained full happiness has won full salvation. The requirements for happiness are those of salvation."[26]

The practices of the Church were outlined in his second series of lectures. John described how LDS practices were designed to refine each aspect in attaining the object of happiness. Topics included caring for body and mind, nourishing emotions, spiritual enrichment, family, social welfare, economic security, the Church and the state, ordinances and related activities, and the daily life of a Latter-day Saint.

The organization of the Church was carefully explained in his third series of lectures, which covered general priesthood responsibilities, divisions in the priesthood, territorial divisions of the Church, administrative practices, judicial provisions, obtaining forgiveness, temple work, and the work of the auxiliary organizations.

Explanations of the Church was the subject of his fourth series. He briefly described Church explanations that enhance understanding of perplexing concerns and give reassurance and hope for the future. His subjects included the unity and contents of the universe, the mystery of origin, the plan of salvation, laws of progression, functions of the Church, universal salvation, filling God's plan, and the Articles of Faith.

The origin of the Church was explained in his final series of lectures in the first two quarters. The topics he chose to address were the course of the gospel on earth, restoration of the Church of Christ, laying the foundations of the Church, settlement in the Intermountain West, after Brigham Young, and recent history (1928–1936).

In the spring quarter, Widtsoe taught from the Doctrine and Covenants. He presented the unique tenets of Latter-day Saint beliefs to the students at USC, which, in the spring quarter, brought an increased number of non-LDS students. From his outlines and from a written transcript of his lectures, G. Homer Durham, Widtsoe's son-in-law and former president of Arizona State University, compiled a book entitled *The Message of the Doctrine and Covenants.* Durham explained, "It represents an opus magnum, he delivered in lectures at the university, April through early June, 1936, but not completed or 'polished' in his own inimitable manner for publication. What I have done is to edit and organize the transcript of these lectures into chapter divisions. They follow, in order, the lectures and materials as delivered and recorded in those days, April-June 1936, at the University of Southern California."[27]

When Elder Widtsoe returned to Salt Lake City for general conference in April 1936, the *Deseret News* again published an interview:

> "Our experiments in religious education on the Pacific Coast are going very successfully. Our work along religious education lines will probably continue for a long time at the educational institutions on the Pacific coast, where it will grow in momentum and interest. The Latter-day Saints in California are faithful, devoted people, and they are prospering. Through their splendid preparatory work we have been able not only to continue our classes at the U.S.C., but also to organize and teach the Latter-day Saint students at the U.C.L.A. and Los Angeles Junior College, who hold weekly meetings to discuss religion.

Dr. Widtsoe with officials of the University of Southern California in the School of Religion at USC.

Students of these institutions who are members of the Church show a very great interest in the gospel. And they are eager for it."

Paying tribute to Elder Widtsoe and his work in religious education in Los Angeles, President Cannon said that "Dr. Widtsoe has lightened up the whole outlook of the Church in California, especially at the USC among both students and professors. The course in the Doctrine and Covenants last week had a registration of more than 90—it will soon reach well over 100—and is rated as the largest theological class, and the largest class irregardless of the number of students attending the university."[28]

At the end of the year John reported to the First Presidency that university credit had been given for the study of Mormonism taught under university sponsorship in university classrooms. The Church and its teachings had gained a high degree of respect and influential friends. Many nonmembers—indeed, more than half of the morning class—had learned about the Church. Some had been baptized, and many had sought John out to express appreciation for learning the program of a sane and practical church. "The registered attendance was 169," John wrote, "with nearly twice that many as occasional visitors. Nearly all of those students were members of the Church; though some non-Mormons, including a graduate working for the Ph.D. degree, were registered for credit in the course."[29] His report included successes in the Deseret Clubs at three other institutions. He particularly requested that an office be established at UCLA, where classes had attracted thirty students. Out of a concern for costs, he wrote, "Our young people represent the real Church problem in Los Angeles. Every effort should be made to hold them."[30] He strongly urged that the experiment be continued, though expectations about attendance should be modest, concluding, "The experiment in religious education undertaken by the U.S.C. is the greatest educational venture of my day. May it prosper."[31]

SIDE-EFFECTS AND AFTERMATH

Whenever President Heber J. Grant was in Los Angeles, he stopped at USC for a visit with Elder Widtsoe, which had a powerful impact on John's colleagues in the experiment. He wrote to President Grant:

> After you left the luncheon which we both attended last week the conversation for several minutes was directed upon you. The chairman said, "there goes a real statesman." Another answered and said, "If our country could have such men in office all would be well." A third volunteered, "I hope the time may come when such men may be called to public service in our land." Of course I was very pleased, and wanted to tell you about it. . . . The University people are beginning now to plan for next year and we shall have to decide what we desire to do with regard to the coming year.[32]

At USC Widtsoe had shared the message of the restoration and mingled closely with prominent religious leaders, key faculty members, the dean of the School of Religion, and President von KleinSmid. He was invited to faculty luncheons, lectures, and dinners, and he frequently met with school officials to discuss religion.[33] He was satisfied that the teachings of Joseph Smith were being taught at USC without the Mormon label.[34] Many of the best books on the Church, as selected by Dr. Widtsoe, were put in the main collection of the university library.[35]

In 1936 G. Byron Done was called to be Widtsoe's successor. As Paul H. Dunn reported, this was "a position which he held for approximately twenty years, from 1936 to 1956. During that time, with one or two exceptions, he pretty well managed the whole program, taught the classes, met the students, and conducted the activities."[36]

Done followed Widtsoe's program of instruction and even used his outlines and lecture notes.[37] The LDS classes continued to be successful, but waning interest and slackening enrollments among the other groups severely dampened the hopes of university officials and brought an end to their visionary experiment. Its demise was caused by the inability of most of the church groups to attract sufficient support for their classes, not by USC's retreat from their plan to grant credit for those classes. By 1941 only two of the groups qualified for credit by the university. Done wrote to the Church commissioner of education, Dr. Franklin West, "At the University of Southern California I now have two classes in Mormon philosophy and practice for which credit is given. With the exception of the group led by Dr. Polyzoides, our church is the only one granted this permission. The basis of the grant is that of increased attendance."[38]

Though the credit experiment failed, John's work launched the establishment of Institutes of Religion across California. Historian Leonard Arrington noted, "The first Institute to be established outside the intermountain area was at the University of Southern California in Los Angeles; it was founded under the direction of Dr. John A. Widtsoe in 1935."[39] John's sentiments are a fitting summation of his USC work and its aftermath: "Theology became our best loved subject. It formed our outlook upon life; and made us more sensitive to right and wrong. It shaped our characters and conduct in life. From my own experience and from the observation of the lives of those who have had parallel training in secular and sacred subjects, I have been throughout life an unchanging, firm believer in religious education for youth."[40]

39

EDITOR OF THE
IMPROVEMENT ERA

J OHN A. Widtsoe had a natural gift for writing. It was so natural that it set him as far above his peers as did his work in chemistry. "English was always a favorite subject," he recalled. "In it I did well. I wrote for our College newspaper, the *Harvard Crimson,* and our magazine, the *Harvard Advocate.* One of my stories was selected by the *Boston Herald* in the special graduation issue, as a representative of the literary efforts of the class. When I graduated, I had the chance to enter the editorial employ of the *Youth's Companion,* in that day the foremost magazine for youth."[1]

In his years as chemist and director of the Utah Experiment Station, John authored nearly a hundred station bulletins, circulars, and reports on the latest developments of scientific agriculture. As the bulletins were primarily intended for professionals in agriculture, John felt they didn't reach a wide enough audience, so, he wrote, "to secure even closer contact with the farmer and his family, three of us, Lewis A. Merrill, J. Edward Taylor, and I, founded an agricultural weekly, *The Deseret Farmer.*"[2] It was a popular journal, helpful and useful to the everyday farmer and farm family.

Before John's appointment as *Improvement Era* editor, he worked closely with associate editors as an author. He was also a regular contributor to the *Utah Genealogical and Historical Magazine.* His first experience with the direct responsibilities for a regular Church publication came with his assignment to edit the *Latter-day Saints' Millennial Star.*

REORGANIZATION OF THE IMPROVEMENT ERA

On 23 April 1935, the First Presidency announced that Elder Widtsoe would be associated with President Grant as editor of the *Improvement Era* and that he would assume the active editorial direction of the magazine.[3] In a pamphlet entitled *The Era Campaign 1935–36, Instruction and Information for Stake and Ward Directors,* they expressed the opinion that the *Era* had taken its greatest forward stride with the appointment of Elder Widtsoe as joint editor with President Grant. President Grant grew fond of labeling the *Era* "the Voice of the Church."[4]

The *Deseret News* was equally enthusiastic: "In the hands of Dr. Widtsoe as active editor, it is expected that the Church magazine will move steadily forward. . . . Dr. Widtsoe has a sympathetic understanding of the problems facing Church members and particularly the young people."[5] With John guiding the destiny of the magazine, it was acknowledged that "President Grant, who has always had the keenest interest in the magazine's welfare, will be able in the councils of the general authorities to give more and more guidance to the periodical."[6]

Other *Era* appointments included Harrison R. Merrill and Elsie Talmage Brandley, associate editors; George Q. Morris, general manager; Clarissa A. Beesley, associate manager; and J. K. Orton, business manager.[7] For many years the annual June conference was the rallying point of the Young Men's and Young Women's MIA and the time for launching the annual subscription drive for the *Era.* In the 1935 June conference, a ward from Salt Lake City performed a musical dramatization entitled "*Era* Melodies" in which they paraded across the stage some highlights from the contents of the *Era* for the coming year. In that conference John gave an address entitled "A Forward Look with the *Improvement Era.*" In it he discussed his editorial ambitions and vision for the magazine: "We believe in eternal progression, in everlasting development, in the highest type of evolution, and when this Church stands still in the application of its fundamental principles or of its organization, it is in danger. . . . The *Era* has changed to meet the needs of the day. The same eternal principles have been taught, the same fine testimonies of the truth have been borne, but the methods of approach have changed."[8]

John heralded the need of a magazine in the Church. Kept conveniently before the people, it would be the greatest force for determining the thinking and practices of Church members.

> *The Era,* I hope, will be the voice of this great Church, as never before. . . . It must be as a living voice, appearing monthly, telling every reader that which is in the mind of the Church as a whole. We cannot get along without such a voice; it would be impossible.

> Another thing enters into the *Era* editorial plan. . . . The gospel . . . is a system of philosophy, which if applied to human lives will bring about individual and community happiness. It is so organized, devised . . . by the application of the principles of the gospel.

> A third principle must be kept in mind in planning for the contents of the *Era.* . . . When I shut my eyes and look back, I can hardly believe that this is the world into which I entered; it has changed so. . . . There is a new body of knowledge built upon the old. One of the important things for Latter-day Saints is to keep up with the procession of thought, of knowledge of the new things that come.

> There is an important fourth principle to keep in mind. The *Era* must supply entertaining material in the imaginative field—the field of art if you choose. Stories, poetry, pictorial art, must have their place in our magazine to serve a very vital need of the normal intelligent person.

> Here are the four *Era* objectives: To be the voice of the Church; to be the interpreter in gospel terms of world events; to keep the readers abreast of increasing knowledge, and to supply the entertainment that comes from stories, poetry, and art. How nearly we can reach our *Era* ideals can not be foretold. . . . The Church has large numbers of gifted, trained members in every field of human activity. Surely, with

your help and theirs we can make our *Era* . . . a magazine, unique in its mission and great in its service.[9]

John's assignment as joint editor marked a new emphasis for the *Era,* and with it came many changes and heightened ambitions for the whole *Era* family. The inside front cover of the September 1935 issue heralded, "*The Improvement Era* Now Becomes More Than Ever THE VOICE OF THE CHURCH. To the stakes of Zion from New York to Hawaii, to the Missions in the most distant parts of the earth, the Gospel message is to be carried each month by this splendid missionary magazine."[10] Photographs of Grant, Widtsoe, and Merrill headed the page with a note that clarified President Grant's role as chief editor, explaining that Widtsoe was "recently assigned to the Active Editorial direction of our magazine. . . . There are already several excellent American family magazines in circulation. There can be no good reason for adding another to an already cluttered market, unless it has a specific purpose or message for its readers. In the case of the *Era,* this purpose must be the purpose of the Priesthood Quorums, the Mutual Improvement Associations, the Department of Education, and the Music Committee—the strengthening of the faith of the members in the restored Church of Christ, and the promulgation among all readers of the truths and principles of the Gospel."[11]

A wide range of interests mixing Church subjects with cultural, economic, governmental, historical, scientific, fictional, poetic, and pictorial were to be considered for publication under six broad areas of interest: (1) The Voice of the Church, (2) Interpreting World Movements, (3) Applying the Gospel to Human Life, (4) Keeping Abreast of Current Knowledge, (5) Supplying the Need for Creative art, and (6) Miscellaneous.[12]

Two unexpected events quickly followed that had a powerful impact on the operations of the *Era.* First, in August, Elsie Talmage Brandley, the highly esteemed associate editor, died. Though only 38 years old, the passing of her strong voice brought a flood of letters and poems in her honor, some of which were published. Second, on 12 September, the First Presidency announced that Elder Widtsoe would move to Los Angeles for a year's appointment to teach LDS religion classes for academic credit at the University of Southern California. These two events pressed for immediate attention to organizational adjustments that exceeded those already being anticipated with Widtsoe's appointment as editor.

John had the highest regard for his co-workers at the *Era*. He wrote, "When Brother Merrill retired to give his whole time to his work at the B.Y.U., Richard L. Evans, later a member of the First Council of Seventy, was made managing editor; and Sister Brandley, who died in the midst of her life's best years, was succeeded by Marba Cannon Josephson. Better people could not have been found for the positions."[13]

Just three days before John's departure for Los Angeles, President Grant called a meeting in the board room of the Church Administration Building to make critical decisions relating to the management of the *Era* while John was still in Salt Lake City. In attendance, besides Elder Widtsoe, were David O. McKay of the Sunday School superintendency, Albert E. Bowen and Franklin L. West of the YMMIA presidency, Ruth May Fox and Clarissa A. Beesley of the YWMIA presidency, and Franklin S. Harris and Stringham Stephens of the *Era*. Several needs were discussed, but most urgent was the decision that a full-time associate editor be secured. The final decision was left pending, but the direction was clear to all. Harrison R. Merrill, then the part-time associate editor, was to be given his choice to remain with the *Era* on a full-time basis or to assume full-time teaching responsibilities at Brigham Young University. If the latter was his choice, Richard L. Evans was recommended as the new full-time associate editor.[14] In a letter to Elder Widtsoe, written the following day, Merrill indicated a preference for his faculty assignment at BYU, affirmed the desirability of a full-time person to replace him at the *Era*, and expressed his personal approval of the Evans recommendation. Because plans for each issue of the *Era* were laid several months in advance, the separation of Merrill was somewhat protracted.

When Merrill's decision was made, John grew anxious for closure on the Evans appointment. The separation caused by the USC experiment only increased his anxiety. Evans had served in the European Mission and had helped edit the *Millennial Star* when elders Talmage and Widtsoe were its editors and presidents of the European Mission. Appointing a good associate or managing editor was particularly crucial, because John felt that with the *Era*, "perhaps the biggest work . . . is in the business department,"[15] which he had little time for, especially when he was two states away.

From their first meeting in the European Mission Office in December 1927, the relationship between John Widtsoe and Richard Evans was like that of a father and son. Evans's feelings were stated in a letter:

> Many times I have berated you for trusting your fellowmen too far, for not taking time out to look after your own financial interests, for being too generous and free hearted and too easily imposed upon, for giving of yourself fully in all things as you have done and for being so unbelievably considerate of others that your own plans and comforts and wishes have gone by the way—but all the time I have been chiding you I have been secretly envying you and hoping and praying that somehow I could bring my own spirit to the foothills of such heights as yours has soared.
>
> I know that you have had your reward here and that what awaits you hereafter will be limited only by the ability of the Lord Himself to bestow blessings upon those He loves and those who love Him. There's no man who ever lived whose company I enjoy more, whose presence I would rather live in, and whose confidence I would rather have. Not having known my own father I can say these things to you with full truth and an overflowing heart.[16]

In the six-month wrestle Evans had over accepting the assignment, several letters passed between them while Widtsoe laid the program of the Church before the world in the halls of USC. They both awaited Merrill's separation and other appropriate changes. In a personal letter, John wrote of some of those changes and of his expanding views of the *Era*. A glimpse is given of the gentle manner with which he strode through difficulties and of his ever-present interest in the media mission of the Church:

"Get a nice soft pillow and 'sit on your trunk.' You will not have to sit on it much longer, but while you are there you might just as well enjoy it." He urged patience with the reminder that Merrill was free to decide between full-time employment at BYU or full-time employment at the *Era.* The decision was obviously difficult to make. John added, "Brother Merrill . . . is showing the finest spirit imaginable—I really admire his attitude." The indications given to Widtsoe were that Merrill would return to BYU and that Evans would step into the position. He wrote:

> I am very happy to think of your coming association with *The Improvement Era,* without casting any adverse reflection on the splendid work done by those laboring in its behalf the last few years. I believe, also, that it will be a good thing for you. It is difficult to look into the future, to know effects from causes, but considering everything, health, peace of mind, an opportunity for possible advancement, I am inclined to the belief that the change will be a desirable one for you. Perhaps your destiny is not to make so much money, but to do a greater work in some other way. Why quarrel with destiny.
>
> There is much to be done for the *Era.* There is a long possibility it can be made into a magazine of much importance beyond the borders of our own people, but it is certain that it can be made even more serviceable than it has been to the members of the Church.
>
> You know how happy I shall be while I may be connected with the *Era* to labor with you in a modest way, and I am sure that as your associates become acquainted with you, you will win much love from them.[17]

Admiration and gratitude abound in the warm response Evans sent a week later. It is addressed to "Mother and Father Widtsoe." The letter affectionately illustrates the power of Widtsoe's impact on the direction Evans's life followed. As always, a touch of humor added glitter to written word and the affected heart:

> The information contained in Dr. Widtsoe's letter with regard to the *Era* situation was the news I had been waiting for. I can't tell you why exactly, but I have been more anxious to get into that work for the past sixty days than I have been for any undertaking or opportunity that I remember in all my life. I advised my family and some of the "higher ups" here of the impending change, and they were all

happy for me, because they know that I have been discontented and restless for a long time. Unfortunately, however, the good news didn't last long, and today I received my first disappointment in connection with it.

I went to A. E. Bowen's house . . . and before I left he asked me if I hadn't done some wondering about the silence that had followed my conference with him and George Q. Morris, and I admitted that I had. He went to President Grant's office yesterday on other business, and the President told him to "wait a few minutes" on the *Era* change. . . . A. E. looked supremely disgusted when he told me of the situation, and when A. E. Bowen looks supremely disgusted there ain't any further way of looking disgusted, because even when A. E. looks mildly disgusted, it's supreme. . . .

I haven't any desire to have the *Era* job if the Lord doesn't want me to have it. I don't even want it if Heber J. Grant or John A. Widtsoe don't want me to have it. But I want to be sure that it's the Lord or Heber J. Grant or John A. Widtsoe and not a "combination in restraint" of something or other.

I have absolutely no desire in the world except to serve in the capacity of my greatest usefulness and I'm not doing that now, and no one knows it as well as I do. And so if the *Era* job is one of those "might have been's" the thing for me to do is to engage in some thinking and some looking around. I have sacrificed ambitions and cherished hopes before, and I can do it again. My big projecting jaw is set pretty firmly tonight, and I am prepared to pay what it costs to get out of the rut I'm in, and my very good and charming wife is right with me.[18]

Evans's fear over the snag that developed is a good indication of the interest he had and his intent to accept the offer. His spiritual qualifications for the *Era* are demonstrated in his desire to have the approval of President Grant, of Elder Widtsoe, and of God. Five days after Evans sent his letter, a telegram from A. E. Bowen arrived: "I have seen Presidency everything satisfactory arranged regarding Evans."[19] In spite of the telegram, the drama over Evans's official appointment continued to unfold in Salt Lake City. In a subsequent letter to Widtsoe, Evans reported that when Bishop Sylvester Q. Cannon heard about the presidency's plan to move Evans from KSL to the *Era*, he expressed serious opposition to President Grant out of concern for the operations of the KSL radio station. In a conversation with Evans that afternoon, Cannon assured Evans that his opposition had thwarted the plan, especially in the mind of Elder McKay. After considerable discussion with Evans, Cannon softened his opposition and agreed to meet with the presidency and withdraw his objections. Elder Bowen confirmed that Cannon's remarks had delayed plans. As the hours passed, Evans grew more restless over the matter and in due time asked Cannon if he had spoken with the presidency as he had agreed. Cannon answered that he had tried but was unable to reach them and that he was leaving for California the next morning. In a letter to Widtsoe, Evans described the anxiety Cannon had raised and the course he followed thereafter:

> I thanked him, and told him I would probably go over and correct the situation myself. Accordingly, I arranged an appointment with President Grant and when I told him what I had come for he chuckled, and advised me that Bishop Cannon had just beat me by about two minutes. I haven't seen the Bishop since. I hope he "ain't sore."
>
> President Grant was very warm and cordial and friendly, and chatted with me at some length about things in general. A week later, yesterday, he came to my office here at KSL and advised me that he had seen Brother Merrill and had arranged for me to open all the time I could with him during the next month or so. He called in Earl Glade while he was here and advised him that they were taking me over there. Earl said, "Why President Grant we think a great deal of this man." President Grant replied;—"So do we, that's why we're taking him." That settled that. President Grant also advised Mr. Glade in my presence that "the Presidency is united in the opinions that I should continue to handle the Tabernacle broadcast." That settled that. Taking it all in all, it was a very fine day.
>
> And so this morning I met in the *Era* with A. E., George Q., Lucy Grant and Harrison Merrill and was officially inducted into the preliminaries with due ceremony. The situation is not quite as favorable as it would have been a month ago, because I am more or less obligated to see the station through the holiday rush and will not have time to spend with the *Era* that I would like to, but Harrison does not

seem to be in any big hurry, and I believe he would stay on into part of January if it proved to be advantageous for me and the *Era*.[20]

When the offer was finally extended to Evans, he had to make one of the most difficult decisions of his life. He had developed an illustrious radio career as producer and announcer of important and popular programs for KSL, the radio voice of the Church. Three years later, in accepting his call to the First Council of the Seventy, he shared some personal feelings about his call to the *Era*:

> It has been a gratifying experience to me to be associated in the editorship of the *Improvement Era*. I struggled with myself for more than six months from the time the Presidency first called me over and suggested that I take the editorship of this magazine, until the time that it was actually undertaken. They did not make their request in the nature of a call. They left it entirely to my judgment, and it took me six months to reach the conclusion that they would not have called me over there if they had not wanted me to do it; but this realization finally settled upon my consciousness and I made the change for what reason I did not know at the time. I was very grateful that the Presidency have left me some radio activity, because it has meant much to me and I feel that the results are gaining.[21]

Finally the Evans appointment was complete and his attachment to the *Era* begun. This brought John and Richard into another relationship they both treasured, and the combination became a rich blessing for the Church. Indicative of that blessing are remarks Elder Mark E. Petersen made in general conference thirteen years later. He spoke of the love Church members have for the words of the General Authorities, especially the Prophet. After deliberating on the difficulty of the president of the Church in reaching the spreading membership, he offered some consolation: "But President [George Albert] Smith is the editor of *The Improvement Era*, and every month there is an editorial from him in *The Improvement Era*. . . . I wouldn't for anything miss the editorials that appear there under the name of the President of this Church."[22] That sentiment has grown as Church membership has increased and the importance of an attractive printed voice has grown with every expansion in membership.

Elder Petersen added, "President Smith is assisted in the editorship of *The Improvement Era* by Dr. John A. Widtsoe and President Richard L. Evans. These men are a great inspiration to the Church. You are in excellent company when you are in their presence, and if you want to have their influence about you and the children in your home, then take *The Improvement Era.*"[23] About a year after these sentiments were expressed, it was announced that "Richard L. Evans of the First Council of the Seventy, who since February of 1936 has been managing editor of the magazine, has been advanced to the position of editor along with President George Albert Smith and Elder John A. Widtsoe."[24]

THE EDITOR AS MANAGER

The calling as editor of the *Improvement Era* required knowledge and strict orthodoxy on the doctrinal and spiritual underpinnings of the Church. It required management skills that assured balanced representation, effective expression, attractive presentation, and efficient fiscal control without undue strain on fiscal resources.

John's call required constant vigilance and active involvement in managing the many tasks associated with producing, promoting, publishing, and distributing a magazine of the size and scope of the *Improvement Era.* In the first few months of his appointment, he familiarized himself with its many operations and the people responsible for its production. He held meetings with the heads of the auxiliaries and organizations that used the *Era* as their official voice. He met with the members of the editorial staff to review plans and develop strategies to optimize the contents and resources for upcoming issues and to make assignments to solicit articles and other important information. In that early transition stage especially, he was under heavy pressure from other Church responsibilities. He was still commissioner of education and was deeply involved with the summer school for seminary, institute, and religion teachers of the Church. There were pressing demands from his assignment as chair of a committee that led to the formation of the Radio, Publicity, and Mission Literature Committee.

Frequent stake conference visits and mission tours drew heavily on his time and energy. Meetings were required with the First Presidency and Quorum of the Twelve. He had talks to prepare; articles, lessons, and books to write; and the piles of letters to be answered seemed never to end. His recent return from Europe made life with his family of more pressing importance. Anna and her children needed exceptional nurturing, and the problems of getting their house returned to habitable status required much attention.

In the midst of all of these demands there came the call from the First Presidency to be the professor of Mormonism at USC. From his office at USC he continued to manage the *Era,* patiently awaiting the organizational changes decided upon by the First Presidency and carefully doing the work of the editor. He received many drafts of articles and spent many hours each week reading, editing, and commenting on them. Suitable letters to contributors were carefully crafted so as not to offend or curtail their interest, even when articles were rejected.

John's career in the state's college and university had established many significant contacts, whom he saw as a ready source of stimulating, insightful, instructive, and inspirational articles. Many of his files contain requests for articles from those contacts, including several notable university presidents. John pursued these contributions with a vigorous vision of what could become of the *Era:* "I really believe that anyone who contributes to the circulation of the *Era* is blessing the people. We do not read enough and we do not read enough of the right kind of literature. I only wish that we might make the *Era* more successful and useful and more acceptable to the people than it is."[25] He used his eloquent style and witty charm to invite authors to contribute:

> *The Improvement Era* is hungry for a message from you. An article of about two thousand or three thousand words would be greatly appreciated.[26]

> *The Improvement Era* has a good strong appetite. It is hungry. For some time it has had a desire for another flash from the Eternal Semaphore.[27]

> You are hereby appointed an accomplice with me to secure for the *Era* an article or more from your father. If I were you I should cer-

tainly select for my own use the tremendous sums that he will receive from the *Era* for the articles.[28]

> College presidents are notoriously free from pressing duties. Therefore, I take the liberty of asking the important question, is it not time to write an article or two for *The Improvement Era?*[29]

A particularly interesting example that marked the beginning of one of the most illustrious and fruitful careers with the *Improvement Era* is an exchange with the Nibley family. Alex Nibley, Hugh Nibley's father, begged Widtsoe to request that Hugh prepare some material for the *Era*, particularly about things that happened around 600 B.C. At the bottom of the letter is a handwritten postscript asking Widtsoe not to let Hugh know that his father was behind it.[30] Naturally, he could not refuse the invitation, so he wrote to Nibley:

> I have been thinking about you lately and have come to the con-clusion that a man who is learning as much as you are should be pass-ing some of it on to his fellow men. I mean not only in the . . . sacred places on the academic campus, but in the columns of the great mag-azine known as "*The Improvement Era.*" Now do not smile when I speak of "*The Improvement Era*" as a great magazine. It is serving a very fine purpose, has a reading circle of about one hundred fifty thou-sand, and above all is an organ of the Church to which you belong and which brought your family into this western land of America.
>
> Choose some subject of general appeal—something that will interest the common man. A lot of things happened some four to six hundred years before Christ which have a deep meaning to the Latter-day Saints. You spoke to me about your work in the philosophical and historical field of that period. Can we count on you to prepare such an article?[31]

No Church scholar had a more fruitful career with the *Improvement Era* than Hugh Nibley. Under John's leadership the *Era* expanded its emphasis on commercial advertising and the use of graphic media to add to readership appeal. Nibley remarked, "He took a very active hand in those things. Very visible. He was good!"[32] Numerous letters from Widtsoe advised authors not to be "too heavy" in their articles.

In meetings with Widtsoe (or managing editor Richard L. Evans), this matter was always addressed. Nibley recalled, "His advice to me always amused me. He used to tell me, oh, he thought I was too high falutin', 'Always write as if you were addressing the tiredest farmer in _____ . Now the tiredest farmer in _____ would make it very simple and I'll tell you it wouldn't really be worth addressing. It wouldn't be much. So I did not heed that advice, but he would always say it just the same."[33]

When asked, "What is the best counsel Elder Widtsoe ever gave you, other than to marry Phyllis?" Nibley gave away one of the secrets of his remarkable career: "The best counsel he gave me, produce! produce! produce! You have to have somebody producing here. You can't just talk about things, you have to produce."[34]

Some of the tasks of the editor were lifted from John's shoulders while he served at USC, particularly after Evans was appointed, but he still received many articles which he carefully edited.[35] In his files are copies of thousands of letters to contributors with encouraging comments and helpful critiques. Most often his comments were brief and simple: "Too condensed," "Too heavy," or "Not at a good level for young readers." Sometimes he included comments about doctrinal errors or an indication that they would like to use the article at a more appropriate time.[36] As the *Era* grew in popularity, critiques and correspondence became an ever larger task. He wrote, "*The Improvement Era* receives seven hundred to nine hundred contributions a month. It can use a scant twenty or twenty-five. In making selections such material is chosen as seems best to fit the needs of the magazine. Hundreds of most excellent articles that should see the light of day must be returned since the magazine only has a certain limited amount of space."[37]

As John traveled on stake conference visits or other Church assignments, he kept a sharp eye out for noteworthy stories. Writing to Neils Peterson, he asked: "When I attended the regional conference of the Church in Richfield some time ago, you said, as I remember, that you have been a ward teacher for sixty-five years. Could you give us some information about this long record of service? We should like to secure it."[38] Within the week he received the information. "Your letter of May 29th, containing information about your life and your ward teaching experiences, was received today. Thank you for your help. The letter has gone over to the *Era* staff. An article will probably be written concerning your untiring activities."[39] A tribute to Peterson's achievement appeared in the October issue on the Presiding Bishopric's page: "This is the longest continuous record in ward teaching yet to be reported to the presiding bishop's office. It is believed to be an all-church record in this activity."[40]

Through all of his editing activities, John maintained constant contact with his joint editor, President Grant, whose interest in the *Improvement Era* never waned.[41]

John loved working with the youth and felt a great responsibility to them. In a letter to President Ruth May Fox and counselors of the YWMIA, he said, "I am more and more convinced that our young people from twelve to eighteen years need renewed attention, under the changing educational and social conditions of this day."[42] But he also wanted the *Era* to continue to become the "voice of the Church." He wrote to Richard L. Evans, "I am delighted that President Grant OK'd the title page and table of contents. If he really means that *The Improvement Era* is to be the Church magazine, that is the voice of the Church, we have an obligation, an opportunity of great value to all concerned."[43]

There were regular meetings of the general *Era* committee. Frequently discussions arose as to the level of writing. It was unanimously felt that contributors must avoid being "too heavy" in their published pieces. There were discussions about the use of fiction. *True Story* was a popular magazine, and they considered copying some of its format to increase popularity, especially among the youth. John asked some key questions: "Is it love of fiction or love of sex that makes that magazine so popular?" . . . "Is poor fiction better than no fiction?"[44] From this discussion the decision was made not to include fiction. In addition, the First Presidency and the Council of the Twelve felt that all articles should be signed by the author so that responsibility for all published material might be fixed.

The *Improvement Era* progressed exceptionally well. Every element of the magazine was carefully managed to maintain the highest standards.

As the quality of the magazine increased, so did its circulation. Ten years after John's appointment, the circulation had skyrocketed to more than 100,000.[45] Elder Evans wrote to Elder Widtsoe on that accomplishment:

> With your characteristic generosity you attached a note to the copy of the auditor's statement which you returned a few days ago which, addressing me said: "You have reason to be very happy and may I say proud that the *Era* can show such a report."
>
> Of course, that is the type of thing that you would always say, being the sincerely generous gentleman that you are—but with something of a conscience still left, I can't let the remark pass without reminding myself and you and all whom it may concern that the rebirth of the Era began with your association with it, some months before mine, in your vision, your editorial contributions, your alert interests, your policies, your name, and your encouragement have been real factors in the success of recent years.[46]

When John left Salt Lake City to teach at USC, he did not have the close contact with the *Era* that he desired, but he still kept his hands on the controls. Harrison R. Merrill, the managing editor when John left, constantly sought his advice: "You have probably received . . . the *Improvement Era*. Mrs. Josephson and I will await your reaction in fear and trembling, but hopeful that we have succeeded in making a magazine which you and our people will enjoy. If it isn't right the mistakes are of the head and the printer and not of the heart."[47]

That significant success was quickly achieved is evident in a tribute published in the *Deseret News* in April 1937: "With the April issue of *The Improvement Era*, the once-small 'Voice of the Church' has struck a new note to proclaim its presence among the great institutions of the World, and with the same gesture, it takes another big step in a steady advance toward becoming a class publication of the highest rank."[48] The tribute praised its professional makeup and treatment of information: "The noteworthy feature of the current issue is its presentation of articles pertaining to the Church which are not only of wide public interest but which have already received the attention of political, economic and social observers of national prominence."[49]

40

THE EDITOR AS WRITER

As valuable as John A. Widtsoe's experience, skills, and ideas were as a manager, his greatest contributions were the writing he did for the *Era*. Over his years as editor, he contributed almost 650 *Era* entries. These include 75 influential feature articles, 90 sensitive editorials, 173 carefully prepared articles answering difficult doctrinal and Church history questions under the title "Evidences and Reconciliations," and 310 book reviews encouraging the Saints to study good books and guiding them to particularly valuable ones. Almost every issue contained tasteful and articulate entries of particular note about needful topics addressing the needs of the many audiences the *Era* served. The avid readership bespoke the ongoing impact John had on the lives and thoughts of Church members for many years.

John's love of writing was expressed especially well in a letter to Edwin F. Reed: "In 1921 I retired from the Presidency of the University of Utah because of a call to serve in the Church to which I belong. I have been a member of the Council of the Twelve Apostles since that time; and among my various incidental labors is editorial work in connection with *The Improvement Era*, to which you refer. The writer's itch has troubled me from my boyhood; so naturally I have enjoyed and am enjoying the work with the magazine."[1]

Many letters of thanks and inquiries about things he had written remain in his files. He wrote, "I am grateful to you for what you say about my editorial work in the *Era*. Sometimes I attempt to say things in such a way as to stir the thinking of the people and in some cases this has happened. Indeed, I am more concerned about developing the thinking habits among our people than to feed them facts which are easy to receive when they are furnished by someone else."[2] Thousands of letters from across the Church praised his writing and expressed personal reactions and sincere appreciation.

A military chaplain wrote a letter of thanks to the entire *Improvement Era* production staff, adding, "Brother Thornton Y. Booth, with whom I am closely associated recently stated: 'Dr. Widtsoe's power with the pen is a wonderful influence for good in the Church today,' and to me your writings have always seemed to verify this statement 'The pen is mightier than the sword.' Especially helpful to us in the army Church work were two of your editorials in the September and November *Eras*. *The Era* is our most favored magazine reading. Its value to soldiers cannot be over estimated."[3]

INDEPENDENT FEATURE ARTICLES

Many of John's independent articles reflect developments in the Church and events, concerns, or advancements in the larger society. Most of them centered around important Church doctrine, programs, and practices. A half dozen of them focused attention on aspects of the Word of Wisdom. Several grew out of John's interests in science, chemistry, ecology, and irrigation. Some came as a result of the fears, threats, and trials of World War II. There were also many about important Church leaders. His files contain countless letters of appreciation for the information in these articles.

EDITORIALS

Editorials were much more frequent in the early years of John's assignment, being replaced in later years by his book reviews and series of evidences and reconciliations. His ninety editorials covered many topics, most centering on doctrinal teachings and admonitions. Many were tributes to Church leaders. Anniversaries and recognition celebrations were often noted; concerns of world citizenship were frequently a focus. Typical reactions to John's editorials are conveyed in the words of Marba Josephson, the *Era's* associate editor: "So many people have commented on your last editorial that I thought I should like to tell you how favorably it has been received here at home and how I am equally sure that it will be received with like favor in other places. One woman, who is very well-read, said it was the best editorial that she ever read. It appealed to me especially because of the consequences of the imagery which I am sure will make young people shudder away from evil."[4]

President Heber J. Grant also paid tribute: "I cannot tell you how much I appreciate the editorials that you are writing for *The Improvement Era* from time to time, as well as the articles which you contribute to that magazine."[5]

BOOK REVIEWS

"Off the Bookrack" was a regular column that published more than three hundred book reviews through which John sought to help the membership of the Church keep up with world events and viewpoints. He wrote most about the latest releases on Church history, biography, and doctrine. Next in frequency were books on nutrition, health, and the Word of Wisdom; these enumerated many findings in secular studies that overlapped Church teachings. The third largest group dealt with books on agriculture, chemurgy (biochemical engineering), and practical applications of scientific discoveries to aid the Saints in improving farm operations. Following this were book reviews on discoveries about ancient American peoples, beliefs, archaeological sites, and evidences of the Book of Mormon.

The longest of John's reviews was published in the March 1946 issue on the book *No Man Knows My History*.[6] Its emphasis and temper are outgrowths of John's devotion to the Prophet Joseph Smith and his credentials as an avid student of the life of the Prophet:

This purported history of Joseph Smith is really an attempt to portray Joseph Smith as a deceiver. No effort is made to *prove* him a fraud; it is merely asserted in the preface and in chapter one that he was such, much after the practice of other, earlier, defamers of the Prophet. Then, having made the assertion, every act in the Prophet's life is set forth as the product of a dishonest man, who knew that he was acting out a lie. That is not acceptable historical writing.

There is a labored aim to give the book a scholarly color, by numerous footnotes, some from doubtful sources. But as these are examined, nothing new is found. Everything in the book has been presented by other writers in the large anti-Mormon field of writing. A worthy enemy often contributes something new. Not so in this book. Few, if any, of the untruths Mormon-haters have dished out during the last century are missed, but nothing new has been added.[7]

After an assessment of the character of the book's sources, John used a particularly negative description of the Prophet's true character attributed to Brigham Young to expose the book's fallacies. No one at that time knew Brigham's teachings better than John. He wrote, "Such unfairness illustrates the venomous temper of the author."[8] His summary assessments reflect a seldom-seen side of John A. Widtsoe. He sought always to put a positive light on things, particularly scholarly matters, and rarely can one find in his work a whisper of contempt for scholarship and opinion. John's review continued:

A fair historian seeks the full story, and tries to see both sides. This of course could not be done by an author who declares the subject of the book from the beginning to have a dishonest motive. . . . As a history of Joseph Smith the book is a flat failure. It may find favor with some salacious-minded enemies of the Church. It will be of no interest to Latter-day Saints who have correct knowledge of the history of Joseph Smith, and who are surfeited with shallow treatments of their faith, and who know by heart the untrue charges against Joseph Smith which are retailed anew by this book. The author might have produced a near "definitive" history of Joseph, instead of another tirade, however thinly veiled, against the Mormon faith.[9]

John wrote a follow-up article in his "Evidences and Reconciliations" column that same month titled "Is the 'History of Joseph Smith' Trustworthy?" In it he traced the careful efforts of the Prophet to keep the commandment in *Doctrine and Covenants* 21:1 through an accurate history and personal journal of the events that occurred. He also described the activities of many who were associated with keeping and compiling that history who, by their sheer number, assure an accurate telling of the history:

> At length, beginning in 1904 the work was published in modern book form, forming the first six volumes of the projected full history of the Church. In the successive printings, conflicts of dates were rectified, errors corrected, and later discovered materials added. The 1904 edition is also well annotated. So well has the work been done, and so carefully has the truth been respected, that writers and speakers for and against Mormonism have used it fully as a sound historical document. The "history" is really a compilation. It is the journal of the Prophet, interlarded with available, original documents, including the revelations to the Prophet. His own comments generally serve to tie the documents together in historical form. The wealth of original documents makes the volumes of double interest and importance.[10]

John carefully pointed out how many parallel accounts, independently given by close associates of Joseph Smith, eliminate questions of fraud and deceit. With an eye on the cursory neglect of these volumes and the many false charges in *No Man Knows My History*, John added, "To call witnesses liars is an easy way to write history, but it is not in harmony with the accepted canons of historical writing. Yet such breaches of historical study and writing make the foundation of anti-Mormon books, of which there are many."[11]

In January 1947 he published a review of *New Riches from the Soil*,[12] by Wheeler McMillen, the president of the National Farm Chemurgic Council and editor of the *Farm Journal*, noting, "The progress of chemurgy is the theme of this fascinating book. Chemurgy is the development of new industrial uses for farm grown materials, and the establishment of new farm crops. It is the association of science, industry, and agriculture for the common good. . . . The book itself reads better than most fiction."[13]

John often reviewed books connected to ancient America. He was especially enthusiastic in his review of Francis W. Kirkham's *A New Witness for Christ in America:* "The historical proof of the truth of the Book of Mormon has never been presented more fully or convincingly than in this book. This second revised edition contains much new confirmatory material, based upon new information. Students of the Book of Mormon, at home or in the mission field, in facing opposition to the Book of Mormon, or to increase their testimony of its truth, need to know the facts and theories set forth in this volume. It is a notable book."[14]

ARTICLES IN SERIES

The Articles of Faith. Beyond the individual articles, editorials, and critiques, Elder Widtsoe made valuable contributions in writing several series of articles, one of which was on the Articles of Faith. The series began in the April 1935 issue and continued through 14 articles ending in the October 1938 issue. The Articles of Faith are statements of the basic tenets of Latter-day Saint belief. A committee of the Sunday School made a request to have a course on the Articles of Faith approved for the missionary class. Approval by the Council of the Twelve was acknowledged in a letter from Widtsoe in early March of 1935: "Whether the book is to be printed as a book, in a cheap edition or divided into four parts, to follow the quarterly system now in vote, is a matter that may be decided by your committee and the Sunday School administration. The preparations of outlines, to guide the teachers in this important course, is now in the hands of your Committee."[15]

In the following month the *Era* published the first lesson, "We Believe." An excerpt indicates John's thoughts on the series: "Two words, 'We believe,' introduce each, save one, of the Articles of Faith. These are words which in all ages have made human history. As men have believed they have lived, labored, and died. When men's beliefs have conformed to truth, peace and prosperity have entered the world; when false, darkness, hate and chaos have ruled. 'As a man thinketh in his heart, so is he;' but as a man believes, so does he. The potency of life lies in our beliefs."[16] He further explained the significance of the series: "In the Articles of Faith, prepared to present only fundamental doctrine, lie imbedded every vital Gospel principle of human action."[17] Clarifying the significance of knowledge, belief, and faith, he wrote, "Indeed, the Prophet could have said truthfully at the beginning of each statement, 'We know.' Knowledge, properly tested, becomes belief. Belief, put to the test of prayer and human use, in turn becomes faith, which is the higher, perfected knowledge."[18]

The series was so well liked that it was repeated as a course manual several times in subsequent years. The Special Interest Committee of the MIA obtained permission to publish the series as a course manual. They wrote, "The committee feels that the material here presented will not only serve special interest groups in their study program, but that it will have wide appeal for individuals and families, for missionaries and leaders in the various auxiliaries of the Church, and for people not affiliated who are interested in knowing what the Latter-day Saints believe."[19]

The series was published as a priesthood manual at least three times. Each one used the exact text of the *Improvement Era* series but added materials relevant to its audience. In 1959 the series was put into a manual for use of the priesthood and published in Portuguese.

Evidences and Reconciliations. From his youth and early education in Norway, John was the consummate student and questioner, the ultimate seeker after truth, all truth, whether of science, of life, of observation, of the gospel and religion, or of the spirit. A significant experience with such seeking during the early stage of his career set his compass in an important direction, one he would follow the rest of his life. It came in an interview with his stake president in Logan when he was called as elders quorum instructor: "It has seemed to me that the next few minutes changed the course of my life."[20] That course found much of its fruition in his *Era* years and the series he wrote and dedicated to "a generation of seekers after truth,"[21] especially those driven a little beyond the ordinary.

John's files at the Agricultural College, the university, the State

Historical Society, and the Historical Division of the Church contain an ongoing exchange with thousands of people, as much about gospel concerns as scientific matters. In his later years as editor of the *Millennial Star,* John tested the written word as a way to provide thoughtful and satisfactory answers to common and generally pertinent questions. His reputation as an outstanding teacher and skillful communicator peaked coincidentally with his *Era* appointment.

The *Era* was the most suitable means for circulating answers to the most important and most frequently asked questions from readers. Responding regularly to the common concerns of Church members was a natural way of fulfilling the *Era's* mission to be the "voice of the Church." In a tract written to interested souls of different faiths, John wrote, "Clear and sensible answers to many questions asked by men throughout the ages have made the Latter-day Saints spiritually intelligent and contented. Truth feeds the spirit of man."[22]

The questions asked in the varied congregations all across the Church, as John filled his many assignments, provided a natural barometer of the interests of Church members generally. A sample list of the questions he answered demonstrates that he endeavored to address fundamental and difficult questions honest seekers were asking:

> What is the attitude of the Church Toward Science? (October 1938.)
>
> In the event of the death of the President of the Church, The Council of the Twelve Apostles takes over the Presidency of the Church. Does this Council possess the necessary power? Can this practice be confirmed by revelation? (October 1938.)
>
> Does the Church receive revelations today as it did in the days of Joseph Smith? (November 1938.)
>
> What are the facts concerning the Adam-God myth, so frequently mentioned by enemies of the Church? (November 1938.)
>
> How Old is the Earth? (December 1938.)
>
> Where are the Lost Tribes of Israel? (January 1939.)
>
> Does the Payment of tithing cause Economic Distress? (February 1939.)
>
> How did the Earth come into being? (February 1939.)
>
> What is the Origin of Life on earth? (March 1939.)

Is it Wrong to Doubt? (April 1939.)

How do you account for Gospel Resemblances in Non-Christian Religions? (June 1939.)

To What Extent Should the Doctrine of Evolution be Accepted? (July 1939.)

Does Higher Education tend to Diminish Faith in the Gospel? (August 1939.)

Are the Early Books of the Bible (the Pentateuch and Joshua) Historically Correct? (September 1939.)

Did the Sun Stand Still Upon Gibeon? (October 1939.)

How Trustworthy is Science? (November 1939.)

What is the difference between the Holy Spirit and the Holy Ghost? (December 1939.)

Why did Joseph Smith, the Prophet, need the help of the Urim and Thummim? (January 1940.)

The series began in October 1938 and continued until after John's death in 1952, the last three being published in 1953. There were 173 in the series, almost 12 per year over a 15-year duration, or about one a month for the remainder of his life. Though the questions were difficult, and full answers were of necessity somewhat complicated, John's friendly, concise, precise, and easily understood responses took the sting out of many of the troublesome issues. John's opinion of the validity of the series is contained in two letters. He wrote, "'Evidences and Reconciliations' in the *Improvement Era* is being carried on for the benefit of a large number of our intelligent young people and older people for that matter who ask questions in all seriousness and are entitled to modern up-to-date answers harmonizing to our Gospel views."[23] "The whole series entitled Evidences and Reconciliations which, placed upon my shoulders, is a result of the numerous questions which our young people in this modern day are asking. It seemed wiser and better to answer those questions as far as we are able to do so than to leave them under a halo of mystery. It is better to say 'we do not know' than to evade the question."[24] Many things pointed to this time of increased inquiry. Global crises such as war and depression gave rise to deep questions. Church members in large numbers were or had been involved with college and university life, which encouraged inquiry and exposed them to new interests, new questions, and seeming conflicts. It was a time that begged for Widtsoe's devotion, Widtsoe's mind, Widtsoe's experience, and Widtsoe's pen to help fill voids.

Another view of the origin of "Evidences and Reconciliations" comes from Hugh Nibley:

> [Widtsoe] was perpetually on the alert for issues in which he could contribute. That is, for any sign of trouble or injury like that, he was alert and didn't hesitate to step in, and before it was too late, he didn't stand around, he stopped controversy, arguing, and bitterness before it could get very far. He used to get in those things—you see, that's the trouble, he never held back, he never hesitated to take the sides, either side, he never hesitated. Everybody else hesitates a little and thinks about that next week, but I've never known the doctor to postpone anything like that. When an issue came up he would take it up like (snapping his fingers). . . . We'll put it on the agenda and talk about it next week, no, never with him.[25]

The great bulk of the questions were modest and sincere inquiries submitted by members who wanted to increase their understanding and deepen their faith, testimony, and comprehension. But some inquiries carried doubt and acrimony. One letter was in response to Widtsoe's answer to: "Does Higher Education Tend to Diminish Faith in the Church?"

> You list four major causes for the loss of faith by those who, attending higher institutions of learning, drift away from the teachings of the Church. May I be permitted to offer a comment? The causes you give for this drifting are: (1) Starvation of faith through lack of study and practice of the gospel teachings, (2) imitation of those having improper habits of life, (3) immorality and (4) failure to see the real relation that religion bears to all truth. It seems to me that these are defensive or apologetic reasons, reasons which any religious organization would give to explain why its members, pursuing higher educational goals, sometimes lose their fervor for, or enthusiasm of faith in their church. If another church, say Catholic, made such an explanation, would we not accuse it of rationalizing, of trying to

attach the blame on its starving member, thus acquitting itself for any culpability? May there not be another cause for this "loss of faith" and may not this cause lie in our failure to understand the psychology involved in the process?

May it not be that in our zeal to maintain our *changeless* gospel we have shut our eyes to truths because they "spring up from the earth" rather than "come down from heaven?"

Sometimes the fact that one does not have the same religious conceptions that he had in early childhood and youth causes his former friends and associates to believe and to say that he has drifted away from the light. . . . Surely studying mathematics would change his mathematical conceptions. Could it be possible that studying, re-examining one's religious conceptions, would result in their being changed? May not change sometimes be growth? May not one committed to the philosophy of a changeless gospel mistake healthy growth for irreligion? . . . Those who have rebelled against the religious *status quo* have been persecuted and even martyred but a later generation has built shrines at their sepulchers.[26]

Widtsoe had great empathy for earnest seekers holding onto faith in the face of seemingly severe tests. He responded:

I quite agree with the general spirit of your comments. I shall be very pleased to have the opportunity of a face to face conversation with you about this subject. Letter writing, unless carefully done is always likely to be somewhat misleading. May I say, however, that two principles which you touched upon in your letter are fundamental in Mormon thinking. First, that there are certain changeless principles upon which the whole structure of Mormonism is built and second, that the application of these principles as in human life change as human needs change. That is, the Gospel, as understood by the Church, is an unchanging system of truths ever changing in its application to the ever changing conditions of life.

Young college students frequently fail to make the discrimination between foundation principles and their application; between primary principles and derivative functions.

You draw some illustrations from the field of science. There we have the same distinction: facts of observation, correct as far as human powers go and inferences or the explanation of these facts changing with the increasing knowledge.

Mormonism invites examination, but it knows quite well that if friend or foe really wants to understand the restored Gospel he must look for its truths and not for its weaknesses in proclaiming or using that truth. The men within my acquaintanceship who, with academic training have drifted away from full practice of Church principles, have seldom thought the matter through. They have splashed about on the surface until the beauty of the depths have become obscure. As for myself, once having been established within my own mind the certainty of the fundamental principles of Mormonism I prefer to follow the Church. Shall we talk this matter over in person?[27]

The year after John began his "Evidences and Reconciliations" series, he was asked to write a lesson manual for the adult department of the MIA. The first part of the manual focused on applying the Articles of Faith to everyday life. The second part was a reprint of his essays in the "Evidences and Reconciliations" series. The manual was titled *Current Gospel Questions.*[28]

Richard L. Evans undertook the task of compiling the "Evidences and Reconciliations" series into book form in 1943. The first sixty-eight selections in the series were put into the volume essentially as they were written for the *Era*. In his foreword Evans wrote:

> Books come into being in many different ways—some because writers choose to write, and some, like this one, because readers make insistent demands. . . . That the series filled an urgent need is attested by the fact that requests for permanent compilations began to increase as the writings progressed through the months—thus repeating the experience of other writers who, by reason of demand, have been obliged to publish their serial efforts in book form. . . . Widtsoe has the stimulating manner of a true teacher, the open mind of a true scholar, the engaging charm of a true gentleman, and the true humility of a man of God. His pen, sparing in its use of words and direct in its approach, is nevertheless colorful in expression—and it quickly focuses attention on fact, avoiding unsupportable generalization. With this brief glimpse of a man and his work, neither of which needs introduction, it is gratifying to bring this volume to the readers who have

asked for it and to the many students, both of science and religion, who will find in it many "aids to faith in a modern day."[29]

Evans took charge of assembling and publishing the book, and with the help of the *Era* staff, he saw to its completion. In a copy of this volume, kept close to Evans's desk, is inscribed:

> Dear Richard: This book has been made possible by your suggestion and labor. Its mechanical beauty of type, paper, arrangement, cover and jacket reveal your innate feeling for and sense of the beautiful in thought, word and form.
>
> To me this volume is another evidence of your goodness to me. No son could do more than you have done for me in our association together. This I appreciate beyond ordinary expression. I recognize your gifts, service to the world and to your people; and rejoice in the abundant share of your affections bestowed on me.
>
> Before you lies a long, increasingly distinguished career, in which your inborn and trained powers and your unusual wisdom will have full play. Your every attainment gives me gladness.
>
> Thank you again. The Lord bless you. Affectionately, John A. Widtsoe.[30]

In this volume Evans arranged the 68 essays under twelve topic headings: The Approach to Truth (10 essays), Revelation (9), The Bible (5), Science (7), Salvation (3), Priesthood (7), Church Organization (3), Church Practice (4), Marriage and the Family (4), Evil (5), Life Hereafter (4), and Miscellaneous (7). Interest in this compilation was so great that a similar publication of John's answers since 1943 was undertaken four years later. Another fifty "Evidences and Reconciliations" were grouped under ten subject headings and published in a volume bearing the title *Gospel Interpretations*. The headings indicate the emphasis he gave to questions in those four years: The Godhead (3), The Divine Purpose (5), The Unchanging Gospel (4), Free Agency (3), Church Practice (6), Joseph Smith (10), The Word of Wisdom (5), Delusions (4), Brigham Young and the Pioneers (4), and Miscellaneous (6).

In another four years an additional forty-three were published in a third volume. They were also compiled under ten headings: The

Godhead (2), Church Doctrine (7), Priesthood (2), The Law of Progress (3), Intelligence (4), The Book of Mormon (3), Joseph Smith (4), Free Agency (2), The Gospel on Earth (9), and Miscellaneous (7). The preface states, "The hundreds of questions that arrive annually are in the main serious inquiries into gospel lore and are so treated. They often reflect the confusion of thought in the secular world, but are an honest intelligent search for truth. The intelligence of the Church is at a high level. We should thank the Lord for the earnest seekers after gospel truth. They are as cement in preserving the integrity of the Church of Jesus Christ of Latter-day Saints."[31]

The series concluded with Widtsoe's death in 1952. In 1960 the executives of Bookcraft made arrangements with G. Homer Durham, son-in-law to the Widtsoes, to condense the material into one volume that would be a popular and lasting standard reference book in the homes of Church members worldwide.[32] They indicated that Elder Widtsoe had expressed an interest in having a single volume of his explanations available to the Saints: "Thus completed is the original plan arranged with the author. Three single volumes have preceded. These predecessors represented a printing of available articles, each of which was written, usually a month apart, over the last fifteen years of the author's life. Always recognized was the need for compiling the project into a single volume. This obligation has now been accomplished."[33]

The volume contained 107 of the original 173 evidences and reconciliations that John authored. This volume has continued to be popular even though its answers are a half-century old.

There are many letters of appreciation to Elder Widtsoe for the "Evidences and Reconciliations" series from all quarters of the Church. Earl J. Glade, manager of the KSL radio station, wrote that the series was such "an inspiration that it is constantly piling up the great obligation which I already feel toward you. You certainly have my profound gratitude."[34]

How the Desert Was Tamed. The year 1947 was a monumental celebration of the centennial of the arrival of the Saints in the Salt Lake Valley. John's contribution to the celebration was a series of essays about how the pioneers tamed the desert. His tribute was written in seven parts and twelve chapters between the months of January and July, in recognition of those who made the trek between 1847 and 1869, when the railroad was completed. His desire was to look beyond the well-known accomplishments to the principles the Saints followed to tame their arid lands:

> As these principles, which lie imbedded in the work of the pioneers, were used, conquest and progress raised their heads. It is curious that in the abundant literature concerning the settlement of the Great Basin of North America, and the surrounding territory, only scattered attempts have been made to discover the real causes of the success attending the pioneers in their battle with arid conditions. We have been content to know what they did, rather than how the thing was done.
>
> This essay grew out of an attempt to dissect the pioneer achievements and to discover one by one the causes, which acting together, made "the desert blossom as the rose." As these were revealed, they were, as might be expected, simple, and of general use, and known from antiquity. They reveal, also, the things of the spirit which made the pioneers willing to risk their lives and happiness in the westward venture.[35]
>
> This is a life-giving theme, to which scholars should give profound study. This essay or sketch is but a brief approach to the subject.[36]

Another of John's manuals, *Your Questions Answered,* was the result of a careful investigation of the interests of young adult members of the Church: "As a result of a survey . . . it was found that the prevailing desire of this age group was to know the answer to perplexing doctrinal questions and problems which they meet daily in schools and associations. . . . Consequently, the M Men-Gleaner committee asked Dr. John A. Widtsoe of the Council of the Twelve, to prepare twenty-two lessons designed to satisfy the inquiry of these young people."[37]

Growing out of the same inquiring interest came an assignment to republish *A Rational Theology.* Amid all these duties, perhaps seeking repose in his early days, he produced *In the Gospel Net,* the life story of his mother and the first volume of his autobiography. It is a story so inspirational that the Relief Society strongly urged its publication: "We are so happy to know that we shall have the sketch of your mother for our next course. We understand that you are preparing this for us, and are writing to ask if we may have it not later than the last of November, as we wish to send it in time for translation which is necessary in the European Missions."[38] In spare moments John and Leah continued their work on a modern and informed interpretation of the Word of Wisdom. When it was near completion, he submitted it to members of his quorum for review and refinement. Through the Melchizedek Priesthood Committee, they requested that the book be adapted as the lesson manual for the priesthood quorums. John replied, "This was wholly unexpected by me. Naturally, however, after the decision was made the matter went out of my hands; the book is being printed by the Deseret News Press for the Deseret Book Company."[39]

The magnitude of work behind the hundreds of written contributions John made to the *Improvement Era*, independent of his many other assignments, is evidence of his zeal. He said as his career with the *Era* drew to a close, "I want to say to you frankly that I have nothing to recommend me except one thing—and thousands of men can say the same thing—I have done a day's work all the days of my life; and if that can be spoken of me, I shall be quite satisfied."[40]

Bryant S. Hinckley added this accolade:

> One is impressed with the quality and amount of work he can do. He is a prodigious worker and his work is of the highest order. He has the rare capacity for seeing things in their proper relation and the ability to express himself with clearness and beauty. His name will stand forever among the distinguished scholars and educators in the Church. The depth of his understanding, the breadth of his tolerance, the effectiveness and wisdom of his diplomacy are all evidences of real superiority. From his boyhood, he has been active in the organizations of the Church and is one of the best informed men in the Church on doctrines and organization. His theological writings would constitute a library.[41]

41

THE WORD OF WISDOM

JOHN narrowed his expertise in physical chemistry to agricultural chemistry and finally to the chemistry of foods and nutrition. Leah's route was more direct. From her mother, Susa, she inherited an emphasis on practical education for women. In 1896–97, Susa persuaded BYA president Benjamin Cluff to allow Leah to teach women a course in domestic science. When Leah finished, she returned from the Pratt Institute to establish the Domestic Science or Home Economics Department at BYA.

John's learning thrived in the laboratories of the ACU in Logan while Leah's matured in the Pratt laboratories in Brooklyn.

While there she wrote an essay about Pratt aimed at giving young LDS women an appreciation for the opportunities offered in domestic science. Pratt was "one of the few—and perhaps the most advanced and best known—schools in which the problem of woman's work in life is dealt with and studied in a systematic and scientific manner and with other collegiate courses." The main building housed the Department of Domestic Arts, which, Leah wrote, covered "the sanitary, hygienic, and chemical departments of life . . . as well as the more practical problems of hygienic and economic cooking."[1] Instruction included courses in chemistry, biology, bacteriology, diet calculation, and home sanitation. Leah felt "there can be no purpose more noble, more soul satisfying, more God-given than to be the mistress and intelligent maker of a happy home."[2]

The early belief that good animal nutrition depended on the proper ratio between proteins and carbohydrates took John to Göttingen. The next steps in nutritional science focused on the proper level of energy (heat) in food and recognition of the importance of calories. In 1912 vitamins were discovered. Scholars have noted that nutritional discoveries flourished from the 1880s to the 1930s, when the Widtsoes were at their prime academically.[3] John wrote, "Fortunately, my wife, in this riot of new nutritional knowledge, was a trained Home Economist who saw as I did the meaning of the Word of Wisdom in terms of the new knowledge, and its confirmation of the truth of the restoration of the gospel of Jesus Christ. So as time permitted we have worked together on this subject throughout the years."[4] John later added, "During the many years of deep study and interest in the health field, the preventive side, I have given occasional lectures on the subject, my wife, hundreds."[5]

For many years their Farmer's Institutes were outlets for their ideas. In 1903 Leah conducted the first Women's Institute in Utah. It considered three topics: home economics, nutrition, and health.[6] In the years that followed, she promoted legislation through Senator Reed Smoot that would grant research money for the home economics programs she had pioneered. Senate Bill S7006 was prepared by Smoot in 1911. It was revised in S280, which became part of the Purnell Act that provided equal funds for the study of home and agriculture at land-grant colleges. Her efforts led to other bills that involved teaching family science, consumer education, and vocational guidance.[7]

John's work with the Extension Service led to the program of county extension agents. He sent Luther Winsor to the Uintah Basin as the first county extension agent in the United States. With Leah's persuasion, John soon concluded, "If a county agent were desirable to help the farmers, would not an agent to help the women be equally desirable?"[8] Soon home demonstration agents were in nearly every Utah county. Amy Lyman was "the first one in the procession of such workers in the United States."[9] To further promote home economics in Utah, John ordered the construction of the Woman's Buildings for Domestic Arts and Sciences at the Agricultural College and the University of Utah.[10]

In Leah's ninety-first year, she restated her belief about nutrition: "We shouldn't be sick, the Lord didn't intend it. . . . people shouldn't be sick. The Lord gave us the Word of Wisdom to keep us well and if we're sick, its our own fault, because we don't know any better. I have reached 91 years and I haven't an ache or a pain in any part of my body. . . . I've outlived my grandparents, and my parents by 15 years, and I attribute it to my observance of the Word of Wisdom."[11]

Leah felt Church members did not regard the Word of Wisdom as highly as other revelations from God. In her mind, happiness, joy, and salvation should begin with good physical health. She took pleasure in relating one of John's encounters in front of the Church Administration Building with an elderly brother: "'Dr. Widtsoe, your book is alright, but I think it's a mistake to ask the Priesthood to study it. The Relief Society ought to be studying this book.' My hubby said, 'Brother so and so, did you ever read the Word of Wisdom?' 'Why' he said, 'of course I did, Dr. Widtsoe.' My hubby said the first sentence says it is given to the Council of High Priests and all Saints who are and can be called saints."[12]

The Widtsoes were so identified with the Word of Wisdom that some jokingly called it the "Word of Widtsoe." Leah disliked that reference, and when their book *The Word of Wisdom, a Modern Interpretation* was due for another printing, she would not proceed without approval from the first Presidency. Each of the presidency wrote a strong letter of endorsement urging that the book be updated and reprinted. Leah recorded, "And then I wrote a letter to Joseph Fielding Smith, because he's pretty dear to me. I said if it didn't have his approval and the Twelve, I wasn't going to reprint it." President Smith replied: "My only regret, Sister Widtsoe, is that our people don't live it; your book is as appropriate today as when it was written."[13]

Leah taught, "The greatest reward of keeping these laws of health and refraining from undermining practices is the mastery which man acquires over his body, and the self-control which he develops and maintains. The power of the human will to say 'no' to evil, and 'yes' to good is the supreme test of mortal achievement. When so exercised, one may know that mortal life is being lived in its fullness."[14]

Over many years John wrote articles and editorials as background for his Word of Wisdom text. In "The Chemistry of Digestion," he wrote about understanding the relationship of our bodies to the food we put into them, noting, "The young people of Zion, especially, who desire to be receptive to every prompting of the Spirit, should inform themselves of every fact, the possession of which will enable them to keep their bodies in such a condition that the Spirit can work its will without hindrance."[15]

In "The Food of Man," he emphasized that "almost everything that the human mind has penetrated is better understood by the mass of mankind, than the true nature, use, and effect of the food we eat. . . . In the Word of Wisdom lie the germs of many important principles that will be developed by the workers in science, and then be brought into our daily lives to give health and strength to our bodies."[16]

In a Word of Wisdom tract, John described the scientific confirmation that physical health is mostly related to blood chemistry. "In the true Gospel of Jesus Christ," he wrote, "the sanctity of the body is second only to that of the spirit. It is the duty, as well as the desire, of every person to preserve his physical health, so that he may live out most completely the destiny of his existence. . . . The rewards of obedience to this divine law are appealing: Health of body, mental strength, endurance, protection against the devastating scourges of the earth, and an understanding peace of mind."[17]

In 1932, the centennial commemoration of the Teetotalism movement begun in Preston, England, John identified four features that distinguish the Word of Wisdom from Teetotalism and other health movements. First, rather than having arisen in the minds of devout men, it became a concern under divine mandate. Second, it came from the Master of Truth rather than the opinion of men. Third, it was wonderfully confirmed by the new science of nutrition. Fourth, it makes direct and definite promises to those who heed it. "Joseph Smith did not borrow the ideas in the Word of Wisdom from contemporary or earlier movements," he wrote. "They came by inspiration from on high. Latter-day Saints may well use the Lord's code of health, the Word of Wisdom, as a mighty evidence of the divine inspiration of the Prophet Joseph Smith."[18]

In 1936 John wrote an editorial response to answer an avalanche of questions about the effects of cola drinks. They were rapidly becoming the preferred beverage of a great many people, including Latter-day Saints. In his response he named many varieties and wrote, "Cola drinks contain the drug, caffeine. For that reason, every argument used against coffee and tea, and some other arguments, may be used against cola drinks, and all other beverages containing caffeine, even in small amounts. They are determined habit formers and may lead to the coffee and tea habit. They injure human health."[19]

In another article he defended the use of whole wheat and explained scientifically why wheat is the grain of choice for man.[20] In another he labeled alcoholism "a disease of the human will."[21] In his *Improvement Era* years, he critiqued dozens of books about foods, health, and nutrition.

THE WORD OF WISDOM, A MODERN INTERPRETATION

When the Widtsoes returned to Salt Lake City in 1933, they embarked on a book on the Word of Wisdom. Because of their heavy assignments between 1933 and 1937, work on the book was slowed, and at times they thought to pass the baton on to others:

> As the years increased we tried to find some competent and willing person to show how the general principles of the Word of Wisdom corresponded with those of the modern experimentally established science of nutrition. Several doctors (M.D.) desired to help, but found not time. Finally, an assignment to do some work at the University of Southern California gave me the opportunity. My wife joined in. I took the negative teachings of the Word of Wisdom, she took the positive aspects. The book was written as our crowded lives permitted.[22]

When the manuscript was complete in October 1937, President Grant requested a copy. Widtsoe sent a cover letter, writing, "A few years ago, Leah and I decided to collect and organize the wealth of knowledge bearing upon the Word of Wisdom. It was entirely a work of love, which we might not have undertaken had we foreseen the great amount of labor and expense involved. Yet, our people needed the help. . . . I am quite aware that gossip has charged Leah, perhaps myself, with being extreme in our Word of Wisdom views. That is unjust. It has hurt us, but we have never attempted to correct gossip, so have tried to forget it."[23] The letter concludes with his testimony of the Prophet Joseph Smith and a request: "It would please us much to be allowed to dedicate the book to you—the foremost defender, in the history of the Church of the Word of Wisdom."[24] President Grant replied, "It will be a real pleasure to me, Brother Widtsoe, to have you dedicate your book to me. I am grateful beyond expression for your constant work in the interest of the Church, for your wonderful labors in preparing yourself for the battle of life."[25]

On 21 October Joseph Fielding Smith sent two pages of suggestions and concluded, "This work is needed immediately and should be published as soon as possible."[26] On 25 October formal approval came from President McKay: "Elders Joseph F. Merrill, Charles A. Callis, and Albert E. Bowen, acting under appointment, report that they have read your manuscript entitled THE WORD OF WISDOM—A MODERN INTERPRETATION, with very great interest and found it to be an ably written exposition of the Word of Wisdom as seen in the light of a multitude of confirmatory evidence furnished by modern science. . . . We are therefore pleased to give our consent to the publication of this book."[27]

In a letter to President Nephi L. Morris, John expressed his gratification that "the committee recommended that it be used as a text for the Priesthood. I am not sorry that this was done, for the revelation was given to a quorum of the Priesthood first, and through them to the Church, so perhaps it is wise to have the Priesthood give attention to their work for a passing year."[28]

In the preface John detailed his and Leah's three objectives: "First, to make clear the meaning of the Word of Wisdom in terms of modern knowledge. Second, to show that the learning of the last century confirms the teachings of the Word of Wisdom. Third, to furnish information for the guidance, through proper nutrition, of those who seek to retain, improve or recover their health."[29] A personal note was added for the reader:

> More than a generation ago the authors of this book sought out and studied with the world's leaders in the sciences underlying nutrition, and have been connected at various times since then with the scientific and practical aspects of the subject. Out of this life-long, intimate association with the Word of Wisdom and the sciences back of it have come two main convictions: that this health code promotes human welfare; and that the full accord of the Word of Wisdom with advancing science is a convincing evidence of the divine inspiration of the Prophet Joseph Smith.[30]

NEGATIVE ASPECTS AND WARNINGS

In the first of nineteen chapters, John included the full text of the Word of Wisdom from Doctrine and Covenants 89. However, he divided it into four sections: I. "Introduction," which includes verses 1–4 and comprises chapters 2–4 of the book. II. "Negative Health Factors," which includes verses 5–9 and chapters 5–7. III. "Positive Health Factors," which includes verses 10–17 and chapters 9–16. IV. "Rewards," which includes verses 18–21 and chapters 2 and 18.

The second chapter, "Need of Health Information," presents data from the first three decades of the twentieth century. The figures were impressive and brought out two comments from the Widtsoes: "Even the partial observance of the Word of Wisdom has affected notably and favorably the comparative health status of the Latter-day Saints."[31] But "it is evident that the people of the Church are not observing fully all the factors of health as given in the Word of Wisdom, else they would have an even greater immunity from all diseases."[32] "Too much of the modern food supply comes from tin cans or packages, for often women as well as men work in factories and offices, and the can opener is coming to be the most used kitchen implement."[33]

Chapter 3, "The Order and Will of God," reviews the origin of the revelation. Widtsoe wanted people to understand that the revelation was an answer to a specific prayer by Joseph Smith that arose out of tobacco abuses in council meetings of the priesthood. To the seeming contradictions in language, Widtsoe felt the overriding statements were that it was received by revelation and it showed forth "the order and will of God (verse 2)." Regarding the meaning of "adapted to the capacity of the weak and weakest of all saints who are or can be called saints" (verse 3), he wrote, "A person who cannot obey a temporal law, such as the Word of Wisdom, seldom can obey spiritual laws, which reach more profoundly into the nature of man. That is, those who are living the high spiritual laws of the Gospel, true saints, must have achieved sufficient desire and power of will to obey the temporal commandment known as the Word of Wisdom. Unless they have done so, the spiritual integrity of such persons may be called into question."[34]

In chapter 4, "Evils and Designs," Widtsoe called attention to the Lord's warning against conspiring men who would deceive innocent people on matters injurious to their health.

Chapter 5, "Alcohol," and chapter 6, "Tobacco," are two of the longest chapters in the book. Information on these two topics is so advanced now and their detriments so widely known that it is unnecessary to add Widtsoe's views here. Chapter 7, "Hot Drinks," covers the third category of forbidden products and was and is the most contested of the nineteen chapters.

A detailed analysis of the composition of tea and coffee and the effects of those substances on the human body and mind are the heart of this chapter. Following that is information on cola drinks, cocoa, and chocolate. Of cola drinks he wrote, "Every argument used against coffee and tea, and some other arguments, may be used properly against the cola drinks. They are only cold coffees. The fact that the drug is added in a crystallizing condition, not surrounded by other insoluble substances as in nature, makes them more dangerous than the ordinary coffee or tea, since they are absorbed into the blood stream more quickly and completely."[35]

John's discussion of cocoa and chocolate may be less popular than his teachings about cola drinks. He reported that cocoa beans, from which chocolate is made, contain theobromine, a close relative of caffeine. Perhaps as dangerous as theobromine, he wrote, are the sugary preparations that accompany it in chocolate mixes. They "are a menace to human health. Theobromine acts upon the body, especially upon the kidneys, very much as does caffeine. While it does not have as strong an effect upon the central nervous system, it is more irritating to the kidneys."[36] He was especially concerned about the danger chocolate poses to children. Experiments had shown that it reduces the availability of needed calcium and phosphorus, especially in the digestion of milk. "The chocolate milk used extensively for school children should be eliminated. To thus adulterate nature's finest food for children seems almost criminal."[37] A fitting conclusion to his discussion of these matters is this statement:

> That the expression "hot drinks" was used in the Word of Wisdom rather than "coffee and tea," is notable; for by so doing a host of other injurious habit-forming beverages now used (or that may be used) become subject to the Word of Wisdom. Indeed the use of the words "hot drinks" implies a knowledge beyond that possessed by man when the Word of Wisdom was received. It is remarkable indeed that Joseph Smith could so boldly declare himself against coffee and tea, as against all similar beverages, at a time when the world's learning could not safely make the statement.[38]

POSITIVE ASPECTS AND BLESSINGS

The remaining chapters were largely Leah's work. Her discussion follows wise counsel: "It is more important to keep the body well nourished, thereby to prevent all unnatural cravings for injurious substance, than to try to cure injurious habits of food and drink once formed. 'Prevention is better than cure.'"[39] In chapter 8 Leah wrote that the three functions of food are: (1) "To build and repair the tissues of which the body is composed," (2) "to maintain body temperature," and (3) "to furnish energy for work."[40] This was followed by a discussion of the six groups of food constituents. She concluded, "The essential thought remains, that to abstain from the things forbidden in the Word of Wisdom as injurious to health is not sufficient; *it is equally important* to partake of foods that build the body properly and meet bodily needs. Men may heed the laws of life and live; or they may ignore or pervert them and suffer disease and finally perish."[41]

That physical man is formed out of the dust of the earth is a scientific reality as well as a religious notion. Chapter 9, "Out of the Ground," details the necessary trace minerals needed for the body to perform all of its functions well. "The practice of the principles indicated in the Word of Wisdom provides all the necessary mineral elements necessary for full health."[42]

In chapter 10, "All Wholesome Herbs," Leah clarified that *herbs* in 1833 meant all plants that were good for mankind. Scientific analyses reviewed in this chapter revealed that vegetables and fruits contain "all the necessary food substances, and that they are rich in minerals. They are also the best sources of vitamins. It is now conceded that vegetables and fruits are of first importance in maintaining full health."[43] To any who wondered if she advocated a strictly vegetarian diet, she wrote:

> Let it be understood that the Word of Wisdom is not a Vegetarian document. If one wishes to live without meat or animal food, one must do it on one's own volition and with great intelligence and understanding if health is to be maintained. If one uses meat it must be used sparingly and in winter or famine only, as stated in this wise law of health. They who wish to be well and gain the promised rewards stated in the Word of Wisdom, must obey all of the law, not just part of it as suits their whim or their appetite, or their notion of its meaning.[44]

In "In the Season Thereof," Leah warned about the loss of vitality (vitamins) that accompanies the processing of foods and the consequent malnourishment. The chapter includes a detailed analysis of the source of each of the known vitamins and the devitalization that occurs in their processing and storage. She wrote, "Most impressive is the fact that all the truths discovered regarding the importance of vitamins in man's diet conform so strictly to the instructions given in the Word of Wisdom: 'Every herb and every fruit in the season thereof' and this long before the science of modern nutrition was born. No man of his own wisdom could have foretold the findings of modern science as did the

Prophet in this inspired document. To follow its teachings literally is to find health and joy of body and mind and soul."[45]

In chapter 12 Leah wrote about grains. She commended the use of home or neighborhood mills, because from them the vitamins are the most potent and the nourishment and flavor are at their peak. She argued against the use of refined sugar and taught that the needed sugars for man could be obtained from grains and natural fruits. She condemned the use of chocolate and noted that the healthiest races of men do not know what sugar is nor the many diseases linked to it. "Everyone should use intelligence and demand that foods shall be used as nature intended and that dependence shall not be placed on devitalized foods or a 'broken staff.' Again the Word of Wisdom points the way to health and happiness; and again the prophetic power of Joseph Smith is made evident."[46]

"Wheat for Man," a specific instruction in the Word of Wisdom, is the subject of chapter 13 and a powerful argument against bleached flour and white bread.

A chapter entitled "Meat—Sparingly" contains an excellent discussion of man's need for protein and where it is best obtained. Another chapter, "Healthful Drinks," contains a strong appeal for the intake of a substantial amount of water and the use of natural juices from fruits, vegetables, and grains. "Prudence and Thanksgiving" brought out the word *moderation* as an essential principle in human activity. Near the end of the book Leah turned her attention to "Rewards," as the Word of Wisdom is "a principle with a promise" for the "benefit" of man. She described four rewards: "First, strength and vigor of body; second, protection against disease; and third, the possession of knowledge and wisdom, even 'hidden treasures of knowledge.' A fourth reward is implied, namely 'temporal salvation,' in which may be included economic welfare."[47] The book ended with this testimony:

> The followers of the restored Gospel of Jesus Christ are grateful for the gift of this Law of Health, and offer it to all the world as one means by which full health may be owned by all men. The rewards of obedience to this divine law are appealing. Health of body, mental strength, endurance, protection against devastating scourges of earth,

economic security, social welfare, treasures of knowledge, spiritual development and an understanding peace of mind. Were this law fully kept a new compelling power for good would arise in earth.[48]

Reviews and Reactions

The *Deseret News* published a review of the book, noting:

> Though one might consider himself thoroughly familiar with the Word of Wisdom, as this section is known among the Church membership, yet a study of this new book vitalized this law of health and creates a will to do in the reader.
>
> We used the word *study* advisedly. Though the book is entertaining to the point that it is fascinating to read yet the nature of its contents bears more thorough study to become familiar with its contents to the extent that the principles discussed will become a part of one's life. For this reason its current use as a study course by the Melchizedek Priesthood Quorums of the Church can readily be endorsed.
>
> To understand the ultimate purpose of this book the reader must be acquainted with the objectives of the authors. Between the covers of the book are the gems of a life-time of gleaning in the world's largest centers and among the works of the best international minds in the field of health and nutrition.[49]

In the Widtsoe papers are hundreds of letters responding to John's writing on the Word of Wisdom. Most are complimentary, some seek further verification, and some are contentious.

A former European missionary had developed a good business as a distributor of Coca-Cola. He wrote to John, seeking advice about discontinuing his employment in light of the book. John replied, "The question you put to me is difficult to answer. It would be better, no doubt, if the world did not use any such beverages. However I cannot advise you to give up your position. You are not the manufacturer of the beverage and probably have no reason to advocate its use if you are acting as a distributor. If the composition of Coca Cola were known . . . publicly . . . it would be easier for you and all interested in such questions."[50]

In response to a query on the Widtsoes' financial interest in the book, John wrote, "Ordinarily, nothing is said about such matters—we are all happy to do all we can for the advancement of the cause of the Lord—but your direct question leads me to break that rule. . . . I may say that to secure the information for which the book is based, cost me several hundred dollars, which I hope will be paid back to me. Judging from past experience, that will probably be all."[51]

Asked about the meaning of the Church's teaching on "health in the navel," John wrote, "It is through the navel that the unborn babe receives its very life; the region of the navel in [the] human body after birth represents the most important organs of living and continued life. Clearly the expression is a symbol of profound meaning dealing with the giving of life, the preservation of life and the continuation of life."[52]

A protest was lodged against an advertisement for "Globe A Pancake and Waffle flour" in the *Improvement Era,* of which Widtsoe was editor: "I would like to know the reason for such an ad, in view of the fact that I have been studying and quoting your works for some time. For my reference, I use your own book. . . . As an editor, do you believe in practicing your own words, or are we as a people more interested in making money?"[53] Widtsoe replied, "The warning given in the Word of Wisdom book . . . is one that should be heeded. It does not say there, as I remember, that waffles must not be eaten, but tells of the effects they have upon the human body. I practice the Word of Wisdom the best I can, and knowing what I know I use my judgment in giving attention to any kind of advertised foods. You must do the same."[54]

John responded to praise from a stake president with a valuable insight: "It has always been a comfort to me that the findings of science do not clash or quarrel with our beliefs as Latter-day Saints. At times when the theories are set up there may be an apparent discord but with the facts themselves there is never anything but harmony. All truth flows from the same source, and truth, as it has been so well said, cannot quarrel with itself."[55]

How to Be Well

Five years after their book was published, Leah completed its companion volume, *How to Be Well: A Health Handbook and Cook-book Based on the Newer Knowledge of Nutrition.* John wrote in the foreword:

"This volume is really an outgrowth of *The Word of Wisdom, a Modern Interpretation*, written by us jointly. It was evident to us, as to numerous correspondents, that all nutritional problems must at last be solved in the kitchens of the world. Hence, the heavy labor and toil to produce this book was undertaken."[56] *How to Be Well* contains more than a thousand recipes that are in agreement with sound human nutrition. Hence, "it is a handbook for the kitchen of every intelligent, health-loving woman."[57]

The first seven chapters are filled with basic information on the food necessities in good nutrition. Emphasis is placed on the use of menus in assuring health and interest. The greatest part of the book is given to recipes. Leah added chapters on leftovers and preparing lunches for school or business, healthy food preparation for special occasions, entertaining, company meals, parties, and Church dinners and picnics.

The response to the book was satisfactory: "It is a scholarly production and contains very vital material that should be read by every prospective housewife, as well as those who have already received the responsibility of conducting a home."[58] After using the book, one woman wrote of marked improvements in her persistent kidney problems.[59]

Over the years the use of cola drinks was the most common concern. In many cases Widtsoe simply called it "cold coffee." To a bishop who questioned advertisements for Coca-Cola in the *Deseret News*, John replied, "Why the Deseret News advertises Coca Cola I am not able to tell you, you must write to them directly. However, pay no attention to the advertising. Refrain from the use of Coca Cola and tell your members to do so. The beverage is injurious to the human organs."[60]

John was a little disappointed but generally pleased with the reception of Church members toward the *Word of Wisdom*. He wrote, "There is a gradual change in the thinking of people with respect to nutrition. I suppose we can't expect anything else. Evolution is better than revolution ordinarily."[61]

To the end of their lives John and Leah taught the importance of the principles of the Word of Wisdom. Their writings removed ignorance about the divinity of the revelation. More important than the health the revelation assures was its confirmation of the divine call of the Prophet Joseph Smith. John wrote:

> It is a marvelous thing that a boy of western New York, untaught in the ways of the world, unacquainted with the sciences of this day, unfamiliar with the universities and the learning thereof, should be able to speak in such a manner, at a time when science was in its swaddling clothes, and to be found correct in his teaching and in full harmony with the most recent findings of modern science. We are very grateful that wherever we turn in the history of the Prophet Joseph Smith we find evidences of the divine wisdom and inspiration in all that he did.[62]

42

STAKE CONFERENCE VISITS

V ISITS to stake conferences across the Church were wonderful opportunities for John to get well acquainted with a great many Church members and to feel the pulse of the people. It was especially good for getting personally acquainted with the stake presidents and their families. Almost every week for the years he spent in Salt Lake City he was off on another stake conference adventure. This chapter chronicles those adventures with the business, the problems, the concerns, the questions, and the communications that surrounded them. Each event shown here represents dozens, perhaps a hundred more.

Efficient Church-wide organization is a prerequisite to the unity and central direction of the Church. For many years John was the organizational spokesman of the Church through his Melchizedek Priesthood manual, *Priesthood and Church Government*. It gave a description of stakes as a key element in the organizational system the Lord provided. His contemporary descriptions are a fitting introduction to this chapter.

> The Church, outside of the mission field, is territorially divided into "Stakes of Zion." The word stake as here used is a figure of speech, referring to the stakes driven into the ground to support the tent and its hangings. (Isaiah 54:2, 3.) They shall be called stakes, for

the curtains or the strength of Zion. D&C 101:21. . . . The Prophet Joseph uses this term in a sense entirely new from its common acception. A "Stake" of Zion is a geographical, numerical and governmental division of the Church. . . . The simple fact is, the stakes are merely subdivisions of the government of Zion. They did not exist until after Church government was established, but were afterwards erected out of the territorial and spiritual domain of the Kingdom. They were thus "consecrated" to be a strength in the government of Zion, and an extension of her borders.[1]

Each stake was a branch of Zion with the full program of the Church in operation. Each stake was also a "defense and a refuge" where safety and direction was provided. Merrill J. Bateman wrote, "In the revelation on Church organization and government . . . Church members were instructed to 'meet in conference once in three months, or from time to time as said conferences shall direct or appoint; and said conferences are to do whatever church business is necessary to be done at the time'" (D&C 20:61–62).[2] In 1877 the First Presidency refined these instructions and outlined a major reorganization that set up the program of quarterly conferences in effect when Elder Widtsoe was one of the Twelve.

In the years of John's service as an apostle, stake quarterly conferences were the primary Sabbath life of all members of the Twelve. In *The Acts of Modern Apostles,* William Talbot wrote, "All the Apostles spent a great deal of time visiting the quarterly stake conferences as designated in the Latter-day Saint scriptures. Numerous reports illustrate the energy spent by this Quorum in its responsibility to the members in their organized wards and stakes. During this period of growth and missionary success, administration over the expanding Church demanded much of the Apostles' time and effort."[3]

In John's early years, the number of stakes was still relatively small, and a quarterly visit from an apostle was the common practice. The increases in the number of stakes given in the statistical reports of the annual general conferences of the Church during John's apostolic years accentuate the increasing strain quarterly conferences put on the Twelve. At the end of his first year, 1922, there were 87 stakes. By the time John returned from his European mission, in 1934, the number had grown to 110. Between 1936 and 1949, the most active years of John's quarterly conference visits, the number swelled to 172. By the time of his death, the number of stakes exceeded 200.

To be out among the Saints, always ready to edify and inspire, was a welcome duty of the Twelve, but it came with a heavy load of other executive assignments and normal family duties. John wrote, "The membership of the Church have little conception of the work resting upon their sustained leaders. With stake conference appointments, correspondence, visitors, and numerous committee appointments, the whole week is taken. There is no Sabbath, or day of rest."[4] John had a lot of energy, and he worked hard, but even for him this was a great strain. He wrote, "[I] did not really know the meaning of intensive continuous effort until called to the apostleship. As a job, no sane man could wish for the position."[5] Another reflection is insightful: "I had had much freedom of initiative. Ample secretarial help had been mine. I had been in executive positions, with power to decide and act. Now, I was told where and when to go, and pretty much what to do. I was given for some years only part time secretarial service, which of course limited my productive power. As the years went on, duties increased, until there was really no time for recharging the mind with ideas or thinking out problems."[6] Nevertheless, he knew well the value of regular conferences:

> A new generation is always rising who need to be taught the gospel, and the older generation must be refreshed in their faith. Then warnings must be given against new designs of the evil one to lead people astray. As the years bring new problems, their solution by gospel use must be explained. Teaching, encouraging, warning, interpreting must, for the safety of the Church, be a continuous process. In the stake quarterly conferences, the visiting member of the General Authorities can reach more people with his message than at any other time, except at general conferences. And, it has been surprising how new, often unexpected, questions and problems arise with the passing of the years.[7]

In 1940 there were 130 stakes requiring 520 quarterly conferences.

The schedule was made to spread the Twelve as far as possible through those conferences.[8] However, one of the Twelve continually served as the European Mission president, and each of the remaining eleven were assigned to make at least one annual month-long tour of the Church's missions. This effectively left ten of the Twelve for stake visits, assuming good health and normal operations. To cover the 520 quarterly conferences with ten apostles in 52 weeks required each of them to attend a stake conference every week. With two Sundays given to general conferences, another to Christmas, and another lost to vacations or ill health, by 1940 it was impossible to follow the quarterly conference custom.

John immediately took on the assignment: "The second week-end after my ordination and a week before I was sustained by the people, I was asked to conduct a stake quarterly conference. It was the beginning of a continuous succession of such appointments."[9] Preparation time, travel time, and Church business associated with the conference meant that a large part of almost every week was taken up with a conference visit. John protested: "In my experience, there should be one Sunday in the month free from a conference assignment, else the man is likely to grow stale in his work; his health may be impaired; and his family suffer from his steady absence from home. If a person give himself to the work of the conference—council meetings, visits with the people, preaching and ordinations, it takes about two days thereafter to return to normal. Meanwhile office duties have accumulated and there is no time to rest. It is exhausting work. And when men pass 70, the number of required visits should be reduced."[10]

PROCEDURES, PREPARATIONS, AND PLANNING

Most quarterly conferences were Saturday and Sunday events, but frequently there were also Friday meetings, and occasionally they ran into Monday or Tuesday. Usually notice was given two weeks in advance of the conference but not always.[11] John frequently had a week or less to prepare.[12] These were difficult problems, not in line with his usual management style.

Upon receiving a conference assignment, John typically wrote to the stake president, notifying him of the conference and specifying what information he would like to have ready or what assignments he would like to have made in connection with it. He would request information on any special needs or conditions in the stake. Sometimes he suggested meeting schedules.[13] John was generous in acknowledging help from the stake president. A typical note reads, "Such careful work as you are doing should help me in making the conference successful."[14] His customary attention to detail was not diminished by tight deadlines: "When we were talking matters over in the office did I mention to you that we should have a loud speaker in the pulpit? It would improve the service very much. I recall dimly that you said you had one, but if you haven't you can rent one for the meetings."[15]

Conflicting demands put on the Twelve when assigned to visit a stake sometimes required adjustments in conference plans. John wrote to one stake president:

> As perhaps you know, I am the visitor to your conference next Saturday and Sunday. Unfortunately, one of the most important meetings of the executive committee of the Church Board of Education occurs on the Friday. I shall therefore be prevented from taking this evening's train which would land me in Portland either Friday night or Saturday morning. Instead, I shall take the 8 o'clock train Friday evening, but shall not arrive in Portland until 8:40 P. M. Saturday–too late to attend your Priesthood meeting. I regret this very much, but in considering the matter, it would seem that the urgency of the meeting here tomorrow justifies missing your Priesthood meeting. Will you please, therefore, conduct the Priesthood meeting as outlined in the program. I shall be with you all day Sunday and longer if needed.[16]

TRAVEL ARRANGEMENTS

Train travel was the most common means of getting to quarterly conferences. But even with its legendary history for on-time operation, leisurely efficiency, and a certain amount of charm, it was a persistent hindrance in the lives of the Brethren. Talbot noted the growth trends outside the intermountain area: "Ward and stake organization and conference visits which occupied such a vast amount of the Quorum's time were now extended throughout the world as the Saints both decreased their migration to the tops of the mountains and moved from the strongholds of the Church to other areas. Evidence of this trend is indicated in the figures that show 90 percent of the total membership of the Church living in Utah, Idaho, and Arizona in 1900, but only 65 percent living in this area by 1947."[17] In 1920, the year before John's call to the Twelve, there were 3,697 Church members living in California. By 1950, there were 102,000.[18] Similar increases were occurring in Arizona and the Pacific Northwest. The number of stakes to be visited and the distance to each of them increased rapidly. A few excerpts from John's correspondence gives an accurate picture of his encounters with this problem. To the president of the St. Joseph Arizona Stake he wrote, "Yesterday I received the appointment to visit your Stake Conference on February 22 and 23. I shall take my wife along, according to present plans and shall leave here Thursday evening, the twentieth arriving in Thatcher sometime Saturday afternoon. The following Saturday and Sunday I am appointed to be at the Southern Arizona Stake Conference and shall have to discover the best way of getting there immediately after your Conference. Perhaps you know about the time tables."[19] This was the first leg of a tour that kept him on the road for several weeks. Of similar arrangements he wrote:

> Of course, you know by this time that I am to visit your stake next Saturday and Sunday. It pleases me greatly, for I like to meet with the good people of Idaho Falls. I expect to leave Salt Lake on the 8:00 morning train. At Pocatello I will change to one of the buses and reach Idaho Falls between 4:00 and 5:00, I believe.
>
> I do not want to return on that inhuman train to Pocatello, which means that conference visitors have to sit up until one or two o'clock in the morning, so I will stay over until Monday morning and then move homeward. I shall be very pleased to do as in the past—occupy a room in one of your hotels, or stay anywhere else you may desire. I am bringing along some work with me to fill up spare time.[20]

> I've been appointed to attend the next Teton Stake quarterly conference. I expect to leave on next Friday evening's train, and will

come to Driggs by rail, arriving there according to the time table at 10:20 A.M. Saturday. . . . Because of a trip I will have to make to Las Vegas, I may have to leave as early as I can after the conference.[21]

> My wife and I will leave Salt Lake City for New York in the Los Angeles Limited, Train number Two, on the morning of May 9th. That, I think, will bring us to New York on May 11th in time for the Stake Conference on May 13th and 14th. I shall be very happy to take part in your conference proceedings. I know we enjoyed our last conference attendance there. Since we have a stake conference the following 20th and 21st, we shall remain in New York to see the sights and take a little rest until about May 19th or possibly May 20th.[22]

Greater problems seemed to occur on the return trips. On returning from one conference John reported, "The train did not leave Pocatello until well after ten o'clock, and I reached home a little after four o'clock in the morning. It is the last time during the war time that I am going to trust myself to number thirty-four. I believe that is the name of the train."[23] "The train leaving Denver and I arrived in Salt Lake City three hours late. I barely made connection with the young couple who were about to be married."[24] Often the return to Salt Lake City took so long that the Twelve were unable to get a proper night's sleep before the new week began.

As the years passed, trains were replaced by automobiles for conferences a few hours away from Salt Lake City. As often as practicable, the conference visitors drove together. Quite typical is the request in a letter to Thomas Martin from Milton Bennion, the general superintendent of the Sunday Schools: "We find by the announcements that Dr. John A. Widtsoe is appointed to quarterly conference at Big Horn Stake August 25 and that thus far no one is appointed to go with him. I have just talked with him telling him you may be interested in visiting Big Horn Stake for the Sunday School and might be able to drive. . . . He suggests that we notify you at once and ask you to communicate directly with him in regard to the matter."[25]

Weather conditions were generally a concern: "It was a real disappointment to me not to be able to attend the Wayne Stake Conference last Sunday. The climatic conditions, from all we can learn, would have made it somewhat hesitant for city people like myself to go over the mountain. It was decided in the interest of safety that the trip be not taken. . . . Weather conditions frequently upset the best laid plans in this mountainous country."[26]

The exhausting work took its toll on John's health. He wrote to one correspondent, "Your letter of August 17 reached me in Safford, Arizona. However, I left Salt Lake with a wounded foot, which developed into a very deep sore before I reached Arizona. Because of this condition I was called home and am still in bed. They do not know whether I will be able to fill the appointment to San Francisco or not."[27] Traveling and unfamiliar surroundings also had a detrimental effect on Leah. More than once she slipped in an unfamiliar bathtub and broke several ribs.

In 1948 John suffered a debilitating eye condition that severely limited his ability to fulfill his responsibilities. Harold L. Snow, one of his eye doctors, wrote a troubled letter to President George Albert Smith giving his professional opinion that John would come to great harm if he continued making conference visits before the eye was substantially healed. John heeded his doctor's advice, noting, "I don't want to take any unnecessary chances and if, by avoiding the strain of conferences, travel and two days of steady preaching, I can protect my health and the other eye, it would seem wise to do so."[28] It took almost a year for the eye to heal to the point that he could resume his quarterly conference appointments.

John loved to meet with the Saints. He wrote:

> They are good people, none better, or sweeter in their lives. They have a clear active faith, based upon an intelligent use of their powers. They are rooted in the truth, sure of their task and destiny, free from downcast faces. They are sons and daughters of God, of his very nature and being. Officers and people alike are full of the spirit of sacrifice for the upbuilding of the kingdom of God on earth. They toil to make today joyous that tomorrow might bring us nearer to this great objective. There is a world view and consciousness, a conception of eternal meanings and realities, that make the humble men and women

assembled at the conferences a great people. They seem always to give more than they receive. It is a heavy responsibility to stand as a teacher before such assembled hosts of Zion.[29]

John's other apostolic duties did not stop while he was on the conference road. He often wrote in his announcement letters to stake presidents that he would "[bring] along some work . . . to fill up spare time."[30] On long trips he was always careful to arrange for his mail to be forwarded to him. He tried to take care of as much business as possible while gone. Firsthand experience with the amount of work involved in the apostleship led him to reflect on the administrative organization of the Church:

> The recent appointment of five assistants to the Twelve indicates the growing need of help. The First Quorum of Seventy will no doubt be called into being to help meet the situation. And while policies will always be concentrated in the First Presidency, the Twelve, and other members of the General Authorities, there must be less such concentration of the work of carrying out policies. Thousands of men and women may be called to assist, as in the auxiliary organizations which have shown themselves capable of doing effective, dependable work. . . .
>
> Undoubtedly, as time goes on, more and more responsibility will rest upon the stakes. Self-government must be read into the dry roots of the restored church of Christ. That is voiced clearly by the fundamental revelations upon which the Church rests. Men to fill stake and ward offices must be chosen with greater care and deliberation, under the guidance of the spirit. Then they may safely be trusted to carry on the latter-day work with occasional help and supervision from the General Authorities.[31]

He further proposed:

> A good development for the stakes to stand upon their own feet at one or two conferences in the year. A delayed train made me late to a stake conference. The president, a prince in Israel, expressed his joy at my arrival, by saying that during the twenty-five years of his stake presidency, only at one conference had they been without a visitor from headquarters. The next day, when he was in a reminiscent mood,

I asked him how they fared at the one conference when they were alone. He answered, with moistened eyes at the memory, that at no other conference in the stake had they had "such an outpouring of the Holy Spirit." It was a natural consequence. They leaned for help upon the Lord and his spirit, rather than upon men.[32]

DIVIDING AND CREATING STAKES

Making the decision to divide stakes was not easy. Often most difficult was the separation of people it required in the spread of the kingdom. The wards and branches around Hollywood, California, were a closely watched early model of Church settlement. On 1 October 1939, elders Widtsoe and Merrill organized the new Pasadena Stake, located in Alhambra and made up of 3,813 members. The former Pasadena Stake was renamed the San Fernando Stake, headquartered in Burbank. In meetings leading up to the actions reported in the *Improvement Era*, there were discussions connected with that change, and similar changes made years earlier. A letter written by Preston Richards, the man who opened the door to the USC experiment, is a good measure of the concern that arose among many people. Richards referred to a statement made by President David O. McKay when the Pasadena Stake was formed from the Hollywood Stake:

> President McKay stated in the afternoon session of the conference in which the action was taken that the members in the Hollywood Ward were being called on a mission to contribute members enough to help establish that stake. . . . The members of the Hollywood Ward have felt ever since that President McKay meant just what he said. . . . They are inquiring "when will our mission be ended."
>
> While new adjustments are being made in stake lines they are naturally asking that question now and they are naturally wondering why they are asked to travel ten miles through a narrow pass in the mountains to attend stake meetings when they could travel four and one-tenth miles to the Hollywood Stake House over one hundred roads and avenues that are open to them, avoiding traffic congestion. . . .
>
> When you made the statement last night that the time would never come when Hollywood Ward would be returned to Hollywood

Stake I wondered how President McKay's inferential promise to the people could ever (be) fulfilled. I have been puzzled to know what to say and I should appreciate it if you could give me a suggestion as to just how to answer this inquiry because I am sure that we will be confronted with it frequently.[33]

John responded, stating that President Grant felt that because the Hollywood Stake presidency was concerned about the costs of maintaining the Hollywood unit, "action has been taken which may leave Beverly Hills Ward in Hollywood Stake."[34]

A month later John wrote another letter to Richards, noting, "In some respects I am glad that I was away during the last month for otherwise I might have been sent down to continue the work of changing names and organizing new stakes in the Los Angeles section. Apparently . . . the cannonading is all over and peace again reigns upon the Western front. . . . It may be the very best thing to have Beverly Hills Ward in the old Hollywood Stake, which, as I understand it, is now Los Angeles Stake."[35]

Prior to a stake division in Oakland, John wrote to the stake president, "Would it be possible, when I arrive, to have a map of the district, showing the proposed division of the stake, and some one to take me around so I can get the information necessary to make a proper report to the Brethren when I return?"[36] He repeated the practice of using maps in numerous division decisions.

Another interesting and complicated stake division included much of the population of Ogden, Utah. John wrote to the First Presidency and the Twelve:

The 10th Ward is suffering from over population—about 1,600 members. While there are geographical difficulties in the way of division, they may be overcome. The Ward should be divided. I suggest that the Presidency give this matter early and earnest attention. There is only one patriarch, and he is not in good health, in this Stake of about 7,500 members. One or two more patriarchs would help meet the needs of the Stake. I looked over the material at hand, as best I could, and had several promising men speak. . . .

It would seem to me that the North Weber Stake with about

7,500 members is soon ready for division. There are fifteen wards and branches in the Stake. Perhaps the whole Ogden situation might be gone over with the view of organizing one or more stakes there, thus lessening the labors of the presiding brethren in the Stakes, and securing greater activity and supervision among the people.[37]

After careful analysis and broad consultation, John reported to the Brethren.

> After considering these conditions and consulting with Church members in Ogden we recommend that 1) each of the four Ogden stakes be divided into two stakes. 2) That each division occur within the present boundaries of the stakes concerned. 3) That the wards be assigned to each stake approximately as indicated on the accompanying sheet subject to such rearrangement as may be found desirable after further consultation with the authorities of each stake. 4) That Mt. Ogden stake be divided at the Mt. Ogden stake conference, December 6 and 7, 1941; and that the other stakes in question be divided at their next Melchizedek priesthood conferences. 5) That the larger wards be divided, but that ward division be left, after stake division, for the study and recommendation of the Stake authorities.[38]

From the statistical information on each prospective stake's demographic alignment, careful examination of Church expansion throughout Ogden continued. John acquired area maps and drew prospective division lines showing the numbers of members and the locations of prospective leaders in each of the wards and stakes that would result.[39] The divisions did occur, in fact, very much as John had suggested.

REORGANIZING STAKE PRESIDENCIES

Next to stake divisions, reorganizing stake presidencies was probably the most difficult task in quarterly conference assignments. The reorganizations associated with the divisions in the Ogden area stakes illustrate the effort that went into finding the right man to be the new stake president and the process of making that selection. Two examples demonstrate the communication that was routinely followed. The first is an excerpt from a letter regarding the first of the Ogden reorganizations just referred to. The second involved a stake in Burley, Idaho.

Would it be convenient for you to arrange for meetings with yourself first and a little later with yourself and your counselors, sometime during the afternoon? Further, could a High Council meeting be held as early as possible, perhaps 5 or 6 o'clock, so that there will be sometime between adjournment of that meeting and beginning of the Priesthood meeting, for work in connection with the division of the stakes? If I am not asking too much, if someone of your official body who happens to have a Saturday afternoon off could be with me to meet some of the people of the Stake, it would be helpful. Meanwhile I hope we can talk over the details when I meet you or your representatives toward 1 P.M. at the hotel.[40]

Brother Clifford E. Young and I have been appointed to be present at the coming Quarterly Conference of Burley Stake. We have been informed already that, much to our regret, the Stake Presidency is going to be released. We hope that you will be able to give us all possible help in making a new selection. We shall be glad to meet you alone some time Saturday afternoon. Then, we should like to meet you and your counselors about 5 o'clock Saturday afternoon; and, an hour or so before the priesthood meeting, we shall be glad to meet with the High Council. If you could arrange these meetings, we will appreciate it very much.[41]

It was customary to keep the business of reorganizing a new stake presidency confidential to avoid speculation. However, often astute members could predict such actions by the public announcements carried in the papers. It also appears that Elder Widtsoe was known for his involvement in these affairs. One friend wrote, "[I] see by the paper you and Elder Kimball are to be at Idaho Falls Sunday. I am wondering if I am making the right guess, due to the fact that you two 'war horses' as they used to call good missionaries in the mission field, are going to be there, if that don't mean a change in the Stake Presidency. I have watched with interest where you have taken the lead in a good many Stake organizations, and reorganizations."[42]

After his return to Salt Lake City, John always wrote a letter of reassurance and counsel to the newly called president; for example, "Congratulations upon your appointment to be Stake President in

North Idaho Falls Stake. As I told you last Saturday and Sunday, I am sure that you will fill the office with the greatest credit to yourself, and that much good will come to the stake through the administration of its affairs. The Lord was present in making your selection; but more about that when I have a chance to see you."[43]

John felt responsible for the preparation of those he called into this service. He preferred face-to-face discussions, but his letters are a valuable means of demonstrating what he, through vast experience, saw as the opportunities and duties of stake presidents. Typical of the counsel he gave and the confidence he expressed over the years are these excerpts from letters he sent Earl S. Paul in 1941 and John P. Lillywhite in 1944:

> Stake Presidents should take no action or initiative in any venture without full consultation with their Counselors. The President and his Counselors should be as one in planning for the welfare of the Stake, and in executing the plans that may be approved. This makes it necessary that the Presidency hold frequent and regular meetings: preferably weekly; and that in these meetings, all matters that may later be presented to the High Council, be fully discussed. With the same spirit, all things pertaining to the business of the Stake should be laid by the Presidency before the High Council for discussion and approval. Safety lies in full and complete understanding among the Presidency and the High Council. To ignore these properly constituted authorities of the Stake weakens their desire and power to serve.[44]

> Do not hesitate to make use of men and women who may not be so well known, but who may develop into very competent helpers. As I looked over the congregation last Sunday, it seemed to me that I saw scores of young people and middle-aged people, possessing much ability, and who, when worked into service, will prove themselves as valiant helpers. This applies also to bishops, who are often very much inclined to let some people sleep, as it were, for long periods of time.

> You know the gospel very well. People like to hear you explain it. There undoubtedly will be opportunities in wards and elsewhere when you can take the time to make expositions of gospel principles. But in

general, in conferences particularly, the preaching presidents, which applies to you and your counselors and to the High Council, is not best. There are sacrament meetings and preaching meetings where there is ample opportunity to explain the doctrines of the Church. In conferences generally the program is crowded. Many like to appear. That is also a good word to pass on to administrative workers in the stake.[45]

Further insight into John's feelings about stake and ward leaders and the service they can provide is contained in an interview by Harold Lundstrom that was published in the *Deseret News, Church Section,* under the title "Elder Widtsoe Reviews Life of Gospel Service":

> First, the leaders of the wards and stakes can actually become the leaders of the world if they will live righteously and prepare for their work. When anyone in the Church receives a call for any service, he must prepare himself, certainly nothing hinders the program and progress of the Church more than an unprepared worker, be he an executive or a teacher.
>
> Stake leaders, I think, shouldn't overburden their workers with too many assignments. Give each person a responsibility in which he has an interest and then let him become a specialist.
>
> Workers themselves should not take on too many things, either. They must toil for perfection in their work and strive to become specialists. This will help the Church prosper with its program, too.
>
> The Church leaders set up guide posts and every worker must heed them, of course. But if a lay member sees a way of improving something, he should feel free to discuss the change with the proper authorities. He must keep in mind that he should not change the program without permission and be sure that his criticism is constructive and in the spirit of the Gospel. Faultfinding as such absolutely has no place in the Church.
>
> And when changes are necessary to give certain individuals broader experience, executives should explain carefully to the person why the change is being made. But as a general rule there should not be much change when workers are doing their work well.[46]

Elder Widtsoe also had words of counsel to those being released:

May I say first that your service to the Church has not yet come to an end. However, as for the division of the wards, I have never yet been assigned to divide a ward or a stake, without finding that many of the people were in opposition to it, and also that after it had been done, evidence of its desirability has become evident. The stake president, of course, would have to struggle with the question; but when a ward gets to be more than 650 in size, some members of the Church, who otherwise would be active, are left without a Church job.

Recently in dividing Liberty Stake one of the wards was also divided, really in opposition to the judgment of several of the prominent people in the ward. Just the other day one of the members called in to tell me that since the division nearly as many people attend meetings in each ward as attended in the combined ward formerly. In addition, tithing and other evidences of faith in each ward have increased greatly.[47]

I quite realize that when a man has served for many years in a position, no matter how ready he may be to lay down the burden of the office, the actual severance of old ties is always a shock. However, in your case, the memory of the happy associations, the great service you have rendered the people of the Stake and the high esteem in which you are held by your co-workers and the love that is felt for you by the brethren in the Priesthood, will, I know, in a measure take away the inevitable sting of the parting from old duties.[48]

I am back in the office for a few moments, and cannot refrain from extending to you congratulations not only upon your long service in the cause of the Lord, but upon the manner in which you assisted us in dividing North Weber Stake and finding new officers for the Stake. Thank you also for the good meal which you insisted in serving us Sunday and for the transportation and for the telephone calls and for the many other things that made the occasion operate smoothly.[49]

Customary Conference Meetings

In addition to the general meetings associated with the quarterly conference visits, there were usually meetings with the Sunday School,

YMMIA and YWMIA leaders, genealogical meetings, missionary meetings, Aaronic Priesthood meetings, and "Mothers and Daughters" meetings. Sometimes special needs required a Friday night meeting on welfare, stake divisions, or new Church programs. Unless a more senior member of the Twelve accompanied him to the conference, John presided over the meetings and was the main speaker in all sessions. Frequently he had stake and ward leaders report on their stewardship in the priesthood session, and he warned them to be prepared to speak in the general meetings.[50] But the primary responsibility for speaking and giving instruction always fell on him. Usually he delivered a prepared message, but he often found that "the spirit of prophecy has been in evidence; and the fulfillment of words uttered has been witnessed. In speaking to the saints, planned discourses have often been forgotten, and another theme, later found to be needed, has come into mind."[51]

His prominence in agriculture, education, and other community interests often presented conflicting engagements as he traveled from community to community on conference visits. Usually the demands of the conferences were so heavy that he was unable to meet other engagements, though occasionally he allowed them to interrupt his conference schedule. Often close friends and valued acquaintances invited him to special firesides with a select group of friends. To one such request John responded, "It would be a great pleasure for me to be present at one of your fireside meetings. However, both Sundays that I expect to be in California are Conference Sundays, and both stakes have evening meetings—one in San Bernardino, and the other in South Los Angeles Stake."[52]

His visits also gave him direct familiarity with the people—their spiritual, social, and economic security. He could feel, firsthand, what their needs were and what he ought to address, as shown in this excerpt from a general conference address:

> Those of us who are fairly certain to be called upon at these conferences are torn between two desires: To bear testimony under the influence and inspiration of these vast gatherings to the truth of the restored Gospel; or to speak to some subject that seems of importance,

perhaps of vital importance, to the Latter-day Cause. For this occasion I have chosen the latter course, and should like to discuss with you during the time allotted me, the reading habit, and especially the practice of the regular reading of the scriptures. It may not be directly a spiritual theme; but I have been impressed from my visits among the Stakes of Zion that it is one that needs to be called to the attention of the Latter-day Saints.[53]

ORDINATIONS, SETTINGS APART, AND PRIESTHOOD BLESSINGS

In the decades of John's apostolic ministry, he ordained and set apart many members of the priesthood. He also gave countless blessings of comfort, guidance, and healing.

John hated to disappoint anyone who sought a blessing, as shown in this note: "It grieves me to have to say in answer to your letter of February 4th that the heavy snowfall made automobile [travel] dangerous the days that the Wayne Stake conference was held. Consequently, I did not visit the conference as expected. However, I shall probably be assigned to the conference next time, and shall make a special effort to meet your father and to bless him. Meanwhile I will place his name on the temple prayer roll of the Presidency and the Twelve."[54]

John made only a few brief mentions of this part of his conference ministry in his autobiography: "There are other miracles, thousands of them, healing the sick, guidance in human affairs, and others, that proclaim the reality of the gift of the priesthood of God—the power and authority of God."[55] "In short, the years have witnessed miracles, comparable with those of the Bible, and more of them. In the midst of such experiences, there was the compelling belief that the affairs of righteous people are directed by the powers that issue from the unseen world, from the place where God and Christ dwell."[56]

In his comments on the thousands of miracles he witnessed, John made specific mention of those involving "healing the sick" and "guidance in human affairs." Guidance was often given as general counsel under the inspiration of the Spirit. Elder LeGrand Richards, then presiding bishop of the Church, reported one such incident:

One of the most interesting things that has occurred to me during this Conference was a visit at the Presiding Bishop's Office of one of my former associates in the Church who was recently appointed a Patriarch and set apart and ordained by Dr. Widtsoe. He told me of how he felt his inability to meet that wonderful calling until he was blessed by Brother Widtsoe, and then he told of the joy he had had in giving blessings to the young people in the Church and of the manifestations that had come to him. Among other things he said that while he was blessing one young man he saw an evil spirit standing by his side, and the impression came to him that the evil spirit was listening to what was being said so that he would know what his mission in life was, that he might try to destroy that mission.[57]

Joseph L. Wirthlin reported in general conference in October 1947:

I had related to me a rather interesting story of a humble man who lives in the state of Arizona; it is as follows: Dr. John A. Widtsoe of the Council of the Twelve had been visiting in the Snowflake Stake and among other counsel he gave to the brethren was this: "Why don't you drill wells that you might bring more of this arid land under cultivation?"

President Flake of the presidency pondered over the counsel given, and he came to the conclusion that a servant of God had spoken and that it would be wise to follow such counsel. Going to a neighboring town he endeavored to secure the services of a well driller. And the driller said, "Yes, I will drill you a well. I assume you want the usual size pipe, six or eight inches." President Flake said: "No, I want a twelve-inch pipe." The well driller replied: "Man, you are foolish. There isn't enough water in this country to fill a twelve-inch pipe, and furthermore, I wouldn't take your money to drill a well of that size because it would be a waste of money." And so he refused to drill the well.

But, undaunted, President Flake went to another well driller in a neighboring community. He told the man what he wanted. The man said: "Well, it seems foolish, but nevertheless if you want to spend the money, I will drill the hole and put a twelve-inch pipe in it."

A site was selected for the well on a piece of arid land adjacent to Snowflake, Arizona, and drilling operations were commenced.

After the men had drilled for a few days, a government man came along, and he said: "Mr. Flake, I think you are foolish in drilling for water here. I am quite sure that you won't find any. It is my judgment had you gone over here a short distance the possibilities are that you might have found a little water."

But again, undaunted and believing implicitly in the counsel of one of God's servants, the drilling continued and after reaching a depth of two hundred feet, a flow of water was struck in sufficient amount to fill the twelve-inch pipe up within sixty feet of the surface. The ground was broken, cultivated, and crops were planted. A pump was placed on the well, and it delivered nine hundred gallons a minute. This year the crops grown on what was arid land two years ago will pay for the drilling of the well and the pumping equipment installed.

President Flake further indicated that the volume of water has been sufficient, not only to take care of this year's crop, but also will be sufficient to irrigate a total of 175 acres.

President Flake followed the counsel of one of Christ's apostles and received the blessing for obedience rendered, which brings us to the conclusion that we should hearken always to the voices of the prophets to the end that the windows of heaven will be open to us— spiritually and temporally.[58]

John always tried to give suitable instruction and training to those whom he ordained or set apart. Sometimes these callings occurred under unexpected circumstances, often with a touch of humor. On one such occasion Elder Widtsoe and the mission president were making arrangements to create a new branch:

On May 13, 1940, W. Aird MacDonald, President of the California Mission, and Elder John A. Widtsoe, of the Quorum of the Twelve Apostles, and their wives, came to Placerville for the purpose of organizing the Placerville California Branch, which would be a dependent branch in the El Dorado District of the California Mission.

The four walked into the Green Line Food Store located on Main St. in Placerville; owned and operated by Clyde Curtis. They waited for Clyde to finish waiting on a customer and then shook hands with him. Brother Curtis had known President MacDonald as the Stake

President when he and his family lived in Oakland, prior to his move to Placerville. Pres. MacDonald said, "Clyde, We have come to Placerville to organize a branch and you are to be the president. I wasn't taking any chances on your going out of town, so I never told you. The meeting is called for tonight at the Shakespeare Club House and the missionaries are out now inviting all the members, so we expect to see you there."

President MacDonald conducted the meeting, under the direction of Elder Widtsoe, and the congregation, by show of hands, unanimously sustained Clyde F. Curtis, as president of the Placerville, California Branch, of the Church of Jesus Christ of Latter-Day Saints. President MacDonald then turned and told President Curtis that he would have to select his counselors and then went on talking to the congregation. In just a few minutes, Pres. MacDonald turned around and asked Pres. Curtis for the names. Clyde replied that he thought he'd have some time to think about it and President MacDonald said, "No, Let's have them now." Clyde wrote two names down on a piece of paper, and handed them to him. Leo Cheney, former bishop of the Homestead Ward of Oakland, was read as the 1st counselor and U. John Fox, a recent convert from South Dakota and recently from Pocatello, Idaho, was read in as the 2nd counselor. Being familiar with Church procedure, Brother Cheney stood up, but Brother Fox was so shocked by all of it, that he could not close his mouth or stand up. After what seemed like ages, he weakly said, "But I'm only a priest." Elder Widtsoe quickly spoke up and said, "That can quickly be taken care of." The two were sustained as the counselors of the new Placerville Branch. (John Fox later became Bishop of the Yuba City Ward). Everyone in the branch had to hold more than one calling because there were not enough members to fill all the positions.[59]

John also had advice about physical facilities: "You need a new meeting house or a larger hall for conference and for recreational purposes. It should be one of the main attempts to the stake to secure such a building."[60] And he often passed on practices he found of value:

> In my visit to the Alberta Stake I found that an experiment is in progress with which we should be familiar. The membership of the Melchizedek Priesthood quorums is divided into two groups—Junior

and Senior. A chairman of the Stake Melchizedek Priesthood Committee explained that they felt that by allowing the younger men to sit together as a class and the older men as a corresponding group that better progress would be made in the quorums. Both the Junior and the Senior group are following the regular courses of study.

I did not dissuade them from the experiment, because it seemed to me to be wholly experimental and perhaps out of it might come valuable information to help guide the quorums generally throughout the church.[61]

There was often Church business to do with land purchases, building construction, or program expansion. In a 1939 letter to James L. Dunford, John wrote, "I have a Pasadena Conference for the 19th, and some other work after that in connection with the Brigham Young film being made by one of the Hollywood companies."[62] "Today I received notice that I am to be in attendance at the next Oakland Stake Conference, September 26 and 27. I have some work in connection with our Welfare investigations, relating especially to dehydrated foods, which will take one or two days of my time."[63] In 1941, while organizing the Reno Stake, John carefully investigated the prospects of establishing an Institute of Religion program at the University of Nevada.[64]

ACCOMMODATIONS

Conference arrangements usually included some special effort in finding and preparing a suitable place for John to stay. Most often the stake president made the best possible arrangements. But John never took such preparations for granted. When Leah accompanied him, he was even more thorough, as shown in this note: "I have the appointment to visit Provo Stake next Saturday and Sunday. I shall be south of Provo most of Saturday, but shall return to Provo in time for the Priesthood meeting Saturday night. I think my wife will be along. Could you make arrangements for us to stay somewhere, either at a home or hotel overnight."[65] A hotel seems to have been the option he most preferred, though he often stayed with the stake president and was always agreeable to any decision the president made.

If the area he was visiting was unfamiliar, he had to rely even more on the hospitality of the stake president. "At last I am back in the office safely after engaging in a long railroad trip on delayed trains. I want to thank you very sincerely for your courtesies to me while in Oakland. A dinner in the charming little place was delightful and our conversation and experience together will long be remembered. I only regret that conference periods are so crowded that one can only begin to talk over subjects of interest."⁶⁶ "This is a delayed but equally hearty note of thanks to you both for your hospitality to me while I was attending your recent Pocatello Stake conference. I was very tired Saturday, but was much refreshed by the good night's sleep in the comfortable bed and room that you provided me. I also enjoyed the midnight supper and the equally good breakfast, as well as the hurried-up dinner at luncheon time, which we imposed upon you."⁶⁷

The hospitality afforded by most stake presidents built relationships that John valued: "This is just a word to thank you in behalf of Sister Widtsoe and myself for the excellent entertainment at your house during the recent Stake Conference. We very much enjoyed renewing our acquaintanceship a little more intimately, and of course a comfortable bed and the excellent meals, one indeed a banquet, made our stay very enjoyable. We shall long remember your hospitality."⁶⁸

AFTER THE CONFERENCE

Following each conference there was a stream of letters. Occasionally they were written on a Monday or a Wednesday, but a quick examination of John's correspondence reveals that the great majority of his letters were written on Tuesdays. Much of Monday was occupied with the trip home and any emergencies that had arisen in his absence.

Accommodation, meals, transportation, laundry, and every other offer of help was greatly appreciated, and from the thousands of letters he wrote expressing thanks, it would seem that he missed no one. As impressive as that is, equally so is the fact that there is not even a hint of a form letter or common wording. Each person was individually remembered, and due apology for the imposition he caused was humbly expressed. Usually he tried to add a dose of humor: "Will you please see to it that the weather is such that I won't have to buy a quilt to wrap myself in as I did on my last visit to your stake?"[69] Often a copy of one of John's books accompanied his letter. Most received either *A Rational Theology, What is Mormonism, In Search of Truth*, or a centennial tract.[70]

On the other side of the coin, John received countless letters following his conference visits, thanking him for his talks, his counsel, his kindness, or his blessing. One from a stake president summarizes the view all held of his visits: "In behalf of our Stake Presidency, the High Council and the people of our stake we thank you sincerely for your visit with us at our Conference. Many of our members have expressed themselves as most happy and encouraged by your fine messages and the spirit of Good Will and kindly interest which you always have with you. I am sure that you did all of us a real service and strengthened us for the months that are ahead."[71]

43

BEGINNINGS OF
THE WELFARE PLAN

THOSE who were raised under the tutelage of the generation that bore the burden of the Great Depression have a strong understanding of the privation felt far and wide. They also understand that the starkness of the depression began in 1929. John A. Widtsoe "was appointed to the Church Security Committee" in a regular temple meeting of the Twelve and the First Presidency on 21 October 1937.[1] That seems significantly late to those who remember the reverberations of the darker years, showing the need for a deeper understanding of the Church's efforts at temporal security for its members.

While discussions of Church-wide relief programs continued in the presiding quorums, direct relief measures in the deeper years of the depression were largely left to local ward and stake leaders. The "Church Security Program" was initiated with a survey conducted in September 1935, and its name was changed to the "Church Welfare Plan" in the April 1938 general conference. The survey showed that 16.3 percent of the Church population (80,553 people) were assisted by public sources. Another 1.6 percent (7,907) were on Church relief. It was further found that of those combined figures, about 13,500 were unemployed, while the other 75,000 were working in "depression-inspired projects." It also showed that perhaps as many as 16,500 did not need the assistance they were given.[2]

Because bearing one another's burdens and comforting those who stand in need of comfort represent the temporal covenant of Church membership, meeting the temporal needs of Church members is directly ascribed to the Presiding Bishop's Office. Sylvester Q. Cannon, the presiding bishop in 1938, pledged from the pulpit at general conference to do everything possible to see to the needs of Church members, primarily by providing the means to enable them to help themselves.

The federal relief plans of President Franklin D. Roosevelt and Congress, with the twin goals of relief and recovery, were running out of steam by 1935 when Roosevelt urged Congress to cease its direct federal relief programs. Federal actions in the winter of 1935–36 made it apparent that though some of the work programs would continue, direct relief was being turned over to state and local entities. Former Church historian Leonard J. Arrington described the Church's reaction to those indications: "It seems clear that this intended shift of the burden of relief from the federal government to the states and localities was the immediate factor which led L.D.S. officials to announce the Church Security Program in April 1936. Aware that the local governments in Utah and surrounding states were not in a position to assume a large burden of this nature, the church established the Security Program to assure that at least its own faithful members were taken care of."[3]

The "so-called dole" and other abuses of government assistance were of great moral concern to Church leaders, yet the prospective curtailment of those programs caused great anxiety for both members and nonmembers. Counsel from Church leaders centered on these concerns and seemed to speed Church action. Arrington concluded, "The sequence of events at the time of its establishment makes it clear that the Church Security Program was essentially a reaction to the prospective curtailment of federal relief. Each time there was uncertainty as to the amount and extent of federal relief assistance, the church renewed its efforts to strengthen its own program of relief."[4]

Many of the actions taken by local bishops and stake presidents were innovative and effective in meeting immediate needs for food, shelter, and temporary employment. Many stakes in Salt Lake City and elsewhere developed work projects for unemployed members. Some stakes even organized cooperative exchanges with nearby farmers to provide food essentials. Richard Cowan, a modern historian, noted, "The Pioneer Stake, also in Salt Lake City, was probably hardest hit by the depression. Under the leadership of Stake President Harold B. Lee, a stake storehouse was established for the benefit of the poor. It was stocked with goods produced on a variety of stake projects or donated by Church members."[5] When the First Presidency was ready to inaugurate the plan, they called Harold B. Lee into a special meeting on 20 April 1935. They picked a Saturday morning when presidents Grant and McKay could spend the entire morning with Lee. Lee was given the charge to expand the kinds of things his stake had done into a Church-wide program. He reported, "I was astounded to learn . . . that for years there had been before them, as a result of their thinking and planning and as the result of the inspiration of Almighty God, the genius of the very plan that is being carried out and was in waiting and preparation for a time when in their judgment the faith of the Latter-day Saints was such that they were willing to follow the counsel of the men who lead and preside in this Church."[6]

Harold B. Lee initially felt that the Saturday meeting had intruded on the precious time of the Brethren, but he later realized:

> They were instructing, encouraging, and outlining what I was supposed to do. . . . I prayed most earnestly. I had started out with the thought that there would have to be some new kind of organization set up to carry forward the Welfare Program. . . . My spiritual understanding was opened, and I was given a comprehension of the grandeur of the organization of the Church and the Kingdom of God, the likes of which I had never contemplated before. The significant truth which was impressed upon me was that there was no need for any new organization to do what the Presidency had counseled us to do. It was as though the Lord was saying: "All in the world that you have to do is to put to work the organization which I have already given."[7]

On 15 April 1936, after a year of consultation, the First Presidency

The Church Welfare Committee in 1939. Left to right: Harold B. Lee, Albert E. Bowen, Henry D. Moyle, Melvin J. Ballard, John A. Widtsoe.

asked Lee to begin his program at once. To give the committee Church-wide authority, they appointed Melvin J. Ballard, a member of the Twelve, to chair the Church Security Committee. Before long they created four subcommittees: (1) Agriculture, (2) Church Beautification, (3) Finance-Cooperative Security Corporation, and (4) Industries and New Projects. With this division of their work, the organization was expanded to include John A. Widtsoe as one of three advisors from the Twelve:

> Appointment of Elder John A. Widtsoe, of the Council of the Twelve, to a post of official connection with the Church Security Program was announced today by the First Presidency.
>
> Elder Widtsoe will become one of the three Council of Twelve advisors to the general committee and will directly supervise three important fields of agriculture, it was announced. Elder Melvin J. Ballard and Albert E. Bowen form the remainder of the advisory group from the Council of the Twelve.
>
> Elder Widtsoe will be in a position to correlate this experimental work of the Church Security Program with the work of the experimental and research departments of . . . three big educational institutions. He will have at his disposal the material of the American Farm Chemurgic Council.

With these qualifications in which he has been trained for many years, Elder Widtsoe will devote much of his time to the development of the agricultural program of the Church Security organization.[8]

As the advisor to the agriculture subcommittee, John was to oversee a survey of private and public lands that could be purchased, settled, and well run by Latter-day Saint families. The survey was also to determine the number of LDS families who had the desire to settle and farm the lands the committee discovered. Those lands and the prospective families were to be reported to proper Church officers. Additionally, the agriculture subcommittee was to advise welfare committee officials on favorable ways of placing those families on the farms and on obtaining full cooperation from the agricultural colleges and county agents in teaching effective farm practices. Finally, they were to learn about new crop uses and favorable outlets for farm produce.[9]

After being called to an advisory status on the Church Security Committee, John became exceptionally devoted to the plan and one of its best spokesmen. In its fulfillment, the two aspects of his life, agricultural expert and apostle, came together with great strength. As formally introduced to Church members, "The program has two objectives, one of which is immediate and the other ultimate."[10] The "immediate objective" was to create a surplus of basic commodities and provide employment for all able persons receiving assistance by 1 October 1936. The "ultimate objective" was to "take care of all of its people exclusive of government relief and to assist them in placing themselves on a financially independent basis."[11] Newspaper accounts clarified John's role in the plan: "Elder Widtsoe will take active charge of three definite fields of agriculture on behalf of the general committee. These will include the improvement of standard and quality of farm produce; and through proper and intelligent use of fertilizers to increase the quality of farm production; and to study the use of surplus commodities through a program being developed by the Farm Chemurgic Council."[12]

Shortly after his call, in an *Improvement Era* article John refined the objectives of the plan and acknowledged that both immediate objectives had been well met. He also identified the specific work he had been called to do:

The Security Program of the Church of Jesus Christ of Latter-day Saints has three objectives: First to supply food, clothing and shelter to faithful Latter-day Saints, who are unable through their own efforts to secure these necessities of life; second, to find employment for those now unemployed, who are capable of laboring; third, to improve the conditions of those who may be employed, but whose income is so meager as to furnish the bare necessities, not the comforts of life. These objectives may be summarized as charity, self-support, and progressive improvement of existing conditions.

The attempt to find worth-while, permanent employment for the unemployed, and to better the conditions of those whose scanty earnings are insufficient for ordinary human comforts, of necessity brings the Program into the field of agriculture. Indeed, from Latter-day Saint farms came the vast majority of the food supplies provided for the destitute of the Church during the last two years. The Church has always held that a stable, enduring civilization rests upon a body of men and women who own and till the soil—who make their living by farming; and is proud to know that the majority of its members are tillers of the soil. Moreover, leading students of the subject believe that the profession of farming is a good business, and an excellent mode of living, compared with the many pursuits of man.

The statement may be well defended, if necessary, that farming as a business, if practiced properly, provides great certainty of food and health and increasing economic substance. As a mode of living, the most important consideration of life, farming is unsurpassed. Individually and socially, morally and spiritually, life under the open sky, in constant touch with the elemental forces of nature, gives strength, endurance, and permanence. Crime is not bred on the farm; and the clean blood of the farm is drawn upon continuously to maintain the vigor of the cities.[13]

On 5 December 1937, a conference on rural life was held at the Utah State Agricultural College in Logan. John gave an address about the desirability of rural life in which he presented some figures that defined the problem he was trying to deal with as agriculture advisor to the Church Security Committee: "Our agricultural production in dollars . . . is not larger this year than it was in 1910. Our rural indebtedness is six times as great as it was in 1910."[14] Church security sought to relieve the problems these figures illustrated by helping people sustain themselves and prosper: "In this program agriculture seems of primary importance in solving present difficulties. . . . Agriculture is first a business and secondly a mode of living. . . . If that which any man does for a living is just a business, he is an unsuccessful man."[15] To promote the desirability of a life in agriculture, John detailed several advantages of the "business" and the "mode of living" aspects: "I set up for you here four distinct advantages of agriculture as a business: Security of food, security of health, a reasonable security of wealth and the possibility of cooperation." As to advantages as a mode of living, he identified intellectual growth, the safe development of family and home, the opportunity of cooperation with fellow farmers, the moral value of rural living, and the spiritual aspects of close communion with the unseen world.[16] He concluded with ten statements about how agricultural success as a business and a mode of living could be achieved. No one knew those essentials better than he. As noted, in 1937 the majority of Church members were farmers, and farming was good business. The task John saw for agriculture, in light of the "ultimate objective" of their financial independence, was reduced to five points in a major article he wrote to the Church: (1) "There must be a new spirit of conservation of our resources, of soil, water, and money." (2) "More profitable crops must be grown." (3) "There must be more cooperation among farmers in the production and marketing of crops." (4) "Men must be helped to own farms." (5) "Farm life must be made attractive."[17]

The principles on which the welfare plan was built are spiritual. In general conference Elder Widtsoe once said, "Every man worthy of life desires to be able to sustain himself and a family of his own. . . . In our welfare program the need of caring for the poor, necessary and beautiful as it is, is less important than the attempt to find ways and means to enable the poor to provide for themselves, and to raise the standard of living of all to meet their natural wants properly."[18] In another address he raised some baseline questions: "What about our neighbor? Are we solicitous of his welfare? Do we look charitably upon his weaknesses? Do we recognize his virtues without jealousy? Do we try to love him?"[19]

In a 1938 *Improvement Era* editorial, John wrote about spiritual principles of the welfare plan that have frequently been used in teaching welfare doctrine through the decades:

> Eternal principles must guide us in our efforts, else the results will be temporary. That is the first and most important consideration.
>
> WORK, or industry, is the basis of economic safety. True wealth is produced by the intelligent application of human labor to the resources offered by earth, and in no other way.
>
> THRIFT is a companion principle to WORK. Wealth, won by intelligent industry, whether much or little, should be used with discriminating care. It must be cherished as the product of life's best possessions, which are: Opportunity for industry, strength to labor, and time in which to work. Wealth must not be wasted, or spent in useless pursuits. Waste is an evil second only to idleness.
>
> A third principle completes the supporting pillars of a safe economic structure. Men must live within the means obtained from their productive labor. That is, DEBT must be avoided. Economic prosperity requires that men go without things rather than to go into debt for them.
>
> Add to these principles FAITH and trust in the Lord, OBEDIENCE to His commands, and PRAYER to Him for help. . . . Let it ever be remembered that only the Lord can give security to human kind. Man can only advance one another's welfare. Therefore, the name Church Welfare Plan is preferable to Church Security Program.
>
> These principles of economic security and progress must be applied by each individual for himself in his life's endeavors. SELF-EFFORT is the key to self-development and personal progress. The only dependence should be self-dependence, under God's will. Self-help brings greatest happiness.
>
> To prevent an economic depression or to rise out of one is the personal concern of every individual. The long history of the race shows that individual self-effort, coupled with self-reliance, is always victorious. If it does not yield great wealth, it makes big men.[20]

In his book *Priesthood and Church Government*, Widtsoe devoted considerable space to the priesthood's obligations to the aims of the

Welfare Program. As he did so, he taught all of the Saints many of the nuts and bolts of the program. For example:

> Every quorum of the Priesthood should have a project of its own. Such projects should have for their objective, the taking care of those within their quorum first, and then the supplying of material assistance to those elsewhere who may not be so favored. Assistance in building homes, aiding in the cultivation of farms, saving of mortgaged homes from foreclosure, counseling with quorum members who need wisdom and direction from those more experienced, all these and many other matters are practical applications of the Gospel of Jesus Christ that will be made when Priesthood quorums sense their responsibility to the members of their quorum, and when they come to realize the full meaning of the word of the Lord that: "Men should be anxiously engaged in a good cause, and do many things of their own free will, and bring to pass much righteousness; for the power is in them wherein they are agents within themselves. And inasmuch as men do good they shall in nowise lose their reward [D&C 58:27–28]."[21]

Elder Rudger Clawson, president of the Council of the Twelve, wrote in the preface of the 1939 Melchizedek Priesthood study course, *Priesthood and Church Welfare,* "The Latter-day Saints' Welfare Plan, divinely inspired, is now under way in the wards, stakes and missions of the Church. The rate of progress will depend to a large degree upon the actual support given it by the Quorums of the Priesthood. It seemed wise, therefore, to devote the quorum class periods for one year to a consideration of the meaning, problems and opportunities of the Plan."[22]

THE NATIONAL FARM CHEMURGIC MOVEMENT

Providentially, the agricultural needs John identified fit closely with interests he had developed in a new movement that began on 7–8 May 1935 in Dearborn, Michigan, under the title National Farm Chemurgic Council.[23] On 10 February 1937, officials across the state formed the Utah Farm Chemurgic Council, the second state council so organized. Elder Widtsoe was made the permanent chairman, and President Grant, the honorary chairman.[24] In May, President Grant and John A. Widtsoe gave prepared addresses in the third Dearborn meetings of the National Council.[25] A few weeks later John was placed on the permanent board of directors for the National Farm Chemurgic Council.[26] He explained the connection between chemurgy and Church security:

CHEMURGY, a new word, has been compounded by the eminent chemist Dr. W. J. Hale from the Greek words for chemistry and work, and may be said to mean chemistry at work. It was coined to serve a nation-wide movement to connect agriculture and industry, through the aid of chemistry, for the benefit of both. Farm Chemurgic aims to find, develop and establish crops which by chemical processes may be used in industry. It is a movement which may rise to prime importance for American prosperity.

Two major questions in this discussion arise: How may the farmer receive a more adequate return for his labor? What shall be grown on the lands now set free or not needed for food production? Farm Chemurgic answers that the way out is by the closer association of farm and factory, with the aid of chemistry, through the establishment of crops that may be used in other than the present food and clothing industries. Likewise, American industry which has been upset by new methods and machines would also profit by the use of farm products in its manufacturing processes. Perhaps right there is the key to the rehabilitation and permanent security of industry. The failure of agriculture to connect more closely with industry by the use of the organic products of the farm has been and is increasingly a major cause of our present economic difficulties.

Economic success on the farm depends on securing the largest crop and monetary returns for the land and machinery used and for the time consumed in production. Large acre yields with good, steady prices, determine the farmer's economic welfare. To achieve this happy condition, especially in the West, under irrigation, the farmer must first grow crops of high acre value, intensive crops; second, crops that may be held over a season should market prices be unfavorable; and third, crops that may be manufactured. Industry meets the first and third requirements, and often the second, for the crops needed by industry are usually intensive crops, and it can well use in one year crops of the preceding year. Agriculture has need of industry. Indeed, it is doubtful, if in our age, agriculture can continue on its present scale as a profitable enterprise without industrial cooperation. With such cooperation it may possibly be largely expanded.[27]

In a conference on chemurgy in the Pacific Northwest, John described to other agricultural experts five things that had to be done in Utah to obtain optimal success in agriculture: "First, we must find new uses for old crops; second, we must encourage, by means of propaganda, the use of crops that are now already being manufactured; third, we must discover new crops that may be manufactured; fourth, we must care for the wastes on the farm; fifth, we must find outlets for farm surplus through chemurgical means."[28]

William J. Hale and Carl B. Fritsche, deemed the founders of chemurgy, visited President Grant and Elder Widtsoe in Salt Lake City in November 1936. The four had become friends in the earlier meetings in Michigan. The *Deseret News* reported, "The visitors praised highly the Church Security Program, which takes a similar road out of depression difficulties. Scientific development of the soil, to get the most out of it at the least expense is the aim of the council, which is striving at once to educate the farmer on the most efficient methods of cultivation and to insure the industrial use of American farm products."[29]

At the National Farm Chemurgic Council meetings in 1937, President Grant spoke on "Character Building Through Self Help." After an impressive review of pioneer survival in early Utah, he concluded, "I have aimed to show two things—first, that our people who settled . . . the 'valleys of the mountains' had sterling character, indomitable will, great courage, and abundant energy, and if I have reached my aim, I have also shown to you that in so far as these things came from their own efforts, they were the result of self-help, but they believed, and we believe that God was with them, and that without this divine help, they would not have succeeded."[30]

Their involvement in the beginnings of chemurgy brought President Grant and Elder Widtsoe national attention. One author described the prime movers in a brief history of chemurgy. She wrote, "There's Henry Ford, cupping his ear to catch the conversation of his table companion, Dr. Heber J. Grant, the tall and grizzled patriarch who is president of the

Latter Day Saints, and whose eighty years stretch back to a time when, he remembers, it was usual for him to have to remove his hat to prove Mormons are not horned devils."[31] After describing several other prominent attendees, she added, "There is Dr. John A. Widtsoe, the fatherly little man with the white-tufted chin, who directed the Utah Experimental Station, headed the School of Agriculture in Brigham Young University, presided over the Utah Agricultural College and the University of Utah, sits on the Council of Twelve of the Mormon Church, and carried the chemurgic torch in the West."[32] Another time the *National Chemurgic Digest* compiled a feature article titled "Friend of Chemurgy: John A. Widtsoe."[33] After a brief biography, it stated, "As one of the General Authorities of his Church, he has traveled the world furthering the cause which his widowed mother accepted in Norway. As part and parcel of that gospel he has preached the principles of sound agriculture. As a chemist he early saw the great contribution which agriculture should make to industry; and, in turn, the significant contribution which industry can make to agriculture."[34]

Just after his appointment to the board of governors of the National Farm Chemurgic Council, John wrote to Harold B. Lee, "As you know, we are all working as rapidly as we can to set up an agricultural program for the Church Security Committee. You know how slowly the work has developed the last few weeks, though it looks very promising at the present moment. However, there are some things which should be acted upon soon." Several projects were pursued. Some proved profitable and some did not, but all of them achieved the main objective of the Welfare Plan; they all provided valid work opportunities for those receiving assistance from the Church.

Armed with the optimism of farm chemurgy, John concentrated on elevating a career in agriculture to the status of providing financial independence. In the October 1937 general conference he said:

> The tilling of the soil has ever been recognized as the basis of national welfare. It is the basic industry of humanity. Without it mankind could not survive. The physical toil which formerly accompanied farming could, if farming were managed properly, disappear with the invention and introduction of farm machinery. Work is not

undesirable; it accompanies all success. The drudgery charged against farm life may in our day be eliminated by proper planning and systematic approach to farm tasks. Advancing science has accumulated a body of knowledge concerning the production of plants and animals, which has raised agriculture, from the point of view of organized knowledge, to one of the best established of professions. Our institutions of learning, notably the agricultural colleges, give unsurpassed training for life on the farm. A person should train for agriculture as for any other profession.

It was J. W. Sanborn, first president of the Utah State Agricultural College, who went back to his native New Hampshire, and converted, by modern methods, worn out, deserted farms into prosperous, money making enterprises. And he assured me that he won unsurpassed joy in the labor.

My spirit thrilled to the young missionary who said to me, "My brother and I are poultry producers. The flocks of poultry are keeping me on this mission. When I am released, I shall go back to that business. It is good enough for me." It is a source of satisfaction to me to know that perhaps two-thirds of the Latter-day Saints are farmers, tillers of the soil, keepers of flocks, producers of the world's first necessity, food. We may get along without many things but food we must have.[35]

CHURCH WELFARE PROJECTS AND FARMS

As the program developed, it became more and more a regular part of Church operations. The Presiding Bishopric, with the general committee, prepared a complete budget of the welfare needs of the Church a year in advance. A provision for dairy and poultry products, livestock, meat, fish, vegetables, fruit, sugar, household supplies, drugs, sugar beets, wheat, barley, oats, alfalfa, cotton, and clothing was included. After approval at the general and stake levels, the stake welfare committee made assignments to the wards and local priesthood quorums. The assessment was presumed voluntary. "Many wards have purchased farms or ranches from which to produce their share of the budget. Other wards rely upon priesthood quorums and individuals to produce a portion of the ward's budget. The women's Relief Society in every ward in the Church, so far as we know, have in the final analysis produced a very substantial part of this budget."[36]

In 1937 the Deseret Clothing Factory was established to manufacture LDS garments and similar knitted items while providing additional employment opportunities for many Church members who were unemployed. Additional developments brought forth another important resource for many Church members:

> Under the authority of the L. D. S. Church Welfare Plan, an organization, Deseret Industries, has been established [on Saturday 13 August 1938]. The purpose of the venture is to collect articles no longer needed or used by a household, to renovate them for use where they may be needed, and to place them on sale at low prices at convenient points. It is a salvaging and manufacturing enterprise of real utility.
>
> Deseret Industries aims to accomplish four things: First, those who have will be given another type of opportunity to help those who have not. Second, waste will be reduced by keeping our possessions in use as long as possible. Third, the work of renovation will employ many now unemployed. Fourth, articles in common use, of good quality, will be available at a low cost.
>
> The enterprise, approved by the First Presidency, will be under the general direction of the Church Welfare Committee. A board of directors will have supervising control, and a corps of trained workers, selected from among the unemployed, will give immediate attention to the work to be done. Ward, stake, and regional committees will foster the project.[37]

TO THE WORK AT HAND

John A. Widtsoe's first few months in the advisory assignment focused on his survey for suitable farm lands and qualified people to take them over. Besides working to help Church members establish their own successful farms, he was immersed in overseeing farms operated by the welfare committee to provide work opportunities for people receiving Church assistance. The Church ran thirty-five all-purpose farms; five citrus, walnut, and olive farms; several hog, beef, poultry, and honey ranches; a coal mine; a soap manufacturing plant; a knitting factory; sixty-five canneries; several large dairies; and some large mills.[38] John proved to be an invaluable and irreplaceable asset in determining what projects would be successful and what land could support such projects.

John frequently taught the Saints about the agricultural undertakings of the welfare committee. One of his talks was entitled "Origin, Organization, Functions, Policies and Procedures of our Agricultural Advisory Committees, and Stake Regional Agricultural Committees."[39] Speaking opportunities frequently arose. Often they went through Harold B. Lee, the managing director of Church Welfare. Typically, Lee wrote, "As you know, I have been advised by President McKay or President Clawson that the East Central Utah Region, that is the Provo Region, have arranged a general meeting . . . at the College Hall of the Brigham Young University at 2:00 o'clock P.M. at which they are desirous of having you speak on the subject, 'Projects Through Priesthood Quorums.' From my previous discussions with them I am sure they are desirous of having this talk applied particularly to agricultural projects."[40]

By midsummer 1938, Widtsoe sent Lee some specific recommendations that reflect the activity of the agriculture subcommittee. The two most urgent matters opened his letter:

> First, the finding and listing of suitable land opportunities for those of our people who ought to go on the farm. Until this is done, proper offerings can not be made. Whatever offerings are made should be presented to the people within the next sixty days so that consideration and preparation may be made for the next agricultural season.
>
> Second, of urgent consideration, . . . even of more immediate need than the listing of suitable agricultural lands, is the preparation of the fruit crop of this season for the market and the finding of market outlets for the crop. According to all reports Utah will have a bumper peach crop and good apple and pear crops. Upon the proper preparations of these crops for the market, depends an increased income to the farmers of Utah of tens of thousands, perhaps of hundreds of thousands of dollars. To secure such preparation, grading, etc. units must be installed within the next few days.[41]

A few months later Lee wrote back, "I have known of the extensive investigations that have been made in the state of Utah, and I believe that most of the members of the Committee also know of your activities in making these investigations. It seems to me that we already have in our possession enough information about land opportunities in the state of Utah and elsewhere to enable us to map out some very definite policies and to proceed to take the first steps toward the solution of our general problem. I am with you 100% in your conclusions and the position you have taken thus far relative to these matters."[42]

EXTENDING THE REACH

There was more than a natural connection between John's assignment on the welfare committee and his editorship of the *Improvement Era*. He wrote, "For some time I have been wondering why the Church Welfare Program should not take a page or more every month . . . for putting its case before the people. I know that there are many circulars sent . . . [to] those who are officially connected with the movement. . . . Meanwhile with our fifty-three thousand circulation there might be a chance of reaching a tremendous body with the Welfare Program."[43]

His most effective welfare teaching occurred in conjunction with countless stake conferences he presided over. Each conference had a welfare session and sometimes a separate day. Often he learned of improvements that could be made in projects the stakes had promoted, and as often he was able to help stakes with special needs. When visiting one stake, he helped them buy and stock a 100-acre farm to be used for welfare work.[44] While in San Diego he held a "spirited" meeting with the San Diego Stake and then examined their agricultural project of three years, consisting of sixteen acres of carrots and other vegetables that they provided to the poor. John thought that every stake needed to have a similar farm.[45] In the Grantsville Stake there was "an excellent representation of sisters, but a very poor one of the male members until toward the end of the meeting." John continued, "Three bishops, I think, were present five or ten minutes after the time of opening, but all were present at the end. The excuse was that the cows needed milking, the chores needed to be done, and they could not get there earlier."[46]

John encountered a new project in the Panguitch Stake in April. After a "fine" welfare meeting in which he learned that the members had already fulfilled the assignments given them by the Welfare Committee, John reported, "I was interested to note that every ward had been assigned a certain number of ducks. I looked in vain for duck ponds; and since water is very scarce in that locality, there probably will not be very many built. Some of the welfare workers suggested that since ducks appear to do well in that climate, they undertake a duck project. . . . Now every ward is raising a certain number of ducks. For one, I like new ideas and the trying out of new crops. And ducks taste good when roasted properly."[47]

The deprivations of the depression quickly became the deprivations of the Second World War, and many of the farms had to yield young men to the cause of peace. John saw the cessation of hostilities as a boon to agriculture:

> The majority of the service men of the Church have come from the farm. They are acquainted with rural conditions. It would be wise to encourage them to return to the farm. They would make no mistake if they do so. Modern agriculture has become a profession of equal dignity with the older, so-called, learned professions. It is good business, if practiced properly. It has the unequaled power to yield daily, sane joy to the farmer and his family. And from generation to generation it builds men and women of strength for the world's service. If the family farm is too small to be divided, lands may yet be obtained. Such opportunities are usually known in every community. Communication with the agricultural committee of the welfare program will reveal many localities where lands may be obtained under conditions that may be met by our young men. Our western lands are far from being fully occupied.[48]

Albert E. Bowen broadened the call for new farmers as he summarized many of the efforts of the agricultural committee ten years after the security program began:

> If people in distress were to be helped to self-maintenance, agriculture was a prospective road for any fitted by experience and capacity. The committee accordingly amassed a vast lot of information

about the location and quality and desirability of lands open to acquisition in one way or another. They asked stakes to list possibilities in their own localities and the number of people they severally had who were looking for opportunities on the land. Inquiries were directed to the central committee who made available its cumulated data as well as offering advice and counsel to inquirers.

Some unsuited to agricultural pursuits were dissuaded from embarking upon what would seem to be unfruitful ventures. Others were guided in their selection of location in light of their tastes and experiences and the nature of agricultural pursuits possible in different places. It is reported that over 100,000 acres of available land were obtained and several thousand members were assisted in finding profitable farming locations. Four separate projects, comprising an aggregate of 21,935 acres were acquired and sold out to families in farm-size parcels and on such terms as they could meet. . . . Some of the purchasers failed, as is inevitable, but others, better suited, took their places and they seem now all to be well on the way to meeting their payments and becoming independent land owners. Their payments generally are current.

Besides that there is a project comprising 5,670 acres acquired by gift from President Grant which is operated on a lease basis by the Elders quorums of a stake which has furnished an avenue of employment to some quorum members and a considerable fund for the quorum's use among its own group. A half dozen other families have been set up on an 1,800 acre tract also acquired through Welfare aid and gives promise of successfully setting these families on a permanent basis.[49]

Over the years, John helped stakes produce sugar beets, milk cows, alfalfa, grains, potatoes, cotton, oranges, beans, tomatoes, squash, and apples. Through it all, he helped people overcome hunger and humiliation and worked to instill in them the desire to help each other and themselves. The plan also let Church members put eternal principles into action. Thus John was able to combine his professional passion—helping farm workers achieve greater productivity and esteem—with his high ecclesiastical call.

44

RESCUING THE
EUROPEAN SAINTS

The experiences in self-sufficiency and self-government that John A. Widtsoe urgently sought to provide during his tenure as European mission president proved exceptionally valuable to the European Saints. Near the end of 1938, just five years after the Widtsoes left Europe, Adolf Hitler amassed his troops on the German-Czech border. The First Presidency immediately ordered the evacuation of all missionaries from Germany and Czechoslovakia. After the crisis eased, some missionaries returned.[1] But less than a year later, Hitler turned his attention to Poland. The war John so feared and often spoke of seemed imminent. On 24 August 1939, the First Presidency again ordered the evacuation of missionaries from Germany and Czechoslovakia. A week later, 1 September 1939, Germany invaded Poland, and World War II began. Soon thereafter all foreign missionaries were evacuated from Europe, and the European Saints were left on their own to uphold the kingdom. Historian Richard O. Cowan wrote, "Although there were some isolated exceptions, the Saints' faithful adherence to Church doctrines and procedures was actually strengthened during the war. In several areas the contribution of tithes and fast offerings and the attendance at Church meetings increased. In Switzerland local missionaries gave two evenings per week and succeeded in baptizing more converts than the full-time missionaries had done just before the outbreak of the war. . . . During prewar years mission presidents had actively prepared the Saints for just such an eventuality."[2]

A report given in the April 1941 general conference is an official view of Church progress in those trying times. More than a year had passed since the 699 American missionaries were evacuated. At that time, capable local brethren carried the work on quite successfully, but mobilization for war took nearly all the brethren of military age to the front, and the work fell to elderly brethren and the sisters. All Church meetings continued with appropriate adjustments:

> In spite of these handicaps, progress is being made. The district and annual conferences are being held. Limited missionary work is being done. . . . Baptisms are reported from all the missions. Tithing and Fast Offerings are being paid, collections of food and clothing are made . . . and the less fortunate of the members are being well cared for.

The following paragraph, taken from the Norwegian Mission Report, is typical of reports from a number of the missions:

> Many of the Saints have lost all they own—home, property, work. All they have left is the clothes they wear. Many have taken part in the fights, but their lives are spared. These hardest afflicted of the Saints have not lost their faith. They have seen that even if they have lost everything else, God has saved their lives. . . .
>
> The conditions of the British Mission are about the same. All the branches are functioning and we have had no casualties or damage within the last two months. . . .
>
> Except in Paris, France, the headquarters of all the missions, including the Czechoslovakian and Palestine-Syrian Missions, are being maintained as usual, and very encouraging reports are being received from all the Acting Mission Presidents. They all say: "Don't worry about us, we are all right—we have the Gospel."[3]

Starvation, sickness, exposure, and lack of clothing and basic necessities characterized the lives of many of the Saints across Europe. "The exact number of people killed because of World War II will never be known. Military deaths probably totaled about 17 million. Civilian deaths were even greater as a result of starvation, bombing raids, massacres, epidemics, and other war-related causes. . . . Battles were waged on frozen fields in the Soviet Union, below the surface of the Atlantic Ocean, and in the streets of many European cities."[4]

During those trying years, many efforts were made to maintain communication with the Saints in the war zone. Thomas E. McKay was European mission president when the missionaries were evacuated. He read from a letter he had received from the Swedish Mission:

> I hereby forward the statistical and financial reports for the months of June and July. . . . I am particularly thankful to our Heavenly Father that we also, in our country, have been able to hold our meetings and conferences. June 23–27 we held our great M.I.A. conference in Goteborg. . . . I have received deplorable information from Norway. . . . It is also now clear to me that a great need of provisions exists and that the aged, especially, are hard hit. I have therefore decided to go to Oslo, if permission can be had for traveling abroad, to personally find out what can be done. Presumably the Church here in our country must try to organize some source whereby our members in the Norwegian mission can be assisted.[5]

Arthur Gaeth, former German missionary and president of the Czechoslovakia Mission, was a European news analyst and correspondent. He described some of the things he observed: "Through the faithful payment of tithing the mission office was maintained on a solid financial basis and now has a healthy bank account. Some of the Brno Church members were bombed out, but generally the Latter-day Saint people in Czechoslovakia fared much better than those in Germany."[6] Gaeth gave a vivid picture of the extent of the need for fuel: "On the Sunday after Christmas I drove my jeep through the ruins of Berlin. I had lived in the capital as a missionary and had last seen it in the summer of 1938. The *Tiergarten,* always a landmark, was only a mass of stumps. People badly needing winter fuel had raided the majestic old trees and cut them down when they were not smashed in the week-long struggle so furiously fought in the park."[7]

Trying to convey the exemplary and refreshing faith of Saints under severe afflictions, he described a group of LDS women in Frankfurt who met in the mission home every Sunday in fasting and prayer: "Thirty-six of them were crowded into the small air raid shelter under the home while three bombs dropped about them but broke no windows in the house. On another occasion, however, a near-miss struck in the court-yard and carried away a wall of the house. The mission home lost every door casing and window when the Germans themselves destroyed the bridge across the Main on the Schaumainkai corner before the home."[8] Church leaders carefully monitored reports of the suffering of the Saints and searched for ways to relieve them: "Elder John A. Widtsoe reported that he had received a letter from the president of the northernmost branch of the Church in Narvik, Norway, who reported the destruction of his home and the death of his wife as a result of the bombing. Near the close of the letter, this man said that if any of the Brethren had a pair of shoes or two of his size, he could use them very well. He said fur-ther that his children had no clothing."[9]

From Denmark, Brother Orson West wrote, "I beg to inform you that as far as food is concerned we can get along. Our people in Norway and Finland need it much more than we do. We would be more than happy, however, to receive, underwear, shirts, stockings, and socks. Especially the babies need these things very much. It is almost impos-sible to buy babies' clothing." From the East-German Mission, Brother Herbert Klopfer wrote, "Had two wonderful meetings today. At two P.M. just a priesthood meeting with forty-five present. At four we held a memorial service in honor of President Grant. There were at least two hundred fifty to three hundred present in a hall big enough to hold one hundred seventy-five. It was just as full of spirit as it was of people. The old mission home at Händelallee is a pile of rubble."

From the Netherlands Mission, Brother J. Schipaanboord wrote, "We have endeavored to keep the right course. . . . Owing to the food scarcity, many of the faithful Saints had to be supported by money or in kind. You no doubt know that the mission house in The Hague had to be evacuated, and we finally moved and rented a place in Utrecht." From Czechoslovakia, Brother Joseph Roubiek wrote, "It has been a ter-rible time. We have remained faithful however, and we await you. . . .

Here there is great need and distress, great hunger among the people. The Saints, however, have continued to enjoy the blessings of the Lord. Their testimonies of the truthfulness of the gospel have not wavered, even in the worst moments of the great conflict."[10] Similar reports were read from the French, Norwegian, Swiss, West German, and Austrian missions.

When the war ended, much of the suffering continued and even intensified. Elder Ezra Taft Benson reported, "Great tracts of once fertile and productive land [are] lying idle. The anomaly of land idle, and people starving because there was no seed to plant, no machinery with which to plant, cultivate and harvest, and no power because power machinery had been destroyed and horses killed during the bombing and many others killed and eaten for human's food!"[11]

Frederick Babbel, Elder Benson's secretary, saw firsthand how extensive the suffering really was, and he heard much more from the victims or their family and friends. Max Zimmer of the Swiss Mission reported to him about a suffering sister:

> She had burlap sacks wrapped around her feet and legs in place of shoes. Even these were now in shreds. Her clothing was patched and tattered. As I looked at her purple-grey face, . . . I was looking at a person in the advanced stages of starvation. . . .
>
> This good sister had lived in East Prussia. During the final days of the frightful battles in that area, her husband had been killed. She was left with four small children, one of them a babe in arms. Under the agreements of the occupying military powers, she was one of 11 million Germans who was required to leave her homeland and all her basic possessions, and go to Western Germany to seek a new home. She was permitted only to take such bare necessities, bedding, etc. as she could load in her small wooden-wheeled wagon—about sixty-five pounds in all—which she pulled across this desolate wasteland of war. Her smallest child she carried in her arms while the other small children did their best to walk beside her during this trek of over a thousand miles on foot.
>
> She started the journey in late summer. Having neither food nor money among her few possessions, she was forced to gather a daily subsistence from the fields and forests along the way. She was also

constantly faced with dangers from panicky refugees and marauding troops.

Soon the snows came and temperatures dropped to about 40° below zero. One by one her children died, either frozen to death or the victims of starvation, or both. She buried them in shallow graves by the roadside, using a tablespoon as a shovel. Finally, as she was reaching the end of her journey, her last little child died in her arms. Her spoon was gone now, so she dug a grave in the frozen earth with her bare fingers.[12]

President George Albert Smith described an enormous problem of the theft of relief packages by military officials: "Those that represent the Russian Government will just take it, no matter what quantity it is, and dole out just enough to keep people from starvation."[13] A deeper view is a story of privation among the children: "By the way, there was another thing in that letter—and I want to be sure I get it right, because it was astonishing to me. He told how much milk the small children were permitted to have. Perhaps I cannot turn to it in this letter in a hurry, but the small children have nothing else but just a small portion of milk once a day."[14]

Times were desperate, and the need was great. Winston Churchill gave an official view in a letter to President Franklin D. Roosevelt about people in Holland who were starving as the war was nearing its end:

The plight of the civil population in Occupied Holland is desperate. Between two and three million people are facing starvation. We believe that large numbers are dying daily, and the situation must deteriorate rapidly now that communications between Germany and Holland are virtually cut. I fear we may soon be in the presence of tragedy.

Eisenhower has plans prepared for bringing relief to the civil population when Western Holland is liberated, and we have accumulated the stocks for this purpose in suitable proximity. But if we wait until Holland has been liberated this help may come too late. There is need for action to bring immediate help, on a far larger scale than is offered by the Swedish relief scheme.[15]

As winter began closing in, everyone realized that fuel for heat and avoidance of disease in their weakened state became primary. Then, food and clothing were not their greatest need. An *Improvement Era* article further described their plight:

> Perhaps the most critical need facing Europe is fuel. It is necessary that the little available be used for the running of trains and the factories. Homes and dwelling places are not heated or heated poorly, and the slightest use of hot water is a luxury. There is little fuel even for cooking. In many of the overrun countries the stoves, even pots and pans, were taken by the Nazis for the making of munitions. Unless the people are immediately clothed against the cold winter, suffering will be intense. . . .
>
> Realizing that this is a real opportunity to help our brothers and sisters, the directing heads of the program are anxious that the best of clothing and shoes be donated. How bitter their disappointment will be, and how imprudent to waste time and money, if articles are sent that are not serviceable.
>
> While the dire need for clothing and bedding is being met, food is also being shipped in increasing amounts during the winter. The harvest in Europe has been poor and small this fall. The diets of all have been meager and insufficient for adequate nutrition. The greatest need is for fats. Most of the fats available during the past war years have been used in the making of ammunition. The welfare program will endeavor to supply this lack through the various meat-producing projects. The second need is for vitamins. For some years at least two stakes have produced vitamins as their part of the budget assignment. In addition to their production, it will be necessary to make commercial purchases to supply the demand.[16]

On 7 May 1945, Germany surrendered. On 14 May 1945, President Grant died at age eighty-eight. On 2 September 1945, Japan surrendered. Restoring order to the Church in the affected countries and rescuing the many Saints from their suffering there became the responsibility of President George Albert Smith. Formal action for devising a plan began on 18 October 1945 in the temple meeting of the Twelve and the First Presidency. John wrote in his journal, "Was called to go with Thomas E. McKay to European Missions."[17] The *Deseret News* reported two difficult assignments given to Elder Widtsoe two days later:

Most important of the steps being taken to lend spiritual and temporal succor to the Saints in the war-ravished countries, was the appointment of two of the general authorities to go immediately to Europe. Elder John A. Widtsoe of the Council of the Twelve, and Elder Thomas E. McKay, assistant to the Council of the Twelve, both of whom have had wide experience in Europe, received this assignment from the First Presidency.

They expect to make contact with all European missions and to direct aid to individual Saints who are reported to be suffering from lack of food and clothing. Elders Widtsoe and McKay expect to be gone for several months, possibly a full year, on this assignment. They are to go alone as soon as the transportation can be arranged.

Other action to assure relief from suffering of members of the Church in Europe was taken this week by a committee of Church leaders assigned the task of finding ways and means to send food and clothing to those in need. This committee is headed by Elder Widtsoe who is assisted by Elder Harold B. Lee of the Council of the Twelve and managing director of the Church Welfare Program. . . .

It is expected that the next few weeks will see several appointments of mission presidents to European countries for a full opening up of the missions there. The two general authorities will assist these new presidents in the reorganization of their missions, help make contact with the Saints and assist in the spiritual and temporal rehabilitation of 30,000 members of the Church in Europe.[18]

On the basis of acquaintance and experience, elders Widtsoe and McKay were obvious choices. Of all people, John best knew the location, status, and amounts of food items, clothing, and other provisions available to be sent to suffering Saints in Europe. No one could more efficiently gather those materials and have them ready for shipping. The problems came after that point. Mail and delivery systems had been destroyed by the war. In most countries military transport was the only thing available. Limits were quickly set: eleven pounds per person per week combined of food, clothing, and provisions. A mission to Washington to overcome the shipping problems became more urgent than the one to Europe. Again John made the connections. Before setting out for Washington and then to Europe, he went for a physical examination. His journal entries detail what happened:

> October 29: Gone over by Dr. W. R. Calderwood and by Dr. H. Z. Lund. Both found all organs in good condition except blood pressure nearly 180mm. Both declared against European trip.
>
> October 30: 9:30—with Dr. Lund—same blood pressure, 178 mm. Left w. Prest. Geo. Albert Smith, Elder Thos. E. McKay & Joseph Anderson for Washington, D. C.
>
> November 3 At 10:45 A.M.—20 minutes with Prest. Harry Truman of U. S. Then 45 min. w. Anderson, Secy of Agrl.[19]

In general conference, October 1947, President George Albert Smith gave an account of the 3 November 1945 meeting with President Truman:

> When the war was over, I went representing the Church, to see the president of the United States. When I called on him, he received me very graciously—I had met him before—and I said: "I have just come to ascertain from you, Mr. President, what your attitude will be if the Latter-day Saints are prepared to ship food and clothing and bedding to Europe."
>
> He smiled and looked at me, and said: "Well, what do you want to ship it over there for? Their money isn't any good."
>
> I said: "We don't want their money." He looked at me and asked: "You don't mean you are going to give it to them?"
>
> I said: "Of course, we would give it to them. They are our brothers and sisters and are in distress. God has blessed us with a surplus, and we will be glad to send it if we can have the co-operation of the government."
>
> He said: "You are on the right track," and added, "we will be glad to help you in any way we can."
>
> I have thought of that a good many times. After we had sat there a moment or two, he said again: "How long will it take you to get this ready?"
>
> I said: "It's all ready."
>
> The government you remember had been destroying food and refusing to plant grain during the war, so I said to him:
>
> "Mr. President, while the administration at Washington were

Most of the members of the Church Welfare General Committee and their advisors, about 1950.

advising the destroying of food, we were building elevators and filling them with grain, and increasing our flocks and our herds, and now what we need is the cars and the ships in order to send considerable food, clothing and bedding to the people of Europe who are in distress. We have an organization in the Church that has over two thousand homemade quilts ready."

The group that sang for you this morning, the Singing Mothers of the Relief Society, represent that organization. They had two thousand quilts made by their own hands ready to ship. The result was that many people received warm clothing and bedding and food without any delay. Just as fast as we could get cars and ships, we had what was necessary to send to Europe.[20]

For several days they called on every agency and embassy that could assist them in opening transportation and delivery of relief supplies to the needy. On 13 November 1945, John noted:

The call to Europe has come. Whether it can be realized, no one can foretell just now. Conditions are difficult over there; travel especially so. Not only that, but permission to go into certain countries, unless the work is connected with military forces, is not easily obtained. We have spent about ten days in Washington meeting with a large number of officials, and know pretty well what we can do to assist immediately our needy saints abroad. They are not so greatly under the need of food, although they do not have enough to eat; but they are in dire need of clothing against the coming winter, since fuel is so scarce to be unobtainable. We are pushing on with all our might here to meet these needs.[21]

On 19 November he wrote to Hugh B. Brown, president of the British Mission.

The Brethren have asked me and Brother Thomas E. McKay to take a trip to Europe. I think the plan is to have me stay there only a very short time. However, no plans have matured so far. Brother McKay, because of his heart ailment will probably not be able to go. The doctors have been advising me not to try the trip under the unfavorable conditions that exist in Europe. What President may decide I do not know. It may be that someone else will have to be appointed. However, I shall be more than happy, as you know, to render some more service to the European people.[22]

In mid-December he wrote to R. B. Summerhays, "It is not at all likely that I shall leave for Europe, if I do leave at all, for some months yet. We are engaged here in shipping materials to European countries, which is probably better service just now than to be over there meeting all manner of inconveniences and impossibilities in our work. However, we shall see what happens."[23] George Albert Smith recorded in his journal, "J. A. [Widtsoe] feels too shaky to go . . . high blood pressure and hardening of the arteries."[24] John was nearly seventy-four. On 22 December he recorded in his journal, "10:30 A.M., meeting of presidency & Twelve. I was released from European trip. E. T. Benson sent instead."[25] Two carefully documented books tell about the mercy mission President Benson filled in 1946.[26] His experiences shed further light on the role John had in that rescue. On the day of his release John wrote to Hugh B. Brown:

This forenoon I was released from my appointment to go to Europe at this time. While this, in a way, is a disappointment to me, I believe it is for the best interest for all concerned. Brother McKay has been released also because of physical condition and I think I have been released primarily because of my age, with an occasional rise in blood pressure, and the doctors think it might not be advisable for me to meet the hardships of Europe at the present time. Ordinarily, under the old conditions, a trip to Europe would be nothing more than a pleasure trip, as you know. Now conditions are different, especially if effective work is to be done. While I feel just as peppy as ever, and have about the same working capacity, I realize that the years do take their toll, and that there is no use defying nature. So perhaps by this action I shall live a little longer, and that is worthwhile also. Nevertheless, I would not be surprised if, when conditions change, I may not again put my feet on European soils.[27]

The journal reads, "I was released from my European trip"; he was not released from the rescue mission. Two weeks later, on 7 January 1946, he wrote, "The trip to Europe has become a trip to Washington in return. It is very unlikely that I shall go there in the very near future. At this end we are handling relief for the European saints. Great quantities of material are being sent out."[28] The First Presidency described the change in the *Deseret News* for 19 January: "Developments have made it seem both desirable and wise to release Elders John A. Widtsoe and Thomas E. McKay from their call to the European Mission in order that they might supervise the collection and forwarding of relief materials to Europe, and to call Elder Ezra T. Benson to preside over that mission."[29] Of his efforts John said, "At this end I am looking after the forwarding of welfare material to the saints in Europe. You may be sure that we are not idle."[30] He maintained his focus on delivering relief to the starving Saints in Europe.

45

THE LAST FOUR YEARS

———————◼———————

Until 1948, John spoke highly of a life marked by unusually good health: "My birthdays are anniversaries that come around quite regularly once a year. But I am glad to meet them, for so far I have been able to extend a hand of friendship to them, since I am still in good working condition."[1] The year 1948 began normally, with stake conferences in the South Davis, Rexburg, Sharon, and Portneuf stakes. Committee work continued at full pace, the *Improvement Era* required a constant vigil, and John oversaw a new Swedish translation of *In the Gospel Net*. His compulsion for acquiring genealogical books also continued. "Herewith is a catalog of second-hand books from Oslo, Norway," he wrote. "I have put a mark against those that are most important. Some of these may already be in the library, since I picked up all available when I was in Norway last. Some months ago . . . we had word . . . that a big series of district histories in Norway of incalculable value to genealogists, were obtainable for a sum of under one hundred dollars. This set is now becoming very rare and is increasing in price."[2]

Bad weather caused the cancellation of stake conference the first weekend of February, giving John time to prepare for a few weeks of stake conferences in Canada. He and Leah spent the next four weekends in

Lethbridge, Edmonton, Raymond, and Cardston. Sometime during this conference tour, the first serious attack on John's health took place. Sight in his right eye was suddenly, though painlessly, obscured. He wrote to a doctor friend, "A hemorrhage in my right eye is the trouble. Whether it is going to be absorbed or will remain to trouble me indefinitely of course no one knows. I am leaving . . . for a few weeks' rest in the hope that the avoidance of any kind of strain and tension will help speed the recovery."[3] The possibility of a similar hemorrhage in his left eye heightened concern.

John took prescribed measures the best he could. He wrote to George F. Richards, president of the Quorum of the Twelve, "I have just come from the doctor concerning an eye trouble. . . . Under his orders I shall . . . have to ask you to excuse me from all the stake appointments during March. I hope by that time the condition will be improved. I am sorry, but I am sure you would want me to let you know."[4] On 15 March John and Leah left home to spend two weeks in Arizona to relieve strain and lower his blood pressure. He wrote, "I have suffered some serious eye trouble, which I am trying to correct. Whether I succeed or not will depend upon time and the blessings of the Lord."[5] In April John returned to Salt Lake City for general conference. In his address he twice alluded to the "light" of truth as the only light one may rely on.[6] About that time John received a special assignment from President George Albert Smith. He wrote back:

> Few assignments could please me more than the privilege to write the story of Joseph Smith. I shall be glad indeed to undertake the work with such strength and time as I may have. . . . It was Joseph Smith, his story and his work, that brought me into the Church and primarily which has held me in the Church. He is an astonishingly great figure. I should want to handle it as an interpretation of his life, proclaiming his prophetic power and leadership. I would want to write about him as a Prophet of God. . . . With a good secretary to help me, and in the hope that my eyesight may improve, it would be possible to do the work effectively and efficiently.[7]

Following the conference, John and Leah went to Westwood Village and the shadows of UCLA for six weeks. He wrote, "The doctors are prescribing sea level and freedom from the daily routine. I shall not be idle. I am taking some work with me that I trust will have value to the great cause."[8] While in Westwood, John frequently visited the home of Dr. Harold L. Snow, who oversaw his progress. After his return to Salt Lake City, John wrote to Snow, "I am feeling very well indeed, thanks to you and others, after the long rest I had. My eye is, of course, pretty much the same . . . completely useless so far. . . . The psychological effect of being with you . . . has not been the least valuable remedy that you applied."[9]

A newspaper announced their return in time to celebrate their golden wedding anniversary: "The Widtsoes observed their half century day in the best of health—and in that warm and markedly pleasant radiancy for which they are loved throughout the Church. . . . As demonstrated in their public lives, so have their private and family lives been the personification of service for the betterment of mankind. Their influence for good has extended far beyond that of the ordinary mortal for the Church library of a Latter-day Saint is not complete without its 'Widtsoe shelf.'"[10]

Dr. Snow wrote to President George Albert Smith about John's condition and stated his belief that recovery would be hindered by the strain of stake conferences and mission tours. John informed Dr. Snow of President Smith's response: "He was very gracious and suggested that week-end trips to the stakes might be greatly reduced. He still more graciously left the matter largely with myself. So, I shall act upon his advice, and follow yours also. I find that I feel very well, except that I am inclined to tire rather more readily than in the past. Both eyes are about as they were. The bad eye bad and the good eye doing pretty good work."[11]

In August John wrote Dr. Snow, "I am leaving instantly for a genealogical convention. . . . My eye is about the same. I think it is clearing up a little at the edges. The other eye is as usual, though it does seem to me that the cloud that hangs down over it in part has been increasing lately. Yet, it gives me no special trouble."[12]

John wrote to President Smith, "Dr. Homer E. Smith, who looks after my eyes here, [is] trying to guard against the hemorrhage in my other eye which is none too good. Of course, I regret this. I have never been a shirker, but I have enjoyed working hard and long."[13] He was grateful that President Smith had assigned him to write a book about Joseph Smith, as the work helped compensate for the guilt of missed conference visits.

At the time of the October general conference, John gave the nationwide "Church of the Air" address, "Hunger in the Midst of Plenty." In it he compared the plights of physical hunger in a day when agriculture was thriving to the spiritual hunger in a day when gospel truths had been restored.

In 1948, despite his weakened condition, John published ten articles in the "Evidences and Reconciliations" series, three editorials in the *Improvement Era,* and thirty-eight book reviews. This was a challenging year for the other Brethren, who were trying to keep up with the fervent pace of quarterly conferences. President David O. McKay and elders Spencer W. Kimball and Ezra Taft Benson experienced health problems that kept them from conference visits for several weeks, intensifying the strain on healthy members of the Quorum of the Twelve.

The quarterly conference problem influenced the decision to call assistants to the Twelve in 1941, and it became part of lengthy discussions in considering the authority of members of the First Council of the Seventy (seven presidents of the Seventy). Because John had written *Priesthood and Church Government,* he was viewed as an expert on priesthood matters. When President George Albert Smith asked for counsel in expanding the role of the Seventy, John replied, "In continuation of your discussion last night with Elder Joseph Fielding Smith and myself. Five suggestions have been made to lighten the burdens of the General Authorities in serving the rapidly growing church." The suggestions included giving stake presidents authority to ordain bishops, reducing stake conferences to two per year, calling more assistants to the Twelve as the need arose, creating a general priesthood board with members who could be assigned to visit conferences, and organizing the First Quorum of the Seventy and calling men to it as the needs of the Church required. John added, "There is a difference between priesthood and office in the priesthood. Normally, every priesthood holder functions in the office conferred upon him; but, since he holds the priesthood, whether an elder, seventy or high priest, he may be called by proper authority to perform any administrative work in the Church."[14]

As 1949 began, John wrote that he was yet "hoping so to live as to not lose all [his] sight."[15] Work on the Joseph Smith book progressed. Several articles in his "Evidences and Reconciliations" series focused on the Prophet's life. As John was scheduled to give another series of radio addresses, he likewise chose Joseph's work as his general topic. The addresses ran weekly from 2 January through 3 July 1949. He wrote to a listener, "I am glad that some good is being done by the radio talks which I have given in the last few weeks. Joseph Smith is a great subject. There is some talk of compiling the talks into book form. Of course, if that is done I must add a little more material than that which can be given during the period at my command—until the end of June."[16] To another in Mexico he wrote, "It occurred to me that when my turn came to take over the radio addresses that perhaps the best thing I could do would be to talk about Joseph Smith, prophet of God. After all, with him we began our history; without him we have nothing left."[17]

The addresses focused on the theological significance of Joseph Smith's experiences. They discussed concerns about witnesses, persecution, evidences of the Book of Mormon, Church organization, and other subjects. Some episodes examined the unique teachings Joseph Smith introduced, the premortal life, the destiny of mankind, plural marriage, and the eternal family unit. Several addresses considered how the Prophet received revelations.[18]

A few weeks into the addresses John wrote, "The good eye is doing pretty well. . . . If it were not for the mirages of the bad eye clouding that which the good eye sees, vision would at least be a little clearer. I am trying to be as careful as I can. I read very little and write very little. I am giving the radio addresses Sunday evenings, the preparations of which require a certain amount of reading and writing."[19]

Midway through the radio addresses, A. H. Reiser of Deseret Book contacted John: "We hope you are considering publishing your radio addresses on the Prophet Joseph Smith in book form. We shall be pleased if you will give us opportunity to publish it. The Prophet is one subject about which Latter-day Saints cannot hear too much from the authorities of the Church. My own enthusiasm for him and my admiration for your gift of language leading me to believe that your addresses in book form would be deeply appreciated by the Latter-day Saints."[20]

John agreed. In the preface of the book he wrote, "Joseph Smith has perplexed the world. He taught a consistent authoritative theology, known only in fragments in his day, that answers satisfactorily the deep questions of the soul. He set up under this theology an understandable system of practices for human good. Besides, he left convincing evidences of the truth of his claims." John also wrote that President George Albert Smith "was eager that anything new about Joseph Smith, in fact or presentation, provided it rests on truth, be given to the world. The commission given more than three years ago has guided the pen in the preparation of this volume."[21]

When the book was finished, John wrote to President Smith, "I have prepared the book with a series of radio addresses. . . . Relatively little attention has been paid to time and places, but much to what the Prophet actually did in his life and left for us. It has been a great joy to work with Joseph Smith over this period. As you learn to know him more intimately he rises to a gigantic stature. I know of none like him since the days of Christ."[22]

John was also heavily involved in helping with arrangements for the centennial celebration of the Church in Scandinavia. In November he finished proofreading a reprint of *Under the Midnight Sun,* the history of missionary work in Scandinavia. He wrote to the committee chair, "I suggested to them [mission presidents] . . . they could honor the memory of the pioneers that brought the gospel to Scandinavia . . . make the jubilee one of high and intense proselyting activities. The condensation of the history of Scandinavia is well underway, under the direction of Albert L. Zobell, Jr. I shall have some of the workers in the building go over it for its value."[23] In general conference he said, "One hundred years ago at this conference, the brethren then in authority . . . sent out a small army of men into the world to preach the gospel. These were scattered far and wide. Some went into the non-English speaking parts of Europe and there founded missions which are celebrating this year

John and Leah in Whitingham, Vermont, for the unveiling of the plaque noting Brigham Young's birthplace

the hundredth anniversary of their beginning. Rich harvests were gathered. Through the years since that time a stream of men and women, lovers of truth, have flowed from those countries to us here."[24]

As 1950 began, in part to alleviate strain on John, Richard L. Evans was made a co-editor of the *Improvement Era* with John and President George Albert Smith.[25] In May, John and Leah traveled to conferences in the New York Stake and in Washington, D.C., so they could accompany President George Albert Smith to Brigham Young's birthplace, Whitingham, Vermont, for the dedication and unveiling of a statue in his honor. On their return they stopped in Washington, D.C., to dedicate a statue of Brigham Young for the Capitol Statuary Hall. John and Leah were grateful representatives of the Brigham Young family.

After John's return to Salt Lake City, his interests turned to what was to be his last trip to Europe. He telegraphed the European mission presidents about "a conference . . . to convene in Copenhagen, Wednesday, July 5. Please be present. Your wife is, of course, invited to come along to discuss women's problems in the mission. You should arrive Tuesday, so that the work can begin Wednesday morning. President Sorenson will seek room for us. We shall have a happy time together. Bring your problems along."[26] From Copenhagen he visited Norway, Sweden, and Britain.

Leah stayed at home, and John missed her very much. He wrote, "Dearest Sweetheart: The work is progressing, surprisingly well. I suppose as time goes on methods will improve, but comparing conditions with those of 17 years ago there has been little change. . . . This trip has been quite worthwhile . . . but it has been harder than necessary . . . because of my worry over you, and because I have been alone. A kiss for you over space. Love you always—John."[27]

For six lonely weeks in Europe, John's health held up remarkably well. When he returned home, he learned that the reprint of *The Word of Wisdom, a Modern Interpretation* was nearly completed, and that the *Chemurgic Digest* for August, with his picture on the cover, described him as one of the key chemurgic figures in America.[28]

John reported on his trip in October general conference: "It was my privilege to be sent to Scandinavia . . . I suppose, because I am able to speak a little of the tongues of those countries. I came back feeling thrilled with the manner in which the gospel had developed and spread from the humble beginnings of a hundred years ago in those countries." With understandable pleasure John then spoke of his homeland:

> Norway is a long country, nearly a thousand miles long. Up in the icy north, we have two or three branches, one very recently established, and I was pleased to find in Oslo, which is nearly at the south end of the country, people who had come from the far north to celebrate and to thank the Lord for the coming of the gospel to their land. The same happened in Sweden: also in Denmark, which is a small country. All had a very large representation of their Church members in attendance at the celebrations. There was a spirit of faith and devotion like that we have here today. Many people had traveled hundreds of miles to sit by one another in meetings like this and to listen to discourses on the simple principles of the gospel of the Lord Jesus Christ.[29]

In association with general conference, John's CBS "Church of the Air" address was entitled "Fear." He said, "We must be vocal in our opposition to evil, we must be eager to cast evil out from among us. In the home circle, in our churches, in our places of toil, wherever we walk and talk, as members of society and as citizens of our land, we must stand as enemies of evil. There must be no yielding to the whisperings from the dungeons of existence. Then the Lord will add his power and his blessings; fear will flee. We need everywhere throughout our sunlit land men who are strong enough for righteousness to face the enemy."[30] It was a stirring address for any age.

In the days before April general conference in 1951, George Albert Smith passed away and David O. McKay succeeded him as president of the Church. Stephen L Richards was called into the First Presidency, so John assumed the second position in the Quorum of the Twelve, sitting next to his quorum president, Joseph Fielding Smith. He said to the Saints, "My dear brethren and sisters . . . I confess that standing before such an audience, I feel a sobering effect. Brigham Young felt it in his day. He declared that since we are all children of God, there is within each one of us a part of God's very nature, and that to stand before a great group of Latter-day Saints, the accumulation, so to speak, of their godliness, lifts a man to a feeling that he stands before the great dignity of the Maker of us all."[31]

After the conference ended, John wrote to President McKay about a remarkable experience during the Solemn Assembly:

> Twice in my official Church experience my emotions have interfered with my assignments. The first time was at the dedication of the Idaho Falls Temple when I found it somewhat difficult to speak because of an emotional upheaval. The second time was at the Solemn Assembly meeting of last week when you requested me to offer the benediction.
>
> I had been listening to you very carefully when a curtain seemed to roll up before me. I had a vision of the future of the great latter-day cause with a certain assurance that that which had been done at the meeting was acceptable to the Lord and would receive His mighty blessings. The close contact for the moment, with the great unseen

world, touched my emotions and I am afraid that the closing prayer that I offered was somewhat halting. I want you to know why it was so, and to apologize, if one should apologize for such experiences. Perhaps I did not quite carry out what you had in mind. However, the testimony of the Divine approval of that which had been done leaves only joy in my heart; and no regret for the momentary contact with the unseen world.[32]

President McKay responded, "Your graciousness in having taken the time to express in writing your affectionate confidence and unqualified support has given us more encouragement and hope than you can possibly realize. Gratefully, I acknowledge your heartfelt approval and proffered cooperation."[33]

In August, John received a special invitation from the Canadian government. With President McKay's blessing, he accepted. The Canadian papers recorded, "Dr. John A. Widtsoe . . . has been appointed to a Canadian government commission to investigate feasibility of a large irrigation project in the wheat province of Saskatchewan. He will advise the Canadian government as to whether the proposed $100,000,000 project would yield 'economic and social returns to the Canadian people commensurate with the cost.'"[34]

John felt rich renewal in his old love of reclamation and wrote that the endeavor was "really a study of the economic future of the provinces under a low rainfall."[35] He was the only member of the three-man commission familiar with irrigation, and hence the sole voice to determine the amount of good the water retention could do for agriculture in the region. He noted, "It has been found that the enlivening power of water used in irrigation increases the crops many-fold and what is better, permits a close settlement, and in time the building of a state. There is water aplenty in the land of our neighbors to the north. . . . The problem is how to use that water on the dry lands of Alberta, Saskatchewan, and other neighboring provinces, to build the Dominion of Canada, now great, into a greater country."[36]

Before leaving for Canada, John addressed a matter important to President McKay: "When President Heber J. Grant was approaching his 80th birthday the Improvement Era staff conceived the project of presenting him on that day a book containing extracts from his writings. This we did and the book that came out, *Gospel Standards*, gave President Grant much joy and gave us, the staff, much joy also in giving our senior editor the Prophet of his day the satisfaction that came to him from the collection of his uttered words. The Improvement Era staff would like to do for you and your writings what was done for President Grant and his writings."[37]

Gospel Ideals: Selections from the Discourses of David O. McKay was the title given to the book. It was published less than two years after John first approached President McKay.[38] The greater burden of the work was shouldered by John, G. Homer Durham, and Richard L. Evans. In the acknowledgments, Elder Evans wrote, "To Dr. John A. Widtsoe goes the credit for initiating this work. The line of communication between the President of the Church and the people was dear to his heart. Even though he passed away before publication was completed, Dr. Widtsoe guided the formative stages of this book and proposed and planned its final presentation to honor President David O. McKay on the occasion of his eightieth birthday anniversary."[39]

As the Canadian commission moved forward, John foresaw a collision with general conference. He wrote to President McKay, "The work there may so develop as to prevent me from attending the General Conference. Public meetings have been called, some of them about the time of the Conference, and other matters at that time are in sight. May I then be excused from the Conference if it seems desirable to me 'to remain on the job'? It will be a disappointment to me for the General Conferences always leave me stronger."[40]

John and Leah enjoyed getting acquainted with Canada and her citizens. They attended the opening of Parliament and other international gatherings. A dispute on the location of the dam halted John's work for a time, and nearly a year passed before he finished his work. Elder Hugh B. Brown shared an account of the esteem those citizens gained for John:

> It was in Canada, his last trip to Canada. They came to our home. He had been with a group of eminent scholars, they had toured part of the country because he was on a commission, a royal commis-

sion, if you please, to make a report to the government. And one of the men who was in his group later said to me, 'There is the most remarkable man I've ever met, and he's married to a woman who is his mate and his match.' He said we were out in the backwoods, so to speak, although woods is not quite the word in Western Canada; but we were in a little farm house, and the man that owned it wasn't home, and we were obliged to spend the night there. And he says, 'Imagine my surprise when this man, Doctor Widtsoe took off his coat, rolled up his sleeves and prepared a meal for us, and served it.' He said, 'I've never seen anything like that in my life coming from a man of that stature.' And then he added, 'His stature seemed to stretch as he served us.'"[41]

John was away on church business on 31 January 1952. Leah, not knowing it would be his last birthday, sent an appropriate message: "To my Darling, who has brought into my life the greatest joys earth has to give. All my love—Leah."[42] Soon thereafter they learned that John had a seriously diseased prostate. From that point his health declined dramatically.

April general conference was very significant to John. He had missed the last conference, and he was getting weaker. In his address he summed up his work, his life, and his testimony:

> It has always been a curious thing to me . . . how we were led by the hand of God . . . over the deserts and over the mountains to be settled in this country. But our people came here and for the first time in the history of civilization demonstrated that a successful manner of community living might be built with the irrigation ditch. The Lord guiding us took us to a protected home . . . he made us teachers of the world in these twin arts of successful soil conservation. In this state, from which we have spread over the west and are spreading over the world, has come the birth of modern irrigation. Most countries which lie in part under low rainfall have sent agents or representatives here to find out what we did and how we did it, and whether they can do it also.
>
> But you know there is a great symbolism in irrigation. As a life-long student of the subject I have always been impressed by the fact that the dry desert soil contains nearly all the elements of fertility. All

that it needs is the enlivening power of a stream of water to flow over that soil. Suddenly the land begins to yield, and it becomes powerful. Is it not so in our spiritual lives, I wonder? Men according to our theology are children of God not created under the old idea, but being literally children of Almighty God, contain all the elements under the law of eternal progression that will lead them into the likeness of their Father in heaven. When this being, this divine being, because in one sense we are all divine, is touched by the power of the Holy Ghost, the Holy Spirit, the power that flows from God, suddenly a man blossoms into a new life, new possibilities arise, new powers develop. That transformation is marvelous. I have seen it in the mission field, where I first heard the gospel. I have seen it here at home. I see it every day. Every person has a measure of God's Spirit given to him. We are all in God's presence through his Holy Spirit.

The weavers of the midlands in England, the coal miners of Wales, the fishermen in Norway, the trudging farmers of Denmark, very common ordinary people, who accept the gospel from the lips of some humble Mormon missionary become so changed by those enlightening truths of the gospel that they are not the same people any longer. They have been fertilized, so to speak, by the Spirit of God that flows from eternal truth, just as in irrigation the barren, dry soil is fertilized by diverting the stream of water from the irrigation ditch onto the thirsty land.

I remember the man who baptized me into the Church, a very common, ordinary man to begin with, a ropewalker with a jug of beer two or three times a day, a glass of whiskey a little later, and a cud of tobacco mostly all day long, living a useless, purposeless life, except for three meals a day, and the satisfaction of some of the carnal appetites. He heard the gospel and accepted it. It was good. It was something he had been longing for. The man grew in power and stature in the Church. As I recall it, he filled five or six missions and presided over one of the missions of the Church. He was the same man, with the same arms, same feet, same body, same mind, but changed because of the Spirit that comes with the acceptance of eternal truth. But remember, when irrigation began in Utah, it was a struggle with the earth. It required toil. The water did not flow down these canyon streams to the farms just by asking it to do so, but men dug and drilled and shoveled and made canals. And so to get that spiritual stream that I have been talking about, it must be sought for; it must be fought for; it must be labored for. It will come, but we must ask for it and seek it and labor for it. Then comes that great change—an overwhelming change. It changes men to a Godlike phase of life and living.

Let us determine to cling to our heritage here in this land where we were led by the guiding power of God, and may the descendants of our pioneer fathers refuse to sell their birthright for gold lest it turn to a "mess of pottage." May we remember our heritage in this Church of land, of water, and of spiritual power, I pray in the name of the Lord Jesus Christ. Amen.[43]

When October general conference came, John was too ill to attend. In opening remarks President David O. McKay said, "We are sorry that Elder John A. Widtsoe is unable to be with us this morning. We hope that the Lord will bless him sufficiently to join us later in the sessions of this conference."[44] John was not able to attend any of the sessions, though in a few days he was able to go on an automobile ride with friends.[45]

John was also able to conclude his work in Canada. He wrote to the prime minister, "The work on the South Saskatchewan River to which you appointed me a little more than a year ago has now been completed. Mr. Richardson, the secretary, has just left me here with the report such as it will in substance appear in print. I am grateful to have had this opportunity of serving the great Canadian Nation; thankful to you for your personal good will and attention."[46] The report recommended further investigations before proceeding with a dam. It was one of the last documents John signed. Six years later, the Canadian government, in light of a terrible drought, moved forward in building the dam the commission had carefully studied.

John's health was deteriorating rapidly. He was scheduled to speak at BYU, but he wrote to President Wilkinson, "As Sister Feik has already notified you, under the circumstances I think it would not be wise for me to address the students tomorrow. Give me a little later date. My malady is of such that I suffer from intense pain at certain times. I believe I am gradually overcoming this."⁴⁷ In place of John's address, President Wilkinson read to the students from *In a Sunlit Land,* John's newly published autobiography. John's health continued to decline, and about three weeks after his letter to President Wilkinson, his kidneys shut down. The next week was most difficult, but he was continually comforted by Leah, who stayed at his bedside. Loved ones, the Brethren, and close friends visited him as often as he could endure. Finally, on 29 November 1952, in the comfort of his home and family, John's call to mortality ended. Leah described his last year and the trial his passing was to her:

> My husband has not been well since last January and while he has not been desperately ill or bedridden I have spent my time helping him to finish some literary work he has desired much to do as well as added burdens because of his physical condition. Until his 80th birthday he had what seemed to be perfect health except for an occasional attack of laryngitis due, no doubt, to his many calls for using his voice in his public work. In the last year or two he has known that he had a beginning prostate gland trouble. After his birthday last January the doctors discovered that it was quite serious but preferred not to operate because of his age; so gradually his health has deteriorated until about a week before his passing his kidneys became ineffective and his last week only was spent in bed.
>
> It has been a most difficult year as you may guess for our lives have been so much one and so happy that it has been very difficult for me to face reality. However the gospel helps greatly. I don't know what people do who do not have our understanding of life hereafter with its continuation of family relations and joys, with ever increasing learning, intelligent activity and happiness.⁴⁸

> When my hubby passed away, I needn't tell you how upset I was. I felt—oh for a year I never stepped inside of the Church Office Building. So Homer Durham, Dr. G. Homer Durham, my son-in-law and my eldest daughter, Anne Wallace, were responsible for what happened to all the manuscripts and private material that were in my husband's office. I don't know what became of any of it. They knew, I wasn't interested in what was left of him. In those days I was busy,

I guess, with other kinds of thoughts. Took me over a year to get on my feet after his passing. Because we were always very intimate, we worked together as pals and we were great lovers, to the end of the journey.[49]

The *Deseret News* announcement of his death read, "Dr. John A. Widtsoe, 80, since 1921 a member of the Council of the Twelve Apostles, Church of Jesus Christ of Latter-day Saints, and a leading educator and writer, died of uremia at his home, 1425 Sigsbee Ave., Saturday at 8:30 A.M."[50] The funeral was held the following Tuesday, 2 December 1952, in the Salt Lake Tabernacle. President David O. McKay conducted and gave the closing address. President Steven L Richards, counselor in the First Presidency, gave the invocation. Excerpts from impressive letters and telegrams were read by President McKay.[51] Addresses were given by Franklin S. Harris, Richard L. Evans, and J. Reuben Clark, also a counselor in the First Presidency. Joseph Fielding Smith, president of the Quorum of the Twelve, gave the benediction.

All of the speakers had known John intimately for many years. Each of them remembered parts of his life that, combined, provided a fitting review and final tribute. President Harris said, "Dr. Widtsoe's ability to win order out of chaos, simplicity out of complexity, light out of darkness, hope out of despair, and faith out of doubt, was soon recognized beyond the walls of the institution where he served. In the three institutions of Utah . . . he was not only a skilled administrator and organizer, but he also personally stimulated thousands of men and young women to make the most of themselves."[52]

Richard L. Evans added, "These two together came into my life a few months after they had lost their last son. . . . Deep disappointment and sorrow ensued, but no bitterness. Instead they took unto themselves yet other sons, who most kindly they encouraged and lifted on their way in life." Speaking further of John and Leah, Elder Evans added, "And all this he shared with the wonderful companion of his life. From their first days together, nearly sixty years ago, to these last difficult but devoted days, I have never seen a sweeter association. Eternity is little enough for such completeness of companionship as theirs has been." Of John's faith he said, "There are some men in whom faith in things not seen, comes very close to certain knowledge, so close indeed that there is little or no room between the two; and in him there was such faith."

President Clark said, "I think I can summarize my own view about him and his work . . . by saying that where other men saw blind forces at work and at play, he saw God. And throughout his life, as I see it, he brought to bear the full treasure house of his great knowledge in the field of science, to advance the cause of our Heavenly Father. That was the key to his work throughout life." President McKay saw another image: "It has been said that many men know how to flatter, few men know how to praise. Elder Widtsoe is one of the rare men that knew how to praise. It is that quality, I think . . . that has encouraged and stimulated many students who sought Brother Widtsoe's advice, and were encouraged thereby to press on to achievement."

In the benediction, President Smith gave one last view: "And we who have been closely associated with him, the lives of the members of the family, because we miss him, because we loved him, because he was faithful and true to every covenant and obligation. Our lives have been enriched by his example and by his teachings, for he was true. No influence of evil influenced him, or caused him to falter, or turned him from the path of truth."[53]

Epilogue

FAMILY MEMORIES

IN *the Gospel Net,* John's tribute to his mother, is a beautiful story of family love as John learned it. It was a life with plenty of hardships to strengthen bonds and mold character.[1] Next to John's relationship with God, deep and abiding family love was the largest stone in the foundation of his life. It was equally so with Leah. Their greatest sadness in life, their cross, was the death of their five children and the inability to perpetuate that family love in the Widtsoe name.

"The Love Story" is the title of the twenty-first chapter in John's autobiography. In it he wrote, "Without a love story, life, whatever its outward achievements, would be a succession of drab, listless days. With love, as I have found, the humblest life and the meanest task become glorious. Whether love found me, or I found love, matters little. Love and I have built a happy life."[2] That chapter tells of his meeting Leah, their bantering, their courtship, their falling in love, their marriage, and their children.

The life of John and Leah Widtsoe is a living lesson in successful marriage. John wrote, "Our home life was always ideal. There were no storms, and few differences. Love tempered every action. There were

John and Leah in their Sigsbee Avenue home near the end of John's life.

many guests, but they were not allowed to interfere with our method of living. We were Latter-day Saints, and ordered our home accordingly."[3]

It may be said that John lived the lives of several men. His accomplishments are a measure of devotion and good management. That the Widtsoes' love story was not adversely affected by those accomplishments is the best measure of that devotion and management. John wrote, "We tried to be together as much as possible, for thereby love is nurtured. Long separations are never good in married life. Yet my Church work was such that we were parted nearly one half of our days. But most separations were short, therefore tolerable. When long trips were in view, we went together, to share like experiences, and to be together for Love's sake. Too many marital rifts occur because the effect of separation is not understood. That is one reason why I kept out of clubs. If I had free time, it could best be spent at home."[4]

Changes in John's responsibilities required substantial relocations for long periods. Through those changes, John wrote, "Our love . . . was not affected. It grew with time. Today, after half a century, it is real and living, and as full of charm and romance as ever. May I borrow Mark Twain's phrase and say that wherever Leah is there is Eden. This is the best chapter of the story of my life."[5]

Bits and pieces of their love story show the feelings they held and their gentle touch in expressing them. Following their first summer in Cambridge, they wrote many letters, which grew in size as the months passed. They competed openly in a teasing effort to make each letter longer than the last received. In one of them John wrote a revealing, heartfelt answer to a question Leah had put to him: "'Which would I rather be? An old man's darling or a young man's slave?' Why neither. I should prefer to be a young woman's sweetheart. Were I a young lady I should want to be the darling of the man I loved, be he young or old; but nobody's slave."[6]

In sharing more direct feelings, he wrote, "I said of your eight-page letter that it was not half-enough. You sent me 17 pages—one page more than twice the first. It was real cute, but I can not say that it is enough. You can never write enough. When you have not the time and inclination to write long letters why write short ones—of course the longer are preferred. When you are real busy, even your 'Leah' enclosed in an envelope and mailed to me will show me I am still remembered. I am lonesome 18 out of the 24, the others I sleep."[7] They were lovers in bloom, and lovers they would ever be with never a fear of expressing their devotion.

With that same gentle-heartedness, at age seventy-eight John wrote a note on his office stationery:

> Journal entries for Christmas, 1950.
> For *Leah*—Queen of hearts—No! Of my heart!
> Arranged in ascending order of importance
> 1. Miscellaneous
> • Pair of slippers
> • Paint remover—not for range
> • copy of the Christmas number of the London Illustrated News
> • box of thin shelled nuts—to be cracked carefully, by hand,—
>   no fragments on the floor

- collection of Southwest offerings *when it comes*
2. A Chinese carpet, to match the wall paper in the dining room. Oh! Hand tufted! Can be walked on
3. A big refrigerator—Admiral—May need Dramamine
4. A check for $25.00—disgustingly small after 53 years.
5. A gossamer box full of love—careful, it's alive!
6. A lover, real and yours, named John.

I guess # 6 will make up for the others.[8]

Sprinkled throughout their married correspondence are dozens of letters, mostly written during prolonged church assignments. Most begin "Dearest One," and most mention real loneliness in the absence of the other. The interest in long letters and gentle expression lingered in both of them over the years.

Romantic moments were part of their daily lives. On their Holy Land tour in 1933, Leah wrote, "The sadness of fate; the loveliest sea voyage imaginable and John and I both had such huge cold sores that we could not kiss! The voyage ended as all things must—most enjoyable. The blue blue of the Mediterranean is incomparable unless with Bear Lake at its best."[9]

Other than John and Leah's parents and children, no one knew the couple better than Richard L. Evans. In remarks about John, after reviewing his many successes, Elder Evans gestured to Leah and said, "In all this, it should surely be said here that this lovely companion, this gracious lady by his side has been a great factor. I have never seen a sweeter association nor a more congenial companionship nor a more complete understanding between husband and wife. It has been an inspiration to observe over the years."[10] John Wallace, a grandson, described Richard's relationship: "Suppers were always basically a family affair. We ate upstairs. Incidentally, the only person that ever had a key to our house, besides Mother and Eudora, was Richard L. Evans. Every night on the way home from work, we'd hear the key in the door: 'Here comes Uncle Dick.' He would pull up a chair and sit down at the table—he'd never eat—and they would just have a grand old time chatting, every night that we were there. I don't think he ever went home without stopping in to see Grandpa and Grandma or Mother."[11]

The tradition of telling their love story has been passed to their grandchildren, of whom there are only six, three each from Anna and Eudora. Because of Anna's early divorce, she and her three children spent many years in the basement of the Sigsbee Avenue home with Grandma and Grandpa Widtsoe. When asked about that relationship, one of them, Peggy, said, "He was the only father I ever knew. Mother was divorced before I was born. He was just a grandpa—just a dear, loving grandpa. He would come in after work, and Grandma and the ladies would be getting dinner on and he'd be reading the newspaper. I would just go barreling in and jump in his lap. He'd sit there with his arms around me. He'd talk about Hans Christian Anderson. Oh, my goodness! He was another Hans Christian Anderson! He would spin the most marvelous tales of fairies and gnomes and princesses. They had trolls under bridges, and I would just be off in this world. To this day I believe in fairies and gnomes because they're so real to me from that. I didn't know he was busy. I thought he was always just waiting for me to climb up in his lap." John Wallace added, "He read to us a lot. And he liked to tell stories, I mean real stories. He was just a great friend, a great companion."

George reported, "I was told that my grandfather was a remarkable person, was a bright person, and yet what I knew of my grandfather wasn't this austere, distant legend but a cuddly, warm human being. I remember sitting on his lap and being hugged by him and feeling the warmth of his body and letting me kind of just crunch into him. I also have memories of his taking me to the first Mighty Joe Young movie in the late forties. I remember his taking me to Walt Disney movies as they would either recycle or come out for the first time. I think my first *Snow White and the Seven Dwarfs* or even *Bambi* was with my Grandfather Widtsoe."

Joanne has an envelope containing a letter from her grandfather. On it she has written, "This is my most cherished possession." She was once working in the Grand Canyon area, and John wrote to her about their life at home. He encouraged her to read about the canyon's history, adding, "Someday go out to Point Sublime when the evening shadows fall into the canyon and dream about life and its mystery." He closed, "Be a good girl, as good as you have been."

John Wallace remembered his grandfather's love of nature: "On trips he was a marvelous gardener. If we were driving down through Utah, he would tell us what those plants were and what we could do with that soil. Soil growing those plants would produce this. Watering would help this. Then we'd get into geology, and then botany. It was just a marvel. If we were in the mountains, he could tell us about the folding and layers. Yes, there was a creation. No, it didn't happen in seven days. No, it didn't happen in seven thousand years. There was an element of evolution, as there still is. Things change, things evolve. Mountains move around, streams change in their course. Time is measured only by man."

In describing one of her favorite memories, Joanne said, "Farr's Ice Cream and the Bluebird [Cafe] in Logan. Grandpa was driving, and the car started to change lanes to go into Farr's Ice Cream, and Grandma, in the back seat, said, 'John, I forbid you to go in that store.' And the car kept going this way [motioning]. 'John I forbid you.' And then he would say, 'I can't help it, Leah. The car's just turning.' And when I was driving, once in Logan when Grandpa wanted to turn into the Bluebird, the same thing happened there." The grandchildren remember the almost weekly ice cream trips: "He would always say, 'Just stop for ice cream on South Temple there.' So we always did, and it was just absolutely a rule, a routine that we went through. We would turn in, and Grandma would say, 'Oh, Father, oh, Daddy, you are not taking these children to get them more sugar again!' And he'd say, 'Well, Leah, I am not driving, the car just turned in here, and there is just no point in being here if we are not going to go in. Besides, we have to think a little bit scientifically. We have to make this a scientific experiment. We have to go in and do a test to see if the ice cream is as good this week as it was last week. The only way we will ever know that is to go in there and find out for ourselves; this is in the interest of science that we are doing this.' 'Oh, Father, oh, Daddy, I wish you wouldn't do this.' He said, 'It is where the car is; we will just have to go in.'"

Asked if her grandfather was a fanatic on the Word of Wisdom,

Peggy said, "I think everybody knew that was Grandma's area more than Grandpa's. We were not allowed to have white flour! But it was because Grandma wouldn't allow it. Grandpa would walk over to the bakery and get his white flour, then come to our house. We'd all sit around and have milk and dunk it. When Grandma wasn't looking, he would do that. But she was total about the whole thing. The fun we'd have together eating it far outweighs whatever detriment there would be due to the extra sugar." Considering the idea of extremism, she added, "I think he could see the wisdom, and he knew she was right, but he definitely was not an extremist. The only thing I knew him to be extreme about, and he was adamant about this, but then he was in the Twelve: He'd go over to Z C [ZCMI]—they have that little lunchroom in there—and he'd go over there for lunch often. He always ordered root beer or something, and they would try to serve it to him in a Coca-Cola glass, and he would say, 'No I will not drink this out of the Coca-Cola glass.' He used to tell us, 'Just trust me on this. It is important to avoid the very appearance of evil.' But he said, 'If I did that just once, people would assume I was drinking a Coca-Cola. And I'm telling people this is harmful; I feel that it really is. And I could not then, in good conscience, do that.' Even if nobody was looking, he would never have done that."

At other times John did family things that were not strictly in line with Leah's views of nutrition and the Word of Wisdom. George said, "I have memories of going out because mother would tell me that he was coming for breakfast on Saturday morning, and I would go out, because we lived just two blocks from them, and he would walk along Reservoir Park and then up Butler Avenue, and he would come in, and often we'd have pancakes or waffles because my grandmother didn't like to use syrup very much. And that was a fun aspect." Joanne added, "Grandma and Grandpa had a girl named Berle living with them. Berle used to just tie me in knots because she would be so bossy to Grandpa and wouldn't let him eat anything. So he would walk over to the Crystal Palace Market, go to the back, and get these square crumb-cakes made with flour and a little bit of sugar on top and a quart of milk, walk around the corner (because we were right in back of the Crystal Palace), open

the door, and say, 'Berle told me I can't have these; can I have them?'"
John Wallace remembered, "Several times on Douglas [Street] we
would be home and Grandpa would walk over to 5th East on 2nd South
to get a haircut. Across the street was a bakery. Grandma didn't support
sweets. Although we had cakes, they were whole-wheat cakes, and pie
crusts were whole-wheat pie crusts. He would come over with a little
bag of chocolate eclairs, and he'd sit down and eat chocolate eclairs
with milk."

Things were always fun with John and Leah, even the teasing about
sugar and flour. Especially fun were the memories of birthdays and celebrations and times at the family cabin. George said, "I have extraordinary memories of his capacity to celebrate birthdays and holidays. And
there was something almost like a festival or celebration just to be in his
and my grandmother's presence." Peggy remembered it as almost magic:
"In Brighton, by our cabin, we had a little sacred grove, a fairy glen, and
that's where fairies lived. And there was a rock, and if you wrote something to the fairies that you really wanted them to bring and put it under
that rock, it was always there the next morning. I don't know how
Mother did it, because I never remember anything we asked for not
being there in the morning, and that's how I knew for sure that Grandpa
was right, that there really were fairies, because he brought things that
you could never get down at the city and Grandma and Grandpa's. You
would never ask for candy down there, but you could ask for it in
Brighton. It always came."

Peggy remembered a bear story: "I don't know how old I was, but
Grandpa and I were hiking up the hill in back of the cabin. We went up
quite a ways and saw a bear, and it really scared both of us, especially
Grandpa. He said, 'Honey, run down. Be very careful not to trip and
fall—I'll be right in back of you.' But he wouldn't get ahead of me or
anything, and he'd say, 'Let's just get out of here.' And I remember running as fast as we both could down that hill. That's probably why I'm
still scared of bears to this day. . . . I couldn't run very fast, but he was
either holding my hand or was right in back of me, saying, 'Now be careful, we don't want to fall, but let's hurry, let's run, but don't fall.'"

John Wallace shared another Brighton memory: "Grandpa had a

close relationship with all of his missionaries, and they would frequently come over. They and their wives would go to the family cabin in Brighton. They'd all have their musical instruments, and they'd spend hours singing and then taking these long hikes. There was no big rush to get down to church like there is now. They would have church on the porch. A number of times, Grandpa would take all the boys and leave at midnight on Saturday and hike to the top of sunset peak and just have a testimony meeting up there."

Carolyn prized a memory of her grandfather: "He gave me a sense of place and an identity, which I always pinpoint to Temple Square. It was a feeling of ownership, that this was my people. And his accessibility—he would interrupt anything to let us run in, to greet us and have us kiss not one cheek but both, because the other would be sad if it were not kissed as well." Of Leah, Carolyn said, "I thought of [Grandma] as a *grande dame*! She really had style! She was wonderful. She recognized in me a tendency to vanity—desiring more than I could have—and she told me that she would support the purchase of anything that I would make. I've been a knitter ever since, because she was someone who would finance my means to an end of having."

Doralee shared more memories: "I wanted to be a great writer when I was young; I still would like to be a great writer. And so I was very diligent, and I wrote a whole lot of poems one year—in school—just little ditties. And for a surprise, he had these little poems published—my poems! And he titled the book *Wooing the Muse at Twelve*. He gave me a huge box of the books, which I shared. Another thing that I remember is that we were asleep upstairs on Christmas Eve. I remember walking downstairs and seeing Santa in Grandpa's chair, and he said, 'What are you doing up? I think you'd better go back to bed if you want to have a present for Christmas.' That's very clear in my mind, and we have that chair now."

Grandma's "bedroom talks" are also favorite memories with the grandchildren. Peggy recalled, "She had her bedroom talks, but she only did it in private. She would never do it in front of anyone. If she saw something that she thought wasn't kind or wasn't good behavior or something, she would take us into the bedroom and shut the door, and she would always sit down so that our knees were almost touching, take your hand, and look right in your eye, and say whatever it was." Joanne added, "I was always going into the bedroom. We would go in there, and she would lay down the law about whatever it was that I had done, and I was always doing something. Once we went into that bedroom and shut that door, nobody ever heard anything more about it. Grandma never mentioned it again."

Even early on, the grandchildren were aware that in addition to John's being their grandpa, there was something great and special about him. George remembered, "The study that I showed you at Sigsbee Avenue, from the outside—somehow from very early toddlerhood I was taught that was a special room and wasn't a place for me to play, but it was a place where important things called ideas and writing and thinking took place."

When Peggy was asked if she ever felt she had lived under a spotlight, she recalled, "The only time was when there was a big ski meet in Salt Lake, but the big events were going to be on Sunday, and I wanted to go. Mother said, 'Oh, Peggy, you cannot do that to your grandfather. You know what people will say.' And I said, 'Well, lots of people won't even know.' And she said 'Oh, they will know.' And so I went to Grandpa, and I said, 'Oh, Grandpa, please, please, Grandpa, please! If you just knew.' My little sixteen-year-old heart was just broken at the thought of missing; everybody was going to go. I said, 'Oh please, please, Grandpa, oh, please say I can go. Life as I know it will be over if I cannot go up there on a Sunday.' And I thought surely he would understand, and I'm sure he did. And he said, 'Oh, oh, honey. I wish I could make that decision for you, and I can't. You are the only one that can make that decision, and I want you to know that whatever decision you make, I know that will be right for you, and I will love you and support you. But I can't. I wish I could. I wish I could make it for you, and I can't. But you do what seems best to you, and we'll be fine with it.' I couldn't go. How do you go after that?"

Peggy shared another perspective: "I got to the Y, and a lot of people—students, when they found out who Grandpa was—expected me to know more than I did, and I was embarrassed that I didn't know more than I did."

When asked about any intimidation family members might have felt because of their famous father, George said, "Let me just mention about her [Eudora], in terms of the adoration she felt for her father. I don't think, when he was in town, that a day went by that there wasn't at least a brief phone call. And cards on holidays—not just to her and my father but to us too, for our special days. He was a wonderful dad, and that was clear to me. And my father used to say to me sometimes—we talked about intimidation about his Ph.D. and his greatness and so forth—my father said the hardest thing about following John A. Widtsoe was his ability to love, appreciate, celebrate, and be emotionally present. He didn't use those words, but he was saying he was a hard act to follow."

Among all the memories were great teaching moments. Peggy recalled, "One time in high school, my girlfriends asked, 'Did you ever play with the Ouija board?' We did a couple of times. We'd say, 'Oh, Ouija, Ouija, will so-and-so ask me to the dance, or does so-and-so like me, oh, Ouija?' We thought it was fun, and Grandpa found out, and he called me in and said, 'Oh, honey, please, I have to tell you that is going to be one of Satan's tools. He does not have a body. Satan and his legions will do anything to get hold of a body. It's their only way, because they are forbidden to have one. Please, please, you just do not know the risk you are taking. If you do anything that has anything to do with Lucifer or Satan, you will be opening yourself up to his influence. Please have a healthy respect for Lucifer. He is the son of the morning, and he's intelligent, and please do not underestimate him.'"

Peggy described another memorable lesson: "We were going to go down to California—Grandma and Grandpa, Mother and Joanne, and I were going to go down and see my brother John because he would be shipped overseas. It might be the last time we would see him, so we were going down to spend Christmas with him. We had our gifts and the suitcases. We always had a family prayer before we traveled anywhere. We would kneel down and have a family prayer. Then, we were all out in the car. Grandpa went in the house for one last final check. He was in there for the longest time, and Grandma was saying, 'Oh, I hope Daddy comes soon. We will miss our train.' Grandpa came out, and he said, 'We can't go.' I looked at him, and he said, 'I don't know why, but we can't go.' I was just looking at Mother and Grandmother and thinking *'Do something! We can't let this stand; I mean, we are on our way there!'* What I remember so clearly is Mother and Grandma saying, 'All right, then, let's stay home and have Christmas here.' Grandpa just had this strong prompting that we weren't to go. They didn't argue; they didn't question it. Grandma took off her hat, and we went in. I was thinking, 'Wait, wait! Say something to him! We have got to go!' We sat around and laughed and played Flinch. Two or three days later, we learned why we weren't supposed to be on that train. There was some big trellis over a ravine, and the trellis was broken, and the train went down, and many, many people were killed. That was the train we would have been on."

Each of the grandchildren had special memories of the love, affection, and intimacy John and Leah shared. Joanne recalled, "The living room had a fireplace at one end. They got a love seat just big enough for two. I remember they put it in front of the fireplace. We'd come up, and their kitchen door, you could open it a little. And we'd look in there, and the two of them would be there talking, the fireplace going, and music playing from somewhere—the two of them just sitting there. Oh, I always knew they loved each other."

George remembered the romantic love: "I am keenly aware of the friendship and the respect and affection, really, truly the deep romance that existed between my grandparents. I do have visible memories of sitting on the floor, leaning into their couch, and watching them hold hands while the fire was burning and they were talking." Getting more specific he said, "She often referred to him, in addition to her colleague and her husband, as her lover. And that was said in the best sense of that word. It reminded me to a degree of the comment that's in the *Richard L. Evans Quote Book*: 'The greatest gift that a man can give his children is the knowledge that he loves their mother.' I think throughout all the cousins and all the generations, that you would sense that.

There was deep friendship, deep affection, deep romance, deep respect. What a marvelous example that is for any marriage, including our own."

George told of Leah's longing to have another child after having lost four babies. It is a mother's special pleading, like that of Hannah of old: "Following the death of child number six, when she was the president's wife at Utah State, she consecrated some time to work in the temple and became a set-apart temple worker in the Logan Temple. In due course she became pregnant and therefore always felt that my mother was her 'temple child.' As the temple child, my mother had been 'forced' to give Marsel a kiss in the coffin. And that had really frightened her—not that she didn't love him, but she had a sense of not wanting to deal with death. She didn't want to see an angel, didn't want to see a spirit. Many years later, with that as a background, that she was not someone who sought those kinds of experiences, she and Father were permitted to be at the first dedication service of the renovated Logan Temple. And that had been the place—the temple child story. She said that during the very sacred Hosanna Shout, she quietly and calmly noted a shaft of light coming through a window in the celestial room where they were. She looked over and saw both of her parents, not as elderly, but as her parents, younger people, yet with an eternal sense about them, smiling at her and holding hands. She said they didn't say a thing, but she felt the love and message of approval. And she said, 'It was not frightening, it was not scary, it was incredibly peaceful.'"

NOTES

CHAPTER 1

1. Widtsoe, *Gospel Net,* 17.
2. "Vikings," *World Book 1998 Multimedia Encyclopedia,* Deluxe Edition, CD-ROM.
3. *Encyclopaedia Britannica,* 17:582.
4. *Encyclopaedia Britannica,* 17:582.
5. *Encyclopaedia Britannica,* 17:583.
6. *Encyclopaedia Britannica,* 17:582.
7. Widtsoe, *Gospel Net,* 17.
8. Widtsoe, *Gospel Net,* 37.
9. Widtsoe, *Gospel Net,* 41.
10. Widtsoe, *Gospel Net,* 42.

CHAPTER 2

1. Widtsoe, *Gospel Net,* 49–50.
2. Widtsoe, *Gospel Net,* 53–54.
3. Widtsoe, *Sunlit Land,* 2.
4. Widtsoe, *Sunlit Land,* 1.
5. Widtsoe, *Gospel Net,* 57.
6. Widtsoe, *Sunlit Land,* 2.
7. Widtsoe, *Gospel Net,* 59.
8. Widtsoe, *Gospel Net,* 58.
9. Widtsoe, *Sunlit Land,* 3.

CHAPTER 3

1. Widtsoe, *Sunlit Land,* 4.
2. Widtsoe, *Sunlit Land,* 3.
3. Widtsoe, *Gospel Net,* 62.

4. Widtsoe, *Gospel Net,* 65.
5. "Trondheim at that time, was notorious as the headquarters of Mormon persecution. The authorities had gone to the extreme. They arrested and severely punished some of our sisters because they left the Norwegian church, accepted Mormonism, and were baptized into this new church. Among these sisters were Marit Greslie and Mrs. Olsen, two sisters who later came to Logan and were married to respectable men, and Lena Christensen who later came to Salt Lake City. These sisters were imprisoned and sentenced to five days' imprisonment with a diet of bread and water. I was also called to the court house at the trial and had to answer many questions put to me by the chief of police. Several of the questions were of such a nature that I did not feel under any obligation to answer them, which did not bring the chief into the best of humor. As a result, the police chief promised me that he should not forget me. He was very bitter in his feelings

towards the Saints." (Anthon L. Skanchy, "A Brief Autobiographical Sketch of the Missionary Labors of a Valiant Soldier for Christ, Part II," trans. and ed. John A. Widtsoe [1915], 12.)

6. Widtsoe, *Gospel Net*, 67.
7. Widtsoe, *Gospel Net*, 68–69.
8. Widtsoe, *Gospel Net*, 68.
9. Widtsoe, *Sunlit Land*, 6.
10. Widtsoe, *Gospel Net*, 70–71.
11. Widtsoe, *Gospel Net*, 72.

CHAPTER 4

1. Widtsoe, *Sunlit Land*, 7.
2. Widtsoe, *Sunlit Land*, 8.
3. Widtsoe, *Gospel Net*, 80.
4. Ben Hite, "How I Began Life," *Deseret News*, 29 January 1922.
5. Widtsoe, *Gospel Net*, 81.
6. John A. Widtsoe, "The Lost Goldpiece," *Children's Friend*, September 1947, 369.
7. Widtsoe, *Gospel Net*, 82.
8. Widtsoe, *Sunlit Land*, 13–14.
9. Widtsoe, *Gospel Net*, 84.

CHAPTER 5

1. Widtsoe, *Sunlit Land*, 13.
2. Widtsoe, *Sunlit Land*, 14.
3. Widtsoe, *Sunlit Land*, 15.
4. Peterson, *History of Cache County*, 124–25.
5. Widtsoe, *Sunlit Land*, 11–12.
6. Widtsoe, *Sunlit Land*, 18.
7. Widtsoe, *Gospel Net*, 87.
8. Widtsoe, *Sunlit Land*, 10.
9. Widtsoe, *Gospel Net*, 89.
10. Widtsoe, *Gospel Net*, 87.
11. Olsen, *Logan Temple*, 11–12.
12. Olsen, *Logan Temple*, 12.
13. Olsen, *Logan Temple*, 23.
14. Widtsoe, *Gospel Net*, 87–88.
15. Widtsoe, *Gospel Net*, 153–54.
16. Widtsoe, *Gospel Net*, 154.
17. Widtsoe, *Gospel Net*, 88.
18. Olsen, *Logan Temple*, 137–39.
19. Olsen, *Logan Temple*, 146–52.
20. Olsen, *Logan Temple*, vii.

CHAPTER 6

1. Widtsoe, *Sunlit Land*, 8.
2. Ben Hite, "How I Began Life," *Deseret News*, 29 January 1922.
3. Widtsoe, *Evidences and Reconciliations*, 3:204–6.
4. Widtsoe, *Sunlit Land*, 19.
5. Widtsoe, *Sunlit Land*, 20.
6. Widtsoe, *Sunlit Land*, 20.
7. "A Blessing given by Patriarch Ola Nilson Liljenquist on the head of John Andreas Widtsoe, Logan City, November 30 1888," John A. Widtsoe Collection, LDS Church Archives.
8. "A Blessing given by William J. Smith, Patriarch upon the head of John Andreas Widtsoe son of John Widtsoe and Anna Gaarden, Logan, 21 May 1889," John A. Widtsoe Collection, LDS Church Archives.
9. Widtsoe, *Gospel Net*, 94.
10. Widtsoe, *Sunlit Land*, 19.
11. In the Brigham Young College Deed of Trust, cited in Peterson, *History of Cache County*, 203–4.
12. Ironically, John A. Widtsoe, one of its highest acclaimed graduates, was the Church commissioner of education who had to announce and implement the Church Educational System's board of trustees decision to close BYC.
13. Widtsoe, *Sunlit Land*, 21.
14. Widtsoe, *Sunlit Land*, 21.
15. Widtsoe, *Sunlit Land*, 24–25.
16. Widtsoe, *Sunlit Land*, 22.
17. Widtsoe, *Sunlit Land*, 23–24.
18. Widtsoe, *Sunlit Land*, 17–18.
19. Ward, *A Life Divided*, 10.
20. *Young Woman's Journal*, May 1892, 340.
21. Ward, *A Life Divided*, 24.
22. Ward, *A Life Divided*, 29.
23. Widtsoe, *Sunlit Land*, 26.
24. Widtsoe, *Sunlit Land*, 26.
25. Widtsoe, *Gospel Net*, 95.
26. Widtsoe, *Sunlit Land*, 27.

CHAPTER 7

1. Widtsoe, *Sunlit Land,* 28.
2. Eliot, *Harvard Memories,* 5. Spelling and punctuation standardized.
3. Eliot, *Harvard Memories,* 11.
4. "When Darwin's 'Origin of Species' began to rock the western world in 1859, his friends Asa Gray and Jeffries Wyman, who were already evolutionists, became (with some reservations) converts to natural selection, but Louis Agassiz continued to assert the permanence of type inculcated by his master Cuvier. Agassiz promptly became a hero to the clergy, and until his death in 1873 he remained the rallying point of the opposition. Josiah Parsons Cook and 'Fanny' Bowen were also anti-Darwinians. It is said to have been a combination of clerical and classical influence that prevented John Fiske, the brilliant young convert to Darwinism who graduated in 1863, from obtaining a Harvard tutorship. Young Nathaniel S. Shaler, however, was appointed University Lecturer in 1864, although satisfied by geological evidence of the essential truth of Darwin's theories; the fear that 'Darwinism' would contaminate undergraduate morals was responsible for this discrimination." (Morison, *Three Centuries of Harvard,* 308.) "The Lawrence Scientific School was full of sparkle, with Agassiz denouncing and Gray defending Darwinism, and Jeffries Wyman giving a course of lectures on Comparative Anatomy and Embryology with the facts so cunningly arranged that the audience supplied the 'missing links.'" (Ibid., 306.) "From these brief summaries, it is clear that John A. Widtsoe was surrounded by many of the best minds on both sides of the debate over evolution. His success in his many science classes attests to his weighing as heavily as any member of the church all of the issues it presents to religion." (Ibid., 306–8.)
5. Bailyn et al., *Glimpses of the Harvard Past,* 77. Bailyn et al. gave evidence for the problems increasing numbers brought to the college: "Here are the actual statistics. The teachers of professorial grade in Harvard College grew from 45 in 1868–1869, the year before Eliot came in, to 90 in 1888–1889, and then to 194 in 1908–1909, when Eliot went out; and for comparative purposes to 469 in 1928–1929, when Lowell's presidency was waning in turn. As for undergraduates, there were 570 in 1868–1869, 1215 in 1888–1889, 2277 in 1908–1909, and 3486 in 1928–1929."
6. Widtsoe, *Sunlit Land,* 34.
7. Morison, *Three Centuries of Harvard,* 343.
8. Bailyn et al., *Glimpses of the Harvard Past,* 77.
9. Morison, *Three Centuries of Harvard,* 397.
10. Widtsoe, *Sunlit Land,* 28. John recorded in his journal that the trip cost $120.
11. Morison, *Three Centuries of Harvard,* 69.
12. Bailyn et al., *Glimpses of the Harvard Past,* 78.
13. Widtsoe, *Sunlit Land,* 30.
14. "Widtsoe Upholds Standards Maintained by Utah Schools," *Salt Lake Tribune,* 26 November 1921.
15. Widtsoe, *Sunlit Land,* 31.
16. Widtsoe to Heber J. Grant, 20 October 1937, John A. Widtsoe Collection, LDS Church Archives.
17. Widtsoe, *Sunlit Land,* 31–32.
18. Widtsoe, *Sunlit Land,* 32.
19. Widtsoe, *Sunlit Land,* 36.
20. Widtsoe, *Sunlit Land,* 250–51.
21. Widtsoe, *Sunlit Land,* 251.
22. Widtsoe, *Sunlit Land,* 36–37.
23. Widtsoe, *Sunlit Land,* 37.
24. Widtsoe, *Sunlit Land,* 34.

25. Widtsoe, *Sunlit Land,* 35.
26. Widtsoe, *Sunlit Land,* 37.
27. Widtsoe to Leah Eudora Dunford, 25 December 1893, Leah Widtsoe Collection, LDS Church Archives.
28. Tanner, *A Mormon Mother,* 136.
29. Tanner, *A Mormon Mother,* 140.
30. Widtsoe, *Sunlit Land,* 37–38.
31. Susa Young Gates to Widtsoe, 10 December 1892, Leah Widtsoe Collection, LDS Church Archives.
32. Widtsoe, *Sunlit Land,* 37–38.
33. Widtsoe, *Sunlit Land,* 229.
34. Widtsoe to Willard Croxall, 3 July 1893, John A. Widtsoe Collection, LDS Church Archives.
35. Widtsoe, *Sunlit Land,* 229–30.
36. Oral History Interview with Leah Eudora Widtsoe, 11 February 1965, 28–29, Leah D. Widtsoe Papers, BYU Special Collections.
37. Widtsoe, *Sunlit Land,* 230.
38. Widtsoe, *Sunlit Land,* 230.
39. Widtsoe, *Sunlit Land,* 231.
40. Widtsoe, *Sunlit Land,* 231–32.
41. Widtsoe, *Sunlit Land,* 232.
42. Widtsoe, *Sunlit Land,* 232.
43. Widtsoe to Leah Eudora Dunford, 25 December 1893, Leah Widtsoe Collection, LDS Church Archives.
44. Widtsoe to Leah Eudora Dunford, 25 December 1893, Leah Widtsoe Collection, LDS Church Archives.
45. Widtsoe to Leah Eudora Dunford, 16 September 1893, Leah Widtsoe Collection, LDS Church Archives.
46. "Lunatics about Leah," Widtsoe Papers, 14–15, Utah State Historical Society. Below it he wrote, "*The manuscript doth here affirm that a thought of the woman, Leah Dunford, caused the writing of the above."
47. Widtsoe, *Sunlit Land,* 32.
48. Widtsoe, *Sunlit Land,* 39–40.
49. Widtsoe, *Sunlit Land,* 40.
50. Susa Young Gates, "A Union of Art and Science," an announcement for the *Young Woman's Journal,* 1898, Widtsoe Papers, Utah State Historical Society.
51. "Elder Widtsoe Is New Hall of Fame Inductee," *Church News,* 12 January 1986, 6.
52. Widtsoe, *Sunlit Land,* 39.
53. *Record of the Class of 1894,* 286.
54. *Record of the Class of 1894,* 592–96.
55. Widtsoe, *Sunlit Land,* 40.

CHAPTER 8
1. Ronald W. Walker, "Crisis in Zion: Heber J. Grant and the Panic of 1893," *Sunstone,* May 1985, 70–78.
2. James E. Talmage to Widtsoe, 8 February 1894, LDS Church Archives.
3. James E. Talmage to Widtsoe, 8 February 1894, LDS Church Archives.
4. Benjamin Cluff, Jr., to Widtsoe, 29 March 1894, LDS Church Archives.
5. J. H. Paul to Widtsoe, 12 March 1894, LDS Church Archives.
6. The titles *Agricultural College of Utah* (ACU) and *Utah Agricultural College* (UAC) are used interchangeably through the literature and histories of the college. Most official is the title *Agricultural College of Utah* (ACU). Frequently *Utah Agricultural College* (UAC) is used in the sources cited, and therefore it appears that way in this manuscript.
7. J. H. Paul to Widtsoe, 19 June 1894, LDS Church Archives.
8. Lindsey, *Pullman Strike,* 1.
9. Widtsoe to J. H. Paul, 11 July 1894, LDS Church Archives.
10. *Minutes of the Board of Trustees of the Agricultural College of Utah,* Book 1, 228.
11. Widtsoe, *Gospel Net,* 96.
12. Widtsoe, *Sunlit Land,* 41.
13. "A Bright Young Man," *Logan Journal,* 1 September 1894, 8.
14. Widtsoe, *Gospel Net,* 98.
15. Widtsoe, *Sunlit Land,* 50–51.
16. Widtsoe, *Sunlit Land,* 52.

17. Journal History of the Church, 11 April 1898.
18. Ricks, *Utah State Agricultural College,* 24–26.
19. Widtsoe, *Sunlit Land,* 46–47.
20. Widtsoe, *Sunlit Land,* 47.
21. Simmonds, *Pictures Past,* 12.
22. "Agricultural Experiment Station," *Logan Republican,* 1 January 1904, 6.
23. Widtsoe, *Sunlit Land,* 42–43.
24. The Utah Agricultural College Experiment Station, *Bulletin No. 35,* inside cover.
25. The Utah Agricultural College Experiment Station, *Fifth Annual Report,* 26.
26. Widtsoe, *Sunlit Land,* 47–48.
27. Widtsoe to George H. Brimhall, 20 September 1904, Brimhall Presidential Papers, BYU Special Collections.
28. Widtsoe to Lyman H. Rich, undated, Widtsoe Family Collection, Utah State Historical Society.
29. Widtsoe, *Sunlit Land,* 50.
30. Widtsoe, *Sunlit Land,* 50.
31. Widtsoe, *Sunlit Land,* 50.
32. "Lucerne," *Utah Church and Farm,* 28 July 1894, 30.
33. Widtsoe, *Sunlit Land,* 48.
34. The Agricultural College of Utah Experiment Station, *Bulletin No. 48* and *Bulletin No. 58.*
35. The Agricultural College of Utah Experiment Station, *Bulletin No. 48,* 68–69.
36. Board of Trustees Minutes, 4 February 1900, Utah State Agricultural College, 1:541–42.
37. Franklin S. Harris, "Apostle John Andreas Widtsoe," *Young Woman's Journal,* June 1921, 321.
38. Widtsoe, *Sunlit Land,* 48.
39. Richard S. Van Wagoner, "The Lehi Sugar Factory—100 Years in Retrospect," *Utah Historical Quarterly,* 59:195.
40. Ellsworth, *Utah's Heritage,* 383.
41. The Utah Agricultural College Experiment Station, *Eighth Annual Report,* 1 July 1896–30 June 1897, 12–13.
42. Ellsworth, *Utah's Heritage,* 374.
43. The Utah Agricultural College Experiment Station, *Seventh Annual Report,* 1 July 1895–30 June 1896, 19.
44. Widtsoe, *Sunlit Land,* 49.
45. Widtsoe, *Sunlit Land,* 46.

CHAPTER 9

1. Widtsoe, *Sunlit Land,* 232.
2. John A. Widtsoe, *Lunatics About Leah,* the title penned on a handwritten volume introduced as "A reminiscence of six weeks in Cambridge, Mass, during the summer of 1893, for Leah Dunford, from Her Friend." An introductory page written as if it were found a hundred years later, states: "Lunar Inspirations and Other Lunatics. Found in the ruins of the Harvard College Library, Recently Uncovered and Edited by Professor A. B. C. Def, G. H. As a psychological study. . . ." The preface states, "The manuscripts found here seemed to show the varying mental states of the author during a period that gave to him the society of a woman who evidently appealed strongly to all his senses." Widtsoe Family Collection, Utah State Historical Society.
3. Susa Young Gates to Widtsoe, 7 January 1928, Widtsoe Family Collection, Utah State Historical Society.
4. Susa Young Gates, *The Life Story of Brigham Young* (London: Jarrolds Publishers, 1930).
5. Oral History Interview with Leah Eudora Widtsoe, 11 February 1965, Leah D. Widtsoe Papers, BYU Special Collections.
6. Leah D. Widtsoe to Susa Young Gates, 26 October 1929, Widtsoe Family Collection, Utah State Historical Society.

7. Mary Jane Woodger, "Leah Widtsoe: Pioneer in Healthy Lifestyle Family Education," *Journal of Family and Consumer Sciences*, 92:50–54.

8. Oral History Interview with Leah Eudora Widtsoe, 11 February 1965, 29, Leah D. Widtsoe Papers, BYU Special Collections.

9. Leah D. Widtsoe, "Home Economics at B.Y.U.," 2, Leah D. Widtsoe Papers, BYU Special Collections.

10. Virginia F. Cutler, "Leah Dunford Widtsoe (1874–1965)" a tribute written to accompany a special program, perhaps a commencement, in which Leah's work and memorabilia were exhibited and awards were given in her name. Also, "Sketch of Leah Eudora Dunford Widtsoe," unknown author, Leah D. Widtsoe Papers, BYU Special Collections.

11. "Home Economics at B.Y.U.," 2.

12. "Home Economics at B.Y.U.," 2.

13. "Home Economics at B.Y.U.," 3.

14. "Home Economics at B.Y.U.," 4.

15. "Home Economics at B.Y.U.," 4.

16. "Home Economics at B.Y.U.," 5.

17. An author on Susa's life noted her closeness to Leah in these concerns: "Of the five children who survived to adulthood, Susa's eldest daughter Leah Dunford Widtsoe (1874) was her mother's literary collaborator, confidante, and close friend. She graduated as valedictorian of her class from the University of Utah in 1896, receiving the Normal Diploma. She continued her study in home economics at the Pratt Institute in Brooklyn, New York, the foremost school in the United States at this time for home economics. She was the first western graduate of the school." Carolyn D. Person, "Susa Young Gates," in *Mormon Sisters*, 198–223.

18. "Home Economics at B.Y.U.," 6.

19. Transcript of a microfilm copy of the catalog for 1897–98, Leah D.

Widtsoe Papers, BYU Special Collections.

20. "Home Economics at B.Y.U.," 8.

21. Widtsoe, *Sunlit Land*, 234.

22. Leah explained, "You see, that was what the Home Economics did, united Domestic Science and Domestic Arts. At first they were separate, lady's work and cooking. But it was dubbed Domestic Science later. That term had just been coming into use, you see and Home Economics was entirely new out west here. It was ridiculed by most everybody, and it was Home Economics in the school where I studied. Of course, it should be that when I started a department of my own." Oral History Interview with Leah Eudora Widtsoe, 11 February 1965, 25, Leah D. Widtsoe Papers, BYU Special Collections.

23. "Home Economics at B.Y.U.," 8.

CHAPTER 10

1. Minutes of the Board of Trustees of the Agricultural College of Utah, 29 April 1898, 474–75.

2. *Record of the Class of 1894*, 593.

3. Widtsoe, *Sunlit Land*, 53.

4. Widtsoe, *Sunlit Land*, 232.

5. Widtsoe, *Sunlit Land*, 232–33.

6. Oral History Interview with Leah Eudora Widtsoe, 11 February 1965, 23–24, Leah D. Widtsoe Papers, BYU Special Collections.

7. Widtsoe, *Sunlit Land*, 233–34.

8. Susa Young Gates, "A Union of Art and Science" (typed copy), Widtsoe Collection, Utah State Historical Society.

9. Oral History Interview with Leah Eudora Widtsoe, 11 February 1965, 26, Leah D. Widtsoe Papers, BYU Special Collections.

10. Widtsoe, *Sunlit Land*, 53.

11. Widtsoe, *Sunlit Land*, 238.

12. Oral History Interview with Leah Eudora Widtsoe, 11 February 1965,

Leah D. Widtsoe Papers, BYU Special Collections.

13. Widtsoe, *Sunlit Land,* 62–63.
14. Brubacher and Rudy, *Higher Education in Transition,* 175.
15. Brubacher and Rudy, *Higher Education,* 176.
16. Brubacher and Rudy, *Higher Education,* 177.
17. Brubacher and Rudy, *Higher Education,* 179.
18. Anke Dannenberg, MCSI, "Göttingen online!—history," 10/23/99, www.goettingen.de/eng/geschich/index.htm, 3.
19. Widtsoe, *Sunlit Land,* 64.
20. Widtsoe, *Sunlit Land,* 55–56.
21. Widtsoe, *Sunlit Land,* 56.
22. Widtsoe to M. F. Pack, 28 September 1907, Widtsoe Presidential Papers, USU Special Collections.
23. Widtsoe to Grandma Young, 3 April 1899, John A. Widtsoe Collection, Utah State Historical Society.
24. John A. Widtsoe, a handwritten manuscript biography of Anna's first three years, John A. Widtsoe Collection, Utah State Historical Society, 6.
25. John A. Widtsoe, a handwritten manuscript biography of Anna's first three years, John A. Widtsoe Collection, Utah State Historical Society, 8–9.
26. Widtsoe, *Sunlit Land,* 57.
27. Widtsoe, *Sunlit Land,* 66.
28. Widtsoe, *Sunlit Land,* 66.
29. Widtsoe, *Sunlit Land,* 67.
30. Widtsoe, *Sunlit Land,* 68.
31. Widtsoe, *Sunlit Land,* 68–69.
32. Widtsoe, *Sunlit Land,* 60.
33. Widtsoe, *Sunlit Land,* 58.
34. Widtsoe, *Sunlit Land,* 70.
35. Widtsoe, *Sunlit Land,* 70. The minutes of the board of trustees, 4 February 1900, list Widtsoe's as the last of eight applications read to the board.
36. Minutes of the Board of Trustees of the Agricultural College of Utah, 11 June 1900, 11–13.
37. Widtsoe, *Sunlit Land,* 71.

CHAPTER *11*

1. Widtsoe to Presiding Bishop W. B. Preston, undated, Widtsoe Family Collection, Utah State Historical Society.
2. Widtsoe, *Sunlit Land,* 81.
3. The Utah Agricultural College Experiment Station, *Twelfth Annual Report,* 1 July 1900–30 June 1901, vii.
4. Widtsoe, *Sunlit Land,* 73.
5. Widtsoe to L. M. Winsor, 10 June 1910, Widtsoe Presidential Papers, USU Special Collections.
6. From a transcript of an oral interview with Richard Welling Roskelley, 14 November 1979, in Special Collections at USU, ref. file MS509. "When he was appointed director of the experiment station here in the spring of 1900, he said he didn't know very much about what the problems of agriculture were. He got in a buggy and drove from Logan to Kanab, over to St. George and back up this way. It took him about 4 months to do it, and he did not spend one night in a hotel, or eat one meal in a restaurant. Rather, he lived right with the farmers and learned from farmers what their problems were. And he said, 'Brother Roskelley, when I got back I knew what our experiment station should be working on.'" Widtsoe described going to the field to find the works that needed Station research again when he was appointed college president. "When he was appointed president of the university, in 1907 to 1916 he went out and did the same thing as president of the university. Again he stayed with people and asked them what were the kinds of things they thought the

university should be doing to serve them in their rural communities, on their farms, in their families and everywhere else. He told me again that 'When I got back I knew what the job of the university was.' This put him in a position to tell some of the teachers what they ought to be doing and he told some of them if they really wanted to find out anything they should go out and live with the people and learn their problems. That way they could really get first hand information about how to improve agriculture and other conditions."

7. M.C. Merrill, O.W. Israelsen and Byron Alder; Circular #39, Utah Agricultural Experiment Station, Logan, Utah, December 1918, 4.

8. Widtsoe, *Sunlit Land*, 79.

9. John A. Widtsoe, "A Word to Our Boys about 'Farming,'" *Deseret Farmer*, 30 November 1905, 9.

10. Widtsoe, "A Word to Our Boys about 'Farming,'" 9.

11. "Of Interest to the Farmers Only," *Logan Republican*, 13 March 1903, 1.

12. "Important Experiments," *Logan Republican*, 29 June 1904, 1. The article reported that Utahns interested in the progress of agriculture could not have a more instructive or interesting day than one with a visit to the experimental farm of the ACU.

13. John A. Widtsoe, "The Right Way to Irrigate," *Bulletin No. 86*, The Agricultural College of Utah, Logan, Utah, 1903, 57.

14. Israelsen and Hansen, *Irrigation Principles and Practices*, 236–37.

15. Widtsoe, *Dry Farming*, 8–10.

16. Utah Agricultural College Experiment Station, *Bulletin No. 39*, 9, in BYU's Harold B. Lee Library under *Utah Experiment Station Bulletins Nos. 1–50*.

17. See The Agricultural College of Utah Experiment Station, *Bulletin No. 80*, "Irrigation Is Harmful Unless It Is Done in the Proper Way," *Logan Republican*, 30 April 1904, 1; Experiment Station of the Agricultural College of Utah, *Circular No. 2* (Provo, Utah: Skelton Publishing).

18. "Of Interest to the Farmers Only," *Logan Republican*, 13 March 1903, 1.

19. John A. Widtsoe and Lewis A. Merrill, "Arid Farming or Dry Farming," *Bulletin No. 75*, Experiment Station of the Agricultural College of Utah, Logan, Utah, January 1902, 115.

20. "The Dry Farms," *Logan Republican*, 15 July 1903, 6.

21. Widtsoe, *Sunlit Land*, 80.

22. John T. Burns to Widtsoe, 12 September 1911, Widtsoe Presidential Papers, USU Special Collections; F. H. Perry to Widtsoe, 15 October 1907, Widtsoe Presidential Papers, USU Special Collections.

23. Lewis A. Merrill, "The Drouth of 1910," *Deseret Farmer*, 13 August 1910, 1917.

24. Widtsoe, *Dry Farming: A System of Agriculture for Countries Under a Low Rainfall* (New York: Macmillan, 1911); *The Principles of Irrigation Practice* (New York: Macmillan, 1914).

25. His book on dry farming was translated into Spanish and was used in Spain and its colonies, and into French, and France used it in its African colonies. For evidence of Hungarian and Australian involvement, along with South African, see Widtsoe to John T. Burns, 7 September 1911, Widtsoe Presidential Papers; and Widtsoe to Charles Cristadoro, 12 June 1911, Widtsoe Presidential Papers, USU Special Collections. His involvement in the United States has already been noted. He was extensively involved with both individuals and the Dry-farm Congress in Canada. He had people

from at least the countries of Mexico and Brazil contact him for help in dry farming, as can be seen in letters: Widtsoe to Eugenio Dahne, 10 December 1910, Widtsoe Presidential Papers; and Warren Longhurst to Widtsoe, 6 November 1908, Widtsoe Presidential Papers, USU Special Collections, along with many other letters.

26. J. W. Paxman to Widtsoe, 11 July 1912, Widtsoe Presidential Papers, USU Special Collections.
27. Charles S. Peterson, "Cholera, Blight, and Sparrows: a Look at Utah's First Agricultural Agents," *Utah Historical Quarterly*, vol. 57, no. 2 (1989): 139.
28. Ellsworth, *Utah's Heritage*, 375–76.
29. Utah State Department of Agriculture, *Utah Agricultural Statistics 1984*, 9–11.
30. "A. C. of U. Notes," *Logan Republican*, 22 October 1904, 1; "A. C. at World's Fair," *Logan Republican*, 30 July 1904, 1.
31. The Agricultural College of Utah Experiment Station, *Thirteenth Annual Report*, x, 1 July 1901–30 June 1902.
32. Widtsoe, *Sunlit Land*, 78.
33. "Important Experiments," *Logan Republican*, 29 June 1904, 1.
34. The Utah Agricultural College Experiment Station, *Seventh Annual Report*, 1 July 1895–30 June 1896, 19–20.
35. Widtsoe, *Sunlit Land*, 78.
36. "Farmers Institutes," *Logan Republican*, 11 November 1903, 1. The appreciation many farmers felt for the help of the college and the Experiment Station is expressed in a letter written to the *Deseret Farmer:* "Professors J. A. Widtsoe and Robert S. Northrop of the Agricultural College made us a very pleasant call yesterday as they were passing through our city on their way home from the Dixie capital,

where they had been in the interests of the experiment farm that is located in that vicinity. They were much pleased with the move that our people are making in the interests of arid farming, and assured us that it would be a paying proposition. They expressed a willingness to do everything in their power to help us to make the move a success, and said that when we get the farm ready for seeding they will help us with their advice in the selection of seed and also let us know where it can be obtained." *Deseret Farmer*, 13 April 1905, 4.

37. Widtsoe, *Sunlit Land*, 78.
38. For a few examples see "Agricultural College of Utah," *Deseret Farmer*, 15 September 1904, 4; "Agricultural Education," *Deseret Farmer*, 6 April 1905, 5.
39. Widtsoe, *Sunlit Land*, 79.
40. Charles S. Peterson, "Cholera, Blight, and Sparrows: a Look at Utah's First Agricultural Agents," *Utah Historical Quarterly*, vol. 57, no. 2 (1989): 139–40.
41. "Agricultural Experiment Station," *Logan Republican*, 1 January 1904, 6.
42. Ellsworth, *Utah's Heritage*, 374.
43. "Worth of the A.C. of U.," *Logan Republican*, 4 January 1905, 4.
44. Ellsworth, *Utah's Heritage,* 377.
45. Widtsoe, *The Principles of Irrigation Practice*, 472.
46. Widtsoe to David A. Burgoyne, February 25, 1938, John A. Widtsoe Papers, LDS Church Archives.
47. See chapter 13 for a full discussion of the controversy leading to the dismissal.
48. Widtsoe, *Sunlit Land*, 86–87.
49. Widtsoe, *Sunlit Land*, 86.

CHAPTER *12*

1. Rex E. Lee, "Of Circles, Bells, and the College That We Love," Annual University Conference, Brigham

Young University, 28 August 1989, 16.

2. Wilkinson, *Brigham Young University*, 1:484.

3. Bok, *Beyond the Ivory Tower*, 61.

4. Bok, *Beyond the Ivory Tower*, 62.

5. George H. Brimhall to Widtsoe, 16 September 1904, Brimhall Presidential Papers, BYU Special Collections.

6. George H. Brimhall to Widtsoe, 16 September 1904.

7. Widtsoe to George H. Brimhall, 20 September 1904, Brimhall Presidential Papers, BYU Special Collections.

8. G. Homer Durham transcript of "The Pocket Diary of John A. Widtsoe," 15 July 1905, 32, MSS Sc 1629, BYU Special Collections. Hereafter referred to as Pocket Diary.

9. Allen, *The History of Psychology at Brigham Young University*, 48.

10. Wilkinson, *Brigham Young University*, 1:461.

11. Horrocks, *Agronomy and Horticulture at BYU*, 9.

12. Horrocks, *Agronomy and Horticulture at BYU*, 16–17.

13. *Deseret Farmer*, 27 July 1905, 5.

14. Franklin S. Harris to Leah Widtsoe, 8 June 1933, Harris Presidential Papers, BYU Special Collections.

15. Widtsoe, *Sunlit Land*, 91.

16. Widtsoe, *Sunlit Land*, 95.

17. Franklin S. Harris, "Apostle John Andreas Widtsoe," *Young Woman's Journal*, June 1921, 321.

18. George H. Brimhall to John J. Starley, 2 November 1906, Brimhall Presidential Papers, BYU Special Collections.

19. Henry Peterson to George H. Brimhall, 3 December 1906, Brimhall Presidential Papers, BYU Special Collections.

20. E. E. Balcomb to George H. Brimhall, 11 May 1907, Brimhall Presidential Papers, BYU Special Collections.

21. George H. Brimhall to J. M. Tanner, 8 December 1905, Brimhall Presidential Papers, BYU Special Collections. There is some confusion about whom this letter is really to. It is addressed to "Dear Brother" but says, "We appeal to you, as General Superintendent of the Church School System." J. M. Tanner was the general superintendent of the Church School System at the time the letter was written. Furthermore, the letter notes that its recipient would have more personal influence with Widtsoe than anyone else. Tanner would easily fit this description. Also, there is record of a reply to this letter that is generally believed to be from Tanner. However, the initials at the top of pages two and three are G. R. F. Just who G. R. F. could be is not known. Despite this, most of the evidence points toward this letter being intended for Tanner.

22. J. M. Tanner to George H. Brimhall, 27 December 1905, Brimhall Presidential Papers, BYU Special Collections.

23. "Remarks by Franklin S. Harris," in *In Memoriam*, 16.

24. Widtsoe, *Sunlit Land*, 90.

25. Clifton Kerr, "My most influential teacher," *Deseret Church News*, 12 July 1980, 2.

26. Franklin S. Harris to Widtsoe, 18 February 1933, Harris Presidential Papers, BYU Special Collections.

27. Widtsoe, *Sunlit Land*, 81.

28. Pocket Diary, 21 February 1906, 44.

29. Pocket Diary, 19 March 1906, 45.

30. George H. Brimhall to Superintendent J. M. Tanner, 22 February 1906, Brimhall Presidential Papers, BYU Special Collections. On 2 March 1906, President Brimhall reported the enrollment at 225, George H. Brimhall to Hinckley, Brimhall

Presidential Papers, BYU Special Collections.

31. First Presidency to George H. Brimhall, 6 January 1906, Brimhall Presidential Papers, BYU Special Collections.

32. William H. Homer, Jr., to George H. Brimhall, 9 May 1906, 19 January 1906; George H. Brimhall to William H. Homer, Jr., 8 January 1906; Brimhall Presidential Papers, BYU Special Collections. *Deseret Farmer,* 18 January 1906, 1.

33. George H. Brimhall to A. A. Hinckley, 6 February 1906; George H. Brimhall to L. A. Merrill, 30 March 1906; L. A. Merrill to George H. Brimhall 3 April 1906; Brimhall Presidential Papers, BYU Special Collections. Also Pocket Diary, 13 February 1906, 43.

34. George H. Brimhall to J. M. Tanner, 20 March 1906, Brimhall Presidential Papers, BYU Special Collections.

35. Pocket Diary, 3 January 1906, 41. 30 January 1907, 63.

36. George S. Taylor to Widtsoe, 1 October 1906, Brimhall Presidential Papers, BYU Special Collections.

37. Widtsoe to George H. Brimhall, 17 August 1907, Brimhall Presidential Papers, BYU Special Collections.

38. *BYU Quarterly,* 1 November 1905, 13.

39. *BYU Quarterly,* 1 November 1905, 13.

40. Pocket Diary, 19 October 1906, 57; 10 January 1907, 62; 15 March 1907, 66.

41. "Oral History Interview with George Richard Hill," 3, UA OH 18, BYU Special Collections.

42. Widtsoe to George H. Brimhall, 15 January 1909, Brimhall Presidential Papers, BYU Special Collections.

43. Horrocks, *Agronomy and Horticulture,* 167.

44. Horrocks, *Agronomy and Horticulture,* 168.

45. Horrocks, *Agronomy and Horticulture,* 47, 71.

46. Ernest L. Wilkinson to Leah D. Widtsoe, 1 December 1952, Wilkinson Presidential Papers, BYU Special Collections.

47. Pocket Diary, 31 January 1907, 63.

48. *BYU Quarterly,* vol. 2, no. 4, 1 February 1907, 14–16.

49. Wilkinson, *Brigham Young University,* 1:463.

50. Pocket Diary, 14–15 December 1906, 60.

51. *BYU Quarterly,* 1 November 1905, 12.

52. George H. Brimhall to unknown person, 22 February 1906, Brimhall Presidential Papers, BYU Special Collections.

53. George H. Brimhall to E. Snow, 25 October 1906, Brimhall Presidential Papers, BYU Special Collections.

54. *BYU Quarterly,* vol. 2, no. 4, 1 February 1906, 6.

55. George H. Brimhall to James W. Paxman, 19 December 1906, Brimhall Presidential Papers, BYU Special Collections.

56. Pocket Diary, 1 February 1907, 63.

57. *BYU Quarterly,* 1 November 1905, 3–9.

58. *Deseret Farmer,* 30 November 1905, 9.

59. *BYU Quarterly,* 1 November 1905, 12.

60. *Deseret Farmer,* 25 August 1906, 4.

61. *Deseret Farmer,* 16 June 1906, 1.

62. George H. Brimhall to Henry Peterson, 30 October 1906, Brimhall Presidential Papers, BYU Special Collections.

63. George H. Brimhall to E. Snow, 25 October 1906, Brimhall Presidential Papers, BYU Special Collections.

64. Widtsoe to George H. Brimhall, 17 August 1907, Brimhall Presidential Papers, BYU Special Collections.

65. Widtsoe, *Sunlit Land,* 73.

66. George Whitehead to Widtsoe, 26 November 1905; A. L. Neff to George H. Brimhall, 4 January

1906; S. L. Swenson to George H. Brimhall, 11 January 1906; Mamie Ollerton to George H. Brimhall, 22 November 1906; Brimhall Presidential Papers, BYU Special Collections.

67. Pocket Diary 24 January 1907, 63, and *Deseret Farmer,* 26 January 1907, 1, 3, 10, 11, 14.

68. Pocket Diary, 12 December 1905, 40; 16 June, 15 November, 31 December 1906, 50, 59, 61 respectively.

69. Pocket Diary, 28–29.

70. Pocket Diary, 8 September 1905, 35. Also George H. Brimhall to J. M. Tanner, 20 March 1906, Brimhall Presidential Papers, BYU Special Collections.

71. George H. Brimhall to J. M. Tanner, 8 December 1905, Brimhall Presidential Papers, BYU Special Collections.

72. George H. Brimhall to J. M. Tanner, 8 December 1905, Brimhall Presidential Papers. See note 22. This was a real concern for Brimhall, who had to release three professors a few years later because he felt they weren't teaching science based on revelation. For information on this, see *Brigham Young University,* 1:419–32.

73. "Introduction" to the John A. Widtsoe Memorial Scholarship Foundation, Wilkinson Presidential Papers, BYU Special Collections.

74. Pocket Diary, 31 December 1906, 61.

75. Pocket Diary, 21 March 1907, 66.

76. Widtsoe to George H. Brimhall, 13 April 1907, Brimhall Presidential Papers. BYU Special Collections.

77. Wilkinson, *Brigham Young University,* 1:463, n. 7.

78. Diary of George H. Brimhall, 14 March 1906, 186, Brimhall Presidential Papers, BYU Special Collections.

79. Pocket Diary, 7 March 1906, 44.

80. Pocket Diary, 29 April 1907, 68.

81. Pocket Diary, 29 April 1907, 68.

82. Pocket Diary, 28 June 1907, 71.

83. Pocket Diary, 29 June 1907, 71.

84. Pocket Diary, 27 August 1906, 54.

85. Pocket Diary, 28 August 1906, 54.

86. Further evidence of Widtsoe's grief can be seen from the next two days in his diary. The day after the funeral he wrote, "Wandering. Wrote Lesson 6 for Young Ladies. Work does not relieve me." He spent time wandering on the next day, too. See Pocket Diary, 27—31 August 1906, 54.

87. Pocket Diary, 25 October 1906, 57.

88. Pocket Diary, 30 May 1907, 69.

89. Widtsoe to George H. Brimhall, 17 August 1907, Brimhall Presidential Papers, BYU Special Collections.

90. Widtsoe to George H. Brimhall, 21 December 1907, Brimhall Presidential Papers, BYU Special Collections.

91. George H. Brimhall to Widtsoe, 19 August 1907, Brimhall Presidential Papers, BYU Special Collections.

92. George H. Brimhall to Widtsoe, 17 December 1907, Brimhall Presidential Papers, BYU Special Collections.

93. George H. Brimhall to Widtsoe, 15 February 1909, Brimhall Presidential Papers, BYU Special Collections.

94. Widtsoe to George H. Brimhall, 15 January 1909, Brimhall Presidential Papers, BYU Special Collections.

95. Amos N. Merrill to George H. Brimhall, 20 February 1909, Brimhall Presidential Papers, BYU Special Collections.

96. George H. Brimhall to Widtsoe, 22 March 1921, Brimhall Presidential Papers, BYU Special Collections.

97. Widtsoe to George H. Brimhall, 17 August 1907, Brimhall Presidential Papers.

98. Pocket Diary, 26 June 1907, 71.

CHAPTER *13*

1. Whitney, *History of Utah,* 4:624–26; Alter, *Utah, the Storied Domain,* 2:285–86; Carter, *Our Pioneer Heritage,* 10:337–39.
2. *Constitution of the State of Utah* (Salt Lake City, 1895), Article X, Section 4.
3. Heber M. Wells, the state's first governor and Cutler's immediate predecessor, was also concerned about duplication. He sought to resolve the problem by bringing the two governing boards together in a special meeting. See Board of Regents Minutes, University of Utah, 24 January 1903.
4. Herschel Bullen, Jr., "The University of Utah–Utah Agricultural College Consolidation Controversy 1904 to 1907 and 1927," 2, manuscript in author's possession.
5. *Senate Journal,* 408.
6. *Senate Journal,* 402.
7. *Senate Journal,* 403–4.
8. *Senate Journal,* 403; see also *House Journal,* Joint Senate and House Bill No. 1, 1905, 647.
9. *Summary of the Majority Report of the College Commission 1906,* Papers of John A. Widtsoe, Special Collections, Utah State University, 10. Also in Herschel Bullen, Jr., "The University of Utah–Utah Agricultural College Consolidation Controversy 1904 to 1907 and 1927," 5, manuscript in author's possession.
10. Herschel Bullen, Jr., "The University of Utah–Utah Agricultural College Consolidation Controversy 1904 to 1907 and 1927," 11–12, manuscript in author's possession.
11. Director William Peterson, as quoted in Ricks, *Utah State Agricultural College,* 59.
12. Ricks, *Utah State Agricultural College,* 62.
13. Ricks, *Utah State Agricultural College,* 63.
14. J. W. Woolf to Widtsoe, 8 January 1910, Papers of John A. Widtsoe, Special Collections, Utah State University.
15. Widtsoe to J. W. Woolf, 20 January 1910. Papers of John A. Widtsoe, Special Collections, Utah State University.
16. Widtsoe to J. W. Woolf, 20 January 1910.
17. In June 1905, Professor Merrill was so opposed to Kerr's policies that he sent a letter of resignation to the board of trustees. Days later, he sent a letter to Kerr seeking to withdraw his resignation. In his appeal, he wrote, "Why am I singled out? Surely you don't mean to infer that I alone am the offender, because John A. Widtsoe is just as deep in this as I am." *Logan Journal,* 17 June 1905, 1.
18. "A Sensible View of the College Situation," *Logan Journal,* 16 May 1905, 1.
19. Minutes of the Board of Trustees, Utah Agricultural College, 2 June 1905, 143.
20. In a letter to George H. Brimhall, president of Brigham Young University, 3 May 1905, Widtsoe wrote what appears to be the acceptance of a job offer made vocally at a prior time. It says, "I am now ready to accept the proposition that you made some days ago. . . . My term of office in the A. C. U. closes Sept. 1st, 1905." Widtsoe to George H. Brimhall, 3 May 1905, Brimhall Presidential Papers, BYU Special Collections.
21. "Row in State Institution," *Salt Lake Tribune,* 3 June 1905, 2.
22. Minutes of the Board of Trustees, Utah Agricultural College, 5 June 1905, 147.
23. Minutes of the Board of Trustees, Utah Agricultural College, 8 July 1905, 153.

24. Minutes of the Board of Trustees, Utah Agricultural College, 8 July 1905, 157.

25. Minutes of the Board of Trustees, Utah Agricultural College, 8 July 1905, 157.

26. Melvin C. Merrill, "Another Agricultural College Graduate Favors Consolidation," *Deseret Farmer*, 29 September 1906, 12. See also *Deseret Farmer*, 22 September 1906, 13–14.

27. "A Difference," *Deseret Farmer*, 25 August 1906, 5.

28. Joseph F. Merrill, "Urges Consolidation," *Deseret Farmer*, 1 September 1906, 3.

29. *Logan Journal*, as quoted in *Deseret Farmer*, 8 September 1906, 4.

30. *Deseret Farmer*, 8 September 1906, 4.

31. *Senate Journal*, Seventh Session of the Legislature of the State of Utah, 1907 (Salt Lake City: Century Printing Company, 1907) 353.

32. Herschel Bullen, Jr., "The University of Utah–Utah Agricultural College Consolidation Controversy 1904 to 1907 and 1927," 17, manuscript in author's possession.

33. Herschel Bullen, Jr., "The University of Utah–Utah Agricultural College Consolidation Controversy 1904 to 1907 and 1927," 22, manuscript in author's possession.

34. *Logan Journal*, 21 March 1907, 1.

35. Minutes of the Board of Trustees, Utah Agricultural College, 28 March 1907, 226.

CHAPTER 14

1. Widtsoe, *Sunlit Land*, 99–100.

2. Widtsoe, *Sunlit Land*, 102–3.

3. "The Record of President John A. Widtsoe Described by a Correspondent," *Deseret Evening News*, 12 February 1916, 4–5.

4. Ricks, *Utah State Agricultural College*, 72.

5. "The Record of President John A. Widtsoe Described by a Correspondent," *Deseret Evening News*, 12 February 1916, 4.

6. "Good for the College—and for Utah," *Intermountain Republican*, 29 March 1907, 4.

7. Minutes of the Board of Trustees of the Agricultural College of Utah, 23 April 1907, 243.

8. Oral interview with Richard Welling Roskelley by the USU Sociology Department, 10–11, USU Special Collections.

9. Biennial Report of the Board of Trustees of the Agricultural College of Utah, 1911–1912, 4, Widtsoe Presidential Papers, USU Special Collections.

10. "President Widtsoe Praised in England," *Salt Lake Tribune*, 13 August 1916.

11. Widtsoe, *Education For Necessary Pursuits*, 32.

12. Widtsoe, *Education For Necessary Pursuits*, 22.

13. Widtsoe, *Education For Necessary Pursuits*, 28–29.

14. Widtsoe, *Education For Necessary Pursuits*, 30.

15. Widtsoe to the Board of Trustees, 30 November 1907, 2, Widtsoe Presidential Papers, USU Special Collections.

16. Widtsoe, *Sunlit Land*, 103.

17. Widtsoe to R. J. Gordon, 17 November 1908, Widtsoe Presidential Papers, USU Special Collections.

18. Widtsoe, *Sunlit Land*, 121.

19. Joseph T. Kingsbury to Widtsoe, 14 December 1908, Widtsoe Presidential Papers, USU Special Collections.

20. "Conclusions Reached at a Conference between the Presidents of the University of Utah and the Agricultural College of Utah," 10 December 1913, Widtsoe

Presidential Papers, USU Special Collections.

21. Joseph T. Kingsbury to Widtsoe, 19 February 1915, Widtsoe Presidential Papers, USU Special Collections.

22. "Widtsoe Expresses Thanks for Welcome," *Salt Lake Tribune,* 1 March 1916, 3.

23. Widtsoe to the Board of Trustees, 30 November 1907, 2, Widtsoe Presidential Papers, USU Special Collections.

24. Widtsoe to the Board of Trustees, 30 November 1907, 2, Widtsoe Presidential Papers, USU Special Collections.

25. Widtsoe to the Board of Trustees, 30 November 1907, 2–3, Widtsoe Presidential Papers, USU Special Collections.

26. Ricks, *Utah State Agricultural College,* 85.

27. Widtsoe to the Board of Trustees, 30 November 1907, 3, Widtsoe Presidential Papers, USU Special Collections.

28. Widtsoe to the Board of Trustees, 30 November 1907, 3, Widtsoe Presidential Papers, USU Special Collections.

29. Widtsoe to Bishop John M. Holladay, 24 June 1908, Widtsoe Presidential Papers, USU Special Collections.

30. Widtsoe to Franklin S. Harris, 25 October 1910, Widtsoe Presidential Papers, USU Special Collections.

31. "The School of Agriculture," Widtsoe Presidential Papers, USU Special Collections.

32. Biennial Report of the Board of Trustees of the Agricultural College of Utah, 1911–12, 5.

33. Biennial Report of the Board of Trustees of the Agricultural College of Utah, 1911–12, 13.

34. Biennial Report of the Board of Trustees of the Agricultural College of Utah, 1911–12, 9–10.

35. See handwritten history of the college in Widtsoe Presidential Papers, USU Special Collections.

36. Widtsoe to All Friends of the State School at Cedar City, 21 July 1913, Widtsoe Presidential Papers, USU Special Collections.

37. Report on Summer School, Widtsoe Presidential Papers, USU Special Collections.

38. Widtsoe to Dr. George Thomas, 13 July 1909, Widtsoe Presidential Papers, USU Special Collections.

39. Biennial Report of the Board of Trustees of the Agricultural College of Utah, 1911–12, 5.

40. Widtsoe, *Sunlit Land,* 108.

CHAPTER *15*

1. Ricks, *Utah State Agricultural College,* 84.

2. Widtsoe, *Sunlit Land,* 112.

3. Widtsoe to Erastus Peterson, 23 August 1907, Widtsoe Presidential Papers, USU Special Collections.

4. Widtsoe to the President and Executive Committee of the U.A.C. Student Body, 29 May 1915, Widtsoe Presidential Papers, USU Special Collections.

5. "The Record of President John A. Widtsoe Described by a Correspondent," 11 February 1916, Journal History of the Church, 4.

6. Ernest L. Wilkinson to Noble White, 30 November 1953, Wilkinson Presidential Papers, BYU Special Collections.

7. Widtsoe to Lydia Sventzer, 10 September 1910, Widtsoe Presidential Papers, USU Special Collections.

8. Widtsoe to Alma Andreasen, 10 September 1910, Widtsoe Presidential Papers, USU Special Collections.

9. Widtsoe to J. LeRoy White, 6 November 1912, Widtsoe Presidential Papers, USU Special Collections.

10. Widtsoe to Ernest Mohr, 20 April

1914, Widtsoe Presidential Papers, USU Special Collections.

11. Widtsoe to Juanita Johnson, 31 July 1909, Widtsoe Presidential Papers, USU Special Collections.

12. Widtsoe to J. E. Blair, 31 July 1909, Widtsoe Presidential Papers, USU Special Collections.

13. Widtsoe to S. Jackson Major, 3 July 1909, Widtsoe Presidential Papers, USU Special Collections.

14. Widtsoe to G. Merle Taylor, 14 September 1910, Widtsoe Presidential Papers, USU Special Collections.

15. Widtsoe to Lucy Williams, 13 September 1907, Widtsoe Presidential Papers, USU Special Collections.

16. Widtsoe to Lorin T. Oldroyd, 19 January 1911, Widtsoe Presidential Papers, USU Special Collections.

17. Widtsoe to Grant Costley, 9 February 1909, Widtsoe Presidential Papers, USU Special Collections.

18. Widtsoe, *Sunlit Land,* 107.

19. Biennial Report of the Board of Trustees of the Agricultural College of Utah, 1914, as quoted in Ricks, *The Utah State Agricultural College,* 78.

20. Ricks, *Utah State Agricultural College,* 79.

21. Widtsoe to Maud May Babcock, 17 April 1911, Widtsoe Presidential Papers, USU Special Collections.

22. Widtsoe to Franklin S. Harris, 25 October 1910, Widtsoe Presidential Papers, USU Special Collections.

23. Louis F. Boyle to Widtsoe, 3 March 1909, Widtsoe Presidential Papers, USU Special Collections.

24. W. S. Langston to Widtsoe, 12 May 1913, Widtsoe Presidential Papers, USU Special Collections.

25. Widtsoe to Franklin S. Harris, 20 April 1911, Widtsoe Presidential Papers, USU Special Collections.

26. Widtsoe to C. N. Jensen, 22 October 1908, Widtsoe Presidential Papers, USU Special Collections.

27. Widtsoe to John Dern, 24 September 1914, Widtsoe Presidential Papers, USU Special Collections.

28. Biennial Report of the Board of Trustees of the Agricultural College of Utah, 1911–12, 6.

29. Biennial Report of the Board of Trustees of the Agricultural College of Utah, 1913–1914, as quoted in Ricks, *The Utah State Agricultural College,* 80.

30. Widtsoe to J. E. Hickman, 16 April 1909, Widtsoe Presidential Papers, USU Special Collections.

31. Widtsoe, *Sunlit Land,* 146.

32. Widtsoe, *Sunlit Land,* 89–90.

33. Widtsoe to I. B. Evans, 10 June 1909, Widtsoe Presidential Papers, USU Special Collections.

34. Widtsoe to Harrison Dale, 30 April 1910, Widtsoe Presidential Papers, USU Special Collections.

35. Widtsoe, *Sunlit Land,* 105.

36. Widtsoe to Hazel Guldbraudsen, 10 September 1910, Widtsoe Presidential Papers, USU Special Collections.

37. "Address delivered by Dr. John A. Widtsoe before the International Congress of Farm Women, October 26th, 1912," Widtsoe Presidential Papers, USU Special Collections. In today's world it would be easy to view such statements as implying that Widtsoe believed that women were not capable of the same work as men, or were unequal. This is far from the truth. Two things must be kept in mind that will enable the reader to see the liberating ideas Widtsoe held on women. First, his ideas were very progressive for the time. He fought a strong fight for women to obtain an education when many still felt it was not a proper course. Second, Widtsoe was the president of an agricultural college and was working for industrial education. Farming families had to divide the work

between the man in the field and the woman in the home. Farming during that era required a great amount of physical strength and exertion, and much of the work emphasized the physical differences between men and women.

38. Widtsoe, *Education for Necessary Pursuits,* 34–36.

39. Widtsoe, *Education For Necessary Pursuits,* 83.

40. Minutes of the Board of Trustees Meeting, Utah Agricultural College, 23 April 1907, 244.

41. Widtsoe to Mrs. Byron Cummings, 29 October 1908, Kerr Presidential Papers, USU Special Collections.

42. Widtsoe, *Education for Necessary Pursuits,* 30.

43. Widtsoe, *Education For Necessary Pursuits,* 38.

44. From unknown worker to Irma Mathews, 1 October 1913, Widtsoe Presidential Papers, USU Special Collections.

45. Widtsoe, *Sunlit Land,* 116–17.

46. Widtsoe, *Sunlit Land,* 109.

47. Lewis A. Merrill, "The College Extension Work," *Deseret Farmer,* 27 August 1910, 3.

48. See ad from *Vernal Express Print,* Widtsoe Presidential Papers, USU Special Collections.

49. Merrill, "The College Extension Work," 3.

50. Henry Peterson to George H. Brimhall, 3 December 1906, Brimhall Presidential Papers, BYU Special Collections. The letter says, "Last Saturday evening I heard a lecture here by Pres. Andrews of the U. of Neb. He says that in connection with their course in Agriculture they deliver lectures in the railroad towns of his state. They do it in this way. The R. R. Co. furnishes a car large enough for 75 to 100 men. Into this the lecturer puts his specimens of soils etc. and starts out. The R. R. Co. sends him gratis from station to station where he lectures from 30 to 45 minutes. In this way they cover the state and much good is accomplished. I wonder if the R. R. Co's of Utah would not cooperate with you there. It would help the farmers, the railroads, and the University."

51. Widtsoe to Thomas Smart, 11 February 1911, Widtsoe Presidential Papers, USU Special Collections.

52. "Farm Is Abandoned," *Logan Journal,* 4 May 1916, 1.

53. Widtsoe, *Sunlit Land,* 109–10.

54. "A. C. Catalogue Issued from Press," *Logan Journal,* 20 May 1916, 1.

55. Widtsoe, *Sunlit Land,* 114.

56. Charles S. Peterson, "Cholera, Blight, and Sparrows: a Look at Utah's First Agricultural Agents," *Utah Historical Quarterly,* vol. 57, no. 2 (1989): 140.

57. E. G. Peterson to Widtsoe, undated, Widtsoe Presidential Papers, USU Special Collections.

58. E. G. Peterson to Widtsoe, undated, Widtsoe Presidential Papers, USU Special Collections.

59. Widtsoe, *Education for Necessary Pursuits,* 46–48.

60. Biennial Report of the Board of Trustees of the Agricultural College of Utah, 1911–12, 10.

61. Undated letter from the office of the *Deseret Farmer,* Widtsoe Presidential Papers, USU Special Collections.

62. Widtsoe to Joseph T. Kingsbury, 19 June 1914, Widtsoe Presidential Papers, USU Special Collections.

63. Widtsoe to "Editor of the News," 17 November 1915, Widtsoe Presidential Papers, USU Special Collections.

64. E. G. Peterson to Widtsoe, 139–40.

65. Ellsworth, *Utah's Heritage,* 374.

66. Widtsoe to the Board of Trustees, 30 November 1907, 4–5.

67. Widtsoe to Jeremiah W. Sanborn, 28 June 1909, Widtsoe Presidential Papers, USU Special Collections.

68. Widtsoe to T. H. Harris, 7 January

1909, Widtsoe Presidential Papers, USU Special Collections.

69. Widtsoe to John C. Sharp, 10 April 1912, Widtsoe Presidential Papers, USU Special Collections.

70. Widtsoe to Ellen Huntington, 28 September 1912, Widtsoe Presidential Papers, USU Special Collections.

71. "A. C. Catalogue Issued from Press," *Logan Journal,* 20 May 1916, 1.

72. Ricks, *Utah State Agricultural College,* 84.

73. "The Record of President John A. Widtsoe Described by a Correspondent," 11 February 1916, Journal History of the Church, 4.

74. Osborne Widtsoe to chairman graduate employment committee at UAC, 1 March 1911, Widtsoe Presidential Papers, USU Special Collections.

75. Widtsoe, *Sunlit Land,* 115.

76. Widtsoe to A. S. Condon, 29 October 1907, Widtsoe Presidential Papers, USU Special Collections.

77. Widtsoe to Franklin S. Harris, 20 April 1911, Widtsoe Presidential Papers, USU Special Collections.

78. Biennial Report of the Board of Trustees of the Agricultural College of Utah, 1911–12, 11.

79. "The New President of the University of Utah," Journal History of the Church, March 1916, 9.

80. J. W. Paxman to Widtsoe, 11 July 1912, Widtsoe Presidential Papers, USU Special Collections.

81. John A. Widtsoe, "The Conquest of Drouth," Journal History of the Church, February 1913, 22–23.

82. Widtsoe to John Burns, 7 September 1911, Widtsoe Presidential Papers, USU Special Collections.

83. Franklin S. Harris, "Apostle John Andreas Widtsoe," *Young Woman's Journal,* June 1921, 321.

84. L. H. Bailey to Widtsoe, 18 May 1909, Widtsoe Presidential Papers, USU Special Collections.

85. Widtsoe to L. H. Bailey, 10 May

86. Widtsoe, *Dry Farming: A System of Agriculture for Countries Under a Low Rainfall* (New York: Macmillan, 1911).

87. Widtsoe, *Dry Farming,* vii.

88. E. W. Hilgard to Widtsoe, 4 April 1911, Widtsoe Presidential Papers, USU Special Collections.

89. John T. Burns to Baron Paul Inksy, 9 May 1911, Widtsoe Presidential Papers, USU Special Collections.

90. John T. Burns to Widtsoe, 13 March 1912, Widtsoe Presidential Papers, USU Special Collections.

91. "Elder Widtsoe Is New Hall of Fame Inductee," *Church News,* 12 January 1986, 6.

92. Widtsoe, *Sunlit Land,* 118.

93. Widtsoe to Richard Young, 14 May 1912, Widtsoe Presidential Papers, USU Special Collections.

94. Widtsoe to William Spry, 7 October 1912, Widtsoe Presidential Papers, USU Special Collections.

95. Widtsoe, *Sunlit Land,* 117.

96. Widtsoe to L. H. Bailey, 27 February 1911, Widtsoe Presidential Papers, USU Special Collections.

97. Widtsoe, *The Principles of Irrigation Practice.*

98. Richard R. Lyman to Widtsoe, 4 March 1915, Widtsoe Presidential Papers, USU Special Collections.

99. "Remarks by Franklin S. Harris," in *In Memoriam,* 18.

100. A. W. Israelsen to Widtsoe, 16 July 1913, Widtsoe Presidential Papers, USU Special Collections.

101. Susa Young Gates to Leah Widtsoe, 8 June 1909, Widtsoe Presidential Papers, USU Special Collections.

102. Widtsoe to Joseph F. Smith, 22 October 1910, Widtsoe Presidential Papers, USU Special Collections.

103. G. Ilclin to Widtsoe, 24 August 1911, Widtsoe Presidential Papers, USU Special Collections.

104. Widtsoe to C. N. Jensen, 23 March

1915, Widtsoe Presidential Papers, USU Special Collections.

105. Widtsoe to W. S. McCornick, 31 May 1911, Widtsoe Presidential Papers, USU Special Collections.

106. Widtsoe to John Dern, 18 May 1911, Widtsoe Presidential Papers, USU Special Collections.

107. Widtsoe, *Sunlit Land,* 123.

108. Widtsoe, *Sunlit Land,* 124.

109. Widtsoe, *Sunlit Land,* 124.

110. Widtsoe, *Sunlit Land,* 238.

111. Widtsoe, *Sunlit Land,* 124–25.

112. "Remarks by Franklin S. Harris," in *In Memoriam,* 16.

113. Widtsoe, *Sunlit Land,* 125–27.

114. "Dr. Widtsoe's Resignation is Received By Board," Journal History of the Church, 8 February 1916, 2.

115. "Prest. Kingsbury to Retire from the University," Journal History of the Church, 20 January 1916, 5.

116. "Dr. Widtsoe's Resignation is Received By Board," Journal History of the Church, 26 January 1916, 3.

117. "U.A.C. Faculty Resolutions," *Logan Journal,* 10 February 1916, 1.

118. Peterson, *History of Cache County,* 139.

119. Franklin S. Harris, "Apostle John Andreas Widtsoe," *Young Woman's Journal,* June 1921, 322.

120. "The New President of the University of Utah," Journal History of the Church, March 1916, 12.

CHAPTER 16

1. Wells, "Historic Sketch," *Improvement Era,* June 1925, 714.

2. Wells, "Historic Sketch," *Improvement Era,* June 1925, 715.

3. Wells, "Historic Sketch," *Improvement Era,* June 1925, 715.

4. Widtsoe, *Sunlit Land,* 94.

5. Widtsoe, *Sunlit Land,* 155.

6. John A. Widtsoe, "M Men, Gleaner Girls, Noblesse Oblige!" *Improvement Era,* June 1947, 384.

7. Widtsoe, "M Men, Gleaner Girls, Noblesse Oblige!" *Improvement Era,* June 1947, 384.

8. Joseph F. Smith, *Gospel Doctrine, Sermons and Writings of President Joseph F. Smith,* John A. Widtsoe, ed. (Salt Lake City: Deseret News, 1919), introduction, v.

9. Widtsoe Journal, 27 September 1909. On 29 September he added, "Work on notes for Origin of Man." On 30 September he wrote, "Came to Salt Lake on Morning train. Committee on Evolution w. Apostle Whitney, Dr. Talmage & Dr. Brimhall."

10. Widtsoe to David O. McKay, 19 September 1914, John A. Widtsoe Collection, LDS Church Archives.

11. John A. Widtsoe, "Joseph F. Smith—An Appreciation," *Improvement Era,* November 1914, 39.

12. Widtsoe, "Joseph F. Smith—An Appreciation," 41–42.

13. Edward H. Anderson to Widtsoe, 15 October 1914, John A. Widtsoe Collection, LDS Church Archives.

14. Diary of Franklin Stewart Harris, 1 November 1918, Friday, 242.

15. Widtsoe, "Joseph F. Smith—An Appreciation," *Improvement Era,* November 1914, 44–45.

16. As quoted in Ronald W. Walker, "Crisis in Zion, Heber J. Grant and the Panic of 1893," *Sunstone,* May 1985, 76. Walker's article notes: "The depression paralyzed the Church. By late June cash donations had almost ceased. On July 1 the Church failed to meet its payroll, forcing General Authorities to draw their living allowances in tithing commodities. In Salt Lake City, mission president J. Golden Kimball described himself at 'the *end* of the rope' and pled for *'anything'* to aid him in returning to his Church assignment in the southern states."

17. James B. Allen and Glen M.

Leonard, *The Story of the Latter-day Saints* (Salt Lake City: Deseret Book, 1976), 458–59.

18. Harrison R. Merrill, "40 Years of Service," *Improvement Era,* November 1937, 679.

19. Harrison R. Merrill, "40 Years of Service," *Improvement Era,* November 1937, 679.

20. Heber J. Grant, "A Greeting to the Youth of the Church," *Improvement Era,* July 1941, 393.

21. Heber J. Grant, "A Greeting to the Youth of the Church," *Improvement Era,* July 1941, 393.

22. Harrison R. Merrill, "40 Years of Service," *Improvement Era,* November 1937, 680.

23. Conference Report, October 1902, 87. In Smith, *Gospel Doctrine,* 488.

24. "First Presidency Declaration of the Place and Privileges of the Young Men's Mutual Improvement Association," June Conference, 5 June 1909. In Smith, *Gospel Doctrine,* 489.

25. John A. Widtsoe, "A Voice From the Soil," *Improvement Era,* December 1898, 108–9.

26. John A. Widtsoe, "A Voice From the Soil," *Improvement Era,* December 1898, 109.

27. John A. Widtsoe, "A Voice From the Soil," *Improvement Era,* December 1898, 109.

28. John A. Widtsoe, "A Voice From the Soil," *Improvement Era,* December 1898, 110.

29. John A. Widtsoe, "A Voice From the Soil," *Improvement Era,* December 1898, 114.

30. John A. Widtsoe, "We Walk by Faith," *Improvement Era,* June 1900, 563.

31. John A. Widtsoe, "We Walk by Faith," *Improvement Era,* June 1900, 563–64.

32. John A. Widtsoe, "We Walk by Faith," *Improvement Era,* June 1900, 569.

33. Edward H. Anderson to Widtsoe, 20 February 1901, John A. Widtsoe Collection, LDS Church Archives.

34. Edward H. Anderson to Widtsoe, 13 August 1900, John A. Widtsoe Collection, LDS Church Archives. The articles referred to are "Two Unseen Friends," *Improvement Era,* November 1900, 17; "One of Aristotle's Elements," *Improvement Era,* December 1900, 131; and "Liebig and Lawes," *Improvement Era,* January 1901, 196.

35. Joseph F. Smith to Widtsoe, 24 September 1903, John A. Widtsoe Collection, LDS Church Archives.

36. John A. Widtsoe, "Joseph Smith as Scientist," *Improvement Era,* November 1903, 1.

37. John A. Widtsoe, "Joseph Smith as Scientist," *Improvement Era,* November 1903, 8.

38. John A. Widtsoe, "Joseph Smith as Scientist, II. The Persistence of Matter and Force," *Improvement Era,* December 1903, 82.

39. John A. Widtsoe, "Joseph Smith as Scientist, II. The Persistence of Matter and Force," *Improvement Era,* December 1903, 82–83.

40. The series "Joseph Smith as Scientist" was published in the *Improvement Era* from 1903 to 1904 when Dr. Widtsoe was director of the Agricultural Experiment Station. The general board of the YMMIA arranged for it to be published as their course manual in 1908 and 1920. Four editions of *Joseph Smith as Scientist* have since been published, in 1920, 1964, 1990, and 1997.

41. An entry in the Journal History of the Church, dated 11 April 1898, reads, "Professor J. A. Widtsoe presented to the First Presidency the Mss of an elaborate concordance of the Doctrine and Covenants, which he had prepared with great labor and completeness, and offered it as a gift to the church, hoping that it would prove

acceptable and useful. The Presidency thankfully accepted the gift in behalf of the Church, and expressed the belief that it would prove very useful."

42. John A. Widtsoe, "Lord Kelvin, the God-Fearing," *Improvement Era*, April 1908, 401.

43. John A. Widtsoe, "Lord Kelvin, the God-Fearing," *Improvement Era*, April 1908, 403–4.

44. John A. Widtsoe, "Lord Kelvin, the God-Fearing," *Improvement Era*, April 1908, 402–3.

45. Clark, *Messages of the First Presidency*, 4:200 (see also endnote 9).

CHAPTER *17*

1. Chamberlain, *The University of Utah*, 323.

2. Chamberlain, *The University of Utah*, 323.

3. Chamberlain, *The University of Utah*, 326.

4. Chamberlain, *The University of Utah*, 326.

5. Chamberlain, *The University of Utah*, 328.

6. Chamberlain, *The University of Utah*, 331.

7. Chamberlain, *The University of Utah*, 335.

8. Chamberlain, *The University of Utah*, 336–37.

9. Chamberlain, *The University of Utah*, 338.

10. Minutes of the Board of Regents, 20 January 1916.

11. Minutes of the Board of Regents, 20 January 1916.

12. Minutes of the Board of Regents, 20 January 1916.

13. "President J. T. Kingsbury Will Probably Resign," *Utah Chronicle*, 20 January 1916, 1.

14. "Four Regents Protest against Selection of Dr. John A. Widtsoe," *Utah Chronicle*, 24 January 1916, 4.

15. "Four Regents Protest against Selection of Dr. John A. Widtsoe," *Utah Chronicle*, 24 January 1916, 1.

16. Chamberlain, *The University of Utah*, 340.

17. Minutes of the Board of Regents, 20 Janurary 1916.

18. "Four Regents Protest against Selection of Dr. John A. Widtsoe," *Utah Chronicle*, 24 January 1916, 1, 4.

19. "Alumni Adopt Resolutions Condemning Regents' Action," *Utah Chronicle*, 7 February 1916, 4.

20. Minutes of the Board of Regents, 20 January 1916.

21. Minutes of the Board of Regents, 20 January 1916.

22. Widtsoe, *Sunlit Land*, 125.

23. Widtsoe, *Sunlit Land*, 125–26.

24. "Widtsoe Accepts Presidency of the University," *Utah Chronicle*, 10 February 1916, 1, 3.

25. "Widtsoe Explains Resignation to Aggie Students," *Utah Chronicle*, 7 February 1916, 2.

26. Widtsoe to F. J. Alway, 17 February 1916, LDS Church Archives.

27. "Widtsoe Accepts Presidency of the University," *Utah Chronicle*, 10 February 1916, 1.

28. "The Record of President John A. Widtsoe Described by a Correspondent," *Deseret Evening News*, 12 February 1916, 4.

29. "Vote to Support New President," *Utah Chronicle*, 25 February 1916, 2.

30. Joseph T. Kingsbury to Widtsoe, 21 January 1916, LDS Church Archives.

31. Widtsoe to Joseph T. Kingsbury, 26 January 1916, LDS Church Archives.

32. Widtsoe to D. R. Allen, 26 January 1916, LDS Church Archives.

33. L. H. Bailey to Widtsoe, 25 February 1916, LDS Church Archives.

34. Widtsoe to L. H. Bailey, 1 March 1916, LDS Church Archives.

35. Widtsoe to W. M. Jardine, director, Kansas Experiment Station, 9

February 1916, LDS Church
Archives.

36. A. E. Winship, *Journal of Education,*
3 February 1916, as cited in Edward
H. Anderson, "The New President
of the University of Utah,"
Improvement Era, March 1916, 457.

37. Anderson, "The New President,"
447.

38. Heber J. Grant to Widtsoe, 26
January 1916, LDS Church
Archives.

39. Widtsoe, *Sunlit Land,* 127.

40. Widtsoe to the Board of Regents of
the University of Utah, 11 May
1916.

41. Widtsoe to Major Richard W.
Young, 10 August 1916.

CHAPTER *18*

1. "Education Is Need of State," *Salt
Lake Tribune,* 17 December 1920, 8.

2. "Education," undated, Widtsoe
Presidential Papers, U of U Special
Collections. More broadly he wrote:
"Let it never be forgotten that the
future of free America lies in the
hands of its educators." Widtsoe,
Sunlit Land, 152.

3. Widtsoe to LeRoy E. Cowles, 25
October 1919, Widtsoe Presidential
Papers, U of U Special Collections.

4. Widtsoe to C. W. Porter, 20
November 1919, Widtsoe
Presidential Papers, U of U Special
Collections.

5. John A. Widtsoe, "President's
Address at the First Faculty Meeting
of the Autumn Quarter, Tuesday,
September 23, 1919," *Bulletin of the
University of Utah,* vol. 11, no. 5, 6.

6. Widtsoe to Reed Smoot, 11
September 1919, Widtsoe
Presidential Papers, U of U Special
Collections.

7. Widtsoe to Waldemar VanCott, 26
April 1920, Widtsoe Presidential
Papers, U of U Special Collections.

8. Widtsoe, *Sunlit Land,* 132.

9. Conference Report, April 1951, 99.

10. Widtsoe, *Sunlit Land,* 134.

11. "Dr. Widtsoe Sees Bright Prospects,"
Utah Chronicle, 17 May 1916, 1.

12. Widtsoe, *Sunlit Land,* 134.

13. Widtsoe to Waldemar VanCott, 26
April 1920, Widtsoe Presidential
Papers, U of U Special Collections.

14. "No Change in Faculty Personnel,"
Utah Chronicle, 6 March 1916, 1.

15. Widtsoe, *Sunlit Land,* 132–33.

16. "President Asks Faculty for
Suggestions," *University Chronicle,* 8
February 1917, 1–2.

17. Widtsoe, *Sunlit Land,* 134–35.

18. *Regulations of the Faculty of the
University of Utah,* undated,
Widtsoe Presidential Papers, U of U
Special Collections.

19. See "Meeting of the Administrative
Council," 2 April 1920, Widtsoe
Presidential Papers, U of U Special
Collections.

20. An example can be seen when
President Widtsoe read a letter from
a professor to the deans' council.
See "Meeting of the Deans'
Council, 29 October 1920, Widtsoe
Presidential Papers, U of U Special
Collections.

21. Widtsoe to F. W. Reynolds, 20
November 1919, Widtsoe
Presidential Papers, U of U Special
Collections.

22. Widtsoe to Maud May Babcock, 24
April 1920, Widtsoe Presidential
Papers, U of U Special Collections.

23. Widtsoe to F. W. Reynolds, 11
February 1921, Widtsoe Presidential
Papers, U of U Special Collections.

24. H. L. Marshall to Widtsoe, 16 June
1920, Widtsoe Presidential Papers,
U of U Special Collections.

25. Widtsoe, *Sunlit Land,* 132–33.

26. Widtsoe to Oscar G. Russell, 17
March 1919, Widtsoe Presidential
Papers, U of U Special Collections.

27. Widtsoe, *Sunlit Land,* 137–38.

28. Widtsoe, *Sunlit Land* 137.

29. Widtsoe to Louisa McCready, 14
June 1920, Widtsoe Presidential
Papers, U of U Special Collections.

30. Widtsoe to Milton Bennion, 4 February 1920, Widtsoe Presidential Papers, U of U Special Collections.

31. Widtsoe, *Sunlit Land,* 150.

32. John A. Widtsoe, "President's Address at the First Faculty Meeting of the Autumn Quarter, Tuesday, September 23, 1919," *Bulletin of the University of Utah,* vol. 11, no. 5, 4–6.

33. John A. Widtsoe, "The Early Years," in *University of Utah Centennial Commencement Proceedings, the State University in American Education* (Salt Lake City: University of Utah Press, 1950), 31.

34. Widtsoe to the Members of the Faculty of the University of Utah, Widtsoe Presidential Papers, U of U Special Collections.

35. Widtsoe, *Sunlit Land,* 133.

36. "President Widtsoe Defines Attitude toward Students," *Chronicle,* 2 October 1916, 1.

37. "President Widtsoe Welcomes Students," *Utah Chronicle,* 21 September 1916, 1.

38. Widtsoe to E. D. Fisher, 13 February 1920, Widtsoe Presidential Papers, U of U Special Collections.

39. Widtsoe to Milton A. Melville, 7 September 1920, Widtsoe Presidential Papers, U of U Special Collections.

40. Widtsoe to John W. Dayley, 17 September 1919, Widtsoe Presidential Papers, U of U Special Collections.

41. Widtsoe to Joseph Grue, 28 August 1919, Widtsoe Presidential Papers, U of U Special Collections.

42. Widtsoe to George V. Morris, 20 December 1920, Widtsoe Presidential Papers, U of U Special Collections.

43. Widtsoe to W. Taylor Parkinson, 24 August 1920, Widtsoe Presidential Papers, U of U Special Collections.

44. "Seniors Receive Prexy's Greetings," *Chronicle,* 9 May 1917, 4.

45. Widtsoe to Whom It May Concern, 4 February 1920, Widtsoe Presidential Papers, U of U Special Collections.

46. Widtsoe to Phi Alpha Epsilon Fraternity, 30 April 1919, Widtsoe Presidential Papers, U of U Special Collections.

47. Widtsoe to R. W. Sandowsky and members of the Skull and Bones Society, 17 March 1919, Widtsoe Presidential Papers, U of U Special Collections.

48. John A. Widtsoe, "President's Address at the First Faculty Meeting of the Autumn Quarter, Tuesday, September 23, 1919," *Bulletin of the University of Utah,* vol. 11, no. 5, 4–5.

49. Widtsoe to Fred Meissner, 25 March 1920, Widtsoe Presidential Papers, U of U Special Collections.

50. T. S. Parmelee to Widtsoe, 17 December 1919, Widtsoe Presidential Papers, U of U Special Collections.

51. Widtsoe, *Sunlit Land,* 138.

52. Widtsoe, *Sunlit Land,* 138.

53. Widtsoe, *Sunlit Land,* 139.

54. John A. Widtsoe, "The Worth of Souls," *Church Service on Genealogical Committees,* 231.

55. Richard L. Evans, "Dr. John A. Widtsoe 75th Birthday Anniversary, 3 January 1947."

56. Franklin S. Harris, "Remarks," in *In Memoriam of John A. Widtsoe* (Salt Lake City: Bookcraft, 1952), 17.

57. David O. McKay, "Closing Remarks," *In Memoriam,* 25.

CHAPTER *19*

1. Widtsoe, *Sunlit Land,* 139–40.

2. Chamberlain, *University of Utah,* 348.

3. "Regents and President Asked to Inaugurate Military Training," *Utah Chronicle,* 22 March 1917, 1.

4. *Chronicle,* 22 March 1917, 2, in Chamberlain, 349–50.

5. "Over 100 Names Now on Request

for Training," *Utah Chronicle,* 29
March 1917, 1.

6. "Regents Boost Commerce and
   Army Science," *Utah Chronicle,* 2
   April 1917, 1.

7. Minutes of the Faculty, 26 May
   1917, in Chamberlain, 352.

8. L. Ames Brown, director of the
   Division of Publicity, to Widtsoe, 11
   September 1917.

9. Widtsoe to L. Ames Brown, 11
   October 1917.

10. C. F. Homer, director of publicity,
    Treasury Department, to Widtsoe, 3
    October 1917.

11. John A. Widtsoe, "The Cause of the
    War," An address delivered at the
    annual MIA Conference, 7 June
    1918, cited from *Improvement Era,*
    October 1918, 1,032–37.

12. Chamberlain, *The University of
    Utah,* 351.

13. "The Four-Quarter Plan of
    University Operation During the
    War and After," *Journal of the
    National Education Association,* vol.
    12, no. 4, December 1917, 295.

14. O. J. Grimes to Widtsoe, 10 October
    1918, Widtsoe Presidential Papers,
    U. of U. archives.

15. Widtsoe to O. J. Grimes, 15 October
    1918, Widtsoe Presidential Papers,
    USU Special Collections.

16. Widtsoe to E. G. Gowans, 27
    November 1918, Widtsoe
    Presidential Papers, U of U Special
    Collections.

17. Widtsoe to Dr. Claxton, 19 February
    1918, Widtsoe Presidential Papers,
    U of U Special Collections.

18. Widtsoe for the "Payroll Builder," 17
    July 1918, Widtsoe Presidential
    Papers, U of U Special Collections.

19. Chamberlain, *The University of
    Utah,* 356.

20. Chamberlain, *The University of
    Utah,* 356.

21. Widtsoe to John S. White, 29
    January 1919, Widtsoe Presidential
    Papers, U of U Special Collections.

22. Governor Bamberger to Widtsoe, 4

December 1918, Widtsoe
Presidential Papers, U of U Special
Collections.

23. Widtsoe to Governor Bamberger, 7
    December 1918, Widtsoe
    Presidential Papers, U of U Special
    Collections.

24. Chamberlain, *The University of
    Utah,* 351–52.

25. Widtsoe to William H. King, 10
    December 1918, Widtsoe
    Presidential Papers, U of U Special
    Collections.

26. Minutes of the Board of Regents, 17
    December 1918, as quoted in
    Chamberlain, 357–8.

27. Widtsoe to Faculty Member, 25
    January 1921, Widtsoe Presidential
    Papers, U of U Special Collections.

28. "Influenza 1918," 1998. In the
    American Experience [database
    online]. PBS, 1998—[cited 19 July
    2001]. Available from www.pbs.org/
    wgbh/amex/influenza/filmmore/
    description.html.

29. Widtsoe to James H. Moyle, 27
    February 1919, Widtsoe Presidential
    Papers, U of U Special Collections.
    [flu file].

30. Chamberlain, *The University of
    Utah,* 356–7.

31. Widtsoe, *Sunlit Land,* 140.

32. Widtsoe to Daniel F. Jauntzen, 3
    February 1919, Widtsoe Presidential
    Papers, U of U Special Collections.

33. General Bulletin No. 32 from the
    University of Utah President's
    Office, 2 February 1920, Widtsoe
    Presidential Papers, U of U Special
    Collections.

CHAPTER 20

1. John A. Widtsoe, "President's
   Address at the First Faculty Meeting
   of the Autumn Quarter, Tuesday,
   September 23, 1919," *Bulletin of the
   University of Utah,* vol. 11, no. 5,
   2–3.

2. John A. Widtsoe, "The University

of Utah," *Improvement Era,* July 1920, 13.

3. Widtsoe to A. L. Beeley, 25 August 1919, Widtsoe Presidential Papers, U of U Special Collections.

4. John A. Widtsoe, "President's Address at the First Faculty Meeting of the Autumn Quarter, Tuesday, September 23, 1919," *Bulletin of the University of Utah,* vol. 11, no. 5, 3.

5. Widtsoe to Walter J. Crocker, 6 December 1920, Widtsoe Presidential Papers, U of U Special Collections.

6. Widtsoe to E. H. Beckstrand, 24 November 1919, Widtsoe Presidential Papers, U of U Special Collections.

7. Widtsoe to Thomas Varley, 10 November 1920, Widtsoe Presidential Papers, U of U Special Collections.

8. Widtsoe to Joseph F. Merrill, 23 November 1920, Widtsoe Presidential Papers, U of U Special Collections.

9. Widtsoe to Joseph F. Merrill, 17 April 1920, Widtsoe Presidential Papers, U of U Special Collections.

10. Widtsoe to C. E. McClung, 14 June 1920, Widtsoe Presidential Papers, U of U Special Collections.

11. Widtsoe to LeRoy E. Cowles, 11 February 1921, Widtsoe Presidential Papers, U of U Special Collections.

12. Widtsoe, *Gospel Net,* 96.

13. "No Change in Faculty Personnel," *Utah Chronicle,* 6 March 1916, 3.

14. John A. Widtsoe, "President's Report," *Bulletin of the University of Utah,* July 1920, 27–28.

15. John A. Widtsoe, "President's Address at the First Faculty Meeting of the Autumn Quarter, Tuesday, September 23, 1919," *Bulletin of the University of Utah,* vol. 11, no. 5, 1–2.

16. Widtsoe, *Sunlit Land,* 135.

17. "Education for Adults," 25 September 1919, Widtsoe Presidential Papers, U of U Special Collections.

18. "Extension Courses 1919–1920," 23 September 1919, Widtsoe Presidential Papers, U of U Special Collections.

19. "Extension Division, University of Utah," flyer without date, Widtsoe Presidential Papers [in 2 December 1919 packet, ext. file]; letter from unknown person to Widtsoe, 5 May 1919, Widtsoe Presidential Papers, U of U Special Collections.

20. E. H. Beckstrand to Widtsoe, 20 October 1919, Widtsoe Presidential Papers, U of U Special Collections.

21. Widtsoe to F. W. Reynolds, 5 February 1920, Widtsoe Presidential Papers, U of U Special Collections.

22. F. W. Reynolds to Widtsoe, 2 February 1920, Widtsoe Presidential Papers, U of U Special Collections.

23. Widtsoe, *Sunlit Land,* 135.

24. Widtsoe to J. H. Moyle, 22 April 1920, Widtsoe Presidential Papers, U of U Special Collections.

25. Extension Division to Teachers of Box Elder County, 8 January 1920, Widtsoe Presidential Papers, U of U Special Collections.

26. "Extension Division, University of Utah, Short Term Extension Courses," flyer without date, Widtsoe Presidential Papers, U of U Special Collections.

27. F. W. Reynolds to Widtsoe, 11 February 1921, Widtsoe Presidential Papers, U of U Special Collections.

28. John A. Widtsoe, "Education Is Need of State," *Salt Lake Tribune,* 17 December 1920, 8.

29. John A. Widtsoe, "Education Is Need of State," *Salt Lake Tribune,* 17 December 1920, 8.

30. Widtsoe to J. H. Paul, 25 June 1921, Widtsoe Presidential Papers, U of U Special Collections.

31. Widtsoe to A. C. Rees, 10 February 1919, Widtsoe Presidential Papers, U of U Special Collections.

32. Widtsoe, Fiftieth Commencement Addresses, 27.

33. Widtsoe to George Thomas, 13 June 1919, Widtsoe Presidential Papers, U of U Special Collections.

34. Widtsoe to Fred J. Pack, 13 June 1919, Widtsoe Presidential Papers, U of U Special Collections.

35. F. W. Reynolds to Widtsoe, 10 February 1921, Widtsoe Presidential Papers, U of U Special Collections.

36. John A. Widtsoe, "Utah As a Playground," *Salt Lake Tribune*, 25 April 1920, Magazine Section, 1, 5.

37. Widtsoe to Reed Smoot, 3 January 1921, Widtsoe Presidential Papers, U of U Special Collections.

38. See Widtsoe to E. O. Leatherwood, 11 June 1920, Widtsoe Presidential Papers; Widtsoe to Barton Warren Evermann, 27 June 1919, Widtsoe Presidential Papers; Widtsoe to American Nurses Association, 2 April 1920, Widtsoe Presidential Papers, U of U Special Collections.

39. Widtsoe, *Sunlit Land*, 148–49.

40. Widtsoe to Department Heads, 3 December 1919, Widtsoe Presidential Papers, U of U Special Collections.

41. B. A. Fowler to Widtsoe, 10 January 1918, Widtsoe Presidential Papers, U of U Special Collections.

42. Extension Division to the Teachers of the State, Widtsoe Presidential Papers, U of U Special Collections.

43. "Draft," in E. E. Ericksen to Widtsoe, 22 October 1919, Widtsoe Presidential Papers, U of U Special Collections.

44. Widtsoe to members of the faculty, employees of the University and Officers and Members of the Student Body, 21 April 1920, Widtsoe Presidential Papers, U of U Special Collections.

45. Widtsoe to A. M. Merrill, 13 December 1920, Widtsoe Presidential Papers, U of U Special Collections.

46. Widtsoe to G. N. Child, 22 January 1920, Widtsoe Presidential Papers, U of U Special Collections.

47. Widtsoe to G. N. Child, 22 January 1920, Widtsoe Presidential Papers, U of U Special Collections.

48. Minutes of State Board of Education, 8 April 1920, Widtsoe Presidential Papers, U of U Special Collections.

49. Milton Bennion to Widtsoe, 27 January 1920, Widtsoe Presidential Papers, U of U Special Collections.

50. Widtsoe to Milton Bennion, 27 December 1919, Widtsoe Presidential Papers, U of U Special Collections.

51. Widtsoe to Milton Bennion, 27 December 1919, Widtsoe Presidential Papers, U of U Special Collections.

52. Widtsoe, "The University of Utah," 13.

53. "Summer Outdoor Art School," 29 March 1921, Widtsoe Presidential Papers, U of U Special Collections.

54. Widtsoe to A. D. Bevan, 6 March 1916, Widtsoe Presidential Papers, U of U Special Collections.

55. Widtsoe, *Sunlit Land*, 136.

56. Widtsoe to L. J. Muir, 28 January 1921, Widtsoe Presidential Papers, U of U Special Collections.

57. Widtsoe, *Sunlit Land*, 139.

58. Widtsoe to P. L. Campbell 21 October 1920, Widtsoe Presidential Papers, U of U Special Collections.

59. Widtsoe to F. W. Reynolds, 2 September 1920, Widtsoe Presidential Papers, U of U Special Collections.

60. Widtsoe to A. C. Carrington, 10 April 1920, Widtsoe Presidential Papers, U of U Special Collections.

61. Widtsoe to A. C. Carrington, 10 April 1920, Widtsoe Presidential Papers, U of U Special Collections.

62. John A. Widtsoe, "President's Address at the First Faculty Meeting of the Autumn Quarter, Tuesday, September 21, 1920," *Bulletin of the University of Utah*, vol. 11, no. 7, 3.

63. Widtsoe to Carrington, 10 April 1920, Widtsoe Presidential Papers, U of U Special Collections.

64. John A. Widtsoe, "President's Address at the First Faculty Meeting of the Autumn Quarter, Tuesday, September 21, 1920," *Bulletin of the University of Utah*, vol. 11, no. 7, 2.

65. Widtsoe to Gerald Lambert, 5 April 1920, Widtsoe Presidential Papers, U of U Special Collections.

66. John A. Widtsoe, "Education is Need of State," *Salt Lake Tribune*, 16 December 1920, 8.

67. John A. Widtsoe, "President's Address at the First Faculty Meeting of the Autumn Quarter, Tuesday, September 21, 1920," *Bulletin of the University of Utah*, vol. 11, no. 7, 3.

68. Widtsoe to A. C. Carrington, 4 November 1920, Widtsoe Presidential Papers, U of U Special Collections.

69. Widtsoe to LeRoy Cowles, 11 February 1921, Widtsoe Presidential Papers, U of U Special Collections.

CHAPTER 21

1. Widtsoe to E. H. Beckstrand, 5 February 1920, Widtsoe Presidential Papers, U of U Special Collections.

2. Widtsoe to A. C. Carrington, 4 November 1920, Widtsoe Presidential Papers, U of U Special Collections.

3. Widtsoe to Joseph F. Merrill, 23 October 1919, Widtsoe Presidential Papers, U of U Special Collections.

4. Widtsoe, "The University of Utah," 14.

5. Widtsoe, *Sunlit Land*, 136–37.

6. Widtsoe, "The University of Utah," 13.

7. Widtsoe, *Sunlit Land*, 137.

8. Widtsoe, *Sunlit Land*, 142.

9. Horace H. Cummings to Widtsoe, 14 June 1919, Widtsoe Presidential Papers, U of U Special Collections.

10. Widtsoe, *Sunlit Land*, 143.

11. Widtsoe, *Sunlit Land*, 143–44.

12. Widtsoe, *Sunlit Land*, 143.

13. Widtsoe, *Sunlit Land*, 146.

14. Widtsoe, *Sunlit Land*, 152.

15. Widtsoe to Walter W. Davis, 3 February 1920, Widtsoe Presidential Papers, U of U Special Collections.

16. Widtsoe, *Sunlit Land*, 141.

17. Widtsoe to E. G. Peterson, 22 May 1919, Widtsoe Presidential Papers, U of U Special Collections.

18. Widtsoe, *Sunlit Land*, 153.

19. Widtsoe, *Sunlit Land*, 154–55.

20. Franklin S. Harris, "Apostle John Andreas Widtsoe," *Young Woman's Journal*, June 1921, 320.

21. Widtsoe, *Sunlit Land*, 154.

22. Widtsoe, *Gospel Net*, 130.

23. Widtsoe to J. M. Macfarlane, 15 August 1919, Widtsoe Presidential Papers, U of U Special Collections.

24. Widtsoe to Percy Shelly, 15 October 1919, Widtsoe Presidential Papers, U of U Special Collections.

25. Widtsoe to A. C. Carrington, 10 April 1920, Widtsoe Presidential Papers, U of U Special Collections.

26. Widtsoe to A. C. Carrington, 10 April 1920, Widtsoe Presidential Papers, U of U Special Collections.

27. Widtsoe to A. C. Carrington, 10 April 1920, Widtsoe Presidential Papers, U of U Special Collections.

28. Arthur L. Beeley to Widtsoe, 16 June 1920, Widtsoe Presidential Papers, U of U Special Collections.

29. Widtsoe to David O. McKay, 11 March 1921, Widtsoe Presidential Papers, U of U Special Collections.

30. Widtsoe to Thomas A. Beal, 21 November 1919, Widtsoe Presidential Papers, U of U Special Collections.

31. Widtsoe, *Sunlit Land*, 151.

32. Franklin S. Harris, "Apostle John Andreas Widtsoe," *Young Woman's Journal*, June 1921, 322.

33. Widtsoe, *Sunlit Land*, 156–57.

34. "Widtsoe Named L. D. S. Apostle," *Salt Lake Tribune*, 18 March 1921.

35. "Widtsoe Named L. D. S. Apostle," *Salt Lake Tribune*, 18 March 1921.

36. Widtsoe to the Honorable Board of Regents, 11 April 1921, Widtsoe Presidential Papers, U of U Special Collections.

37. Widtsoe to the Honorable Board of Regents, 11 April 1921, Widtsoe Presidential Papers, U of U Special Collections.

38. "Retiring President of State University Bids School Farewell," *Deseret News*, 27 May 1921, 2.

39. Widtsoe to the Members of the Faculty of the University of Utah, 30 June 1921, Widtsoe Presidential Papers, U of U Special Collections.

40. "High Honorary Degrees Conferred on Our Prominent Men of Utah," *Deseret News*, 11 June 1921.

CHAPTER 22

1. *Teachings of the Prophet Joseph Smith*, 74.

2. Widtsoe, *Sunlit Land*, 160.

3. Widtsoe to Rev. Edwin T. Lewis, 31 October 1921, John A. Widtsoe Collection, LDS Church Archives.

4. Franklin S. Harris, "Apostle John Andreas Widtsoe," *Young Woman's Journal*, June 1921.

5. George H. Brimhall to Widtsoe, 22 March 1921, Brimhall Presidential Papers, BYU Special Collections. The letter went on to say, "When the late 'Uncle Jesse' [Knight], vice-president of our Board, pressed me for an expression of my choice of a man to build up our School, I saw 'John A. Widtsoe.' You will remember how I pled with you to stay with us and lead us on years ago, and he, believing that nothing was too good for the Brigham Young University, was working to that end."

6. Widtsoe, *Sunlit Land*, 160–61.

7. John Andreas Widtsoe, *Harvard Class of 1894—Report XIV*, 595.

8. David O. McKay to Widtsoe, 9 February 1922, John A. Widtsoe Collection, LDS Church Archives.

9. Ole Gulbrandsen to Widtsoe, 19 March 1921, John A. Widtsoe Collection, LDS Church Archives.

10. "Filling the Ranks of Leadership," Journal History of the Church, 18 March 1921.

11. Widtsoe to Florence Willard, 13 May 1921, John A. Widtsoe Collection, LDS Church Archives.

12. Widtsoe to Frank M. McVey, 20 May 1921, John A. Widtsoe Collection, LDS Church Archives.

13. Franklin S. Harris, "Apostle John Andreas Widtsoe," *Young Woman's Journal*, June 1921, 320–21.

14. Widtsoe to M. R. Hovey, 17 June 1921, John A. Widtsoe Collection, LDS Church Archives.

15. Widtsoe to Col. and Mrs. Howard Rand Perry, 20 May 1921, John A. Widtsoe Collection, LDS Church Archives.

16. Widtsoe, *Sunlit Land*, 161–62.

17. Widtsoe, *Sunlit Land*, 161–62.

18. Widtsoe, *Sunlit Land*, 238.

19. Widtsoe to Heber J. Grant, 12 September 1923, John A. Widtsoe Collection, LDS Church Archives.

20. Widtsoe to Rose Widtsoe, 11 March 1921, John A. Widtsoe Collection, LDS Church Archives.

21. Charles A. Callis to Widtsoe, 14 July 1922, John A. Widtsoe Collection, LDS Church Archives.

22. Grace E. Callis to Widtsoe, 15 July 1922, John A. Widtsoe Collection, LDS Church Archives.

23. Widtsoe to Elenor Wilkinson, 18 October 1926, John A. Widtsoe Collection, LDS Church Archives.

24. Widtsoe to Lewis J. Wallace, 5 October 1927, John A. Widtsoe Collection, LDS Church Archives.

25. Marsel Widtsoe to Leah Widtsoe, 23 February 1926, Widtsoe Family Collection, Utah State Historical Society.

26. David O. McKay to Widtsoe, 31 May 1924, Widtsoe Family Collection, 4, Utah State Historical Society.

27. Widtsoe to Heber J. Grant, 24 September 1924, John A. Widtsoe Collection, LDS Church Archives.

28. Franklin S. Harris to Widtsoe, 31 January 1923, John A. Widtsoe Collection, LDS Church Archives.

29. Widtsoe to F. P. Nash, 21 April 1923, John A. Widtsoe Collection, LDS Church Archives.

30. Widtsoe to George Stewart, 4 June 1926, John A. Widtsoe Collection, LDS Church Archives.

31. Everett G. Ward to Widtsoe, 1 June 1922, John A. Widtsoe Collection, LDS Church Archives.

32. Widtsoe to B. J. Stewart (PTA President of the William M. Stewart School), 28 May 1923, John A. Widtsoe Collection, LDS Church Archives.

33. Widtsoe to Joseph W. Smith, 20 June 1923, John A. Widtsoe Collection, LDS Church Archives.

34. Widtsoe to the Family of J. M. Tanner, 19 October 1927, John A. Widtsoe Collection, LDS Church Archives.

35. Susa Young Gates to Widtsoe, 31 January 1922, John A. Widtsoe Collection, LDS Church Archives. The rest of the letter reads, "You have had many blessings voiced to you many promises made, much foretold. But there is one promise I feel to make which you shall prove in your life work: Many paths, of duty, of fame, of achievement will open to your willing and highly trained footsteps. Men, good and otherwise, will cry, 'lo here,' and 'lo there!' Many great and glorious works, of voice and pen, of organization and arrangement avail your creative powers. But you will find your greatest achievement, your most profound inspiration will flow from and follow you whenever you lift your voice, weild [sic] your pen, or set your organizing hand to the cause of Salvation for the Dead. The living have many advocates— the dead have so few. Whatsoever you greatly desire, seek at the Alter steps. I feel sure your mother has obtained permission to visit you— and me—this day. And together we bless you with wisdom and light, with joy in travail and power in achievement. We hail you as one of those great intelligences whom god saw and chose, before the earth was formed, for His leaders. Be of good courage—the Lord is with you. Osborne shall not forget to visit you. By way of caution: at time harden your heart. Waste not your vitality on lesser matters and men. Who and what are the lesser things? Only God and experience may answer. Now, let this suffice. I am Your grateful and loving Mother Young-Gates."

36. Widtsoe to Isaac K. Russell, 26 February 1921, LDS Church Archives.

37. "Splendid Tribute Is Paid Founder of State Sunday," *Deseret News*, 4 June 1923.

38. Widtsoe to John T. Miller, 14 October 1925, John A. Widtsoe Collection, LDS Church Archives, LDS Church Archives.

39. Widtsoe to Fenton Dunning, 5 August 1926, John A. Widtsoe Collection, LDS Church Archives.

40. Widtsoe to Heber J. Grant and Councilors, 15 March 1927, John A. Widtsoe Collection, LDS Church Archives.

41. Widtsoe to Isaac K. Russell, 3 November 1926, John A. Widtsoe Collection, LDS Church Archives.

42. C. L. Olsen to Widtsoe, 1 February 1921, John A. Widtsoe Collection, LDS Church Archives.

43. Report written by Widtsoe, John A. Widtsoe Collection, LDS Church Archives.

44. Widtsoe to Franklin S. Forsberg, 28 January 1927, John A. Widtsoe Collection, LDS Church Archives.

45. Widtsoe to Franklin S. Forsberg, 28 January 1927.
46. Widtsoe to First Presidency, 25 March 1926, John A. Widtsoe Collection, LDS Church Archives.
47. Widtsoe to Oluff I. Peterson, 12 October 1921, John A. Widtsoe Collection, LDS Church Archives.
48. Widtsoe to Heber J. Grant, 5 May 1923, John A. Widtsoe Collection, LDS Church Archives.
49. Widtsoe to Heber J. Grant, 5 May 1923.
50. Widtsoe to John Wells, 23 January 1922, John A. Widtsoe Collection, LDS Church Archives.
51. John A. Widtsoe, "Wonderful Opportunities for Education in Church of Jesus Christ of Latter-day Saints—Gospel's Scope Embraces All Truth," address given in Salt Lake City to Liberty Stake on 23 October 1921, as reported in *Deseret News,* 21 November 1921.
52. Widtsoe to Leland H. Monson, 3 June 1924, John A. Widtsoe Collection, LDS Church Archives.
53. Widtsoe to Leland H. Monson, 3 June 1924.

CHAPTER 23

1. See Allen, Embry, and Mehr, *Hearts Turned to the Fathers.*
2. John A. Widtsoe, "The Opening of Our New Home," *Utah Genealogical and Historical Magazine* (hereafter UGHM), April 1934, 56.
3. Widtsoe, *Sunlit Land,* 176–77.
4. Widtsoe to Nellie T. Taylor, 9 November 1921, John A. Widtsoe Collection, LDS Church Archives.
5. Widtsoe to Harry H. Russell, 28 March 1923, John A. Widtsoe Collection, LDS Church Archives.
6. Widtsoe to Nellie T. Taylor, 27 March 1923, John A. Widtsoe Collection, LDS Church Archives.
7. *Teachings of the Prophet Joseph Smith,* 356.
8. *Teachings of the Prophet Joseph Smith,* 193.
9. John A. Widtsoe, "What Is Our Personal Obligation for the Salvation of the Dead?" in *Gospel Interpretations,* 98–99.
10. John A. Widtsoe, "Purpose of the Family Organization," UGHM, June 1923, 81.
11. John A. Widtsoe, "The Worth of Souls," *Millennial Star* 96 (1 March 1934): 132–34.
12. John A. Widtsoe, "The Beginnings of Modern Temple Work," *Improvement Era,* October 1927, 1,076, 1,079.
13. John A. Widtsoe, "Temple Worship," UGHM, April 1921, 54.
14. John A. Widtsoe, "Genealogical Activities in Europe," UGHM, July 1931, 105.
15. Widtsoe, "Temple Worship," UGHM, April 1921, 62. A similar reference to temples in earlier ages and other cultures suggests an important connection to modern temple work:

   "All people of all ages have had temples in one form or another. When the history of human thought shall be written from the point of view of temple worship, it may well be found that temples and the work done in them have been the dominating influence in shaping human thought from the beginning of the race. Even today political controversies are as nothing in determining the temper of a people, as compared with religious sentiments and convictions, especially as practiced in the temples of the people.

   "In every land and in every age temples have been built and used. In China, age old with four thousand years of written history; in India; on the islands of the sea; in South America; in North America; in Africa and in Australia; everywhere there are evidences of

the existence and use of temples."
(Ibid., 52).

16. Widtsoe, "Temple Worship," 53–54.
17. See "The Biennial Meeting of the
Genealogical Society of Utah,"
UGHM, July 1910, 140.
18. John A. Widtsoe, "The
Genealogical Society's Quarterly
Meeting," *UGHM,* January 1911,
46.
19. Widtsoe, "Work for the Dead," 33.
20. See Widtsoe, "Temple Worship,"
53–54: "Those who understand the
eternal nature of the gospel—
planned before the foundation of
the earth—understand clearly why
all history seems to revolve about
the building and use of temples."
21. Widtsoe, "Temple Worship," 53.
The critical emphasis the Prophet
Joseph Smith put on temple and
genealogical work is further attested
in an address by Widtsoe to the
Liberty Stake Genealogical
Convention on 24 May 1922: "It is
sufficient for us to remember that
temple work for the living and for
the dead was the burden of the
thought and labors of the Prophet
Joseph Smith from the day when
the Angel Moroni first stood before
him and told him of the things that
were to be, up to the last day of the
Prophet's life. The principle of
salvation for the dead received
foremost consideration by the
prophet because of its close and
intertwining relationship to all other
principles." John A. Widtsoe,
"Fundamentals of Temple
Doctrine," *UGHM,* July 1922, 129.
  An outstanding essay by
Widtsoe reviewing Joseph's
involvement in the beginnings of
modern temple work was published
in October 1927; see Widtsoe,
"Beginnings of Modern Temple
Work," *Improvement Era,* October
1927, 1,073–79.
22. John A. Widtsoe, "The Meaning

and Importance of Records,"
UGHM, July 1920, 97.
23. Widtsoe, *Sunlit Land,* 177.
24. Widtsoe, "Temple Worship," 64.
25. Widtsoe, "Temple Worship," 56.
26. Widtsoe to Maud May Babcock, 14
December 1921, John A. Widtsoe
Collection, LDS Church Archives.
27. Allen, Embry, and Mehr, *Hearts
Turned to the Fathers,* 95.
28. Allen, Embry, and Mehr, *Hearts
Turned to the Fathers,* 97.
29. Widtsoe, "Purpose of the Family
Organization," 81.
30. See Allen, Embry, and Mehr, *Hearts
Turned to the Fathers,* 98.
31. Allen, Embry, and Mehr, *Hearts
Turned to the Fathers,* 97–98.
32. See Archibald F. Bennett, "The
Growth of the Temple Index
Bureau: World-Wide Clearinghouse," *Improvement Era,* April
1936, 218.
33. Widtsoe to Heber J. Grant, 15
November 1921, John A. Widtsoe
Collection, LDS Church Archives.
34. See Widtsoe to First Presidency, 13
January 1922, John A. Widtsoe
Collection, LDS Church Archives.
35. John A. Widtsoe, "Fundamentals of
Temple Doctrine," *UGHM,* July
1922, 130–34. A powerful editorial
by Widtsoe summarizing these same
fundamental principles was
published in the *Millennial Star* in
1929: "Salvation for the Dead,"
Millennial Star 91 (19 September
1929): 600–601.
36. John A. Widtsoe, "Serving Our
Dead," *Millennial Star* 89 (4 August
1927): 483.
37. Widtsoe, "Serving Our Dead,"
Millennial Star, 484.
38. See Allen, Embry, and Mehr, *Hearts
Turned to the Fathers,* 112.
39. See Widtsoe to Superintendent
Adam Bennion, 13 May 1921, John
A. Widtsoe Collection, LDS
Church Archives.
40. Widtsoe to Louie B. Felt, 26 July

1922, John A. Widtsoe Collection, LDS Church Archives.

41. Widtsoe to George D. Kirby, 24 February 1923, John A. Widtsoe Collection, LDS Church Archives.

42. John A. Widtsoe, "Lessons In Genealogy," *UGHM*, January 1925, 33.

43. John A. Widtsoe, "Lessons In Genealogy," *UGHM*, January 1925, 33.

44. See John A. Widtsoe, "Report of Dr. John A. Widtsoe's Visit to Scandinavia," *UGHM*, January 1924, 11–16.

45. See John A. Widtsoe, "Report of Dr. John A. Widtsoe's Visit to Scandinavia," *UGHM*, January 1924, 15.

46. John A. Widtsoe, "Genealogical Activities in Europe," *UGHM*, July 1931, 100.

47. John A. Widtsoe, "Genealogical Activities in Europe," *UGHM*, July 1931, 101.

48. The Church's recent move toward constructing many smaller temples, making the temple more accessible to all Church members, is further evidence of this need.

49. See Widtsoe, "Beginnings of Modern Temple Work," *Improvement Era*, October 1927, 1,079.

50. See John A. Widtsoe, "Obtaining Scandinavian Genealogies," *UGHM*, January 1928, 1–8.

51. Editorial from the *Millennial Star*, "European Program for Genealogical Study, Research and Exchange," *UGHM*, January 1930, 34.

52. Editorial from the *Millennial Star*, "European Program for Genealogical Study, Research and Exchange," *UGHM*, January 1930, 35.

53. Allen, Embry, and Mehr, *Hearts Turned to the Fathers*, 105.

54. Widtsoe to F. W. Smith, 13

September 1923, John A. Widtsoe Collection, LDS Church Archives.

55. Widtsoe to Susa Young Gates, 25 June 1925, John A. Widtsoe Collection, LDS Church Archives.

56. Widtsoe to Susa Young Gates, 8 August 1927, John A. Widtsoe Collection, LDS Church Archives.

57. "Lesson Course: Methods of Genealogical Research," *UGHM*, July 1935, 139.

58. John A. Widtsoe, "Elijah, the Tishbite," *UGHM*, April 1936, 54.

59. John A. Widtsoe, "The Urgency of Temple Service," *UGHM*, January 1937, 5.

60. See Allen, Embry, and Mehr, *Hearts Turned to the Fathers*, 133.

61. John A. Widtsoe, "The Temple Calls," *Improvement Era*, April 1943, 224.

62. John A. Widtsoe, "The Way of Salvation," *Improvement Era*, May 1943, 278–79.

63. Allen, Embry, and Mehr, *Hearts Turned to the Fathers*, 177.

64. John A. Widtsoe, "Universal Brotherhood Will Save the World," *Improvement Era*, May 1950, 429.

65. John A. Widtsoe, "Universal Brotherhood Will Save the World," *Improvement Era*, May 1950, 430.

66. Widtsoe, *Sunlit Land*, 176.

67. John A. Widtsoe, "Looking toward the Temple," *Improvement Era*, October 1962, 710.

68. John A. Widtsoe, "Looking toward the Temple," *Improvement Era*, October 1962, 765.

CHAPTER 24

1. Widtsoe to Leah Eudora Widtsoe, 2 July 1923, LDS Church Archives.

2. *Messages of the First Presidency*, Vol. 5, 225.

3. Heber J. Grant, Anthon H. Lund, Charles W. Penrose, First Presidency *Improvement Era*, February 1921, 354–55. See also James R. Clark,

Messages of the First Presidency,
5:188–89.

4. Heber J. Grant to Reed Smoot, 25
April 1921, Smoot Papers, BYU
Special Collections.

5. Heber J. Grant to Reed Smoot, 25
April 1921, Smoot Papers, BYU
Special Collections.

6. Heber J. Grant to Reed Smoot,
August 24, 1921, Smoot Papers,
BYU Special Collections; see
Messages of the First Presidency, Vol.
5, 202.

7. Reed Smoot to Heber J. Grant,
September 7, 1921, Smoot Papers,
BYU Special Collections.

8. Reed Smoot to Heber J. Grant,
September 7, 1921, Smoot Papers,
BYU Special Collections.

9. Reed Smoot to Heber J. Grant, 19
February 1922, Smoot Papers, BYU
Special Collections.

10. Heber J. Grant to Reed Smoot, 1
April 1922, Smoot Papers, BYU
Special Collections.

11. Widtsoe to Heber J. Grant, 27 June
1923, LDS Church Archives. He
added, "I believe the most
convincing testimony that has come
to me during the last two years or
more as I have sat in intimate view
of the making of the policies of the
Church is that God is at the helm,
and that the man who stands at the
head of the Church is deeply blessed
with prophetic power. I need not
add a word to tell you how happy
this testimony makes me as
evidence crowds upon evidence."

12. Widtsoe to Leah Eudora Widtsoe, 1
July 1923, LDS Church Archives.

13. Widtsoe to Leah Eudora Widtsoe, 2
July 1923, LDS Church Archives.

14. Widtsoe to Leah Eudora Widtsoe, 2
July 1923, LDS Church Archives.

15. Widtsoe to Leah Eudora Widtsoe, 3
July 1923, LDS Church Archives.

16. Widtsoe to Leah Eudora Widtsoe,
12 July 1923, LDS Church
Archives.

17. Smoot Journal, Book 33, 81.

18. Smoot Journal, Book 33, 85.

19. Smoot Journal, Book 33, 87.

20. Widtsoe to Leah Eudora Widtsoe,
21 July 1923, LDS Church
Archives.

21. Smoot Journal, Book 33, 89.

22. Widtsoe to Leah Eudora Widtsoe,
21 July 1923, LDS Church
Archives.

23. Smoot Journal, Book 33, 93–94.

24. Smoot Journal, Book 33, 97–98, 27
July 1923.

25. Smoot Journal, Book 33, 105.

26. Reed Smoot to Heber J. Grant, 3
November 1923, Smoot Collection,
BYU Special Collections.

27. Reed Smoot to Heber J. Grant, 5
November 1923, Smoot Collection,
BYU Special Collections.

28. Widtsoe to Leah Eudora Widtsoe,
12 July 1923, LDS Church
Archives.

29. Widtsoe to Leah Eudora Widtsoe,
12 July 1923, LDS Church
Archives.

30. Widtsoe to Leah Eudora Widtsoe,
12 July 1923, LDS Church
Archives.

31. Widtsoe to Leah Eudora Widtsoe,
12 July 1923, LDS Church
Archives.

32. Widtsoe to Leah Eudora Widtsoe,
15 July 1923, LDS Church
Archives.

33. Widtsoe to Leah Eudora Widtsoe,
15 July 1923, LDS Church
Archives.

34. Widtsoe to Leah Eudora Widtsoe,
15 July 1923, LDS Church
Archives.

35. Widtsoe to Leah Eudora Widtsoe,
21 July 1923, LDS Church
Archives.

36. Widtsoe to Marsel Widtsoe, 8
November 1923, Widtsoe Family
Collection, Utah State Historical
Society.

37. Widtsoe to Marsel Widtsoe, 2,
Widtsoe Family Collection, Utah
State Historical Society.

38. Widtsoe to Marsel Widtsoe, 4,

Widtsoe Family Collection, Utah State Historical Society.

39. Widtsoe to Heber J. Grant (undated, but appears to be written as a note to the 21 August 1923 letter), John A. Widtsoe Collection, LDS Church Archives.

40. Widtsoe to Heber J. Grant (same letter as footnote 39), John A. Widtsoe Collection, LDS Church Archives.

41. Widtsoe to Heber J. Grant, 21 August 1923, John A. Widtsoe Collection, LDS Church Archives.

CHAPTER 25

1. *Calgary Daily Herald,* 11–19 August 1921, also *Farm and Ranch Review,* 15 August 1921, John A. Widtsoe Collection, LDS Church Archives.

2. *Yakima Morning Herald,* 29 October 1921, John A. Widtsoe Collection, LDS Church Archives.

3. "Colorado River Compact Terms Are Suggested," *Salt Lake Tribune,* 29 March 1922.

4. Olson, *Colorado River Compact,* 73.

5. Olson, *Colorado River Compact,* 492.

6. "Colorado River Compact Terms Are Suggested," *Salt Lake Tribune,* 29 March 1922.

7. *Deseret News,* 28 March 1922, John A. Widtsoe Collection, LDS Church Archives.

8. "Utahns Explore Wonder Section of State, Dr. Widtsoe Relates Impressions of Trip," *Deseret News,* 25 September 1922.

9. *Salt Lake Telegram,* 21 November 1922, John A. Widtsoe Collection, LDS Church Archives.

10. *The New Mexican,* date unknown, LDS Church Archives.

11. Article I of the Compact, Appendix II—Exhibit A, Olson, *The Colorado River Compact,* 225–29.

12. Article IV of the Compact, Appendix II—Exhibit A, Olson, *The Colorado River Compact,* 225–29.

13. *Federal Reclamation by Irrigation, Report of the Committee of Special Advisors on Reclamation,* U.S. Government Printing Office, Department of the Interior, Washington D.C., 1921, 24.

14. Widtsoe to Marsel Widtsoe, 8 November 1923, Widtsoe Family Collection, Utah State Historical Society.

15. *Federal Reclamation by Irrigation, Report of the Committee of Special Advisors on Reclamation,* U.S. Government Printing Office, Department of the Interior, Washington D.C., 1921, 25.

16. *Utah Farmer,* 22 September 1923, John A. Widtsoe Collection, LDS Church Archives.

17. *Federal Reclamation by Irrigation, Report of the Committee of Special Advisors on Reclamation,* U.S. Government Printing Office, Department of the Interior, Washington D.C., 1921, 121.

18. "Transcript of Salt Lake Hearings," 17 January 1924, entry 40, box 5, RG 115, 547, National Archives Rocky Mountain Region, Denver (hereafter cited as RG 115).

19. Minutes of the Special Advisors on Reclamation, 10 April 1924, entry 40, box 14, RG 115, 168.

20. Minutes of the Special Advisors on Reclamation, 18 October 1923, entry 40, box 14, RG 115, 8.

21. Minutes of the Special Advisors on Reclamation, 8 December 1923, entry 40, box 14, RG 115, 71.

22. Minutes of the Special Advisors on Reclamation, 5 January 1924, entry 40, box 14, RG 115, 98.

23. "Transcript of Salt Lake Hearings," 17 January 1924, entry 40, box 5, RG 115, 9.

24. "Transcript of Salt Lake Hearings," 17 January 1924, entry 40, box 5, RG 115, 16–17.

25. "Transcript of Salt Lake Hearings," 17 January 1924, entry 40, box 5, RG 115, 343–44.

26. *Federal Reclamation by Irrigation, Report of the Committee of Special Advisors on Reclamation,* U.S. Government Printing Office, Department of the Interior, Washington D.C., 1921, xi.

27. President Calvin Coolidge, The White House, 21 April 1924, *Report of the Committee of Special Advisors on Reclamation,* ix.

28. Committee of Special Advisors, *Report of the Committee of Special Advisors on Reclamation,* xii.

29. Committee of Special Advisors, *Report of the Committee of Special Advisors on Reclamation,* xiv.

30. *Federal Reclamation Laws Annotated,* US. Department of the Interior, U.S. Government Printing Office, Washington, D.C., 1943, 272–83.

31. The scholars quoted are Dorothy Lampen, Michael C. Robinson, James R. Klugar, Lawrence B. Lee, and Donald Swain. For more thorough descriptions, see Brian Q. Cannon, "'We Are Now Entering a New Era': Federal Reclamation and the Fact Finding Commission of 1923–1924," *Pacific Historical Review,* American Historical Association, Pacific Coast Branch, 1997, 187–88.

32. Elwood Mead to Widtsoe, 15 September 1924, Entry 7, box 229, RG 115.

33. Widtsoe to Elwood Mead, 24 September 1924, Entry 7, box 229, RG 115.

34. Elwood Mead to Thomas E. Campbell and Widtsoe, 24 December 1924, Entry 7, box 229, RG 115.

35. Hubert Work to Thomas E. Campbell and Widtsoe, 30 January 1925, entry 7, box 229, RG 115.

36. Widtsoe to Hubert Work, 2 April 1925, Entry 7, box 229, RG 115.

37. Widtsoe to Elwood Mead, 24 April 1925, Entry 7, box 229, RG 115.

38. Widtsoe to Elwood Mead, 29 May and 3 June 1925, Entry 7, box 229, RG 115.

39. Widtsoe to Elwood Mead, 29 May and 3 June 1925, Entry 7, box 229, RG 115.

40. *Deseret News,* 8 July 1925, 1.

41. *Deseret News,* 8 July 1925, 1.

42. "A Letter on Reclamation," paper and date not indicated, LDS Church Archives.

43. Widtsoe to Elwood Mead, 8 August 1925, entry 7, box 226, RG 115.

44. Widtsoe to Elwood Mead, 8 August 1925, entry 7, box 226, RG 115.

45. Widtsoe, *Sunlit Land,* 182.

46. Widtsoe, *Sunlit Land,* 182.

47. John A. Widtsoe, *Success on Irrigation Projects,* iii.

48. *Deseret News,* 27 May 1926.

49. Widtsoe, *Sunlit Land,* 138.

50. "Mead, Work in Meeting Give Saints Tribute," *Deseret News,* 20 April 1925, 1.

51. Widtsoe, *Sunlit Land,* 182–83.

52. *Great Falls Daily Tribune,* Editorial page, LDS Church Archives.

53. *Great Falls Daily Tribune,* Editorial page, LDS Church Archives.

54. *Lethbridge Herald,* 30 January 1926.

55. "Russia Will Use Irrigation to Put End to Famines," *Deseret News,* 25 October 1926.

56. Widtsoe to George H. Dern, 7 October 1927, LDS Church Archives.

57. Widtsoe to George H. Dern, 7 October 1927, LDS Church Archives.

CHAPTER 26

1. Widtsoe Journal, 26 January 1922: "Temple meeting. Abt. 3:30 P.M. Pres. Heber J. Grant nominated me to be Commissioner of Education vice D. O. McKay who had made the suggestion. I was taken by surprise. God give me strength to do my work well."

2. Widtsoe Journal, 1 April 1925.

3. *Improvement Era,* March 1922, 472.

4. Orson F. Whitney to Widtsoe, 20 February 1922.

5. John A. Widtsoe, "The Church School System," *Improvement Era*, September 1923, 1,012.

6. John A. Widtsoe, "The Church School System," *Improvement Era*, September 1923, 1,012.

7. Widtsoe to Frank Warren Smith, 8 March 1922, John A. Widtsoe Collection, LDS Church Archives.

8. Widtsoe to Franklin S. Harris, 16 May 1921, John A. Widtsoe Collection, LDS Church Archives.

9. Widtsoe to Edward E. Domm, 26 June 1924, John A. Widtsoe Collection, LDS Church Archives.

10. John A. Widtsoe, "The Church School System," *Improvement Era*, September 1923, 868.

11. Widtsoe to Edward E. Domm, 26 June 1924, John A. Widtsoe Collection, LDS Church Archives.

12. "The Church School System ," *Improvement Era*, September 1923, 1,011.

13. John A. Widtsoe, "Educational Comparisons," Editor's Table, *Improvement Era*, June 1923, 744.

14. John A. Widtsoe, "The Educational Level of the Latter-day Saints," *Improvement Era*, July 1947, 444.

15. Hughes and Lancelot, *Education—America's Magic*, 40–41, in *Improvement Era*, July 1947, 446.

16. Hughes and Lancelot, *Education—America's Magic*, 40–41, in *Improvement Era*, July 1947, 446.

17. John A. Widtsoe, "Wonderful Opportunities for Education in Church of Jesus Christ of Latter-day Saints—Gospel's Scope Embraces All Truth," address given in Salt Lake City to Liberty Stake on 23 October 1921, as reported in *Deseret News*, 21 November 1921.

18. Widtsoe, *Sunlit Land*, 218.

19. Widtsoe to David O. McKay, 12 May 1923.

20. Widtsoe to Henry Goddard Leach, 9 May 1927, John A. Widtsoe Collection, LDS Church Archives.

21. John A. Widtsoe, "Right Education as a Force in Obedience to Law," *Improvement Era*, November 1922, 74–75.

22. John A. Widtsoe, "Right Education as a Force in Obedience to Law," *Improvement Era*, November 1922, 77.

23. John A. Widtsoe, "The Church School System," *Improvement Era*, August 1923, 863.

24. John A. Widtsoe, "The Church School System," *Improvement Era*, August 1923, 863.

25. John A. Widtsoe, "Serve your 'Own Generation,'" *Improvement Era*, July 1938, 393.

26. John A. Widtsoe, "The Church School System," *Improvement Era*, August 1923, 865.

27. Widtsoe to Henry Goddard Leach, 9 May 1927, John A. Widtsoe Collection, LDS Church Archives.

28. John A. Widtsoe, "How the Desert Was Tamed," part v, *Improvement Era*, May 1947, 305–6.

29. John A. Widtsoe, "How the Desert Was Tamed," part v, *Improvement Era*, May 1947, 306.

30. John A. Widtsoe, "How the Desert Was Tamed," part v, *Improvement Era*, May 1947, 306.

31. Widtsoe to Heber J. Grant, 27 June 1923, John A. Widtsoe Collection, LDS Church Archives.

32. John A. Widtsoe, "The Church School System," *Improvement Era*, September 1923, 1,013.

33. "Religious Education Great Need of Hour; Convention Decision," *Deseret News*, 8 April 1923.

34. "Plans for Church Schools Outlined by Elder Widtsoe," *Deseret News*, 27 January 1923.

35. Widtsoe to C. D. Steiner, 30 January 1923.

36. Widtsoe, *Sunlit Land*, 171.

37. Widtsoe, *In Search of Truth*, 11.

38. Widtsoe, *In Search of Truth*, 14.

39. Widtsoe, *In Search of Truth*, 16.
40. Widtsoe, *In Search of Truth*, 17–18.
41. Widtsoe, *In Search of Truth*, 17–18.
42. Widtsoe, *In Search of Truth*, 19–21.
43. Widtsoe, *In Search of Truth*, 22.
44. Widtsoe, *In Search of Truth*, 23.
45. Widtsoe, *In Search of Truth*, 32.
46. In Widtsoe, *In Search of Truth*, 40.
47. Widtsoe, *In Search of Truth*, 37.
48. Widtsoe, *In Search of Truth*, 37.
49. Widtsoe, *In Search of Truth*, 39.
50. Widtsoe, *In Search of Truth*, 44.
51. Widtsoe, *In Search of Truth*, 48.
52. Widtsoe, *In Search of Truth*, 49.
53. Widtsoe, *In Search of Truth*, 53.
54. Widtsoe, *In Search of Truth*, 54.
55. Widtsoe, *In Search of Truth*, 55.
56. Widtsoe, *In Search of Truth*, 56.
57. Widtsoe, *In Search of Truth*, 59–60.
58. Widtsoe, *In Search of Truth*, 61.
59. Widtsoe, *In Search of Truth*, 64–65.
60. Widtsoe, *In Search of Truth*, 71.
61. Widtsoe, *In Search of Truth*, 68.
62. Widtsoe, *In Search of Truth*, 69.
63. Widtsoe, *In Search of Truth*, 70.
64. Widtsoe, *In Search of Truth*, 71.
65. Widtsoe, *In Search of Truth*, 73.
66. Widtsoe, *In Search of Truth*, 77.
67. Widtsoe, *In Search of Truth*, 80.
68. Widtsoe, *In Search of Truth*, 78–79.
69. Widtsoe, *In Search of Truth*, Prefatory Note.
70. Heber J. Grant to Widtsoe, 22 December 1931, John A. Widtsoe Collection, LDS Church Archives.
71. "Presentation and Closing Remarks of Dr. John A. Widtsoe. Seminary Teachers' Summer School, 13 July 1934," 4, John A. Widtsoe Collection, LDS Church Archives, 4.
72. Presentation and Closing Remarks of Dr. John A. Widtsoe, 5–6.
73. Widtsoe to Principals and Faculties of the Senior Seminaries, 13 April 1934, John A. Widtsoe Collection, LDS Church Archives.
74. Widtsoe to Principals and Faculties of the Senior Seminaries, 19 May 1934, John A. Widtsoe Collection, LDS Church Archives.
75. Widtsoe to Principals and Faculties of the Senior Seminaries, 19 May 1934, John A. Widtsoe Collection, LDS Church Archives.
76. "Opening Remarks by Dr. John A. Widtsoe, Seminary Teachers' Summer School, 12 June 1934," 1–2, John A. Widtsoe Collection, LDS Church Archives.
77. Widtsoe to G. T. Harrison, 27 June 1934, John A. Widtsoe Collection, LDS Church Archives.
78. "Opening Remarks by Dr. John A. Widtsoe, Seminary Teachers' Summer School, 12 June 1934," 1.
79. "Opening Remarks by Dr. John A. Widtsoe, Seminary Teachers' Summer School, 12 June 1934," 1.
80. "Opening Remarks by Dr. John A. Widtsoe, Seminary Teachers' Summer School, 12 June 1934," 5.
81. "Opening Remarks by Dr. John A. Widtsoe, Seminary Teachers' Summer School, 12 June 1934," 8–9.
82. "Man and the Gospel, Seminary Summer School 1934," 2, John A. Widtsoe Collection, LDS Church Archives.
83. "Man and the Gospel, Seminary Summer School 1934," 2–3, 15, John A. Widtsoe Collection, LDS Church Archives.
84. "Man and the Gospel, Seminary Summer School 1934," 32, John A. Widtsoe Collection, LDS Church Archives.
85. "Man and the Gospel, Seminary Summer School 1934," 56, John A. Widtsoe Collection, LDS Church Archives.
86. "The Temple Endowment," Seminary Summer School, 19 June 1934, 3, John A. Widtsoe Collection, LDS Church Archives.
87. "The Temple Endowment," Seminary Summer School, 19 June 1934, 3, John A. Widtsoe Collection, LDS Church Archives.
88. "The Temple Endowment," Seminary Summer School, 19 June

1934," 3, John A. Widtsoe Collection, LDS Church Archives.

89. "Presentation and Closing Remarks of Dr. John A. Widtsoe. Seminary Teachers' Summer School, 13 July 1934," John A. Widtsoe Collection, LDS Church Archives.

90. "Presentation and Closing Remarks of Dr. John A. Widtsoe. Seminary Teachers' Summer School, 13 July 1934," 1, John A. Widtsoe Collection, LDS Church Archives.

CHAPTER 27

1. Widtsoe, *Gospel Net*, 99.

2. Widtsoe, *Sunlit Land*, 235.

3. Widtsoe Journal, 15 May, 23–31, June 7, 1927.

4. Widtsoe Journal, 29 September 1927.

5. Widtsoe, *Sunlit Land*, 189.

6. Widtsoe to F. W. Smith, 16 September 1927, John A. Widtsoe Collection, LDS Church Archives.

7. Widtsoe to Mrs. Ambrose P. Merrill, 22 August 1927, John A. Widtsoe Collection, LDS Church Archives.

8. Widtsoe to Daniel J. Lange, 7 November 1927, John A. Widtsoe Collection, LDS Church Archives.

9. Leah D. Widtsoe to First Presidency, 16 September 1933, Widtsoe Family Collection, Utah State Historical Society.

10. Widtsoe to James E. Talmage, 1 November 1927, John A. Widtsoe Collection, LDS Church Archives.

11. Conference Report, October 1927, 24.

12. Conference Report, October 1927, 24–26.

13. "European Mission Changes," *Deseret News*, 1 October 1927.

14. Franklin S. Harris to Widtsoe, 1 October 1927, Harris Presidential Papers, BYU Special Collections.

15. "Welcome, President Widtsoe!" *Millennial Star*, 22 December 1927, 808–9.

16. Conference Report, April 1934, 113.

17. Conference Report, April 1934, 113.

18. Widtsoe to Heber J. Grant, 13 January 1928, John A. Widtsoe Collection, LDS Church Archives.

19. Widtsoe to David O. McKay, 1 February 1928, John A. Widtsoe Collection, LDS Church Archives.

20. Widtsoe to Heber J. Grant and Counselors, 28 February 1928, John A. Widtsoe Collection, LDS Church Archives.

21. Susa Young Gates to Widtsoe, 17 October 1928, Susa Young Gates Collection, Utah State Historical Society.

22. Widtsoe to Mr. and Mrs. Jacob F. Gates, 19 November 1928, Susa Young Gates Collection, Utah State Historical Society.

23. Widtsoe to James E. Talmage, 20 July 1929, John A. Widtsoe Collection, LDS Church Archives.

24. John A. Widtsoe, "The European Mission in 1928," *Millennial Star*, vol. 91, no. 9, 138–39.

25. Widtsoe to J. Reuben Clark, Jr., 25 January 1929, John A. Widtsoe Collection, LDS Church Archives.

26. Widtsoe to First Presidency, 1 August 1928, John A. Widtsoe Collection, LDS Church Archives.

27. Widtsoe to W. S. Wanlass, 4 January 1929, John A. Widtsoe Collection, LDS Church Archives.

28. See Widtsoe to Heber J. Grant, 31 December 1929, John A. Widtsoe Collection, LDS Church Archives.

29. John A. Widtsoe, "Headquarters of the British Mission," *Millennial Star*, vol. 91, no. 8, 9.

30. Widtsoe to Heber J. Grant, 3 July 1930, John A. Widtsoe Collection, LDS Church Archives.

31. Widtsoe to First Presidency, 3 May 1929, John A. Widtsoe Collection, LDS Church Archives.

32. Widtsoe to the Jacob F. Gates Family, 4 May 1929, John A.

Widtsoe Collection, LDS Church Archives.

33. Susa Young Gates to Eudora Widtsoe, 23 January 1929, Widtsoe Family Collection, Utah State Historical Society.

34. Susa Young Gates to Widtsoe, 19 August 1929, Susa Young Gates Collection, Utah State Historical Society.

35. Widtsoe to Susa Young Gates, 3 October 1929, Susa Young Gates Collection, Utah State Historical Society.

CHAPTER 28

1. Widtsoe, *Sunlit Land,* 202.

2. Widtsoe to Robert W. Major, 27 January 1932, John A. Widtsoe Collection, LDS Church Archives.

3. Widtsoe to Mr. and Mrs. A. E. Bowen, 13 March 1929, Susa Young Gates Collection, Utah State Historical Society.

4. Widtsoe to First Presidency, 2 September 1929, John A. Widtsoe Collection, LDS Church Archives.

5. Arnold D. White, Oral interview by Wayne A. Jacobson, The James Moyle Oral History Program, LDS Church Archives, 68–70.

6. Arnold D. White, Oral interview, 68–70.

7. "Another Mormon Speaks Out," *Sunday Mercury and Sunday News in England,* 5 February 1928.

8. "Old Mormon Bogey Dead, Girls Not the Only Attraction," *Sheffield Daily Independent,* 9 April 1928.

9. "Granddaughter of Brigham Young Preaches to Mormon Church at Varteg; Man with Nineteen Wives and Fifty-six Children," *Free Press of Monmouth Shire,* 9 November 1928.

10. Widtsoe to Reed Smoot, 17 July 1928, John A. Widtsoe Collection, LDS Church Archives.

11. Widtsoe to First Presidency, 3 May 1929, John A. Widtsoe Collection, LDS Church Archives.

12. Arnold D. White, Oral interview 69.

13. "The Mormons Are Here: A Frank Talk, Two Apostles Who Forgot," paper name unknown, 8 September 1929, John A. Widtsoe Collection, LDS Church Archives.

14. "The Mormons Are Here: A Frank Talk, Two Apostles Who Forgot," paper name unknown, 8 September 1929, John A. Widtsoe Collection, LDS Church Archives.

15. John A. Widtsoe, "Europe in the Melting Pot," *Improvement Era,* November 1929, 9.

16. Widtsoe to Mr. and Mrs. A. E. Bowen, 13 March 1929, Susa Young Gates Collection, Utah State Historical Society.

17. Widtsoe to Mr. and Mrs. A. E. Bowen, 13 March 1929, Susa Young Gates Collection, Utah State Historical Society.

18. Widtsoe to Mr. and Mrs. A. E. Bowen, 13 March 1929, Susa Young Gates Collection, Utah State Historical Society.

19. John A. Widtsoe, "The First Word of Wisdom Exhibit," *Improvement Era,* November 1930, 13–14.

20. Widtsoe to F. W. Smith, 14 January 1931, John A. Widtsoe Collection, LDS Church Archives.

21. Widtsoe to Heber J. Grant, 15 March 1929, John A. Widtsoe Collection, LDS Church Archives.

22. Widtsoe to Joseph Quinney, Jr., 10 August 1931, John A. Widtsoe Collection, LDS Church Archives.

23. Widtsoe to Evan L. Christiansen, 13 March 1934, John A. Widtsoe Collection, LDS Church Archives.

24. Widtsoe to Harden Bennion, 7 February 1933, John A. Widtsoe Collection, LDS Church Archives.

25. Widtsoe to Joseph F. Merrill, 24 November 1933, John A. Widtsoe Collection, LDS Church Archives.

26. Widtsoe to John A. Hofstead, 27 January 1932; John A. Hofstead to Widtsoe, 19 February 1932; John A.

Widtsoe Collection, LDS Church Archives.

27. Arnold D. White, Oral interview 67.

CHAPTER 29

1. Widtsoe to Susa Young Gates, 2 March 1928, Susa Young Gates Collection, Utah State Historical Society.

2. Susa Young Gates to Widtsoe, 10 March 1928, Susa Young Gates Collection, Utah State Historical Society.

3. Widtsoe to Susa Young Gates, 29 September 1928, Susa Young Gates Collection, Utah State Historical Society.

4. Susa Young Gates to Widtsoe, 17 October 1928, Susa Young Gates Collection, Utah State Historical Society.

5. Widtsoe to Susa Young Gates, 19 November 1928, Susa Young Gates Collection, Utah State Historical Society.

6. Harold J. Shepstone to Widtsoe, 7 February 1929, John A. Widtsoe Collection, LDS Church Archives.

7. Widtsoe to Harold J. Shepstone, 22 February 1929, John A. Widtsoe Collection, LDS Church Archives.

8. Harold J. Shepstone to Widtsoe, 12 March 1929, John A. Widtsoe Collection, LDS Church Archives.

9. Widtsoe to Harold J. Shepstone, 12 March 1929, John A. Widtsoe Collection, LDS Church Archives.

10. Widtsoe to Harold J. Shepstone, 27 August 1929, John A. Widtsoe Collection, LDS Church Archives.

11. Harold J. Shepstone to Widtsoe, 29 August 1929, John A. Widtsoe Collection, LDS Church Archives.

12. Widtsoe to Susa Young Gates, 14 October 1929, Susa Young Gates Collection, Utah State Historical Society.

13. Widtsoe to Susa Young Gates, 14 October 1929, Susa Young Gates Collection, Utah State Historical Society.

14. Harold J. Shepstone to Widtsoe, 28 November 1929, John A. Widtsoe Collection, LDS Church Archives.

15. Harold J. Shepstone to Widtsoe, 11 December 1929, John A. Widtsoe Collection, LDS Church Archives.

16. Susa Young Gates to Widtsoe, 23 December 1929, Susa Young Gates Collection, Utah State Historical Society.

17. Widtsoe to Harold J. Shepstone, 4 January 1930, John A. Widtsoe Collection, LDS Church Archives.

18. Widtsoe to Harold J. Shepstone, 9 January 1930, John A. Widtsoe Collection, LDS Church Archives.

19. Widtsoe to Susa Young Gates, 1 May 1930, Susa Young Gates Collection, Utah State Historical Society.

20. Widtsoe to Susa Young Gates, 1 May 1930, Susa Young Gates Collection, Utah State Historical Society.

21. Widtsoe to Susa Young Gates, 1 May 1930, Susa Young Gates Collection, Utah State Historical Society.

22. Widtsoe to Susa Young Gates, 5 June 1930, Susa Young Gates Collection, Utah State Historical Society.

23. Susa Young Gates to Widtsoe, 7 July 1930, Susa Young Gates Collection, Utah State Historical Society.

24. Widtsoe to Susa Young Gates, 2 October 1930, Susa Young Gates Collection, Utah State Historical Society.

25. Leah Widtsoe to Susa Young Gates, 24 October 1931, Susa Young Gates Collection, Utah State Historical Society.

26. Leah Widtsoe to Susa Young Gates, 24 October 1931, Susa Young Gates Collection, Utah State Historical Society.

27. Widtsoe, *Sunlit Land*, 201.

28. Widtsoe, *Sunlit Land*, 200–201.

29. Leah Widtsoe to Mr. and Mrs. G. B. Shaw, 19 October 1933, Widtsoe Family Collection, Utah State Historical Society.

30. Widtsoe to Heber J. Grant, 15 March 1929, John A. Widtsoe Collection, LDS Church Archives.

31. Susa Young Gates to Widtsoe, 19 August 1929, Susa Young Gates Collection, Utah State Historical Society.

CHAPTER 30

1. Widtsoe, *Sunlit Land,* 197–98.

2. Widtsoe, *Sunlit Land,* 224.

3. John A. Widtsoe, "The Gospel and Health: a Study Course for the Mutual Improvement Associations in the British Mission of the Church of Jesus Christ of Latter-day Saints" (Liverpool, England: 1928).

4. John A. Widtsoe, "The Gospel and Health," *Millennial Star,* 11 October 1928, 648.

5. Widtsoe, preface to "The Gospel and Health: a Study Course."

6. Widtsoe, preface to "The Gospel and Health: a Study Course."

7. John A. Widtsoe, "Schnaps," *Millennial Star,* 16 August 1928, 520.

8. John A. Widtsoe, "The Word of Wisdom in the Market Place," *Millennial Star,* 19 January 1928, 40–41.

9. John A. Widtsoe, "Is My Body My Own?" *Millennial Star,* 31 August 1933, 568–69.

10. John A. Widtsoe, "Word of Wisdom Lessons," *Millennial Star,* 14 February 1929, 104.

11. Leah D. Widtsoe, "Relief Society Course of Study for 1929," *Millennial Star,* January 1929, 35.

12. Relief Society Course of Study for 1929, 36.

13. Relief Society Course of Study for 1929, 36.

14. Leah D. Widtsoe, "Word of Wisdom Lessons (No. 1)," *Millennial Star,* January 1929, 37.

15. Leah D. Widtsoe, "Word of Wisdom Lessons (No. 2)," *Millennial Star,* February 1929, 42–43.

16. Leah D. Widtsoe, "Word of Wisdom Lesson (No. 2)," *Millennial Star,* February 1929, 42; Hyrum M. Smith and Janne M. Sjodahl, *Doctrine and Covenants Commentary* (Salt Lake City: Deseret Book, rev. ed., 1954) 571.

17. Leah D. Widtsoe, "Word of Wisdom Lessons (No. 3)," *Millennial Star,* March 1929, 102–3.

18. V. H. Mottram, "Food and the Family," in Leah D. Widtsoe, "Word of Wisdom Lessons (No. 5)," *Millennial Star,* May 1929, 215.

19. Leah D. Widtsoe, "Word of Wisdom Lessons (No. 6)," *Millennial Star,* June 1929, 329.

20. Leah D. Widtsoe, "Word of Wisdom Lessons (No. 8)," *Millennial Star,* August 1929, 457.

21. Leah D. Widtsoe, "Word of Wisdom Lessons (No. 9)," *Millennial Star,* September 1929, 521.

22. Leah D. Widtsoe, "Word of Wisdom Lessons (No. 10)," *Millennial Star,* October 1929, 587.

23. Leah D. Widtsoe, "Word of Wisdom Lessons (No. 11)," *Millennial Star,* November 1929, 666.

24. Leah D. Widtsoe, "Word of Wisdom Lessons (No. 11)," *Millennial Star,* November 1929, 666.

25. Leah D. Widtsoe, "Word of Wisdom Lessons (No. 12)," *Millennial Star,* December 1929, 741–42.

26. Leah D. Widtsoe, "Word of Wisdom Lessons (No. 12)," *Millennial Star,* December 1929, 745.

27. Widtsoe to First Presidency, 19 February 1930, John A. Widtsoe Collection, LDS Church Archives.

28. The other two sections of the manual were "Theology," prepared by Weston N. Nordgren, and "Literary," prepared by Alvin G. Pack (John A. Widtsoe, "Relief

Society Course of Study," *Millennial Star,* 13 March 1930, 168).

29. Leah D. Widtsoe, "Relief Society, The Lessons for 1930," *Millennial Star,* January 1930, 7.

30. Leah D. Widtsoe, "Word of Wisdom Lessons (No. 11)," *Millennial Star,* 17 October 1929, 665.

31. "No Vitamins in Tea," *Deseret News,* 13 August 1929, in "Word of Wisdom Lessons (No. 11)," *Millennial Star,* 10 October 1929, 663.

32. John A. Widtsoe, "Water, Whisky, Wealth, Health," *Millennial Star,* 5 September 1929, 568.

33. John A. Widtsoe, "History and the Word of Wisdom," *Millennial Star,* 3 November 1932, 712.

34. Arthur Gaeth, "Experiences on Tour With Lecture Include Contact With Police," *Deseret News,* 8 February 1936, 8.

35. John A. Widtsoe "The First Word of Wisdom Exhibit," *Improvement Era,* November 1930, 14.

36. John A. Widtsoe, "The First Word of Wisdom Exhibit," *Improvement Era,* November 1930, 14.

37. John A. Widtsoe, "The First Word of Wisdom Exhibit," *Improvement Era,* November 1930, 14.

38. John A. Widtsoe, "Temperance and man's Free Agency," *Millennial* Star, 22 February 1934, 117.

39. John A. Widtsoe, "Close of the Word of Wisdom Exhibition," *Millennial Star,* 6 November 1930, 777.

40. Widtsoe to F. W. Smith, 14 January 1931, John A. Widtsoe Collection, LDS Church Archives.

CHAPTER 31

1. Widtsoe to First Presidency, 5 May 1929, John A. Widtsoe Collection, LDS Church Archives.

2. Widtsoe, *Sunlit Land,* 190–91.

3. "Now Comes Call to Young Missionary to Labor in Another Field," part of a series entitled "A Missionary's Odyssey," *Deseret News,* Saturday, 15 February 1936, 8.

4. "Now Comes Call To Young Missionary," 8.

5. Arthur Gaeth, "A Missionary's Odyssey," *Deseret News,* 14 December 1935.

6. Arthur Gaeth, "A Missionary's Odyssey," *Deseret News,* 25 January 1936.

7. Arthur Gaeth, "A Missionary's Odyssey," *Deseret News,* 8 February 1936.

8. Spencer L. Taggert, "The First Czecho-Slovak Temple Excursion," *Utah Genealogical Magazine* 26 (1935), 183. The phrase was taken from a statement from Widtsoe in the Czechoslovakian Mission History, 20 December 1931.

9. Arthur Gaeth, "A Missionary's Odyssey," *Deseret News,* 23 February 1936.

10. Arthur Gaeth, "A Missionary's Odyssey," *Deseret News,* 23 February 1936.

11. Arthur Gaeth, Oral History, interview by Ronald G. Watt. Denver Colorado, 1976. Typescript. The James Moyle Oral History Program, LDS Church Archives.

12. Widtsoe Journal, 22–24 July 1929.

13. Widtsoe to Joseph Quinney, Jr, 5 August 1929, John A. Widtsoe Collection, LDS Church Archives.

14. Arthur Gaeth, "A Missionary's Odyssey," *Deseret News,* 7 March 1936.

15. Minutes of the Dedicatory Services of the Czechoslovak Mission, 24 July 1929, John A. Widtsoe Collection, LDS Church Archives.

16. Arthur Gaeth, "What a Day to Open a Mission! But the Sun Broke Through the Clouds," *Deseret News,* 7 March 1936.

17. Arthur Gaeth, "What a Day to Open a Mission! But the Sun Broke

Through the Clouds," *Deseret News,* 7 March 1936.

18. Arthur Gaeth, "What a Day to Open a Mission! But the Sun Broke Through the Clouds," *Deseret News,* 7 March 1936.

19. John A. Widtsoe, "Opening the Gospel Doors to the Slavs," *Improvement Era,* December 1929, 117–19.

20. Widtsoe, "Opening the Gospel Doors to the Slavs," 117–19.

21. Taggert, "The First Czecho-Slovak Temple Excursion," 184.

22. Widtsoe to First Presidency, 30 July 1929, John A. Widtsoe Collection, LDS Church Archives.

23. Anthony W. Ivins to Widtsoe, 17 February 1930, John A. Widtsoe Collection, LDS Church Archives.

24. Arthur Gaeth, "A Missionary's Odyssey," *Deseret News,* 14 March 1936.

25. One of these is in a letter addressed to Dr. Vaughn N. Pond of Twin Falls, Idaho, dated 30 March 1965. The account quoted in the letter is credited to T. R. Holt, former president of the Lewiston Idaho Stake. "Prophecy of Elder John A. Widtsoe Prague Czecho Slovakia, August 1932." The critical excerpt is: "Communism is the work of the Devil. The Lord is using it to break down the hold of the Catholic and Russian Orthodox churches over the minds of men. When Communism has completed its task of breaking this hold, it will pass out of existence almost over night. And then the Church will send missionaries by the hundreds into the Slavic lands of Europe, including the mother land of Russia." The second account was given as part of a Gospel Doctrine Sunday School lesson by Martin C. Ririe of the Dixie Downs 4th Ward on 4 February 1990. The quote is taken from his missionary journal dated 10 July 1932. "Communism is

the work of the Devil, from his evil empire. The Lord is using it to break down the hold of the Catholic and Russian Orthodox Churches' teachings over the minds of men. When Communism has completed its task of breaking this hold, it will pass out of existence almost overnight. And then the Church of Jesus Christ of Latter-day Saints will send missionaries by the hundreds into the Slavic Lands of Europe, including the Motherland of Russia." Copies are in the possession of the author.

26. Conference Report, April 1931, 108.

27. Conference Report, April 1931, 108.

28. Conference Report, April 1931, 108.

29. Gaeth Oral History, 3.

30. Gaeth Oral History, 4.

31. Widtsoe Journal, 23 March 1931.

32. Widtsoe, *Sunlit Land,* 191.

33. Arthur Gaeth, "In Central Europe's Lonely Democracy," *Improvement Era,* January 1937, 14.

34. Conference Report, April 1940, 51–52.

CHAPTER 32

1. European Mission Presidents Conference Minutes, 27 August 1928, John A. Widtsoe Collection, LDS Church Archives.

2. European Mission Presidents Conference Minutes, 27 August 1928.

3. Program Suggestions for the European Mission Presidents Conference for 1929, John A. Widtsoe Collection, LDS Church Archives.

4. Widtsoe to First Presidency, 16 October 1929, John A. Widtsoe Collection, LDS Church Archives.

5. Office of the First Presidency, Salt Lake City, Utah, October 18, 1929, to Presidents of the European

Missions, *Messages of the First Presidency,* 5:268–69.

6. Widtsoe to First Presidency, 19 February 1930, John A. Widtsoe Collection, LDS Church Archives.

7. Minutes of the Conference of the Presidents of the European Missions, July 5–15 1932, 11, John A. Widtsoe Collection, LDS Church Archives.

8. Clifton Kerr, "My most influential teacher," *Church News,* 12 July 1980, 2.

9. Minutes from the Conference of the Presidents of the European Missions, June 18–28 1930, John A. Widtsoe Collection, LDS Church Archives.

10. Minutes from the Conference of the Presidents of the European Missions, June 18–28 1930, 26.

11. Kerr, "My most influential teacher," 2.

12. Arnold D. White, Oral interview by Wayne A. Jacobson, The James Moyle Oral History Program, LDS Church Archives, 4, 65–66.

13. Widtsoe to First Presidency, 12 January 1932, John A. Widtsoe Collection, LDS Church Archives.

14. "Comparative Report of Missionary Activities of the European Mission in May, 1933," Widtsoe Collection, Utah State Historical Society.

15. Widtsoe to First Presidency, "Report of the European Mission President for 1932," John A. Widtsoe Collection, LDS Church Archives.

16. Widtsoe to Joseph H. Merrill, 1933.

17. John A. Widtsoe, *The Successful Missionary: Letters to Elders in the Field,* European Mission, 295 Edge Lane, Liverpool, England, 1932, 83 pages.

18. Arnold D. White, Oral interview, 3.

19. Widtsoe, *The Successful Missionary,* 10.

20. Widtsoe, *The Successful Missionary,* 12.

21. Widtsoe, *The Successful Missionary,* 16.

22. Widtsoe, *The Successful Missionary,* 17.

23. Widtsoe, *The Successful Missionary,* 51.

24. Widtsoe to Susa Young Gates, Susa Young Gates Collection, 2 March 1928, Utah State Historical Society.

25. "Oral Interview With David M. Kennedy," 66, LDS Church Archives.

26. George Romney, "My Most Influential Teacher, *Church News,* 1 October 1977, 2.

27. Widtsoe to Robert H. Summers, 15 August 1933, John A. Widtsoe Collection, LDS Church Archives.

28. Widtsoe to Elsa Vera Edmond, 15 August 1933, John A. Widtsoe Collection, LDS Church Archives.

29. Oral interview With David M. Kennedy, 67.

30. Arnold D. White, Oral interview, 3.

31. Arnold D. White, Oral interview, 67–68.

32. Sam Therman to Widtsoe, 21 January 1930, John A. Widtsoe Collection, LDS Church Archives.

33. James E. Talmage to Widtsoe, 24 August 1928, John A. Widtsoe Collection, LDS Church Archives.

34. Widtsoe to the young men of the University Ward Missionary Class, c/o Lyman Pettit, 19 November 1930, John A. Widtsoe Collection, LDS Church Archives.

35. Evans, *Richard L. Evans,* 35.

36. Richard L. Evans to Leah D. Widtsoe, 7 January 1931, Widtsoe Family Collection, 4, 11, Utah State Historical Society.

37. Evans, *Richard L. Evans,* 36.

38. Oral interview With David M. Kennedy, 67–70.

39. George Romney, "My Most Influential Teacher," 2.

CHAPTER 33

1. Arnold D. White, Oral interview by Wayne A. Jacobson, The James

Moyle Oral History Program, LDS Church Archives, 2–3.

2. Minutes of Mission Presidents' Conference, 27 August 1928, John A. Widtsoe Collection, LDS Church Archives.

3. Minutes of Mission Presidents' Conference, 27 August 1928.

4. Widtsoe to Susa Young Gates, 3 October 1929, Susa Young Gates Collection, Utah State Historical Society.

5. Widtsoe to R. Stoof, 3 August 1929, John A. Widtsoe Collection, LDS Church Archives.

6. Widtsoe to First Presidency, 2 September 1929, John A. Widtsoe Collection, LDS Church Archives.

7. Widtsoe, *Sunlit Land,* 193.

8. Minutes of Mission Presidents' Conference, 27 August 1928.

9. White, Oral Interview, 4.

10. Widtsoe, *Sunlit Land,* 195.

11. Widtsoe to Heber J. Grant, 13 October 1930, John A. Widtsoe Collection, LDS Church Archives.

12. White, Oral Interview, 65.

13. Widtsoe, *Sunlit Land,* 196–97.

14. Widtsoe, *Sunlit Land,* 192.

15. White, Oral Interview, 65.

16. Widtsoe to First Presidency, 19 February 1930, John A. Widtsoe Collection, LDS Church Archives.

17. Widtsoe, *Sunlit Land,* 192–93.

18. Widtsoe to First Presidency, "1932," John A. Widtsoe Collection, LDS Church Archives.

19. Conference Report, April 1932, 52.

20. Conference Report, October 1933, 78.

21. Conference Report, October 1934, 61.

22. Conference Report, October 1934, 76.

23. William A. Dawson to Widtsoe, 25 November 1929; poem by Arvilla Smith; John A. Widtsoe Collection, LDS Church Archives.

24. Widtsoe to First Presidency, 29 August 1931, John A. Widtsoe Collection, LDS Church Archives.

25. Widtsoe to Heber J. Grant, 3 July 1930, John A. Widtsoe Collection, LDS Church Archives.

26. Widtsoe, *Man and the Dragon.*

27. Widtsoe to First Presidency, 4 September 1930, LDS Church Archives.

28. Widtsoe, *Sunlit Land,* 194.

29. Widtsoe to G. N. Holtenstrom, Fred Tadje, Arthur Gaeth, and Golden L. Woolf, 6 January 1931, John A. Widtsoe Collection, LDS Church Archives.

30. Francis W. Kirkham to Widtsoe, undated, John A. Widtsoe Collection, LDS Church Archives.

31. Weston Nordgren to Widtsoe, 19 December 1932, John A. Widtsoe Collection, LDS Church Archives.

32. Widtsoe, *Sunlit Land,* 194–95.

33. Widtsoe to Susa Young Gates, 2 October 1930, Susa Young Gates Collection, Utah State Historical Society.

34. John A. Widtsoe, *Success on Irrigation Projects.*

35. Franklin S. Harris to Widtsoe, 4 November 1927, Franklin S. Harris Papers, BYU Special Collections.

36. Widtsoe to Heber J. Grant, 26 October 1928, John A. Widtsoe Collection, LDS Church Archives.

37. Widtsoe to First Presidency, 2 February 1929, John A. Widtsoe Collection, LDS Church Archives.

38. Susa Young Gates to Widtsoe, 7 January 1928, Susa Young Gates Collection, Utah State Historical Society.

39. Widtsoe to T. Albert Hooper, 10 February 1930, John A. Widtsoe Collection, LDS Church Archives.

40. Lorenzo W. Anderson to Widtsoe, 22 November 1930.

41. T. Albert Hooper to Widtsoe, 31 May 1932, John A. Widtsoe Collection, LDS Church Archives.

42. Heber J. Grant to Widtsoe, 17 April 1929, John A. Widtsoe Collection, LDS Church Archives.

43. Heber J. Grant to Widtsoe, 22

December 1931, John A. Widtsoe Collection, LDS Church Archives.

44. Heber J. Grant to Widtsoe, 28 February 1932, John A. Widtsoe Collection, LDS Church Archives.

45. Heber J. Grant to Widtsoe, 17 May 1933, John A. Widtsoe Collection, LDS Church Archives.

46. Heber J. Gates to Widtsoe, 20 September 1930, Susa Young Gates Collection, Utah State Historical Society.

47. White, Oral Interview, 4.

48. See John A. Widtsoe, "European Program for Genealogical Study, Research and Exchange," *Utah Genealogical and Historical Magazine*, vol. 21, January 1930, 33–35, and John A. Widtsoe, "Genealogical Activities in Europe," *Utah Genealogical and Historical Magazine*, vol. 22, July 1931, 96–106.

49. See Widtsoe to George Albert Smith, 21 April 1932, and two letters dated 25 April 1932, John A. Widtsoe Collection, LDS Church Archives.

50. Widtsoe to Max Zimmer, 26 August 1931, John A. Widtsoe Collection, LDS Church Archives.

CHAPTER 34

1. Widtsoe to Heber J. Grant, 3 July 1930, John A. Widtsoe Collection, LDS Church Archives.

2. Widtsoe to Joseph Fielding Smith, 28 August 1930, John A. Widtsoe Collection, LDS Church Archives.

3. Widtsoe Journal, 24 October 1930.

4. Widtsoe to First Presidency, 11 November 1930, John A. Widtsoe Collection, LDS Church Archives.

5. Widtsoe to Melvin J. Ballard, 5 December 1930, John A. Widtsoe Collection, LDS Church Archives.

6. Widtsoe to Heber J. Grant, 3 July 1930, John A. Widtsoe Collection, LDS Church Archives.

7. Widtsoe to First Presidency, 4 September 1930, John A. Widtsoe Collection, LDS Church Archives.

8. Widtsoe to George Thomas, 21 November 1930, John A. Widtsoe Collection, LDS Church Archives.

9. Susa Young Gates to Widtsoe, 20 September 1930, Susa Young Gates Collection, Utah State Historical Society.

10. Widtsoe, *Sunlit Land*, 198.

11. Widtsoe to Susa Young Gates, 2 February 1931, Susa Young Gates Collection, Utah State Historical Society.

12. Conference Report, April 1931, 5–14. This was an official statement of the president of the Church to the Church members and to the detractors of the Church on the subject of plural marriages. It should be noted that President Grant states that the statement he read to the conference had been "unanimously approved" by the First Presidency, the Council of the Twelve Apostles, the Presiding Patriarch, the First Council of Seventy, and the Presiding Bishopric before being read to the conference. Also, as indicated, the general conference approved it unanimously.

13. Conference Report, April 1931, 54.

14. "Salvation for the Dead," *Millennial Star*, 91, 19 September 1929, 600–601.

15. Widtsoe to Joseph Quinney, Jr., 20 May 1931, John A. Widtsoe Collection, LDS Church Archives.

16. Widtsoe to First Presidency, 12 January 1932, John A. Widtsoe Collection, LDS Church Archives.

17. Widtsoe to Joseph Quinney, Jr., 10 August 1931, John A. Widtsoe Collection, LDS Church Archives.

18. Susa Young Gates to Widtsoe, 29 August 1931, Susa Young Gates Collection, Utah State Historical Society.

19. Widtsoe to James E. Talmage, 10 March 1930.

20. Widtsoe to Susa Young Gates 23

October 1929, Susa Young Gates Collection, Utah State Historical Society.

21. Susa Young Gates to Widtsoe, 17 October 1928, Susa Young Gates Collection, Utah State Historical Society.

22. First Presidency to Council of the Twelve, First Council of the Seventy, and Presiding Bishopric, 5 April 1931, John A. Widtsoe Collection, LDS Church Archives.

23. Susa Young Gates to Widtsoe, 2 January 1931, Susa Young Gates Collection, Utah State Historical Society. "B. H. Roberts wrote a very biased letter to the Presidency concerning Joseph's sermon and article which was published in our Genealogical Magazine, taking issue with Joseph as he does with nearly everybody on earth. But I think the Presidency will not do very much about it. What a peculiar man B. H. is and how he needed an intelligent Latter-day Saint wife to knock off the corners of his peculiarities so that he could use all his brilliant faculties instead of only a part of them to build up righteousness in the earth."

24. Widtsoe Journal, 26 March 1931.

25. Widtsoe Journal, 7 April 1931.

26. Susa Young Gates to Widtsoe, 29 August 1931, Susa Collection, Utah State Historical Society.

27. James E. Talmage to Widtsoe, 27 August 1931, John A. Widtsoe Collection, LDS Church Archives.

28. James E. Talmage to Widtsoe, 27 August 1931, John A. Widtsoe Collection, LDS Church Archives.

29. Widtsoe to Rudger Clawson, 9 September 1931, John A. Widtsoe Collection, LDS Church Archives.

30. Widtsoe to Rudger Clawson, 9 September 1931, John A. Widtsoe Collection, LDS Church Archives.

31. Widtsoe to Joseph Fielding Smith, 15 September 1931, John A.

Widtsoe Collection, LDS Church Archives.

32. Susa Young Gates to Widtsoe, 10 October 1931, Susa Young Gates Collection, Utah State Historical Society.

33. Widtsoe to Susa Young Gates, 30 October 1931, Susa Young Gates Collection, Utah State Historical Society.

34. Susa Young Gates to Widtsoe, 17 November 1931, Susa Young Gates Collection, Utah State Historical Society.

35. James E. Talmage to Widtsoe, 18 November 1931 John A. Widtsoe Collection, LDS Church Archives.

36. Joseph Fielding Smith to Widtsoe, 12 November 1931, John A. Widtsoe Collection, LDS Church Archives.

CHAPTER 35

1. Mark B. Garff, "The Danish Mission," *Improvement Era,* May 1932, 401.

2. Widtsoe to Joseph Quinney, Jr., 10 August 1931.

3. Janne M. Sjodahl to Widtsoe, 4 November 1931, John A. Widtsoe Collection, LDS Church Archives.

4. Arnold D. White, Oral Interview by Wayne A. Jacobson, The James Moyle Oral History Program, LDS Church Archives, 66.

5. Widtsoe to First Presidency, 12 January 1932, John A. Widtsoe Collection, LDS Church Archives.

6. Widtsoe to Susa Young Gates, 30 October 1931, Susa Young Gates Collection, Utah State Historical Society.

7. Widtsoe to First Presidency, 9 October 1931, John A. Widtsoe Collection, LDS Church Archives.

8. Widtsoe to First Presidency, 12 January 1932, John A. Widtsoe Collection, LDS Church Archives.

9. Widtsoe, *Sunlit Land,* 190.

10. Widtsoe, *Sunlit Land,* 199.

11. Widtsoe to First Presidency, 19 March 1932, John A. Widtsoe Collection, LDS Church Archives.

12. White, Oral Interview, 1–2.

13. White, Oral Interview, 2.

14. Widtsoe to First Presidency, 2 July 1932, John A. Widtsoe Collection, LDS Church Archives.

15. Widtsoe to First Presidency, Report of the European Mission President for 1932, John A. Widtsoe Collection, LDS Church Archives.

16. Widtsoe to Mr. and Mrs. A. E. Bowen, 5 December 1932, John A. Widtsoe Collection, LDS Church Archives. He concluded his letter, "You must have had 'a hot time in the old town.' May the Lord over-rule the result to the good of the Church."

17. Widtsoe to First Presidency, Report of the European Mission President for 1932, John A. Widtsoe Collection, LDS Church Archives.

18. Widtsoe to First Presidency, Report of the European Mission President for 1932, John A. Widtsoe Collection, LDS Church Archives.

19. Widtsoe to A. E. Bowen, 5 December 1932, John A. Widtsoe Collection, LDS Church Archives.

CHAPTER 36

1. M. Cowey (Essex England) to Widtsoe, 8 January 1933, John A. Widtsoe Collection, LDS Church Archives.

2. Anthony W. Ivins to Widtsoe, 9 January 1933, John A. Widtsoe Collection, LDS Church Archives.

3. Widtsoe to Anthony W. Ivins, 25 February 1933, John A. Widtsoe Collection, LDS Church Archives.

4. Widtsoe to Anthony W. Ivins, 25 February 1933, John A. Widtsoe Collection, LDS Church Archives.

5. Cowan, *Church in the Twentieth Century,* 163.

6. Widtsoe to Samuel O. Bennion, 11 March 1933, John A. Widtsoe Collection, LDS Church Archives.

7. Widtsoe to Samuel O. Bennion, 11 March 1933, John A. Widtsoe Collection, LDS Church Archives.

8. Heber J. Grant to Leah D. Widtsoe, 13 October 1933, in Cowan, *Church in the Twentieth Century,* 164.

9. Widtsoe to Mr. and Mrs. Alvin G. Pack, 2 March 1933, John A. Widtsoe Collection, LDS Church Archives.

10. Widtsoe to George Thomas, 28 April 1933, John A. Widtsoe Collection, LDS Church Archives.

11. Widtsoe, *Sunlit Land,* 207.

12. Widtsoe Journal, 16 May 1933.

13. Widtsoe, *Sunlit Land,* 208.

14. Widtsoe Journal, 21 May 1933.

15. Widtsoe, *Sunlit Land,* 216.

16. Widtsoe Journal 24 May 1933.

17. S. D. Yoffe to Widtsoe, 12 October 1930, John A. Widtsoe Collection, LDS Church Archives.

18. S. D. Yoffe to Widtsoe, 12 October 1930, John A. Widtsoe Collection, LDS Church Archives.

19. Widtsoe to Editor of *Hasedah,* 27 January 1932, John A. Widtsoe Collection, LDS Church Archives.

20. Widtsoe, *Sunlit Land,* 211.

21. Widtsoe to First Presidency, 5 June 1933, John A. Widtsoe Collection, LDS Church Archives.

22. See Secretary of Widtsoe to John Anakin of Haifa, Palestine, 8 June 1932, John A. Widtsoe Collection, LDS Church Archives.

23. Gates to Dear Family and Best of Friends, 1933, Susa Young Gates Collection, Utah State Historical Society.

24. Howard M. Cullimore to Widtsoe, 27 May 1933, telegram number 1, John A. Widtsoe Collection, LDS Church Archives.

25. Howard M. Cullimore to Widtsoe, 27 May 1933, telegram number 2, John A. Widtsoe Collection, LDS Church Archives.

26. Widtsoe to Jacob F. Gates and

Family, 4 June 1933, Susa Young Gates Collection, Utah State Historical Society.

27. Widtsoe Journal, 30 May 1933.

28. Widtsoe to Dr. J. E. Volcani, 10 July 1933, John A. Widtsoe Collection, LDS Church Archives.

29. Widtsoe to Jacob F. Gates and Family, 4 June 1933, Susa Collection, Utah State Historical Society.

30. Widtsoe Journal, 11 June 1933.

31. Widtsoe Journal, 16 April 1931. (In Salt Lake City) "Booth monument Met w. D. O. McKay & J. E. Talmage abt. Monument for J. Wilford Booth. Visit from Sister J. Wilford Booth."

32. Widtsoe, *Sunlit Land,* 210.

33. Widtsoe, *Sunlit Land,* 210.

34. Widtsoe to Chaim Weizmann, 2 December 1933, John A. Widtsoe Collection, LDS Church Archives.

35. Heber J. Grant to Widtsoe, 17 May 1933, John A. Widtsoe Collection, LDS Church Archives.

36. Widtsoe to Heber J. Grant, 9 June 1933, John A. Widtsoe Collection, LDS Church Archives.

37. First Presidency to Widtsoe, 25 August 1933, John A. Widtsoe Collection, LDS Church Archives.

38. Conference Report, October 1933, 53.

39. Widtsoe to Anthony W. Ivins, 24 July 1933, John A. Widtsoe Collection, LDS Church Archives.

40. Widtsoe to R. M. Bryce Thomas, 2 October 1933, John A. Widtsoe Collection, LDS Church Archives.

41. Widtsoe to Don MacDalton, 5 September 1933, John A. Widtsoe Collection, LDS Church Archives.

42. Benjamin R. Birchall to the Widtsoes, 16 October 1933, John A. Widtsoe Collection, LDS Church Archives.

43. Hettie H. Harper to Widtsoe, 12 September 1933, John A. Widtsoe Collection, LDS Church Archives.

44. Widtsoe to Bishop James H. Wallis, 26 August 1933, John A. Widtsoe Collection, LDS Church.

45. Widtsoe to First Presidency, 31 August 1933, John A. Widtsoe Collection, LDS Church Archives.

46. Widtsoe Journal, 16 September 1933.

47. M. H. Knudson to Widtsoe, 5 October 1933, John A. Widtsoe Collection, LDS Church Archives.

48. Widtsoe to Joseph F. Merrill, 1933, John A. Widtsoe Collection, LDS Church Archives.

49. Widtsoe to Joseph F. Merrill, undated, John A. Widtsoe Collection, LDS Church Archives.

50. Widtsoe to Joseph F. Merrill, undated, John A. Widtsoe Collection, LDS Church Archives.

51. Widtsoe to Joseph F. Merrill, undated, John A. Widtsoe Collection, LDS Church Archives.

52. Widtsoe to Joseph F. Merrill, undated, John A. Widtsoe Collection, LDS Church Archives.

53. Joseph F. Merrill to First Presidency, 12 October 1933, John A. Widtsoe Collection, LDS Church Archives.

54. "As We Part—We Remember," *B.M.A.* [British Missionaries Association] *Harbinger,* vol. 16, 15 October 1933, WC, LDS Church Archives.

55. "The King's Image," *B.M.A.* [British Missionaries Association] *Harbinger,* vol. 16, 15 October 1933, WC, LDS Church Archives.

56. "The King's Image," *B.M.A.* [British Missionaries Association] *Harbinger,* vol. 16, 15 October 1933, WC, LDS Church Archives.

57. Widtsoe Journal, 14 October 1933.

58. Widtsoe Journal, 28 October 1933.

59. Widtsoe Journal, 28 October 1933.

60. Widtsoe Journal, 5 November 1933.

61. Widtsoe to Lloyd Garison, 11 April 1934, John A. Widtsoe Collection, LDS Church Archives.

62. Widtsoe to F. W. Smith, 5 February 1934, John A. Widtsoe Collection, LDS Church Archives.

63. Conference Report, April 1934, 113.

64. Conference Report, April 1934, 113.

65. Conference Report, April 1934, 113.

66. Conference Report, April 1934, 113.

67. Widtsoe, *Sunlit Land,* 203.

CHAPTER 37

1. *Improvement Era,* June 1922, 735.

2. *Improvement Era,* June 1922, 735.

3. Earl J. Glade, "Preaching the Gospel through the Radio," *Improvement Era,* January 1925, 243.

4. Glade, "Preaching the Gospel," 245.

5. Conference Report, October 1924, 11.

6. Conference Report, October 1927, 25.

7. Widtsoe, *Sunlit Land,* 202.

8. Widtsoe to Mr. and Mrs. A. E. Bowen, 13 March 1929, Susa Young Gates Collection, Utah State Historical Society.

9. Widtsoe to Mr. and Mrs. A. E. Bowen, 13 March 1929, Susa Young Gates Collection, Utah State Historical Society.

10. Conference Report, October 1930, 8.

11. Conference Report, April 1931, 57.

12. Conference Report, April 1934, 114.

13. Rudger Clawson to Widtsoe, 26 February 1934, John A. Widtsoe Collection, LDS Church Archives.

14. George S. Romney to Widtsoe, 5 April 1934, John A. Widtsoe Collection, LDS Church Archives.

15. Joseph Daynes to Widtsoe, 11 April 1934, John A. Widtsoe Collection, LDS Church Archives.

16. LeGrand Richards to Widtsoe, 13 April 1934, John A. Widtsoe Collection, LDS Church Archives.

17. Marden Broadbent to Widtsoe, 14 April 1934, John A. Widtsoe Collection, LDS Church Archives.

18. Report of the LDS Church Publicity Bureau, undated, John A. Widtsoe Collection, LDS Church Archives.

19. Glen F. Harding to Widtsoe, 16 August 1934, John A. Widtsoe Collection, LDS Church Archives.

20. See Ora F. Pate, "Suggested Material for a Book of Mormon Lecture," and Ora F. Pate, "Suggestions for Detailed Arrangement of Book of Mormon Film," John A. Widtsoe Collection, LDS Church Archives.

21. Minutes of the meeting of Mission Presidents with the Missionary Committee of the Council of the Twelve, 8 April 1935, John A. Widtsoe Collection, LDS Church Archives.

22. Conference Report, October 1948, 112–13.

23. Widtsoe to First Presidency, 29 January 1935, John A. Widtsoe Collection, LDS Church Archives.

24. LeGrand Richards to Widtsoe, 19 February 1935, John A. Widtsoe Collection, LDS Church Archives.

25. Widtsoe to Don B. Colton, 30 April 1934, John A. Widtsoe Collection, LDS Church Archives.

26. Widtsoe to Rulon S. Howells, 27 June 1934, John A. Widtsoe Collection, LDS Church Archives.

27. Widtsoe to Howard M. Cullimore, 17 July 1934, John A. Widtsoe Collection, LDS Church Archives.

28. Committee on Mission Publicity to Rudger Clawson and Members of the Council of the Twelve, 24 September 1934, John A. Widtsoe Collection, LDS Church Archives.

29. Widtsoe to LeGrand Richards, 29 August 1934, John A. Widtsoe Collection, LDS Church Archives.

30. Committee on Mission Publicity to Rudger Clawson and Members of the Council of the Twelve, 24 September 1934, John A. Widtsoe Collection, LDS Church Archives.

31. Widtsoe to David O. McKay, 19 September 1935, John A. Widtsoe Collection, LDS Church Archives.

32. Widtsoe to David A. Smith, 20 September 1935, John A. Widtsoe Collection, LDS Church Archives.

33. Cowan, *Church in the Twentieth Century*, 163.

34. Dew, *Go Forward with Faith*, 88.

35. In Elder Widtsoe's correspondence over the years that followed Hinckley's employment, there are many references to the work he was editing and producing. It is evident that Widtsoe thought highly of Hinckley's ability and his dedication to the work of the committee. The following are samples of many letters: Widtsoe to Bishop John Wells, 11 September 1935: "He has done a fine piece of work." Widtsoe to Elias S. Woodruff, 17 September 1936, complimentary reference to his work on a new "Elder's Guide." Widtsoe to Stephen L Richards, 27 October 1936: "Brother Hinckley's work has been well done. He should be congratulated upon his success in preparing the manuscript."

36. Widtsoe to Wilford A. Hinkson, 18 April 1944, John A. Widtsoe Collection, LDS Church Archives.

37. Conference Report, October 1946, 14.

38. Widtsoe to Steven L Richards, 16 October 1937, John A. Widtsoe Collection, LDS Church Archives.

39. Widtsoe to John Wells, 11 September 1935, John A. Widtsoe Collection, LDS Church Archives.

40. Cowan, *Church in the Twentieth Century*, 165.

41. Dew, *Go Forward with Faith*, 94.

42. John A. Widtsoe, "What Is Man?" *Deseret News*, 10 October 1936.

43. "Peace Keynotes 110th Semi-annual Conference," *Improvement Era*, November 1939, 670.

44. "Church of the Air," *Improvement Era*, April 1946, 194.

45. John A. Widtsoe, "Hunger in the Midst of Plenty," *Improvement Era*, November 1948, 693.

46. John A. Widtsoe, "Be of Good Courage," *Improvement Era*, January 1951, 20–21, 35.

47. Widtsoe to Eugene Watkins, 28 December 1943, John A. Widtsoe Collection, LDS Church Archives.

48. John A. Widtsoe, "An Understandable Religion—Can the Unseen World Be Known?" *Deseret News*, 8 January 1944.

49. Widtsoe to N. B. Lundwall, 14 March 1944, John A. Widtsoe Collection, LDS Church Archives.

50. Widtsoe to C. V. Hansen, 1 June 1944, John A. Widtsoe Collection, LDS Church Archives.

51. John A. Widtsoe, *An Understandable Religion* (Independence, Missouri: Zion's Printing and Publishing Company, 1944).

52. Gordon B. Hinckley to Widtsoe, 29 May 1942, John A. Widtsoe Collection, LDS Church Archives.

53. Widtsoe to Steven L Richards, chairman of the Church Radio and Publicity Committee, 4 February 1937, John A. Widtsoe Collection, LDS Church Archives.

54. Widtsoe to Steven L Richards, 27 July 1939, John A. Widtsoe Collection, LDS Church Archives.

55. "Expo Will Hear Great Choir Sing," *San Diego Union*, 9 November 1936; "Mormon Day at the Fair," unknown newspaper, John A. Widtsoe Collection, LDS Church Archives.

56. Widtsoe to Steven L Richards, 26 March 1935, John A. Widtsoe Collection, LDS Church Archives.

57. Widtsoe to Elias Woodruff, 17 September 1936, John A. Widtsoe Collection, LDS Church Archives.

58. Dew, *Go Forward with Faith*, 102.

59. A. H. Reiser to Widtsoe, 25 May 1936, John A. Widtsoe Collection, LDS Church Archives.

60. Widtsoe to Steven L Richards and Members of Church Radio, Publicity and Mission Literature Committee, 1 April 1937, John A.

Widtsoe Collection, LDS Church Archives.

61. Widtsoe to Steven L Richards, 10 May 1937, John A. Widtsoe Collection, LDS Church Archives.

CHAPTER 38

1. Radio address, "Developing World Neighbors through the Churches," von KleinSmid Papers, USC Archives.

2. Widtsoe, *Sunlit Land,* 173.

3. University of Southern California Bulletin, School of Religion, 1935–1936, vol. 30, no. 15, 25.

4. The *Daily Bruin* (UCLA student newspaper) of 13 January 1932 credited Richards with being a legal advisor of Secretary Knox and the man who drew up the 16th and 17th amendments of the U.S. Constitution.

5. Preston D. Richards to Widtsoe, 31 July 1935, Preston D. Richards Papers, BYU Special Collections.

6. Preston D. Richards to Widtsoe, 19 August 1935, Preston D. Richards Papers, BYU Special Collections.

7. Preston D. Richards to Widtsoe, 12 September 1935, telegram, Preston D. Richards Papers, BYU Special Collections.

8. Widtsoe to Preston D. Richards, 12 September 1935, telegram, Preston D. Richards Papers, BYU Special Collections.

9. Oral interview with Paul H. Dunn, in Rimington, *Vistas on Visions,* 70. "While pursuing my doctoral studies beneath the arches of the von KleinSmid Center I became aware of the high esteem in which he is held. Those arches are symbolic of his influence over the university through his forty-three years as President and Chancellor. It was especially gratifying to learn of his interest in the work Widtsoe began and therefore severely disappointing to discover that his papers with the correspondence conveying that interest were destroyed."

10. Widtsoe to Preston D. Richards, 12 September 1935, Preston D. Richards Papers, BYU Special Collections.

11. Widtsoe to Preston D. Richards, 12 September 1935, Preston D. Richards Papers, BYU Special Collections.

12. "Dr. Widtsoe Named Church Teacher at U.S.C.," *Deseret News,* 14 September 1935.

13. "Dr. Widtsoe Named Church Teacher at U.S.C.," *Deseret News,* 14 September 1935.

14. Widtsoe to Elias S. Woodruff, 19 September 1935, John A. Widtsoe Collection, LDS Church Archives.

15. Widtsoe, *Sunlit Land,* 173.

16. Widtsoe to Leo J. Muir and David H. Cannon, 12 September 1935, Richards Papers, BYU Special Collections.

17. Widtsoe to First Presidency, 28 October 1935, John A. Widtsoe Collection, LDS Church Archives.

18. Widtsoe to First Presidency, 28 September 1935, John A. Widtsoe Collection, LDS Church Archives.

19. Widtsoe to First Presidency, 28 September 1935.

20. First Presidency to Widtsoe, 3 October 1935, telegram, John A. Widtsoe Collection, LDS Church Archives.

21. Widtsoe to First Presidency, 28 October 1935, John A. Widtsoe Collection, LDS Church Archives.

22. Heber J. Grant and David O. McKay to Widtsoe, 8 November 1935, John A. Widtsoe Collection, LDS Church Archives.

23. "Success Crowns Church Religion Class at USC," *Deseret News,* 26 December 1935.

24. John A. Widtsoe, "A Notable Experiment in Religious Education," *Improvement Era,* January 1936, 8–11.

25. Widtsoe, *Program of the Church, 3,* 11–13.
26. Widtsoe, *Program of the Church, 28.*
27. Widtsoe, *The Message of the Doctrine and Covenants,* vi.
28. "Religious Courses Get Fine Support," *Deseret News,* 4 April 1936.
29. Widtsoe to First Presidency, 16 June 1936, John A. Widtsoe Collection, LDS Church Archives.
30. Widtsoe to First Presidency, 16 June 1936, John A. Widtsoe Collection, LDS Church Archives.
31. Widtsoe to First Presidency, 16 June 1936, John A. Widtsoe Collection, LDS Church Archives.
32. Widtsoe to Heber J. Grant, 12 March 1936, John A. Widtsoe Collection, LDS Church Archives.
33. Miscellaneous documents, John A. Widtsoe Collection, LDS Church Archives.
34. Widtsoe to First Presidency, 28 October 1935, John A. Widtsoe Collection, LDS Church Archives.
35. Widtsoe to First Presidency, 28 October 1935, John A. Widtsoe Collection, LDS Church Archives.
36. Oral interview with Paul H. Dunn in Rimington, *Vistas on Visions,* 72.
37. G. Byron Done to Widtsoe, 2 April 1937, John A. Widtsoe Collection, LDS Church Archives.
38. G. Byron Done to Franklin West, 14 November 1941, in Rimington, *Vistas on Visions,* 3.
39. Leonard J. Arrington, "The Founding of the L.D.S. Institutes of Religion," *Dialogue: A Journal of Mormon Thought* 2/2, 1967. "It is a paradox that men will gladly devote time every day for many years to learn a science or art; yet will expect to win a knowledge of the gospel which comprehends all sciences and arts, through perfunctory glances at books or occasional listening to sermons. The gospel should be studied more intensively than any school or

college subject. They who pass opinion on the gospel without having given it intimate and careful study are not lovers of the truth, and their opinions are worthless." Widtsoe, *Evidences and Reconciliations,* 16–17.
40. Widtsoe, *Sunlit Land,* 24–25.

CHAPTER 39
1. Widtsoe, *Sunlit Land,* 33.
2. Widtsoe, *Sunlit Land,* 78–79.
3. An Announcement flyer, John A. Widtsoe Collection, LDS Church Archives.
4. Pamphlet, John A. Widtsoe Collection, LDS Church Archives.
5. "Church Official Named to Editorship with Pres. Grant," *Deseret News* 23 April 1935.
6. "New Officials of The Improvement Era," *Improvement Era,* June 1935, 367.
7. "New Officials of The Improvement Era," *Improvement Era,* June 1935, 367.
8. Widtsoe, "A Forward Look with The Improvement Era," An address given in the 1935 M.I.A. June Conference, in a pamphlet entitled *The Era Campaign 1935–36,* John A. Widtsoe Collection, LDS Church Archives.
9. Widtsoe, "A Forward Look."
10. *Improvement Era,* September 1935, inside front cover.
11. *Improvement Era,* September 1935, inside front cover.
12. *Improvement Era,* September 1935, inside front cover.
13. Widtsoe, *Sunlit Land,* 174.
14. Minutes of a meeting held 18 September 1935, John A. Widtsoe Collection, LDS Church Archives.
15. Widtsoe to Superintendent Elbert R. Curtis and President Bertha S. Reeder, 27 June 1949, John A. Widtsoe Collection, LDS Church Archives.
16. Richard L. Evans to Widtsoe on his

70th birthday, 31 January 1942, John A. Widtsoe Collection, LDS Church Archives.

17. Widtsoe to Richard L. Evans, 2 November 1935, John A. Widtsoe Collection, LDS Church Archives.
18. Richard L. Evans to Widtsoe, 10 November 1935, John A. Widtsoe Collection, LDS Church Archives 4.
19. A. E. Bowen to Widtsoe, 15 November 1935, telegram, John A. Widtsoe Collection, LDS Church Archives.
20. Richard L. Evans to Widtsoe, 5 December 1935, John A. Widtsoe Collection, LDS Church Archives.
21. Conference Report, October 1938, 91.
22. Mark E. Petersen, "Builders of Faith," *Improvement Era,* November 1948, 698, 758.
23. Mark E. Petersen, "Builders of Faith," *Improvement Era,* November 1948, 758.
24. John A. Widtsoe, "The Era Grows," *Improvement Era,* January 1950, 22.
25. Widtsoe to E. J. Sorenson, 20 August 1943, John A. Widtsoe Collection, LDS Church Archives.
26. Widtsoe to Joseph J. Cannon, 4 November 1935, John A. Widtsoe Collection, LDS Church Archives.
27. Widtsoe to Leo J. Muir, 4 November 1935, John A. Widtsoe Collection, LDS Church Archives.
28. Widtsoe to Marion E. Taylor, 18 November 1935, John A. Widtsoe Collection, LDS Church Archives.
29. Widtsoe to Franklin S. Harris, 30 October 1935, John A. Widtsoe Collection, LDS Church Archives.
30. Alex Nibley to Widtsoe, 15 July 1936, John A. Widtsoe Collection, LDS Church Archives.
31. Widtsoe to Hugh Nibley, 28 July 1936, John A. Widtsoe Collection, LDS Church Archives.
32. Oral interview with Hugh Nibley by Alan K. Parrish, 21 February 1997.

33. Oral interview with Hugh Nibley by Alan K. Parrish, 21 February 1997.
34. Oral interview with Hugh Nibley by Alan K. Parrish, 21 February 1997.
35. Widtsoe to H. R. Merrill, 30 November 1935, John A. Widtsoe Collection, LDS Church Archives.
36. See box 114, folders 9 and 10, John A. Widtsoe Collection, LDS Church Archives.
37. Widtsoe to Silcia G. Reeves, 31 July 1942, John A. Widtsoe Collection, LDS Church Archives.
38. Widtsoe to Neils P. Peterson, 25 May 1943, John A. Widtsoe Collection, LDS Church Archives.
39. Widtsoe to Neils P. Peterson, 1 June 1943, John A. Widtsoe Collection, LDS Church Archives.
40. *Improvement Era,* October 1943, 620.
41. See, for example, Widtsoe to Richard L. Evans, 26 March 1936, John A. Widtsoe Collection, LDS Church Archives.
42. Widtsoe to Ruth May Fox and counselors of the YWMIA, 29 March 1935, John A. Widtsoe Collection, LDS Church Archives.
43. Widtsoe to Richard L. Evans, 4 March 1936, John A. Widtsoe Collection, LDS Church Archives.
44. General *Era* Committee Meeting Minutes, 24 November 1936, WC, LDS Church Archives.
45. Widtsoe to E. L. Worth, 27 July 1945, John A. Widtsoe Collection, LDS Church Archives.
46. Richard L. Evans to Widtsoe, 5 August 1942, John A. Widtsoe Collection, LDS Church Archives.
47. H. R. Merrill to Widtsoe, 27 November 1935, John A. Widtsoe Collection, LDS Church Archives.
48. "The Improvement Era," *Deseret News,* 1 April 1937.
49. "The Improvement Era," *Deseret News,* 1 April 1937.

CHAPTER 40

1. Widtsoe to Edwin F. Reed, 16 February 1945, John A. Widtsoe Collection, LDS Church Archives.
2. Widtsoe to Perry Cyress Martineau, 19 June 1937, John A. Widtsoe Collection, LDS Church Archives.
3. Reed G. Probst to Widtsoe, 4 January 1942, John A. Widtsoe Collection, LDS Church Archives.
4. Marba Josephson to Widtsoe, 2 June 1936, John A. Widtsoe Collection, LDS Church Archives.
5. Heber J. Grant to Widtsoe, 18 April 1938, John A. Widtsoe Collection, LDS Church Archives.
6. Fawn M. Brodie, *No Man Knows My History* (New York: Knopf, 1945).
7. John A. Widtsoe, "No Man Knows My History," *Improvement Era,* March 1946, 132.
8. John A. Widtsoe, "No Man Knows My History," *Improvement Era,* March 1946, 133.
9. John A. Widtsoe, "No Man Knows My History," *Improvement Era,* March 1946, 132.
10. John A. Widtsoe, "Is the 'History of Joseph Smith' Trustworthy?" *Improvement Era,* March 1946, 161.
11. John A. Widtsoe, "Is the 'History of Joseph Smith' Trustworthy?" *Improvement Era,* March 1946, 190.
12. John A. Widtsoe, book review of Wheeler McMillen, *New Riches from the Soil: The Progress of Chemurgy* (New York: Van Nostrand, 1946), *Improvement Era,* January 1947, 40.
13. Widtsoe, *New Riches from the Soil,* 40.
14. *Improvement Era,* November 1947, 727.
15. Widtsoe to Brother Judd, 11 March 1935, John A. Widtsoe Collection, LDS Church Archives.
16. Widtsoe, "We Believe," *Improvement Era,* April 1935, 237.
17. Widtsoe, "We Believe," *Improvement Era,* April 1935, 237.
18. Widtsoe, "We Believe," *Improvement Era,* April 1935, 264.
19. *Articles of Faith* (Salt Lake City: Young Men's and Young Women's Mutual Improvement Associations of the Church of Jesus Christ of Latter-day Saints, 1949), foreword.
20. Widtsoe, *Sunlit Land,* 51.
21. Widtsoe, *Evidences and Reconciliations,* 1:v.
22. Widtsoe, *Handbook of the Restoration,* 209.
23. Widtsoe to C. Frank Steele, 2 June 1939, John A. Widtsoe Collection, LDS Church Archives.
24. Widtsoe to Mrs. Marion Cannon Bennion, 10 October 1939, John A. Widtsoe Collection, LDS Church Archives.
25. Personal interview with Hugh Nibley, 18, 21.
26. W. S. Stout to Widtsoe, September 1939, John A. Widtsoe Collection, LDS Church Archives.
27. Widtsoe to W. S. Stout, 8 September 1939, John A. Widtsoe Collection, LDS Church Archives.
28. Widtsoe, *Current Gospel Questions.*
29. Richard L. Evans, "Foreword to the First Edition," *Evidences and Reconciliations,* vii–viii.
30. Evans, *Richard L. Evans,* 36.
31. Widtsoe, *Evidences and Reconciliations,* 2d ed., 3, preface.
32. Widtsoe, *Evidences and Reconciliations,* combined single volume ed., publishers preface.
33. Earl J. Glade to Widtsoe, 26 January 1939, WC, LDS Church Archives.
34. John A. Widtsoe, "How the Desert Was Tamed," *Improvement Era,* January 1947, 14.
35. John A. Widtsoe, "How the Desert Was Tamed," *Improvement Era,* January 1947, 14.
36. John A. Widtsoe, *Your Questions Answered* (Salt Lake City: General Boards of the Mutual Improvement Associations of The Church of Jesus Christ of Latter-day Saints, 1943).
37. Louise Y. Robison, Kate M. Baker,

and Julia A. F. Lund to Widtsoe, 19
October 1937, John A. Widtsoe
Collection, LDS Church Archives.

38. Widtsoe to Elias S. Woodruff,
president of the Central States
Mission, 16 December 1937, John
A. Widtsoe Collection, LDS
Church Archives.

39. *Improvement Era*, January 1953, 59.

40. *Improvement Era*, January 1953, 20.

41. Hinckley, *Hours with Our Leaders*,
75–76.

CHAPTER *41*

1. Leah Eudora Dunford, "A Visit to
the Pratt Institute," *Young Woman's
Journal*, March 1897, 249–59.

2. Leah Eudora Dunford, "A Visit to
the Pratt Institute," *Young Woman's
Journal*, March 1897, 259.

3. E. Neige Todhunter, "Chronology of
Some Events in the Development
and Application of the Science of
Nutrition," *Nutrition Reviews*,
Volume 34, Number 12 (December
1976), 353–65.

4. Widtsoe, *Sunlit Land*, 220–21.

5. Widtsoe, *Sunlit Land*, 226.

6. Mary Jane Woodger, "Leah Widtsoe:
Pioneer in Healthy Lifestyle Family
Education," *Journal of Family and
Consumer Sciences*, 92:51.

7. Woodger, "Leah Widtsoe: Pioneer,"
53.

8. Widtsoe, *Sunlit Land*, 115.

9. Widtsoe, *Sunlit Land*, 221.

10. "When I came to the University of
Utah the same poor preparation for
woman's work was observed. Shortly
before I left, one of the large
buildings was remodeled for a
woman's building. For some time
only a part of the building was used
as intended—it was planned to use
the entire building or build a new
one as need might arise. It is now so
used. Modern classrooms and
laboratories should be available for
the special instruction that every

girl should have." Widtsoe, *Sunlit
Land*, 224.

11. Oral History Interview with Leah
Eudora Widtsoe, 11 February 1965,
1, 4, 9, Leah D. Widtsoe Papers,
BYU Special Collections.

12. Oral History Interview with Leah
Eudora Widtsoe, 11 February 1965,
6, Leah D. Widtsoe Papers, BYU
Special Collections.

13. Oral History Interview with Leah
Eudora Widtsoe, 11 February 1965,
7, Leah D. Widtsoe Papers, BYU
Special Collections.

14. Leah D. Widtsoe, "Religion and
Health," *Millennial Star*, April 1930,
283.

15. John A. Widtsoe, "The Chemistry of
Digestion," *Improvement Era*, June
1901, 564.

16. John A. Widtsoe, "The Food of
Man," *Improvement Era*, August
1901, 769–73.

17. John A. Widtsoe, "The Word of
Wisdom," *Millennial Star*, Volume
92, 591–92 (7 August 1930).

18. John A. Widtsoe, "History and the
Word of Wisdom," *Millennial Star*, 3
November 1932, 714.

19. John A. Widtsoe, "Caffeine in Cola
Drinks," *Improvement Era*,
November 1939, 659.

20. John A. Widtsoe, "The Staff of Life,
The Case for Whole Wheat Bread,"
Improvement Era, December 1945,
742.

21. John A. Widtsoe, "Is Alcoholism a
Disease?" *Improvement Era*, August
1947, 508.

22. Widtsoe, *Sunlit Land*, 224–25.

23. Widtsoe to Heber J. Grant, 20
October 1937, Widtsoe Family
Collection, 1, Utah State Historical
Society.

24. Widtsoe to Heber J. Grant, 20
October 1937, 2. In a letter to Elias
S. Woodruff, president of the
Central States Mission, who had
hoped to publish the book, Elder
Widtsoe wrote, "I fear that I have
not quite made clear to you that the

manuscript on the Word of Wisdom prepared by myself and my wife, when examined by a committee of the Twelve, was selected as the Priesthood course of study for 1938. This was wholly unexpected by me. Naturally, however, after the decision was made the matter went out of my hands; the book is being printed by Deseret News Press for the Deseret Book Company." Widtsoe to Elias S. Woodruff, 16 December 1937, John A. Widtsoe Collection, LDS Church Archives. Franklin S. Harris, president of BYU, also sought to publish the book and offered money to cover research expenses. Franklin S. Harris to Widtsoe, 6 August 1937, Widtsoe Collection, Utah State Historical Society.

25. Heber J. Grant to Widtsoe, 29 October 1937, Widtsoe Family Collection, Utah State Historical Society.

26. Joseph Fielding Smith to Widtsoe, 21 October 1937, Widtsoe Family Collection, Utah State Historical Society.

27. David O. McKay to Widtsoe, 25 October 1937, Widtsoe Family Collection, Utah State Historical Society.

28. Widtsoe to Nephi L. Morris, 7 April 1938, John A. Widtsoe Collection, LDS Church Archives.

29. Widtsoe and Widtsoe, *Word of Wisdom*, v.

30. Widtsoe and Widtsoe, *Word of Wisdom*, v-vi.

31. Widtsoe and Widtsoe, *Word of Wisdom*, 9.

32. Widtsoe and Widtsoe, *Word of Wisdom*, 11–12.

33. Widtsoe and Widtsoe, *Word of Wisdom*, 6.

34. Widtsoe and Widtsoe, *Word of Wisdom*, 21.

35. Widtsoe and Widtsoe, *Word of Wisdom*, 87.

36. Widtsoe and Widtsoe, *Word of Wisdom*, 88.

37. Widtsoe and Widtsoe, *Word of Wisdom*, 88.

38. Widtsoe and Widtsoe, *Word of Wisdom*, 90.

39. Widtsoe and Widtsoe, *Word of Wisdom*, 93.

40. Widtsoe and Widtsoe, *Word of Wisdom*, 96–97.

41. Widtsoe and Widtsoe, *Word of Wisdom*, 99.

42. Widtsoe and Widtsoe, *Word of Wisdom*, 119.

43. Widtsoe and Widtsoe, *Word of Wisdom*, 122.

44. Widtsoe and Widtsoe, *Word of Wisdom*, 137.

45. Widtsoe and Widtsoe, *Word of Wisdom*, 196.

46. Widtsoe and Widtsoe, *Word of Wisdom*, 211.

47. Widtsoe and Widtsoe, *Word of Wisdom*, 276–77.

48. Widtsoe and Widtsoe, *Word of Wisdom*, 288.

49. "New Word of Wisdom Book is Excellent Treatment of Word of Wisdom," *Deseret News*, 22 January 1938, John A. Widtsoe Collection, LDS Church Archives.

50. Widtsoe to Clyde B. Crow, 4 January 1936, John A. Widtsoe Collection, LDS Church Archives.

51. Widtsoe to James L. Graham, 25 January 1938, John A. Widtsoe Collection, LDS Church Archives.

52. Widtsoe to W. H. Stewart, 9 April 1938, John A. Widtsoe Collection, LDS Church Archives.

53. E. H. Ahlens to Widtsoe, 8 December 1938, John A. Widtsoe Collection, LDS Church Archives.

54. Widtsoe to E. H. Ahlens, 27 December 1938, John A. Widtsoe Collection, LDS Church Archives.

55. Widtsoe to Leo J. Muir, 2 August 1938, John A. Widtsoe Collection, Utah State Historical Society.

56. John A. Widtsoe, in Leah D. Widtsoe, *How to Be Well*, 6.

57. Leah D. Widtsoe, *How to Be Well,* 6.

58. Thomas C. Romney to Widtsoe, 28 January 1944, John A. Widtsoe Collection, LDS Church Archives.

59. Mrs. J. Lanell Foote to Widtsoe, 20 April 1950, John A. Widtsoe Collection, LDS Church Archives.

60. Widtsoe to Syerl Dennis, 9 September 1949, John A. Widtsoe Collection, LDS Church Archives.

61. Widtsoe to Henry F. Gordon, 9 March 1950, John A. Widtsoe Collection, LDS Church Archives.

62. John A. Widtsoe, "Temperance and Man's Free Agency," *Deseret News,* 27 June 1934.

CHAPTER 42

1. Widtsoe, *Priesthood and Church Government,* 184–5, 286–7.

2. Merrill J. Bateman, "Stake Conference," in *Encyclopedia of Mormonism,* 1:308–9.

3. Talbot, *Acts of the Modern Apostles,* 242.

4. Widtsoe, *Sunlit Land,* 163.

5. Widtsoe, *Sunlit Land,* 164.

6. Widtsoe, *Sunlit Land,* 163.

7. Widtsoe, *Sunlit Land,* 166.

8. See "The Stake Conference Schedule: 1940," John A, Widtsoe Collection, LDS Church Archives.

9. Widtsoe, *Sunlit Land,* 164.

10. Widtsoe, *Sunlit Land,* 165.

11. For an example, See George F. Richards to Widtsoe, 2 January 1946, John A. Widtsoe Collection, LDS Church Archives. There are hundreds of these letters in Widtsoe's archival collection.

12. Widtsoe to Newel Steed, 9 May 1941, John A. Widtsoe Collection, LDS Church Archives, Widtsoe to James M. Smith, 13 February 1947, John A. Widtsoe Collection, LDS Church Archives.

13. See Widtsoe to Arvel L. Child, 28 December 1949, John A. Widtsoe Collection, Archives.

14. Widtsoe to Laurence S. Burton, 28 January 1947, John A. Widtsoe Collection, LDS Church Archives.

15. Widtsoe to Myron B. Child, 18 October 1949, John A. Widtsoe Collection, LDS Church Archives.

16. Widtsoe to M. L. Dean, 18 May 1939, John A. Widtsoe Collection, LDS Church Archives.

17. Talbot, *Acts of the Modern Apostles,* 238.

18. Cowan and Homer, *California Saints,* 419.

19. Widtsoe to James M. Smith, 13 February 1947, John A. Widtsoe Collection, LDS Church Archives.

20. Widtsoe to David Smith, 15 March 1945, John A. Widtsoe Collection, LDS Church Archives.

21. Widtsoe to Albert Choules, 18 September 1944, John A. Widtsoe Collection, LDS Church Archives.

22. Widtsoe to William F. Edwards, 26 April 1950, John A. Widtsoe Collection, LDS Church Archives.

23. Widtsoe to President and Mrs. H. W. Henderson, 18 November 1942, John A. Widtsoe Collection, LDS Church Archives.

24. Widtsoe to President and Mrs. E. E. Drury, Jr., 17 October 1944, John A. Widtsoe Collection, LDS Church Archives.

25. Milton Bennion to Thomas L. Martin, 9 August 1946, John A. Widtsoe Collection, LDS Church Archives.

26. Widtsoe to Alma Taylor, 12 November 1947, John A. Widtsoe Collection, LDS Church Archives.

27. Widtsoe to Mrs. Ethelyn O. Greaves, 25 August 1939, John A. Widtsoe Collection, LDS Church Archives.

28. Widtsoe to Harold Snow, 3 August 1948, John A. Widtsoe Collection, LDS Church Archives.

29. Widtsoe, *Sunlit Land,* 167.

30. Widtsoe to David Smith, 15 March 1945, John A. Widtsoe Collection, LDS Church Archives.

31. Widtsoe, *Sunlit Land,* 163–65.

32. Widtsoe, *Sunlit Land*, 166.
33. Preston Richards to Widtsoe, 2 October 1939, Preston D. Richards Collection, BYU Special Collections.
34. Widtsoe to Preston Richards, 10 November 1939, Preston D. Richards Collection, BYU Special Collections.
35. Widtsoe to Preston Richards, 18 December 1939, Preston D. Richards Papers, BYU Special Collections.
36. Widtsoe to Eugene Hilton, 12 June 1945, John A. Widtsoe Collection, LDS Church Archives.
37. Widtsoe to First Presidency and Council of the Twelve, 18 June 1940, John A. Widtsoe Collection, LDS Church Archives.
38. Widtsoe to Rudger Clawson and members of the Twelve, 3 December 1941, John A. Widtsoe Collection, LDS Church Archives.
39. See John A. Widtsoe Collection, LDS Church Archives.
40. Widtsoe to William H. Reeder, Jr., 4 December 1941, John A. Widtsoe Collection, LDS Church Archives.
41. Widtsoe to Robert O. Hatch, 28 August 1942. See also Widtsoe and A. E. Bowen to Claudius Harshi, 7 October 1942, John A. Widtsoe Collection, LDS Church Archives.
42. William M. Hansen to Widtsoe, 26 September 1945, John A. Widtsoe Collection, LDS Church Archives.
43. Widtsoe to Henry Ray Hatch, 4 October 1945, John A. Widtsoe Collection, LDS Church Archives.
44. Widtsoe to Earl S. Paul, 30 December 1941, John A. Widtsoe Collection, LDS Church Archives.
45. Widtsoe to John P. Lillywhite, 14 November 1944, John A. Widtsoe Collection, LDS Church Archives.
46. Harold Lundstrom, "Elder Widtsoe Reviews Life of Gospel Service," *Church News*, 3.
47. Widtsoe to S. Norman Lee, 1 December 1944, John A. Widtsoe Collection, LDS Church Archives.
48. Widtsoe to President and Mrs. George Key Hyde, 17 July 1940, John A. Widtsoe Collection, LDS Church Archives.
49. Widtsoe to Thomas M. Irvine, 20 January 1942, John A. Widtsoe Collection, LDS Church Archives.
50. O'Douglas Barnes to Widtsoe, 12 May 1940, John A. Widtsoe Collection, LDS Church Archives.
51. Widtsoe, *Sunlit Land*, 242.
52. Widtsoe to Darlene Sheranian, 16 January 1945, John A. Widtsoe Collection, LDS Church Archives.
53. Conference Report, April 1939, 19.
54. Widtsoe to Mrs. Roger W. Rundquist, 9 February 1948, John A. Widtsoe Collection, LDS Church Archives.
55. Widtsoe, *Sunlit Land*, 167.
56. Widtsoe, *Sunlit Land*, 242–43.
57. Conference Report, April 1940, 131.
58. Conference Report, October 1947, 126.
59. Holland, *Sierra Saints*, 77–78.
60. Widtsoe to President and Mrs. Wilfred L. Hickison, 3 October 1947, John A. Widtsoe Collection, LDS Church Archives.
61. Widtsoe to Melchizedek Priesthood Committee, 6 March 1940, John A. Widtsoe Collection, LDS Church Archives.
62. Widtsoe to James L. Dunford, 8 June 1939, John A. Widtsoe Collection, LDS Church Archives.
63. Widtsoe to Eugene Hilton, 17 September 1942, John A. Widtsoe Collection, LDS Church Archives.
64. Widtsoe to Frank L. West, 14 February 1941, John A. Widtsoe Collection, LDS Church Archives.
65. Widtsoe to Charles E. Rowan Jr., 16 September 1942, John A. Widtsoe Collection, LDS Church Archives.
66. Widtsoe to W. G. Harmon, 30 September 1942, John A. Widtsoe Collection, LDS Church Archives.

67. Widtsoe to President and Mrs. J. O. Anderson, 14 May 1945, John A. Widtsoe Collection, LDS Church Archives.

68. Widtsoe to President and Mrs. Charles E. Rowan, Jr., 17 April 1947, John A. Widtsoe Collection, LDS Church Archives.

69. Widtsoe to Levi S. Udall, 6 November 1940, John A. Widtsoe Collection, LDS Church Archives.

70. See "List of gift books and pamphlets to be sent," John A. Widtsoe Collection, LDS Church Archives.

71. Charles W. Dunn to Widtsoe, 8 December 1942, John A. Widtsoe Collection, LDS Church Archives.

CHAPTER 43

1. Widtsoe Journal, 21 October 1937, 744.

2. Leonard J. Arrington and Wayne K. Hinton, "Origin of the Welfare Plan of The Church of Jesus Christ of Latter-day Saints," *BYU Studies*, vol. 5, 1964, 67–85.

3. Leonard J. Arrington and Wayne K. Hinton, "Origin of the Welfare Plan of The Church of Jesus Christ of Latter-day Saints," *BYU Studies*, vol. 5, 1964, 75.

4. Leonard J. Arrington and Wayne K. Hinton, "Origin of the Welfare Plan of The Church of Jesus Christ of Latter-day Saints," *BYU Studies*, vol. 5, 1964, 77.

5. Cowan, *Church in the Twentieth Century*, 140.

6. Cowan, *Church in the Twentieth Century*, 142–43.

7. Cowan, *Church in the Twentieth Century*, 143.

8. "Official Will Direct Agricultural Activities," *Deseret News*, 22 October 1937.

9. Stewart, Walker, and McGavin, *Priesthood and Church Welfare*, 36.

10. Henry A. Smith, "Church-wide Security Program Organized," *Improvement Era*, June 1936, 337.

11. Henry A. Smith, "Church-wide Security Program Organized," *Improvement Era*, June 1936, 337.

12. "Official Will Direct Agricultural Activities," *Deseret News*, 22 October 1937.

13. John A. Widtsoe, "Agriculture and the Church Security Program," *Improvement Era*, January 1938, 8–9.

14. John A. Widtsoe, "The Philosophy of Rural Life," address at the L.D.S. Institute of Religion, USAC, 5 December 1937, 1, copy in author's possession.

15. John A. Widtsoe, "The Philosophy of Rural Life," address at the L.D.S. Institute of Religion, USAC, 5 December 1937, 2, copy in author's possession.

16. John A. Widtsoe, "The Philosophy of Rural Life," address at the L.D.S. Institute of Religion, USAC, 5 December 1937, 3–4, copy in author's possession.

17. John A. Widtsoe, "Agriculture and the Church Security Program," *Improvement Era*, January 1938, 8–9.

18. Conference Report October 1940, 64.

19. Conference Report October 1939, 99.

20. Stewart, Walker, and McGavin, *Priesthood and Church Welfare*, 20–21.

21. Widtsoe, *Priesthood and Church Government*, 154.

22. Stewart, Walker, and McGavin, *Priesthood and Church Welfare*, 1.

23. John A. Widtsoe, "What is Farm Chemurgic?" *Improvement Era*, January 1937, 4.

24. "New Chemurgy Leaders Push Utah Program," *Deseret News*, 11 February 1937.

25. "Pres. Grant, Dr. Widtsoe To Talk In East," *Deseret News*, 14 May 1937.

26. "Utahn Given High Position," *Deseret News*, 20 July 1937.

27. Widtsoe, "What is Farm Chemurgic?" 4.

28. Stewart, 201–3.

29. "Chemist Hits Scarcity Idea of Production," *Deseret News,* 16 November 1936.

30. "Colonizing Success Laid to Initiative and Self-Help," *Deseret News,* 27 May 1937.

31. Borth, *Pioneers of Plenty,* 144.

32. Borth, *Pioneers of Plenty,* 145.

33. "Friend of Chemurgy: John A. Widtsoe," *National Chemurgic Digest,* 4/8, August 1950.

34. "Friend of Chemurgy: John A. Widtsoe," *National Chemurgic Digest,* 4/8, August 1950, inside cover.

35. Conference Report, October 1937, 64.

36. Henry D. Moyle, "Ten Years of Church Welfare," *Improvement Era,* April 1946, 209, 244.

37. John A. Widtsoe, "Deseret Industries," *Improvement Era,* September 1938, 544.

38. Bowen, *Church Welfare Plan,* 99.

39. Program of the meeting of Stake and Regional Agricultural Advisory Committees, 8 April 1939, John A. Widtsoe Collection, LDS Church Archives.

40. Harold B. Lee to Widtsoe, 2 February 1938, John A. Widtsoe Collection, LDS Church Archives.

41. Widtsoe to Harold B. Lee, 14 June 1938, John A. Widtsoe Collection, LDS Church Archives.

42. Harold B. Lee to Widtsoe, 2 September 1938, John A. Widtsoe Collection, LDS Church Archives.

43. Widtsoe to Harold B. Lee, 27 November 1941, John A. Widtsoe Collection, LDS Church Archives.

44. Widtsoe to the General Church Welfare Committee, 29 January 1947, John A. Widtsoe Collection, LDS Church Archives.

45. Widtsoe to the General Church Welfare Committee, 16 March 1943, John A. Widtsoe Collection, LDS Church Archives.

46. Widtsoe to the General Church Welfare Committee, around 1 April 1943, John A. Widtsoe Collection, LDS Church Archives.

47. Widtsoe to the General Church Welfare Committee, 29 April 1943, John A. Widtsoe Collection, LDS Church Archives.

48. Conference Report, October 1944, 50.

49. Bowen, *Church Welfare Plan,* 98–99.

CHAPTER *44*

1. Cowan, *Church in the Twentieth Century,* 176.

2. Cowan, *Church in the Twentieth Century,* 183.

3. Conference Report, April 1941, 12–13.

4. "World War II (1939–1945)," *World Book 1998 Multimedia Encyclopedia,* Deluxe Edition, CD-ROM.

5. Thomas E. McKay, general conference address, October 1943.

6. Arthur Gaeth, "The Saints in Central Europe," *Improvement Era,* March 1946, 148.

7. Gaeth, "The Saints in Central Europe, 148.

8. Gaeth, "The Saints in Central Europe, 148.

9. Benson, *A Labor of Love,* 1–2.

10. Conference Report, October 1945, 78–79.

11. Conference Report, October 1952, 119.

12. Babbel, *On Wings of Faith,* 40–41.

13. Conference Report, April 1948, 178.

14. Conference Report, April 1948, 178.

15. Churchill, *The Second World War,* 468–69.

16. "The Church Welfare Program Helps European Saints," *Improvement Era,* December 1945, 747.

17. Widtsoe Journal, 18 October 1945, 927.

18. "Church Sends Aid to Europe," *Church News,* 20 October 1945, 1, 5.

19. Widtsoe Journal, 29 October–3 November 1945, 928.

20. Conference Report, October 1947, 5–6.

21. Widtsoe to Mrs. Robert R. Bowen, 13 November 1945, John A. Widtsoe Collection, LDS Church Archives.

22. Widtsoe to Hugh B. Brown, 19 November 1945, John A. Widtsoe Collection, LDS Church Archives.

23. Widtsoe to R. B. Summerhays, 10 December 1945, John A. Widtsoe Collection, LDS Church Archives.

24. Gibbons, *George Albert Smith,* 302.

25. Widtsoe Journal, 22 December 1945.

26. Frederick W. Babbel, *On Wings of Faith* (Salt Lake City: Bookcraft, 1972). Ezra Taft Benson, *A Labor of Love* (Salt Lake City: Deseret Book, 1989).

27. Widtsoe to Hugh B. Brown, 22 December 1945, John A. Widtsoe Collection, LDS Church Archives.

28. Widtsoe to George L. Zundale, 7 January 1946, John A. Widtsoe Collection, LDS Church Archives.

29. "Elder Benson Prepares to Preside in European Mission," *Church News,* 19 January 1946.

30. Widtsoe to Grover C. Dunford, 21 January 1946, John A. Widtsoe Collection, LDS Church Archives.

CHAPTER 45

1. Widtsoe to Ralph B. Jordan, 3 February 1944, John A. Widtsoe Collection, LDS Church Archives.

2. Widtsoe to Archibald F. Bennett, 15 January 1948, John A. Widtsoe Collection, LDS Church Archives.

3. Widtsoe to Lloyd L. Cullimore, 12 April 1948, John A. Widtsoe Collection, LDS Church Archives.

4. Widtsoe to George F. Richards, 4 March 1948, John A. Widtsoe Collection, LDS Church Archives.

5. Widtsoe to S. Norman Lee, 9 April 1948, John A. Widtsoe Collection, LDS Church Archives.

6. Conference Report, April 1948, 148–49.

7. Widtsoe to George Albert Smith, 14 April 1948, John A. Widtsoe Collection, LDS Church Archives.

8. Widtsoe to George F. Richards, 16 April 1948, John A. Widtsoe Collection, LDS Church Archives.

9. Widtsoe to Harold L. Snow, 16 June 1948, John A. Widtsoe Collection, LDS Church Archives.

10. Harold Lundstrom, "Elder, Mrs. Widtsoe Note Golden Wedding," *Church News,* 6 June 1948.

11. Widtsoe to Harold L. Snow, 1 July 1948, John A. Widtsoe Collection, LDS Church Archives.

12. Widtsoe to Harold L. Snow, 13 August 1948, John A. Widtsoe Collection, LDS Church Archives.

13. Widtsoe to George Albert Smith, 11 August 1948, John A. Widtsoe Collection, LDS Church Archives.

14. Widtsoe to George Albert Smith, 23 December 1948, John A. Widtsoe Collection, LDS Church Archives.

15. Widtsoe to C. Frank Steele, 18 February 1949, John A. Widtsoe Collection, LDS Church Archives.

16. Widtsoe to Jessie D. Barrow, letter without date, John A. Widtsoe Collection, LDS Church Archives.

17. Widtsoe to President and Mrs. Farnsworth, 14 February 1949, John A. Widtsoe Collection, LDS Church Archives.

18. John A. Widtsoe, *Joseph Smith, Seeker After Truth, Prophet of God* (Salt Lake City: Bookcraft, 1991).

19. Widtsoe to Harold L. Snow, 3 March 1949, John A. Widtsoe Collection, LDS Church Archives.

20. A. Hamer Reiser to Widtsoe, 9 May 1949, John A. Widtsoe Collection, LDS Church Archives.

21. Widtsoe, *Joseph Smith, Seeker After Truth, Prophet of God,* v–vi.

22. Widtsoe to George Albert Smith, 8 November 1950, John A. Widtsoe Collection, LDS Church Archives.

23. Widtsoe to Horace A. Sorensen, 7 December 1949, John A. Widtsoe Collection, LDS Church Archives.

24. Conference Report, April 1950, 125–26.

25. John A. Widtsoe, "The Era Grows," *Improvement Era,* January 1950, 22.

26. Widtsoe to Samuel B. Bringhurst, 28 June 1950, John A. Widtsoe Collection, LDS Church Archives.

27. Widtsoe to Leah Eudora Widtsoe, 7 July 1950, John A. Widtsoe Collection, LDS Church Archives.

28. *Chemurgic Digest,* August 1950, vol. 9.

29. Conference Report, October 1950, 35–36.

30. Conference Report, April 1950, 187.

31. Conference Report, April 1951, 98.

32. Widtsoe to David O. McKay, April 1951, John A. Widtsoe Collection, LDS Church Archives.

33. David O. McKay to Widtsoe, 25 April 1951, John A. Widtsoe Collection, LDS Church Archives.

34. "Elder Widtsoe Appointed to Canadian Unit, Special to the News, from Ottawa," *Deseret News,* 26 August 1951.

35. Widtsoe, *Sunlit Land,* 184.

36. Conference Report, April 1952, 33.

37. Widtsoe to David O. McKay, 6 September 1951, John A. Widtsoe Collection, LDS Church Archives.

38. *Gospel Ideals: Selections from the Discourses of David O. McKay* (Salt Lake City: Deseret New Press, 1953).

39. *Gospel Ideals,* ix.

40. Widtsoe to David O. McKay, 10 September 1951, John A. Widtsoe Collection, LDS Church Archives.

41. Transcript of "Sister Leah Widtsoe Funeral Services," 20.

42. Leah Eudora Widtsoe to Widtsoe, 31 January 1952, John A. Widtsoe Collection, LDS Church Archives.

43. Conference Report, April 1952, 32–35.

44. Conference Report, October 1952, 7.

45. Eva S. Feik to Marian Morgan, 7 October 1952, John A. Widtsoe Collection, LDS Church Archives.

46. Widtsoe to L. S. St. Laurent, 27 October 1952, John A. Widtsoe Collection, LDS Church Archives.

47. Widtsoe to Ernest L. Wilkinson, 29 October 1952, John A. Widtsoe Collection, LDS Church Archives.

48. Leah Eudora Widtsoe to James Bleakley, 19 December 1952, John A. Widtsoe Collection, LDS Church Archives.

49. Oral History Interview with Leah Eudora Widtsoe, February 11, 1965, BYU Special Collections.

50. "Eminent Scientist Served as USAC, U. of U. Chief," *Deseret News—Telegram,* 30 November 1953.

51. Brief excerpts from those read by President McKay include the following. A. Ray Olpin, president of the University of Utah wrote, "He bequeathed to us his great library on Western history and culture. He built his home on the edge of the campus where he was almost surrounded by students. He was where he could observe affairs at the University close at hand. Yet he always seemed to withhold comment on things which may have displeased him and commended our every effort to maintain high standards of education. And with that we present our resolutions from the faculty." Lewis L. Madsen, president of the Utah State Agricultural College, wrote, "Through his wise and sympathetic teaching, his skill in writing, his power as an administrator, and his inspirational leadership of men and women young and old, he has exerted a many sided influence which will never die." Ernest L. Wilkinson, president of Brigham Young University, wrote, "On behalf

of the university itself—a university whose soul has been enriched by the inspiration and loyalty of you and your devoted husband since your wedding reception, before the turn of the century, in the old College Hall." S. D. Howe, acting prime minister, dominion of Canada, wrote, "The Prime Minister, now in England, is being informed immediately. In the meantime I should like to extend to you on my own behalf and that of all my colleagues our most heartfelt sympathy. Dr. Widtsoe's long and distinguished service in his chosen field will not soon be forgotten." ("Life of Apostle Extolled in Impressive Rites," *Deseret News— Telegram,* 6 December 1952.)

52. "Life of Apostle Extolled in Impressive Rites," *Deseret News— Telegram,* 6 December 1952.

53. "Life of Apostle Extolled in Impressive Rites," *Deseret News— Telegram,* 6 December 1952.

Epilogue

1. John A. Widtsoe, *In the Gospel Net* (Salt Lake City: Improvement Era, 1941).

2. Widtsoe, *Sunlit Land,* 228.

3. Widtsoe, *Sunlit Land,* 237–38.

4. Widtsoe, *Sunlit Land,* 238.

5. Widtsoe, *Sunlit Land,* 239.

6. Widtsoe to Leah Eudora Widtsoe, 16 September 1893, Widtsoe Family Collection, Utah State Historical Society.

7. Widtsoe to Leah Eudora Widtsoe, 16 September 1893, Widtsoe Family Collection, Utah State Historical Society.

8. Widtsoe to Leah Eudora Widtsoe, 25 December 1950, Widtsoe Family Collection, Utah State Historical Society.

9. Leah Eudora Dunford Widtsoe, Biographical Notes from the Register of the Widtsoe Family Collection, Utah State Historical Society.

10. Richard L. Evans address, Sons of the Utah Pioneers luncheon in honor of Dr. John A. Widtsoe, 25 August 1952, Hotel Utah, Widtsoe Family Collection, Utah State Historical Society.

11. All of the interviews in this epilogue were conducted by the author with Widtsoe family members John Widtsoe Wallace, Peggy Thorpe, George H. Durham II, Joanne Koplin, Carolyn Person, and Doralee Madsen. Typescripts are in the possession of the author.

BIBLIOGRAPHY

Allen, James B., and Glen M. Leonard. *The Story of the Latter-day Saints.* Salt Lake City: Deseret Book, 1976.

Allen, James B., Jesse L. Embry, and Kahlile B. Mehr. *Hearts Turned to the Fathers: A History of the Genealogical Society of Utah, 1894–1994.* Provo, Utah: BYU Studies, 1995.

Allen, Mark K. *The History of Psychology at Brigham Young University.* Provo, Utah: BYU Press, 1975.

Alter, J. Cecil. *Utah, the Storied Domain.* Chicago: American Historical Society, 1932.

Babbel, Frederick W. *On Wings of Faith.* Salt Lake City: Bookcraft, 1972.

Bailyn, Bernard, Donald Fleming, Oscar Handlin, and Stephan Thernstrom. *Glimpses of the Harvard Past.* Cambridge, Mass.: Harvard University Press, 1986.

Benson, Ezra Taft. *A Labor of Love.* Salt Lake City: Deseret Book, 1989.

Bok, Derek. *Beyond the Ivory Tower: Social Responsibilities of the Modern University.* Cambridge, Mass.: Harvard University Press, 1982.

Bowen, Albert E. *The Church Welfare Plan.* Independence, Mo.: Zion's Printing and Publishing, 1946.

Brubacher, John S., and Willis Rudy. *Higher Education in Transition: A History of American Colleges and Universities.* New York: Harper and Row, 1968.

Bushman, Claudia L., ed. *Mormon Sisters: Women in Early Utah.* Cambridge, Mass.: Emmeline Press, 1976.

Carter, Kate B. *Our Pioneer Heritage.* Salt Lake City: Daughters of the Utah Pioneers, 1958–77.

Chamberlain, Ralph V. *The University of Utah: A History of Its First Hundred Years, 1850 to 1950.* Salt Lake City: University of Utah Press, 1960.

Churchill, Winston. *The Second World War, Triumph and Tragedy.* Boston: Houghton Mifflin, 1953.

Clark, James R. *Messages of the First Presidency*, 6 vols. Salt Lake City: Bookcraft, 1965–1975.

Cowan, Richard O. *The Church in the Twentieth Century*. Salt Lake City: Bookcraft, 1985.

Cowan, Richard O., and William E. Homer. *California Saints: A 150 Year Legacy in the Golden State*. Provo, Utah: Religious Studies Center, 1996.

Dew, Sheri L. *Go Forward with Faith: The Biography of Gordon B. Hinckley*. Salt Lake City: Deseret Book, 1996.

Donigan, Robert W. *An Outline History of Broadcasting in The Church of Jesus Christ of Latter-day Saints, 1922–1963*. Provo, Utah: 1963.

Eliot, Charles W. *Harvard Memories*. Cambridge, Mass.: Harvard University Press, 1923.

Ellsworth, S. George. *Utah's Heritage*. Salt Lake City: Peregrine Smith, 1981.

Encyclopaedia Britannica. Chicago: R. S. Peale Co., 1892.

Evans, Richard L., Jr. *Richard L. Evans, The Man and the Message*. Salt Lake City: Bookcraft, 1973.

Gates, Susa Young. *The Life Story of Brigham Young*. London: Jarrolds Publishers, 1930.

Gibbons, Francis M. *George Albert Smith, Kind and Caring Christian, Prophet of God*. Salt Lake City: Deseret Book, 1990.

Hinckley, Bryant S. *Hours with Our Leaders*. Salt Lake City: General Boards of the Mutual Improvement Associations of The Church of Jesus Christ of Latter-day Saints, 1941.

Holland, S. Dennis. *Sierra Saints: A Brief History of the Mormons in Western El Dorado County, 1847–1997*. Placerville, Calif.: S. D. Holland Publishing, 1997.

Hughes, Raymond M., and William H. Lancelot. *Education—America's Magic*. Ames Iowa: Iowa State College Press, 1946.

In Memoriam of John A. Widtsoe. Salt Lake City: Bookcraft, 1952.

Israelsen, Orson W., and Vaughn E. Hansen. *Irrigation Principles and Practices*. New York: John Wiley and Sons, 1962.

Lindsey, Almont. *The Pullman Strike*. Chicago: Phoenix, 1964.

Ludlow, Daniel H., ed. *Encyclopedia of Mormonism*. New York: Macmillan, 1992.

Morison, Samuel Eliot. *Three Centuries of Harvard, 1636–1936*. Cambridge, Mass.: Harvard University Press, 1936.

Olson, Reuel Leslie. *The Colorado River Compact*. Los Angeles, Calif.: Neuner Corporation, 1926.

Peterson, F. Ross. *A History of Cache County*. Salt Lake City: Utah State Historical Society, Cache County Council, 1997.

Record of the Class of 1894. Cambridge, Mass.: Harvard University Press, 1944.

Ricks, Joel Edward. *The Utah State Agricultural College, a History of Fifty Years*. Salt Lake City: Deseret News Press, 1938.

Smith, Hyrum M., and Janne M. Sjodahl. *Doctrine and Covenants Commentary*. Salt Lake City: Deseret Book, 1954.

Smith, Joseph. *Teachings of the Prophet Joseph Smith*. Selected by Joseph Fielding Smith. Salt Lake City: Deseret News Press, 1938.

Smith, Joseph F. *Gospel Doctrine: Sermons and Writings of President Joseph F. Smith*. Edited by John A. Widtsoe. Salt Lake City: Deseret News, 1919.

Stewart, George, Dilworth Walker, and E. Cecil McGavin. *Priesthood and Church Welfare.* Salt Lake City: Deseret Book, 1938.

Talbot, William D. *The Acts of the Modern Apostles.* Salt Lake City: Randall Book, 1985.

Tanner, Annie Clark. *A Mormon Mother.* Salt Lake City: University of Utah Library, Tanner Trust Fund, 1983.

Ward, Margery W. *A Life Divided: The Biography of Joseph Marion Tanner, 1859–1927.* Salt Lake City: Publisher's Press, 1980.

Whitney, Orson F. *History of Utah.* Salt Lake City: George Q. Cannon and Sons, 1904.

Widtsoe, John A. *An Understandable Religion.* Independence, Mo.: Zion's Printing and Publishing, 1944.

———. *Current Gospel Questions.* Salt Lake City: General Boards of the Mutual Improvement Associations of The Church of Jesus Christ of Latter-day Saints, 1939.

———. *Dry-Farming: A System of Agriculture for Countries under a Low Rainfall.* New York: Macmillan, 1911.

———. *Education for Necessary Pursuits.* Logan, Utah: Utah Agricultural College, 1913.

———. *Evidences and Reconciliations: Aids to Faith in a Modern Day.* Salt Lake City: Bookcraft, 1943.

———. *Evidences and Reconciliations.* 3 vols. Arranged by G. Homer Durham. Salt Lake City: Bookcraft, 1960.

———. *Handbook of the Restoration.* Liverpool: European Mission, 1930.

———. *In a Sunlit Land: The Autobiography of John A. Widtsoe.* Salt Lake City: Deseret News Press, 1952.

———. *In Search of Truth: Comments on the Gospel and Modern Thought.* Salt Lake City: Deseret Book, 1930.

———. *In the Gospel Net: The Story of Anna Karine Gaarden Widtsoe.* Salt Lake City: Improvement Era, 1942.

———. *Man and the Dragon.* Salt Lake City: Bookcraft, 1945.

———. *Priesthood and Church Government.* Salt Lake City: Deseret Book, 1939.

———. *Program of The Church of Jesus Christ of Latter-day Saints.* Salt Lake City: Department of Education of The Church of Jesus Christ of Latter-day Saints, 1937.

———. *Success on Irrigation Projects.* New York: John Wiley, 1928.

———. *The Message of the Doctrine and Covenants.* Edited by G. Homer Durham. Salt Lake City: Bookcraft, 1969.

———. *The Principles of Irrigation in Practice.* New York: Macmillan, 1914.

———. *The Successful Missionary: Letters to Elders in the Field.* Liverpool: European Mission, 1932.

———. *Your Questions Answered.* Salt Lake City: General Boards of the Mutual Improvement Associations of The Church of Jesus Christ of Latter-day Saints, 1943.

Widtsoe, John A., and Leah D. Widtsoe. *The Word of Wisdom, a Modern Interpretation,* revised edition. Salt Lake City: Deseret Book, 1950.

Widtsoe, Leah D. *How to Be Well: A Health Handbook and Cook-book Based on the Newer Knowledge of Nutrition.* Salt Lake City: Deseret Book, 1943.

Wilkinson, Ernest L., ed. *Brigham Young University, The First One Hundred Years.* 2 vols. Provo, Utah: BYU Press, 1975–1976.

Woodruff, Wilford. *Discourses of Wilford Woodruff.* Edited by G. Homer Durham. Salt Lake City: Bookcraft, 1969.

Young, Brigham. *Discourses of Brigham Young.* Edited by John A. Widtsoe. Salt Lake City: Deseret Book, 1954.

INDEX

Academic administrators, duties of, 175–76

Adam: fulness of gospel possessed by, 305–6; doctrinal controversy regarding, 484

Adult education programs, 260

Adversity: overcoming, 383–84; of European Saints in World War II, 640–41

Agency, 249, 302, 304–5, 312; unrighteous use of, 519–20

Agricultural College of Utah (ACU, UAC; later known as Utah State University), 298; JW accepts job offer from, 82–83; campus (photographs), 84, 132, 133, 181, 183, 189, 191; professors lose jobs at, due to polygamy, 119; founding of, 152; college consolidation controversy at, 151–61; conflicts regarding funding of, 152; expansion of, 154–55; conflicts among faculty of, 154–56; JW dismissed from faculty of, 158–59; president's home at (photograph), 164; government restricts curriculum of, 164; night classes offered at, 166; cooperates with U of U, 167–68; planning for growth of, 168–71; advertising campaign of, 169; increased enrollment at, 169–71; "practical courses" at, 170; elective courses at, 170–71; offers training for teachers, 171; summer school at, 171; moral training at, 173; faculty of, 175–79; domestic science courses at, 180–84; extension division of, 184; growing enrollment at, 188; government funding of, 189; master plan contest at, 190–91; summary of JW's service to, 199–201; JW's contributions to, 222

Agricultural courses taught in Utah high schools, 187

Agricultural engineering, ACU begins teaching courses in, 170

Agricultural Experiment Station, 82, 88; purpose of, 88; JW's work at, 89–90

Agricultural research: JW conducts, 89–93; impact of, 133–34

Agriculture: in Utah, 122–35, 145–46, 200–201; JW's assessment of, 133–35; application of scientific principles to, 138; significance of, 147, 340, 629–30; increased productivity in, 187–88; evidence of God's hand in, 210; water resources and, 338–39; JW reviews book on,

747

Durham, Leah Eudora Widtsoe. *See* Widtsoe, Leah Eudora (Durham)

Education: importance of, 50–51, 76, 174, 230, 290–91; maturity and, 87; practical, 88–89; Germany's influence on, 111; of farmers, 124–27, 628; philosophies of, 137–38, 142, 165–66; goals of, 147; JW's philosophy of, 147, 362–63; government funds allocated to, 154; JW's contributions to, 192; accessibility of, 259–60; JW serves as Church Commissioner of, 289; benefits of, 298; in Utah, 359–60; religion and, 360–61; religious, 363; faith and, 572–74
Educator, role of, 140; JW's prominence as, 201; responsibility of, 230–31; traits of, 237
Election, doctrine of, 305
Electrical power, use of Colorado River to generate, 342
Eliot, Charles W., 58–59
Employment for U of U students, 261
England. *See* Great Britain
Eternal progression, 301–3, 312, 377
Eternity: scientific basis of, 214–16; temple endowment and, 378
Europe: anti-American sentiment in, 116–17; Saints in, 318–20, 460; Church's growing acceptance in, 401; mission presidents' conferences in, 445–46; strengthening Church in, 448–49; training branch leaders in, 461
European Mission, 318; JW called as president of, 383–86; geographical area of, 386; Widtsoes' arrival at headquarters of, 386–87; JW's recommendations regarding, 390–91; division of, from British mission, 390–92; JW tours, 392–93, 446–47; JW works to build Church's image in, 394–402, 404–6; Word of Wisdom exhibits in, 402–4, 426–28; preparing Slavic lands for the gospel in, 429–44; missionaries' responsibilities in, 450–51; branch

and district leadership in, 460; lack of Church manuals in, 461; training local leaders in, 461–62, 489, 495–96, 498; priesthood leadership in, 463–64; JW's success in leading, 465–66; missionary tracts in, 468; lack of temples in, 478; headquarters of, moved from Liverpool to London, 490–92; Church members in, 507–8; auxiliaries strengthened in, 509–10; meeting facilities in, 510; members in, express appreciation, 511; spirituality of Saints in, 514–15; missionaries evacuated from, 636; faithfulness of Saints in, 636–40; suffering of Saints in, 637–42; communication with, during World War II, 638. *See also* individual nations
Evans, Richard L.: JW's friendship with, 458–59; as editor of *Improvement Era*, 551–57; on serving the Lord, 553–54; on call to serve as editor of *Improvement Era*, 556; *Improvement Era* positions held by, 557; compiles *Evidences and Reconciliations*, 574–76; appointed co-editor of *Improvement Era*, 654; speaks at JW's funeral, 663; on JW's marriage, 668; closeness of, to Widtsoe family, 668–69
Evidences and Reconciliations, 569–76; topics discussed in series, 570–76; answers gospel questions, 570–71; publication of, as books, 574–76
Evil, fight against, 655–56
Evolution, 215, 370–72
Exaltation, temple work and, 304–5
Excellence, working toward, 336
Exercise, health benefits of, 419–20
Experience, role of, in mortality, 432
Experiments, agricultural, 143–44

Fact Finding Commission: JW serves on, 342–50; members of (photograph), 344; duties of, 343–44; JW serves as vice chairman of, 345; hosts convention in Salt Lake City, 346–48; submits report of findings,

Church callings:
serves as elders quorum counselor and instructor, 85; prepares concordance for D&C, 85–86; ordained as seventy, 110; writes MIA lessons and priesthood course of study, serves on YMMIA general board, 197; as ward YMMIA president, 203; as YMMIA general board member, 203; writes lessons for youth and Sunday School, 203; confers with First Presidency and apostles, 204–5; writes priesthood manual, 205; attitude of, toward Church service, 384. *See also* Widtsoe, John Andreas: Apostle; Mission president

Education:
gathers funds to attend Harvard, 56; arrival of, at Harvard University, 57; as Harvard student (photograph), 60; takes entrance examinations at Harvard, 60–61; chooses college major, 61; overcomes homesickness, 62; professors and studies of, at Harvard, 62–63; aptitude of, as university student, 63; discusses studies at Harvard, 64; writes for student newspaper, 64; has period of questioning, 65, 78, 209; testimony strengthened, 65; with LDS students at Harvard, 1893 (photograph), 66; research projects of, in chemistry, 75; graduation of, from Harvard, 76; graduation day of (photograph), 77; academic awards received, 76; expresses gratitude for education, 77; enthusiasm of, for research, 113; travels to Europe, 109–10; misses train in Holland, 110; at Göttingen University, 111–17; receives Ph.D., 114–15; lists benefits of European studies, 117; visits Norway, 118. *See also* Widtsoe, John Andreas: Childhood and youth

Family:
meets Leah, 68; develops friendship with Leah, 71; makes journal entry regarding Leah, 72; sends photograph to Leah, 73; has friendly correspondence with Leah, 73–74; writes poem to Leah, 74; makes diary entry regarding feelings for Leah, 95; proposes marriage to Leah, 103; sets date for marriage, 106; wedding day of, 106–7; on Leah's personality, 107–8; and Leah at time of marriage (photograph), 109; first child born to, 113–14; with Leah and first daughter, Anna (photograph), 114; required to remarry Leah in Switzerland, 116–17; son Mark Adriel dies, 148–49; circa 1907 (photograph), 167; after birth of last child (photograph), 168; additional children born to, 197–98; two infant daughters die, 197–98; moves to Salt Lake City: 229; financial sacrifices of, 271–72, 287; mother Anna Karine Gaarden Widtsoe dies, 273; vacation of, in Alaska, 273–74; has automobile accident, 274; celebrates silver anniversary, 287–88; comforts brother's widow, 288; children of, serve missions, 288–89; celebrates fiftieth birthday, 293; visits son Marsel in England, 334–36; counseled to marry rather than serve mission, 380; list of children born to, 381; son Marsel dies, 381–83; concern of, for daughter Anna, 389, 558; concern of, about daughters, 499; places headstone on father's grave, 508; celebrates golden wedding anniversary, 650; marriage relationship of, with Leah, 655, 665–66, 676; tributes from children and grandchildren of, 665–78; and Leah in later years (photograph), 666; correspondence of, with Leah, 667–68; family activities of, 672–73

Mission president:
called as president of European Mission, 318, 385–86; reasons for not serving mission as youth, 380; set apart for mission, 386; as European Mission president (photograph), 386;